Georgiana Lea Morrill

Speculum Gy de Warewyke

An English Poem with Introduction, Notes, and Glossary

Georgiana Lea Morrill

Speculum Gy de Warewyke
An English Poem with Introduction, Notes, and Glossary

ISBN/EAN: 9783744763646

Printed in Europe, USA, Canada, Australia, Japan

Cover: Foto ©Thomas Meinert / pixelio.de

More available books at **www.hansebooks.com**

☞ The Society intends to complete forthwith the Reprints of its out-of-print Texts of the year 1866. Prof. Skeat has sent *Partenay* to press; Dr. McKnight of Cornell is re-editing *King Horn* and *Floris and Blancheflour;* Dr. H. Spies will probably undertake *Seinte Marherete;* and Dr. Furnivall will revise *Hali Meidenhad* and his *Political, Religious and Love Poems* later in 1899, so that the Society may begin 1900 with all its Texts in print.

February 1899. For this year the Original-Series Texts were issued in 1897. Those for 1900 are now ready. The texts of several other works are now printed.

For 1897, the Original-Series Texts are, No. 108, *Child-Marriages and Divorces, Trothplights, Adulteries, Affiliations, Libels, Wills, Miscellanea, Clandestine Marriages,* Depositions in Trials in the Bishop's Court, Chester, A.D. 1561-6, with *Entries from the Chester Mayors' Books,* 1558-1600, ed. Dr. F. J. Furnivall,—a most curious volume, full of the social life of its time;—and Part II of the *Prymer or Lay-Folks' Prayer-book,* edited by Mr. Henry Littlehales, with a Paper by Mr. Bishop on the Origin and Growth of the Prymer.

For 1897, the Extra-Series Texts are LXXI, *The Towneley Plays,* re-edited from the unique MS. by Mr. George England, with sidenotes and Introduction by Alfred W. Pollard, M.A.; LXXII, Hoccleve's *Regement of Princes,* A.D. 1411-12, with 14 *Minor Poems,* now first assigned to Hoccleve, from the DeGuilleville MS. Egerton 615, re-edited from the MSS. by Dr. Furnivall: the latter forms Part III of Hoccleve's Works; LXXIII, Part II of Hoccleve's Works is Hoccleve's *Minor Poems II,* from the Yates Thompson (late Ashburnham) MS., edited by Mr. Israel Gollancz, M.A. This last, the Editor promises forthwith.

The Original-Series Texts for 1898 are Nos. 110, 111,—Part II, Sections 1 and 2, of Dr. T. Miller's *Collations of Four MSS. of the Old-English Version of Bede's Ecclesiastical History.* Another Part will complete the work.

The Extra-Series Texts for 1898 are No. LXXIV, *Secreta Secretorum,* 3 prose Englishings, one by Jas. Yonge with interesting passages about Ireland, edited by Robert Steele, B.A., Part I; and No. LXXV, Miss Morrill's edition of the *Speculum Guidonis* in the Society's Guy-of-Warwick Series. (This latter book was priced only 10s. before its size was known.)

The Original-Series Texts for 1899 are No. 112, *Merlin,* Part IV, Prof. W. E. Mead's *Outlines of the Legend of Merlin,* with Glossary, &c., and No. 113, *Queen Elizabeth's Englishings of Boethius de Consolatione,* Plutarch's *De Curiositate,* and part of Horace, *De Arte Poetica,* edited from the unique MS. (a portion in the Queen's own hand) in the Public Record Office, London, by the late Miss C. Pemberton, with a Facsimile, and a note on the Queen's use of *i* for long *e*.

The Extra-Series Texts for 1899 ought to be the Second Part of the prose Romance of *Melusine*—Introduction, with ten facsimiles of the best woodblocks of the old foreign blackletter editions, Glossary, &c., by A. K. Donald, B.A., if he can be found; and a new edition of the famous Early-English Dictionary (English and Latin), *Promptorium Parvulorum,* from the Winchester MS., ab. 1440 A.D.: in this, the Editor, the Rev. A. L. Mayhew, M.A., will follow and print his MS. not only in its arrangement of nouns first, and verbs second, under every letter of the Alphabet, but also in its giving of the flexions of the words. The Society's edition will thus be the first modern one that really represents its original, a point on which Mr. Mayhew's insistance will meet with the sympathy of all our Members. But if neither of these Texts is forthcoming in 1899, the first Part of Lydgate's englisht *Pilgrimage of the Life of Man,* edited by Dr. F. J. Furnivall, and Miss Mary Bateson's edition of George Ashby's *Active Policy of a Prince,* and englisht *Dicta Philosophorum,* from the unique MS. A.D. 1463, will be substituted for them, and the others will be issued in 1900.

The Original-Series Texts for 1900 will be No. 114, Part IV (the last) of Prof. Skeat's edition of Aelfric's *Metrical Lives of Saints;* and No. 115, *Jacob's Well,* a quaint allegorical treatise on the cleansing and building-up of Man's Conscience, edited from the unique MS. in Salisbury Cathedral, by Dr. J. W. Brandeis, Part I.

The Extra-Series Texts for 1901 will be chosen from Mr. I. Gollancz's re-edition of two Alliterative Poems, *Winner and Waster,* &c., ab. 1360, just issued for the Roxburghe Club; Dr. Norman Moore's re-edition of *The Book of the Foundation of St. Bartholomew's Hospital, London,* from the unique MS. ab. 1425, which gives an account of the Founder, Rahere, and the miraculous cures wrought at the Hospital; or *The Craft of Nombrynge,* with other of the earliest englisht Treatises on Arithmetic, edited by R. Steele, B.A., or *Alexander Scott's Poems,* 1568, from the unique Edinburgh MS., ed. A. K. Donald, B.A.; or *The Sege of Jerusalem,* the alliterative version, edited by Prof. Dr. E. Kölbing.

An urgent appeal is hereby made to Members to increase the list of Subscribers to the E. E. Text Society. It is nothing less than a scandal that the Hellenic Society should have nearly 1000 members, while the Early English Text Society has only about 300!

4   *Texts preparing: The Extra Series for* 1901 & 1902.   *Deguilleville.*

The Original-Series Texts for 1901 and 1902 will be chosen from books already at press: Part II of the *Minor Poems of the Vernon MS.*, edited by Dr. F. J. Furnivall; Mr. Gollancz's re-edited *Exeter-Book*—Anglo-Saxon Poems from the unique MS. in Exeter Cathedral—Part II; Dr. Bruce's Introduction to *The English Conquest of Ireland*, Part II; Dr. Furnivall's edition of the *Lichfield Gilds*, which is all printed, and waits only for the Introduction, that Prof. E. C. K. Gonner has kindly undertaken to write for the book. Dr. G. Herzfeld's re-edition of the Anglo-Saxon *Martyrology* is all in type. Part II of Dr. Holthausen's *Vices and Virtues* needs only its Glossary.

The Texts for the Extra Series in 1901 and 1902 will be chosen from *The Three Kings' Sons*, Part II, the Introduction &c. by Prof. Dr. Leon Kellner; Part II of *The Chester Plays*, re-edited from the MSS., with a full collation of the formerly missing Devonshire MS., by Mr. G. England and Dr. Matthews; the Parallel-Text of the only two MSS. of the *Owl and Nightingale*, edited by Mr. G. F. H. Sykes (at press); Robert of Brunne's *Handlyng Synne*, edited by Dr. Furnivall; Deguilleville's *Pilgrimage of the Life of Man*, in English verse by Lydgate, Part II. (For the three prose versions—two English, one French—an Editor is wanted.) Members are askt to realise the fact that the Society has now 50 years' work on its Lists,—at its present rate of production,—and that there is from 100 to 200 more years' work to come after that. The year 2000 will not see finisht all the Texts that the Society ought to print. The need of more Members and money is urgent.

Before his death in 1895, Mr. G. N. Currie was preparing an edition of the 15th and 16th century Prose Versions of Guillaume de Deguilleville's *Pilgrimage of the Life of Man*, with the French prose version by Jean Gallopes, from Lord Aldenham's MS., he having generously promist to pay the extra cost of printing the French text, and engraving one or two of the illuminations in his MS. But Mr. Currie, when on his deathbed, charged a friend to burn *all* his MSS. which lay in a corner of his room, and unluckily all the E. E. T. S.'s copies of the Deguilleville prose versions were with them, and were burnt with them, so that the Society will be put to the cost of fresh copies, Mr. Currie having died in debt.

Guillaume de Deguilleville, monk of the Cistercian abbey of Chaalis, in the diocese of Senlis, wrote his first verse *Pelerinaige de l'Homme* in 1330-1 when he was 36.[1] Twenty-five (or six) years after, in 1355, he revised his poem, and issued a second version of it, and this is the only one that has been printed. Of the prose representative of the first version, 1330-1, a prose Englishing, about 1430 A.D., was edited by Mr. Aldis Wright for the Roxburghe Club in 1869, from MS. Ff. 5. 30 in the Cambridge University Library. Other copies of this prose English are in the Hunterian Museum, Glasgow, Q. 2. 25; Univ. Coll. and Corpus Christi, Oxford[2]; and the Laud Collection in the Bodleian, no. 740. A copy in the Northern dialect is MS. G. 21, in St. John's Coll., Cambridge, and this is the MS. which will be edited for the E. E. Text Society. The Laud MS. 740 was somewhat condenst and modernised, in the 17th century, into MS. Ff. 6. 30, in the Cambridge University Library:[3] "The Pilgrime or the Pilgrimage of Man in this World," copied by Will. Baspoole, whose copy "was verbatim written by Walter Parker, 1645, and from thence transcribed by G. G. 1649; and from thence by W. A. 1655." This last copy may have been read by, or its story reported to, Bunyan, and may have been the groundwork of his *Pilgrim's Progress*. It will be edited for the E. E. T. Soc., its text running under the earlier English, as in Mr. Herrtage's edition of the *Gesta Romanorum* for the Society. In February 1464,[4] Jean Gallopes—a clerk of Angers, afterwards chaplain to John, Duke of Bedford, Regent of France—turned Deguilleville's first verse *Pelerinaige* into a prose *Pelerinage de la vie humaine*.[5] By the kindness of Lord Aldenham, as above mentioned, Gallopes's French text will be printed opposite the early prose northern Englishing in the Society's edition.

The Second Version of Deguilleville's *Pelerinaige de l'Homme*, A.D. 1355 or -6, was englisht in verse by Lydgate in 1426. Of Lydgate's poem, the larger part is in the Cotton MS. Vitellius C. xiii (leaves 2-308). This MS. leaves out Chaucer's englishing of Deguilleville's *A B C* or *Prayer to the Virgin*, of which the successive stanzas start with A, B, C, and run all thro' the alphabet; and it has 2 main gaps, besides many small ones from the tops of leaves being burnt in the Cotton fire. All these gaps (save the A B C) will be fild up from the Stowe MS. 952 (which old John Stowe completed) and from the end of the other imperfect MS. Cotton, Tiberius A vii. Thanks to the diligence of the old Elizabethan tailor and manuscript-lover, a complete text of Lydgate's poem can be given. The British Museum French MSS. (Harleian 4399,[6] and Additional 22,937[7] and 25,594[8]) are all of the First Version.

---

[1] He was born about 1295. See Abbé GOUJET's *Bibliothèque française*, Vol. IX, p. 73-4.—P. M.
[2] These 3 MSS. have not yet been collated, but are believed to be all of the same version.
[3] Another MS. is in the Pepys Library.
[4] According to Lord Aldenham's MS.
[5] These were printed in France, late in the 15th or early in the 16th century.
[6] 15th cent., containing only the *Vie humaine*.
[7] 15th cent., containing all the 3 Pilgrimages, the 3rd being Jesus Christ's.
[8] 14th cent., containing the *Vie humaine* and the 2nd Pilgrimage, *de l'Ame*: both incomplete.

Besides his first *Pelerinaige de l'homme* in its two versions, Deguilleville wrote a second, "de l'ame separee du corps," and a third, "de nostre seigneur Iesus." Of the second, a prose Englishing of 1413, *The Pilgrimage of the Sowle* (with poems by Hoccleve, already printed for the Society with that author's *Regement of Princes*), exists in the Egerton MS. 615,[1] at Hatfield, Cambridge (Univ. Kk. 1. 7, and Caius), Oxford (Univ. Coll. and Corpus), and in Caxton's edition of 1483. This version has 'somewhat of addicions' as Caxton says, and some shortenings too, as the maker of both, the first translator, tells us in the MSS. Caxton leaves out the earlier englisher's interesting Epilog in the Egerton MS. This prose englishing of the *Sowle* will be edited for the Society by Prof. Dr. Leon Kellner after that of the *Man* is finisht, and will have Gallopes's French opposite it, from Lord Aldenham's MS., as his gift to the Society. Of the Pilgrimage of Jesus, no englishing is known.

As to the MS. Anglo-Saxon Psalters, Dr. Hy. Sweet has edited the oldest MS., the Vespasian, in his *Oldest English Texts* for the Society, and Mr. Harsley has edited the latest, c. 1150, Eadwine's Canterbury Psalter. The other MSS., except the Paris one, being interlinear versions,—some of the Roman-Latin redaction, and some of the Gallican,—Prof. Logeman has prepared for press, a Parallel-Text edition of the first twelve Psalms, to start the complete work. He will do his best to get the Paris Psalter—tho' it is not an interlinear one—into this collective edition; but the additional matter, especially in the Verse-Psalms, is very difficult to manage. If the Paris text cannot be parallelised, it will form a separate volume. The Early English Psalters are all independent versions, and will follow separately in due course.

Through the good offices of the Examiners, some of the books for the Early-English Examinations of the University of London will be chosen from the Society's publications, the Committee having undertaken to supply such books to students at a large reduction in price. The profits from these sales, after the payment of costs arising out of the issuing of such Texts to Students, will be applied to the Society's Reprints. Five of its 1866 Texts, and one of its 1867 (now at press), still need reproducing. Donations for this purpose will be welcome. They should be paid to the Hon. Sec., Mr. W. A. Dalziel, 67 Victoria Rd., Finsbury Park, London, N.

Members are reminded that *fresh Subscribers are always wanted*, and that the Committee can at any time, on short notice, send to press an additional Thousand Pounds' worth of work.

The Subscribers to the Original Series must be prepared for the issue of the whole of the Early English *Lives of Saints*, sooner or later. The Society cannot leave out any of them, even though some are dull. The Sinners would doubtless be much more interesting. But in many Saints' Lives will be found valuable incidental details of our forefathers' social state, and all are worthful for the history of our language. The Lives may be lookt on as the religious romances or story-books of their period.

The Standard Collection of Saints' Lives in the Corpus and Ashmole MSS., the Harleian MS. 2277, &c. will repeat the Laud set, our No. 87, with additions, and in right order. (The foundation MS. (Laud 108) had to be printed first, to prevent quite unwieldy collations.) The Supplementary Lives from the Vernon and other MSS. will form one or two separate volumes.

Besides the Saints' Lives, Trevisa's englishing of *Bartholomæus de Proprietatibus Rerum*, the mediæval Cyclopædia of Science, &c., will be the Society's next big undertaking. Dr. R. von Fleischhacker will edit it. Prof. Napier of Oxford, wishing to have the whole of our MS. Anglo-Saxon in type, and accessible to students, will edit for the Society all the unprinted and other Anglo-Saxon Homilies which are not included in Thorpe's edition of Ælfric's prose,[2] Dr. Morris's of the Blickling Homilies, and Prof. Skeat's of Ælfric's Metrical Homilies. Prof. Kölbing has also undertaken for the Society's Extra Series a Parallel-Text of all the six MSS. of the *Ancren Riwle*, one of the most important foundation-documents of Early English. Mr. Harvey, too, means to prepare an edition of the three MSS. of the *Earliest English Metrical Psalter*, one of which was edited by the late Mr. Stevenson for the Surtees Society.

In case more Texts are ready at any time than can be paid for by the current year's income, they will be dated the next year, and issued in advance to such Members as will pay advance subscriptions. The 1886-7 delay in getting out Texts must not occur again, if it can possibly be avoided. The Director has in hand for future volunteer Editors, copies of 2 or 3 MSS.

Members of the Society will learn with pleasure that its example has been followed, not only by the Old French Text Society which has done such admirable work under its founders Profs. Paul Meyer and Gaston Paris, but also by the Early Russian Text Society, which was set on foot in 1877, and has since issued many excellent editions of old MS. Chronicles &c.

---

[1] Ab. 1430, 106 leaves (leaf 1 of text wanting), with illuminations of nice little devils—red, green, tawny &c.—and damnd souls, fires, angels &c.
[2] Of these, Mr. Harsley is preparing a new edition, with collations of all the MSS. Many copies of Thorpe's book, not issued by the Ælfric Society, are still in stock.
Of the Vercell Homilies, the Society has bought the copy made by Prof. G. Lattanzi.

Members will also note with pleasure the annexation of large tracts of our Early English territory by the important German contingent under General Zupitza, Colonel Kölbing, volunteers Hausknecht, Einenkel, Haenisch, Kaluza, Hupe, Adam, Holthausen, Schick, Herzfeld, Brandeis, &c. Scandinavia has also sent us Prof. Erdmann; Holland, Prof. H. Logeman, who is now working in Belgium; France, Prof. Paul Meyer—with Gaston Paris as adviser; —Italy, Prof. Lattanzi; Hungary, Dr. von Fleischhacker; while America is represented by the late Prof. Child, by Dr. Mary Noyes Colvin, Profs. Mead, Perrin, McClintock, Triggs, &c. The sympathy, the ready help, which the Society's work has cald forth from the Continent and the United States, have been among the pleasantest experiences of the Society's life, a real aid and cheer amid all troubles and discouragements. All our Members are grateful for it, and recognise that the bond their work has woven between them and the lovers of language and antiquity across the seas is one of the most welcome results of the Society's efforts.

ORIGINAL SERIES.

Half the Publications for 1866 (13, 14, 15, 18, 22) are out of print, but will be gradually reprinted. Subscribers who desire the issue for 1866 should send their guineas at once to the Hon. Secretary, in order that other Texts for 1866 may be sent to press.

The *Publications for 1864-1897 (one guinea each year, save those for 1866 now half out of print, two guineas) are* :—

1. **Early English Alliterative Poems**, ab. 1360 A.D., ed. Rev. Dr. R. Morris. 16s. — 1864
2. **Arthur**, ab. 1440, ed. F. J. Furnivall, M.A. 4s. — ,,
3. **Lauder on the Dewtie of Kyngis**, &c., 1556, ed. F. Hall, D.C.L. 4s. — ,,
4. **Sir Gawayne and the Green Knight**, ab. 1360, ed. Rev. Dr. R. Morris. 10s. — ,,
5. **Hume's Orthographie and Congruitie of the Britan Tongue**, ab 1617, ed. H. B. Wheatley. 4s. — 1865
6. **Lancelot of the Laik**, ab. 1500, ed. Rev. W. W. Skeat. 8s — ,,
7. **Genesis & Exodus**, ab. 1250, ed. Rev. Dr. R. Morris. 8s. — ,,
8. **Morte Arthure**, ab. 1440, ed. E. Brock. 7s. — ,,
9. **Thynne on Speght's ed. of Chaucer**, A.D. 1599, ed. Dr. G. Kingsley and Dr. F. J. Furnivall. 10s. — ,,
10. **Merlin**, ab. 1440, Part I., ed. H. B. Wheatley. 2s. 6d. — ,,
11. **Lyndesay's Monarche**, &c., 1552, Part I., ed. J. Small, M.A. 3s. — ,,
12. **Wright's Chaste Wife**, ab. 1462, ed. F. J. Furnivall, M.A. 1s. — ,,
13. **Seinte Marherete**, 1200-1330, ed. Rev. O. Cockayne : to be re-edited by Dr. H. Spies, Ph.D. — 1866
14. **Kyng Horn, Floris and Blancheflour**, &c., ed. Rev. J. R. Lumby, B.D. — ,,
15. **Political, Religious, and Love Poems**, ed. F. J. Furnivall. — ,,
16. **The Book of Quinte Essence**, ab. 1460-70, ed. F. J. Furnivall. 1s. [*In print.*] — ,,
17. **Parallel Extracts from 45 MSS. of Piers the Plowman**, ed. Rev. W. W. Skeat. 1s. [*In print.*] — ,,
18. **Hali Meidenhad**, ab. 1200, ed. Rev. O. Cockayne. — ,,
19. **Lyndesay's Monarche**, &c., Part II., ed. J. Small, M.A. 3s. 6d. [*In print.*] — ,,
20. **Hampole's English Prose Treatises**, ed. Rev. G. G. Perry. 1s. [*In print.*] — ,,
21. **Merlin**, Part II., ed. H. B. Wheatley. 4s. [*In print.*] — ,,
22. **Partenay or Lusignen**, ed. Rev. W. W. Skeat. [*At Press.*] — ,,
23. **Dan Michel's Ayenbite of Inwyt**, 1340, ed. Rev. Dr. R. Morris. 10s. 6d. [*In print.*] — ,,
24. **Hymns to the Virgin and Christ; the Parliament of Devils**, &c., ab. 1430, ed. F. J. Furnivall. — 1867
25. **The Stacions of Rome, the Pilgrims' Sea-voyage, with Clene Maydenhod**, ed. F. J. Furnivall. 1s. — ,,
26. **Religious Pieces in Prose and Verse**, from R. Thornton's MS. (ab. 1440), ed. Rev. G. G. Perry. 2s. — ,,
27. **Levins's Manipulus Vocabulorum, a ryming Dictionary**, 1570, ed. H. B. Wheatley. 12s. — ,,
28. **William's Vision of Piers the Plowman**, 1362 A.D.; Text A, Part I., ed. Rev. W. W. Skeat. 6s. — ,,
29. **Old English Homilies** (ab. 1220-30 A.D.). Part I. Edited by Rev. Dr. R. Morris. 7s. — ,,
30. **Pierce the Ploughmans Crede**, ed. Rev. W. W. Skeat. — ,,
31. **Myrc's Duties of a Parish Priest, in Verse**, ab. 1420 A.D., ed. E. Peacock. 4s. — 1868
32. **Early English Meals and Manners : the Boke of Norture of John Russell, the Bokes of Keruynge, Curtasye, and Demeanor, the Babees Book, Urbanitatis**, &c., ed. F. J. Furnivall. 12s. — ,,
33. **The Knight de la Tour Landry**, ab. 1440 A.D. A Book for Daughters, ed. T. Wright, M.A. 8s. — ,,
34. **Old English Homilies** (before 1300 A.D.). Part II., ed. R. Morris, LL.D. 8s. — ,,
35. **Lyndesay's Works**, Part III. : The Historie and Testament of Squyer Meldrum, ed. F. Hall. 2s. — ,,
36. **Merlin**, Part III. Ed. H. B. Wheatley. On Arthurian Localities, by J. S. Stuart Glennie. 12s. — 1869
37. **Sir David Lyndesay's Works**, Part IV., Ane Satyre of the Three Estaits. Ed. F. Hall, D.C.L. 4s. — ,,
38. **William's Vision of Piers the Plowman**, Part II. Text B. Ed. Rev. W. W. Skeat, M.A. 10s. 6d. — ,,
39. **Alliterative Romance of the Destruction of Troy**. Ed. D. Donaldson & G. A. Panton. Pt. I. 10s. 6d. — ,,
40. **English Gilds, their Statutes and Customs**, 1389 A.D. Edit. Toulmin Smith and Lucy T. Smith, with an Essay on Gilds and Trades-Unions, by Dr. L. Brentano. 21s. — 1870
41. **William Lauder's Minor Poems**. Ed. F. J. Furnivall. 3s. — ,,
42. **Bernardus De Cura Rei Famuliaris, Early Scottish Prophecies**, &c. Ed. J. R. Lumby, M.A. 2s. — ,,
43. **Ratis Raving, and other Moral and Religious Pieces**. Ed. J. R. Lumby, M.A. 3s. — ,,

44. The Alliterative Romance of Joseph of Arimathie, or The Holy Grail: from the Vernon MS.; with W. de Worde's and Pynson's Lives of Joseph: ed. Rev. W. W. Skeat, M.A. 5s. 1871
45. King Alfred's West-Saxon Version of Gregory's Pastoral Care, edited from 2 MSS., with an English translation, by Henry Sweet, Esq., B.A., Balliol College, Oxford. Part I. 10s. ,,
46. Legends of the Holy Rood, Symbols of the Passion and Cross Poems, ed. Rev. Dr. R. Morris. 10s. ,,
47. Sir David Lyndesay's Works, Part V., ed. Dr. J. A. H. Murray. 3s. ,,
48. The Times' Whistle, and other Poems, by R. C., 1616; ed. by J. M. Cowper, Esq. 6s. ,,
49. An Old English Miscellany, containing a Bestiary, Kentish Sermons, Proverbs of Alfred, and Religious Poems of the 13th cent., ed. from the MSS. by the Rev. R. Morris, LL.D. 10s. 1872
50. King Alfred's West-Saxon Version of Gregory's Pastoral Care, ed. H. Sweet, M.A. Part II. 10s. ,,
51. The Life of St Juliana, 2 versions, A.D. 1230, with translations; ed. T. O. Cockayne & E. Brock. 2s. ,,
52. Palladius on Husbondrie, englisht (ab. 1420 A.D.), ed. Rev. Barton Lodge, M.A. Part I. 10s. ,,
53. Old-English Homilies, Series II., and three Hymns to the Virgin and God, 13th-century, with the music to two of them, in old and modern notation; ed. Rev. R. Morris, LL.D. 8s. 1873
54. The Vision of Piers Plowman, Text C: Richard the Redeles (by William, the author of the *Vision*) and The Crowned King; Part III., ed. Rev. W. W. Skeat, M.A. 18s. ,,
55. Generydes, a Romance, ab. 1440 A.D., ed. W. Aldis Wright, M.A. Part I. 3s. ,,
56. The Gest Hystoriale of the Destruction of Troy, in alliterative verse; ed. by D. Donaldson, Esq., and the late Rev. G. A. Panton. Part II. 10s. 6d. 1874
57. The Early English Version of the "Cursor Mundi"; in four Texts, edited by the Rev. R. Morris, M.A., LL.D. Part I, with 2 photolithographic facsimiles. 10s. 6d. ,,
58. The Blickling Homilies, 971 A.D., ed. Rev. R. Morris, LL.D. Part I. 8s. ,,
59. The "Cursor Mundi," in four Texts, ed. Rev. Dr. R. Morris. Part II. 15s. 1875
60. Meditacyuns on the Soper of our Lorde (by Robert of Brunne), edited by J. M. Cowper. 2s. 6d. ,,
61. The Romance and Prophecies of Thomas of Erceldoune, from 5 MSS.; ed. Dr. J. A. H. Murray. 10s. 6d. ,,
62. The "Cursor Mundi," in four Texts, ed. Rev. Dr. R. Morris. Part III. 15s. 1876
63. The Blickling Homilies, 971 A.D., ed. Rev. Dr. R. Morris. Part II. 7s. ,,
64. Francis Thynne's Embleames and Epigrams, A.D. 1600, ed. F. J. Furnivall. 7s. ,,
65. Be Domes Daege (Bede's *De Die Judicii*), &c., ed. J. R. Lumby, B.D. 2s. ,,
66. The "Cursor Mundi," in four Texts, ed. Rev. Dr. R. Morris. Part IV., with 2 autotypes. 10s. 1877
67. Notes on Piers Plowman, by the Rev. W. W. Skeat, M.A. Part I. 21s. ,,
68. The "Cursor Mundi," in 4 Texts, ed. Rev. Dr. R. Morris. Part V. 25s. 1878
69. Adam Davie's 5 Dreams about Edward II., &c., ed. F. J. Furnivall, M.A. 5s. ,,
70. Generydes, a Romance, ed. W. Aldis Wright, M.A. Part II. 4s. ,,
71. The Lay Folks Mass-Book, four texts, ed. Rev. Canon Simmons. 25s. 1879
72. Palladius on Husbondrie, englisht (ab. 1420 A.D.). Part II. Ed. S. J. Herrtage, B.A. 15s. ,,
73. The Blickling Homilies, 971 A.D., ed. Rev. Dr. R. Morris. Part III. 10s. 1880
74. English Works of Wyclif, hitherto unprinted, ed. F. D. Matthew, Esq. 20s. ,,
75. Catholicon Anglicum, an early English Dictionary, from Lord Monson's MS. A.D. 1483, ed., with Introduction & Notes, by S. J. Herrtage, B.A.; and with a Preface by H. B. Wheatley. 20s. 1881
76. Aelfric's Metrical Lives of Saints, in MS. Cott. Jul. E 7., ed. Rev. Prof. Skeat, M.A. Part I. 10s. ,,
77. Beowulf, the unique MS. autotyped and transliterated, edited by Prof. Zupitza, Ph.D. 25s. 1882
78. The Fifty Earliest English Wills, in the Court of Probate, 1387-1439, ed. by F. J. Furnivall, M.A. 7s. ,,
79. King Alfred's Orosius, from Lord Tollemache's 9th century MS., Part I, ed. H. Sweet, M.A. 13s. 1883
Extra Volume. Facsimile of the Epinal Glossary, 8th cent., ed. H. Sweet, M.A. 15s. ,,
80. The Early-English Life of St. Katherine and its Latin Original, ed. Dr. Einenkel. 12s. 1884
81. Piers Plowman: Notes, Glossary, &c. Part IV, completing the work, ed. Rev. Prof. Skeat, M.A. 18s. ,,
82. Aelfric's Metrical Lives of Saints, MS. Cott. Jul. E 7., ed. Rev. Prof. Skeat, M.A., LL.D. Part II. 12s. 1885
83. The Oldest English Texts, Charters, &c., ed. H. Sweet, M.A. 20s. ,,
84. Additional Analogs to 'The Wright's Chaste Wife,' No. 12, by W. A. Clouston. 1s. 1886
85. The Three Kings of Cologne. 2 English Texts, and 1 Latin, ed. Dr. C. Horstmann. 17s. ,,
86. Prose Lives of Women Saints, ab. 1610 A.D., ed. from the unique MS. by Dr. C. Horstmann. 12s. ,,
87. Early English Verse Lives of Saints (earliest version), Laud MS. 108, ed. Dr. C. Horstmann. 20s. 1887
88. Hy. Bradshaw's Life of St. Werburghe (Pynson, 1521), ed. Dr. C. Horstmann. 10s. ,,
89. Vices and Virtues, from the unique MS., ab. 1200 A.D., ed. Dr. F. Holthausen. Part I. 8s. 1888
90. Anglo-Saxon and Latin Rule of St. Benet, interlinear Glosses, ed. Dr. H. Logeman. 12s. ,,
91. Two Fifteenth-Century Cookery-Books, ab. 1430-1450, edited by Mr. T. Austin. 10s. ,,
92. Eadwine's Canterbury Psalter, from the Trin. Cambr. MS., ab. 1150 A.D., ed. F. Harsley, B.A. Pt. I. 12s. 1889
93. Defensor's Liber Scintillarum, edited from the MSS. by Ernest Rhodes, B.A. 12s. ,,
94. Aelfric's Metrical Lives of Saints, MS. Cott. Jul. E 7, Part III., ed. Prof. Skeat, Litt.D., LL.D. 12s. 1890
95. The Old-English version of Bede's Ecclesiastical History, re-ed. by Dr. Thomas Miller. Pt. I, § 1. 18s. ,, (With Reprints of No. 16, The Book of Quinte Essence, and No. 26, Religious Pieces, from R. Thornton's MS.)
96. The Old-English version of Bede's Ecclesiastical History, re-ed. by Dr. Thomas Miller. Pt. I, § 2. 15s. 1891
97. The Earliest English Prose Psalter, edited from its 2 MSS. by Dr. K. D. Buelbring. Part I. 15s. ,,
98. Minor Poems of the Vernon MS., Part I., ed. Dr. C. Horstmann. 20s. 1892
99. Cursor Mundi. Part VI. Preface, Notes, and Glossary, ed. Rev. Dr. R. Morris. 10s. ,,
100. Capgrave's Life of St. Katharine, ed. Dr. C. Horstmann, with Forewords by Dr. Furnivall. 20s. 1893
101. Cursor Mundi. Part VII. Essay on the MSS., their Dialects, &c., by Dr. H. Hupe. 10s. ,,

102. Lanfrank's Cirurgie, ab. 1400 A.D., ed. Dr. R. von Fleischhacker. Part I. 20s. — 1894
103. The Legend of the Cross, from a 12th century MS., &c., ed. Prof. A. S. Napier, M.A., Ph.D. 7s. 6d. ,,
104. The Exeter Book (Anglo-Saxon Poems), re-edited from the unique MS. by I. Gollancz, M.A. Part I. 20s. 1895
105. The Prymer or Lay-Folks' Prayer-Book, Camb. Univ. MS., ab. 1420, ed. Henry Littlehales. Part I. 10s. ,,
106. R. Misyn's Fire of Love and Mending of Life (Hampole), 1434, 1435, ed. Rev. R. Harvey, M.A. 15s. 1896
107. The English Conquest of Ireland, A.D. 1166-1185, 2 Texts, 1425, 1440, Pt. I., ed. Dr. Furnivall. 15s. ,,
108. Child-Marriages and -Divorces, Trothplights, &c. Chester Depositions, 1561-6, ed. Dr. Furnivall. 15s. 1897
109. The Prymer or Lay-Folks' Prayer-Book, ab. 1420, ed. Henry Littlehales. Part II. 10s. ,,
110. The Old-English Version of Bede's Ecclesiastical History, ed. Dr. T. Miller. Part II, § 1. 15s. 1898
111. The Old-English Version of Bede's Ecclesiastical History, ed. Dr. T. Miller. Part II, § 2. 15s. ,,
112. Merlin, Part IV: Outlines of the Legend of Merlin, by Prof. W. E. Mead, Ph.D. 15s. 1899
113. Queen Elizabethes Englishings of Boethius, Plutarch &c. &c., ed. Miss C. Pemberton. 15s. ,,
114. Aelfric's Metrical Lives of Saints, Part IV and last, ed. Prof. Skeat, Litt.D., LL.D. 15s. 1900
115. Jacob's Well, edited from the unique Salisbury Cathedral MS. by Dr. J. W. Brandeis. Part I. 15s. ,,

EXTRA SERIES.

The Publications for 1867-1895 (one guinea each year) are:—

I. William of Palerne; or, William and the Werwolf. Re-edited by Rev. W. W. Skeat, M.A. 13s. 1867
II. Early English Pronunciation with especial Reference to Shakspere and Chaucer, by A. J. Ellis, F.R.S. Part I. 10s. ,,
III. Caxton's Book of Curtesye, in Three Versions. Ed. F. J. Furnivall. 5s. 1868
IV. Havelok the Dane. Re-edited by the Rev. W. W. Skeat, M.A. 10s. ,,
V. Chaucer's Boethius. Edited from the two best MSS. by Rev. Dr. R. Morris. 12s. ,,
VI. Chevelere Assigne. Re-edited from the unique MS. by Lord Aldenham, M.A. 3s. ,,
VII. Early English Pronunciation, by A. J. Ellis, F.R.S. Part II. 10s. 1869
VIII. Queene Elizabethes Achademy, &c. Ed. F. J. Furnivall. Essays on early Italian and German Books of Courtesy, by W. M. Rossetti and Dr. E. Oswald. 13s. ,,
IX. Awdeley's Fraternitye of Vacabondes, Harman's Caveat, &c. Ed. E. Viles & F. J. Furnivall. 7s. 6d. ,,
X. Andrew Boorde's Introduction of Knowledge, 1547, Dyetary of Helth, 1542, Barnes in Defence of the Berde, 1542-3. Ed. F. J. Furnivall. 18s. 1870
XI. Barbour's Bruce, Part I. Ed. from MSS. and editions, by Rev. W. W. Skeat, M.A. 12s. ,,
XII. England in Henry VIII.'s Time: a Dialogue between Cardinal Pole & Lupset, by Thom. Starkey, Chaplain to Henry VIII. Ed. J. M. Cowper. Part II. 12s. (Part I. is No. XXXII, 1878, 8s.) 1871
XIII. A Supplicacyon of the Beggers, by Simon Fish, 1528-9 A.D., ed. F. J. Furnivall; with A Supplication to our Moste Soueraigne Lorde; A Supplication of the Poore Commons; and The Decaye of England by the Great Multitude of Sheep, ed. by J. M. Cowper, Esq. 6s. ,,
XIV. Early English Pronunciation, by A. J. Ellis, Esq., F.R.S. Part III. 10s. ,,
XV. Robert Crowley's Thirty-One Epigrams, Voyce of the Last Trumpet, Way to Wealth, &c., A.D. 1550-1, edited by J. M. Cowper, Esq. 12s. 1872
XVI. Chaucer's Treatise on the Astrolabe. Ed. Rev. W. W. Skeat, M.A. 6s. ,,
XVII. The Complaynt of Scotlande, 1549 A.D., with 4 Tracts (1542-48), ed. Dr. Murray. Part I. 10s. ,,
XVIII. The Complaynt of Scotlande, 1549 A.D., ed. Dr. Murray. Part II. 8s. 1873
XIX. Oure Ladyes Myroure, A.D. 1530, ed. Rev. J. H. Blunt, M.A. 24s. ,,
XX. Lonelich's History of the Holy Grail (ab. 1450 A.D.), ed. F. J. Furnivall, M.A., Ph.D. Part I. 8s. 1874
XXI. Barbour's Bruce, Part II., ed. Rev. W. W. Skeat, M.A. 4s. ,,
XXII. Henry Brinklow's Complaynt of Roderyck Mors (ab. 1542); and The Lamentacion of a Christian against the Citie of London, made by Roderigo Mors, A.D. 1545. Ed. J. M. Cowper. 9s. ,,
XXIII. Early English Pronunciation, by A. J. Ellis, F.R.S. Part IV. 10s. ,,
XXIV. Lonelich's History of the Holy Grail, ed. F. J. Furnivall, M.A., Ph.D. Part II. 10s. 1875
XXV. Guy of Warwick, 15th-century Version, ed. Prof. Zupitza. Part I. 20s. ,,
XXVI. Guy of Warwick, 15th-century Version, ed. Prof. Zupitza. Part II. 14s. 1876
XXVII. Bp. Fisher's English Works (died 1535), ed. by Prof. J. E. B. Mayor. Part I, the Text. 16s. ,,
XXVIII. Lonelich's Holy Grail, ed. F. J. Furnivall, M.A., Ph.D. Part III. 10s. 1877
XXIX. Barbour's Bruce. Part III., ed. Rev. W. W. Skeat, M.A. 21s. ,,
XXX. Lonelich's Holy Grail, ed. F. J. Furnivall, M.A., Ph.D. Part IV. 15s. 1878
XXXI. The Alliterative Romance of Alexander and Dindimus, ed. Rev. W. W. Skeat. 6s. ,,
XXXII. Starkey's "England in Henry VIII's time." Pt. I. Starkey's Life and Letters, ed. S. J. Herrtage. 8s. ,,
XXXIII. Gesta Romanorum (english ab. 1440), ed. S. J. Herrtage, B.A. 15s. 1879
XXXIV. The Charlemagne Romances:—1. Sir Ferumbras, from Ashm. MS. 33, ed. S. J. Herrtage. 15s. ,,
XXXV. Charlemagne Romances:—2. The Sege off Melayne, Sir Otuell, &c., ed. S. J. Herrtage. 12s. 1880
XXXVI. Charlemagne Romances:—3. Lyf of Charles the Grete, Pt. I., ed. S. J. Herrtage. 16s. ,,
XXXVII. Charlemagne Romances:—4. Lyf of Charles the Grete, Pt. II., ed. S. J. Herrtage. 15s. 1881
XXXVIII. Charlemagne Romances:—5. The Sowdone of Babylone, ed. Dr. Hausknecht. 15s. ,,

Works preparing for the " Early English Text Society." 9

XXXIX. Charlemagne Romances:—6. Rauf Colyear, Roland, Otuel, &c., ed. S. J. Herrtage, B.A. 15s. 1882
XL. Charlemagne Romances:—7. Huon of Burdeux, by Lord Berners, ed. S. L. Lee, B.A. Part I. 15s. ,,
XLI. Charlemagne Romances:—8. Huon of Burdeux, by Lord Berners, ed. S. L. Lee, B.A. Pt. II. 15s. 1883
XLII. Guy of Warwick: 2 texts (Auchinleck MS. and Caius MS.), ed. Prof. Zupitza. Part I. 15s. ,,
XLIII. Charlemagne Romances:—9. Huon of Burdeux, by Lord Berners, ed. S. L. Lee, B.A. Pt. III. 15s. 1884
XLIV. Charlemagne Romances:—10. The Four Sons of Aymon, ed. Miss Octavia Richardson. Pt. I. 15s. ,,
XLV. Charlemagne Romances:—11. The Four Sons of Aymon, ed. Miss O. Richardson. Pt. II. 20s. 1885
XLVI. Sir Bevis of Hamton, from the Auchinleck and other MSS., ed. Prof. E. Kölbing, Ph.D. Part I. 10s. ,,
XLVII. The Wars of Alexander, ed. Rev. Prof. Skeat, Litt.D., LL.D. 20s. 1886
XLVIII. Sir Bevis of Hamton, ed. Prof. E. Kölbing, Ph.D. Part II. 10s. ,,
XLIX. Guy of Warwick, 2 texts (Auchinleck and Caius MSS.), Pt. II., ed. Prof. J. Zupitza, Ph.D. 15s. 1887
L. Charlemagne Romances:—12. Huon of Burdeux, by Lord Berners, ed. S. L. Lee, B.A. Part IV. 5s. ,,
LI. Torrent of Portyngale, from the unique MS. in the Chetham Library, ed. E. Adam, Ph.D. 10s. ,,
LII. Bullein's Dialogue against the Feuer Pestilence, 1578 (ed. 1, 1564). Ed. M. & A. H. Bullen. 10s. 1888
LIII. Vicary's Anatomie of the Body of Man, 1548, ed. 1577, ed. F. J. & Percy Furnivall. Part I. 15s. ,,
LIV. Caxton's Englishing of Alain Chartier's Curial, ed. Dr. F. J. Furnivall & Prof. P. Meyer. 5s. ,,
LV. Barbour's Bruce, ed. Rev. Prof. Skeat, Litt.D., LL.D. Part IV. 5s. 1889
LVI. Early English Pronunciation, by A. J. Ellis, Esq., F.R.S. Pt. V., the present English Dialects. 25s. ,,
LVII. Caxton's Eneydos, A.D. 1490, coll. with its French, ed. M. T. Culley, M.A. & Dr. F. J. Furnivall. 13s. 1890
LVIII. Caxton's Blanchardyn & Eglantine, c. 1489, extracts from ed. 1595, & French, ed. Dr. L. Kellner. 17s. ,,
LIX. Guy of Warwick, 2 texts (Auchinleck and Caius MSS.), Part III., ed. Prof. J. Zupitza, Ph.D. 15s. 1891
LX. Lydgate's Temple of Glass, re-edited from the MSS. by Dr. J. Schick. 15s. ,,
LXI. Hoccleve's Minor Poems, I., from the Phillipps and Durham MSS., ed. F. J. Furnivall, Ph.D. 15s. 1892
LXII. The Chester Plays, re-edited from the MSS. by the late Dr. Hermann Deimling. Part I. 15s. ,,
LXIII. Thomas a Kempis's De Imitatione Christi, englisht ab. 1440, & 1502, ed. Prof. J. K. Ingram. 15s. 1893
LXIV. Caxton's Godfrey of Boloyne, or Last Siege of Jerusalem, 1481, ed. Dr. Mary N. Colvin. 15s. ,,
LXV. Sir Bevis of Hamton, ed. Prof. E. Kölbing, Ph.D. Part III. 15s. 1894
LXVI. Lydgate's and Burgh's Secrees of Philisoffres. ab. 1445—50, ed. R. Steele, B.A. 15s. ,,
LXVII. The Three Kings' Sons, a Romance, ab. 1500, Part I., the Text, ed. Dr. Furnivall. 10s. 1895
LXVIII. Melusine, the prose Romance, ab. 1500, Part I, the Text, ed. A. K. Donald. 20s. ,,
LXIX. Lydgate's Assembly of the Gods, ed. Prof. Oscar L. Triggs, M.A., Ph.D. 15s. 1896
LXX. The Digby Plays, edited by Dr. F. J. Furnivall. 15s. ,,
LXXI. The Towneley Plays, ed. Geo. England and A. W. Pollard, M.A. 15s. 1897
LXXII. Hoccleve's Regement of Princes, 1411-12, and 14 Poems, edited by Dr. F. J. Furnivall. 15s. ,,
LXXIII. Hoccleve's Minor Poems, II., from the Ashburnham MS., ed. I. Gollancz, M.A. [*At Press.* ,,
LXXIV. Secreta Secretorum, 3 prose Englishings, by Jas. Yonge, 1428, ed. R. Steele, B.A. Part I. 20s. 1898
LXXV. Speculum Guidonis de Warwyk, edited by Miss R. L. Morrill, M.A., Ph.D. 10s. ,,
LXXVI. Lydgate's DeGuilleville's Pilgrimage of the Life of Man, 1426, ed. Dr. F. J. Furnivall. Part I. 15s. 1899
LXXVII. George Ashby's Active Policy of a Prince, &c., ed. Miss Mary Bateson. 15s. ,,
? Melusine, the Prose Romance, ab. 1500, Part II., Introduction by A. K. Donald. 10s. 1900
? Promptorium Parvulorum, c. 1440, from the Winchester MS., ed. Rev. A. L. Mayhew, M.A. Part I. 20s. ,,

EARLY ENGLISH TEXT SOCIETY TEXTS PREPARING.

Besides the Texts named as at press on p. 12 of the Cover of the Early English Text Society's last books, the following Texts are also slowly preparing for the Society:—

ORIGINAL SERIES.

Thomas Robinson's Life and Death of Mary Magdalene, from the 2 MSS. ab. 1620 A.D. (*Text in type.*)
The Earliest English Prose Psalter, ed. Dr. K. D. Buelbring. Part II.
The Earliest English Verse Psalter, 3 texts, ed. Rev. R. Harvey, M.A.
Anglo-Saxon Poems, from the Vercelli MS., re-edited by I. Gollancz, M.A.
Anglo-Saxon Glosses to Latin Prayers and Hymns, edited by Dr. F. Holthausen.
Aelfric's Metrical Lives of Saints, MS. Cott. Jul. E 7, Part IV, ed. Prof. Skeat, Litt.D., LL.D.
All the Anglo-Saxon Homilies and Lives of Saints not accessible in English editions, including those of the Vercelli MS. &c., edited by Prof. Napier, M.A., Ph.D.
The Anglo-Saxon Psalms; all the MSS. in Parallel Texts, ed. Dr. H. Logeman and F. Harsley, B.A.
Beowulf, a critical Text, &c., edited by a Pupil of the late Prof. Zupitza, Ph.D.
Byrhtferth's Handboc, edited by Prof. G. Hempl.
The Rule of St. Benet: 5 Texts, Anglo-Saxon, Early English, Caxton, &c. (*Editor wanted.*)
The Seven Sages, in the Northern Dialect, from a Cotton MS., edited by Dr. Squires.
The Master of the Game, a Book of Huntynge for Hen. V. when Prince of Wales. (*Editor wanted.*)
Ailred's Rule of Nuns, &c., edited from the Vernon MS., by the Rev. Canon H. R. Bramley, M.A.
Lonelich's Merlin (verse), from the unique MS., ed. by Prof. E. Kölbing, Ph.D.
Early English Verse Lives of Saints, Standard Collection, from the Harl. MS.
Early English Confessionals, edited by Dr. R. von Fleischhacker.
A Lapidary, from Lord Tollemache's MS., &c., edited by Dr. R. von Fleischhacker.

Early English Deeds and Documents, from unique MSS., ed. Dr. Lorenz Morsbach.
Gilbert Banastre's Poems, and other Boccaccio englishings, ed. by a pupil of the late Prof. J. Zupitza, Ph.D.
Lanfranc's Cirurgie, ab. 1400 A.D., ed. Dr. R. von Fleischhacker, Part II.
William of Nassington's Mirror of Life, from Jn. of Waldby, edited by J. T. Herbert, M.A.
A Chronicle of England to 1327 A.D., Northern verse (42,000 lines), ab. 1400 A.D., ed. M. L. Perrin, B.A.
More Early English Wills from the Probate Registry at Somerset House. (*Editor Wanted.*)
Early Lincoln Wills and Documents from the Bishops' Registers, &c., edited by Dr. F. J. Furnivall.
Early Canterbury Wills, edited by William Cowper, B.A., and J. Meadows Cowper.
Early Norwich Wills, edited by Walter Rye, and F. J. Furnivall.
The Cartularies of Oseney Abbey and Godstow Nunnery, englisht ab. 1450, ed. Rev. A Clark, M.A.
The Macro Moralities, edited from Mr. Gurney's unique MS., by Alfred W. Pollard, M.A.
A Troy-Book, edited from the unique Laud MS. 595, by Dr. E. Wülfing.
Alliterative Prophecies, edited from the MSS. by Prof. Brandl, Ph. D.
Miscellaneous Alliterative Poems, edited from the MSS. by Dr. L. Morsbach.
Bird and Beast Poems, a collection from MSS., edited by Dr. K. D. Buelbring.
Scire Mori, &c., from the Lichfield MS. 16, ed. Mrs. L. Grindon, LL.A., and Miss Florence Gilbert.
Nicholas Trivet's French Chronicle, from Sir A. Acland-Hood's unique MS., ed. by Miss Mary Bateson.
Stories for Sermons, edited from the Addit. MS. 25,719 by Dr. Wieck of Coblentz.
Early English Homilies in Harl. 2276 &c., c. 1400, ed. J. Friedländer.
Extracts from the Registers of Boughton, ed. Hy. Littlehales, Esq.
The Diary of Prior Moore of Worcester, A.D. 1518-35, from the unique MS., ed. Henry Littlehales, Esq.
The Pore Caitif, edited from its MSS., by Mr. Peake.

EXTRA SERIES.

Bp. Fisher's English Works, Pt. II., with his Life and Letters, ed. Rev. Ronald Bayne, B.A. [*At Press.*
John of Arderne's Surgery, c. 1425, ed. J. F. Payne, M.D., and W. Anderson, F.R.C.S.
De Guilleville's Pilgrimage of the Sowle, edited by Prof. Dr. Leon Kellner.
Vicary's Anatomie, 1548, from the unique MS. copy by George Jeans, edited by F. J. & Percy Furnivall.
Vicary's Anatomie, 1548, ed. 1577, edited by F. J. & Percy Furnivall. Part II. [*At Press.*
A Compilacion of Surgerye, from H. de Mandeville and Lanfrank, A.D. 1392, ed. Dr. J. F. Payne.
William Staunton's St. Patrick's Purgatory, &c., ed. Mr. G. P. Krapp, U.S.A.
A Parallel-text of the 6 MSS. of the Ancren Riwle, ed. Prof. Dr. E. Kölbing.
Trevisa's Bartholomæus de Proprietatibus Rerum, re-edited by Dr. R. von Fleischhacker.
Bullein's Dialogue against the Feuer Pestilence, 1564, 1573, 1578. Ed. A. H. and M. Bullen. Pt. II.
The Romance of Boctus and Sidrac, edited from the MSS. by Dr. K. D. Buelbring.
The Romance of Clariodus, re-edited by Dr. K. D. Buelbring.
Sir Amadas, re-edited from the MSS. by Dr. K. D. Buelbring.
Sir Degrevant, edited from the MSS. by Dr. K. Luick.
Robert of Brunne's Chronicle of England, from the Inner Temple MS., ed. by Prof. W. E. Mead, Ph.D.
Maundeville's Voiage and Travaile, re-edited from the Cotton MS. Titus C. 16, &c., by Miss M. Bateson.
Avowynge of Arthur, re-edited from the unique Ireland MS. by Dr. K. D. Buelbring.
Guy of Warwick, Copland's version, edited by a pupil of the late Prof. Zupitza, Ph.D.
Liber Fundacionis Ecclesie Sancti Bartholomei Londoniarum : onglisht ab. 1425, ed. Norman Moore, M.D.
Awdelay's Poems, re-edited from the unique MS. Douce 302, by Dr. E. Wülfing.
William of Shoreham's Works, re-edited by Professor Konrath, Ph.D.
The Wyse Chylde and other early Treatises on Education, Northwich School, Harl. 2099 &c., ed. G. Collar, B.A.
Caxton's Dictes and Sayengis of Philosophirs, 1477, with Lord Tollemache's MS. version, ed. S. I. Butler, Esq.
Caxton's Book of the Ordre of Chyualry, collated with Loutfut's Scotch copy, ed. F. S. Ellis, Esq.
Lydgate's Court of Sapience, edited by Dr. Borsdorf.
Lydgate's Lyfe of oure Lady, ed. by Prof. Georg Fiedler, Ph.D.
Lydgate's Reason and Sensuality, englisht from the French, edited by Dr. Sieper.
Lydgate's Dance of Death, edited by Miss Florence Warren.
Lydgate's Life of St. Edmund, edited from the MSS. by Dr. Axel Erdmann.
Richard Cœr de Lion, re-edited from Harl. MS. 4690, by Prof. Hausknecht, Ph.D.
The Romance of Athelstan, re-edited by a pupil of the late Prof. J. Zupitza, Ph.D.
The Romance of Sir Degare, re-edited by Dr. Breul.
Mulcaster's Positions 1581, and Elementarie 1582, ed. Dr. Th. Klaehr, Dresden.
Caxton's Recuyell of the Histories of Troye, edited by H. Halliday Sparling.
Walton's verse Boethius de Consolatione, edited by Mark H. Liddell, U. S. A.
The Gospel of Nichodemus, edited by Ernest Riedel.

The Society is anxious to hear of more early Dialect MSS. John Lacy's copy, in the Newcastle-on-Tyne dialect, 1434, of some theological tracts in MS. 94 of St. John's College, Oxford, is to be edited by Prof. McClintock. More Hampoles in the Yorkshire dialect will probably follow. The Lincoln and Norfolk Wills, already copied by or for Dr. Furnivall, unluckily show but little traces of dialect.

More members (to bring money) and Editors (to bring brains) are wanted by the Society.

Speculum Gy de Warewyke.

Early English Text Society.

Extra Series, LXXV.

1898.

Speculum Gy de Warewyke

An English Poem

WITH INTRODUCTION, NOTES, AND GLOSSARY

HERE FOR THE FIRST TIME PRINTED
AND FIRST EDITED FROM THE MANUSCRIPTS

BY

GEORGIANA LEA MORRILL, A.M., Ph.D.

LONDON:
PUBLISHT FOR THE EARLY ENGLISH TEXT SOCIETY
BY KEGAN PAUL, TRENCH, TRÜBNER & CO.,
PATERNOSTER HOUSE, CHARING-CROSS ROAD.
1898.

Extra Series, LXXV.

R. CLAY & SONS, LIMITED, LONDON & BUNGAY.

To the Memory of
Professor Julius Zupitza
and to
Professor Eugen Kölbing
GRATEFULLY DEDICATED

TABLE OF CONTENTS

	PAGE
PREFATORY NOTE	ix

INTRODUCTION

PART I.

CHAPTER I.	THE GUY SAGA AS ADAPTED TO THE SPECULUM ...	xiii
,, II.	TITLE AND LITERARY NOTICES OF THE POEM ...	xviii
,, III.	DESCRIPTION OF THE MANUSCRIPTS	xxvii
,, IV.	GENEALOGICAL HISTORY OF THE TEXTS ...	xl
,, V.	PRINCIPLES UNDERLYING THE EDITION ...	lviii

PART II.

,, VI.	THE RELATION OF THE SPECULUM TO THE GUY OF WARWICK ROMANCES	lxv
,, VII.	CONCERNING GUY, EARL OF WARWICK	lxxiv
,, VIII.	GUIDO, COUNT OF TOURS	lxxxiii
,, IX.	PRINCIPAL SOURCES OF THE SPECULUM ...	xciii
,, X.	MINOR SOURCES OF THE POEM	cxiv

PART III.

,, XI.	THE METRICAL STRUCTURE OF THE SPECULUM ...	cxxv
,, XII.	THE RIMING STRUCTURE OF THE SPECULUM ...	cxliii
,, XIII.	THE PHONOLOGY OF THE SPECULUM	cxlix
,, XIV.	THE INFLECTION OF THE SPECULUM	clxix
,, XV.	DIALECT AND CHRONOLOGY OF THE SPECULUM	clxxxiv
,, XVI.	AUTHORSHIP OF THE SPECULUM	cxcii

SPECULUM GY DE WAREWYKE

TEXT	3
CRITICAL AND EXPLANATORY NOTES	47
EDITIONS OF MIDDLE ENGLISH TEXTS	103
GLOSSARY	105
INDEX OF PROPER NAMES	116

PREFATORY NOTE

THE following edition of the *Speculum Gy de Warewyke* is indebted for its origin to the kindness of the late Professor Julius Zupitza. The preparation of the volume was begun under Professor Zupitza's immediate direction and personal guidance and was interrupted only by his sad and unexpected death. The name Zupitza, to-day at once an inspiration and a lament, recalls a central figure in English scholarship. Whatever is of worth in these pages, should reverently and gratefully bear tribute to connection with the master student.

The text of the poem has been carefully arranged from six manuscripts on basis of the Auchinleck MS. and was printed in May 1896, an edition having been already completed in German and in English. In harmony with the suggestion of Dr. Furnivall, the work does not present a distinctively critical text, but it aims to mark fidelity to its original, and to avoid arbitrary changes by which a picturesque meaning would be lost or an interesting philological form obscured. Full material for such a text, subject to the judgment of the individual student, is offered in the decisive readings of the various manuscripts of the *Speculum* and in its critical notes. The arrangement of the Introduction needs no explanation. It will be seen that Part I contains a description of the manuscripts of the poem and a critical investigation of its texts. Part II is limited to the examination of its sources and its genesis with reference to history and literature, and particularly to the Guy of Warwick romances. Part III treats of the language, and the metrical and inflectional forms used by the poet, his dialect, and the chronology and authorship of the poem.

It is recognized, that in some decisions there is ground for other opinions than those adopted in these pages. I am aware that there are three readings of no great importance, that might contradict the pedigree of the manuscripts as it stands at present. The question is open to the friendly opinion of the public. The peculiarly individual development of each of the texts has rendered the arrangement of the genealogical tables one of marked delicacy. Some points could have been discussed more briefly than I have judged[1] advisable. Others could have been treated with greater fulness. The enumeration of the Biblical sources of the various passages is not complete, but has received additional references in the explanatory notes. The chapter on inflection could have been enriched by other appropriate illustrations, the phonology with more complete comparison with other M.E. texts, and the analysis of the relationship of the various Guy of Warwick manuscripts could have been more exhaustive, but additional expansion was believed to be beyond the scope of the volume. The present edition seems to set forth the main peculiarities of the poem.

Adequate recognition will, it is trusted, be conceded the *Speculum*, not merely through reverence for antiquity and susceptibility to romance, but through an instinct for the preservation of what is in itself of individual merit. The poem, a quaint conceit of an author of the M.E. period, has an æsthetic value, preserving traces of the *naïve* vigour of pre-conquest literature, and reflecting the culture of the mediæval poet. It is a fair example of the homily of the thirteenth century and gives testimony to the theological status of that period of English life; but, in general tendency, incorporating an episode in the career of the marvellous hero of Warwick, it links itself with the metrical romance. Its text possesses philological interest in its vocabulary through the introduction of rare words, and through its phonology as marked in its rime. The volume opens to the public for the first time manuscripts of unique interest.

I have here to thank the friends[2] of the *Speculum*—among them the most distinguished scholars of the day—for the unselfish interest with which this edition has been favoured. Although foreshadowed by calamity in the loss of Professor Zupitza's genial counsel, my book has matured in auspicious atmosphere through the helpfulness of Professor Kölbing. Professor Kölbing's generosity placed before me his exact and beautiful *fac simile* of one of my texts,[3] when

---

[1] Some allowance must be made for the difficulty of transferring this work from the German edition. Traces of German training, chiefly at the University of Berlin, must be attributed to their proper source.

[2] Thanks are due to the skill and patience of the printers, Messrs. Richard Clay and Sons, and particularly the kindness of Mr. Archibald of their office, for careful execution of trying work.

[3] This edition has been prepared from the MSS. as consulted by the editor.

access to the original was impossible. Putting aside more important work of his own, he showed me the great kindness of reading most carefully many pages of my proof, and he has aided me from the earliest beginning of my work with judicious suggestions, marking the excellence of his skilful and varied scholarship. I have also had the advantage of consultation with Mr. Donald of Gray's Inn. I am deeply indebted for clerical and other service rendered by Mr. Donald. Mention should be made of Zupitza's pupil, Professor Schick, to whom, in April 1894, the interests of my work were intrusted. Traces of Professor Schick's influence, direct and indirect, will be recognized in the Introduction and in the arrangement of the text. I share with all students of English the debt to Professor Wülker and Professor Sievers through their noble contributions[1] to philological investigation, but my obligation is enhanced by the benefit of direct instruction in lecture hall. I am grateful for a few valuable words from Dr. Furnivall, Mr. Henry Bradley, and my earlier critic, Mrs. Truman J. Backus.

Gratitude is to be extended for the courtesy of the officers and attendants in the various libraries[2] where I have had the pleasure of study upon the *Speculum*. I wish to express my obligation to Mr. Bickley and Mr. Herbert of the British Museum, for aid in determining the age of the manuscripts and for other assistance; to Mr. Clark of the Advocates' Library, Edinburgh; and to the librarian of the Princeton University Library, Dr. Richardson, editor of *Liber De Viris Inlustribus*.

I am indebted to Professor J. Ulrich of the University of Zürich, who, having announced[3] in *Englische Studien* his intention of publishing this text from the MSS., yielded in my favour any prior claim to editorship.

GEORGIANA LEA MORRILL.

London, *May 1896*.

[1] The editor is indebted to the valuable works of Professor Skeat, Mr. Gollancz, and Professor Morsbach, editions of special importance to the student of this period of English literary history, and expresses thanks to Miss Edith Luther for kind interest in the *Speculum*.
[2] Here are to be included the *Königliche Bibliothek*, Berlin, the University Library, Cambridge, England, the Library of the Lambeth Palace, and the Astor Library and the Columbia University Library, New York City.
[3] In *Englische Studien*, vol. vii, p. 183.

[The editor begs to state, that a single text of the six employed in the *Speculum Gy de Warewyke* appeared in Horstmann's *Yorkshire Writers*, Vol. II, after the preparation of this edition had been completed, and after the present text had been printed. She believes it to be unnecessary to add, that, on the authority of the most eminent critics, the print of one manuscript alone without reference to the oldest and best transcript is of comparatively small value. Owing to circumstances for which neither editor nor publisher is responsible, interruption of nearly two years occurred in work upon the *Speculum*, after the edition was at press. The volume has been otherwise retarded by the author's absence in America during the printing of the book.]

INTRODUCTION TO THE *SPECULUM*

"sothe stories ben stoken vp and straught out of mynde
and swolowet into swym by swiftenes of yeres.

. . . olde stories of stithe, þat astate helde,
may be solas to sum . . . .

. . . . þat suet after,
to ken all the crafte, how þe case felle,
by lokying of letturs, þat lefte were of olde."[1]

Part I.

CHAPTER I.

THE GUY OF WARWICK SAGA AS ADAPTED TO THE *SPECULUM.*

§ 1. *The Argument of the Main Guy Legend.*

The history of Guy the Earl, in whom the romance and the chivalric glory of Warwick early came to the distinction of letters, has never been fully made clear. His conquests have been magnificently immortalized in verse and tale, and his exploits have become so intimately the poetical treasure[2] of centuries, that the immediate and objective facts of his achievement have been obliterated, and the traces of his true development have been concealed. Yet the documents preserving the incidents of his career have been scrutinized by critics so keen and so illustrious, that to say of Guy of Warwick what is unique and unexpected seems not possible. The tradition marking his romantic life is assimilated with landscape[3] and history in name and event, so that an impression of actual presence is firmly engendered, and to the visitor of modern Warwick Guy is invested with the same proud claim to English fatherhood that is the inheritance of that bright English gem Sidney. To doubt the

---

[1] From the *Destruction of Troy*, verses 11, 12, and 21 ff.
[2] The most exquisite of parchment folios preserve the history of Guy. Incrusted with gorgeous illumination, the Guy documents are in themselves a priceless treasure, as is assured by those of the Royal Library alone.
[3] "On a ryuere syde hys hows he hadde
   (A full holy lyff he there ladde)
   Besydes Warwyke, þat was hys,
   And Gybbe clyf clepyd ys."—Auch. 22, v. 10,527 ff.

genuineness of Guy's adventures impresses one as involving a suggestion of insincerity. The discovery of decisive facts might add to the interest of the romance, localizing current theories in clear-cut environment, but it could not modify the sentiment emanating from Guy the hero. In publishing pseudo-Guy manuscript the *Speculum* deals with fresh material and endeavours to establish the reality of much-debated tradition, but it does not succeed in enlarging the probability of the tale. The Guy history must be regarded as an exotic from the misty shadow-land[1] of fairy knighthood. Guy is the Prince of Romance, brave, strong, beautiful.

In the memory of the people the main current of history was of striking importance. Influenced by the barbaric splendour of the mediæval epic, the conspicuous element in Guy's career centered in warfare. To the English folk of the thirteenth century, as no doubt to their fathers of a more remote period, Guy was known as the conqueror of giant and Saracen, the slayer of boar and dragon. He was famed for romantic connection with the estate of the hereditary Earl of Warwick, and for valiant adventure far from his birthplace. He suddenly appeared in Winchester, found England in extraordinary political condition, and restored civil authority to its earlier vigour. The English, helpless and passive under a foreign enemy, elected Guy leader and gave battle to returning adversaries. The knight single-handed commanded a British victory. Weak points of this conception of Guy were detected, and a later growth presented the legend in a new aspect in English life.

The after-glow in the tradition is the reflection of letters, not the "twilight of ancient memory." A touch of the fanciful illuminates the saga. Not the hero but the heroine becomes the central luminary. Felice, the gracious lady of knighthood, one of the earliest of mediæval women and one of the most lovely, gives character to the narrative. Guy, the subordinate figure, establishes his constancy to Felice by submission. He voluntarily accepts exile, and masks himself as ally to the oppressed. This episode marks "tragic night" for Guy and Felice, the "struggle of might and beauty" in a "world of adversity." In another sense it ushers in the dawn of modern literature[2] in England. These primitive germs have been circulated

---

[1] Cf. Mr. Jacobs's interpretation in the introduction to *Old French Romances*.
[2] The history was "reprinted at the Renaissance, read under Elizabeth," and plays taken from it "supplied matter for popular *Chap Books*, written for the love of the people of merry England."—Jusserand, *A Literary History of the English People*.

under the name Guy. The early Guy poetry continued to be in favour through adaptations emanating from the original names, and ultimately the evolution of a Guy fiction proceeded in prose rather than in verse. Prose writers obtained for Guy the qualities predominant in the novel, or the elements of a genuine tragedy.

A half light of ecclesiastical feeling touches the legend. Guy, the sovereign representative of honour and chivalry, is also the obedient servant of the church. The influence of mediæval Christianity is active, prescribing penitence and penance as atonement for sin. In this influence the province of the *Speculum* is to be accorded. The poem reflects the most charming elements of the main tradition, the religious and the romantic as emanating from Felice. It turns a hallowed religious light on the storied regions of beautiful Warwickshire; it transfigures with a fine spirit of devotion any harshness attending the history of Felice; and, while seeming to encroach upon a distinctly Zupitza province,—for Zupitza's service is almost inseparable from the Guy of Warwick texts,—it exists as an independent literary product. The reader will be stimulated to analyze the relationship of the *Speculum* to the main legend from study of the argument and purpose of the poet as sketched in the following section.

§ 2. *The Motif of the Speculum.*

"See where he rides, our Knight!
Within his eyes the light
Of battle, and youth's gold about his brow."

The *Speculum* presents its hero to the reader at the very point at which the attractiveness of his history culminates. Here Guy's character, a beacon shining at the opening of a national literature, would embody all that is lofty in generous purity and patriotism. In this attitude alone is he designated in the *Speculum*. All dull experiences and all tedious accessories[1] are banished; the *Speculum* exists only as exponent of romantic and chivalric charm. A few words summon its bright picture.

In time of Æthelstan of England a gentle lady, Felice, lived at the castle of Warwick. Guy, enraptured with this sweetest vision, fostered a hope that he might for her sake make chivalric vow of eternal fealty. He pondered in his heart how he could find deeds of greatest prowess With devout prayer, guided by the idealized vision of his lady, Guy rode forth in dauntless courage to deed and

---

[1] See ten Brink, *Eng. Lit.*, vol. i., pp. 246, 247.

to warfare. He did not cease to seek a chance to win a royal accolade. And when the hour of battle came, the sword was drawn in brave fight, and the foe was brought to naught in manful battle. God that guideth all kept Guy in safety, and granted him victory.

The months passed on; Guy's journey was perilous; giants, dragons, and a Saracen host fell in his way. Still his heart did not fail. Felice was ever before him. His bed, a cold stone, was to him the soft and dewy grass. Sleet and snow were the sweet and tender winds; heavy skies, the sunny Maytime. Guy kept faith with devout prayer, and honour came; fair ladies courted his smile; wealth was added to him, the lordship of distant lands, and by the will of God Guy became the most faultless hero of all the earth.

In great joyance he went to England and held bridal with Felice within the castellated walls of Warwick. Title and honour through God of grace descended to Guy, and the days passed merrily. Then it seemed that earth's blisses were complete.

Forty happy days[1] passed; Guy lived joyously with Felice. Then his heart saddened: he recalled the homes darkened, the thousands sleeping in death through his aspiration for honour and for empty title. Remorse gnawed his soul. Repentance and confession alone would atone for this bloody past. Guy had never spared one minute for his soul's health. Sacrifice must compensate for dreadful slaughter. A brief parting from Felice, a farewell to castle tower and to home, and Guy again wandered forth. His robe was grey. He wore a pilgrim's garb. No glittering sword was at his side. With bent head he left home and fatherland. He would visit the sepulchre of Him who parted with life for sinful man's resurrection. Guy forsook the world and served God ever more (*Speculum*, verses 27—36). He lived all in God's law (v. 38). Meanwhile Felice at home sorrowed comfortless. She found consolation only in Divine meditation and in prayer. She daily fed the poor.

Guy in his stern zeal seeks[2] spiritual counsel (*Speculum*, verses 45—64). He turns to Alquin (46—48), Dean of a brotherhood, who led his life in holiness (39—42), and asks counsel to free his soul from the world's guile (52—64). Alquin in joy praises Christ (65—67), grants Guy's prayer, and as spiritual guide shows moral qualities to be discriminated (68—80). The friar-hermit teaches

[1] The length of the period in number of days varies in different accounts.
[2] The transition to the present tense occurs in these paragraphs through the deliberate purpose of the editor.

how to shun the world that "is too much with us." He classifies the virtues and the vices upon well-known standards (81—136) and unfolds a discourse, whose theological tenets will obtain permit to heaven. The knight is directed as to the means of acquiring true wisdom through the saving grace of pain (137—198). His creed is outlined, and he is instructed through reverence to quell rebellious disobedience (199—250). Guy's incentive to endeavour is offered in a picture of the dreadful hour of doom (250—284). Encouragement is bestowed in promises of heaven-bliss; for it is not God's fault, if man commit sin (285—322).

Charity, love to man, is depicted as a prudential motive to the rapture of seeing the eternal God (323—346), an experience already rejoiced in by Abraham and by Moses (347—368), and by other saintly spirits (369—400). The peacefulness of a pure life is contrasted with the terrors of condemnation (401—458). The solace of hope is held forth to Guy (459—496) through the service of prayer and of reading the Holy Scriptures. When we read, God speaks with us; we speak with God, when we pray (497—510). This is followed by instruction regarding peace (511—522), a plea that Guy be merciful (523—550), and an entreaty that he bear misfortune with forgiving spirit (551—568), with patience (569—622), and in humility (623—634).

After a reference to the fall of Lucifer (635—656) and a renewed exposition of humility and compunction of heart (657—698), a vivid description of *gostli siht* (699—752) is supplemented by a petition for spiritual growth through confession (753—784). The various types of shame are classified (785—812). A *naïve* exposition of the Scriptural *wassheþ, and beþ clene* (813—850) introduces an appeal for the achievement of good (851—918). The sermon to Guy concludes with an exhortation to almsgiving (919—946), with practical application through the story of the woman and her miraculous cruse of oil (947—1028), designed to inflame benevolence in the spirit of the penitent knight. Alquin invokes Christ's blessing and calls for the succour and comfort of the Heaven Queen, the Holy Mary (1029—1034).

Guy may be depicted as again going steadfastly forward, continuing his pilgrimage. At last age creeps over the knight, and an old man[1] he drags his way to England. The giant Colbrand worsted, England freed, the weary pilgrim wandered to home, but not to

---

[1] Cf. *The Vision of Sir Launfal*, II. 2, 3 ff.

friends. Alone in solitary cave in pious meditation he lived till death came, and he and Felice were again together. Their faithful spirits were united in peaceful rest.

Thus the narrative suggested by the title of the present volume is briefly outlined. The *Speculum* opens with terse verses, conveying the purpose of the poem (1—26). A friar-hermit then instructs Guy of Warwick (68 ff.) and unfolds the discourse closely outlined in immediate connection with the introductory theme.

In presenting Guy as the subject of theological study, the poet advances an independent moral purpose. He would inculcate the doctrine of the development of power through actual experience, as based upon definite human choice.[1] Guy, craving immortal blessedness, touched a vital theme in the development of character. He would choose eternal life, renounce earth, and win heaven. The problem of earthly choice is the crux untouched by the strong "grasp of centuries," for the Victorian poet[2] also discovers the "gracious lights" of earth only,—

"when a soul has seen
By the means of Evil, that the Good is best."

CHAPTER II.

TITLE AND LITERARY NOTICES OF THE POEM.

§ 1. *Study of the Title of the Poem.*

1. THE title under which the poem of the present edition appears, *Speculum Gy de Warewyke*, is extant in the MS. 525 of the Harleian collection, fol. 53. That *Speculum Gy de Warewyke* designated the text at the period of its authorship, or even that the poet ascribed title to his composition, contemporary history does not determine. Four manuscripts add nothing in proof, three being incomplete. The MS. Bibl. Reg. 17 B. XVII. confirms preference for the element *Speculum*.

Speculum Gy de Warewyke incorporates the exact form of the parchment, but the colophon as justified by the narrative may be

---

[1] See particularly the *Speculum*, verses 215—220.
[2] The mediæval poet brings to mind incidents where the soul is surprised at the judgment, as depicted in Robert Browning's *Easter Day*, sections xvi and xx. Compare v. 551 with 31—32 of the *Speculum*:

"There stood I . . . .
Choosing the world . . . ."

interpreted to read *Speculum Gy[donis] de Warewyke*,[1] *heremite*,[2] *secundum Alquinum*. This modification is not necessary, as is indicated, if punctuation be inserted in the seemingly inaccurate title. *Speculum : Gy de Warewyke* presents a mediæval aspect of the Guy doctrine; it was a received tradition, that the stalwart conqueror of Colbrand was "England's mirror and all the world's wonder." Was it not his high destiny, "to hold, as 'twere, the mirror[3] up to Nature; to show virtue her own feature"? The exact reading of the scribe admits of varied interpretation, subject to individual speculation, whether it be rendered *Mirror to Guy* or *Mirror of Guy*, glorious "myrour" in whom to "sen al" his "socour," or uphold for emulation a national hero as a mirror reflecting an ideal line of conduct. The *Speculum* mirrors the knight himself in his exalted religious consecration. In the idealized glorification of the poet Guy, no longer mortal, becomes *Speculum sine maculâ :*

"Thou mirror,
In whom, as in the splendour of the sun,
All shapes look glorious, which thou gazest on!"

That the poet availed himself of mediæval licence, departed from the rigid application of verses 505, 506, and portrayed his warrior as example to all the world, *A cheef mirour of al the feste*,[4] *An exemplarie, & mirrour*,[5] *Mirrour of wit, ground of gouernaunce*,[6] the MS. itself assumes. Similar appearance[7] repeats itself in the person of the English Sidney, "glorious star" of Penshurst, in intellectual and moral characteristics also "lively pattern . . . lovely joy . . . . . born into the world to show our age a sample of ancient virtue" in chivalric soldiership and princely gentlemanliness. The poetical Mirror[8] is explained again through the language of Langland, v. 181, CXII.; Spenser, *Shepheardes Calendar* for October, v. 93; *Henry V.* ii. Chor. 6; *Gorboduc*, Act I. sc. 3, v. 798.

The excellence of the title in any of its interpretations is evident. Embodying characteristic features of the poem whose hero is Guy of Warwick and in harmony with a popular mediæval phase of literature, *Speculum Gy de Warewyke* places the associated text in

---

[1] The significance of the bracket (]) uniting *Warewyke* and *heremite* seems to be purely connective, and not indicative of couplet formation; cf. Chap. III. 6.
[2] Mediæval genitive equivalent to *heremitæ*.
[3] *Hamlet*, III. ii. 20.   [4] Ch., *The Book of the Duchesse*, v. 974.
[5] Lyd., *Temple of Glas*, v. 294.   [6] *Ibid.*, v. 754.
[7] Pico della Mirandola was likewise Phœnix to his age among his contemporaries.
[8] See *Temple of Glas* 974, with note to 294, p. 92, and Chaucer *Against Women Unconstaunt*, v. 8: *Right as a mirour nothing may enpresse*.

Chapter II.—Study of the Title of the Poem.

its natural environment. The interest of the episode centres in the valiant knight Guy of Warwick, and the name *Speculum* gives to the homily-romance with which the poem is clothed, it is not to be denied, a mediæval charm. In literary worth Guy's sweet English "sarmoun" gains by association with the greater romance. It gains in historical and philological interest through the factor *Speculum*, for thus it links itself with the period of its composition. The term *Speculum* was, in the estimate of Lorentz,[1] applicable to Alcuin's *De Virtutibus et Vitiis Liber*. Lorentz maintains, that the *Liber* was devised as a mirror, and that to the mind of Alcuin it existed as a *Speculum*, where Count Guido could see *was er zu thun und was er zu lassen habe*.[2] Lorentz thus paraphrases liberally the passage, Caput V., lines 5 f. of Alcuin's work, underlying verses 505, 506 united with 71—74 of the present text. Paulin Paris, *Histoire Littéraire de la France*, 1866, Tom. IV., p. 315, refers to the *Liber* in the following words: *qu'il lui servit de miroir, où il verroit d'un coup d'œil ce qu'il auroit à faire, et ce qu'il auroit à éviter*. Yet nowhere is the *Liber* formally termed *Speculum*. But the argument of Lorentz had been anticipated by some hundreds of years, and had been practically applied to the English version addressed to Guy of Warwick. The title *Speculum* is amply supported by the subject-matter of the poem, and *Speculum*, it is believed, could not have been without worth in the sympathies of a mediæval poet.

2. In its brief literary connection the tenth poem of the Auchinleck folio has attained recognition as *Epistola Alcuini*. Kölbing, *Englische Studien*, vol. vii., p. 183, Morley, *English Writers*, vol. iii., p. 281, and Zupitza in private correspondence with the editor, have given sanction to that title. The eminent authority of so illustrious a triumvirate in letters, and the prestige of literary and printed notice, would, at momentary glance, seem to make additional search for the lost heading of the Auchinleck poem unnecessary. But *Epistola Alcuini* names Alcuin's *De Virtutibus et Vitiis Liber* and other treatises[3] ascribed to Alcuin. The following MSS., each an *Epistola*

---

[1] Lorentz, Professor of History at the University of Halle, author of *Alcuins Leben, ein Beitrag zur Staats-Kirchen- und Culturgeschichte der Karoling. Zeit*. Halle, 1829, translated by Jane Mary Slee, *The Life of Alcuin*, and published in 1837. See p. 199.

[2] The exact passage, *Liber* V, is translated as follows: "Here lies the knowledge of true blessedness; for therein, as in a mirror, man may consider himself, what he is and whither he goes," applied by West in *Alcuin and the Rise of the Christian Schools*, 1893, pp. 115 f.

[3] See *Alcuini Epistolæ*, ed. Jaffé-Dummler in *Monumenta Alcuiniana*, pp. 131—897.

Alcuini, obliterate the claims of an English poem to the title *Epistola:* Bodl. MS. *E Musaeo* 214, formerly numbered 68, fol. 51 *b*—fol. 68 *b* ; Bodl. 3558.5, *Catalogus* Bernardi of the Bodleian Library; Cotton Vesp. A. XIV. ; *Epistola Alcuini Levitæ*, i. e. *Diaconi, qui illie in quibusdam epistolis nuncupatur Albinus cum versibus in fine ;* Bibl. Reg. 5. E. IV. and Bibl. Reg, 6. A. XI. (cf. Book Index); and the *Epistola ad Eulaliam*, etc. Apart from primary grounds for discarding *Epistola Alcuini*, the co-existence of numerous distinct works having legitimate claim upon that title, the form itself is not exact. It could be employed only at the cost of the testimony of the poem concerning its contemporary history. Morley's title correctly applied should read *Epistola Alquini* or *Alquyni*. Historically and on basis of the MS. *Alquyn* is the orthography demanded by a work of the period of the *Speculum;* cf. ten Br., *Ch.* § 103; Sievers, § 208; Sweet, *N.E. Gr.* § 779. The name of the Dean is in O.E. *Alhwine, Ealhwine;* Latin period *Alcuinus;* M.E. *Alquin* or *Alquyn*.[1] The poet writes of the author Alquin, *Alquyn* in MSS. $A_2 D H_1 H_2 R$: *Alquih was his rihte-name*, v. 39. Even Latin MSS. of the fourteenth and fifteenth centuries do not hesitate to adopt the orthography Alquin, Alquyn (the distinction *i*, *y* having no philological weight; cf. ten Br. § 9 and § 22 ; Morsb. § 112) in transcripts of the works of Alcuinus Albinus Flaccus ; cf. *Epistola Alquini*, MS. Bibl. Reg. 5. E. iv.; MS. Bibl. Reg. 6. A. xi.; and Lambeth MS. 378, where *in librum alquini, Pro alquino*, etc. occur.

Apart from the misconception liable to result through confliction among texts bearing the same title, the English poem, distinct and individual in character, a new creation, merits distinctive recognition and a specific place in literature. Its value rests neither in its connection with Alcuinus, nor in his theological views. It does not incorporate the philosophy of the schools of Charlemagne. Its interest centres in that vivid personality, that illustrious knight Gy de Warewyke. *Speculum Gy de Warewyke* belongs to the field of literary history, not to theology. It is a member of that greater Romance cycle, whose brilliant hero is Sir Gy.

3. Warton's title ranks the discourse among poems of the ballad order. *Guy and Alquine* has the merit of granting its poem environment in the English Guy legend, classifying it, through analogy, with

---

[1] Over forms of Alcuin's name compare Schönefelder in his monograph, *Alcuin et Charlemagne*, p. 4, and Pertz, *Monum. Germ. Script.*, I, p. 632 ; over its significance, see Hamelin, *Essai sur la vie et les ouvrages d'Alcuin* (1873), p. 10.

Chapter II.—Study of the Title of the Poem.

Guy and Colbronde, Guy and Phelis, Guy and Amarant.[1] Warton was probably indebted to some MSS. Catalogue for the suggestion, perhaps in connection with the heading of the *Catalogue of the Arundel MSS.*, vol. ii, edition of 1832, naming the poem *Gy Earl of Warwyke and Dekne Alquyne.*[2] Warton's title is without authority historical or manuscript. Equally ungrounded is Scott's (also Laing's) title. As "A Moralization upon certain Latin Texts," apparently an invention of Scott (or of Leyden, cf. § 2) to characterize the subject-matter of the selection, it figures in *Sir Tristrem* and also in *A Penni worth of Witte*, etc.

4. The merit accredited to the genus *Speculum* in mediæval literary history is testified to with eloquent voice through its popularity. Hundreds of varieties of the general type are locked up in MS. collections throughout the world. *Speculum Stultorum*, ed. Wright, 1872, depicted in satire English foibles of the 12th century through Nigel Wireker, and the 14th century is resplendent with a glittering array of *Specula*. The position of the *Speculum* in that period is in the technique of theology.[3] The following list of theological *Specula* from MS. works has been collected, but the various Christian attributes associated with the *Speculum* are surprisingly numerous. The *Speculum* links with itself *humanæ salvationis* in a large family of virtues. It is *Speculum Confessionis, Christianorum, Mundi, Philosophiæ, Religionum, Speculatorum, Innocentiæ Devotorum, Contemplationis* (a *Ladder of Perfection*), *Peccatoris*. It is a *Christian Mirror*, a *Mirror for Maydens, Of Penance, Of Sinners, Of Lewd Men and Women, Of Chastite*,[4] *Of the Sacrament, Of Penance, Le Mirouer des Dames, Le Miroir du Monde, Die Sprighel der sonden ... van Jan iof Weert*, a heterogeneous collection[5] indeed, elaborate attributes of a unique type of literature. The *Specula* include all the tenets of Christian doctrine and embrace all aspects of life inspiring to the 14th century mind. The spiritual history of the 15th century is enriched by the exquisite seriousness of a *Speculum of 7 gyftus of the holi gost*, MS. Ff. iv. 9, Camb. Univ.,

---

[1] Percy's *Reliques*. Edition of Walford, 1880. Part II, pp. 329 ff. and 331 ff.
[2] Also description of *The Index to the Arundel and Burney MSS. in the British Museum.*
[3] This distinction applicable to the generic *Speculum* is irrespective of the subject-matter of the individual text.
[4] The *Mirrour of Chaastitee*, MSS. Harl. 2322, 2325.
[5] For MSS. *Specula* compare MSS. Harl. 113, 116, 953, 1255, 1706, 1713, 2339, 2388, 6581, etc.; Add. MSS. 17,539, 22,283, 25,089, 29,951; Royal MSS. 16 E v.; 8 F X.; 5 B IX., etc.

of a *Myrour to deuot peple*, MS. Gg. I. 6, and by a *Speculum etatis hominis*, MS. Gg. IV. 32, whose mirror is depicted twelve times in twelve distinct circles to reflect the twelve ages of man. Bonaventure's "boke that is clepid" *Myrour of the blissid Lif of Jesu Crist* has disseminated its truths through manifold translations,[1] and was printed by Caxton. In MS. Arundel 112, also MS. Arundel 120, the text is embalmed in a paper 4to. of the 15th century entitled: "*The myrour of the blessed lyfe of oure Lorde Ihesu Criste*, translated from the Latin of Bonaventura with some additions by the translator, and a Treatise at the end on the Body of Christ against the Lollards." A Bodleian MS. is an *Apology for a looking-glass* by Apuleius against Æmilian, in English verse. Harley MS. 3277 contributes a paper book, *A Looking glasse for Looveres*, "wherein are conteyned two sortes of amorous passions, the one expressing the trewe estate and perturbations of hym that is overgon with love; the other a flatt defyance to love and his lawes," containing "78 passions or chapters of prose verse." In 1509 the *Ship of Fooles* dimmed the fair radiance of the theological *Speculum* by the profane *Mirour of good Manners*. So late as the 17th century is still to be found the ubiquitous *Speculum*, a spectrum for laymen in the *Mirror for Martyrs* (1601), from the hand of Weever. In *Speculum Crape-Gownorum*, of the Advocates' Library, are "Observations and Reflections upon the late sermons of some that would be thought Goliahs for the Church of England." London, 1682. Berjeau published, 1861, *reproduit, en Fac-simile, Le plus ancien Monument de la xylographie et de la typographie réuni*, *Speculum Humanæ Salvationis*.

The various *Mirrors* belong to a later period. These descendants of the *Speculum* have imbued new life into earlier saintly themes, and *Speculum* no longer suggests *dedly synnes, confessiones* and bands *clericorum* (Arund. 452) for the religious life of the soul, a *Speculum Conscientiæ*,[2] but names worldly activity and profane subjects in its rank and file of *Princely Deedes* (1598), *Constant Penelopes* (cf. Percy's *Reliques*), and *Mirrors of Knighthood*, not to forget Gower's *Speculum* of "Virtues and Vices," *i.e.* Meditantis, and that most "dolefully dreary[3]" *Mirror for Magistrates* (London, 1563), Gascoigne's *The Steel Glas* (1576), his *Glass of Government*, and the

---

[1] Cf. Add. MSS. 11,565, 19,901, 21,106, 22,558, 30,031; Sloane MS. 1785; Cot. Tib. 6, VII.; Harl. 435, 2241, etc.
[2] Cf. MSS. Harl. 5398; Sloane 3551.
[3] Cf. Lowell, *The Old English Dramatists*, "Marlowe," p. 30.

looking-glass of Thomas Lodge and Robert Green: *A Looking Glasse for London and England.* Here could be numbered from every age all those *Specula*, in whose "immortal flowers of poesy,"—

> "As in a mirror, we perceive
> The highest reaches of a human wit."—*Tamburlaine.*

§ 2. *Literary History of the Manuscripts.*

Specific mention of the *Speculum* is to be found in a brief and inexact description of its Auchinleck text,[1] published by Sir Walter Scott[2] in 1804 through the "Introduction"[3] to *Sir Tristrem*,[4] Appendix IV., p. cxii., and reprinted in various subsequent editions,[5] in 1811 and 1819 under the same numbering of the page, in 1806,[6] p. cviii., in 1833, p. 113. After 1811 *Sir Tristrem* was included with its Introduction in the collective editions of Scott's *Poetical Works*, notice of the *Speculum* being printed often with the pagination 112. Compare the edition of 1868, mentioned by Kölbing, *Engl. Stud.* vii., p. 178.

In 1857 David Laing, in his "preface" to *A Penni worth of Witte, Florice and Blauncheflour*,[7] etc., incorporated Scott's Intro-

---

[1] This description plays a minor part as a single detail in a general sketch of the various texts comprising the Auchinleck folio. Scott's summary is still offered in the *MSS. Catalogue* of the Advocates' Library, classifying the Auch. MS.

[2] Reference to the life of Sir Walter Scott, as employed in this edition, is afforded by *Memoirs of the Life of Sir Walter Scott, Bart.*, by John Gibson Lockhart, The Riverside Press, 1881, and by Richard H. Hutton's *Sir Walter Scott* in Morley's *English Men of Letters*, 1878.

[3] Material for this "Introduction" seems to have been collected by John Leyden (d. 1811 in India), the eminent Oriental scholar (cf. Hutton, pp. 65, 66), and the faithful ally of Scott in the transcription of *Sir Tristrem*; cf. Lockhart, vol. ii., p. 54. Leyden aided Scott in the preparation of the *Border Minstrelsy* (see Lockhart, vol. ii., p. 46), and it was Leyden who prepared the bulky transcript of *King Arthour*, a fragment of seven thousand lines (*Life of Scott*, vol. ii., pp. 60, 61), used by Ellis in his *Specimens of Early English Metrical Romances*. Leyden published, on his own responsibility, *The Complaynt of Scotland* (written 1648) in 1802.

[4] *Sir Tristrem;* a Metrical Romance of the Thirteenth Century; by Thomas of Erceldoune, called the Rhymer. Edited from the Auchinleck MS. by Walter Scott, Esq., Advocate, Edinburgh. This work was published the second of May, 1804.

[5] The edition of 1804 comprised but one hundred and fifty copies, to be sold at two guineas a volume. These are now broadly scattered and are difficult of access. Indebtedness is due to the British Museum for the copy used in the preparation of this edition.

[6] Seven hundred and fifty copies of the subsequent edition in 1806 were necessary to satisfy the public demand. These editions heralded that ill-fated connection with Ballantyne, the *Aldiborontiphoscophornio* of Scott.

[7] *A Penni worth of Witte: Florice and Blauncheflour: and other Pieces of Ancient English Poetry*, "Selected from The Auchinleck Manuscript. Printed at Edinburgh, For the Abbotsford Club." 1857. Laing's edition is also with

duction without attributing it to its direct source. Notice of this poem in its Auch. MS. stands on p. xiv., numbered 11, and called "A Moralization upon certain Latin texts," thus retaining Scott's title, and failing to correct his defective enumeration as preserved in *Sir Tristrem*. For recognition of later date the *Speculum* is indebted to Eugen Kölbing, in his exhaustive study of the Romance selections preserved in the Auchinleck MS., *Englische Studien*, vol. vii., pp. 178 ff. Here, p. 183, designated "Epistola Alcuini," occurs the only entirely reliable account of the *Speculum*. Kölbing prints the first ten verses of the poem and the remaining portions of the twenty-five imperfect lines, ll. 1007—1031. The Auchinleck text received casual notice by Warton and by Morley. In Warton's *History of English Poetry*, edited by Hazlitt, vol. ii., p. 29, the *Speculum* is classified as "Guy and Alquine" in a list that, Warton claims, includes the "principal pieces" of the Auchinleck MS. Morley gives a table of the contents of the folio, naming the *Speculum* "Epistola Alcuini," in *English Writers*, vol. iii., p. 281.

But the earliest known reference to the poem, apart from meagre statistics, was furnished by Ritson,[1] two years earlier than the appearance of *Sir Tristrem*. In *Ancient Engleish Metrical Romanceës*,[2] London, 1802, vol. i., pp. xcii. and xciii., Ritson connects with the Canticum Colbrondi (*Geste, Guy and Colbronde*, Percy, *Reliques*, vol. iii., Part 4, page 26; see also pp. 145, 152, and Percy's Folio MS., vol. ii., pp. 509 ff.), "the cream" of the Guy romance,[3] an "old Engleish poem" of the Harley MS. 525, *Speculum Gy de Warewyke* per Alquinum *heremitam* (according to Ritson). Thirty-five lines beginning this MS. were printed in *Germania*, vol. xxi., pp. 366-7, in

---

difficulty accessible. The *Speculum* is indebted to the copy in the library of the British Museum.

[1] The attitude of his contemporaries toward Ritson, "the ill-conditioned antiquary of vegetarian principles," is well known. He was tolerated only by Scott. Leyden's stanzas, characteristic of Ritson, may be recalled:

"That dwarf, he is so fell of mode,
Tho ye shold drynk his hert blode,
Gode wold ʒe never finde."

"That dwarf, he ben beardless and bare,
And weaselblowen ben al his hair,
Like an ympe or elfe;
And in this world beth al and hale,
Ben nothynge that he loveth an dele
Safe his owen selfe."

[2] Of this first edition, the Königliche Bibliothek, Berlin, has preserved the copy referred to in this issue.
[3] Scott, see Lockhart, Il., p. 63.

an article by Prof. Kölbing. Here Kölbing, calling attention to the importance of the Auchinleck text in the Guy of Warwick question, enumerates the other MSS. of the British Museum, the Arundel MS. 140, and the Harleian MS. 1731, but does not mention MS. Dd 11 and MS. Bibl. Reg. 17 B xvii.

Of the various MSS. of the *Speculum* the Harley MS. 525 has represented its text to the general public. This MS. has received the weight of attention in print, and apparently from Harley 525 interest has developed in other transcripts of the same text. The striking feature of the title, the introduction of the name *Guy of Warwick*, and, indeed, the fact of the existence of a title[1] in connection with what is apparently a complete poem,[2] having introduction, conclusion, and colophon, in a well preserved and beautifully written parchment, explain the popularity of MS. Harley 525. Interest in the Auchinleck MS. was awakened through its association with important Romance texts of the same MS. volume. MSS. Harley 1731 and Arund. 140 have received scanty notice, and no printed mention of MSS. Dd 11, 89, and MS. Reg. 17 B. xvii., has been discovered outside of MSS. Catalogues. There is likewise no account to be found of Worseley 67 of this group of texts.

Notices of a hitherto unprinted poem form naturally no imposing list, yet for nearly a century the *Speculum* has been before the public. Its history is nearly contemporaneous with the printed record of the Auchinleck MS. itself. That folio was mentioned first in Percy's *Reliques of Ancient Poetry;* cf. *Engl. Stud.*, vii., p. 178. It is described as a whole, or in application to some individual work, with greater or less regard for detail and accuracy, in the various editions of the Auchinleck texts. Kölbing's valuable publications, *Sir Beues, Arthour and Merlin, Amis and Amiloun, Tristrem*, etc., Zupitza's *Guy of Warwick* (see edition 1875–76), Mall's *The Harrowing of Hell*, the shorter poems through medium of the *Englische Studien*, the editions of Laing, Ritson, and Turnbull, edited privately and for the Maitland Club or the Abbotsford Club, may be consulted,[3] as well as Ellis in *Early English Pronunciation*, vol. ii., pp. 448, 449. So early as the date of Ritson's arrangement of its table of contents in 1792, the youthful Scott,[4] with a "great meikle

---

[1] Other MSS. have no marked individuality in MS. relationship, and could be mistaken in each instance for a continuation of a preceding text, except in case of MS. D. [2] The most conspicuous MSS. are not otherwise complete.
[3] This list is by no means complete.
[4] The correspondence between Scott and Ellis began March 27, 1801, but

nowthorn[1] to rout on," was scouring the Highlands for ancient lays, and searching for "auld Thomas o' Twizzlehope," seeking for the information, that would culminate later in the interchange of enthusiastic letters between the bard of the *Border Minstrelsy* and George Ellis over the identity of Thomas of Erceldoune. Possibly to that year (1792) might be ascribed Scott's earliest study of the Auchinleck texts.

If the date of the publication of the greater romances become the standard, then the *Speculum*, in contrast with the broader popularity of the greater Guy history, has not been late in attaining to the dignity of a distinct edition. *Sir Gij* was completed only in 1891, and *Sir Beues* first in 1894. Bibliography of the poem in its connection with the Guy of Warwick tradition would follow each century of the history of printing in England, beginning with Copland's fragmentary edition, placed in 1560, and ending only with the present decade.

CHAPTER III.
DESCRIPTION OF THE MANUSCRIPTS.

The *Speculum Gy de Warewyke* has been preserved in the following manuscripts, of which to this date there have been no prints:

Auchinleck.

1. A_1. MS. Auchinleck, Advocates' Library, Edinburgh. A parchment folio of the early fourteenth century; c. 1327—1340. Concerning the contents of this valuable romance[2] MS. Kölbing

---

Scott's search for Thomas the Rhymer was under way earlier. In June 1795, Scott, through zeal in literary affairs, had been appointed one of the curators of the Advocates' Library, colleague of David Hume, Lockhart, I., p. 271.

[1] Cf. Shortreed through Lockhart, I. 230.
[2] *Romance* in application to contents. The Auchinleck MS., it will be recalled, is a repository for a vast treasure of M.E. romance. It contains the first English version of the Guy of Warwick legend (*Sir Gij of Warwicke*, Auch., Nos. 22, 23, ed. Zupitza), as well as transcripts of *Sir Beues* (ed. Kölbing), *Sir Tristrem* (ed. Scott and Kölbing), *Florice and Blancheflour* (ed. Hausknecht, *Floris and Blauncheflur*; cf. also *Flóres Saga ok Blankiflúr*, Icelandic version edited by Kölbing), *King Horn* (ed. Wissmann), *Arthour and Merlin* (ed. Kölbing), *Amis and Amiloun* (ed. Kölbing), *The Legend of Gregory*, named one of the "pearls of M.E. literature" (cf. Schulz, *Die englische Gregorlegende nach dem Auchinleck MS.*; Holtermann, *Ueber Sprache . . . der . . Gregoriuslegende*; and Neussell, *Ueber . . . mittelengl. Bearbeitung der Saga von Gregorius*), and thirty-six other selections, chiefly romance poems, whose popularity in the thirteenth and fourteenth centuries is undisputed. They are the "romances of prys" named in Chaucer's often quoted lines, *Sir Thopas* (ed. Skeat), 2087—2089, etc., and a portion of them denounced by Ascham a century later in the

has treated in detail in *Englische Studien*, vol. vii., pp. 178 ff., with reference to the tenth selection, p. 183. The handwriting, distinct and beautiful, is larger than that of other scribes represented in the Auchinleck transcripts and is not to be found elsewhere in the folio; cf. also Scott, *Sir Tristrem*,[1] p. cxiii. The present text is written in carefully outlined double columns, so cramped in space that sometimes the last word, syllable, or letter of the poetical verse is placed above or below the metrical line: lines 66, 113, 267, 277, etc. In its original condition the poem occupied fol. 39a—fol. 48b. There is no title. Folio headings and fol. 48b with concluding lines, ll. 1032—1034, are lost through mutilation[2] of the MS. for illuminations. On fol. 48a parts of twenty-five lines, ll. 1007—1031, have been cut unevenly from the parchment. Subdivision into chapter or section is not indicated. Capitals are used, but they occur without uniformity. Lines 1, 137, 161, and 277 are marked off by large brilliantly coloured introductory letters. Latin quotations are in red ink. The letter beginning each line is ornamented with red. On the margin to the left, recurring frequently at unequal intervals and without reference to subject-matter, is the character '¶' in red: lines 9, 17, 23, 27, etc. Each leaf contains at the top the lower portion of a Roman numeral, 'xv,' in blue ink.

Lines 179, 180; 421, 422; 551, 552; 645, 646; 925, 926, are omitted. The last word of line 232 was not written; *pylt* is supplied in this edition from MS. A_2. There are a few erasures: lines 33, 178, 197, 202, 249, etc. Line 268 occurs a second time, apparently in order to give to *her* a final -*e*, *here*, but the second reading is not

---

Scholemaster, pp. 79, 80 (reprint of Arber), and again by Nash in Greene's *Menaphon*. The "pleasure" of the "booke" "in two speciall poyntes, in open mans slaughter, & bold bawdrye," killing men "without any quarel," such baseness as "the single head of an Englishman is not hable to invent," becomes through Nash the work of "bable booke-mungers," who "endevor but to repaire the ruinous wals of Venus court," "to imitate a fresh the fantasticall dreames of those exiled Abbie lubbers from whose idle pens proceeded those worne out impressions of the feigned no where acts of Arthur of the rounde table, Arthur of little Brittaine, Sir Tristram," etc. He does not "forbeare laughing" in "reding Bevis of Hampton" at "the scambling shyft he makes to end his verses a like"; cf. also Jusserand, *The English Novel in the Time of Shakespeare*, pp. 307, 308.

[1] Compare the preceding section for the corresponding pagination of this citation in the various editions of *Sir Tristrem*, and in Laing's *A Penni worth of Witte*, etc. "It (the tenth selection) is written in a different and larger hand than the preceding and following articles," says Scott.

[2] Cf. *Legendæ Catholicæ*, "A Lytle Boke of Seyntlic Gestes, Imprinted at Edinburgh in the Year of the Incarnation, MDCCCXL.," p. vi., where the editor wishes that the "Vandal" of these "Hagiologies" had been "qualified to chant shrill treble within the choir of the Sistine chapel."

retained, the line being crossed out. A word, syllable, or letter is occasionally written above the line within the verse: lines 47, 71, 101, 164, 178, etc.

MS. A_1 has some peculiarities in orthography and dialect. To be noted is a redundant final *-h*: þeiħ 25, 80, 104, 170, 184, etc.; *nowħ* 348.—*d* in the function of þ: *wid* 84, 93, 181, 334, 370, 372, etc.; þerwid 147; *widinne* 118, etc.; and *widoute(n)* 252, 258, 277, 278, 302, etc.—*z* represents voiceless *s* in plural forms, and at the end and in the middle of a word: *uertuz* (plu.) 71, 79, 325, etc.; in the middle of a word: *lezczoun* 58, 138; *murszere* 284; at the end of the word: *trespaz* : *solaz* 686; *voiz*[1] 446. An abbreviated form occurs: *fint* 785, *tit* 807; cf. also *Streinþe* 305 through vocalization of O.E. *g*. The *-ie* of *mieknesse* 85, although illustrated also in N.E. *thief*, is still not the usual orthography of this word in M.E.; cf. Stratmann, *M.E. Dict*. A_1 has a predilection for the grammatical form *wole*, often where MS. D has *sal(l)*: *wole* or *wolt* 3, 5, 11, 16, 19, 27, 28, etc. Grammatical mannerisms peculiar to A_1 are: *ou* 2, 816, 824, 848, etc.; *beyþere* 952; þeiħ and *hij* are employed side by side: þeiħ 192, 271, 272, 295, 297, 298, etc.; *hij* 186, 267, 277, 279, 280, 281, etc.; *mait* occurs in rime with *caiht* 882. A dialectical peculiarity is the use of *seide, saide* in *R*, replacing *sede* of the original: lines 140, 168, 494, etc.; cf. *Ipotis, seyde* : (*dede*) 285, 461. Various instances occur, where the copyist marked his dialect through the method of representing O.E. *y*, *ȝ*, umlaut of *u*, *ū* : *puite* : *luite* 924; *duire* : *fire* 252; *ipult* : *gilt* 888; *muche* : *-liche* 386, 672, etc. In some details the vocabulary of A_1 is interesting. *ac* is almost uniformly translated in other MSS. of the *Speculum*; cf. 4, 13, 102, etc.; *heinen* is found 627. *emcristene* 9, 334, etc., þisternesse 114, 306, 731, etc., and þolemod 574, 666, etc., are specially the individual property of A_1, although existing in isolated examples in the other texts.

A portion of a Roman numeral fifteen at the top of each folio indicates the position of the *Speculum* in the early arrangement of the Auchinleck transcripts. If *The Legend of Pope Gregory*, bearing the original number VI., the first transcript of the present MS., be numbered 1, the *Speculum* is in natural sequence the tenth collection. This classification presupposes the loss of five poems before the first of the original collection. The numbering 11 employed by Scott and Laing in designating this poem, is due to the unexplained omission

---

[1] See ten Brink, *Verskunst*, § 109, Anm.

of No. 6 in the enumeration of the Auchinleck texts, forming "Appendix IV." of the "Introduction" to *Sir Tristrem*. No. 5 immediately precedes No. 7, and No. 6 is not accounted for in Scott's list. The original numbers follow each other in natural order without interruption.

Although not free from error, yet MS. A_1, the oldest MS. and approximately complete, has transmitted relatively the most correct text. For these reasons it will become the basis of the following edition. Concerning its arrangement as determining the nature of this volume, see chapter v, § 3.

Bibl. Reg. 17 B XVII.

2. **R.** MS. Bibl. Reg. 17 B XVII., Library of the British Museum, London. On vellum, a small quarto; *c.* 1370—1400. The *Speculum* is found fol. 19*a*—fol. 36*a*. It is without heading. A concluding note runs: *Explicit hic speculum vtile istius mundi*. The leaf is written in single columns, and there is irregularity in the introduction of capitals. Coloured initial letters designate important passages of the poem. The Latin passages are, *primâ manu* Mr. Herbert affirms, in black ink on the margin to the right of the body of the text. They are sometimes inclosed with red lines. The poem is complete without breaks of any kind. Lines 45 and 46 are omitted; lines 571 and 572 are transposed; lines 272 and 548 introduce new readings.

Among palæographical characteristics it will be noted, that, in addition to its customary function, *o* becomes often a purely graphical representative of *e* of other MSS. That *o* in this development, corresponding to a normal M.E. *e*, may preserve an essential integral principle of language, is suggested by the forms *hom* and *hore*, O.E. *heom*, *heora* : *hom* 25, 100, 106, 150, etc.; *hore* (poss. plu.) 103, 169, 188, 265, 298, 308, 434, etc.; *hom selue* 443, 485, etc. An interesting dialectical feature of MS. R is the use in unaccentuated position in the inflection of substantives and verbs of -*is*, -*es*, -*id*, -*us*, -*ud*.—*disciplis* 570, but *londus* (plu.) 163; *beris* (3. sing.) 663; *faris* 673; *metis* 549; *lastis* 746; *wasshis* 820; *sittes* 255; *saies* 567; *lyes* 713; *wratthus* 806 are found. To be added also are in the pp. or pret.: ȝarkid 300; *martrid* 610; *honourid* 632; *foulid* 832; *shewid* 361; *tholyd* (-*id*) 590, 594, 605, etc.; *deud* (3 sing. pret.) 528, 531. The inflectional syllable is not expressed: (þou) *dos* 103; (*hit*) *dos* 112; *bes* (*he*) 128; *Gos* (imp.) 448; *shon* : *won* 106, etc.; *vertuz* is preserved by R (cf. § 1) 79, 325. A Northern *til* replaces (*in*)*to* 271; *hethen, henne* 297. Note also the couplet *reide* : *saiede* 494. MS. R adds to the vocabulary of the poem a translation of *pisternesse* in the word *merkenes* 114, 306, 731, etc.

The *Speculum* stands third in a collection of works, many of which are attributed to the authorship of Richard Rolle, the Hermit of Hampole. The last of these is based upon selections from *The Pricke of Conscience*. Mr. Herbert of the Museum called attention to the numbering of the *Speculum* in the *Old Catalogue* published in 1734. There the first three poems, numbered 1, practically 1, 2, and 3, are regarded as a single work. Thus the *Speculum* is not recognized as an individual poem. Number 2 of the *Catalogue* is virtually number 4, fol. 36*b*—fol. 49*a*, and begins: *Alle mighty god*, etc.

Harleian 1731.

3. H_1. MS. Harleian 1731, Library of the British Museum. A paper MS., quarto; *c.* 1440—1460. This text is contained on fol. 134*a*—fol. 148*b*. It opens without title, and ends l. 910, fol. 148*b*, it is to be conjectured, through the loss of two leaves, that contained the remaining verses of the poem. It is written in single columns. The majuscule beginning each line is in black ink, ornamented with red. Large initials showily coloured in red begin lines 1 and 137. The Latin texts are in red. A significant hand in black, partly outlined in red, points out from the margin l. 109: "pride wraþ and enuye." Other references to pride, ll. 635—638, fol. 144*b*, 1—4, are emphasized by means of red interlineations.

Lines 7, 8 and 641, 642 are omitted. Entirely original readings are conveyed by lines 133, 136, 205, 206, 403, 404, 442, 447, 448, 479, 507, 508, 514, 591, 592, and 606; 409 is slightly changed. H_1 shows much diversity in text, and often alters the verse apparently on its own responsibility.

The *Speculum* comprises with the "Pryke of concyence, composed by R., the Hermit of Hampole," an "old English book;" cf. *Catalogue of the Harleian MSS*. A half-effaced note on the fly-leaf has been with difficulty deciphered to read as follows:

Memorandum quod quinto die julij Anno Domini $M^{lo}.cccc^{mo}.lxxiij^o$ *Ricardus Reder de petyrsfeld deliberauit commissario generali diocesis Wintoniensis ij libros.*

A brief description of these three books follows in the customary method of the mediæval period, *viz.* by quoting in each instance the words beginning the second line of the second folio of the volume. The record for the third book is as follows: Tercij libri 2° *folio*, "And Also hov merciful.".. Turning to the second folio of Harleian MS. 1731, the second line stands: "And al so how mercyful god ys at al assay," confirming the characterization of H_1 as the third of the three books delivered to the Commissary-General of the Diocese of Winchester. Richard Ryder was suspected of Lollardism; cf. *Catalogue of MSS.* in the Harleian Collection.

Arundel 140.

4. A_2. MS. Arundel 140, Library of the British Museum. On paper, folio; *c.* 1420—1430. The handwriting is small and is throughout profusely enriched with flourishes. In general characteristics it suggests a text written soon after the middle of the fourteenth century, but water-marks of the paper determine otherwise and on the authority of careful palæographers place its transcript in the fifteenth[1] century. The *Speculum*, written in double columns, extends from fol. 147*a* to fol. 151*d*. The MS. does not record title and concludes abruptly l. 892, fol. 151*d*, probably on account of a missing leaf that contained the end of the poem. Capitals occur without conformity to rule. A_2 begins with a large red letter, and Latin texts are in red.

In addition to the missing conclusion, ll. 893—1034, lines as follows are omitted: 55, 56, 140, 181, 182, 261, 262, 648—653, 678, 679, 840—845. Ll. 141 and 142 are interpolated between ll. 82 and 83, but appear again in normal sequence preceded a second time by l. 82, in place of the omitted line 140 (*vide supra*). Lines 465, 466 omitted after 464 are interpolated between lines 470 and 471. Lines 75 and 76 are transposed. Lines 251 and 834 introduce new readings.

Although MS. A_2 does not record title, the poem[2] is described as *Gy Earl of Warwyke and Dekne Alquyne* in *Index to Arundel and Burney MSS.* and *Catalogue of the Arundel MSS.* in the British Museum, vol. i., 1834. It is preceded by *The Pricke of Conscience*. A_2 is much worn. The leaves are ragged and uneven. The ink is often faded. In some instances individual words are almost illegible. Sometimes a correction in very black ink distinguishes letter or mono-

---

[1] Difference of opinion exists regarding the period of A_2. Some authorities place the text 1450—1480.

[2] A_2 is further classified as "a religious tale in verse."

Chapter III.—*Description of the MSS.* MS. D. xxxiii

syllable. At the top of folio 148 *d* a representation of the word *Iesu* is to be found. At the bottom of the same folio the line beginning fol. 149*a* is transcribed. In orthography preference for -*i* (-*y*) in place of -*e* in inflectional endings is to be recorded.

Dd 11. 89.

5. **D.** MS. Dd 11. 89, University Library, Cambridge. Parchment, quarto, written in single columns; *c.* 1440—1450. This is the first notice in print of Dd 11. The present text, the fourth in the collection, begins fol. 162*b* and ends fol. 179*b*. It is without title. There is a comprehensive gap, ll. 407—475. A capital is occasionally found at the beginning of a line. Capitals introducing lines 1 and 137 are illuminated. Latin texts are in red. Opposite each, on the margin near the edge of the leaf, suggesting irregularity on the part of the copyist, is the key-word or introductory letter in red.

In addition to the loss of verses through the break at the middle of the text, the following lines are omitted: 342, 534, 535, 679, 738. Lines 376, 790, and 925, 926 differ from the versions of other MSS. Lines 167, 168, 201, 202, 303, 304 are transposed, and the Latin text following line 338 is interpolated between 345 and 346.

Dd 11 is immediately preceded by "þe prykke of conciense." On fol. 162*a*, near the bottom of the page, is to be read: "Here endeþe þe sermon þat a clerk made þat was cleput Alquyn To Gwy of Warwyk." This shows impress of the preceding statement: "Here endeþe þe tretys þat ys cald þe prykke off conciense." MS. D betrays carelessness in transcription. At times the scribe might have been without intelligent appreciation of his prototype.

Noteworthy graphically is the service of the same character, apparently þ not only for þ and *y*, but for ȝ of other MSS. Varnhagen, *Anglia*, vol. iv., p. 182, footnote, mentions a similar usage in the Cambridge University MS. Gg. I. 1. Dialectical peculiarities of *D* are interesting. In orthography, the tendency to drop or to add an initial *h* is characteristic of *D*. A redundant *h* is prefixed: *Habraham* (also in H_2) 347; *halyde* 676; *heye* (O.E. *eâge*) 827; *herþe* (*eorþe* in A_1) 296, 375; *halmisdede* 934.—*h* is omitted[1]: *is* (for *his*) 227.—*wh* is employed for *h*: *where* for *were* 59.—*w* for *wh*: *wyche* 80, 140, 287.—*D* uses *f* for *v* (*u* in A_1): *lofe* 697; *lefeþ* 733.—*g* represents *ch* of A_1: *cage* 903; *knowlage* 509; *knowlaging* 725.—An inorganic ȝ is added in the curious form *maytȝ* 1020, 1021, possibly

---
[1] See also Skeat's illustrations from *Havelok*, p. xxxvii.

xxxiv *Chapter III.—Description of the MSS. MS. H_2.*

through analogy with *mayʒt* 863, 864. Compare also *mayt* (*mait*) 344, 881, 882.—*wole* of A_1 is replaced by *sall* (*sal*) 27, 28, 77, 79, 101, 119, 167, 283, 285, 324, 328 (*sul* 265), etc. *D* introduces forms like *gud* (O.E. *gôd*) 29, 40, 57, etc.; *gede* (O.E. *god'*, but cf. *ged dede*, *Anec. Lit.*, 96) 494; *dude* 895; *pute* : *lute* 924; *god hyd* 379; *boys* (i. e. *bush*) 359, 363, 368. Conspicuous grammatical properties are illustrated in MS. D: *kyd* 178; *es* 3, 4, 146, 193, etc.; *chastyn* (inf.) 181; *wemmyd* (pp.) 366; *be tokenes* (3. sing.) 363; *bedes* (1. plur.) 504; *Mit* for *Mihte* 291. *D* retains suffr*and* 587, 597. The vocabulary of *D* often paraphrases reading of other texts, (1) with words of the same general significance : *cheyse* (*shed* A_1) 217; *creatures* (*shaftes* A_1) 781; *pole þi mode* (*þolemod* A_1) 574. (2) Through words of different significance : *vnneþe* (*anuied* A_1) 124; *bodyly* (*mannes* A_1) 388; *mekenesse* (*soþnes* A_1) 664. Study of the dialectical peculiarities of this transcript results in the conclusion that MS. *D* was written by a northern scribe, possibly by a Scotchman.

Harleian 525.

6. H_2. MS. Harleian 525, Library of the British Museum. See Kölbing, *Germania*, vol. xxi., pp. 366, 367. Parchment; quarto of the latter years[1] of the first half of the fifteenth century, *c.* 1440—1450. H_2 is written in single columns. The handwriting, uniformly clear and exact, recalls the Auchinleck transcript. Near the conclusion it varies in size, but there is no indication of a second copyist. Beginning fol. 44*a* and ending fol. 53*a* is the poem of the present issue. Fol. 44*a* is without title. Written in two lines on fol. 53*a* is the colophon : *Explicit Speculum Gy* (not the expected *Gydonis*) *de Warewyke* (the final -*e* very faint and almost illegible) *heremite* secundum (expanded by Ritson to read *per;* by Kölbing,[2] *et*) *Alquinum*, see *A. E. M. Romanceës*, i. xcii., and *Germania*, xxi. 367. *heremite* is written immediately below *Warewyke*. The two words are united by a bracket ( ]). Every verse begins with a capital letter. Instead of the customary introductory illuminated majuscule, large four-cornered blank spaces were left at lines 1, 161, and 283, apparently for illuminations. In the space line 1 a small capital has been inserted, and a small minuscule in each of the other spaces, probably for the instruction of the illuminator. Latin texts are in black.

[1] 1480—1500 is the limit ascribed to H_2 by some authorities. The period is with difficulty exactly defined.
[2] It should be recalled, that Kölbing's note dates an early period in his work, 1876 ; Ritson's, 1802.

Chapter III.—Description of the MSS. MS. H_2.

The twelve lines concluding the poem, ll. 829—840, contain an apostrophe to the Virgin. An extensive gap, ll. 459—814, and the omission of lines 841—1034 characterize MS. H_2. Numerous illustrations of the omission of characteristic readings are as follows: lines 11, 12, 197, 198, 251, 252, 295—300, 305, 306, 309, 310, 357, 358, 435—444, 451, 452, 823—826. Lines 108, 133, 283, 323, 328, 342, 378 (328 in H_2 and 790 in A_1), and 447, 448 have adopted original readings. Lines 111, 112 are transposed. Lines 819, 820, omitted in the normal sequence of the poem, are interpolated between 828, 829. Two lines are interpolated after 160 and 454 respectively, one after 138, one after 322, and three after 4. It may be noted that MSS. D and H_2 often coincide in readings so far as l. 400. Although copyist's errors are few, yet in the transmission of the text, H_2 is in some degree a revision of the original. H_2 deviates through paraphrase of the true text, through use of synonyms of terms offered by other MSS., and it alters the poem by means of omission, amplification, and circumlocution. Illustration occurs as follows: *Waryed gostys* 447 are to suffer, not *hote* (A_1), but *helle fyre* 282, in the *pytte* (*stronge* A_1, *stynkynge* H_1 *fyre*) *of helle* 449, condemned with *angry eye* 446, at the *daye of* (*heie* A_1) *dome* 415. In plea for charity Guy is appealed to as generous friend: *frende so free* 323. Compare also *formeste* (*forme* A_1) 223; *lethere* (*foule* A_1) 72; *to thys goodnesse* (*hem* A_1) 100; *Vucerteynnesse* (*þisternesse* A_1) 114; *maye he be* (*worþ he* A_1) 128. See variants 133, 138, 160, 343, etc.

The inflectional system is governed by uniform laws illustrated in terminations transmitting -*y* for the normal -*e* in unaccented syllables as follows: *godys* (gen.) 38, 81, 139, etc.; *slewthys* 121; *fadyrys* 254, 255; *Londys* (plu.), *rentys* 152, 163; *metys* 155; *synnys* 91; *thewys* 97; *thewys : shrewis* 102; *Savyd* 128; *wykkyd* 116, 122; *fallyn* (inf.) 170; *betyn* 175; *suffyr* 176, 184; *ekyn* 188; *Herkenythe* (imp. plu.) 1, 137; *Wasshythe* 816; *bryngyþe* (3. sing.) 114; *makyþe* 124. Redundant *h* begins a word: *Habraham* (cf. D) 347.—Initial *h* is omitted: *ys* (for *his*) 227.—*f* occurs for *u* (*v*) of A_1: *leffe* 424.—Metathesis exists in *tharlle* 238. H_2 belonged earlier to the Cotton collection. It was in possession of Robert Cotton and bears his autograph.

Besides the MSS. already enumerated, some have been traced that, in description at least, belong in this chapter. MSS. W and B may be introduced with some certainty as giving information regarding the poem.

Worseley 67.

7. W. Worseley 67. See Edward Bernard in *Catalogi Librorum Manuscriptorum Angliæ et Hiberniæ in unum collecti*, 1697. Under *Librorum Manuscriptorum viri nobilis quo maxime merito speramus, Henrici Worseley de Hospitio Lincolensi apud Londinum Catalogus*, p. 213, is to be found what seems to be a reference to the *Speculum*. Number 67, also 6915, classifies an old "book." Its contents are: *Alquin's Advice to Gwy Earl of Warwyk*, and a "treatise[1] in English verse," the *Prykke of conscyence*, standing first in the book. The second selection is incomplete.

This heading, *Alquin's Advice to Gwy*, in English (M.E.), the form *Alquin* in this specific connection, and particularly the attendance of that Achates of the poem[2] of this volume, the faithful "Prykke of conscyence," serve tangibly to link W with MSS. of the *Speculum*, but the associated text has not been hitherto discovered.

The search[3] for the MSS. of the Worseley collection, as well as the actual investigation of a large number of the fifty MSS.[4] of *The Pricke of Conscience*,[5] has been without practical result in the discovery of the Worseley MSS. collectively, or of the "book" numbered 67. The libraries of Lincoln's Inn, of Lincoln Cathedral,[6] of Lambeth Palace, the Bodleian Library, the collections of the

---

[1] Clue to the history of MS. W and MS. B has not been contributed by the *Catalogue of the Library at Abbotsford*, Edinburgh, 1838, *A Catalogue of the Library of the Faculty of Advocates*, Edinburgh, 1838, Laing's *Catalogue of Manuscripts of the Society of the Writers to H. M. Signet in Scotland*, Hickes' *Thesaurus* or *Antiquæ Literaturæ Septentrionalis Libri duo*, nor from the *List of Manuscript Books in the Collection of David Laing*, nor in any of Laing's numerous editions of M.E. poetry; see, for example, *Select Remains of the Ancient popular Poetry of Scotland*, Edinburgh, 1822, *Early Popular Scottish Poetry* re-edited by W. Carew Hazlitt, London, 1895, nor in Stenhouse's *Lyric Poetry*, 1853, Halliwell's various editions, cf. *Reliquiæ Antiquæ*, 1841, nor in the editions of Ellis, Robson, Ritson, or Weber.

[2] See §§ 3—5 of this chapter.

[3] Search, direct and indirect, for possible MSS. of the *Speculum* in libraries of England, Scotland, Germany and France, has been exhaustive and painstaking. Vast labour, and untiring industry and patience, have not been rewarded in the discovery of MSS. beyond the record of the accompanying pages. The undoubted popularity of the poem in the fourteenth and fifteenth centuries suggested the possibility of many transcripts of the original.

[4] See *On Twenty-five MSS. of Richard Rolle's "Pricke of Conscience,"* "Eighteen of them in the British Museum, four in the Library of Trinity College, Dublin, the Corser MS., and two in Lichfield Cathedral Library," by Karl D. Bülbring, M.A., Ph.D., published for the Philological Society, London, 1889-90, p. 1.

[5] Professor Bülbring's list does not include the transcript MS. Dd 11, 89, of the University Library, Cambridge, nor the Lambeth MSS. *Stimulus Conscientiæ* or *the prykke of Conscience*, Nos. 260 (4) and 491 (6); see p. 2.

[6] Both are suggested by the element *de Hospitio Lincolensi* of Bernard's description of Worseley's collection, p. 213.

British Museum, seem none of them to have been the depository of Worseley's books. That in the disposal of the MSS. by auction, Worseley 67 could have passed into the Harleian collection of MSS., could have been numbered anew in that union, and could have become public in *Catalogue* and history as Harley 1731, might be conjectured through some coincidences in the description of the two MSS.; cf. § 3. If that be the case, MS. W has already been described and has been introduced into this work as MS. H_1.

With less reasonableness another MS., Bodley 1731, may be discussed in this connection.

Bodley 1731.

8. **B.** Bodley 1731. *Disputatio inter priorem aliquem & spiritum Guidonis.* See Ritson, *A. E. Metrical Romanceës*, I., p. xciii., edition of 1802. A title of this character, introduced in connection with a description of MS. Harl. 525, suggested at once a transcript of the *Speculum*, but thus far MS. B has proved to be "an empty name," a title existing only on Ritson's page.

Granting the existence of a corresponding text, coincidence in numbering recalls a second time the Harley MS. 1731, and it is to be conceded that Ritson may simply have referred to the MS. H_1. Some confusion in the heading might be assumed to have arisen on ground of erratic orthography,[1] for which Ritson was famed, or through his proverbial inaccuracy.[2] *aliquem* could be reconciled as a typographical error.

On the other hand, Ritson's description may be accounted for on the hypothesis of a manuscript of a different type, but fulfilling quite rationally the conditions of the title. Although the conclusive MS. has not come to light, yet the theory is strengthened through analogy with MS. Bodley 3903, named also by Ritson in the *A. E. Metrical Romanceës*, I., p. xciii. Bodley 3903 bears now the signature Fairfax 23. Here is another Guido, the *dramatis persona* of

---

[1] "Ballantyne," says Scott, "groans in spirit over the peculiarities of his (Ritson's) orthography, which hath seldom been equalled since the days of Elphinstone, the ingenious author of the mode of spelling according to the pronunciation," etc., Lockhart, II., p. 81.

[2] To Ritson's notable inaccuracy Scott refers writing of "many curious facts and quotations, which the poor defunct (*i.e.* Ritson) had the power of assembling to an astonishing degree, without being able to combine anything like a narrative, or even to deduce one useful inference," Lockhart, II., p. 122. Schick adds a word, *Temple of Glas*, p. cxlviii., asserting that Ritson copied "without understanding from headings of MSS. and entries in *Catalogues*,"—and mingled them in new combinations, could probably be added.

a mediæval vision literature, in which the disembodied spirit of Guido of Alet holds communion with a certain friar. Its hero has nothing in common with Guy of Warwick but the name Guy. The *Jahrbuch des Vereins für niederdeutsche Sprachforschung*, vol. xiii. (1887), p. 81 ff., in an article by Brandes entitled *Guido von Alet* and referring to *Arnt Buschmans Mirakel, von W. Seelman herausgeg., Jahrbuch*, vol. vi., 32 ff., treats of literature of this character. Wright discussed the question forty-four years earlier in *St. Patrick's Purgatory*, "an Essay on the Legends of Purgatory, Hell, and Paradise, current during the Middle Ages;" cf. pp. 45-47. The purpose of this dialogue is to enforce the doctrine of transubstantiation. Another branch of the legend[1] is illustrated in Dr. Anne Leonard's Zürich dissertation, *Zwei mittelenglische Geschichten aus der Hölle*, Zürich, 1891, and the cycle of purgatorial literature is enriched by *The Revelation to the Monk of Evesham* (Arber reprint) with its list of *Gesta Purgatoris*, p. 14. Albrecht Wagner[2] in *Tundale*, "das mittelenglische Gedicht über die Vision des Tundalus," "auf Grund von vier Handschriften," pp. iii. ff., cites arguments basing the source of this comprehensive mediæval type in the *Divine Comedy*. He supports his theory on works of Labitte, *La divine comédie avant Dante in Études littéraires*, I., pp. 193—263, and Ozanam, *Dante et la philosophie catholique au treizième siècle*.

MSS. of the Guido controversy are abundant. Many copies of the fundamental Latin text exist, and an English metrical version[3] is extant in MS. Tiberius E vii., to be dated 1350-60. A prose version exists in the Vernon MS. The opening lines of Fairfax 23 are:

"*Incipit disputatio inter quendam priorem et spiritum gwidonis. Augustinus in libro de fide ad petrum dicit: 'miraculum est, quicquam arduum uel insolitum super facultatem hominis.'*"

Compare with this passage the opening sentence of the Berlin MS., Königliche Bibliothek, MS. germ. Quart. 404, Bl. 85a—111b of the fifteenth century:

---

[1] See Furnivall, *Pol., Relig. and Love Poems*, E. E. Text Society, 1866, pp. 93 ff.; Horstmann, *Altengl. Legenden, Neue Folge*, pp. 367 ff.; Halliwell, *Thornton Romances*, p. xxv.; and Halliwell, *Dictionary*.

[2] Wagner claims for Tundale, *eine wahre Sturmflut von lateinischen Handschriften und alten Drucken über Oesterreich, Italien, die Schweiz, Frankreich, Belgien, England, und Irland*; cf. *Visio Tungdali* lateinisch u. altdeutsch, Erlangen, 1882, pp. x. ff. He finds also Spanish, Provençal, Swedish, and Icelandic versions, discussed by Mussafia in *Sulla Visione di Tundalo*, Wiener Sitzungsberichte, philos.-hist. Cl., Bd. 67, pp. 157 ff.

[3] Cf. *De Spiritu Guidonis*, Vesp. E 1., Vesp. A VI., and Add. MSS. 22,283.

Chapter III.—Description of the MSS. MS. B. xxxix

"*Also alse sunte Augustinus seghet in deme boke van deme yeloven to sunte Peter: Eyn wunder is dat geheiten, dat wunderliken schüt boven de naturliken krefften und boven menslike wunder,*" etc.

The corresponding passage is furnished by the Vernon MS., fol. 363. It begins: "*For as muche as seint Austin seiþ to Peter in þe Booc of þe leeue,*" etc. The metrical version, MS. Tiber. E. vii., ll. 2 ff., reads:

> "*and saint Austin, þe doctur dere,
> and oþer maisters mare & myn,
> sais, þat men grete mede may wyn,*" etc.

This Guido[1] leaves no doubt about himself, v. Bl. 99a: "*bin ich Gowido verlost van der pine des vegevurs veir jar dan sich borde.*" The tradition is followed with fidelity in English. MS. Vernon reads: "*ich am þe spirit of Gy & his soule, þat nou late was ded*"; MS. Tiber. E. vii. :

> "*þe voice answerd to him in hy
> and said: I am spirit of Gy,
> þe whilk ʒe wate was newly dede,*" etc.

It is quite as probable that the Guy of MS. B belongs to this family, as that his prior be identified with Alquin of the *Speculum*. The inference that MSS. Bodley 1731 and 3903, *i. e.* Fairfax 23, are the same, is not ungrounded, but their identity has not been proved, and the use of the term Bodley in both connections cannot be indicated to be other than accidental.

Another theory originates in the prolific literature of the tradition.[2] It is possible to explain Bodley 1731 as a composite title representing several MSS., but not belonging necessarily[3] to any of them, a title without an individual text, one of that "jumble"[4] described by Schick, *Temple of Glas*, p. cxlviii. ff., and Lockhart, II., p. 122. It might result not merely from "splitting up one work into several" (Schick, p. cli.), but from the uniting of the titles of the "split portions" of several works into a single heading without definite MS. For Ritson, the "dogmatical little word-catcher," nothing would be easier than to invent such a visionary title.

---

[1] Guido is a "child of the time," see Arnt Buschman, p. 41: *Ich bin eyn geist, ein cristenmenschen,* etc.

[2] See *Sprachforschung*. Seelman enumerates seventeen texts of the *Mirakel*.

[3] Harl. 2379 is a *Liber de Spiritu Guidonis*: *Narratio Legendaria de confabulatione habita inter Animam prædicti Guidonis civis de Alestey (quæ distat ab Avenion 21 miliarijs)*, and states *Guido obijt* 1323. Cotton Vesp. E 1. ends: *explicit . . . disputacio mirabilis inter priorem . . . et inter spiritum . . . Guydonis.*

[4] Scott writes of Ritson's *Essay on Romance and Minstrelsy*, cf. Lockhart, II., p. 122, that it reminds one of "a heap of rubbish, which had either turned out unfit for the architect's purpose or beyond his skill to make use of."

The material is richly provided through a multitude of the paradise-purgatory texts.[1] MS. Cotton Vespasian E. I., fol. 219 ff., is a "*dispucatio mirabilis inter priorem . . . et inter spiritum . . .*", whose hero is *Guydo.*" Number 16, Bibliothek des Gymnasiums Carolinum, Osnabrück; Papierhs. . . D, 76, is a veritable "*Disputatio inter priorem et spiritum Gwidonis.*" A Kiel MS., "Universitäts-Bibliothek, Miscellan. hs. 38, Bl. 175 ff., is "*spiritus Gwidonis . . . et . . . priorem quendam*" (Ritson's *aliquem*?). The Darmstadt MS. 106 is: *eyne disputatie tuschen eyme prior . . . ind eyme geiste . . . Gwido heisch.*

Whether Ritson's Bodley 1731 be actual or imaginary, whether it be but Harl. 1731, or Worseley 67 classified as Harl. 1731 or not, is not clear. That the three be but descriptions of the same MS., and that recognized as MS. Harl. 1731, there is at present no absolute proof. MS. B cannot be traced.

CHAPTER IV.

GENEALOGICAL HISTORY OF THE TEXTS.

I. GROUP Y.

§ 1. *MSS. H_2 and D in distinction from MSS. $A_1 A_2 H_1 R$.*

1. *Resemblances between MSS. D and H_2.*

OF approximately the same age, but differing often in peculiarities of dialect, D and H_2 are undeniably connected in MS. development. Noteworthy is the conspicuous *lacuna* occurring simultaneously in both MSS. Lines 459—475 are wanting, the break marking practically the conclusion of MS. H_2. Of the fifty-one lines, 407—458, omitted in MS. D, twelve are also deficient in MS. H_2. Otherwise coincidences marking the relationship of D and H_2 are chiefly mutilations characterizing the individual word. In this investigation it must be recalled, that the comparison represents but 400 lines, the last reading to be ascribed to the texts in common being line 399.

Among the more conspicuous resemblances[2] is that to be found

---

[1] For the Swedish version see J. A. Ahlstrand in the *Samlingar* utg. af Svenska Fornskrift Sällskapet I. Ll. f. *Guidonis siels openbarelse.*

[2] It will be assumed as understood, that in this discussion only the more conspicuous instances of the mutilation of the archetype are to be regarded as affording conclusive evidence, determinative of the main results of the argument. Naturally nothing else could be possible.

Chapter IV.—Genealogical History of the Texts. xli

in line 180, where inversion of the adverbial phrase occurs in both D and H_2: *þe better for he (þey H_2) sull (shulde H_2) hym knowe*, in distinction from *For þei schold hym þe better knawe* of MSS. A_2H_1R. Line 381 reads *cler and clene*, contrary to *clene and cler* of the fundamental text. Line 393 describes the *sonn* as feminine, preserving *here*, in harmony with the older Germanic (O.E., O.H.G.) usage instead of *his* of MSS. A_1H_1R. Line 186 replaces *haue* with *suffri* (*suffyr* H_2), 195 *blisse* with *wele*, and 266 *turment* with *tournement*. The texts are identical twice in modification resulting from the dialect of the scribes, through the reproduction of *his* by *is* (*ys*), line 227, and *wouh* by *wowe*, line 302, in opposition to all the other MSS. Alterations in individual words occur as follows:

v. 1 to] vnto D.H_2. 32 þe] þis. 141 it] I. 172 And] He. 182 þat] þe. 186 haue] suffri. 195 blisse] wele. 227 his] is. 257 on] at. 266 turment] tournement. 283 nouþe] now. 302 wouh] wowe. 318 ouer] in. It is unimportant as decisive evidence, that lines 167 and 280 translate *Ac* of MS. A_1 *and*, and interpret *here* 308 as *paire*.

MSS. D and H_2 agree through various omissions from the fundamental text. Conspicuous is the loss of *Nay*, line 398, and of so important a word as *sinful* in line 149. Other MSS. contribute the following readings lost to MSS. D and H_2:

v. 8 þu] *om*. D.H_2 (l. *om*. H_1). 23 For] *om*. 31 Hou] *om*. 40 he was] *om*. 41 he] *om*. 149 sinful] *om*. 183 And] *om*. 308 al] *om*. 327 wite] *om*. 398 Nay] *om*.

On the other hand, D and H_2 preserve at the same time mutilations not familiar in other texts. Compare coincidences in D and H_2 as follows:

v. 196 abouten] all abouten D H_2. 207 shalt] shalt man. 224 singyn] first synne. 321 þe] For the (so). 373 and 391 telle] tell it. 399 preued] proued wele. 138 introduces a redundant þe.

With these combinations must be considered all readings in which D and H_2 harmonize with other MSS., particularly in alterations that unite also peculiarities of MS. A_2; cf. § 2. Minor instances of agreement justify the conclusions of the preceding paragraphs, pointing to a common source for MSS. D and H_2.

2. *Differences between MSS. D and H_2.*

MSS. D and H_2 preserving common errors that might be derived from a single source, deviate in important particulars, suggesting that neither text is dependent on the other. MS. H_2 is often corrupt to a degree not shared by MS. D.

a. That MS. D does not have its origin in MS. H_2, is evident from lines interpolated in H_2, that are not to be found in D, e. g. between 4 and 5; 138, 139; 160, 161; 322, 323; from transpositions of H_2 alone, 111, 112; in the omissions not shared by D, lines 11, 12; 197, 198; 295—300; 309, 310; and in revised readings, lines 108, 133, 283, 323, 328, 378. In H_2 lines 829—1034 of the original text are wanting, and a false conclusion not extant in D appears in place of lines 1022—1034. D is complete in this part of the poem, preserving the true conclusion shared by A_1 and R of the opposing group. These two MSS. differ also in the following instances, where MS. D has often preserved the correct reading:

D *not derived from* H_2: v. 8 god ouer] wele god abovyn H_2. 18 In] In to H_2. 19 wole] shall. 21 Ne for] For noo. 22 þe] his. 25 þeih don god] Iesu criste. 26 bouhte] abouȝte. 27 while] stounde. 30 Gy] Sire Gy. 31 On] Vppe on. 35 And] He. 37 in] be. 45 was wel] sone was full. 46 þerfore] And alle. 49 On] Vpon. 52 wel] *om.* 54 us] ouyr vs. 57 Make me] Doo me make. 59 my delit] grete delyte. 61 foule] false. 62 lad] be lyed. while] A while. 63 wole] wolde. 64 þe world] hym. 66 And] And swythe. 72 foule] lethere. 73 don] mynn. 75 now] nowe hem. 84 þe] me. 87 ful] and fulle. 90 vse] doo welle. 96 lyf] lyffe also. 98 Whar þurw] Where with. reche] Areche. 99 so] thus. 101 wicke] othere. 125 Offte] Welofte. 127 turne] flee. 137 sarmoun] lessounne. 138 tell] rede. in my lesczoun] be resounne. 142 reche] Areche. 152 As] *om.* 157 Hele] Helthe. 158 And] *om.* of] also of. 160 worþ] wylle be. 162 muche] ryȝt mochill. 166 halt] haue. 173 And] For. 174 For] *om.* synn] A synne. 178 kudde] shewythe. 181 He wole] *om.* 187 seknesse] stronge syknysse. 188 And] *om.* 189 leuest] be leue. 192 wo] sorowe. 195 þe] þys. 204 is] ther ys. 209 had] ne hadde. 212 ȝif] gaffe. 213 made] shope. owen] *om.* 217 of] *om.* 225 wite] wyte ryȝte. 229 And] *om.* 258 wid oute nay] for soþe too saye. 259 þat] þat afore. 261 þer] Hedyr. adoun] downe. 262 a] ony. 263 nele] þan wyll. 264 man] men. 265 He shal] They shulle þan. fonge] take. 267 ounne] þan on. 273 bileuen] be leuyn. 275 Austin] austyn he. 281 duire] þere endure. 292 tellen] telle ȝow halffe ne. 314 owen] *om.* 329 Hit is loue] Loue welle. 332 þing] *om.* most] mvste nedys. 335 god] *om.* 337 If] For yffe. ful] *om.* 338 wolt]

Chapter IV.—Genealogical History of the Texts. xliii

mvste nedys. *uides*] *tu vides*. 375 Bodiliche] Godlyche. 379 a þing] ys. 390 grete] moche. 392 lef þu] be leue. 396 bodilich] boldelyche. eiȝe] *om*. him] *om*. 397 on] in. 401 þis] yt. 402 ise] here se.

The list might be increased from numberless individual faults for which H_2 alone bears the responsibility.

β. On the other hand, MS. H_2 did not have its origin in MS. D. This is indicated by an altered verse in MS. D, line 376, and in the transposition of lines 167 and 168; 201, 202; 303, 304. *D* has the following readings, not shared with H_2:

H_2 *not derived from D:* v. 2 And] *om*. D. 10 do] do so. 24 and] þen. 27 *and* 28 wole] sal(l). 35 his] eke hys. 40 gode] riȝt gude. 48 kepen] wyten. qued] dede. 53 And] anon. 58 losczoun] a lessoun. 63 þer of] þer for. 70 Alþere] Erle. wole] schal. 71 for to] to þe. 80 Whiche] þe wyche. 82 be my] I þe. 89 ore] lore. 91 sinne] synne haue. 94 wyll be þi] with dede. 95 charyte] chaste. 101 wole] sall. 113 þis] *om*. 119 wole] sall. 124 man] men. anuied] vnneþe. 130 þurw] *om*. 140 þat] *om*. 144 rod] þe rode. 149 Thys ys] It es. 154 faire and bold] and faire bold. 156 litel] leþe. 160 after] *om*. 168 hem] whum. 176 Or] Oþer. 178 hym] man. 182 hem] hym. 183 Many an] A man. hem] hym. 188 all it is] all. here] þaire ioy and. 192 liuede] lybbeþe. 193 þou] es. 194 maitou] þou myȝt ful. 200 wyll] sal. 206 þre] And þre. 212 gaffe] ȝif þe. 214 of his] and heȝe. 215 ȝaf] ȝif. 217 yuel] of euel. for] cheyse. 218 þe] þat. 222 wole] wollen to. 226 yt] he. 230 him] *om*. 232 pylt] put. 236 aftyr] siþþen. 238 in] to. 241 don] idon. 242 his] hym. 244 he] hem. 250 Tyll it] Forto. 254 into] to. ffadyrys ryche] awne fader. 278 point] apoynt. 284 i wole ȝou] *om*. 289 hadde] haue. 312 þov] it. 320 bi] *om*. 321 the] so. 335 Man] þan. 346 wel] *om*. 355 hym] now. 356 of] al of. 359 on] of. 362 And] In. 377 witen] I wyte. 383 breme] beme. 384 here] þaire. 387 sitte] schyne. 388 euere] euereche. mannes] bodyly. 401 þanne] How.

Numerous variations notably distinct in character are sufficient to show that MSS. D and H_2 are not to be ascribed either to the other for ultimate source, but that rather they both descend from a common original represented by D H_2.

§ 2. *MSS.* A_2 *(D* H_2*).*

Some instances occur in which A_2 unites with D and H_2 in reproducing the same antecedent text. Readings pointing to a common original for MSS. $A_2.D.H_2$, apart from the testimony of important coincidences between D and H_2, shown in the preceding section to go back to a common source, are as follows for lines 1—406, 814—828, the portion of the poem covered by the parallel texts.

v. 45 : Off him] þare of $A_2.D.H_2$. 105 is hit] it is. 167 Ac] And. 168 erere] are (eere H_2). 820 doþ] þe. Compare also line 190, where individuality in grouping is marked by divergence common to each of the MSS. of the group, suggesting defect of prototype and an attempted restoration by the individual scribes of Y. Z, on the other hand, preserves one form, *e. g. miht.*

Group Y is distinguished by readings in which mutilation is represented in a slight modification of the basis of the classification through the individuality of the rendering of a single MS. Recalling the tendency of the copyist of the *Speculum* to leave personal impress on his MS. in emendations originating with himself, it will be recognized that the unity of the grouping Y is not necessarily interrupted by divergence on the part of a single member. Such instances are as follows, where two of the MSS. seem to be derived from the source $(A_2.D.H_2)$, common to the three, while $A_1.H_1.R$ (group Z), the opposing element, exists intact :

v. 51 Alquin] sire alquyn $A_2.D$. ffrere Alquyne H_2. 217 shed] for $A_2.H_2$. cheyse D. 321 þe] þe more $A_2.H_2$. so D. 393 sunne his] sonn here $D.H_2$. sonnes A_2. *Perhaps in verse* 100 : wolt hem to, *where A_2 reads* wylt heuen to, D wylt þese to, *and H_2* wylte to thys. Both A_2 and H_2 attest to irregularity in the transmission of text Z.

To these readings can be added all those instances, in which group Y, on one side, is united in internal relationship in opposition to group Z intact on the other, $A_2.D.H_2$ against $A_1.H_1.R$; cf. § 5. This grouping is confirmed by coincidences between single combining pairs of MSS. comprising Y, and suggestive of an archetype $(A_2.D.H_2)$ common to the three texts. The noteworthy agreement marking D and H_2 has been studied, § 1. Coincidence less striking is to be recognized in MSS. A_2 and H_2.

§ 3. *Study of MSS. A_2 and H_2.*
1. *Resemblances between the MSS.*

Resemblance between A_2 and H_2 occurs in line 154, where H_2 and A_2 offer *faire and bold* instead of the correct version, *and faire*

Chapter IV.—Genealogical History of the Texts. xlv

bold. A_2H_2 substitute *hell* for *hote*, line 282, and add *eke* 311, not found in $A_1A_2DH_1R$. A_2 and H_2, line 815, read *euene* for *ene* of $A_1.H_1$. Other points of resemblance are as follows:

v. 40 And] *om.* $A_2.H_2$. 46 þerfore] And. 68 His] þi. 73 don] *om.* 114 man] a man. 149 þis] þis is. 174 a] *om.* 176 pine] paynes. 257 þider] Hedere. 274 men] man. 331 euere] *om.* 372 imeind] I menged. 393 þat] *om.* 456 him] *om.*

2. *Differences between the MSS.*

Abundant proof contradicts any supposition of the origin of A_2 in H_2, or of H_2 in A_2. A_2 could not have been transcribed from H_2, the younger MS. omitting passages extant in A_2. H_2 preserves verses of which A_2 presents no knowledge. A_2 then cannot be conceived as having passed directly to the hands of the scribe of H_2. H_2 shows no impress of the confusion in verses 82 and 140 with the interpolation after 82 characterizing A_2. H_2 preserves lines 55, 56; 181, 182; 261, 262; omitted in A_2. Compare the following minor instances, where H_2 has often the correct version:

MS. H_2 not derived from MS. A_2: v. 18 þurw his] at a A_2. 23 þer] þei. 24 foule] fals A_2. 35 his] all his. 38 al] wele. 53 And] I. 74 on] o þynge. 77 at] *om.* 85 hope] *om.* 94 wyll be þi] to. 97 þewes] vertues. 108 telle] schewe. 128 he] þei. 131 þurw] for. 133 behouythe] I rede. 138 wyll rede] shall say. 143 þat] And þat. 150 it were] *om.* 167 and rede] *om.* 264 þat] *om.* 272 þeih] *om.* 275 austyn he] poul. 308 For al] For. 312 But] For. 353 grette] sawe. 381 clere] *om.* 387 And] *om.* he] it. so] neuer so. 388 Hit] ȝit it. 389 hire] *om.* 393 ȝaf] *om.* here] *om.* 394 tyme] *om.* 395 þane] so. 419 here] *om.* 432 ȝe] þei. 434 for] to. 441 And] *om.* 446 angry] *om.* 449 evene] *om.* pytte] payne. The list might be increased by additional illustration marking the character of MSS. A_2 and H_2.

§ 4. *Relationship between A_2 and D.*

1. *Coincidences in A_2 and D.*

MSS. A_2.D. form a connecting link in the relationship developing the group Y. Line 51 reads for both *sire alquyn* instead of *Alquin* of group Z. *chirche* replacing *clerk*, l. 667, is a marked characteristic of resemblance linking the two texts. A_2 and D combine in the version *mynde* for *mid* (689) of $A_1.H_1$. In addition to the omission of line 679 common to both, other modifications occur as follows:

v. 6 to god] of god A_2.D. 13 Ac] And. 45 war] I war. 53 And] I. 66 he] *om.* 101 þe] *om.* 127 man] a man. 160 ibouht] abought (aboute *D*). 168 erere] are. 226 bouht] a bouʒt. 241 Ac] And. 299 þe] *om.* 306 þisternesse] dirkenese. 315 Ac] And. 321 inwardlichere] inwordelich. 336 Wher] Wheþere. 350 and as] and. 353 on] *om.* (407—475 *mark the comprehensive break in D.*) 480 out] *om.* 507 hit wolen] willen it. 538 Or] Ouþer. 624 And] *om.* 625 wole] nyll. 628 in none] in no. 635 And] For. 675 a] *om.* 684 hit] þat. 689 mid] mynde. 725 gon] agone. 729 riht] ariht. 731 þisternesse] derkenes. 790 me] to me. 804 wole] nyl. 811 is] is þe. 812 man] men. 834 he shal] schall he. 870 and] or. 880 many] man.

Intimate resemblance is marked in line 791 in distinction from the version of group Z: *sinne wrouht*] *foule synne Iwrouʒt*.

2. *Differences between A_2 and D.*

α. A_2 *not derived from D*: That A_2 preserving the oldest MS. of group Y cannot, for this reason, have originated in MS. D nor in MSS. $D.H_2$ singly or combined, is obvious. Nor is it necessary to give detailed proof, that neither of the younger MS. versions can be the source of the other. The independent character of MS. H_2 is clear from § 1 of this chapter. The same section shows also the indebtedness of $D.H_2$ to some common source. That that original is not A_2 is evident from the omission in that MS. of lines 55, 56; 181, 182; 261, 262; preserved in MSS. $D.H_2$, and of lines 648—653; 678; 840—845 of the original, for which MS. D is authority, where H_2 is practically at an end. The transposition of lines 75, 76 in A_2 is not recorded in $D.H_2$, and the altered readings 140, 141, 142, relatively to 82 with interpolations caused $D.H_2$ no difficulty. Instances occur, where A_2 preserves individual errors and D and H_2 retain the correct versions. Some of these passages are indicated in the sections to follow:

β. *D not derived from A_2*: v. 18 þurw his] at a A_2. 24 foule] fals. 59 my ioye] ioy. 74 on] o þynge. 85 hope] *om.* Many similar examples of irregularity in relationship make it evident that none of the MSS. of this group was antecedent for any other. It is fair to attribute them to a common source (A_2 D H_2).

A_2 and H_2 sharing with D a common source, bear trace of the

Chapter IV.—Genealogical History of the Texts. xlvii

original from which the group Y was generated. That A_2 was not the source of a, the transcript common to $D.H_2$, and that a did not serve as original for A_2 is obvious from comparison of the two groups of coincidences, D and H_2 on one hand § 1, and A_2 and H_2, § 3 on the other. Characteristic readings are in each group so uniformly distinct, that the only hypothesis possible must be the supposition of a common source for A_2 and $a = DH_2$, $Y = A_2.D.H_2$. This grouping is represented by some pair of its MSS. throughout the poem. The existence of a group of MSS. Y involves the explanation of a corresponding group Z, to become the subject of the investigation in the section to follow.

II. GROUP Z.
§ 5. *Two Groups of Manuscripts.*

These six existing texts enumerated in the foregoing chapter may be considered to be subdivided into two groups, a group Z embracing MSS. $A_1.H_1.R$, and a group Y embracing MSS. $A_2.D.H_2$. Determinative in this classification are the following coincidences, $A_1.H_1.R$ on one side, and $A_2.D.H_2$ on the other :

v. 40 A *om.*] A ($A_2.D.H_2$) Y.   45 Off him] þare of Y.   182 þat] þe Y.   200 And *om.*] And Y.   222 man] he Y.   240 for euere] euer Y.   299 þe] *om.* Y.   303 kointise] qweyntise Y.   381 clene] cler Y.   From line 407 the continued omission of one MS. of group Y must be recalled, Z being intact. Otherwise the classification remains uninterrupted.   454 whij] *om.* Y.   480 out] *om.* Y.   624 And] *om.* Y.   667 clerk] chirche Y.   675 a] *om.* Y.   684 hit] þat Y.   725 gon] agone Y.   729 riht] ariht Y.   791 sinne] foule synne Y.   804 wolc] nyl Y.   812 man] men Y.   820 doþ] þe Y.   870 and] or Y.   880 many] *om.* Y.

In support of this grouping the transposition of lines 673 and 674 occurs in each of the three members of group Z, the normal sequence being preserved in the grouping Y. Line 679 is omitted entirely in group Y.

These readings, offsetting each other, and in each instance characteristic of a distinct grouping, seem proof that neither group is derived directly from the other. This hypothesis is confirmed by numerous characteristic modifications, interpolations, or omissions distinguishing individual pairs of manuscripts. It may be assumed that both groups are to be referred to a common source $A_1H_1R\ A_2DH_2$ = U, which was perhaps the original text.

§ 6. *MSS.* A_1 (H_1R).

Group Z is characterized by readings in which group Y is in opposition through a slight alteration in the principle on which the classification is based, cf. § 2. Z is an integral group in the following instances, agreeing by means of the readings introduced below:

v. 51 *Alquin.* 217 *shed.* 321 *þe* (*unmodified*). 393 *sunne his.* 100 *wolt hem to.* Group Z deviates slightly, l. 105, in the omission of *hit* in *R*, where otherwise the two groups are intact. In 167, group Y are unanimous in the use of *And*, while $H_1.R$ translate *Ac* of A_1, by the redaction *But*, a characteristic reading of $H_1.R$ not in opposition to the group Z; cf. § 6. Similarly 188 omits *it*, the value of group Z being uninfluenced. 250 has difficulty with an added *to* in *Y*. The line reads in *D For to com* instead of the *Tyll it came to* of $A_2.H_2$, in opposition to group Z, *Til hit com.*

The integral character of group Z is preserved in additional readings:

v. 79 i wolc] I wyll (*with added word*) $A_2.H_2$. I sal D. 94 shal be þi] *altered* $A_2.D.H_2$. 297 parten] *altered* $A_2.D.H_2$. 321 þe] *altered* $A_2.D.H_2$. 353 as on] *altered* $A_2.D.H_2$. 381 cler] *altered* $A_2.D.H_2$. 399 preued] *altered* $A_2.D.H_2$. 449 fyr] *altered* $A_2.H_2$. D *om.* 550 to þe] *altered* Y. 559 in þouht] *altered* Y. 602 vilte] wyte A_2. vilanie? D. 858 þe] is þe A_2. þi D. 872 or] and A_2. oþer D.

To these may be added other passages, which, though varying in some detail, yet do not in general detract from the force of the argument: lines 168, 188, etc. With these coincidences are to be considered those presenting intimate connection within the limits of its immediate group.

§ 7. *MSS.* H_1 and *R* in opposition to *MSS.* $A_1\ A_2\ D\ H_2$.

1. *Coincidences in MSS.* H_1 *and R.*

It is obvious that intimate relationship must characterize *R* and H_1 in common. Although separated by an interval of seventy-five years on general estimate, and at variance in important details, by which each MS. is characterized by mistakes introduced on its own responsibility, yet it must be admitted, that the transcripts *R* and H_1 in noteworthy instances unite in combinations not accounted for in remaining texts. The omission of lines 737—740 is shared in common

Chapter IV.—Genealogical History of the Texts.

by the MSS. Absolutely in opposition to MSS. $A_1.A_2.D.H_2.$ are coincidences in the version of entire lines often broadly different from the same lines in other texts.[1] R and H_1, for instance, omit the line 792, *In word, in dede, and in þouht,* and substitute in its place line 838 of the original text, *Loþly (Lodely* R) *and fele (foule* R) *many oon.* The line 342, omitted in MS. D, is enriched by *with eghen* in $H_1.R$, of which MSS. $A_1.A_2.H_2$ retain no trace; cf. as follows:

  342: þat þou may alday with eghen se. (R)
     whom þou maiste see eche day wiþ yeȝe. (H_1)

The relationship between R and H_1 is attested to by line 488, where the original text has been omitted, and in its place a different version supplied:

  488: Whil that thou may go & se. (R)
     Whilest þou maiste goo & see. (H_1)
     Loke, þat þu þe bise. (A_1A_2D, *om. in* H_1R)

A similar variation exists in line 790, where A_1 and A_2, the two most reliable texts, are answerable for a good reading: *Sitteþ stille, and herkneþ me.* R and H_1 have preserved: *Herken and I wil telle þe.* A modification occurs, line 808, through the insertion of *fire brenne (fyre burne* H_1). 831 alters *wasshe* ($A_1.A_2.D$) to *to wasshe hem.* 716 contributes the version: *I wil ȝow (þe* R) *telle whi & wharfore.* Inversion occurs in both: 671 *bere he] he bere.* Often of minor importance as conclusive proof, yet offering convincing evidence of coincidence in individual words, are illustrations as follows:

R and H_1 agree in introducing a word differing from texts $A_1.A_2.D.H_1$: v. 4 *and* 736 swiþe] ful $H_1.R$. 791 (I)wrouȝt] don $H_1.R$. 242 ȝaf] had. 366 ene] bene. 466 rede] spede. 168 erere] bifore. Of the same general significance are: 178 kudde] kyþeþ. 190 miht] maist. 198 lihtliche] lyȝtly. 293 also] as. 309 mid] with. 330 in] &. 414 þe] Al. 496 þat] þis. 497 þe] þis. 530 Off] On. 725 knowelaching] knowynge. 909 leten and flen] leoue and fle R, leue and flye H_1. *But* translates *Ac* of MS. A_1 in the following instances, where MSS. $A_2.D.H_2$ read invariably *and* or *for* or omit the word. *But* ($H_1.R$) 13, 167, 280, 463, 467, 471, 615, 623, 660, 893. H_1 and R share the translation with A_2, where that MS. seems to have stumbled upon the same interpretation: 583, 619,

---

[1] In general the arrangement of the examples under § 7 is in the order of their importance.

830, 835, 849. *But* also belongs to $H_1.R$ shared with H_2: 241, 293, 315, 347, 434.

(β) A word is added that is wanting entirely in the opposing MSS.: v. 394 *om.*] siþe $H_1.R$. 452 *om.*] haue. 702 *om.*] childe. 553, 689 *om.*] þere. 678 *om.*] al. 907 *om.*] þen. Less important in the argument are the following instances: 106 *om.*] For. 378 *om.*] and. 801 *om.*] for. 830 *om.*] haue.

(γ) MSS. $A_1.A_2.D.H_2$ contain a word not recorded in H_1 and R: v. 190 þu sek] Seek $H_1.R$. 242 his] *om.* 339 For men] Men (Man H_1). 394 swich] *om.* 410 ne] *om.* 524 Nu] *om.* 582 ne] *om.* 617 þi] *om.* 812 þat] *om.* 840 ne] *om.*

To these coincidences may be added all those variations of a trifling character, which though differing slightly, yet may represent a common source: *he* is replaced by *þei* 833, 834; *miht* by *maiste* 859, 864; *Nas þat* by *þat was* 214; *noht* by *wil noȝ* H_1, *wil not* R 312. The list is to be increased by the common readings distinguishing the three MSS. $A_1.H_1.R$; see §§ 5, 6.

2. *Differences between MSS. H_1 and R.*

Incontrovertible points of coincidence between MSS. R and H_1 are counterbalanced by instances of deviation, suggesting that R and H_1 may be ascribed to a common source rather than to a relationship one from the other.

a. *MS. H_1 not the source of MS. R:* R, the older of the two MSS., cannot be derived from MS. H_1. MS. R preserves individual defects not shared by MS. H_1. Compare lines 6, 9, 15, 34, 84, 107, 129, etc. It contains lines omitted in MS. H_1, omits interpolated passages, and makes frequent alterations of the original as follows: lines 204—206; 403, 404; 447, 448; 507, 508; 591, 592; etc. Omissions in MS. H_1, where MS. R retains the correct reading, are: 7, 8; 133; 136; 272; 479, 572; etc.; cf. chap. iii. 3.

β. *MS. R not the source of MS. H_1:* Equally impossible is it that MS. H_1 find source in MS. R. Lines 45 and 46, transcribed by H_1, are omitted in MS. R. Line 272 of R alters the original reading. A multitude of minor examples confirm the testimony of these verses. That H_1 is not derived from R, is shown by the accompanying instances, where H_1 has in general preserved the correct reading, although at times both MSS. deviate from the original.

v. 12 to *om.*] to R. 20 Ne shaltu] þou shalt not. 22 weye] lawe. 26 ful *om.*] ful. 31 on] in. 38 liuede al in] leued wel alle.

Chapter IV.—Genealogical History of the Texts. li

51 þe] þat. 58 don hit write] write hit. 74 on] bothe one. 84 þey] þese thre. 102 beþ noht gode] are swithe. 114 men] mony. to] vnto. derkenes] merkenes. 116 *and* 121 sleuþe(s)] slownes. 117 wel] ful. 124 anuied] fro mynde. 136 ȝe wil] þai wil. 160 shal be] mot be. 161 falle] bifalle. 177 ȝe here] þou here now. (louc)rede] (I) rede. 182 hem] hom to. 185 and *om.*] and. 193 if] if þou. 194 wel] þo better. 196 abouten] hit thorou. 199 Now I wil here of] Here I wil a while. 201 man] more. 220 ȝifte] might. 226 haþ] was ful. 232 he was] was he. 235 for] for þat. 237 bimonie hym] fro hym tane. 241 þurw] for. 244 man] monkynde. 248 And þus] *om.* deiede] with harde deth. 263 nele] wil. 265 He] þai. 271 go] wende. into] til. 278 point] ende. 285 sumwhat] now forthe. 288 eke see] al so sene. 291 ȝit myȝt it] hit might. 297 þat *om.*] þat. 306 ony derknes] merkenes. 315 lat hit noht come] trow þou wel. 316 any] non. 317 he þat] who so. 327 be] may be. 338 his] þat is hisse. 340 myne] my hyne. 387 sitte] is sett. 389 hire] hit. 399 þat] and þat. 410 ifiled] fyled right. 412 þe] and þo. 415 heie] grete. 423 Comeþ] Comes now. 434 al] þat. 435 turne] hym turne. 440 his fet] fete did hom to seke. 452 ȝe] for ȝe han. 456 Off] On. doþ] wolde. 459 Sein] For seynt. 470 He] ȝit. shal] shalt þou. 471 soþfast] stedfast. haue] haue þou. 493 in drede] I þe reide. 500 lesczoun] gods lessone. 502 goddede] blissed dede. 530 wolde] wolde hym. 535 misdoþ] haue misdone to. 536 hit] so hit. 553 Nym] Take mon. 590 suffrerd] for mon he tholyd. 591 was þerto] þere was. 597 eurei] ilk a. 599 a] ony. 612 may ben] is. 616 þe] *om.* 617 manhede] mon. 618 wreche of wrongful dede] vengaunce a non. 623 art so stout] so proude art. 624 and herte] stoute of hert. 643 And so] So. and some] men. 644 inome] taken. 645 þen be] Now be. 648 Or] Or ellis. 649 founde] tane. 665 muche] neuer so mikel. 668 þat] his. 677 humilite] verray humylite. 678 Awey] Alle. 682 wel] ful. 683 of him] *om.* 688 comforti] confort in hye. 689 mid] with. 693 man] a mon.

This comprehensive enumeration of mutilations defacing MS. R seems to indicate beyond all doubt, that H_1 is not derived from R. H_1 could hardly represent a scribe so critical, that he would perfect his text to a degree of exactness indicated in the version of H_1 as outlined in the preceding paragraphs. On the contrary, the transcript H_1 has already established a reputation for erratic readings.

The list of coincidences of MSS. $H_1 R$ must be augmented by the distinct readings of $A_1.H_1.R.$, proving beyond doubt the nearness of the connection. To the differences between the texts could be added those of a trifling character, showing that it is impossible for H_1 to have been derived from R. H_1 and R must then form a class by themselves, to be accounted for as representing a theoretical MS. H_1R not hitherto discovered.

§ 8. *Agreement of A_1R within the Group Z.*

Common readings pointing to a relationship $A_1.R$ are as follows: v. 8 þu *om.*] þu $A_1.R$. 26 hem] *om.* 70 Alþere] Aller. 411 saiþe] seide. 507 willen it] hit wolen. 518 þe] *om.* 563 wele] it. 625 nyll] wole. 635 For (But)] And. 695 sinne] his sinne. 700 nyl] wole. 715 for lore] ilore. 759 I wrouȝht] wrouht. 768 I schryue] shriue. 773 ifounde] founde. 815 euene (bidene)] ene. 876 þu] þat þu. Here may be included the large number of coincidences, in which the only representative of group Y is the MS. D: 915, 916, 919—921, 924, 931—933, 937, 938, 939, 945—948, 951, 952, 954—956, 964, 969, 970, 973, 974, 977, 980, 983, 993, 995, 999, 1000, 1001, 1004, 1005, 1011, 1024, 1031.

A_1 is naturally not copied from R, the younger MS. Neither is R a copy of A_1. This truth is shown as follows:

R not from A_1: v. 22 weye] lawe R. 102 beþ noht gode] are swithe. 116 sleuþe] slownes. 124 anuied] fro mynde. 237 binomen him] fro hym tane. See additional instances to the end of the poem.

Considerable difference between A_1 and R proves that R cannot have been derived from the older MS. A_1. It is equally impossible that transcript (*b*) retaining correct readings transmitted to H_1 and R alike, but not reproduced in A_1, be derived from A_1; cf. ll. 179, 180; 551, 552; 644—646. The list of individual mistakes in A_1, where H_1 and R preserve the correct reading, is sufficiently imposing to corroborate the conclusion that neither R nor its source was derived from A_1. Hence it must be concluded, that A_1 and R, forming with H_1 a MSS. group, go back to a source now lost, but represented by A_1 (H_1R).

Chapter IV.—Genealogical History of the Texts. liii

§ 9. *Agreement of $A_1 H_1$ within the Group Z.*

MSS. A_1 and H_1 agree[1] in unimportant coincidences. 711 and 712 alter the pronouns þou and þe to ȝe and ȝou; 791 substitutes þouh for ȝef. Other minor details are as follows:

v. 17 caught] ikauht $A_1.H_1$. 149 þis is] þis. (407—475 *om. in D*). 413 þat] þis. 450 And *om.*] And (459—814 *om. in H_2*). 549 Sweche (*D.R*)] Alswich. 664 (Latin) "*qui*" *om.* ($A_2.R$)] *qui*. 689 mynde ($A_2.D$)] mid. 713 þe] þat. 731 derkenes] þisternesse. 763 may] miht. 812 men] man. 826 no *om.*] no. 829 Many ($A._2R$)] Many on. 862 nouþere do] don noþer. $A_1.H._1$ agree in opposition to *D.R.* after the conclusion of A_2: v. 892; 893 ne *om.* 900 þe. 904 biþenke.

None of these three MSS. comprising Group Z is directly or indirectly the antecedent of another. A_1 because the oldest text cannot have been derived from *R* or H_1, nor can *R* have been derived from the younger text H_1. Were this not the case, numerous instances of mutilation in A_1 or in H_1 occur, where the third MS. contributes the original reading. Equally impossible is it that *R* or H_1 has origin in A_1; cf. § 5. Instances exist, where H_1 or *R* conveys the correct reading lost in the other MSS. respectively. The results of the argument of § 7 indicate that H_1 and *R* propagate characteristics of a distinct source *b*. Since none of the three MS. texts is derived from any other of the same group, then it must be assumed that they return to a common original $A_1 H_1 R$.

Two groups of MSS. have thus been discovered, each connected in internal characteristics through its representative texts. Additional coincidences indicate other development, suggesting that some scribe had access to more than one MS., and that he modeled his transcript according to the readings of the two texts, with reference at times to one MS., at times to the other. Relationship seems to be indicated between H_2 and *R*.

§ 10. *Coincidences in $H_2 R$.*

In addition to conditions thus indicated, MSS. $H_2.R$ give evidence of common relationship. Both H_2 and *R* add to the text of the other MSS. *grete*, verses 246 and 380, *ryȝt* 171, *yt* 208, þe 229, þane

---

[1] The agreement $A_1 H_1$ is introduced on authority of Professor Schick. This relationship must involve with it other conclusions important in the arrangement of genealogical tables.

261. Both read þou noht forȝete, instead of nis noht forȝete, line 193. Both read in 265, They shulle take here, replacing He shal fonge his. H_2 and R supply Chastyse hem, line 181, for chasten of A_1. Minor resemblances corroborate these conclusions:

v. 74 Bote] But ȝyffe H_2.R. 80 on] on a. 134 bi] with. 159 þis] ytte. 161 falle] be fall. 162 þat] om. 171 halt þer mide] holte þere with ryȝt. 175 mot] mvste. 194 iwite] wete. 208 do] yt doo. 263 nele] wyll. 293 Ac] Butt. 304 And] om. 318 Haþ] He hathe. 355 him sauh] sawe hym. 360 ibrent] brente. 385 wel] wel om. 389 Inwardliche] Inwardly. 432 þat] ȝe. 817 Kindeliche] Kendely.

The greater age of R removes it from the question of source for H_2. The numberless independent readings vouched for by H_2 (cf. § 1) make it evident that H_2 is not copied immediately from MS. R. It seems possible that the scribe of the transcript used by H_2 may have had knowledge of that employed by the scribe of R, particularly since MS. D ascribed with H_2 to a common source marks also an indirect connection with MS. R.

§ 11. The MS. D.

The MS. D united with the MS. H_2 preserves traces of influence binding it to the MS. R, as the accompanying illustrations will indicate. Both D and R supply beme for the original text breme, line 383. Both introduce the reading, line 893, es for no loue no for no instead of nis for loue ne for (acord). D and R read syttes for is, line 908. Other corrupt forms justify the same theory:

v. 33 he] þer he D.R. 58 in] in a. 65 þo] þen. 68 i wole] he wold. 84 bi leue] leue. 165 low] ful lowe. ful] om. 174 do] ido. 508 fonge] fonde.[1]

Lines 107, 133, 145, 149, 274, 289, 344, 549, 757, 771, 785, 857, 866, 885, 900 confirm these conclusions. That, however, MS. D has no very intimate connection with MS. R, is indicated by the number and quality of the readings preserved with A_1 in opposition to differences numerous in comparison with the instances of agreement with R; cf. preceding section, and also lines 944, 963, 967, 978, 987, 990, 996, 1000, 1004, 1020, 1021.

---

[1] The reading of 508 justified by rime and context seems to confirm the hypothesis, that D and R correct mutilations of MSS. $A_1.A_2.H_1.R$. by the form intended by the poet.

Chapter IV.—Genealogical History of the Texts.

§ 12. *The Relationship H_1H_2.*

A relationship $H_1.H_2$ is to be traced in these two texts, justifying the supposition that the scribe of $D.H_2$ had also access to a MS. employed by $H_1.R$ in the grouping Z. H_1 and H_2 in common preserve the line 175, *he motte (mvste) be betyn* in place of *he mot hit beten*. Other verses preserve corrupt passages confirming this relationship. A single word is added in H_1, H_2 in a number of instances, where it is omitted elsewhere:

v. 120 wel $H_1.H_2$. 204 þer is. 268 *and* 402 here. 280 þe. 290 maner. 423 fere] in fere.

A word is altered in opposition to the readings of $A_1.A_2.D.R$: v. 23 it] þer $H_1.H_2$. 55 par] for. 112 ful] myche. 160 eft] after. 178 hem] him. 214 heihe] his. 236 sippen] after. 243 eke] also. 372 þe] his. 407 nu] wel. 817 ofte] oftentyme.

The investigation suggests a connection $H_1.H_2$ between the two pairs of closely related MSS. $H_1.R$ and $D.H_2$, not to be explained on the ground that either member of the two groupings is the source direct or indirect of the other. Nor has a single MS. of the four offered source for any other. See §§ 1, 7.

The imposing breaks in MSS. group $H_2.D$ remove from this group a possibility of origin for the two opposing elements $H_1.R$. The omission of lines 45 and 46 in R and the individual errors of the single MS. gives proof as follows:

H_2 *not derived from MS. R:* v. 13 þis] *om.* R. 19 Al] *om.* 20 Ne shaltu] þou shalt not. 22 weye] lawe. 26 hem] ful. 27 Her of] *om.* 31 on] in. 36 in his seruise] serued hym after. 38 liuede al in] leued wel alle. 41 and] *om.* 58 don] *om.* 84 þise] þose thre. 102 noht gode] swithe. ac] *om.* 105 hit] *om.* 114 Vncerteynnesse] merkenes. 137 lessounne] sarmoun.

A common grouping is not to be ascribed directly to the four MSS., whereby all return to a common original, as will be recognized by the few and unimportant relationships shared by these MSS. in common, as well as by the character of the divergence.

§ 13. *MSS. $D H_1 H_2 R$.*

v. 18 and] *om.* $D.H_1.H_2.R$. 69 nu] *om.* 146 Nis] Es. 214 Nas] was. 327 hu] what. 399 ishewed] schewed.

Here the common relationship $D.H_1.H_2.R$ ends. It does not seem to be sufficiently marked to justify inference of common ancestry, through direct descent for the four MSS. that it comprises.

It is, however, to be supposed, that the mutilations of some common original propagated in the two groups of texts may have distributed themselves in course of development among the later MSS. In some instances agreement among three of the MSS. in question would seem to be derived from a theoretical H_1RDH_2, particularly in the combination of $H_1.H_2.R$. The disagreement of D in these instances could be explained, as it must be in other relationships, by the hypothesis, that the scribe of D used more than one MS. and supplied necessary corrections. On the other hand, it must be remembered, that the corrupt text H_2 gives proof of diligent conjectural emendation from the hand of some individual scribe, irrespective of other MSS.

Group $D.H_1.R$ appears line 198 (l. *om.* in H_2). l. 198 substitutes *Ful* for *Wel*, 293 *wol ȝyf* for *ȝif*, and in the Latin text 554 includes the complete quotation. Other coincidences occur, chiefly omissions from $D.H_1.R$. See as follows minor coincidences:

v. 202 it] and D.H.R. 221 a $(A_2.H_2.)$] *om.* 295 ifere $(A_1.A_2.)$] in fere. 395 þanne] *om.* Other instances are in opposition to $A_1.A_2$ only. 557 do] do to. 604 on] in a. 633 þeih] he. 716 and *om.*] and. 723 ful iwis] altered. 803 iwrouht] wroȝt. 843 Hij] þay. 875 ne *om.*] ne.

On the other hand the following coincidences do not suggest additional hypotheses regarding the genesis of the MSS. The grouping is confined to three of the MSS. investigated. The fragmentary condition of MSS. D and H_2 is to be recalled in the examination of the following illustrations:

Group $D.H_2.R$. v. 4 Ac] Bot $D.H_2.R$. 65 þo] *om.* 80 alle] *om.* 134 his mihte] all his myȝt. 179 here holde] holde here.

Group $D.H_1.H_2$. v. 46 he *om.*] he $D.H_1.H_2$. 125 swiche] *om.* 175 hit] *om.* 185 As] *om.* 320 þu] *om.*

Group $H_1.H_2.R$. v. 132 ne] *om.* $H_1.H_2.R$. 160 ibouht] boȝte. 173 mot] moste. 230 gan (was)] dide hym. 241 And] But. 249 Ibiried] Biryed. 260 a] *om.* 273 euere] for euer. 276 reuliche] ful reuliche. 293, 315, 347, 434 Ac] But. 336 Wher] If. 348 and *om.*,] and. 362 þat ilke] þat. 411 self] him self. 423 fere] in fere. 424 þat] þat to. 455 nelc] wil.

Conclusions derived from this investigation may be briefly summarized. The two principal groups Y and Z are already classified. A_1 and A_2, MSS. representing each of the groups, are the purest texts, and are most nearly alike. H_1 and R show some close relationship setting them apart in a distinct group. D and H_2 belong in a class by themselves. A general agreement is to be marked between these two secondary groups, but they are not derived one from the other, and they do not represent directly a common source. The group H_1 R offers no difficulty. Of the group $D\, H_2$, D is a more exact text than H_2. H_2 is often miserably corrupt, and is the farthest removed from the original. The differences between D and H_2 are to be accounted for in various ways. Some MS. or MSS. must exist between the transcript D and the transcript H_2. The original of H_2 was undoubtedly defective, and H_2 or its antecedent text attempted to correct the errors of its prototype and to preserve a complete poem. The original not being at hand, the copyist tacked on the spurious conclusion characteristic of H_2. The fact of the break in D and H_2 at approximately the same portion of the poem suggests that D had also access to a defective copy. Both MSS. D and H_2 could be referred to a theoretical MS. (a) fulfilling these conditions. MS. (a), a member of group Y, introduced mutilations transmitted in MSS. H_1 R, suggesting that its copyist used also a theoretical MS. representative of (b). MS. D corrected its copy, hence D is at times more or less identical with the original English text. This conjecture seems to explain best the general condition of these MSS.

Collecting the results obtained through each of these separate arguments, the pedigree of the texts of the six MSS. of the *Speculum*, as developed in the course of this investigation, formulates itself into the following genealogical table. It will not be attempted to prove that one or two texts stood between any two of the combining MSS. It is to be believed that MS. H_2 had in its development the combined results of the association of MSS. representing two distinct groups of texts.

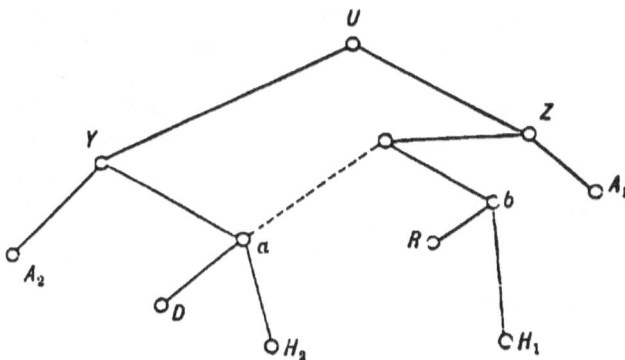

CHAPTER V.

PRINCIPLES UNDERLYING THE EDITION.

§ 1. *The Classification of the MSS.*

The younger and less complete representatives of the MSS. groups classified in the preceding chapter, MSS. H_1 and H_2 with texts often diverging from the original and at times independent in reading, are too imperfect to become the basis of an edition, provided others better adapted to the relationship are to be found. H_2, a late MS. offering a complete poem, not merely introduces new readings and an independent conclusion, but is conspicuous through two unexplained *lacunæ*, comprehending more than half the fundamental text. MS. H_1 has lost its concluding pages. MS. D related to H_2 in the same branch of the family, an older member of the group, is deficient through a break of sixty-eight lines in the middle of the poem and is thus unfitted to become standard for reference. Yet it is not impossible, that these three younger texts may have obtained respectively a reading lost in an older and in some ways a more exact transcript.

MS. R supplying defective portions of the later transcripts preserves also impure readings and dialectical forms not to be reconciled with the original poem. Moreover it seems to be of inferior value, in that it represents a development of a more corrupt branch of the original; cf. MS. H_1 most nearly related. A_2 though imperfect in places, shows little trace of emendation and merits high esteem, but A_2 is also unfortunately incomplete. It has lost not only its conclusion but the one hundred and twenty lines preceding, apparently through no fault of its copyist; cf. chap. iii., 4. MS. A_1 on the other hand deserves in general preference over MSS. $A_2.D.H_1.H_2.R$. MS. A_1 is the oldest transcript. Without important breaks and without interpolations, it offers a version approximately correct. That it is an excellent text, and stands nearest the original in distinction from the other MSS., is assured in its freedom[1] from copyist's errors on the testimony of the parchment, and in the regularity with which it preserves uniform dialectical forms. The fundamental text then, basis of this edition, must be MS. A_1.

---

[1] Yet it must be borne in mind that a scribe who is too intent on his spelling (cf. MS. H_2) and the neatness of his text may give too little attention to his context and the import of what he is writing.

§ 2. *Criticism of Texts.*

Of the two groups of MSS. extant as classified in the preceding chapter, Group Z, represented by MSS. A_1 and R, illustrative of the earlier texts, and by a younger MS. H_1, deserves as a whole precedence over Y. This is clear from the preceding chapter, where, from the readings introduced, it is shown that Z has preserved often the purer text. Group Z contains the two oldest MSS.; Z provides the conclusion, although the same occurs on the authority of one MS. of group Y. A MS. from group Z becomes basis of the edition. That is to say, group Z contains the better readings, and on the whole the fewer erratic forms.

Interpolations of MSS. $A_1DH_1H_2R$ in combined proof are not generally later and corrupt readings, but rather omissions from MS. A_1. Although that MS. preserves the oldest text prepared with considerable exactness, without marked errors detrimental to the main poem, it has simplified its material in passages where even H_1 and H_2, later[1] and often corrupt MSS., combine with better texts in preserving readings lost in MS. A_1. Other texts of the Auchinleck collection are thus shortened and partly altered; cf. Kölbing, *Sir Beues*, p. xli, with reference to *Arthour and Merlin*, p. cliii, and to Bülbring, *Engl. Studien*, vol. xvi, pp. 251 ff. On the other hand the general value and significance of MS. A_1 seems not to be affected by these omissions. That these are first readings and omissions from A_1 is clear. They are introduced in harmonious connection with the subject-matter, and they develop the thought in a way that makes them important to the principal action of the poem. Each of the following couplets adds force to the passage illustrated, and there is nothing in the poet's style to contradict the appropriateness of the reading. Lines inserted after 178 begin a well-defined climax that culminates in line 187. Lines 551, 552 are logically significant in connective and introductory (*i. e.* to paragraph) sense. They, like lines 645, 646, contain vigorous personal application of the truth expounded and add to the dramatic effect of the passage. Lines 645, 646:

"Nowe be þou were, þou proude gome,
þat þou ne be in pryde enome."

Peculiarly representative of the poet, and forcible in the genesis of the poem is the interpolation of one member of group Z, lines 639—640:

---

[1] For a later MS. may be a good copy of a MS. older than any now extant.

> "Out of heuen, þat was so bryȝte,
> Into helle for pride he toke his flyȝte."[1]

Rounding the sentence, in harmony with the context, and characteristic of the style of the poet[2] is the contribution of group Z following line 420:

> "Which shal not be to hem vncowþe,
> For god shal sey it with his mowþe:
> 'Venite, benedicti patris mei.'"

Lines following 160 in MS. H_2 seem in keeping with the dramatic earnestness of the poet:

> "Where be thoo þat thynkyþe þere vpon ?
> I cane nott telle, be seynte John !"

But the textual merit of group Y on basis of its MS. diverging most broadly from the original does not support the introduction of readings of H_2, however well justified they may seem through sentiment. Similarly H_2 in line 323 seems to preserve the meaning of the poet in *Herken now my ffrende so free*. A preferred reading is also that of H_1R in l. 790, *Herken & I wil telle þe*, supported by MS. D, a member of the opposing group beginning *Harkeneþ*; but the wisdom of conservatism has limited the development of these theories to the form of suggestions only.

Particularly at variance with the text are those interpolations that have the tendency to perfect the metre by the substitution of lines of see-saw regularity. The serenity of the verse is consequently marred by a harsh and senseless jingle in contrast with the *naïve* natural grace of the main poem; cf. lines 4—5, 323—324, 454—455, 507—508, and numerous alterations of the entire line, especially in MS. H_2, but also in MS. H_1. In contrast to the freedom and beauty of the original verse these additions are of no value in the textual criticism and are to be rejected as undesirable redaction. Such lines, quoted without reference to the specific MS., are illustrated as follows: 132, 251, 272, 283, 440, 442, 514, 606, 688, 696, etc.

Undoubtedly in minor features[3] an individual MS. may be correct in reading; thus MSS. D and R have preserved *fonde* (*fonge* A_1),

---

[1] Regarding the position of this interpolation as a unit in the integral poem, the editor recognizes grounds for difference of opinion, and in the introduction of the passage is, like Lydgate, open to correction.

[2] The tendency of the poet to clinch his statement with a final expression in summary of his thought is to be marked in this poem.

[3] The discussion of other passages on basis of the two groups of texts might seem desirable in this chapter. The alteration of pronouns by the different MSS. respectively is occasion for investigation, but here the poet himself was

l. 508 satisfactory, as rime and meaning indicate. Line 1029, *he* as preserved by *R* is necessary to the full line, and line 350, *as* and *hem* make two syllables too many for regular scansion; so *nu* in l. 69 is a syllable too much for the metre. *þo*, line 342, and *nost* line 347, are necessary to the meaning.

The testimony of five MSS. for *wyll*, line 2, also *how*, line 267, would perhaps be in opposition to the Auchinleck readings *may* and *what*. To the editor the poetical charm of the Auchinleck rendering was reason for the retention of what may be granted to be on authority of the MSS., a desirable textual alteration.

The question of the legitimacy of the reading *of god*, MSS. A_2D, *god* H_1, om. H_2, lines 6 and 21, is respectfully submitted to the student of textual criticism.

The *Speculum* of this issue would not credit itself as submitting rigorously a critical text. Placing material for thought before its public, it would become groundwork for the investigation of the student of philology.

§ 3. *The Arrangement of the Edition.*

The *Speculum*, as here set forth on basis of MS. A_1, seeks to correct palpable errors[1] extant in the fundamental text. Any attempt at restoration[2] of A_1 is governed by the readings[3] of MSS. A_2, D, H_1, H_2, R, collated separately or with reference to a group-combination. Although members of the family Z preserve nearly complete versions of the original, yet in instance of variance in the MSS., preference is often given to a representative of the group Y. In general a substituted reading presents forms of A_2, the MS.

---

not always exact. Other points have claims to attention, but minor interpolations will generally be recognized as such. The reader is referred to the notes on the poem and the chapter over metre for other questions connected with the criticism of the texts.

[1] Errors in MS. A_1 are chiefly accidental, illustrative of omission rather than of interpolation.

[2] Deficiency is to be recognized through verses that interfere with the scansion, or in instances in which the MSS. are self-contradictory or support one another in obvious error or in mutilation of the archetype.

[3] Avoidable errors in the younger MSS. are notably comprehensive, particularly in MS. D. Among them all haplography and dittography are not common. MS. A_2 is probably answerable for an instance of *skipping* in verses 81 ff. and 140 ff. (chap. III, 4), due probably to *homeoteleuton*. Interpolation and attempt at explanation of unintelligible forms must be attributed to H_2. Intentional error accredited to *mala fides* is to be noted. The scribe often adapts a sentence to a blunder originating with himself or tries to make sense of what he does not understand. Particularly have instances of anacoluthon taxed the grammarian; cf. verses 623—627.

lxii   *Chapter V.—The Arrangement of the Edition.*

second in excellence, or *D*, a MS. affording at times a good text, and often reproducing the original. Hence MS. D supplies lines 1007—1034, imperfect in MS. A_1 through injury to the MS. and wanting in MS. A_2 through loss of leaves. [*pylt*], line 232, has been contributed by A_2, where *put* of *D* is manifestly a mutilation of the first text. On the other hand, MS. R alone preserves [*he*] added line 1029, and necessary to perfect metre on basis of the normal type A. Undoubted blunders of the copyist having been rectified and absolute deficiencies supplied, MS. A_1 has been scrupulously followed. The sources of the present text as thus constructed have been differentiated through the following symbols, by which every deviation from the immediate MS. may be recognized:

(1) Customary italic type, that represents the expansion of a form contracted in the MS.: he*m* 25, Ie*su* 34, eu*ere* 44, u*ertuz* 71, etc., all illustrative of usual methods of MS. abbreviation. (2) Brackets, embracing individual letters, syllables, words, or lines, which have been supplied from other MSS. as conjectural emendations of scribal errors; thus *þiself*[*e*], verse 10, indicates that -[*e*] has been added as the reading of at least three of the MSS., and that the inflectional and metrical value of the verse is improved by the conjecture. On the other hand, while the verse might metrically represent the type C (described chap. xi.), the suffix places it in the normal type A, in agreement with laws presupposed to belong to the *Speculum*. [*nost*], line 347, indicates that an entire word, deficient in MS. A_1, has been inserted within the verse. On this principle the three verses lost in A_1, 1032—1034, are embraced in brackets, showing that this portion of the text is borrowed from MS. D. (3) Parentheses, inclosing a word that should be omitted in text A_1, as inconsistent with meaning, grammatical or metrical form, or historical development. (4) Notes at the bottom of the page, strictly limited to palæographical modifications, important generally to execution alone. So a few instances of dittography are marked in foot-notes, pp. 34, 38, and 40, etc. A foot-note indicates that *þer*, l. 33, is written over erasure in A_1, and that *to*, verse 71, is above the line.

Two necessarily single words united in the MS. (*i. e.* A_1) have been separated. A hyphen identifies the elements of a single word written apart in the MS. Punctuation, paragraphing by the setting in of the line, the introduction of capital letters beginning proper names (*A*lquin 51, *I*udas 129, *G*regory 667) or opening the verse,

Chapter V.—*The Arrangement of the Edition.* lxiii

have been regulated in conformity with harmonious literary usage. Large initial letters correspond to the illuminated capitals of the parchment. The sign ¶ in the MS. is reproduced on the printed page by the same character in the position, relatively to the text, that it occupies on the leaf of the folio. Owing to the abundant failure in the coincidence of the logical and technical paragraphing as presented in the parchment (see lines 9, 48, 57, etc.), the MS. paragraph is not marked by the mechanical setting-in of the line, as is regarded expedient in *Sir Beues.* See also Kölbing, p. xlii., and *Guy of Warwick*, 15th century edition, p. vii. The *Speculum* makes no attempt to introduce the inflectional final -*e*, even when warranted by associated forms, except as an occasional aid to symmetry in metre. Where double thesis can be avoided by the apocope or syncope of the unaccented -*e*, that -*e*, though expressed, is usually to be regarded as silent.

Below the text on each page are given in full the readings of MSS. A_2, D, H_1, H_2, R, arranged as variants and following the leading Auchinleck text in alphabetical order. The orthography is always that of the MS. that first deviates from MS. A_1, be it MS. A_2, D, H_1, H_2, or R. It is hoped that no form conveying difference of meaning has been omitted. Variations purely orthographical or phonetical have in general not been represented. Yet in a few instances graphical or phonetic modifications that seem of peculiar interest are cited among genuine variants, as, for instance: *where,* for *were,* l. 59 in D; *boys, bush,* l. 363 in D; *herth, eorþe* in A_1, l. 375 in D; *hyere,* O.E. *hér,* l. 452 in A_2, H_1. Numberless spirals, curves, twists, and flourishes, and the line crossing *h* or *l* have in general been treated as ornaments, unless the metrical quality of the verse or the inflection demands a final -*e* or -*n*. It is intended, that the variants reproduce exactly the forms of the MSS. without emendations or conjectural readings. An exception is the variant to 524 in H_1, *su[m]what*. A conjecture is also permitted, where minuscules were apparently confused with others having a superficial resemblance to them; cf. variant 602 in D, where -*te* seems confused with -*ie, vilante* for *vilanie,* and 563, -*is* for -*rs, doist* for *dorst?.* The variants bear no alteration in orthography. Punctuation must be looked on as irrespective of the MSS.

The side-notes of the page contain the abstract of the subject-matter; the headlines, a briefer abstract. Alcuin's *Liber* contributes chapter headings in Latin. These are written in italic type on the margin opposite to that containing the brief paraphrase.

Important in the preparation of the edition are the notes, in purpose critical as well as explanatory. Here various textual readings have been discussed and difficult passages, idioms, and usages of the period have been studied through parallel selections from Romance poems and the various homilies of the century. A list of the archaic words of the text, with meanings and verse numbers, is collected in the glossary. If the single word occur more than three times in the same meaning, the sign *etc.* after the third number indicates the fact.

Diacritical marks are introduced into the chapters of the Introduction as follows : a circumflex accent (^) indicates a long syllable in a word of O.E. derivation; a macron (-), a long syllable in a M.E. word or a loan-word of foreign origin; a breve (˘) marks the short syllable in an O.E. or a M.E. word; two dots above a vowel (¨) show that it is to be sounded, below (..), that it is silent; primary stress is denoted by the acute accent ('); secondary stress, by the grave accent (`); the metrical pause, by a period (.); a colon (:) is written between the members of a rhyming couplet; marks of parenthesis () inclose a form not of value in the immediate discussion; < is equivalent to "derived from"; an asterisk (*), a theoretical form.

Apart from reference to the well-known dictionaries[1] of Murray, Bosworth-Toller, Stratmann-Bradley, Kluge, Skeat, Paul's *Grundriss*, Sievers's *Ags. Grammatik*, and the *M.E. Grammatik* of Morsbach, the *Speculum* is frequently indebted to the following works :[2]

E. A. Abbott, *A Shakespearian Grammar.*

B. ten Brink, *Chaucers Sprache und Verskunst.* Leipzig, 1884.

K. Brugmann, *Comparative Grammar of the Indo-Germanic Languages*, Wright, Conway, Rouse, London, 1888—93.

B. Carstens, *Zur Dialectbestimmung des mittelenglischen Sir Firumbras.* Eine Lautuntersuchung. Kiel, 1884.

E. Kölbing, *The Romance of Sir Beues of Hamtoun.* London, 1885—94. (Early English Text Soc., Extra Series, Nos. XLVI., XLVIII., LXV.).

G. Menze, *Der ostmittelländische Dialekt.* I. Vokalismus. Cöthen, 1889.

F. Pabst, *Die Sprache der me. Reimchronik des R. von Gloucester.* Berlin, 1889.

---

[1] These authorities necessary to the specialist in the most primary English study, are too familiar to demand specific description.

[2] Reference in the following edition to any work of the subjoined list will hereafter often cite merely the author's surname, with number of the page quoted for illustration, but without naming specific title.

A. Pogatscher, *Zur Lautlehre der griechischen, lateinischen und romanischen Lehnworte im Altenglischen*, 1888.

J. Schick, *Lydgate's Temple of Glas.* London, 1891 (Early English Text Soc., Extra Series, No. LX.).

W. Skeat, *Principles of English Etymology.* Oxford, 1887–91.

O. Wilda, *Über die örtliche Verbreitung der 12-zeil. Schweifreime in England.*

J. Zupitza,[1] *Alt- und mittelenglisches Übungsbuch.* Wien, 1889.

Part II.

CHAPTER VI.

ON THE RELATION OF THE *SPECULUM* TO THE GUY OF WARWICK ROMANCES.

> "Bove all the knightis that euer weare or shal
> Sir Guy of Warwick beares the coronal."[2]

THE *Speculum* represents the modernized form[3] of the Guy saga, the third working[4] of the material as illustrated in the Copland[5] Guy

---

[1] Naturally frequent reference will be made to Zupitza's editions of the various Guy of Warwick MSS. (Early English Text Society, Extra Series, Nos. XXV., XXVI., XLII., XLIX., and *Sitzungsberichte der phil.-hist. Cl. der kais. Academie der Wiss.*, LXXIV., p. 549), and to Wülker's, Körting's, and ten Brink's histories of English literature.

[2] Selected from the MS. of Lane's Lydgate's *Guy of Warwick, The renowned historic of Sir Gwy, Earl of Warwick,* "surnamed Heremite, begun by Don Lydgatt, monck of St. Edmundes Berye," reworked by John Lane in 1622, but never printed; cf. the Harleian MS. 5243, Lane's Lydgatt's Gwy. It was described and commended by Phillips, the nephew of John Milton. Concerning the "corrected Historic of Sir Gwy," see also Zupitza, *Sitzungsb.*, p. 645, and Turnbull in his edition of the Auchinleck Guy : *The Romances of Sir Guy of Warwick,* Edinburgh, 1840.

[3] Compare date and relative character of material. Minute discussion will be reserved for another occasion.

[4] Cf. Zupitza, *Zur Literaturgeschichte des Guy von Warwick,* Wien, 1873, pp. 632, 635. Lydgate's Guy is probably in one sense an independent text, and the editor would not specify the *Speculum* as necessarily a *third* working of the fundamental legend.

[5] Intermediate in period between the Copland and Lydgate Guys must be recalled the Wynkyn de Worde edition, dated in the Museum collection, 1500; the French text printed à *Paris*, 1525; a later edition (in French) of 1550; and possibly the fragment printed by Sir T. Phillipps, Middle Hill, 1838; cf. Museum text. The brief fragment, three leaves (*Fragmenta Vetusta*) of the W. de Worde edition preserved in the British Museum, Add. MS. 14,408, and the fourth leaf to be found in the Douce Collection 20 of the Bodley MSS., belongs probably to the series associated with *Robert the devyll* of 1510, prose stories printed by Wynkyn de Worde; cf. Jusserand, *The English Novel in the Time of Shakespeare*, p. 64.

lxvi *Chapter VI.—Relation of Speculum to Guy Romances.*

or in Lydgate's Guy. Yet it is to be remembered that the poem of this issue is earlier than the Lydgate text[1] of 1423, or Copland's print[2] of 1560 by the Museum estimate. The *Speculum* supplements the main Guy legend. A chapter lost from some intact version, it is closely interwoven with the thread of the fundamental romance. The "sarmoun" blends with the tale as recorded by Lydgate, the *Lyff of Guy of Warwick*,[3] at the point at which Lydgate's Guy:—

> . . . ."kam to an hermytage,
> where he fond on dwellyng in wyldirnesse.   str. 63[5]
> 64 To hym he drouh besechyng hym of grace."[4]

This "on dwellyng in wyldirnesse" might be recognized as "Alquin," and the "besechyng hym of grace" the plea for "sarmoun" over morality. The event occurred, as in the *Speculum*, when *þe world . . he . . forsok* (v. 33), after Guy had already:—

>   . . ."spedde hym forth for love of Crist Jesu.   str. 24
> 25 Forsook the world onknowe to euery wight,
> Of hih perfeccyoun to leven in penaunce,
> "lefft wyff and kyn and bekam goddis knyght,
> whom for to serve was set all his plesaunce,
> content with lytel (Crist was his suffysaunce)."

Central point[5] of contact determining absolutely immediate time and date of the interview resulting in the discourse to Guy is not definitely chronicled. Conditions of the *Speculum* in source and working display youth[6] rapt to some celestial ecstacy of renunciation. Intuitively a period of irresolution calling for the defining of purpose and determination comes to mind, marking the hour of farewell to Felice, the period of victory over earthly passion. Here belong Alquin's words of courage to the weak soul. The *Speculum* suggests

---

[1] Schick, *Temple of Glas*, pp. civ. and cxii. See Zupitza's date, 1420, *Literaturgeschichte*, p. 648.

[2] The Museum text employed in the arrangement of this edition having lost its first leaves is without date; but compare Copland's prints, *Syr Beuys of Hampton, Syr Degore, Syr Isumbras, The Knight of the Swanne*, etc. of 1560. Copland concludes his task with: Finis. *Laus Deo omnipotenti*. Jusserand dates Copland's print "about 1560," p. 64.

[3] For Lydgate's version see Zupitza, *Sitzungsberichte der philos.-hist. Cl. der kais. Academie der Wiss.* (Berlin, 1874), lxxiv, p. 649, *Acta Guidonis Warwicensis*, "A plesante songe of the valiant actes of Guy of Warwicke."

[4] *Sitzungsberichte (vide supra)*, p. 661, *und Uebungsbuch*, p. 111.

[5] Though infinitely suggestive of the greater subject, this poem purports to attain only to the dignity of the episode. The ten thousand verses (practically 8043, Herbing, p. 12) of more perfect texts have no claim to recognition in the compact exposition of the *Speculum*. Hence comparisons here introduced are in each instance outward from the *Speculum* to associated texts, rather than inward, tracing only the main theme in the brief composition.

[6] Eighteenth century authority is as follows: "You are young and meanly born."—*Chap Book*, 1796.

Chapter VI.—Relation of Speculum to Guy Romances. lxvii

the young energy of a knight in the glow of vigorous manhood. The appropriate passage of Lydgate's version, characterizing a life nearing its "dim goal," is inconsistent with the hypothesis embodied in the *Speculum*, yet in this detail the anachronism[1] could be ascribed to the poetical application of the same incident under diverse treatment of remote ages and different authorship. "So the profound secret purpose of a noble life draws into itself the memories of past joy and past sorrow, and yields them again with chronology lost."[2]

Alquin fills the *rôle* of hermit[3] in another of his functions, in that he becomes Guy's spiritual physician: *i shal nu ben þi leche*, verse 69; *hele of soule i may ou teche*, verse 2. So in Copland's *Guy*, a hermit serves in office of medical adviser:[4]

    1259 "There was a monke behelde him well,
          That could of leche craft some dell."—Copl. p. 15.
    1269 "That Hermite in a little stound
          Looked to Guy and healed his wound."—Copl. p. 15.

The service of hermit as guide, adviser, and healer, is testified to in different versions of the legend. Ample occasion is offered in the early texts for the skill of the physician[5] as counsellor in virtue, but the *Speculum* advances a step beyond other poems in providing tangible personality for a traditional type[6] of mediæval development. The hermit is distinctly named "Alquin."

The sermon also fits well into the narrative, as printed by Copland,[7] in *The Booke of the moste victoryous Prynce, Guy of Warwick* (Imprynted at London in Lothburye, ouer agaynst Saynt Margarit's Church by Wylliam Copland):

---

[1] For Lydgate's well-known tendency to anachronism, see *Schick*, pp. cxxxv, cxxxvi.

[2] Dr. Henry Van Dyke, *The Story of the other Wise Man*, p. 69.

[3] Accounts of Guy's acquaintance with hermits, details of his life history, his "last Will and Testament," his epitaph are abundant; nothing is lacking in the tale, but the name of a hermit never occurs. Alquin is not mentioned.

[4] Compare *Three Early English Metrical Romances*, vol. 1, p. xxxii: "For there were none heremytes in tho dayes, but that they had been men of worshyp and of prowesse, and the heremytes helde grete housholde, and refresshyd peple that were in distresse."

[5] Thus Sir Launcelot came to a "heremyt" and besought aid: *he prayd hym for Goddes sake of socour* (*vide ante*, p. xxx.).

[6] The historian Josephus (b. 37 A.D.) records in the *Life* "by his own Hand" "Tryal" of the doctrines of a famous Master Banus (the *Talmud* names Bani, of "Christ's Disciples"), that led the "Life of a Hermite in Caves and Solitudes."

[7] It is to be noted that the Copland print is without pagination and line-numbers. Parallel passages in Zupitza's *Guy of Warwick*, published in 1875 (E. E. T. S., XXV, XXVI), are often marked at the left of quotations from Copland.

> "And as he rode, by the way
> Besyde he saw a fayre abbay.
> Thyther guy rode well, I wote,
> And there he founde a noble Abbote."—Copl. p. 14.

Copland notes often a visit to a hermit, opportunity for " besechyng of sarmoun," cf. as follows :

> "and the priestes and Clarkes met him with precessyon
> Singing : *te Deum Laudamus*."—Copl. p. 212.

> "To Arderne yede he fast,
> and an Ermitage he founde at last,
> that stoode in wood wylde."—Copl. p. 214.

> "To an Hermite then rode he
> And sayde : 'Hermite, come and go with me.'" . . .
> . . . .
> . . . .
> . . . .

> "The Hermyte sayd : 'gladly perfay.'
> To that Forrest he went with guy."—Copl. p. 14.

> 1247 "To an Hermite then rode Guy,
> That he knew before truely.
> That Hermite in a little stound
> Looked to Guy . . . . . .
> 1269 When he was whole of the Hermite thare,
> His leaue he tooke and forth gan fare."—Copl. p. 15.

Other MSS. versions of the legend enroll pleadings with hermits. MS. Ff. 2, 38, reads as follows (cf. above) :

> "He went to an abbey,
> That was a lytill besyde þe wey.
> The abbot sone he fonde there
> And spake to hym on hys manere."—Ff. 2, 38, v. 1219 ff.

> "Besydes Warwykk go he can
> To an ermyte, þat he knewe or þan."—Auch. v. 10,525.

The language of the entreaty[1] in various accounts of the interview, attests to the symmetry of the development in the various texts, if not to the uniformity of the coincidence in method of address :

G. '75, 1223. "Guy sayd : 'Syr, for charitee.'"—Copl. p. 14.

> " 'Sur,' he sayd, 'saue þe.
> I the bydd, pur charite.'"—Ff. 2, 38, v. 1225.

> "Þat þu wole, par charite."—Auch. 10, v. 55.

> "*Sire cher, par charite.*"—Aug. 28, fol. v. a.

---

[1] The selection proves the uniform conformity of MSS. of different origin to an accepted usage, rather than a striking idiosyncrasy of the Guy texts ; *par charite*, common in address to hermits, presents also forms of entreaty under strong emotion : *Sir Beues*, MS. S, verse 1420, and MS. E, 4004, read :

> v. 1420 : Tel me now pur charyte.
> v. 3164 : For charite ! she seide.
> v. 4004 : And cryede hym mercy pur charyte.

Chapter VI.—*Relation of Speculum to Guy Romances.* lxix

In the different MSS. the motive ascribed to Guy was the same[1]:

"and euer Guy had gode in his thought."—Copl. p. 206, v. 10.

"Therfor y am *purposed* in thought
In godd*is* seruyse now to goo,
To acquite some-what, that y haue mysdoo."—Caius, v. 7426.

. . "in his mynde bethoughte him anone,
That all his lif he wolde chaunge tho,
and in godd*is* seruyse he wolde him do."—Caius, v. 7406.

"All earthly Pleasure he for Heaven forsook."[2]—Epitaph of Guy.

"He thoghte þere wyth all hys myȝt,
To serue hym bothe day and nyght."—Ff. 2, v. 7143.

'All thys worlde y wyll forsake,
And penaunce for my synnes take.
Wende y wyll yn goddys seruyse."—Ff. 2, 7179 ff.

"He þouȝt wiþ dreri mode :

. . . .
For Iesu loue, our saueour,
Neuer no dede he gode."—Auch. 22, v. 16 ff,

"To bote min sinnes ichill wende,
Barfot to mi liues ende."—Auch. 22, v. 10 f.

Corresponding passages in the *Speculum* read :

. . . "on a time he stod in þouht :
Þe worldes blisse him þouhte noht."—Auch. 10, v. 31, 32.

"(And) louede god and his lore,
And in his seruise was euere more."—Auch. 10, v. 35, 36.

Amplification[3] explanatory of the suggestive lines 31—36 of the *Speculum* is supplied by Copland, who describes Guy's self-

---

[1] A later text explains Guy's motive: At the very height of Guy's glory, being exalted to his father's dignities, Conscience biddeth him repent of all his former sins, so Guy resolved to travel to the Holy Land like a Pilgrim. "Ah, Phillis," said he, "I have spent much time in honouring thee and to win thy favour, but never spared one minute for my soul's health in honouring the Lord." After exchange of rings and melting kisses, he departed like a stranger from his own habitation, taking neither money nor scrip with him, and but a small quantity of herbs and roots.—Chap Book, *History of Guy*, of which there seem to be at least twelve editions, one bearing the date 1783; the twelfth appeared in 1790; another was printed for "the company of walking stationers," 1796.

Another account enumerates details as follows: Ruminating on past actions of his Life, and the showers of Blood he had spilt in seeking after Honour, it made him extreamly pensive. He spoke with Felice: "For thy sake, dear Lady, have I waded through Seas of Blood, and with this Hand laid many Thousands sleeping in their silent graves, and spent all the Days of my blooming Youth in seeking that empty Title called Honour." Then after a sad farewell Guy travelled many weary Steps on the Land, pursued his pilgrimage through hardship and danger in the Holy Land with great Devotion. Selected from *The History of the famous Exploits of Guy Earl of Warwick*. Printed for Charles Bates at the Sun and Bible in Pye Corner, near St. Sepulchre's Church.

[2] Cf. Bettesworth's *Guy*, "Epitaph of Guy and Felice."

[3] Weight of the argument based on this parallel is enhanced, if the relative length of the *Speculum* and of the other texts of these selections is to be regarded comparatively.

Chapter VI.—Relation of Speculum to Guy Romances.

abnegation with its ulterior motive.[1] Guy reveals to Felice the reproach of his stricken conscience. Copland states that Guy had :—

> . . . . "bethought him tho,
> how he had done many a man wo,
> 7135 and slayne many a man with his honde,
> Brent and destroyed many a Lande.
>
> 7143 Forth his lyfe therefore guy thought,
> to serue Jesu Crist that him boght.
>
> 7147 'With penaunce amende shall I
> that I haue sinned with my body.'"

The prose version adds : "I am determined to travel for the welfare of my soul, not as before upon my Horse in Armour, but in a Gown of Grey, a Palmer's weed." Then Guy journeys toward the Holy Land, where once Jerusalem's fair city stood.

The *Speculum* in its function of episode makes no further claim to the absolute facts of the greater romance, yet into the suggestiveness of its brief verses it compresses the striking incidents of the fundamental tale. Its service is greater. The spirit of the associated romance is transmitted to the *Speculum*, and is transfused by subtle magic into the very essence of the poem.

The *Speculum*, shaped to the conception of English[2] tradition, is

---

[1] Guy expresses his purpose, in words paraphrasing the record of the *Gesta Romanorum*: "To purchase Heaven I will go pass through Hell."

[2] Whether the origin of the tradition bearing the name Guy be British or Welsh, as in the associated Arthour romance, Saracen, according to Ritson, German, or French, brought from the far East (Herbing, p. 889), as the Furnivall-Hales-Percy text intimates, the immediate Guy typified in this version is English, and the ultimate *motif* is English in the presentation of a national hero. The ballad assumes :

> "An *English-man* I was by Birth ;
> In Faith of Christ a Christian."
>
> "It was an *English-man* all this did do."

Moreover, the distinguishing characteristics of the tale are to be traced to English ground. So the battle with Colbrand was on English soil, according to the poet :

> "and when Guy was on *English* syde,
> Unto worke he gan ryde."
>
> "En Engleterre *feu ico nc.*
> En une ville de *Wallingford*,
> Qu'est pres de *Oxenford*."

Guy's national reputation was English ; cf. Rowlands's Guy. *The famous History of Guy, Earle of Warwicke,* "Great Gvy of Warwick our famous Country man," by Samuel Rowlands, London, ("printed for Edward Brewster at the sign of the Crane in St. Paul's Churchyard," 1682, and published in Glasgow for the Hunterian Club ; Edinburgh print of 1836) asserts that:

> "Great Hercules, if he had breathed on ground,
> When *English* Guy of Warwick liv'd renowned,
> There would have been a combat twixt them two."

The French version of 1525 describes Guy as of English origin : "*Cy com-*

Chapter VI.—Relation of Speculum to Guy Romances.

likewise moulded skilfully to a historical groundwork of facts diametrically opposed in nature and origin. Count Guido,[1] *Guido Comes*, knight of renown, active in war, holding at Tours positions of honour and trust,[2] appeals to Alcuin, Dean[3] of the order of St. Martin[4] 796—804, cultured priest of the school of the palace, preceptor of one greater than Count Guido, superior to youthful neophytes, beloved teacher of the king and emperor[5] Charlemagne, a humble[6] servant consecrated to righteousness. Inspired with religious exaltation through purpose of chivalric glorification of God, Count Guido pleaded for a homily[7] to deepen spiritual consecration under the austerity of war, *Spec.* 49—64 and *Liber*. The devoted friar responded with an exposition of virtue, the *Liber* popular during many ages. There is some ground for believing that the vigilant Count became successor to Alcuin,[8] and to the period of his death was Abbot of the monastery of St. Martin of Tours. The tradition continues to embody with consistent fidelity historical facts of Count Guido's life, for, on authority of Lydgate:—

---

mence *Guy de Warwick chevalier* D'AGLETERRE, *qui en son temps fit plusieurs prouesses et conquestes en* ALLEMAIGNE," etc.

That England claimed the warrior chief seems evidenced in the "address" of the same edition of Rowlands. The first address is "To the Noble English Nation;" the second, "To the Honorable Ladies of England."

[1] In similar guise the exploits of Charlemagne and his retinue of brave warriors are glorified in *Fyrumbras*, or the *Song of Roland* in its various versions, and the victories of King Arthour in his "table round" of noble verse.

[2] Cf. *Liber*, *Epistola Nuncupatoria*, and *Speculum*, verses 27—36. See Adamson under Alcuin in *Dictionary of National Biography* for facts regarding Albinus Flaccus.

[3] As presiding officer of the monastic school Alcuin delighted to be called *Dean*, simple deacon, Migne, vol. i. p. 31, § xxiv.: *beatus Alcuinus in epistolis suis nunquam se monachum, sed vel levitem, vel, quod illo tempore idem significabat diaconum inscribat*, cf. *Speculum*, v. 41.

[4] *Speculum*, verses 37—44.

[5] Alcuin, *Carissime in Christo præceptor* (Ep. 124), was inseparable from Charlemagne in pedagogy, theology, struggles, battles, beloved teacher, theologian, and author. See Schönfelder, *Alcuin*, 1873.

[6] *humillissimus* is the epithet selected by Alcuinus in epitomizing his own character; see *MS. Arundel* 218, fol. 2, where Alcuin is described as *humillissimus levitas in Deo felicitas*, and Monnier, *Alcuin et Charlemagne*, p. 344, *Sa religion et son humilité étaient mal à l'aise au milieu de tout de richesse*. See also Monnier, *Alcuin et son influence littéraire religieuse et politique sur les Franks*, Paris, 1853.

[7] A sermon book was not inconsistent with the times of the great teacher. This form of homily was continued in Germany in ecclesiastical legislation until the close of the fifteenth century; see *Charles I. or Life of Charlemagne*, pp. 85, 86; Werner, *Alcuin und sein Jahrhundert*, 1876, p. 252, and, for the English homily, ten Brink, I. 49, 290, 291; Morley, vol. iii. pp. 350—352.

[8] Alcuin held the highest monastic benefice. As Abbot he enforced the rigorous dispensation of the Benedictine Order; cf. *Ep.* 43.

"the same hermyte with inne a lytel space
by deth is passed the ffyn of his labour,
affter whos day Guy was his successour." str. 64 [5]

Lydgate adds a conclusion suggestive of the reward of piety, interpreting the influence of the discourse, be it *Speculum* or *Liber*, and applicable equally to Count Guido[1] and to Guy. For the "historic" affirms, that Guy of Warwick lived *more and more encresyng in vertu*, 64[1].

The poet thus originates magnificent phantasmagoria. In reckless disregard for local tradition he endows with life a hero of fiction. He bestows on him actual name, rank in actual history, and more than "local habitation." He places him in France. He honours him with conspicuous position in a prominent monastery.[2] He associates him as friend and contemporary of an honoured prelate. He oversteps the limits of time, and places Guy's existence in a definite period a hundred years earlier than the age in which his splendid achievements are uniformly supposed to have enriched his name with glory.[3] In localizing a popular legend, Guy of Warwick is accounted for as an actual hero, Guido of Tours. He lived in the eighth century. The theory of a specific personality for Guy of Warwick is also that of Cornubionsis (Cambrens), Walter of Exeter,[4] Dugdale the historian of Warwickshire, and of Peter Langtoft. If testimony of the *Speculum* be regarded as unauthentic, the delusion, involving the same sense of the reality of the doughty warrior, is

---

[1] The life of the knight was modelled after that of his preceptor. Over the serenity and the spirituality of Alcuin, see West, *Alcuin and the Rise of Christian Schools*, 1893, pp. 115 ff.

[2] The school of the Abbey was, second to the *schola palatina*, the most celebrated in France. Large numbers of distinguished pupils assembled there, among them many foreign students; see Schönfelder, p. 29. It became also a xenodochium for the reception of pilgrims. Not only did Charles I. pass much time in Tours, the queen Luitgarda dying there, but he was constantly patron of the Abbey; Jaffe, *Ep.* 53; Monnier, *Alcuin et Charlemagne*, p. 344; West, p. 64.

[3] Guy's achievement with the famed dragon is described as follows:

"Valiant Guy bestirs his hands,
The Dragon back did shrink.
The giant . . . quaking stands
And knew not what to think.
Guy gets the victory at last,
Which made great Rumbo glad.
He was full glad the fight was fit,
For he before was sad:
The greatful Lion Guy did greet;
When he to him did goe,
And thankfully did lick his feet."

The heroick History of Gvy, Earle of Warwick, by Hvmphrey Crovch, printed for Bell at the East end of the Christ Church, 1655.

[4] Herbing, "*Ueber die Hss. des Guy von W.*," p. 4.

Chapter VI.—*Relation of Speculum to Guy Romances.*

heightened by the revelations of Warwick Castle through the display,[1] in hall and oratory, of trophies testifying to the prowess of some scion of the house of Warwick,[2] nominally the "mightie earle," and through the statue[3] itself at Guy's cliff.

Early literature of the hero ascribes a most realistic actuality to Guy, for example, the ancient ballad,[4] *Bagford Ballads*, vol. ii. p. 19. It describes Guy as one, "Who (for the love of fair Phillis) became a hermit, and died in a Cave of a craggy Rock, a Mile distant from Warwick."

> "And then I lived a hermit's life
> A mile or more out of the town."

The ballad claims:

> "My body in Warwick yet doth lye,
> though now it is consumed to Mould.
> My statue[5] was engraven in stone."

The work is commended in the preface as a theme of wonder for ages long anterior to our own, as portraying the very "locality of the spot" where Guy lived and died. Epitaphs[6] of Guy and Felice record the burial of a knight:

> "Whose great achievments oft perform'd
> Has through Earth's Globe immortalized his Name,
> And given him a never-dying fame."

---

[1] It will be recalled that the exhibition comprises shield, breast-plate, helmet, walking-staff, tilting-pole, and porridge-pot belonging to Guy, the slipper of *pat swete ping*, Felice, and various trophies of contest in tusks of slaughtered boar, ribs of the Dun cow, diagram of the green dragon, *et cetera*, monuments "of lasting Fame of the noble Heroic Champion."

[2] Confusion will not arise between the house of Guy and that of the present representative of the name and title Warwick, whose descent is traced to the biographer of Sidney (*Life of the renowned Sir Philip Sidney*, London, 1652), Elizabeth's favourite, Fulke Greville.

[3] The figure of Guy in the Magdalen chapel is at least in stature worthy the "defender of distressed innocence," comments *The Tourist's Guide to Warwick*, p. 46. In this statue, *diabolicæ staturæ*, Guy is, *non homo! immo potius spiritus diaboli*, says one.

[4] "A pleasant song of the Valiant Deeds of Chivalry achieved by that Noble Knight, Sir Guy of Warwick," "printed at the Angel in Duck-lane, London: where any chapman may be furnished with them, or any other books at reasonable rates." Compare *Roxburghe Ballads*, press mark III. 50, 708.

[5] This statue, according to Dugdale, was erected in honour of Guy of Beauchamp.

[6] Effete philistinism alone would doubt the authenticity of the following noble epitaph, honouring the hero of the Dun cow and the green dragon:

> "Under this marble lies a pair,
> Scarce such another in the world there are,
> Like him so valiant, or like her so fair.
> His actions thro' the world have spread his fame,
> And to the highest honours raised his name;
> For conjugal affection and chaste love
> She's only equalled by the blest above.
> Below they all perfections did possess,
> And now enjoy consummate happiness."
> Finis.

Chapter VII.—*Concerning Guy, Earl of Warwick*.

The assumed identity of Guy of Warwick and of Count Guido is adopted, whether inadvertently or with deliberate intent, in later Latin MSS. of the original *Liber* of Alcuin, absolutely irrespective of the *Speculum;* see MS. e Musaeo[1] 214, formerly No. 68, *Epistola Alcuini leuite Guidoni comiti Warrewici ad eius requisicionem*, fol. 51b—fol. 68b, of the Bodleian Library, Oxford, date *circa* 1450. That, however, the union of Guy and Guido into a single homogeneous unit be justified as historical, independent study of the *dramatis personæ* of the legend and of the *Liber* will aid to disclose. The part played by Count Guido of Tours, under the name of Guy of Warwick, will be considered in the two chapters to follow, in an attempt to interpret the history of the two warriors.

CHAPTER VII.

CONCERNING GUY, EARL OF WARWICK.

> "Come! See the noble Deeds of Warwick's Knight,
> Whose worth within this history is placed
> Like Diamonds, when they're in Gold inchas'd[2]!"

KÖLBING, in *Germania*, vol. xxi. pp. 366, 367, discredits the legitimacy of the impersonation of Count Guido of Tours in the *rôle* of Guy of Warwick, on ground of the anachronism of the one hundred years marking the brilliant piece of bravado characteristic of each of the two men. The English hero is, it must be conceded, of uncertain lineage. Kölbing presents the popular verdict with reference to the period of the proud exploits of Guy the knight.[3] In this aspect the objective point of the narrative is contributed in

---

[1] This Latin MS. is a small quarto described in the *Catalogus Bernardi: Catalogi bibl. MSS. Anglicæ et Hibernæ* (cf. chap. III. 8): see the same Catalogue, Alb. Alcuinus Flaccus, *De Virtutibus & Vitiis Epistola Ejusdem ad Guidonem Comitem Warwicensem*.

[2] Selected from the Bettesworth Guy, "at the sign of the Red Lion on Londonbridge," of 1706, a work dedicated to Mr. Zachariah Heywood, and containing notes from a mysterious unknown.

[3] The various editions of Guy's history, popular during the 18th century, comprise large numbers of "Chap Books," in series combining numerous fascinating tales, *Patient Grissel, History of the Seven Wise Masters of Rome, The Friar and the Boy,* etc. The edition of 1706 contains a "Full and True Account" of Guy's "many Famous and Valiant Actions Remarkable and Brave Exploits, and Noble and Renowned Victories," the history of "his Courtship to fair Phælice—and the many difficulties and Hazards he went through to obtain her Love," "extracted from Authentick Records, and the whole Illustrated with Cuts suitable to the History." Printed by W. O. for E. B., and sold by A. Bettesworth. A fifth edition was published in 1711, a seventh in 1733, and a twelfth, London, 81 Shoe Lane, is without date. The volume is

Chapter VII.—Concerning Guy, Earl of Warwick.

the combat by which the pilgrim, Guy, killed[1] the notable "Gyant of Denmark[2]:

> "that is more dread himselfe alone,
> than a thousande armed Knightes."—Copl. p. 202, v. 29.
> "Colbronde his name is tolde."—Copl. p. 203, v. 3.

About this nucleus has accumulated a cycle of chivalric gests,[3] attributed to Guy, but none of these rival that by which:

> "Guy's courage made the haughty Colebron yield,
> And all the Danish army fly the field!"

---

illustrated with thirteen graphic works of art, the last representing the funeral hearse of the departed heir to glory.

The Bates Guy passed through many editions and was sold for three pence by Charles Bates and Sarah Bates at the Sun and Bible in Guilt-spurr-street, later by Charles Bates at the same stand, where any person may be furnished with all. The Bates Guy seems to have seen numerous editions, one of which has been traced to the date 1680. See print for *Bal. Soc.*, 1871, p. xvii.

Another version printed in Aldermary Churchyard, London, passed through various editions between the years 1780 and 1850. It was sold for two pence. It includes the famous old song, and concludes with an epitaph. It is found in *Garlands and Histories* of 1783. A revised text of the Bettesworth Guy, with a frontispiece, a "*Fac-simile*" of the Statue of Guy in the chapel at Guy's Cliff, was printed by C. Whitingham for John Merridew (Warwick), 1821; and a second revised text is ascribed to J. Beck. It was sold by all booksellers in Leamington and Warwick.

[1] *Sir Beues* [ed. Kölbing], MS. M of the 15th century, claims for *Myles*, son of *Sir Beues*, the later ownership of Colbrand's sword; cf. verses 4169—4170, opening question of analogy with Arthurian *Excalibur*, or finding prototype in the "old mighty sword" of Beowulf:

> "And Myles had Colbrandy's brond,
> That som tyme had Rouland."

[2] Cf. Ritson's version, *A. Eng. M. R.*, vol. iii. p. 348.

[3] The palpable success of great Guy, "exemplarie sparck of christian love," is measured by his biographers in various euphemistic encomiums. Such was his valour in "Quarrels found out for his Recreation," "great Achievements oft performed in fight," that:

> "Pagans trembled at the name of Guy!
> His greatest Foes he always made retire,
> And those that saw him, coud not but admire.
> Nor was there any monstrous Gyant who
> He did not both Engage and Conquer too:
> For Gyants, Dragons, Boar and Dunsmore Cow
> To Guy's all-conquering Arm were forc'd to bow.
> No man could better Love nor better Fight."

The figure of Guy was so imposing that England felt justified in believing "that his glory reached the further corners of the earth." "Jews, Turks, and Infidels, became acquainted with his name" (Aldermary Guy).

> "Erl of Warwyk, named oon the beste knyht
> That was tho dayes . . . ."—*Lydgate*, l. 335.

Even royalty of the English realm did honour to the champion, but modest Guy refused honours, saying: "I am a mortal man, and have set the vain world at defiance."

"At his very birth he looked like a hero," and his "brave Teutonic victories in instances of wicked machinations of evil mind":

> "[Have] through Earth's Globe immortalized his Name."

Chapter VII.—Concerning Guy, Earl of Warwick.

This brilliant struggle, the legendary theme, about which the romance[1] has centered, is that described by Mannyng in the *History of England*,[2] derived from Geoffrey of Monmouth's *Historia Britonum*, of the 12th century, and from de Langtoft's French version of this work, see p. 31:

"Anlaf[3] sent messengers unto Athelstan
And bad him yeld the lond, or find another man
To fight with Colibrant . . . .
. . . .
That was Guy of Warwik, as the boke sais,
Ther he slough Colibrant with hache Daneis."

Such are the records in the various editions of *The History of the famous Exploits of Guy Earl of Warwick:* "His Encountering and Overcoming Monstrous Gyants, and Champions, and his killing the Dun Cow of Dunsmore-Heath, with many other Gallant achievements performed by him in his life, and the manner of his Death." This marvellous version is parodied in the metrical satire, "Guy's Porridge Pot with the Dun Cow roasted whole: An epic Poem, in twenty-five Books. Carefully corrected, and enlarged with many new Passages and additional notes in second edition," Oxford, 1809, ascribed by a pencilling in the Museum copy to the authorship of Landor. The note reads: "By my townsman (Warwick) Walter Savage Landor *versus* Carr," and is signed Dr. Parker.

[1] One of the early accounts describes the event: "Finding his head crowned with silver hairs, after many years travel, he (*i. e.* Guy) resolved to lay his aged body in his native country, and therefore returning from the Holy Land, he came to England, where he found the nation in great distress, the Danes having invaded the land, burning cities and towns, plundering the country, killing men, women, and children, insomuch that King Athelstone was forced to take refuge in his invincible city of Winchester. The Danes drew all their forces hither, and desired that an Englishman might combat with a Dane, and that side to lose the whole, whose champion was defeated. On this, mighty Colbron singled himself from the Danes, and entering upon Morn Hill near Winchester breathing venomous words, calling the English cowardly dogs, that he would make their carcases food for the ravens. Guy hearing proud Colbron could no longer forbear, but on his knees begged the king for a combat. The king liking the courage of the pilgrim bid him go and prosper. Guy walked out the North Gate to Morn Hill, where the giant was, and fought most manfully. He was so nimble, and laid about him like a great dragon, so that he brought the giant to ground."—*The History of Guy Earl of Warwick* (Chap-Book, 1796), p. 21.

Another account explains that: "after the king had been worsted in the combats of the Danes, Colbron, a mighty Gyant of the Danes, advanced to the Walls, bidding Defiance to the English king." When Guy approached, the king said: "Alas, poor Pilgrim, thy aged Limbs are not able to contend with him." "Doubt not, Sire," was Guy's reply, "but the justness of your Cause will add Strength to those Arms which have been used to Conquer." All the English warriors thronged to the walls to behold the event. When Guy had conquered "they on the Wall set up such a shout that echoed to the Clouds." Cf. Bettesworth's Guy.

We learn that "Guy conquered and was entertained with Trumpets, Drums, and other Martial Music."

"Te Deum ont en haut chante
Grand ioye font en la cite."—*Aug.* 77. v. a.

[2] This repository of British fabulous history, *Cronicon sive Historia Britonum*, compiled by the Welsh Monk (Bishop of St. A'aph, d. 1154), was printed in 1508 and translated into English 1718.

[3] O.N. Olafr. Cf. *Bat. of B.*, l. 50.

Chapter VII.—Concerning Guy, Earl of Warwick. lxxvii

Account of the tumultuous departure of the terrified Danes is enrolled by the MS.[1] Cod. Aug. 87. 4. fol. 80:

> .... "Hastiuement hors se vont,
> Passent la mer en lor dromond:
> En Danemarche[2] sont arivez
> Mournes et matz et adoelez."

This inspiring contest places the romance on a historical basis. Colbrand's fight symbolizes the Battle of Brunanburh, commemorated in the poem from the *Chronicle*, the *Battle of Brunanburh*,[3] the song of Æthelstan's Victory, see edition of Wülker, Grein's *Bibliothek der ags. Poesie*, i. p. 37. The *Chronicle* vouches for the date of the fight (cf. Zupitza's *Übungsbuch*, p. 27), *An.* DCCCCXXXVII., although Plummer, in an edition of *Two Saxon Chronicles*, p. 37, dates this battle 938. An old document of the king Æthelstan gives DCCCCXXXVIII, *in quo anno bellum factum est in loco qui bruninga feld dicitur*, cf. Birch, *Cantularium*, Sax, vol. II. p. viii. 937 is the date universally associated with the contest, see Green, *History of the English People*, vol. i. p. 80; Morley, *English Writers*, vol. iii. p. 276. The legend is dated by Lydgate as follows:

> "Fro Cristis birthe complet nyne hundred yeer
> twenty and sevene by computacioun."

The legendary accounts of the fray place Guy's achievement on the same page of history, and unite Guy's master victory with the reign of the English king Æthelstan,[4] 925—941, definitely stated by the song:

> "King Athelstone[5] that tyme was king,
> and, when he heard of Guy's coming,
> He went and met Guy for fayne.
> they kist and wept for ioye certayne."—Copl. p. 31.

---

[1] MS. Cod. Aug. 87. 4 is described as *uralt französisches Liederbuch*, Herbing, *Ueber die Handschrift des Guy von Warwick auf der herzoglichen Bibliothek zu Wolfenbüttel*.

[2] *ofer deop wæter. difelin* (Dublin) *secan.*—*Æthelstan*, 109, 110.

[3] With this century is also associated the Apocryphal poem *Judith* on authority of Groth, *Composition und Alter der Altenglischen Exodus*, 1883; Kluge, *Beiträge*, vol. ix. pp. 448, 449; Luick, *Beiträge*, vol. xi. pp. 490, 491; Lichtenstein, *Zeitschrift für d. Alterthum*, vol. xvi. p. 327; Vigfússon and Powell, etc., *Corpus Poeticum Boreale*, lv., make *Judith* of the same century, perhaps contemporary with the conflict of Guy, or even descriptive of the same *Battle of Brunanburh*, Cook, *Judith*, pp. 2, 8, 11.

[4] Ælfred's "golden-haired grandson" grown to manhood. In childhood he was girded by his king with "sword set in golden scabbard, and a gem-studded belt." Æthelstan's glorious reign attained to the ambitious standard marked for descendants of the race of Ælfred, Green's *History of the English People*, vol. i. p. 79.

[5] There is no mistaking the romancer's period for the immortal Guy: "In the sixth Year of the Reign of King Edgar the Great, this our famous Guy was

lxxviii Chapter VII.—*Concerning Guy, Earl of Warwick.*

So also the Drewry print of the early 18th century: "In the blessed time when Athelstone[1] wore the crown of the English nation, Sir Guy, Warwick's mirror ... was the chief hero of the age." An old song of the *Valiant Deeds of Chivalry by the Noble Knight, Sir Guy of Warwick*, to the tune, "Was ever man?" permits Guy to speak for himself:

"When Athelstone wore the Crown,
I lived here upon the Earth.
Sometime I was of Warwick earl."

Collateral evidence, the Chronicle,[2] substantiates romance: *Her æþelstan[3] cyning . eorla dryhten . beorna beahgifa . his broþor born in the City of Warwick.*" The tradition is modified a little in the Bates Guy, and at variance with the 14th century versions: "In the Reign of *Edgar*, surnamed *Athelstone*, King of the West-Saxons, was born Guyrolous Cassibilanius, vulgarly called *Guy of Warwick.*"

[1] The period is in every detail of the story avowedly that of Æthelstan. Thus the tale narrates that in hour of sorrow, Phillis "sold jewels and costly robes with which she used to grace King Æthelstone's court" (Aldermary Guy). The same text ascribes to Æthelstan the honour of placing in Warwick Castle a representation of the fatal dragon whose head was cut off through Guy's bravery. "The king caused the picture of the dragon, 30 feet in length, to be worked in cloth of arras." It is reported that: "King Athelstone, his Queen, and the chief Nobles and Barons of the land," were present at Guy's wedding. The estate bequeathed to Guy by Earl Roland, when he "resigns this Life for Immortality," is "confirmed by Royal Athelstone."

[2] "A pleasant song of the Valiant Deeds of Chivalry achieved by that Knight Sir Guy of Warwick" reads:

"Nine hundred twenty Years and odd
After our Savior Christ his Birth,
When king Athelstone wore the Crowne,
I lived here upon the Earth."

Thus the ballad supports Lydgate in placing the battle ten years earlier than the accepted date, cf. *The Old Song* enriching the Roxburghe *Ballads*, vol. ii. p. 19: "Ancient Songs and Ballads written on various subjects, and printed between the years 1660 and 1700, chiefly collected by Robert Earl of Oxford, and purchased at the sale of the late Mr. West's library, 1773, and bound in 1774, Museum copy press mark III. 50.708." The public learns that:

"These venerable ancient song-inditers
Soar'd many a pitch above our modern writers;
. . . .
Their words no shuffling double meaning knew:
Their speech was homely, but their hearts were true."

[3] Cf. *Uebungsbuch*, p. 27, or *A.S. Chronicle*, Grein's *Bibliothek der ags. poesie*, ed. Wülker, I. p. 374. Compare Tennyson's translation:

"Athelstan King,
Lord among Earls,
Bracelet-bestower . . .

. . . .
. . . with his brother,
Edmund Atheling,
Gaining a lifelong
Glory in battle,
Slew with the sword-edge
There by Brunanburh," *etc.*

eác. eadmund æþeling . . . . sweorda ecgum. ymbe brunanburh. bordweal clufan.[1] Graphic details of the vigorous pen picture,[2] native characteristics of the skill of the O.E. poet, are lost to the M.E. poem. The mysticism of chivalry replaces the vivid energy of the ancient warrior. The later interest centers in the romantic and sentimental story of Felice. In these immediate details O.E. history does not support M.E. narrative. Fact does not fail in providing the contest. It is described by a series of historians, Wigornensis, Dunelmensis, Malmesbury, Huntingdon, Brompton, Gaimar, but its valiant Warrior Guy is not once mentioned. Guy, the memorable hero, is deficient in every O.E. reference to the battle. On the other hand the M.E. historian did not hesitate to add to the account of the contest manifold embellishments of his own invention.

The working of the material into the Guy tradition seems not to have been coincident with the event. Lydgate alone on ground of traditional literature, an unreliable authority, on support of unreliable historian, ascribes specific source to the M.E. Guy saga. The earliest literary form is attributed by Lydgate to Cornubiensis in a :—

"translacioun . . . .
out of the latyn maad by the cronycleer
callyd of old Gerard Cornubyence.   str. 72[4]
the XI. chapitle of his historyal book."   str. 73[3]

Lydgate's authority is Hearne, *Chronicon sive Annales prioratus de Dunstable*, Appendix XI. *Girardi sive Giraldi Cornubiensis historia Guidonis de Warwick, e cod. MS. in Bibliotheca Collegii Magdalenensis descripta* (Oxford). Cornubiensis has been identified as Giraldus Cambrensis (1146—1216), author of a *History of England*, see Tanner, *Bibliotheca Britannico-Hibernica*. Fabyan, *New Chronicles of England and France*, p. 185, quotes Lydgate's verse as follows: *called of olde Gyrardus Cambrense*. Morley, to the contrary, *English Writers*, vol. iii. p. 276, ascribes the romance to Walter of Exeter, a Cornish Franciscan named by Bale, *Catalogus II.*, p. 44 : *Gualterus de Excestria: apud S. Carocum in Cornubia manens vitam scripsit Guidonis, inclyti olim Warwicensis comitis, libro uno.* A. Tanner, *Die Sage von Guy von Warwick*, pp. 33—34, tries to prove that

---

[1] Historical point of the saga is the battle by which the W. S. king Æthelstan with his brother Edmund, aided by the Mercians, defeated the Danes, combined in forces with the Scotch, at a place, probably Brunanburh, on the western coast of England, in the year 937 (?), Green, *Conquest of England*, p. 254; Wülker, *Grundriss*, 339—342.

[2] Guy's combat recalls to the editor the *Battle of Malden* with its Viking hero rather than the *Battle of Brunanburh*.

Chapter VII.—Concerning Guy, Earl of Warwick.

Gualterus Excestriensis and Giraldus Cambrensis, *alias* Giraldus Cornubiensis (Gerald de Barri ?), are the same historian. Herbing ascribes the legend of Guy to Walter of Exeter (*Ueber die Hss. von Guy*, etc.). Tanner believes that the historian lived in the 12th century. Thus a history is supposed to have been written in the 12th century in which Guy of Warwick is represented as an actual hero, alive in 927, during the reign of Æthelstan, and active in the Battle of Brunanburh. The hero is thus placed in the 12th century, where he has the support, if not of history,[1] again of romance.

Guy has generally been regarded as purely a hero of fiction. Grässe, *Die grossen Sagenkreise des Mittelalters*, traces in the legend a development of the Arthurian saga, in which Guy names Gawain. Guy is described in the *Dictionary of National Biography* as the product of Old English traditions, to which literary form was given by an Anglo-Norman poet; ten Brink, p. 180, agrees in ascribing the work in its first treatment to an Anglo-Norman poet; Zupitza, *Guy of W.*, p. 1, decides that the M.E. versions of the Romances of Guy of Warwick are from the French. This is virtually the opinion of Jusserand,[2] *The English Novel in the time of Shakespeare*, pp. 38, 39, 40. Here *Guy of Warwick* is included in the long list of "poems translated or imitated from French romances," the "awakening" in the palace which the Norman enchanter had doomed to temporary sleep. The author of an article on "Ancient Metrical Romances," *Percy's Reliques*, p. 291, also A. Tanner, p. 47, explain: "These stories were of English invention." "French originals were amplifications of the old English story." The editor, "Introduction" to *Guy and Colbronde*, Hales-Furnivall, *Bishop Percy's Folio MS.*, vol. ii. pp. 509 ff., find the oldest literary form of the Guy history to be purely romance, in literary composition the work of a monk. Guy's desertion of his wife, his asceticism, his remorse, that he has,

"Abbeys brente and citees tane" (MS. Ff. 2. 38),

his penance, are a theme for the sympathies of a monk. He finds the origin of the romance within cloister walls for the amusement and instruction of the brotherhood. Oesterley, *Gest. Rom.*, p. 261, is of the same opinion. A. Tanner (*Sage von Guy von Warwick*, pp. 37, 38) investigates the question, and concludes that Guy of Warwick, his historic warfare, and all his interesting circle are the

---

[1] George Ellis's attempt to identify Guy and Egil is not successful; cf. Turner, Warton, Herbing, and *Egilli Skallagrimii*, ed. Schlegel.
[2] See also *A Lit. Hist. of the Engl. People*, p. 224.

Chapter VII.—Concerning Guy, Earl of Warwick.

product of a wandering minstrel,[1] sung in palace hall or cathedral priory, the material later disseminated as historical fact. He cites in support of this theory an incident from Warton (*History of Engl. Poetry*), where Prior Alexander de Herriard entertained his guest, Adam de Arleton, with the song of Danish Colebrand sung by a minstrel.[2] Tanner's view is confirmed by the essay on the metrical romance (*Percy's Reliques*, p. 290): "The stories of Guy and Bevis were probably the invention of English minstrels." Ritson (*A.E. M.R.*, vol. I. p. xciii) also quotes Warton: "*cantiicum Colbrondi* was sung by a juggler in 1333." Grässe (*vide supra*) finds it one of a cycle of heroic song.

ten Brink, *Gesch. der Eng. Lit.*, p. 180, followed by Körting, *Grundriss*, 89, bases the saga upon "popular traditions of the Middle Ages," and explains Guy's marvellous history as a composite of "local traditions, historical reminiscences, current, fabulous, and romantic themes, and pure invention," a combination of religious and worldly motives delightful to an Age of Chivalry. ten Brink further, p. 246, explains that "probably the poet made use of English local traditions, in which things separated in time and place had already blended." Jusserand, p. 40, virtually similar, claims that all "who had won glory" in England or for England, all "whose fame lingered in ballads and popular songs" served to adorn the metrical

---

[1] Concerning the songs of the monks of a religious house of Eastern England, see ten Brink, *Gesch. der Engl. Lit.*, vol. i. p. 148; and Wordsworth's *Ecclesiastical Sonnet*, XXX:

"Meric sungen muneches binnen Ely,
Tha Cnut chyning reu ther by;
Roweth, cnihtes, noer the land,
And here we thes muneches sang."

"A pleasant music floats along the mere,
From monks in Ely chanting service high,
. . . as Canute the king is rowing by;
. . . . draw near,
That we the sweet songs of the monks may hear.
. . . .
Heart touched . . . .
The royal minstrel . . . .
Gives to the rapture an accordant Rhyme.
. . . . sternest Clime
And rudest Age are subject to the thrill
Of heaven-descended piety and song."

[2] See *Roxburghe Ballads*, vol. vi. p. 733; *Hudibras*, Part I, canto 2, l. 300; Puttenham, *Arte of English Poesie* (1589), p. 57: "antique Eng. romance was sung to the harp at Christmas dinners and brideals"; Corbet, *Iter Boreale* (1582—1635):

"May all the ballads be called in and deye
Which sung the warrs of Colebrand and Sir Guy."

tale, and were regarded as "personal ancestors" of English nobility. In this attempt to give England a national hero and romance a historical background, the chivalric element rules with the poet. A desire must be recognized to idealize the superior merit of resignation to the world and of unwavering piety.

In general, then, it will be seen that the weight of the material of the romance is to be regarded as purely legendary and romantic. Tanner supports his theory of romance origin on basis of the analogy with the romance literature with which the Guy of Warwick is associated: *Hornchild, Ipotis, Sir Tristrem*, and universally *Sir Beuis*,[1] a link by no means to be disregarded. To this day the marvellous exploits of Guy and Bevis are indissolubly united. They present no longer their normal development, but stand for figurative exemplification of prodigious strength; cf. James Russell Lowell in his *Last Poems*, p. 15:

> "Methinks no dragon of the fens
> Flashed huger scales against the sky,
> Roused by Sir Bevis or Sir Guy. . . ."

Sir Beues, Kölbing, p. xxxvii, contributes illustrations attesting to the popularity of the combined elements Guy and Beues. Apart from the oft quoted *Sir Thopas*, v. 188, the partnership occurs *Richard Coer de Lion*, v. 6661; *Speculum Vitæ, Englische Studien*, vol. vii., p. 469, v. 37, 39; *Generides*, A, v. 13 ff. They are joined in various different commentaries, for instance, Taine, *Hist. of Engl. Lit.*, vol. i., p. 100: Arthour, Horn, Beues, Guy of Warwick, "every prince and every people"; cf. Percy's explanation, ten Brink's, etc. In general, then, a purely romantic character[2] must be ascribed the fundamental Guy saga, but that under this popular exterior an actual hero may have been extolled is not impossible.

That this underlying magnate of the romantic world be Count Guido, the investigation from the Guy of Warwick side of the argument does not affirm. Equally ineffectual is an attempt to place the period of the *Speculum*, as represented by Guy, in the time of Guido. The best authority for the date of the literary form of

---

[1] *Sir Beues* goes so far as to cite an exploit of Guy of Warwick, in the contemporary Auchinleck MS., v. 2607:

> "& Gij of Warwik, ich vnderstonde,
> Slouȝ a dragoun in Norþ-Homberlonde."

[2] The metrical tale assumes but a slightly different exterior in the various romances. The main features are the same throughout: a valiant knight, a relentless lady to be won, a world of fight, seas of blood, the knight applauded and rewarded. Cf. *King Horn, Sir Beues*, etc.

the saga places it in the 12th century; cf. *Gesta Romanorum*. To transfer Guy to the battlefield of Brunanburh, there is only the voice of the romancer in authority. The four hundred years between *Liber* and romance are not explained in Guy's history.

The MSS. do not aid in the annihilation of time and distance.[1] The oldest of these is Norman, the Wolfenbüttel Codex, 87. 4, *Augusteorum Guelferbyt.* of the late 13th century. To this century belong the French MSS. 24, 32 in the Bodleian Library. Remaining French MSS. and all the English transcripts are the work of later centuries, the Auchinleck version (No. 23, 24), contemporary with the *Speculum*, being followed by the Caius, Ff. 2. 38 (cf. Zupitza), the Lydgate and the Lane-Lydgate texts. Further, over date see *Chronology of the Speculum*, chap. xv.

That Guy is English and not French, united testimony from all sources evidences, and the poems and tales, the authority most largely quoted, confirm. Generally the scenes of the romance are located in Winchester. Different versions name the exact locality under various names. Winchester is the town of Lydgate and the ballads. Copland places Guy in Wallingford: "*To Wallinford Guy him drew;*" if he were to be located in the Brunanburh fight, then Guy was an Englishman of Lincoln.

A will o' the wisp ever to be pursued, never to be grasped, the investigation[2] of the Guy saga finds only probabilities, never a certainty of relationship. Not one of the lesser of these is the coincidence between the history of Guido and that of Guy. But the investigation has failed to provide historical certainty for the facts proffered by the *Speculum*.

CHAPTER VIII.
CONCERNING GUIDO, COUNT OF TOURS.

". . . . . whose fame
Is couching now with pantherized intent."[3]

COUNT GUIDO was a brilliant light in the local history of Tours, but his splendid deeds seem to have cast no glorifying rays beyond

---

[1] For lists of Guy of Warwick MSS. see Winneberger, *Ueber d. Hss.-Verhält. des Altfr. Guy de W.*, pp. 2, 3, A. Tanner, *Die Sage*, etc., pp. 49—54, and Zupitza, pp. 1, 2 of Introduction.

[2] In the study see Day and Decker's play, 1618—1619, Pepys I. 522, and the Spanish romance *Tirante el blanco*.

[3] *Lines to R. J. Tennant*, from the authorship of Hallam, immortalized in Tennyson's *In Memoriam*.

his own epoch and his own land. Unlike other great commanders, benefactors to home and country, no glowing records illumine his achievements to modern gaze. As an educational medium Count Guido has not contributed forcefully to a later civilization among progressive nations,

"His soul well-knit and all his battles won."

Yet he was conqueror, hero, patriot, and, greatest of all, he possessed a spirit moulded to noble steadiness of purpose and well-balanced in moral force. Count Guido was in real life the benign type and example of the warrior of God in the eternal tragedy of battle.

Important features delineating the history of Count Guido during the lifetime of Alcuin are epitomized in the terse statement of Monnier, *Alcuin et Charlemagne*, p. 35, with reference to the *Liber ad Guidonem*: *Alcuin l'écrivit pour le comte Widon ou Gui, gouverneur de la marche de Bretagne et directeur des biens de saint Martin. Ce seigneur désirait avoir une règle de conduite, qu'il pût suivre au milieu de la carrière des armes.*[1] Hamelin, *Essai*[2] *sur la vie et les ouvrages d'Alcuin*, pp. 102—103, adds: *Il composa ce manuel à la demande du comte Gui, qui, vivant dans le métier des armes, désirait avoir des instructions sur l'art de mériter la gloire éternelle . . . Dans ce livre du guerrier, dans ce livre du grand seigneur, Alcuin prêche la charité, la modestie, la miséricorde, . . . la pratique constante de toutes les vertus.* Completing the picture is the description of Paris, *Histoire Littéraire de la France, publiée*[3] *sous la direction de M. Paulin Paris*, 1866, Tome iv., p. 315: *Ce seigneur (i. e. Widon ou Gui) engagé dans le tumulte des armes et des autres affaires temporelles, l'avoir demandé à l'auteur, à qu'il paroit*, etc.

These succinct passages summarize comprehensive facts[4] in personal character and experience. They prepare for revelation of wonderful military prosperity. Count Guido's chosen pursuit was war. He was esteemed as warrior. Alcuin adapted his counsel to Guido's pursuit, *occupationi, quam te in bellicis rebus habere, Liber*, line 2. A lesser Cæsar, he first conquered the land he was to govern: *Britanniam ingressus, totamque perlustrans, in deditionem accepit*, Mgn.[5] II., col. 444. This illustrious advance of Guido into

---

[1] Selected from the second edition of Monnier's work, Paris, 1864, published with some fragments of a hitherto unedited commentary on Matthew, and some other articles of Alcuin not printed earlier.
[2] *Thèse pour le Doctorat présentée à la Faculté des Lettres.*
[3] Published first M.DCC.XXXVIII.
[4] Cf. *Vita Alchuini*, Jaffé, p. 28; Ceillier, *Hist.*, vol. xii., p. 187.
[5] *Monitum Prævium*, Tom. Sec., p. 5; *Epistola*, vol. ii., col. 643.

Chapter VIII.—Guido, Count of Tours.

Britannia, the subdual of the entire province, with surrender of arms and governmental documents, the glory of adding a province and a people to the territory of Charlemagne, this is for the life of Count Guido the great distinguishing event. Here a battle of Brunanburh, a struggle with Colbrand, is provided, a foe supplied, an Æthelston replaced by a Charlemagne, the conditions of the English saga duplicated on French soil. Not more generously has the valour of Guy of Warwick been sung in English verse, than has the conquest of Guido and the French Britannia been sounded in French history. The chroniclist delights to return to the event: *totamque perlustrans, Britanniæ provincia subiugata, arma ducum in traditionem accepit*, is the refrain of the record of every political event of the day. Cf. Andrea Dv Chesne, *Historiæ Francorvm Scriptores*,[1] Tom. II. III.; Martin Bouquet, *Receueil des Historiens des Gaules et de la France*, MDCCCLXIV, Tom. V. VI.; and numerous chronicles of the period: *Annales de Gestis Caroli Magni Chroniques sur les Gestes de Charlem., De Rebus Gestis Ludovici pii*, and selections *Ex Chronico Elnonensi, Ex Chronico Britannico* (Probat, *Hist. Britanniæ*), *Ex Miraculis Sancti Benedicti, Ex Sigeberti Chronico, Ex Hernianni Chronico*. Records are contributed by Pertz, *Monumenta Germ. Hist.* MDCCCXVI, fol. I., see 80, *Annales Francorum, Annales Bertiani, Capitularia Caroli, Croniques de S. Denis*, &c. The military exploit is without parallel in the age. Various accounts describe conquests over a Saracen foe, *Annales Breves ab Christ.*, DCCVII—DCCXC, p. 40 and p. 59 of a report of the year *Caroli Magni* 798. Here are enrolled statistics of an expedition to the Balearic Islands, laid waste a year earlier by the Saracens.[2] In the defence proffered by the French, and successful, *cum Dei auxilio*, Count Guido has

---

[1] *Opera ac Stvdio Andreæ DV Chesne.*

[2] That the Saracen proselytes of a pseudo-prophet, having conquered Persian host, Grecian phalanx, and Roman cohort, and planted 'standard on the pillars of Hercules' (cf. Washington Irving, *Mahomet and his Successors*, p. 150), dreamed to the day of Alcuin (approximately 800) of the subjection of Europe against the powerful Charlemagne, is to be inferred from the historian's narrative testifying to the incursions of a Saracen foe. That, however, it was again a struggle after the rich treasure of the famed Abbey of Tours, is not probable. It will be recalled that the repulse of the Saracens, completed by Charles Martel in 732, against the accomplished Arab general Abdel Rham, was a final defeat (cf. Freeman, *General Sketch*, p. 119). The Battle of Tours repelled Moslem power with its fierce propagandism, prevented Saracen ascendency in the extreme West, and ended the limitless incursions marked by the burning of the great library at Alexandria, and the military subjugation of the Visigoths succeeding Saracen entry into southern Gaul under El Haur in 710 (cf. also Fisher, *Outlines of General History*, p. 229).

part. *Wido (Guido, p. 59)*[1] *Comes ac Præfectus, qui in marca Britanniæ præsidebat, & vna cum sociis Comitibus Britanniam ingressus, totamque perlustrans, in deditionem accepit; & Regi de Saxonia reuersa arma Ducum, qui se dediderunt, inscripsis Singulorum nominibus præsentauit. Nam his se & terram & populum omnis cuiusque illorum tradidit, & tota Britannorum provincia, quod nunquam antea à Francis fuerat, à Francis subiugata est.*

The exact year of this glorious conquest[2] is not to be stated. For a decade following its occurrence vigilant annals keep fresh its splendour. The description occurs in *Annales de Gestis Caroli imperatoris*, pp. 79, 250, etc.: *ad quem Wido Comes, . . . Nam sociis Comes ille suis compluribus ipsam hoc anno penitus terram lustrauerat omnem, corda domans belli terrore ferocia.* Compare also Bouquet, V., p. 214, *Annales Francorum*, p. 349, etc., the latter confirming the identity of the hero with the words: *Wido Comes, qui marcam contra Britonnes tenebat.* Both historians quoted note an undated definite period, *hoc anno, eodem anno.* The Chronicle seems to have been completed DCCXCI. French Britain must have been in the hands of Guido so early as the date of the writing of the *Liber*, probably earlier. Note also *Ex Hermanni Chronico*, p. 365: *Britannia Cismarina per Wittonem Ducem Caroli subjicitur; Ex Sigeberti Chronico*, p. 378: *Baleares insulæ auxilio Francorum à Saracenis defensantur per Widonem Karoli Ducem Brittones vincuntur, & in deditionem recipiuntur; Chroniques sur les Gestes de Charlem.*, Livre I., p. 247: *Après retourna en France, . . . la chapele s'en ala pour yverner: la celebra la sollempnité de la Nativité & de la Resurrection. Là vint . . . cuens Guis . . . qui gardes des marches de Bretaigne . . . avoit cherchies toutes les contrées des Bretons . . .*

A single defeat is chronicled. The foe congratulates itself on a double glory, in that added to the victory, a powerful adversary, *Guido Comes* has been put to flight: *Guido Cenomannensis Comes sperans cum fortitudine magna vincere in fugam versus est; Brit. Arm.*, p. 219. *Guido Cenoman., Comes, a Lamberte in fugam vertitur; Ex Eutropii Presbyt.*, Tract. p. 298.

Werner ascribes the death of the Count to 814, but another record

---

[1] In the identity of the circumstances detailed, it is curious, that here again fact corresponds to tradition in the Guy history. Both Guys, the legendary Guy and the real Guido, are accredited with conquests against Saracen enemies.

[2] See *Vita Karoli Magni*, pp. 50, 59, 79; *Eginhardi Annales*, p. 214; *Sur les Gestes de Charlemagne*, Liv. I., ch. xi., pp. 247, 248; *Annales Laurissenses*, p. 186.

Chapter VIII.—Guido, Count of Tours.

seems to be connected with Guido. The history of the year 834 contains notice of the lamented death of a Count Guido, killed in a brave fight in defence of the Abbey.[1] In a battle incited by counts Odo and Lambert many illustrious men were slaughtered, among them perhaps Alcuin's Guido.[2] Dv Chesne, *Historiæ,* etc., Tom. III., p. 445, states that a priest escaping announced a cruel fight, and reported to the monks the death of their Abbot: *Teutonem denique Abbatem*[3] *S. Martini, Gvidonem Comitem Cenoman . . . mortem oppetiisse.—Ex. Mirac. s. Bendicti,* p. 213. Great lamentation arose among the sorely afflicted brotherhood, to be read of to this day, a thousand years[4] after these monks on the sunny plains of the Loire sent cries to heaven in bereavement and loss: *Quo nuncio graviter afflicti Fratres, ad Dominum exorandum pro tanta Christiani populi cæde se intentissime conferunt.* The same record is repeated by Bouquet, *Historiens,* etc., Tom. VI., p. 241; *Ex Chronico Engolismensi apud Labbeum,* p. 323; *Ex Chronico Brit.* in Probat, *Hist. Brit.,* p. 351, and *Ex Mirac. S. Benedicti Abbatis,* p. 313. Details of the painful circumstance are to be found *De Rebus Gestis Ludovici Pii,* Liber V., p. 584: *Wido Comes Cenoman. a Ludovico Imperatore . . . mittitur ad inquirendum . . . de beneficiis Ecclesiæ.* The announcement of Guido's death follows: *Guido Comes occiditur pugnando.* Yet through the sacrifice of the valued life of the brave nobleman, the purpose of the mission was accomplished. The Chronicle completes the story: *Quædam Beneficia Ecclesiæ Cennomanicæ restituuntur.* Facts relative to his life are otherwise as limited as they are definite.

That Guido of these historians[5] and Guido of the *Liber* are at times identical, is indicated in statistics contributed occasionally by

---

[1] It will be recalled that St. Martin names the founder of monasticism among the Gauls. Relics of St. Martin were enshrined in a church adjoining the monastery. See Ruskin's account of the saint in *Our Fathers have Told Us,* pp. 23—33.

[2] Alcuin wrote the life of the presiding saint of his monastery, St. Martin.

[3] Fridugis was the pupil named by Alcuin to become his successor, in active superintendence of the Abbey.

[4] Yet from modern literature the history of Count Guido seems to have died with the man. Shadow of inevitable destiny, his aspirations, his battles, the lament of friars, leave but a blank page.

[5] To the Guido of the *Liber* possibility must be conceded of a semi-romantic character introduced by Alcuinus. The type of work illustrated in the *Epistola Nuncupatoria* was popular in the 8th century, and it would be a natural tendency to idealize in the connection, the citizen first in rank as warrior, governor, and patron of the Abbey. Alcuin would thus at the same time pay a graceful compliment to an influential neighbour and follow a popular type of religious literature, where means of attractive form was limited, as in case of the young priests of the Abbey.

Chapter VIII.—*Guido, Count of Tours.*

Migne and by Alcuin in the *Liber*. The source is chiefly the *Annales*[1] *Loiseliani ad annum* DCCXCIX, and details are repeated in some instances in Lorentz's *Alcuins Leben*. Name and associated title are made definite: *Guido (i. e. Wido) Comes*, Mgn. II., col. 444, lines 2, 3; col. 614, line 1; *Wido Landgraf*, Lorz., p. 199. Various positions of honour and responsibility devolved upon Count Guido: *Wido Comes ac Præfectus Brit. limitis*, Eginh. p. 214; *comes qui in Marca Britanniæ præsidebat*, Mgn. I., col. 396, note; *Marca Britanniæ præsidens*, Mgn. I., p. 162; *Markgraf der britannischen Mark*, Lorentz, p. 199; *Rebus St. Martini præfectus*, Mgn. I., col. 276.

Not merely in public relationship is Count Guido introduced. In private capacity he is presented as a loyal citizen. In personal character he was a man of perfect life[2]; he was an incorrupt judge, a trustworthy witness, a faithful ambassador: *Illorum vita a viro perfecto et judice incorrupto et misso fideli Widone audiri potest, qui eorum omnia scrutans agnovit, quid egissent vel qualiter vixissent*, Mgn. I., col. 62; II., col. 444; *judicium ac judicorum æquitate et misericordiæ sedulitate*, Mgn. II., col. 614; *Wido advocatus, Ex Eutropii Presbyteri Tract.*, p. 298. Count Guido was reverenced by his Abbot and Dean. Alcuin appointed him umpire in settlement of a dissension between *episcopum Aurelianensem et fratres Turonenses*, cited in *Epistola* 195, Mgn. I., col. 437. More than once he served as arbitrator in matters of altercation. *In testem vocatur innocentiæ fratrum sancti Martini*, Mgn. I., col. 163. In a vague way Guy of Warwick was also champion of the oppressed; cf. the delivery of the fifteen sons of the aged man in *Guy and Amarant* (Percy's *Reliques*), and numerous instances of the adaptation of semi-selfish motives to an imaginary good, in contrast to this of Guido, based on justice and consecrated zeal.

That Guido had earned the esteem of Alcuin, is evidenced in the history[3] of the *Liber*, a laborious task of affection, undertaken in the

---

[1] Access to these annals has been impossible.

[2] Froben writes of the man; viri perfecti, ac Judicis incorrupti, atque Missi fidelis, Fr. II., p. 5. See also *Diplomata Ludovici Pii Imp.*, p. 834.

[3] Rigid austerity is ascribed to the old age of Alcuin. He forbade his pupils to read the philosophy and poetry of ancient Greece and Rome. To replace the lost texts he multiplied trustworthy copies of religious works. The fame of the school was great for MSS. remarkable for neatness and elegance. Discouragement of secular learning was general at this period; cf. Mullinger, *The Schools of Charles the Great*, pp. 100, 122, and Hallam, *Middle Ages*, chap. ix., part 2. Hraban (d. 856) permitted "a slight tincture of the classical literature," as subsidiary to the religious discipline of the *Scriptoria*.

feeble years[1] of the aged teacher. In enumeration of the works completed *ad extremum vitæ*, the aged preceptor mentions *Liber de Virtutibus et Vitiis ad Widonem sive Wittonem*. The reverential confidence manifested by the Count toward Alcuin is evident in the request for a book to serve as guide for the development of the religious life in period of warfare. To the earnestness and to the practical aspiration of Guido, the words of his entreaty may attest: *postulabat, ut doctrinas vitæ Christianæ suæque conditioni, ac . . . convenientes . . . , ut inter secularia negotia . . libellum . . , ad quem assidue suos actus examinare seque ad æternæ beatitudinis studium excitare posset, Mon. Præv.*, p. 5. Conditions of the entreaty have been found reproduced in the experience of the life of Guy, but the quality of the fervour described in the two episodes is not identical. The *Speculum* portrays mystic purpose, the goal a visionary good. The zeal of Guido is genuine, the seriousness of scholastic growth, and it lacks nothing in definiteness and loyalty to faith.

The immediate home of Guido (Guy's castle?) may have been discovered. *Annales Bert.* (p. 91) accounts for a villa,[2] a country-seat occupied by Count Guido. It bears the name Vendopera: *Wido quidem comes per plures annos tenuerat*. This villa was probably in the neighbourhood of Tours. The Count was a resident of the Marca Britanniæ, possibly of the town of Tours. Britannia is mentioned as *cismarina*, giving assurance of French environment and not of English, should possibility of doubt arise. In this province was situated the Abbey of St. Martin: *Marca Britanniæ cismarinæ, in qua sita civitas et monasterium Turonense*, Mgn. II., col. 444. Alcuin himself (Mgn., p. 659) locates *episcopatus Turonensis, in Gallia*, Mgn. II., col. 659, 660. The name of the villa calls up a picture of summer days outside of the city, amid broad sunny meadows and invigorating breezes; but during the harvest season of active labour, it is not easy to separate Guido from the neighbourhood of the Abbey, with its inspiring master and its administrations "of the honey of the sacred writings."[3]

[1] Alcuin's retreat to the monastery was devised for purposes of rest from active pursuits; Alcuin's own plea to Charlemagne was: "Grant, I pray you, that a weary man may repose himself, that he may pray daily for you, and that he may prepare himself by confession and tears to appear before the eternal judge."

[2] See *Hincmari Remensis Annales*, p. 469: "*villa quæ Vendopera dicebatur, quam piae memoriae Illudowicus imperator sancto Petro tradiderat, et Wido, quidem comes per plures annos tenuerat . . .*"

[3] Alcuin in letter to Charlemagne writes: "To some I administer the honey

Chapter VIII.—Guido, Count of Tours.

Like Guy of Warwick, the fame of Guido was enshrined in metrical composition.[1] Apparently to Count Guido is the following selection from *Carmina Historica, MS. Bibliothecæ Petauij*:

Super Guidonem.
"*Insequor ipse libros, dumque vaco studiis.*
. . . .
Spiritus obtineat, quam merui melius.
. . . .
*Cuius eram Turonensis, ego de nomine Guido,
Gentis Patriciæ, me modo Remis habet,*" etc.

Data of Count Guido's career may be briefly summarized. The exact boundaries of his life are not to be discovered. In 800, approximately the date of the *Liber*, Guido (Wido, Witto, Guy) was possibly in middle life. His achievements, the number and variety of his pursuits, and the offices of honour that he filled, suggest for the period of Alcuin's deanship a man at the height of a prosperous career. The vigour, the activity, and the enthusiasm at this time universally ascribed to Guido, are the *insignia* of one not well advanced in years. In his own century Count Guido seems to have been an imposing figure. In the multitude of affairs in which he was active, his position was uniformly first. In claims of descent his rank socially was hereditary count. In governmental office he presided over the Marca Britanniæ. In military service he was commander. In legal administration he was judge. In theological assembly he was representative. His connection with the venerable

---

of the sacred writings; others I try to inebriate with the wine of the ancient classics. I begin the nourishment of some with the apples of grammatical subtlety: I strive to illuminate many by the arrangement of the stars, as from the painted roof of a lofty palace." This bit of poetical prose, worthy an Elizabethan in graceful selection of terms, is introduced by Craik into his *History of Eng. Lit. and Lang.*, vol. i., p. 46. See *Epistola* 78, Jaffé, p. 345: ". . . *sanctarum mella scripturarum ministrare satago; alios vetere antiquarum disciplinarum mero inaebriare studeo; alios grammaticae subtilitatis enutrire pomis incipiam; quosdam stellarum ordine . . . ceu pictor, cuilibet magnificare domus culmina . . . inluminare gestio.*" See Longfellow, *Outre Mer* (1882), p. 77.

[1] See *Poetæ Saxonici Annal.*, DCCXCIX., Lib. III.; *De Gestis Caroli Magni*, l. 537 ff.:

"*Ad quem (Carolo) Wido Comes cui Brettonum regiones
Commisæ fuerant, gentis tam sæpe rebellis
Detulit arma Ducum, proprio quæ nomine quisque
Inscripto dederat: . . . .
             Francis servire coacti.
Nam sociis Comes ille suis compluribus ipsam
Hoc anno penitus terram lustraverat omnem,
Corda domans belli terrore ferocia grandi.
Et jam perpetuo Brettones jure subacti
Parerent . . . .*"

Abbey during the lifetime of Alcuin was that of patron. His death was grievously mourned with every manifestation of reverence and affection.

Corresponding details mark the life of Guy the Earl. Event corresponds with event in the history of both warriors, yet these two chivalric soldiers of an earlier generation are not the same individual. They present two types, that of the vigorous man of affairs, and that of the dreamer of an imaginary world. Guy of Warwick is not Guy of Tours. Guido, the statesman of profound religious conviction, valiant warrior, honoured citizen, has not been identified with Guy the visionary, Guy the ascetic, the misanthrope, the unpractical knight of tradition. Alcuin is not represented in that high priest of romance, the hermit. It is impossible to explain the intervening years that, according to best reports, exist between the deeds ascribed to the two warriors. The desired unit, a missing link, is not to be discovered in any descendant or friend[1] of Guido the Count, nor is there a trace of reason in carrying Guy back through the century and placing him in the age of Count Guido. Unless some magician with Divine gift grant to Count Guido the roseate glamour of the romancer, and to Guy of Warwick the plain and simple atmosphere of earnest unselfish patriotism and good citizenship, the poet has placed Guido of Tours in a family to which he has no claims of relationship, and Guy of Warwick in a country not his by inheritance.

Practical Interpretation of the Speculum in Application to Guy of Warwick and Guido of Tours.

In the search for the beautiful ideal of knighthood essential features are provided in the bravery, the religious zeal, and probably in the gallantry of Guido the Count. But in his career there is mirrored not even a reflection of the chivalric atmosphere, that

---

[1] Alcuin's Guido cannot be brought into connection with any of the numerous Guidos of his generation. A relationship cannot be traced to Guido, Bishop of Spoleto, to the four hereditary dukes of France, Guidos living at that time, nor to Guido of Soissons, of Rouen, of Auxerre, of Modena; nor is he represented in the fifteen Guidos, dukes, bishops and archbishops distinguished in the 10th century. Gui de Burgagne, celebrating in chanson the expeditions of Charlemagne, seems not to have known Guido of Tours. In none of the distinguished lines of bishops, archbishops, artists, poets, warriors, bearing the family name Guido, has been discovered trace of heredity, direct or indirect, for Guido of Warwick and of Tours. See Wattenbach, *Geschichte des Mittelalters*, and Förstermann, *Namenbuch*.

should environ kinsman to Guy the knight. No beautiful Felice, no sovereign lady, guides the voluntary self-abnegation of the Count. What Guizot says of organized feudalism may be applied to Guy of Warwick. He lived in a Utopia without a date, a drama for which we find in the past neither theatre nor actors. To the true dignity of a lordly Guy, there exists but a tiny germ warmed into activity in the tale of Alexius. Guido the Count typifies, to the contrary, the man who dares to be just, as well as generous. Not a zealot, nor a fanatic, Guido's life is eloquent in deeds, not in dreams.

The *Speculum*, deprived of the glamour of romantic environment, the legitimate inheritance neither of legendary hero nor of historical nobleman, simply an English poem of the 13th century, remains for consideration. The popular *Liber* was adapted to his people by some pious representative of the clergy.[1] This is the explanation for the tenth selection of the Auchinleck folio. A little worldliness tingled in the blood of this priest. His keen poetic sense directed him to grasp at an artistic setting to enliven the monotony of a task imposed in response to conscience and to duty. Sensitive to the charms of poetical art as well as to the atmosphere of his times, fresh from tales of Arthur, of Guy, of Beues, of Ipotis, he grasped at the religious sacrifice ennobled in the primitive Alexius history. Stimulated by zeal for the souls of his flock he attempted to convey interest by giving a sensational exterior to the hackneyed truths of the Dean of the Holy Martin. The element selected to embody his ideal was the bold hero, Sir Guy, the renowned Earl of Warwick. Seeing with the imagination as well as with the material sense, the mediæval poet attempted to establish an easy relationship between romance and theology. Breathing the atmosphere of thought and of knowledge, he lived also the joyous life natural to taste, to culture, and to a clear conscience. His religious nature satisfied, it is not inharmonious that he should execute his task with such ardour, with such skilful adaptation of subject matter that the resulting *sarmoun* should link itself inseparably with literature of two types, and that the imitation should be so clever that hearer and reader alike should be deceived.

The poet's eye for effect, his *naïve* technique, his regard for connection, combined with the sensitiveness of his personality, heighten the impression of a romance of palpable beauty in main

---

[1] See Morley, *English Writers*, vol. iii., p. 364.

facts. The *Speculum* stands as the intense utterance of a poetical temperament, responsive at once to nature and to art, but in touch with earnest daily life. Such utterance meets nature in the reminder that "art is but the masque for nature." Dante speaks for Guido of Warwick and of Tours:

> "Thus hath one Guido from another ta'en
> The praise of speech."

CHAPTER IX.
PRINCIPAL SOURCES OF THE *SPECULUM*.

"Ut of latin ðis song is dragen on engleis speche."

De Virtutibus et Vitiis Liber of Alcuin[1] (*Alcuinus, Flaccus Albinus*) followed with much fidelity is the underlying fundamental source of the *Speculum* in its main outlines. The treatise in its first issue appeared in the edition of A. Dv Chesne, Paris, 1617. It was reprinted by Froben and Migne: *Beati Flacci Albini sev Alcvini Abbatis, Caroli Magni Regis ac Imperatoris, Magistri Opera.*[2] " Cvra ac stvdio Frobenii, S. R. I. Principis et Abbatis ad S. Emmeramvm Ratisbonæ, Tomi Secvndi, Volvmen primvm, M.DCC.LXXVII." The *Liber* is to be found, p. 128 ff. The print of Migne is contained in column 615 ff. of the second volume of Alcuin's works, the one hundred and first of the Series, *Patrologiæ Cursus, Completus* (CI), 1851: *B. Flacci Albini seu Alcuini Opera Omnia*, J. P. Migne.

Alcuin's advice[3] to Count Guido furnished material for numerous Latin MSS. preserved to-day in the libraries of Spain, Italy, France, Germany, Ireland, Scotland, and for many transcripts of greater or less degree of completion and accuracy in libraries of England. Two fragmentary translations[4] in English at the transition stage of the language are extant. One of these, a MS. of the Library of the

---

[1] Glosses representing the *Alcuini Exhortatio* are printed in the well-known Wright-Wülker, *Anglo-Saxon and Old English Vocabularies*, London, 1884, pp. 86 and 87.

[2] This work is characterized further as follows: *Post primam editionem, a viro clarissimo D. Andrea Qvercetano cvratam, de novo collecta, mvltis locis emendata, et opvscvlis primvm repertis plvrimvm aveta, variisqve modis illvstrata*, etc.

[3] See the supplement to *Bibliothèque des Pères Bigne Anciennes leçons de Canisius*, ed. Basnage, Tom. ii., and Ceillier, *Histoire des Auteurs Sacrés et Ecclésiastiques*, Tom. xii. p. 187.

[4] The *Kentish Glosses* preserved in the Cotton MS. Vesp. D vi, printed in Wright's *Vocabularies*, suggest to the reader a possible Englishing of the *Liber* in the ninth century. Regarding these *Alcuini Capitula Theologica ad Guidonem*,

Cambridge University, MS. Ii. 1. 33, has not been favoured with an edition.[1] MS. Vesp. D XIV, fol. 104 *a* ff. was printed by Assmann in *Anglia*, vol. xi. pp. 371 ff. Several facts of correspondence and some instances of omission make it probable that the *Speculum* was constructed directly from a later MS. Deficiency in the poetical treatment of the portion of the subject allotted to the vices (*de Vitiis*), in comparison with the exactness of the discussion of the virtues (*de Virtutibus*) suggests a fragmentary MS. of the original. Although the divergences are at times such as might be involved in shaping a Latin treatise into a metrical composition, with allowance for emotional personal interest, and a conception somewhat dramatic in execution, yet the *Speculum* demands the explanation of a sort of underplot of dramatic fancy, filling out the bleak details of the Latin outline. The poetical orthodoxy of the 13th and 14th centuries required for the complete discharge of duty the narration of the thrilling incident of the first sin, the account of the terrifying horror of the great day of doom, and the expression of the promises of the delights of paradise. To the intense personality of the poet the *Speculum* is indebted for the virtue of the enlivening episode important according to latter-day standards.

Through the individuality of the poet the *Speculum* became alive to the influence of a second source interwoven with the first, and giving tone-quality to the entire work. The real action of the poem centers in the knight Guy. The glorification of Guy of the main Guy of Warwick saga in its current English form, is parallel with the deification of Alexius in the redaction by Konrad von Würzburg. Alexius too left bride and palace to serve God through pilgrimage to Jerusalem. The *Speculum*, as an episode in the main tale, is indebted to a second source in value almost equal with the first, the *Liber*. The origin of the Guy history is prominent in the study of the relationship of Alquin and his *Liber*. The presentation of various episodes of traditional or scriptural origin is also important in the genesis of the *Speculum*. The differentiation of these sources in their various forms may be classified in three elemental groups :

Comitem iisdem Litteris in quibus etiam non nullæ voces Sax. glossatæ; see also Zupitza, *Zeitschrift für deutsches Alterthum, Neue Folge*, Bd. ix.

[1] The chapter *De Scripturarum Lectione* was printed from MS. I by Whelock in *Notes* upon Bede's *Ec. Hist.*, 1643, p. 173, but without connection with the MS. It is also quoted in notes to the second of Soames's Brandon Lectures, MDCCCXXX, *An Inquiry into the Doctrines of the Anglo-Saxon Church*, pp. 92—93. See also *Cat. of MSS. of the University*.

Chapter IX.—*Sources of the Speculum. Alcuin's Liber.*

1. The direct source, the *Liber*, offering frame-work for the complete text.

2. The legendary source, the *motif* directing the work, the Guy saga permeating the entire poem and with delicate subtlety giving personality to the Alexius tale. Thus there exists a link with the literature of Germany, Italy, and Greece, as well as of France, whether it be represented in England or on the continent.

3. Material employed by the poet, derived from various sources, apart from the *Liber* and the Guy saga. Here is to be included the tradition of the bush, the incident of Adam and his fall, of Abraham's interview with the angels, and details borrowed from the Scriptures.

De Virtutibus et Vitiis Liber.

I. *Main Resemblances between Liber and Speculum.*

Epistola Alquini.

"What man that claymeth gentil for to be,
Must . . . . . alle his wittes dresse
Vertu to sewe, and vyces for to fle.
For unto vertu longeth diguitee."[1] . . .

The *Liber*, as reproduced by Froben and by Migne, contains a list of chapters, *Capita*, a dedication with an introduction, *Epistola Nuncupatoria*, predicting the discussion to follow, a treatise on morality described as *De Virtutibus et Vitiis*, and a peroration, *Peroratio*. The different MSS. of the *Liber* are comparatively exact in preserving uniformly the same features, and the *Speculum* incorporates these details with some degree of fulness. It is to be noted, however, that the *Speculum* is authority for a modification of the order of arrangement. The *Epistola Nuncupatoria* of the *Liber* precedes the metrical table of *Capita*. The *Speculum* thus repeats the peculiarities of a single MS., of many brought to the test, namely, MS. *Bibl. Reg.* 6 A. XI. Here the same inversion occurs; there is here, as in the poem, deficiency in the treatise *De Vitiis*, and an appeal invoking divine blessing concludes the MS. text, similar to that marking the *Speculum* in common with numerous M.E. poems of approximately the same date. MS. *Bibl. Reg.* 6 A. XI., as represented by the *Speculum* in method of composition and application of materials, will frequently become the source of the comparison to follow in these pages. This text may be described as follows:

[1] Cf. *Gentilesse, Moral Balade of Chaucer*, Skeat, *The Minor Poems*, p. 195.

xcvi *Chapter IX.—Sources of the Speculum. Alcuin's Liber.*

MS. *Bibl. Reg.* 6 A. XI., Library of the British Museum. On parchment; of the twelfth[1] century. This text begins on fol. 109 *b*, line 28, and ends fol. 120 *b*, line 15. It concludes abruptly with *Capitulum* xxxv., *De quatuor uirtutibus*, and is followed by a distinct treatise, *De elemosina*, beginning fol. 120 *b*, line 16. Line 28, fol. 109 *b* reads: " Incip*it* ep*is*tola alqu*i*ni qua*m* edidit ad Widone*m* Comite*m*." The MS. is occasionally glossed. The leaf is ornamented[2] on the margin to the left.

Further in comparisons important to this issue, the O.E. texts of the *Liber* will be employed as follows:

1. V. MS. Cotton, Vespasian D XIV. 14, of the Museum Library. On parchment: of the twelfth century, Nehab: *Der altenglische Cato*, Berlin, 1879, p. 41. A description of MS. Vesp. D is to be found in the *Catalogue* of Wanley, Hickes *Thesaurus*, Part II., p. 243, quoted in the third volume of the Grein-Wülker, *Bibliothek der Angelsächsischen Prosa; Angelsächs. Homilien und Heiligenleben*[3] (edited by Dr. Assmann), p. 246: *Codex membranaceus in Octavo partim Latine, partim Saxonice diversis temporibus scriptus.* MS. Vesp. D is described by Hickes as *Capita quædam Theologica excerpta ex libro Alcuini*, and has been printed by Dr. Assmann in *Anglia*, vol. xi. p. 371, as *Uebersetzung von Alcuin's De Virtutibus et Vitiis Liber ad Widonem Comitem*. The text occurs third in a volume described as: *Miscellan. Saxonica*. It occupies fol. 104 *a*—118 *b*. The introduction, the lists of vices and virtues, the discussion of the vices, and the *peroration*, are wanting. Sixteen chapters of the original *Liber* are reproduced with marked fidelity.

2. I. MS. Ii. 33, University Library, Cambridge. A small quarto on vellum; probably of the 12th century. MS. Ii has as a whole neither been printed nor received literary notice in print to the date of the present article. As " Theological Extracts from Alcuin's Address to Count Guido of Warwick," it is noted somewhat vaguely in the *Catalogue* of the MSS. of the University Library. Introduction, lists of chapters, discussion of vices, and conclusion are deficient. It contains frequent glosses in Latin. In the history of the transition of the language, MS. Ii may stand a few years nearer the period of the Conquest than does MS. Vesp. D. This fact is at

---

[1] The *Catalogue* ascribes the MS. to the eleventh century.
[2] The decoration consists of grotesque faces in outline, following the text on the left margin.
[3] For information regarding MS. Vesp. D, the editor is indebted to a communication from Dr. Assmann, dated Jan. 12, 1895.

Chapter IX.—Sources of the Speculum. Alcuin's Liber.

once obvious by the large number of weakened inflectional endings presented by *Vesp. D* in contrast with *Ii*. A librarian's note places this MS. "between the earlier copy of Laʒamon, MS. Cot. Cal. A. IX. and the later years of the Abingdon Chronicle." The importance of this testimony will be recognized by the reader.

In the study of the sources of the *Speculum*, the almost slavish exactness of the O.E. translation renders it of little service toward the history of the *Speculum*. The fragmentary condition of the two copies of the O.E. *Liber*, at about the same stage of completion represented in the *Speculum*, as the *Liber* introduces the question as to the character of the MSS. employed respectively by the author of the *Speculum* and by the translator of the *Liber*. That the *Speculum* be derived from an English *Liber* of the period of the Conquest would seem an impossibility; cf. Morsb. § 1, Anm. 1. The link between the two redactions might be explained on supposition that the poet and the translator had access to the same Latin transcript of the original; the divergence in the texts would not seem unnatural, if it be considered that the poet's interest centred in the gallant and romantic warrior, while the translator's zeal found inspiration in the serene orthodoxy of the preceptor of Charlemagne.

The coincidences between *Liber* and *Speculum* are unmistakable in the main outlines of the two compositions. Although the general sequence is not the same, correspondences are significant.

1. *Dedication.*

Dilectissimo Filio suo Widoni Comiti humilis[1] *leuita alchwinus salutem*,[2] MS. R, fol. 109 b, l. 29, is reproduced[3] in the records of the *Speculum*, verses 27—64 of the history of the knight Guy of Warwick. The names of the heroes[4] are identical, *Guy* in both

---

[1] The expansion of contracted forms is indicated by the regular type.
[2] Line 28, fol. 109 b reads: *Incipit epistola alquini quam edidit ad Widonem Comitem*.
[3] Similar features are preserved in MS. Bibl. Reg. 5. E. IV. described: *Alcuini siue Albini Angli ad Guidonem de Virtutibus Liber*, a parchment MS. attributed to the 13th century. This MS. is without heading, and begins *D[i]lectissimo filio Widoni* . . . etc., fol. 97 b. Near the top of the folio is written: *Alcuinus siue Albinus clarissimus*. The peroration is wanting. The text ends fol. 110 b: *Explicit liber Aluuini leuite ad Widonem Comitem* (vide supra, Note). At the conclusion of the volume is a note: *Thy Will be dun ó lorde. Bonum est mihi, Domine*. A bit of a musical staff is inserted into the fly-leaf of the MS.
[4] References occur to folio and line numbering of MS. Bibl. Reg. 6 A. XI. A small number to the right of a word and above it marks the beginning of a line. The orthography is that of the MS. Bibl. Reg. 6 A. XI.

homilies, verse 30 of the *Speculum* and *Guido* represented in the dative *Widoni* (= *Guidoni*). *comes, comiti* (*vide ante*) is þe *eorl*, verses 29, 45, 50, 65, etc. *leuita* is *Dekne* (see Georges, *Lateinisches Wörterbuch*, under *levita*), verse 41. Other correspondences are: *alchwinus* : *Alquin* 39 ; *salutem* : *grete þe wel* 52. *Dilectissimo filio* is at least implied in *fader myn*, v. 52, and is remotely suggested by *leue broþer*, v. 73.

2. *Capitula huius Libri*.[1]

The *capitula* enumerated by Alcuin, are metrically arranged in the list of þewes of the *Speculum*, verses 79—130. The arrangement *De Virtutibus* occurs in both instances first. It is noticeable that of the seventeen moral graces (nominally eighteen) virtually classified in the *Liber*, two are omitted entirely in the enumeration and in the discussion of the *Speculum*, e. g. xvi. *De jeiunio*, and xviij. *De castitate;* two are inverted in this enumeration, e. g. xij. *De penitentia*, and xj. *De confessione*. Verbal correspondences are not exact in three instances of the classification, e. g. v. *De lectionis studio*, replaced by *mieknesse*, ix. *De pacientia*, *Loue of herte* (*ful of pite*), and xv. (12 of the *Speculum*) *De timore domini*, is inadequately presented in *penaunce*. Otherwise the list of þewes of the 'Introduction' to the *Speculum* is the same as that *De Virtutibus* of the *Liber*, and exists in the same order, as the subjoined table will indicate. The orthography of MS. Bibl. Reg. 6 B. XI. is in general preserved. The number of the chapter in the sequence of the *Liber* is inclosed in marks of parenthesis.

DE VIRTUTIBUS.

LIBER.			SPECULUM.	
Virtutes.			þewes to heuene reche.	
i. De sapientia	1.	(1)	Wisdom	v. 81
ij. De fide	2.	(2)	Trewe bileue	83
iij. De caritate	3.	(3)	charite	83
iiij. De spe	4.	(4)	Stedefast hope	85
			mieknesse	85
v. De lectionis studio.	14.	(5)	(reding of lesczoun)	(500)
vj. De pace	5.	(6)	Pes	86
vij. De misericordia	6.	(7)	merci	86
viij. De indulgentia	7.	(8)	forʒifnes	86

[1] Cf. MS. Bibl. Reg. 5. E. IV.

Chapter IX.—*Sources of the Speculum. Alcuin's Liber.*

LIBER.		SPECULUM.	
ix. De pacientia	8. (9)	Loue of herte, ful of pite (god suffraunce)	87 (571)
x. De humilitate	9. (10)	verray humilite	88
xi. De compunctione cordis	10. (11)	repentaunce	91
xij. De confessione	12. (12)	shrifte of mouþe	94
xiij. De penitentia	11. (13)	sorwe at þin herte rote	93
xiiij. De non tardando conuerti ad dominum		(sped þe faste) (In gode weyes) penaunce	(865) (865) 92
xv. De timore domini	15. (14)	(Drede of god)	(883)
xvi. De jeiunio			
xvij. De elemosinis	13. (15)	almes dede and charite	95
xviij. De castitate			

The presentation in the *Speculum* of the second division of the table of contents of the *Liber* is by no means so exact as that of the first portion. The enumeration of the vices is incomplete, and the order of the original is not observed. From the following table it will be evident, that of the sixteen vices considered in the *Liber* (properly fourteen; cf. xxvj and xxvij) again two are deficient, *e. g.* xxiiij (6) *De iracundia*, and xxxiiij (16) *De cenodoxia*, and no attempt is made to preserve the sequence of the *Liber*. *Wicke sleuþe* 116 does not occur in Alcuin's list. In the parallel to follow, Roman numerals represent the *Liber*, Arabic the *Speculum*. Parentheses indicate the sequence of the *Liber*. Otherwise the order of the *Speculum* is illustrated.

DE VITIIS.

Vitia.		*wicke þewes.*	
xix. (1) De fraude cauenda	5. (1)	tricherie	v. 110
xx. (2) De iudicibus	4. (2)	Fals iugement	110
xxj. (3) De falsis testibus	6. (3)	Fals witnesse	111
xxij. (4) De inuidia	3. (4)	enuie	109
xxiij. (5) De superbia	1. (5)	Pride[1]	109
xxiiij. (6) De iracundia			
xxv. (7) De humana laude non querenda	7. (7)	þis worldes blisse Loue not to muche	113
xxvj. (8) De perseuerantia boni operis			

[1] See *Caput xxxv. & primo de Superbia.*

c   *Chapter IX. Sources of the Speculum. Alcuin's Liber.*

xxvij. (9) De viij⁽ᵗᵒ⁾ uiticijs[1] principalibus	(9) þe wicke þewes	101
xxviij. (10) De gula	9. (10) glotonye	115
xxix. (11) De fornicatione	10. (11) leccherie	116
xxx. (12) De auaricia	8. (12) Auarice	115
xxxi. (13) De ira	2. (13) wraþþe	109
xxxij. (14) De accidia	11. (14) Accedie	117
xxxiij. (15) De tristicia	12. (15) Wanhope	126
xxxiiij. (16) De cenodoxia *id est* uana gloria[2]		

3. *Epistola Nuncupatoria.*

Counterpart of the *Epistola Nuncupatoria* is to be traced in the *Speculum* as follows:

(*a*) Certain entreaties and promises are recorded in both texts:

Liber.	*Speculum.*
fol. 109 *b*, l. 30: Memor peticionis ³¹tue.	v. 46. wille to him bar.
fol. 109 *b*, l. 31: qua me obnixe fla³²gitasti.	v. 47. tok his red.
fol. 110 *a*, l. 1: exhortamentum (aliquod ... exhortamentum, *Pero.*).	v. 53. preie þe for godes loue.
fol. 110 *a*, l. 4: tam honeste peticioni.	v. 59. were my ioye.
	v. 60. a gret profyt.
fol. 109 *b*, l. 31: promissionis mee. (sicut petisti, *Pero.*).	v. 68. His preie i wole do.

(*b*) Both Guido (also Guy) and Guy of Warwick had been occupied with war and the affairs of the world. The facts recorded in the *Liber* and in the various descriptions of Count Guido, the friend of Alcuin, are of the nature of those associated with Guy of Warwick in the marvellous versions of his famous exploits. The *Speculum* does not claim to convey a record of the military achievements of the knight, but all that portion of his history is written between the lines of the present poem. The Latin treatise describes a hero of the character of Guy of Warwick, and provides ground in practical life for deeds corresponding to those for which Guy was famed.

[1] Read *octo uicijs*.   [2] *id est* uana gloria *is glossed*.

Chapter IX.—*Sources of the Speculum. Alcuin's Liber.*

fol. 109 *b*, 1. 32 : tue occupationi, qu*am* te in bellic*is* (becill*is in the MS.*) reb*us* habere nouim*us*.—fol. 110 *a*, 1. 9 : sciens te in multis secularu*m* reru*m* cogitatio[10]nib*us* occupatum. Unde p*re*cor s*an*c*tum* salutis tue (*vestræ*, Froben) desideriu*m*.—l, 11: anim*us* exterioribu*s* fatig[12]at*us* molestiis.

The design of the *Speculum* in the conception of the identity of þe *eorl*, the genuine Guy of Warwick, and Guy of the *Liber*, is clear :

v. 29 : an eorl of gode fame.—v. 32 : þe worldes blisse.—v. 33 : þe world . . . he forsok.—v. 61 : þe world . . .—v. 62 : Haþ me lad . . .—v. 64 : þe world forsake.

The resemblance becomes more evident after reference to the English legends (edited by Zupitza) :

Sir Gij. Auch. MS. :
   Hou he hadde euer ben stro*n*g werrour. str. 21, v. 7,
   . . . in wer shadde ma*n*nes blode
   Wiþ mani a griseli wounde . . .

Caius MS. :
   That he come neu*er*e in noo fighte. v. 7401.

MS. Ff. 2. 38 :
   And how he had many slane
   And castels a*nd* toures many tane, v, 7135.

(*c*) The wish of each knight is the same and is recorded in practically the same words ;

brevi sermone conscribere.   v. 57 : Make me a god sarmoun.
                             And don hit write i*n* lesc-
                             zoun.
huius sermonis.   v. 137 : Herkne to my sarmoun.

The peroration (cf. Froben) strengthens the impression of the request : *Hæc tibi brevi sermone . . . dictavi*, l. 1.

(*d*) Both texts mention the purpose of this discourse :

fol. 110 *a*, 1 : ut haberes (*habeas*, Froben) iugit*er* [2]int*er* man*us* (in manibus) pat*er*ne admonicion*is* sententias, in quib*us* teipsu*m* [3]*con*-siderare potuisses (*debuisses*, Fr.), atque ad eterne beatitudinis exci-tare stu[4]diu*m*.—l. 11 : ut anim*us* . . . habeat, in q*u*o gaudeat, *seem to correspond to* v. 56 : in amendement of me.—v. 59 : ioye and delit.—v. 60 : a gret p*ro*fyt.—v. 48 : To kepen his soule from the qued.

(*e*) That the request was granted, each author is authority :

Chapter IX.—*Sources of the Speculum. Alcuin's Liber.*

1, 2: sicut petisti, dictavi (Peroratio).   v. 68 : His preie i wole do.
v. 69 : i shal ben þi leche.

(*f*) The *Speculum* proceeds to outline details characteristic of the discourse:

v. 70 : Aller furst i wole þe teche,
Faire uertuz for to take.

v. 73 : þat maitou noht don, leue broþer,
Bote þu knowe on and oþer,
I shal þe now shewe boþe.

v. 77 : And at the beste i wole biginne.

Compare with these verses selections from Chapter XXXV. *De quatuor uirtutibus*, fol. 120 *a*, l. 19 : Primo sciendum *est*, quid sit uirt*us*, and under *Peroratio Operis* (cf. Froben) l. 3 : [1]in quo possis teipsum considerare, quid cavere, vel quid agere debeas.

It is interesting to find the counterpart of *par charite*, v. 55; l. 14 of the *Liber, Epistola Nuncupatoria*, reads : (tamen certissime scito) sanctæ caritatis (vigore eosdem esse dictatos).

4. *Discussion of Alquin's Moral Virtues.*

It has been seen, that the *Speculum* preserves characteristic features of the *Liber*. The following abstract will show from the body of the discussion, that the narrative sets forth faithfully the main conception of that treatise. The passages incorporated indicate not merely, that the parallel versions correspond, but that they are often identical. The discussion of the *Epistola*[1] proper, *i. e.* the *Liber de Virtutibus*, is briefly epitomized in the *Speculum*. The exactness of the redaction is apparent from the fact that the coinciding passages exist in both texts almost line for line, so far as the connection is adduced. The accompanying tables will affirm that, although mechanical subdivision is lacking, as true poetic feeling would dictate for a metrical composition, yet verses 137—922 may be regarded as divided into sixteen minor parts corresponding to sixteen of the eighteen (nominally eighteen) chapters of the *Liber de Virtutibus*. The digression to be noted in the discussion as in the list of virtues, is the omission of Chapters XVI. and XVIII., *De jeiunio* and *De castitate*. Chapter XVII. is represented in

---

[1] Concerning the literature of the *Epistola*, see ten Brink, *Eng. Lit.*, vol. i. p. 115, with reference to the *motif* of the Alexander saga: *Epistola Alexandri ad Magistrum suum Aristotelem*, etc.

Chapter IX.—*Sources of the Speculum. Alcuin's Liber.*

name only. Chapters I. III. IV. V. XIII. and XV. bear the closest relationship to the *Liber*. The O.E. version of the *Liber* (cf. Assmann, *Anglia*, vol. xi. p. 371), *Uebersetzung von Alcuin's De Virtutibus et Vitiis Liber ad Widonem Comitem*, Vesp. D. 14 (fol. 104 a) will become a third element in the comparison. The more important instances of agreement are indicated on the pages to follow.

The method of arrangement needs no explanation. Each of the three texts follows its manuscript. Capitals and punctuation have been used irrespective of original, but the orthography of the MSS. is in general not altered. Occasionally a variant representing the Cambridge MS. I. is to be noted. At times the reading of Froben (Fr.) indicates the *Liber* in its current version. Otherwise the readings of the editions of Froben and of Migne have not been introduced into these pages. Dr. Assmann follows the Vespasian MS. with exactness.

civ   Chapter IX.—Sources of the Speculum.   Alcuin's Liber.

Epistola[1] Alquini ad Guidonem[3] Comitem De Virtutibus	Speculum Gy de Warewyke De Virtutibus	Liber[2] Alcuini ad Guidonem[3] Comitem De Virtutibus
MS. BIBL. REG. 6 A. XI.	MS. AUCH. 10.	MS. COT. VESP. D. 14.
Capitulum .i.	Verses 70, 74, 139—198.	[1.]
De sapiencia.	Wisdom (v. 139).	De Scientia.
[fol. 110 b.]		
l. 1. Primo (primum, Fr.[5]) omnium querendum est homini, que sit uera scientia.	v. 70. Aller furst i wole þe teche.	1. Ærost ealro þinʒen æʒhwylce mæn is to secene, hwæt seo soðe wisedom [is] (smodere, I.[5])
ll. 4, 5. Sapientia perfecta est deum colere.	v. 74. Boþe þu knowe on and oþer.	
	v. 82. V so wel	5. (And) seo fullfremede snytere is, þæt man ʒode þeowiʒe.
ll. 5, 6. Quia in his duobus uita beata adquiritur, sicut psalmista ait:	v. 139. (also 81) Wisdom in godes drede.	
	v. 141. Tweie þinges it wole þe teche,	6. Þurh þa twa þinʒ byð þæt eadiʒe lif beʒeotan, swa se sealmscop cwæð.
l. 6. Diuerte a malo, & fac bonum.	v. 142. Whar þurw þu miht to heuene reche:	
l. 7. Hec (non, Fr.) etiam sufficit cuiquam mala non facere.	v. 143. (þat is), lat þi sinne, and do god.	7. ʒeeerr fram yfele and do ʒod.
	v. 145. Ac to lato þi sinne al onliche,	8. Buten tweone ne mæʒ nane mæn to ecere hæle ʒehelpen, þæt he yfeles ʒeswica,
l. 10. Virtus boni operis fructus eterne beatitudinis.	v. 146. Nis noht inouh, sikerliche.	*bute he ʒod do[10]; he byð eadiʒ on ecnysse.
	v. 147. Þu most don god forþ þerwiþ,	
	v. 148. If þu wolt haue merci and griþ.	13. ... ʒodes weorcas is wæstme .. ecen eadiʒnysse.
Capitulum .ij.	Verses 201—218.	[2.]
De Fide.	Þi bileue (v. 201).	De Fide.
l. 11. Sed hec cognitio diuinitatis & sciencia ueritatis, per fidem discenda est[12] catholicam.	v. 203. Man, þi bileue shal be so:	14. Ac þeos oncnawednysse þære ʒodcundnysse and þære soðfæstnysse wisedom is to leorniʒen þurh þone rihtne ʒeleafe.
	v. 204. Þat o god is and no mo.	
Capitulum .iij.	Verses 324—346.	[3.]
De caritate.	Of charite (v. 324).	De Caritate.[6]
sine qua nemo deo placet.		
l. 21. In preceptis uero Dei caritas optinet principatum.	v. 325. Off alle uertuz hit is hext,	27. On eallen ʒodes bebodan seo soðe lufe hæfð þone ealdordom.

[1] Selections from MS. Bibl. Reg. 6 A. XI. in the Museum.
[2] Compared with MS. Vesp. D. 14. in the Museum, introduced here with an occasional variant from Camb. MS. Ii. I. 33.
[3] MS. Widonem.   [5] Froben's edition of 1777.
[4] I = Camb. MS.   [6] De uera Karitate in Ii.1 om. in V.

Chapter IX.—*Sources of the Speculum. Alcuin's Liber.*

Epistola.	Speculum.	Liber.
l. 21. Sine cuius *perfectione* nichil *deo* pla[22]cere posse. Paulus testatur.	v. 326. And godes wille hit is next. v. 345. (Þis seiþ) Sein Powel (*and*) bereþ witnesse.	28. (Buten) þære fullfremednysse goðe naht lichigen ne mæig . . . . [29]Paulus se apostol þuss cwæð (*wrde I.*) . . .
l. 25. Diliges Dominum Deum tuum ex toto corde tuo, & ex tota anima tua, & ex tota [20]mente tua.	v. 329. (Hit is), loue god ouer alle þing, v. 330. In þouht, *in* dede, *and* in speking.	33. Lufe þinne drihten[1] god of[2] eallre þinre sawle,[3] *and* of eallen þine mode.
l. 26. Addidit quoque: *Secundum* (Secundum autem, *Fr.*) simile *est* huic.	v. 332. An oþer þing þu most do:	34. Oðer is þyssen gelic:
l. 26. Diliges proximum tuum, *sicut* te [27]ipsum. In hoc cogn[22]oscent omnes.	v. 333. Þu most loue, hu so hit be, v. 334. Þin emcristene forþ wid þe.	35. Lufe þinne nexte swa swa þe sylfne. 42. On þan oncnaweð mænn, *þæt* ge byð mine þeignes.
[fol. 111*a*], l. 1. Qui diligit deum (Dominum, *Fr.*) diligat & proximum suum (*om. Fr.*). l. 2. Sciat omnem christianum recte proximum dici.	v. 337. If þu louest god ful iwis, v. 338. Þu most louen alle his. v. 341. (But þu) loue þe cristene þat bi þe be . . .	45. Se þe god lufige, 45. he eac lufige his þone nextan. 47. Wyte he swyðe rihtlice ælcne Cristena mann beon his nexto.
Capitulum .iiij. *De spe.*	*Verses* 459—478. *Hope to god* (v. 461).	[4.] *De Spe.*
l. 11. Ne[12]mo igitur quamuis ingenti peccatorum pondere prematur, de bonitate diuine [13]pietatis desperare debet.	v. 468. Þouh man be charged, sikerli v. 469. Wiþ grete sinnes heuie and sore, v. 470. He ne shal despeire neuere þe more...	61. Ne sceal nan mann, þeh he seo ofsett mid unʒeme byrdene his synnen, ʒeortreowigen beo þære æwfæstnysse þære godcundan mildheortnysse.
l. 13. *sed* spe certe misericordie illius indulgentiam sibi cotidi[14]anis deprecari lacrimis.	v. 471. Ac soþfast hope haue, to winne v. 472. Godes *merci* of his sinne v. 473. Þurw skrifte of monþe *and* repentaunce.	63. ac mid witendan[4] hyhte *and* mid dæiʒhwamlice tearen him forgyfonysse biddan . .
(cotidianis.) l. 14. Quam recte sperare possunt, si *ab* accione praui operis [15]cessaburt.	v. 475. ʒif þu dost þus, bi day and niht . . . v. 461. Hope to god, *and* do god, v. 465. For alone to hope, widoute goddede, v. 466. Is ydel hope, (so god me rede).	(mid dæighwamlice.) 64-5. Forþan þe swyþe rihtlice he mæig him forgyfonysse wenen . . . þære yfelre weorcan. . . .

[1] *MS. V has* drihten.   [2] *Here MS. I reads:* ealra þinre heortan.   [3] ormetre *in I.*   [4] god *in I.*

cvi Chapter IX.—*Sources of the Speculum. Alcuin's Liber.*

Epistola.	Speculum.	Liber.
Capitulum .v.	Verses 497—510.	[5.]
De lectione.[1]	Reding of lescoun (v. 500).	De Scripturarum Lectione.
l. 21. Sanctarum lectio scripturarum diuinæ est.... In his [20]enim quasi in quodam speculo homo seipsum considerare potest, qualis sit, [22]uel quo tendat.	v. 505. Holi writ is oure myrour, v. 506. In whom we sen al vre socour...	76. On þan halȝen ȝewriten se mann hine sylfne mæiȝ sceawiȝen swa swa on hwylcen sceawere.
l. 24. Qui uult cum deo semper [23]esse, frequenter debet orare, frequenter & legere.	v. 497. Man, if þu wolt þe world forsake, v. 499. Þu most ben ofte in orisoun v. 500. And in reding of lescoun.	81. Se þe wyle simle mid ȝode beon, 81. He sceal him oft ȝebiddan and he sceal oft halȝe ȝewriten rædan.
l. 25. nam cum oramus, ipsi cum deo loquimur.	v. 503. And we wid him, ful iwis, v. 504. Whan we him bisekeþ þat riht is.	82. Forþan þe þonne we us ȝebiddað, we spekað to ȝode.
l. 26. *Cum uero legimus, Deus nobiscum loquitur.*	v. 501. Wid us god spekeþ, whan we rede v. 502. Off him and of his goddede.	83. And þonne we halȝe lech rædað, ȝod specð to us.
Capitulum .vj.	Verses 511—522.	[6.]
[fol. 111 b.] De preceptis pacis.[2]	· Pes and loue (v. 514).	De Pace.
l. 5. Saluator ad patrem rediens quasi speciale donum (munus, Fr.) discipulis pacis dedit[6] precepta dicens.	v. 517. For Iesu Crist hit seiþ ful wel:	100. Se hælend ... sealde ... bebodan and þuss cwæð.
l. 9. "Beati pacifici," quoniam filii dei uocabuntur.	Beati pacifici, quoniam filii Dei uocabuntur.	104. Eadiȝe byð þa ȝesibsume forþan þe heo byð godes bearn ȝeceide.
l. 9. En filius dei incipiþ uocari, qui pa[10]cificus esse iam cepit.	v. 522. For godes children men shal hem calle!	106. se byð ȝodes bearn ȝeceid se þe wyle ȝesibsum beon.
	v. 520. Iblessed be, þat makeþ pes.	
Capitulum .vij.	Verses 523—550, 567, 568.	[7.]
De misericordia.	Of merci (v. 524).	De Misericordia.
l. 24. Precipuum *est* misericordiæ bonum, de qua ipse ait saluator.	v. 526. Man, þu most ben merciable.	126. Mildheortnysse is swyðe helic god [Beo þære se hælend sylf cwæð].
· l. 26. Ergo dimittat homo temporale debitum, ut [27]mereatur recipere eternale bonum.	v. 549. "Alswich met as þu metest me, v. 550. Alswich i wole mete to þe." v. 567. ... "He þat wole no merci haue,	130. Ac forlæte se man nu þa hwilwendlice scylde to þan, þæt he ȝeearniȝe to onfoone þæt ece ȝod.

[1] *De lectionis studio*, Fr. [2] *De pace*, Fr.

Chapter IX. Sources of the Speculum. Alcuin's Liber. cvii

Epistola.	Speculum.	Liber.
l. 29. Quo modo a deo misericordiam expectat, qui cru³delis est in conservos suos?	v. 559. And þu, þat art so cruwel in þouht v. 560. And wolt to-merci herkne noht, v. 561. What wole hit helpe in eny stede v. 562. Þe holi paternoster bede?	136. Hwu mæȝ se him ænȝne mildheortnysse wenen to ȝode, se þe byð wælreow on his efenþeowwes?
l. 31. Ad ³² misericordie opus optimo nos in euangelio dominus exemplo roborauit, ubi ait.	v. 568. On ydel doþ he merci craue." v. 565. And þe holi lok of soþnesse v. 566. Þerof berþ god witnesse v. 567. And seiþ: (Ho þat wole no merci haue).	140. Drihten sylf us eac swyðe æðelice trymede to mildheortnysse weorcan on þan ȝodspelle, þa þa he cwæð.
Capitulum .viij. De indulgentia. [fol. 112 a.] l. 12. (Dominus in euangelio dicit): Dimitite, et dimittetur uobis.	Verses 551—566. Forȝifenesse (v. 683). v. 555. (Þu seist: "Swete Lord,) forȝine þu me, v. 556. Þat i haue gilt aȝeines þe, v. 557. Riht as i do alle þo, v. 558. Þat me hauen ouht misdo.	[8.] De Indulgentia. 160. (Drihten cwæð): Forȝyfeð, þonne byð eow forȝyfen.
Capitulum .ix. De pacientia. l. 27. In pacientia enim uestra (dicitur in euangelio) possidebitis animas uestras. l. 27. In omni enim ²⁹ uita humana pacientia necessaria est. l. 29. & paciencer tribulationes, quæ nobis eueniunt, ³⁰ sufferre necesse est. l. 28. Sicut itaque pacienter sufferre debemus in³⁰iurias ab aliis in nos delatas ita.	Verses 568—622. Of god suffraunce (v. 571). v. 568. In paciencia uestra possidebitis animas uestras. v. 571. (And) bad hem ben of god suffraunce v. 572. In alle manere destourbaunce. v. 585. And, ȝif þe falleþ trauail on honde, v. 587. Off al þis þu most suffraunt be. v. 599. (And), ȝif a man þurw his power, v. 600. Doþ þe wrong on corþe her, v. 612. . . . . . ben here þolemod, v. 613. To suffre wrong and vnriht.	[9.] De Pacientia. 185. Þurh eower ȝeðyld ȝe mugen habben eower sawle hæle. 186. On callen þæs mannes life ȝeðyld is neodðearflice to habbene . . . swa us is eac neod ðearf, þat we eall þa broca and þa ȝoswync, þe us on . . arefnen. 187. swa we seulen ȝeðyldelice arefnen þa teonen þe us oðre mænn doð.
[fol. 112 b.] l. 11. Sine ¹² ferro uel flammis martyres esse ¹² possumus, si pacientiam ueraciter in animo ser¹³ uamus cum proximis nostris.	v. 610. He may be martyr, trewcliche, v. 611. Widoute shedinge of mannes blod, v. 612. Þat may ben here þolemod. . . .	209. We muȝe beon martires buten irene and leȝe, ȝyf ȝe þa ȝeðyld soðfæstlice on ure mode ȝehealdeð mid uren þan nextan.

cviii   *Chapter IX.   Sources of the Speculum.   Alcuin's Liber.*

Epistola.	Speculum.	Liber.
Capitulum *x*.	Verses 623—678.	[*10.*]
De uera[1] *humilitate.*	*Þe vertu of humilite* (v. 658).	*De Humilitate.*
l. 16. Quanta sit uirtus,[2] uera humilitas facile ex uerbis domini agnoscitur.[3]	v. 657. Ac, if þu coueyt knowe and se þe uertu of humilite!	216. We maȝen oncnawen, ... hwu mycel þæt maȝn is eadmodnysse.
L. 17. (Omnis) qui se exaltat, humi[19]liabitur, *et qui* se humiliat, exaltabitur.	v. 658. *Qui se exaltat, humiliabitur, et qui se humiliat, exaltabitur.*	217. Æle[4] þe hine sylfne upp aheð, he byð ȝeeadmodod.
l. 18. Humilitatis passibus ad celi culmi[12]na conscenditur.	v. 630.	219. Wið eadmodnysse stapen we muȝen to heofone hehnysse ȝestton.
l. 19. *quia deus excelsus non superbia sed humilitate attingitur.*	v. 631. Þe milde þurw his humilite.	220. Þone hlchne ȝod ne mæȝ hine man
l. 25. Per superbiam mirabilis angelorum creatura cecidit de celo.	v. 632. Ful heie honoured þeih sholen be.	þurh oferrmeta ȝeræcen, ac þurh eadmodnysse.
[fol. 113 *a*.] l. 5. Qui (enim) sine humilitate bona opera agit, in uento [6]puluerem portat.	v. 633. For þeih sholen be drawen on heih	231. Þurh oferhyde seo wunderlice ȝesceaft ænȝlen feoll of heofone.
	v. 634. And wonye ȝol swiþe neih.	253. Se þe buten eadmodnysse ȝod deð, he
	v. 635. And pride, it is so foul a last,	byð ȝelic þan þe on mycele winde dust berð.
	v. 636. þat out fro heuene he was cast.	
	v. 664. *Qui sine humilitate uirtutes ceteras congregat, est quasi, qui in uento puluerem portat.*	
Capitulum *xi*.	Verses 679—752.	[*11.*]
De compunctione cordis.	*Aferd of trepaz* (v. 685).	*De Compunctione Cordis.*
l. 15. Compunctio cordis ex humilitatis uirtute nascitur.	v. 679. A god þing is humilite!	268. Seo onbrerdnysse þæs mannes heortan cumeð of eadmodnysse.
	v. 680. Off him comeþ verray charite,	269. *and of þære onbrerdnysse ondetnysse.*
	v. 681. And penaunce, and eke shrift.	*And of þære andetnysse cumeð seo dædbote, and of þære soðe dædbote cumð seo forȝyfonysse þære ȝylten.*
l. 15. De compunctione con[16]fessio peccatorum [17]delictorum. De penitencia uera prouenit .. indulgentia.	v. 683. And of him forȝifnesse of sinne.	
Capitulum *xij*.	Verses 753—784.	[*12.*]
[fol. 113 *b*.] *De confessione.*	*To Shrifte* (v. 761).	*De Confessione Peccatorum.*
l. 8. Ore a[12]tem confessio [9]fit ad salutem.	v. 768. Loke, þat þu be ofte shriue, ...	309. Seo andetnysse þæs muðes becumeð þære sawle to hæle.
	v. 774. For hit may hele dedli wounde.—	
	v. 795. And ne sparest for shame ne for eiȝe,	
l. 10. Qui autem confessus fuerit & reliquerit ea, misericordiam consequetur.	v. 796. Þat þu hit nilt in shrifte seie,	312. Se þe heo ȝeandetteð *and* forlæteð, sone he beȝytt ȝodes mildheortnysse.
	v. 797. Off god þu miht wel littliche	
	v. 798. Forȝifnesse haue, sikerliche.	

[1] *om. in Fr.*   [2] *veriæ humilitatis virtus, Fr.*   [3] *cognoscitur, Fr.*   [4] *Ii reads:* æle man .. ȝehyneð.

Epistola.	Speculum.	Liber.
Capitulum .xiij.		
De penitentia.	*Verses 815—850.*	[*13.*]
	Wille to leue sinne (v. 839).	*De Penitentia.*
1. 31. Cuius ipse Saluator in euangelio uirtutem ostendit ²²dicens:	v. 815. Iesu spak *and* seide ene.	345. Dære soðen dædbote mæign ... hælend sylf on his godspelle æteowde.
[fol. 114 *a*.] 1. 3. Lauamini (dicit Dominus per ysayam prophetam) & mundi estote. Lauatur itaque, & mundus est, qui *et* preterita plangit, et iterum flenda non admittit.	(v. 814. *Lauamini, et mundi estote.*) v. 816. Wassheþ ou, *and* beþ clene. v. 839. ȝif þu hast wille to leue þi sinne, v. 841. Of þin eiȝen þe hote teres, v. 843. Hij wolen make god acord v. 845. And make þe clene of þi sinne.	351. *And* drihten cwæð þurh Isaam: Aðweað eow *and* byð clæne.
6. Lauatur, & *non est* mundus, qui plangit ⁵*quod* gessit & *post* lacrimas (*erasure*) delicta reuertuntur.	v. 825. Summe wassheþ, ac noht ariht. v. 827. Þe hote teres of mannes eiȝe, v. 818. Makeþ clannere þan any liȝe.	354. Beo þan mannen, þe heora synnen (beweþeð, *and* eft æfter) þan wope þa ilca synne wyrceð.
1. 6. Fili, peccasti, *dicitur in scriptura sancta,* no ⁷adicius iterum, ... *sed de* pristinis deprecare, ut remittantur.	v. 837. Man, þouh þu haue sinne don, v. 839. ȝif þu hast wille to leue þi sinne, v. 840. Þat þu no more ne come þerinne, v. 841. Of þin eiȝen þe hote teres ... v. 845. (And) make þe clene of þi sinne.	358. Ȝif þu sume synne dest. 359. Ne ȝeech þu þa synne mid aðre synnen. 359. ac þu ȝod ȝeorne bide. 360. Þæt he þa ȝefremda synne forȝyfe.
1. 22. In hac ²³uita tantum penitencie (penitenti, *Fr.*) patet libertas. Post mortem ucro unlla correctionis est ²³licentia.	v. 859. While þu art on liue, þu miht worche v. 860. Godes werkes of holi churche, v. 861. And, certes, whan þat þu art ded, v. 862. Þanne maitou don noþer god ne qued.	385. On þysser wurlde is se friȝdom dedbota, æfter deaðe nis nane mænn nan bote ȝelefd.
Capitulum .xiiij.	*Verses 853—882.*	[*14.*]
De non tardando conuerti ad deum.	*Worche godes werkes (v. 859—60).*	*De Conuersione ad Dominum.*
1. 24. Fili, ne tardes conuerti ad Dominum (Deum, Fr.).	v. 864. (While þu miht gon *and* se), v. 865. In gode weyes speð þe faste.	388. (Sune), ne elca þu na to ȝode to ȝecerran.

Epistola.	Speculum.	Liber.
[fol. 114 b.] l. 18. ne si, dum potest noluerit, omnino cum ᵗᵒtarde uoluerit, non possit.	v. 881. Þerfore worch, while þu mait, v. 892. For sodeyueliche þu miht þe caiht.	390. Se þe elcað, þæt he to ᵹode ne ᵹecerð, he deð on plih[t] his aᵹene sawle, forþan þe se deað hit na elcað.
		[15.]
Capitulum .xv. *De Timore domini.*	*Verses* 883—918. *Drede of god (v. 883).*	*De Timore Domini.*
l. 20. Inicium sapientie timor domini. l. 20. Magna est cautela peccati dei semper presentiam timere (Deum semper praesentem timere, *Fr.*).	*Inicium sapiencie, timor domini.* v. 883. Drede of god in alle þing v. 884. Off wisdom is þe biginning.	434. ᵹodes eᵹe is se frume wisedom. Ælc mann simle ᵹode andweardnyss ondrade.
	v. 885. And many hauen of god drede. v. 907. And so he shal casten his loue	436. Se þe fulfremedlice him ᵹod ondrædeð, he hine sylfne swyðe ᵹeornlice wið synne healdeð.
21. Qui perfecte deum timet, diligenter se a peccatis custodit.	v. 908. To Iesu Crist, þat is aboue, v. 909. And leten and flen sinful dede.	
l. 25. *Alius est* timor seruorum. l. 25. Serui enim propter ²⁸tormenta dominos timent.	v. 890. As hit doþ here bi þe bonde : v. 891. Þe bonde nele noþer loude ne stille. v. 892. Don noht aᵹein his lordes wille—	443. oðer hyð þære þeowen [eᵹe]. 444. Þa þeowwes heom ondrædeð heora hlafordes for wite.
l. 26. Si filii dei sumus, timeamus ²⁷ eum ex caritatis dulcedine, *non* de timoris amaritudine.	v. 897. And ᵹit hit fareþ bi man also, v. 898. Þat spareþ more sinne to do, v. 899. For þe doute of gret pining, v. 900. Þan for þe loue of heuen king.	445. Nu we ᵹodes bearn synden ᵹeceiᵹde, ondræde we us hine of þære soðe lufe swetnysse, na of þæs eᵹes biternysse. 448. He ᵹeðenceð, þæt he ᵹodes andweardnysse nahwyder besleon ne mæiᵹ.
l. 29. & a facie tua quo fugiam ?	v. 904. To biþenke him on godes face.	
[fol. 115 a.] l. 7. Sic timeamus deum, ut diligamus eum, quia perfecta caritas foras mittit timorem seruilem.	v. 909. And leten and flen sinful dede, v. 910. Boþe for loue and eke for drede.	466. Swa ondrædon we us ᵹod, þæt we hine lufiᵹen forþan þe seo fulfremede lufe ut adrifð þone þeowlice eᵹe.
		[16.]
Capitulum xvii. *De elemosinis.*	*Verses* 919—1028. *Of almesdede (v. 922)*	[*De Eleemosynis.*]

5. *Discussion of Alquin's "wicke þewes."*

The portion of Alcuin's subject-matter, that he described as *De Vitiis*, seems to have been by no means attractive to the poet. That those moral disorders were omitted from the discussion[1] entirely and are contained in the metrical enumeration poorly classified and in a fragmentary condition, may be accounted for on ground of a fragmentary MS. The *Epistola Nuncupatoria* of the *Speculum* has treated concerning a few facts of the manual *De Vitiis*. Additional trace of the original is found as follows:

CAPITULUM .XXXIJ.
De Accidia: Accedie.

Liber.	*Speculum.*
fol. 119 b, l. 9. Accidia est pestis.	v. 117. Accedie is a wel foul sinne.
l. 14. De qua nascitur¹⁵ somnolencia. pigricia operis boni.	v. 121. Accedie is as sleuþes broþer.
	v. 124. And makeþ man anuied to do god.

CAPITULUM .XXXIIJ.
De Tristicia: Shame.

l. 22. Tristicie duo sunt genera.	v. 785. Tweye manere shame men fint in boke.
unum salutiferum,	v. 786. þat oþer to sauuacioun.
alterum pestiferum.	v. 787. þat on (goþ) to dampnacioun.
l. 22. Tristicia salutaris²³ est	v. 799. þis ilke shame, be my croun.
quando de peccatis suis	v. 800. Draweþ al to sauuacioun.
anima contristatur peccatoris	
et ita contristatur	v. 794. At þin herte sore agramed,
ut confessionem	v. 795. And ne sparest for shame,
et pe²⁴nitenciam agere querat.	v. 796. þat þu hit nilt in shrifte seie.

---

[1] The poet of the *Speculum* did not always follow his original in the actual arrangement of the chapters. With verses 765—766, 779—782, compare l. 300 ff., Caput xv.: *Qui erubescit in conspectu hominis peccare, quanto magis debet erubescere in conspectu Dei iniquitatem agere.* Cf. MS. R, Cap. xiii., fol. 114 a: *Qui peccata sua occultat et erubescit salubriter confiteri;* Cap. xii., fol. 113 b, ll. 23—25: *Deum quem testem habet item habebit eum ultorem.*

Verses 859 ff. of the *Speculum* recall l. 34, Caput xvii., although included under *Caput* xiii. of the poem: *In vita tua benefac animæ tuæ,* ... *quia post mortem non habes potestatem bene faciendi.*

6. *The Benediction of the Speculum.*

Verses 1029—1034 *of the Speculum.*

The poetical invocation of divine blessing on the poet and his public, the ordinary M.E. formula, meets counterpart in the various MSS. of the *Liber*. The agreement of MS. Reg. 6 A. xi. is as follows:

fol. 109 *b*, l. 28. Auxiliante v. 1028. To þat blisse he vs bryng,
   Domino.
nostro (iesu Cristo qui
cum patre & Spiritu Sancto)
uiuit *et* regnat[16] *per* in-   v. 1029. þat is king ouer alle þyng
finita secula seculorum, amen.   v. 1034. Amen. Amen. So mot
                                          it be.

With these versions may be compared the concluding passage of MS. Ii. 1. ff.:

"Se heofenlice fæder (*and* þe sunu *and* þe halʒa ʒost) ʒeunne us þæt we moton þer ece lif ʒeearnian (*and* ʒe trymme on ̀us þo rihtan ʒe leafan *and* ʒescylde us wið deofles costnunʒa *and*) þæt . . . we moton mid him wunian þær he lifað *and* rixað on ealra worulde woruld abutan ende, Amen."

Add. MS. 18,338 of the Museum, a vellum·octavo of the 10th century called *Isidori Episcopii Liber Officiorium de ecclesiasticis officiis, Breviarum Alcuini* concludes *gloria coronabitur. Amen.* MS. Kk. VI. 19, and MS. Mm. VI. 12, of the University Library, Cambridge, have the same ending, *perpetua coronabitur gloria, Amen.* With these is to be compared the *Speculum*, 1029, 1030, and 1034 :

" *To þat blisse he vs bryng,*
Þat is king ouer alle þyng.
Amen. Amen. so mot it be."

The *Speculum* is quite independent in the additional element of the glorification of the Virgin, verses 1031, 1032 :

"And ʒeue us grace, while we be here,
To serue hym *and* hys moder dere."

An amplification is preserved in MS. H_2 (fol. 53 *a*), 832—835, with fuller detail, marking a monkish environment for MS. H_2.

MS. Bibl. Reg. 5 E. iv. adds the unique and charming *benedicite* (fol. 110 *b*) : cum angelis dei perpetualiter possidere dignus efficietur.[1]

---

[1] *Explicit liber Aluuini* (MS.) *leuite ad Widonem comitem.*

II. *Main Differences between Liber and Speculum.*

Distinct points of agreement marked in the *Speculum*, preserving introduction, arrangement, and main outlines of the *Liber*, have been discovered. On the other hand the two works are distinct from each other in important characteristics. These occur:

1. In the specification and discussion of the moral vices (*De Vitiis*, i. e. *wicke þewes*, v. 101) through deficiency in the original material, or through modification to be credited to the poet.

2. In the section *De Virtutibus*, large portions of the *Liber* are omitted from the *Speculum*, where the Latin author developed his theme consistently with his text, producing a moral, not a liturgical work.[1]

3. In portions of the *Speculum*, *De Virtutibus*, *Whar þurw þu miht to heuene reche*, v. 80, for which the *Liber* is not responsible, and where the poet interweaves episodes of different character.

The preceding section indicates that the *Liber* is the immediate source of the *Speculum*, directing the trend of the argument. Yet but one hundred and fifty of the eight hundred and ninety verses represented in the accompanying tables are to be accounted for through the *Liber*. The larger portion of the *Speculum* is thus not to be discovered in the pages of the *Liber*, but deviates materially from the original composition. Allowing for the variation natural to the metrical arrangement of an underlying prose work devoted to the same current of thought, it must be conceded that after the first one hundred and thirty-seven verses, the *Speculum* exists as a free production of an English redactor. The poet followed his source as conscientious principle seemed to direct, but he modelled his material according to his inspiration and enlivened his theology with incident and episode not connected with the principal action of the work. He improved dull passages, adapting them to the sympathies of the English people.

If the *Speculum* be regarded as an independent unit, its immediate sources must be looked for elsewhere or traced through representative passages. No English work has been found, that, as a whole, can be held responsible for the incidents with which the *Speculum* is enriched. The various categories of vices and virtues characteristic of the Middle Ages add nothing to the proof of the *Liber*, and they are themselves indebted elsewhere for origin. The interesting French

[1] See *Moralia Opuscula*, Froben II, p. 2.

Chapter X.—*Theological Sources of the Speculum.*

treatise, *Somme des Vices et des Vertues* (Frère Lorens 1279), also called *Somme le Roi* or *Miroir du Monde* (ed. F. Chavannus, *Documentes publiés de la Suisse romande*, IV.) is distinct in itself and in its descendants. The *Aʒenbite*, Chaucer's *Persones Tale*, and the later text, *Confessio Amantis*, have no immediate connection with the exposition for Guy. Caxton's print, *The Book Ryal*, *The Book for a Kyng*, based on the ten commandments, the twelve divisions of the Creed, and the seven gifts of the Holy Spirit, is a distinct treatise. Compare also Kläber, *Das Bild bei Chaucer*, pp. 337 ff. Equally distinct are *Vices and Virtues* (Stowe MS. c. 1200), edited by Holthausen, E.E.T.S., and all the various enumerations in the different collections of Homilies, the editions of Morris for the E. E. T. S., Nos. 29, 34, 49, and 53. It is hardly necessary to look for the source of the *Speculum* in a French original. The somewhat large number of words of French origin, in comparison with other texts of the period, *Aʒenbite* through Danker's summary in *Die Laut- u. Flexionslehre d. mittelkent. Denkmäler nebst roman. Wörterverzeichnis* and *Poema Morale*, for example, are to be attributed to the vocabulary of the first source of the text, the *Liber;* however to the contrary[1] see Einenkel, *Anglia*, vol. v., pp. 91 ff. Sturmfels in *Anglia*, vol. viii. p. 205, aims to prove, that in the first half of the 13th century but few A.F. words or derivatives are to be traced in any theme.

An original for the *Speculum* as a specific unit not being discovered, the history of salient passages is to be investigated. The text itself guides uniformly to the clerical literature of the Middle Ages, through allusion to St. Austin (St. Augustine), to Gregory, and to the Scriptures.

CHAPTER X.

MINOR SOURCES OF THE *SPECULUM.*

§ 1. *Minor religious Sources.*

1. *Indebtedness to St. Augustine.*

WITH Chapter XVI. (verse 919) the influence of the *Liber* ends abruptly. With verse 947 the poet transfers his study to another type of popular didactic literature. The *naïve* and charming account of *Eliʒe* is to be recognized as a favourite theme with St. Augustine.

[1] *Die zahl der französischen wörter hängt ab vom stande der verfasser, nicht vom stoff der behandelten gegenstände*, . . .

Chapter X.—Theological Sources of the Speculum.

It is the subject of more than one discourse attributed to that divine. Passages from the *Speculum* may be compared with the fortieth discourse (*Sermo* XL. § 2) of Augustine (see Migne):

St. Augustine. Sermo XL. § 2.	Speculum. Verses 947—970.
jubetur Elias.	v. 950. Spak to Eliȝe þe profete.
ibi pascatur a vidua.	v. 951. To a pore widewe he him sende.
ad eum Dominus	v. 949. Hou Iesu Crist, houre louerd swete ...
dixit: . . . . "Vade	v. 953. (He seide): "Eliȝe, þu shalt fare
in Sareptam.	v. 954. Into Sarepte.
ego mandavi viduæ, ut te pascat ibi."	v. 955. þer is a widewe, þat shal þe fede."
beatus Elias viduam illam inveniet.	v. 959. þe widewe he mette.
aqua se lavaret,	v. 963. A dishful water she sholde him ȝiue.
cum ab ea	v. 969. "Do," he seide, "bi my red,
cibum petet.	v. 970. Bring me wid þe a shiue bred!"
"Vade," inquit, "mihi prius fac!"	v. 982. "Abid," he seide, "er þu go!"
ex eo quod habes, ministra.	v. 983. "First, þerof mak me mete,
inopiam noli timere,	v. 984. And, whan þat i hit haue iete,
	v. 985. Off þat bileueþ, þu shalt make."
non deficientem farinam.	v. 1000. "þi mele ne shal wante noht,
ubi oleum infunderet, tandiu oleum crevit."	v. 1001. And þin oyle shal waxen, sikerli!"
talis ist nativera	v. 1005. Now þu miht knowe in þi mod,
veræ charitatis, ut erogando, crescat.	v. 1006. þat in almesse dede is double god.

Chapter X.—*Theological Sources of the Speculum.*

To Augustine[1] is to be ascribed the comparison embodied in the Latin texts following verse 664 of the *Speculum*, *Sermones*, vol. iii. p. 353, fol. 654, also employed by Gregory:

Qui sine humilitate uirtutes ceteras congregat, est quasi, qui in vento puluerem portat (see edition of Migne).

Augustine's discourses in common with others of the age expound Biblical passages subject to the exegesis of the theologian of the *Speculum* and of English priests of associated literature. Cf. for instance *Sermones* 297, 302, 303, 304, etc., in connection with chapters x, v, i and vii.

2. *Biblical Sources.*

Under the fanciful exaltation, the decorative incidents of the Guy saga is to be discovered a solid texture of Biblical passages so skilfully interwoven, that at first their presence is not to be imagined. Some of them are as follows:

Lines 143—147, *Psal.* xxxiv. 14; xxxvii. 27; *Is.* i. 16, 17; *Amos* v. 15; *Rom.* xii. 9; 1 *Pet.* iii. 11. ll. 148—160, 1 *Cor.* iii. 19. ll. 201—204, *Hebr.* xi. 6. l. 204, *James* ii. 19. ll. 223 ff., *Gen.* iii. 6 ff. ll. 215—220, *Gen.* iii. 22. l. 238, *Gen.* iii. 19. ll. 255, 256, *Matt.* xx. 23; 326, 1 *Cor.* xiii. 13. ll. 329—334, *Luke* x. 27. ll. 329, 330, *Matt.* xxii. 37; *Mark* xii. 31. l. 334, *Matt.* xix. 19; xxii. 39. ll. 346, 352, *Gen.* xviii. 2, 3. ll. 355, 360, *Ex.* xix. 18, 20. ll. 393—397, 1 *Cor.* xiii. 12. l. 412, ff., *Matt.* v. 8. ll. 461—465, *James* ii. 20, 22, 24, 26. l. 518, *Matt.* v. 9. l. 539 ff., *Zech.* vii. 9; *Rom.* ii. 1. ll. 543, 545, *James* ii. 13; *Matt.* v. 7. ll. 535—542, *Mark* xi. 25; *Col.* iii. 13. l. 535, *Eccles.* xxviii. 2—4. ll. 549, 550, *Matt.* vii. 1, 2; *Luke* vi. 37. ll. 555—557, *Matt.* vi. 14.

---

[1] Augustine's sermons preserve other passages suggestive of the *Speculum*: "*Vade, et affer me pusillum ut manducem*"; "*morituram, se dicit, cum consummaverit, quod remansit*",.. "*cum suis filiis moritura...*," etc. "*Benedixit...Elias...hydriam...farinæ et capsacem olei,*" etc. Traces of the *Vulgata* are to be noted in the account preserved by the *Speculum*:

v. 10: "*Cumque venisset ad portam,... apparuit ei... vidua..., vocauit eam, dixitque ei: 'Da mihi paululum aquæ in vase vt bibam.'*"
v. 11: "*Cumque illa pergeret vt afferret, clamauit... dicens: 'Affer mihi... buccellam panis...'*" v. 12: "'... non habeo panem, nisi quantum pugillus farinæ... & paululum olei in lecytho... faciam illum mihi & filio meo... moriamur.'" v. 13: "'*mihi primum fac... tibi... postea...*'"
v. 16: "*farina non defecit, & lecythus olei non est imminutus...*" See *Vulgata* of MDCLXXXVIII. *Liber III.*, REGUM verses 10—16.

The same theme is employed by Gregory, *Hom. in Ezechielem*, Lib. I Hom. IV. Tom. II. col. 808, but marks no resemblance with the version of the present poem.

ll. 559—568, *Matt.* vi. 15. ll. 568 ff., *Luke* xxi. 19. ll. 624—632, *Matt.* xxiii. 12; *Psal.* cxxxviii. 6. ll. 630—634, *Matt.* xxiii. 12; *Luke* xiv. 11; xviii. 14; *James* iv. 6, 10. l. 782, *Num.* xxxii. 23; *Is.* lix. 15; *Prov.* xiii. 21. ll. 814, 816, 824, 848, *Is.* i. 16; 2 *Kings* v. 12, 13. *Ezek.* xvi. 9; *Acts* xxii. 16. ll. 854, 878, *John* xii. 35. ll. 855—857, *John* ii. 35. ll. 861, 862, *Eccles.* ix. 10; *John* ix. 4. l. 883, *Psal.* cxi. 10; *Prov.* i. 7. ll. 949, 1004, 1 *Kings* xvii. 9, 16.

The text underlying verses 168—176 recalls *Prov.* xxix. 23: *A man's pride shall bring him low*, see *Is.* ii. 17; *Prov.* xvi. 18, and *Job* viii. 13:

> *So are the ways of all that forget God;*
> *And the hope of the unholy shall perish.*

Verses 177—188 describe the compensations of adversity suggested by *Heb.* xii. 6: *Whom the Lord loveth, he chasteneth*. See also *Job* v. 17; *Deut.* viii. 5; *Ps.* xciv. 12; *Prov.* iii. 12. The passage carries the mind to verses 837—846 embodying the text,[1] *Psal.* cxxvi. 5: *They that sow in tears shall reap in joy.*

Texts in which God is symbolized by fire (v. 359): *Heb.* xii. 29; *Ps.* xcvii. 3; *Hab.* iii. 5; *Is.* lxvi. 15.

In the Latin texts cited, the *Vulgata* is generally followed throughout the *Speculum*. A few orthographical deviations are to be noted; cf. l. 630, *Matt.* xxiii. 12. l. 554, *Matt.* vi. 12. l. 782, *Mark* iv. 22; *Matt.* x. 26; *Luke* viii. 11, 12, etc.

3. *Indirect Sources of the Speculum.*

Sources of the *Liber* as employed by Alcuin may be regarded as having a secondary and indirect value in the composition of the *Speculum*. Alcuin's *Liber*, apart from the fact that it stands as the product of the great learning and the high spiritual development[2] of

---

[1] Cf. Shakspere, *King Richard III.* iv. 4:
"The liquid drops of tears, that you have shed,
Shall come again, transform'd to orient pearl."
For verses 454, etc., 544, etc., cf. *Merch. of Venice*, iv. 1:
"In course of justice, none of us
Should see salvation."
King Rich. II., v. 3:
"I pardon him, as God shall pardon me."
King Henry VIII., ii. 1:
"I free forgive, as I would be forgiven."

[2] The MS. Jun. 23, Bibl. Bod. preserves some account of the teacher Alcuin. He "ferde siððan on sæ to þa snotcran cyninge Karulus ȝehaten. se hæfde

Chapter X.—Theological Sources of the Speculum.

the eminent teacher, is indebted largely to the theological fathers of the day, for Alcuin was rarely original.[1] Alcuin was a living exponent of modern doctrines. His life marked "self-reverence, self-knowledge, self-control." Added to his sense of responsibility and of consecration he desired to be of service to humanity in promulgating the impressions and vital doctrines of those, whose theology he studied. Accordingly it is not surprising that the *Liber*, and indirectly the *Speculum*, should mirror the fundamental moral truths of Gregory, Augustine,[2] Prosper, Isidore, Bede, and that with Hraban he should find, "Prudence,[3] justice, bravery, temperance," the root and foundation of all virtue. It is not strange, that the contemplations of Alcuin should be flavoured largely with the Christian ethics of Cassian, and that the fidelity of Alcuin to his original should be reproduced in the English poem. In this connection compare passages of the *Speculum*, verses 785 ff., with Cassian over Tristitia: *Tristitiæ genera sunt duo, unum quod vel iracundia desinente vel de illato damno ac desiderio præpedito cassatoque generatur; aliud, quod de irrationabili mentis anxietate seu desperatione descendit.* For additional discussion of this question see Max Förster, *Ueber d. Quellen von Ælfrics Exeget. Hom. Catholicae, Anglia*,[4] vol. xvi. (1892), p. 47.

In purpose and dedication, the address to Guido, nominally Guy of Warwick through the *Speculum*, is to be traced in the work of Jonas of Orleans: *De Institutione Laicali*, Book III. Here Matfred[5] of Orleans receives instruction at his own request for guidance in Christian life. In the classification of the eight fundamental sins, Theodulph and Prosper[3] are in agreement with Cassian.[6]

---

myclene cræft for ȝode *and* for worulde. To þam com albinus se æþela lareow *and* on his anwealde ælþeodiȝ wunode on sancte Martines mynstere *and* þær maneȝa ȝelærde mid þam heofonlican wisdome þe him ȝod forȝeaf."

[1] See Guizot, *Civ. in France*, Lect. XXI.
[2] Dedication of *Com. on John* to Gisela preserves Alcuin's tribute to other authors for help in "expounding holy words of the gospel," and first of all to Augustine.
[3] *quatuor principales: Prudentia Tristitia Fortitudo, Temperantia*, Caput XXXV. l. 3; also Gregory (ed. Migne), Tom. VI. col. 20.
[4] Ælfric's familiarity with the works of Alcuinus is attested to through Ælfric's translation of the *Interrogationes Sigewulfi in Genesin*; see editions of MacLean and Mitchell.
[5] *Dilecto in Christo Mathfredo Jonas in Domino perpetuam salutem*, Migne, Tom. CVI. col. 121.
[6] Werner, *Alcuin u. sein Jhlt.*, p. 254.

Chapter X.—*Traditional Sources of the Speculum.*

§ 2. *Traditional Sources.*

1. *The Alexius Motif.*

Guy's entreaty for counsel has been recognized in the *Liber*; the epexegetical source has been determined; the ascetic factor of the poem, providing romantic and sentimental environment for the ethical theme of Alquin, is to be traced. The legend stands out from inter-workings of Biblical themes, nomadic doctrines, the inheritance of all liturgical and homiletical literature, and finds ulterior source through the investigation of that greater Guy of Warwick saga, in whose atmosphere rests the *Speculum*. In the *motif* of the *Speculum* an element in contrast with the *Liber*, is to be recognized, overshadowing in charm that marked by historical reminiscence. In distinction from the superannuated military glory, that stirred the hearts of the ancestors of modern England, it is the *leit motif* of poem as well as saga, in which present interest attains its highest expression. In the *Speculum* is blended the radicalism and the romanticism of tradition. The minstrel re-echoes the melody of earlier song no longer in familiar tongue. The essential spirit of the poem culminates in a single incident with its outlying episodes, that of the sacrificial resignation of bride in religious consecration. Here Guy of the legend is in confliction with another personality, for, whether the exterior of the saga be endowed with the fine figure of the warrior Guy or mark the features of the priestly saint Alexius, it envelops one underlying kernel. From the fundamental germ of the English Guy history has emanated an opposite type of literature recognized in many languages, a traditional history, which may in general be described as *Cançun de saint Alexis*. Through this agent the ascetic factor of the *Speculum* is to be separated from its Guido-individuality, and the *Speculum*, as a member of the Guy family, is to be regarded as the after-play of an Alexius germ wandered to England. In both are to be recognized the same characteristics; here are the same joyous wedding, the same pilgrim wanderings, and death under the same exaggerated resignation.[1]

The earliest redaction of this material is a life of the saint: *Vita auctore anonymo conscripta. Ex codice nostro membranaceo Ms.*

---

[1] See Dr. Furnivall's edition of the Alexius miracle published for the E. E. T. S. The scope of the present volume limits mention of Alexius texts to fundamental editions. No saga has a literature more comprehensive, extending to all the languages of Europe, and comprehending all types of composition, even *dramma musicale* and *tragédie* (*Le charmant Alexis*).

antiquissimo Hieronymi de Gaule, Geldriae Cancellario, cum aliis collata, found in the collection of the Bollandists, and supposed to have been printed in 1636, *in Rom typis Francisci Corbelletti* from ancient MSS. of the venerable monasteries of St. Boniface and St. Alexius. This text was given to the public by Pinius in the *Acta Sanctorum Julii*. 1725, *Tomus* IV., pp. 238—270, with the title *De S. Alexio Confessore*. The *Vita* was also included in an incomplete form, by Massmann in the following work: *Sanct. Alexius Leben in 8 gereimten mhd. Behandlungen ; nebst geschichtlicher Einleitung, sowie deutschen, griechischen und lateinischen Anhängen.* Quedlinburg u. Leipzig, 1843, cf. pp. 167—171.

Johannes Pinius assumes as undoubted, that the nationality of Alexius as well as this recognition of his history was Roman. His opinion is stated in the title of his edition: *De S. Alexio Confessore, Romae, vel, ut alia acta ferunt, Edessae in Syria.* Pinius bases the entire history on a Greek canon of the 9th century, whose author was St. Joseph.

Gaston Paris, *La Vie de saint Alexis publ. par Gaston Paris et Léopold Pannier*, Paris, 1872, discovers the Guy-Alexius germ in a Syrian legend embodied in literary form by a priest of the church at Edessa, extolling the monastically upright life of a pilgrim to that church, the son of an industrious and virtuous family of Constantinople. He explains the alleged Roman ancestry through accident. The incident carried to Rome by Bishop Sergius became associated with the church of Boniface by Pope Benedict. There the narrative acquired local flavour, and became so genuinely acclimated as an episode of Roman history, that the death of the saint is actually ascribed to the 5th century; cf. *Monograph* by Du Chesne, p. 163.

The earliest presentation of the theme is to be attributed to a Latin MS. written probably in Rome, a transcript of an older text. Thus the Guy of Warwick saga was extant among the Romans, and rests not necessarily on Roman tradition, but on a Roman source developed also in England.

And here again it bespeaks an earlier generation in tradition; but all actual material in ages to follow, whether it be Greek, German, Provençal, or Norman, or French and English promulgated on British soil, returns to Roman ancestry. In all MS. forms, the Alexius narrative embodies a Latin original transcribed in Italy. In its branches are to be recognized the features of the Guy legend, resignation and renunciation, voluntary poverty, the atoning pilgrimage, the return to native land, the acceptance of alms from the fair hands of the forsaken bride, a moment of final recognition before both martyr and martyr's bride become united in death. These familiar lineaments are to be discovered in the history of Guy of Warwick. The link[1] connecting the two episodes is probably French on English ground. The characteristic modifications of the later versions of the history were collected on English shores, but the *Speculum* is undoubtedly indebted directly to a legend bearing the name Guy of Warwick.

2. *Minor Traditional Sources.*

A parallel expression introducing the account of the fiery bush, symbolical of the purity of the Virgin (*Speculum*, verses 355—368), occurs in *The Prymer* or *Lay Folks Prayer Book*,[2] edited by Littlehales, 1895, in the "Hours of the Blessed Virgin" as follows, p. 24: *Bi þe buysch, þat moises siȝ vnbrent, we knowen þat þi preisable maidenhede is kept.* . . . "*Thou art the bosche of Synay*," Shoreham's line, *Poem to Mary*, Wright, p. 131, recalls l. 112 of *Marien Rosenkranz:*

"*Se ys de bush her moysy,*" . . . etc.

The figure is used by Jacob Ryman, compare Zupitza's note, str. 3, v. 1 ff. *Archiv*, vol. xciii, p. 309. Chaucer employs the metaphor in the *Prioresses Tale, Prologue:*

"O mooder mayde! o mayde mooder free!
O bush vnbrent, brenning in Moyses syghte,
That rauysedest doun fro the deitee."—str. 3, v. 1657 f.

But these lines were probably written later than the twelfth stanza of *An A. B. C.* (cf. Skeat, xlvii), *La Priere de Nostre Dame*,[3] str. 12, v. 89 ff., where the theme is developed with some fulness of incident:

"Moises, that saugh the bush with flaumes rede
Brenninge, of which ther never a stikke brende,
Was signe of thyn unwemmed maidenhede.
Thou art the bush on which ther gan descende
The Holy Gost, the which that Moises wende
Had ben a-fyr; and this was in figure."

---

[1] A genealogical table showing the connection between the two developments of the saga as represented by Guy and Alexius might be in order here; but it seems to reserve the discussion for a separate article, particularly since Professor Zupitza has investigated so carefully the Guy MSS.; see *Zur Literaturgesch. des G. v. Warwick.*

[2] E. E. Text Society, Extra Series, cv.

[3] Skeat, *Minor Poems*, pp. xlvii—xlviii and p. 4; Skeat's *Chaucer*, vol. I., p. 266.

cxxii   *Chapter X.—Traditional Sources of the Speculum.*

Skeat cites Chaucer's original from De Deguileville's[1] *Pélérinage de l'Ame*, Part I. *Le Pélérinage de la Vie humaine*, edition[2] of Paul Meyer, MS. 1645, Fonds Français, in the National Library, Paris. The exposition of the *Speculum* seems to stand as near the text of Deguileville as does the Chaucerian quotation, as will be seen from a comparison with the selection as contained in Stürzinger's print[3] of *Le Pélérinage de Vie Humaine*, "final assault of the 7 deadly sins":

> "Moises vit en figure
> Que tu virge neto et pure,
> Ihesu, le fil Dieu, concëus.
> Un buisson contre Nature
> Vit qui(l) ardoit sans arsure.
> C'es tu, n'en sui point decëus.
> Diex est li feus qu'en toi ëus
> Et tu buisson des recrëus
> Es pour temprer leur ardure.
> A ce vëoir, Virge, vëus
> Soie par toi et recëus."——v. 11,025, etc.

The application to the virgin cannot possibly have originated with Deguileville,[4] for it had been given literary form fully two centuries earlier by Walter von der Vogelweide,[5] see *Leich*, edited by Wilmanns, Halle, 1869; p. 31 f., v. 37 ff.:

> "Ein bosch der bran, dâ nie niht an besenget noch verbrennet wart:
> breit[6] unde ganz beleip sin glanz vor fiures flamme und unverschart
> daz ist diu reine maget alleine, diu mit megetlîcher art
> Te kindes muoter worden ist
> An aller manne mitewist,
> und wider menneschlîchen list
> den wâren Krist
> gebar, der uns bedâhte."

Compare *Lobgesang auf Maria*, edited by A. Jeitteles from Innspruch and Breslau MSS., *Germania*, vol. xxxi., pp. 299, 300, v. 167 ff.:

> "du grüener busch, den Moyses sach
> vol flammen, dem doch niht geschach,
> unversenget bleip er gar:
> daz bezeichent offenbâr,
> dar du meit blib unde wære,
> dô du daz ôsterlamp gebære,
> daz für uns geopfert wart
> an daz criuze, Marjâ zart."[7]

---

[1] It will be noted that the orthography of Skeat following Meyer is here employed; see Morley: *Eng. Writ.*, ii. 204.
[2] Copied by Skeat from Furnivall's *One-text Print of Chaucer's Minor Poems*, Part I., p. 84.   [3] Printed for the Roxburghe Club, 1893.
[4] Varying forms are not necessary to the purpose of the *Speculum* in the selection of the passage.
[5] To this selection and to Böddeker's *Ballad* attention was called by Professor Kölbing, to whom thanks are due.
[6] *grüen* according to Bartsch's print of the poem in Pfeiffer's *Deutsche Classiker des Mittelalters*, Leipzig, 1877, vol. i., p. 169.
[7] Zingerle (*Zeitscr. für d. Philologie*, vol. vi., p. 377) ascribes this text to the fifteenth century.

Chapter X.—Traditional Sources of the Speculum.

See footnotes, p. 299 : *Dasselbe Bild in Erl.* 283, 115, *im Melker Marienl.* 117, str. 2, *sowie im Arnsteiner Marienleich* 110, 44 ff.

A *Carroll* in *Jahrbuch für Romanische und Englische Literatur*, Neue Folge, Bd. II., 1875, pp. 92, 93, *Das wunder der Incarnation*, edited by Böddeker in *Englische Lieder u. Balladen aus dem 16. Jahrhundert*, reads as follows:

> "Another signe behold and se:
> Vpon this maid virginite.
> Trulie of hir was ment
> This fierie bushe that was so bright
> To Moises did give suche a light,
> And not one leafe was brent."—str. 4, v. 21.

Skeat, *Prioresses Tale*, p. 144, notes an illustration in an *Alliterative Hymn*, quoted in Warton's *Hist. of Engl. Poetry* (ed. Hazlitt), vol. ii. p. 284, str. ii. v. 2 : *Heil, bush brennyng that never was brent.*

In the discovery that the fiery bush is symbol of the spotless purity of the Virgin, the passage differs from the broad-spread interpretation of the prodigy. The traditions of "bush on fire," conspicuous in all stories of the rood-tree from the days of Cynewulf and Elene to the 14th century, and later[1] in their multitudinous accumulations of gleanings through the Middle Ages, unite in regarding the bush as symbol of divine Presence. A frequent mediæval application of the Biblical passages, Exodus iii. 2—6 ; Mark xii. 26 ; and Acts vii. 30, is embodied in lines from *Legends of the Holy Rood, The Story of the Rood Tree*, p. 73 :

> "For suth, he said, þi wandes mene
> þe trinite þam thre bitwene."

Compare Napier, *History of the Holy Rood-tree*, E. E. Text Society, 103, and *Legends of the Holy Rood, Symbols of the Passion and Cross-Poems*, edited by R. Morris, E. E. Text Society, 46.

Intermediate between the two versions[2] comes Maundeville's interpretation of the expressive Biblical image in *The Voiage and Travaile* of Sir John Maundevile, Kt., ed. Halliwell, London, 1839 ;

---

[1] The "fierie bush" is to this day in current use in figurative language. Dr. Ripley discovered in Transcendentalism "the fair tree of mysticism," a "burning bush" of revelation and sorrow, see Sanborn's *Henry D. Thoreau* in Charles Dudley Warner's "American Men of Letters" (1882), p. 143.

[2] The prodigy is not interpreted as symbolical in Book II. *Of the Jewish Antiquities of Josephus* (ed. Roger L'Estrange, London, 1702), chap. xii., p. 48, where the record stands: "A *Fire* seen in a *Bush*, the *Bush* burning, the Flame fierce and violent, and yet neither Leaves, Flowers, nor Branches blasted or consum'd." The "surprize of it struck *Moses* with astonishment." The "Voice that spake to *Moses* out of the fiery *Bush*" commanded him "to depend upon the Assistance of an Almighty Power."

the text is included in *Early Travels in Palestine*, Bohn's Antiquarian Library, Messrs. George Bell and Sons:

"And the Mount of Synay is clept the Desert of Syne, that is for to seyne, the Bussche brennynge: because there Moyses sawghe oure Lord God many tymes, in forme of Fuyr brennynge upon that Hille; and also in a Bussche[1] brennynge, and spak to him."—p. 58, ed. Bell, p. 42.

"Also behynde the Awtier of that Chirche is the place where Moyses saughe oure Lord God in a brennynge Bussche."—p. 59, Bell, p. 43.

"And a lytille aboven is the Chapelle of Moyses, and the Roche where Moyses fleyhe to, for drede, whan he saughe oure Lord face to face."—p. 62, Bell, p. 44.

Maundeville attempts no explanation of the miracle, leaving the interpretation to the theologian and mystic.

Verses 347—354 contain the exposition of Gen. xviii. 2. See also Hebrews xiii. 2. The same passage is presented in Maundeville's description of Hebron (see Halliwell):

"And in that same Place was Abrahames Hous: and there he satt and saughe 3 Persones, and worschipte but on; as Holy Writt seythe, *Tres vidit et unum adoravit:* that is to seyne; *He saughe 3 and worschiped on.*"—p. 66, Bell, p. 47.

The same general theme is discussed by Orrm as follows, verses 19,385, etc., cf. ed. of Holt:

> "Nan mann ne mihhte næfre sen
> Allmahhtiȝ Godd onn erþe,
> Wiþþ erþlic eȝhe off erþliȝ flæsh.

19,429.   Whatt Abraham, whatt Moysæs,

> . . . .
> Ne sæȝhenn þeȝȝ nohht Drihhtin Godd
> Inn hiss goddcunnde kinde!
> Na fuliȝwiss, ne sahh himm nan
> Wiþþ erþliȝ flæshess eȝhe,
> Þatt wise þæt himm enngless sen
> Inn hiss goddcunnde kinde."

---

[1] Maundeville reports the exhibition of the bush which was "burnt and was not consumed, in which our Lord spoke to Moses," shown at the church of St. Catherine, see edition of Bell, p. 43. "And thanne thei schewen the Bussche, that brenned and wasted nought, in the whiche oure Lord spak to Moyses."—Halliwell, p. 60.

Part III.

CHAPTER XI.

ON THE METRICAL STRUCTURE OF THE *SPECULUM*.

The *Speculum Gydonis* may receive investigation on basis of laws governing the lyric verse of Chaucer. The *Speculum*, representing the pre-conquest rather than the modern side of the mediæval period, marks itself as a distinct type in the growth of language. On authority of Chaucerian study noteworthy questions of mechanical form may be classified. The poem is to be studied with reference to the development of the riming vowel, its phonology, its quality and quantity, and the method of its introduction in the riming system used by the poet. Attention will be directed to the poet's use of open and closed *e-* and *o-* sounds in rime combination, to his representation of the development of O.E. *-y* (*-ȳ*), umlaut of *-u* (*-ū*), and to his arrangement of rimes in the relationship of *-y* : *-ye*, and *cons* : *cons* + *e*.

§ 1. *The Strophe.*

Two lines joined by final rime form the strophe. Compared with the *Poema Morale*, in septenar, and with *On God Ureisun of Ure Lefdi* in mixed verse, where the completion of the strophe marks also the limit of the sentence, the verse may be regarded as presaging the "run-on" line of the Elizabethan drama. Sentence structure is in no way impeded by mechanical verse form. At times the riming characteristic of the strophe is continued through two consecutive couplets, developing the scheme $a\,a\,a\,a$. This illustrates no unusual phenomenon in M.E. versification: *Sir Beues* 633—6, 749—52, 893—6, etc., see Kölbing, p. xi.; *Havelok* 17—20, 37—40, etc.; *Sir Fyrumbras*, see Zupitza, *Übungsbuch*, p. 107, 1138—41, 1144—47, and also in the cæsural rime 1138—41, etc.; *Poema Morale*, 3—6, 75—80, 233—36, etc. The *Speculum* contains illustration through the following instances: (-*ay*) 249—52, (-*erë*) 353—56, (-*é*) 389—92, (-*é*) 401—4 (*ney* : *say* 403—4 in H_1), (-*ë*) 533—36, (-*er(ë)*) 779—82, (-*iht*) 855—58, (-*edë*) 1025—28, as well as in (-*ē*) 549—52, (-*omë*) 643—46. Purely accidental or resulting from the momentary impulse of the poet, successive couplets united by the same riming syllable do not present strophic formation.

cxxvi *Chapter XI.—Metrical Structure of the Speculum.*

§ 2. *Construction of the Verse.*

The normal line contains four stressed syllables with regularly alternating thesis, fulfilling Ruskin's requirement for the "chief poetry of energetic nations." It produces the conventional iambic tetrameter. A final unstressed syllable is admissible. The scheme thus develops a catalectic or a hypercatalectic verse; a metrical pause occurs generally after the second arsis. The same technique is employed in *Guy of Warwick*, the first 7306 lines of the Auchinleck text (cf. Zupitza's edition, and Kölbing, *Sir Beues*, p. xi.), in *Sir Beues*, verses 475—4620 (Auch. MS.), in *Owl and Nightingale*, *King Horn*, and in a multitude of like works. Although following the accentual system of versification imitated from French poetry (cf. Pl. *Grdr.*, vol. ii., p. 1042, § 33), yet the verse partakes of the character of the native English short-line couplet.[1] This is recognized through the logical significance of its stress, through freedom in the development of unstressed syllables, and through incidental return to a modification of the elemental alliterative construction. As medium for the expression of his own personality, external form must be considered to a degree subservient to the moral emotion of the poet. The merit of this quality in the verse is emphasized by contrast with the evenly accentuated measures of the phonetician Orrm, or of the "moral[2] Gower." There the quantitative standard of the Latin model[3] is exemplified with painful exactness. Lines from Orrm, in septenar, Gower, and the author of the *Speculum*, both in tetrameter, placed side by side, display to an advantage the pleasing dignity, the thoughtfulness, and the melody of the verse of the present text. Compare as follows, where the opening verses of the *Ormulum* serve as characteristic of the poem:

---

[1] The short riming couplet is to be regarded as first consistently and regularly employed in a metrical *Paternoster* composed in the south of England in the second half of the 12th century, see ten Brink (ed. Kennedy, 1889), p. 156, and also p. 267.

[2] See Chaucer's dedication of *Troilus* to
". . . moral Gower . . . . . .
To thee and to the philosophical Strode."

Radulphus Strode nobilis poeta has earned attention from Dr. Furnivall and a notice from Gollancz, in *Pearl*, pp. l., li. See also Morley's edition of *Confessio Amantis*, p. xiv.

[3] The *Poema Morale*, illustrating to a degree principles of classical accentuation in respect to precision in the alternation of the stressed and the unstressed syllable, is to be distinguished from the *Speculum*, where the English element predominates.

Chapter XI.—Metrical Structure of the Speculum.

> þiss bóc iss némmnedd Órrmulúm,
> forrþí þatt Órrm itt wróhhtë,
> annd itt iss wróhht off quáþþrigán,
> off góddspellbókess fówwrë.—*Orrm*. ll. 1—4.

> Sometímë lích úntó þe cóck,
> Sometíme untó þe laüërock.[1]—*Gower*, p. 266.

As representative then of the element distinctively English, the verse is subject to modifications dependent on conditions in the thesis and upon various readings made possible through elision, slurring, and the interpretation attributed to the syllabic value of final -*e*. Through diversity in arrangement of syllables of this order the line seems at times too short for the scheme to which it belongs, at times too long. After making due allowance for instances of apocope, syncope, elision by synalepha or ecthlipsis, for the doubling of the unstressed syllable, or for its omission, still the verse contains uniformly four metrical divisions. Every line of the poem can be resolved into a four-stressed verse. For instance, verse 124 reads smoothly under five-syllabic ictus as follows: *And mákëþ mán · anúiëd tó do gód*. With aid of syncope of *e* in *makeþ* and of a double thesis in the first foot, the normal four-stressed measure is attained: *Ănd mălĕþ mán · anúiëd tó do gód*. It is also secured by means of the double thesis in the fourth measure: *And mákëþ mán · anúied tŏ dŏ gód*. With verse 124 compare *Leg. of G. Women*, Recension B, v. 91: *And mákęth hit sóune · aftér his fingeringe*.[2] Verse 329 adapts itself to Gower's standard (the first thesis being deficient[3]) arranged in quantitative pentameter: *Hít is, · lóuë gód ouer állë þíng*. Corrected by H_2, it conforms to the four-beat line. The vigour of the preferred arrangement is apparent: *Hít is, lóuë gód · ouer állë þíng*. The flexible thesis is answerable for similar irresoluteness in verses 232, 398, 670, 847, 959, 973, etc.

In all the texts verses apparently devised for the three-accentuated measure occur, giving the copyist opportunity for amplification of the material. That the poet be answerable for the deficiency, decision cannot be ventured. Copyist alone would hardly incur the

---

[1] Gower's *Confessio Amantis, Tales of the Seven Deadly Sins*, edited by Henry Morley, LL.D., London, 1889, p. 266 (Book V., v. 274).

[2] This scansion presupposes that metrical and word accent do not necessarily fall together. Otherwise the following arrangement is to be adopted:
And máketh hit sóune · áfter his fingeringe.

[3] Naturally Gower never permitted himself the license of the omission of the "up-beat" in the first or the second section of the line according to models of versification purely English in origin.

responsibility of the fundamental mass of deviation. Line 107, *Herkne noupe : to me*, was source of uneasiness to the scribe. Each remodelled the line, to adapt the unstressed measure to the requirements of the tetrameter. Lines omitting the unstressed syllable in the first or the fourth measure have apparently but three metrical divisions. Lines 81 (also 139) and 704 appear, at hasty glance, as follows: 81 (139), *Wisdóm in gódës drédë;* 704, *Dóþ a lítel trespás;* but a preferred reading ranks them in type D: *Wís-dóm · in gódës drédë, Dóþ a lítel · trés-pás.*

In no instance is the principle of the verse necessarily to be regarded as altered by the poet to introduce new rhythms, trimeter or pentrameter, for purpose of added impressiveness, as has been attributed to *Sir Beues*[1] (cf. Kölbing, p. xi.), see line 1376, *þát i sé · nŏw hére*, or 1383, *Lŏ hér, · þe king Ermin*. The *Speculum* does not illustrate the practice of the Elizabethans in modifying its accepted standard to portray solemnity, as for instance under the presence of supernatural beings (see Abbott, §§ 504, 507, 509, etc.), illustrated by Shakspere, *Macbeth*, IV. i. 20; *Rich. III.*, IV. 4, 75.

§ 3. *Metrical Types of the Speculum.*

"So pray I god, that none ...
Ne thee mis-metre, for defaute of tunge."[2]

In general the characteristics of the verse-system of the *Speculum* may be classified metrically according to the following scheme:

A. *A* marks the typical and fundamental line of the poem, the four-accented measure, constructed regularly as it is described in the preceding section. *A* conveys the intended movement of the original verse. To this line as a standard all other lines must be referred in metrical classification. Modifications of type A are presented developing a system,[3] which comprises four additional types of verse structure.[4] Under type A all lines will be classified, that may not be arranged in the remaining four divisions of the subject. The type is abundant in the *Speculum*. The representative verse is as follows:

---

[1] These verses could probably be adapted to the tetrameter on the hypothesis of a monosyllabic arsis, the thesis being replaced by an emphatic pause: *þát i sé · nów-hérē; Lŏ-hér · þe king Ermin*, the effect of slowness and solemnity being still attained.
[2] Chaucer, *Troilus*, v. 1809.
[3] Cf. Schick, pp. lvii ff.
[4] The standard verse of the accentual system is to be regarded as uniformly the metrical couplet of four stressed syllables to the line.

Chapter XI.—Metrical Types of the Speculum.

v. 17. *For, whán þe wórld · þe háþ ikáuht.*—31. *Hou ón a time · he stód in þoúht.*[1]—32. *þe wórldës blíssę · him þóuhtë nóht;* cf. 8, 9, 10, 13, 14, 33, etc. The verse may have a final unstressed syllable, *i. e.* a feminine ending: v. 2. *And hélę of sóulę · i máy ou téchë.*—3. *þat í wole spéke, · it is no fáblë.*—4. *Ac hít is swípë · prófitáblë;* cf. 6, 11, 12, 15, 16, 20, 22, etc.

The number of verses to be ascribed to type A varies, being increased or diminished according to the standard determining the logical significance of the unaccented syllable at the caesura and in the first measure. Confliction often exists between *A* and some other distinct type. Examples could be cited in which an unaccented final syllable may be slurred, apocopated, or syncopated at the caesura in favour of the rhythm, and conducive to type A. On the other hand, poetical license permits the sounding of a final *-e* or *-en*, otherwise silent, at the caesura. Under these conditions types A and C have equal claims to the same verse. Because of the flexible accentual quality of the language at this period and the license permissible in the thesis, ultimate decision in classification on basis of a specific type must be influenced by personal taste, guided by a sensitive ear for rhythmical harmony, and governed by the individual judgment as to the standard employed by the poet. Compare paragraphs to follow over types B, C, D, and E.

B. *B* serves as a variation of the verse structure A, by which a redundant syllable is introduced before the caesura,[2] giving in that position a thesis of two syllables (*i. e.* a trisyllabic measure), the *Speculum* thus presenting a development of the epic caesura. *B* is not well illustrated by the poet. It does not approach the Romance standard (Italian, French, Provençal) of popularity supported by the verse of five measures (cf. Schick, p. lvii.) preserving similar construction. The added variety and melody produced by this type as developed in the five-accentuated line of Chaucer and of the Elizabethan dramatist (cf. Abbott, § 454) is to be attained for the shorter verse by other means. Supposing the accent to have passed to the first syllable in instance of *séruise (seruíse?)*, verse 36 illustrates the use of the epic caesura (type B): *And ín his séruise · was éuere mó.* Otherwise v. 36 is to be classified under the fifth type (E): *Ănd ín his serуíse · was éuere mó.* The preservation of line rime v. 495

---

[1] Read *Hòu ón a time* with fluctuating accent.
[2] *i. e.* trochaic caesura, the first section of the line preserving a feminine ending.

gives the epic cæsura: þere í þe fíndë · í wóle þe bíndë. See also verses 826 and 955. Type B is combined with a trisyllabic foot at the beginning of the verse: v. 357. At thē mount of Sýnăy[1] · bĭ óldë dáwë.—959. At þĕ ʒáte of þe cítē · þĕ widewe he métte. With monosyllabic first measure: 303. Wít and kúnnĭng · ǎnd kóintĭsē, though the reading Wít and kúnnĭng · and kóintĭse (qwéyntĭse, MSS. A₂DH₂) merits recognition. Probably in this class is 157: Héle of bódi · in bón and húidë, permitting the hiatus to exist at the cæsura. Note, however, instances[2] of double thesis in third foot as follows:

v. 347. Abrahám him sáuh, · ǎc þŭ nóst noht hóu.—381. God is so cléng · ǎnd sŏ clér a þíng.—551. Forʒéue, þou mún, · fŏr þĕ lóue of mé. With a final unstressed syllable: 847. Nu ʒé muwę witen, · whǎt ĭt ís to ménë.[3]—549. Álswich mét · ǎs þŭ métëst mé. —362. And himsélf · ĭn þǎt ǔlkë sǐhtë. Additional illustrations of the trisyllabic third measure are: *41, *341, *350 (A_1), 608, 652, 813, 1033.

Under B the number of illustrations is increased by instances in which an unaccented -e (-en) is sounded before the cæsura, but generally final -e will be elided or apocopated in favour of the fundamental type A. Accepting rigidly the inflectional laws attributed to the poet, the following lines may be read by type B: 52, *64, 101, 181, 240, 522, 533, 747. Suppression of the final syllable at the cæsura converts into type A many verses otherwise to be cited under B (see under A): 2, 3, 15, 16, 26, 31, 32, 44, 59, 60, 76, 77, 83, 85, etc. Slurring or syncope will remove from B some illustrations: 12, 13, 345, 424, etc. Verse 94 opens a question treated under declension of substantives, that of the inflectional final -e in dative forms in the singular: And shrífte of móuþĕ · shǎl bé þi bótë. Type B removes all difficulty from the acceptance of this -ë in the present instance, though verse 94 may naturally be interpreted (cf. Decl.): And shrífte of móuþę · shǎl bé þi bótë, avoiding the awkward effect of the break at the middle of the short verse.

Verse 123 possibly belongs to type B: Hĭt ís a dérnĕ · mŏurnĭng in mód; but it seems to provide an instance of double thesis in the fourth measure, rather than at the cæsura: mŏurnĭng in mód; though here the question of fluctuating accent merits consideration.

[1] This reading presupposes that Synay received the accentuation familiar in modern English.
[2] An asterisk marks the number of a verse containing a principle of metrical structure in addition to the one specifically illustrated.
[3] Epic cæsura, if the reading be witĕn.

Chapter XI.—Metrical Types of the Speculum.

mourning is undoubtedly the form to be read, verse 125 *mourninge*: (*springe*). For modern use of the epic cæsura, compare the musical application of Coleridge, *Christabel* (ed. Morley, p. 287), Part I., v. 2: And frŏ́m her kĕ́nnĕl · bĕnéath the rŏ́ck.—Part II., v. 121: She shrănk and shŭddcrĕd · ănd săid agáin. Lyric cæsura characterizes verse 999: Ne drĕ́d þe nŏ́ht, womman, · in þi þŏ́uht. Compare also verse 232.

C. Type C produces in the four-stressed system a verse corresponding to the Lydgatian type in the five-beat measure. It completes the rhythm by substitution of a rest for a sound, a dignified and vigorous means of poetical emphasis. The thesis is wanting in the cæsura, so that the third measure consists of arsis only, two stressed syllables meeting in the middle of the line. Compare Schipper, *Engl. Metrik*, vol. I., p. 37, and Schick, p. lviii. This type seems to have been pleasing to the poet; cf. as follows:

v. 204: þat ó god ís · ánd no má.[1]—215. And ȝáf to mán · fré power.—405. Ȝif þu wolt sén · in þi siht.—613. To súffrĕ wróng · ánd vnríht.—615. Ac swich a fiht · is vnméþ. Other illustrations are: 224, 332, 452, 453?, 454, 503, 719, 726, 918.

It is to be conceded, that in some instances other hypothesis is possible. Uncertainty in the classification of the syllable producing the thesis results in alternative readings for some of the lines previously cited. Following type A with omission of the thesis in the fourth measure are the following versions of lines 204, 224, 613 and 615:

v. 204: þat ó god ís // and nó · mó.
v. 224: þat éuere síngyn // bí · gán.
v. 613: To súffrĕ wróng // and ⅴn · ríht.
v. 615: Ac swich a fiht // is ⅴn · méþ.

v. 719 may be read: Whérþurw þú miht · in þi mód. A question of emphasis modifies the absolute classification of other verses. 332 may receive the interpretation // þu móst · dó in its second section; 453. // fro ȝóu · gón; 454. // haddę ȝé · nón.

Combining with unstressed final syllable occur, v. 105: þanne ís hit gód, · þát þu shónë.—438. þat slówën hím · þurw enúië.—446. Wid stërnë vóiz · ánd wid hetë. Additional illustrations are: 24, 25?, 35, 75, 100?, 227, 253, 498, 583, 766, 832, 909, 960, 1025. Type C produces, in combination with the acephalous verse

---

[1] MSS. H₁ and H₂ attempt to preserve type A by the modification of the construction of verse 204; H₁ and R of verse 452; D and R of verse 615.

(type D), the effect of two short acephalous verses, the half line following the cæsura having the general character of the type[1] in the principle of the full acephalous line: 323. *Hérknë nú · állę to mé.*— 461. *Hópę to gód · ánd do gód.*—80. *Whichę þeih béþ · álle on rëwë.*—90. *Ʒít þu móst · vse móre.*—927. *Gód seiþ pús · in his lóre.* Other examples are: 445, 448, 816, 824, 848, 864, 919, 927, 983, 1026. Uncertainty characterizes also the illustrations of this paragraph. The meaning of the poet may have demanded the following arrangement:

v. 445: Þánnę wole gód // to hém · séië.
v. 448: Góþ anón, // goþ nú · góþë.
v. 461: Hópę to gód // and dó · gód.
v. 494: Óff þis wórd // þat gód · séidë.
v. 816: Wássheþ óu, // and béþ · clénë. 824, 848.
v. 983: First, þeróf // mak mé · métë.

Verse 498 is removed from type C by MSS. D and H₁ through the reading: *Ánd to Iésu Críst þe táke.* 919 passes also to type D on the supposition of fluctuating accent: *Léuë frénd // hèrknë to mé.* 881 may be removed from type C on ground that it contributes illustration of the retention of the imperative ending in weak verbs: *þérfore wórch[ë], // whilę þu máit.* 983 may be read: *First, · þerof // mák me mëtë.*

Type C is enriched by the uniform observance of established poetical laws,[2] particularly in the elision (apocope) of final -e in the cæsura. Yet if it be granted, that through the influence of the metrical pause a syllable be preserved, that would otherwise be suppressed, numerous lines belonging to type C, under rigid adherence to the metrical and inflectional system of the poem, may be read according to type A or type D. With the following lines may be compared v. 217, *Leg. of G. Women:*

v. 145: Ac to láte þi sínnë · ál onlíchë;
v. 294: I shál ʒou shéwë · ín þis plácë;
v. 311: Bóþę þe pórë · ánd þe ríchë.
v. 217: With flórouns smálë · ánd I shál nat lýe.—
Leg. of G. Women.

---

[1] The "up-beat" (*auftakt*) is thus omitted at the beginning of each of the two sections of the verse.

[2] The evolution of type C may possibly be accredited to the influence of the acephalous verse, as well as to the increasing tendency toward the weakening of the O.E. full endings and the ultimate loss of the inflectional final -e. Cf. *Schick*, p. lviii.

Chapter XI.—Metrical Types of the Speculum. cxxxiii

Skeat does not accredit Chaucer with the metrical suppression of -e in the cæsura, *Prioresses Tale*, p. lxii. The poet of the *Speculum* may at times have availed himself of the same licence. He has done so in other measures; cf. 279. *shōlën · wilnën éuerë.*—297. *shōlën · pártën hénnë.*—316. *hém · shal wántën óuht.* Similar instances are not wanting in the third measure: verses 109, 145, 179, 273, etc. A larger number of lines, where conflicting vowels do not coalesce, may be studied under *Hiatus* (cf. § 8). *Sir Beues* illustrates type C, MS. A, 475—4620; v. 485: *Bóutę þow mé · tó him tákë*; cf. 747, 801, 839, 916, 936, etc., and *Pearl* 60[1].

D. *D* classifies a line iambic in movement, but beginning with a single stressed syllable.[1] The first measure consists of arsis alone, the German *auftaktlose verse* or *verse mit fehlendem auftakt*. It is employed by Skeat as the "clipped line," *Leg. of G. Women*, pp. xxxv., xxxvi., by Schick as the "acephalous line," *Temple of Glas*, p. lviii.; cf. also ten Brink, § 299, and Sidney Lanier, *The Science of English Verse*, p. 139. The *Speculum* is rich in illustration. Compare as follows:

v. 7. *þús shal bén · þi bíginning.*—128. *Sáuuëd wórþ he · néuere mó.*—137. *Hérknë nów · to mý sarmóun.* Other instances with unstressed final syllable: v. 1. *Hérknëþ állë · tó my spéchë.*—29. *Óff an éorl · of gódë fámë.*—39. *Álquin wás · his ríhtë námë*, and as follows: 18, 28, 30, 39, *41, 49, 51, 54, 57, 62, 63, 70, 71, 74, 76, *80, *81, 82, 83, 84, 85, 86, 87, 91, 100?, *107, 109, 111, 112, 115, 116, 120, 122, 129, 137, *139, 140, 141, 155, 157, 161?, 164, 177, 187?, 196, 223, 228, 251, etc.

Of the couplet of four measures as employed by Chaucer, type D occurs in *The Hous of Fame;* cf. verses 58, 61, 86, 103, 105, 133, 172, 173, etc. In the Chaucerian pentameter Skeat discovers many illustrations; see *Leg. of G. Women*, pp. xxxv., xxxvi., and note to verse 67; *Prioresses Tale*, p. lxvi. The second system of versification *Sir Beues* uses D, verses 475(1)?, 476(2), 479(5), 481(7), 485(11), 487(13), etc. It existed in the earliest mediæval English versification, in the *septenarius* of the *Poema Morale;* cf. verses 1, 4, 5, 6, 7, 11, 12, 13, etc. Milton[2] makes happy application of the principle in *L'Allegro*, 19, 21, 25, 26, etc., *Il Penseroso*, 17, 32, 34, etc., and it finds expression in *Vision of Sin*, part II. (see Skeat). Freedom in

---

[1] *I. e.* monosyllabic first measure.
[2] See ed. Browne, vol. i, pp. 30, 34, *English Poems by John Milton*.

this construction is attributed to the great Elizabethan master, Abt, § 479.

Group Y of the *Speculum* often seeks to remove the monosyllabic first measure by the introduction of an unstressed syllable beginning the line. The effort of H_2 at reconstruction of the metre is to be noted. Verse 7 accomplishes this by the introduction of *ys;* v. 18 replaces *In* with *Into;* v. 30 writes *Sire Gy* for *Gy;* v. 49 has *Vpon* for *On;* v. 54 *ouyr vs* for *us;* v. 57 *Doo me make* for *Make me;* v. 74 *But ȝyffe* for *Bote;* verses 28, 39, and 41 are not altered in the first measure.

E. The first measure of type E is represented by a thesis of two syllables, *i. e. verse mit doppeltem auftakt*. In contrast with the five-stressed measure, where the type is not uniformly well represented, many verses of the *Speculum* may be read according to this model:

v. 341. *Bŭt þŭ lóue · þe crístene þat bí þe bé* (MS. A₁).—504. *Whăn wĕ him bisékëþ · þát riht ís.* With unstressed final syllable: v. 21. *Nĕ fŏr lóuę to gód · ne fór his éiȝë.*—36. *Aňd in his seruise · was éuerë móre.*—37. *Á gŏd mán þer wás · in þilkë dáwë.*—754. *Aňd öf nédful þing · i wóle ȝou téchë.*—1006. *þăt in álmessę déde · is dóublë gód.*—1013. *Iň ánóþer stéde · i háue witnéssë.* Additional instances are: 124?, 143, 145, *232, 280, 284, 329, 340, 465, 507, 535?, 564, 565, 567, *581, 582, 683, 779, 793, 795,* 835, 859, 936, 940, *959, 966, 975,? 976.

A_2 preserves in verse 149 the reading of *A* in distinction from *E*, *þis is* being read *þis'* (*þis͡is*). Verses 341 and 504 were much tampered with by the scribes (cf. variants) in aspiration toward type A.

By the omission of *þat*, v. 1006 conforms to the fundamental type on basis of MS. R in opposition to A_1 and *D*. Contrary to other MSS., perhaps quite by accident, 92 (= 474) falls into type A in MS. A_2 reading: *And rédy þárę · to dó penáuncë*. The verse is otherwise indefinite in classification, the criterion being *redi*. Accenting the second syllable type E is illustrated. A preferred form places the verse under *A* with double thesis in the second measure.

v. 1020. *Also ófte as þóu · maytȝ ȝéuë óuht*, is excluded from type E, if *Also* be regarded as a single syllable; cf. Chaucer, Genl. Prolog. v. 730. *For thís ye knówen also* (= *als*) *wél as Í.*

The classification distinguishing any one of these individual types is not absolute. A verse admits of various readings according to

Chapter XI.—Metrical Types of the Speculum. cxxxv

varying interpretations of its meaning or its external structure. So 569, belonging apparently to *C*, admits of restoration to type A by the substitution of the dissyllabic *louërd* for *lord* of text A_1 :

  Houre swétë lórd · ín his spéchë. (C)
  Houre swétë lóuerd · ín his spéche. (A)

Similarly, by granting a dissyllabic pronunciation to *eorl*, *rl* being pronounced with a svarabhakti vowel *rël*, type C is converted into type A; cf. verses 45, 50, and 65:

  v. 45. Off hím þe éorl · wás wel wár. (C)
    Off hím þe éor[ĕ]l · wás wel wár. (A)

In opposition to the hypothesis that *eo* is a dissyllable, is the reading of verse 29, *Óff an éorl of gódë fúmë*, and the monophthongic use of *eo* in *eorþe*, possessing the metrical value of *erþe*, compare *eorþe* 296, 375, 397, 600, 604, 735, with *erþe* 382 and 589.

Type C often depends for its classification on the interpretation of the poet's intended meaning. In verse 100, grant that the poet wished to make *þu* conspicuous, and type C is assured; but D is quite possible on supposition of the poet's desire to emphasize the condition presented through *if* in the first measure, with added weight of stress on the idea of the wish suggested in *wolt;* cf. Abt, § 484.

  If þú wolt hém · tó þe tákë. (C)
  If þu wólt hem · tó þe táke. (D)

Type C is peculiarly influenced by the -*ë* at the cæsura. Thus verses 10 and 14 are the property of *C*, if the -*e* of *self*[*e*] be silent (cf. MS. A_1). Interpreting *þiselfë* and *himselfë* as original forms, the normal type claims the verse. The fluctuation between *A* and *C* is illustrated, verse 253, in the copyist's versions of the vigorous *steih: To héuene he stéih · þúrw his míhtë*. The five texts add a final -*ë*, supplying the more melodious *stéyë* (A_2) or *styë* (H_2).

Inflectional forms of the verb, to be regarded as monosyllabic or dissyllabic, open another channel for inexactness, thus *louëst* or *louest* is the reading of v. 13, v. 337, etc. Whether the arsis fall on the first or the second syllable of *redi* determines the classification of verses 92 (= 434); cf. type E.

After making allowance for elision, synizesis, hiatus, and slurrings of all kinds, there still remain verses that are uncertain in metrical structure.[1] Chaucer's pronunciation of *persones* justifies

---

[1] The peculiarly independent nature of each of the individual MSS. of the *Speculum* renders the question opened in textual and metrical study exceptionally perplexing.

the scansion of v. 206 : *þré persónes · in trinité*, with which compare v. 73 of the *Clerkes Tale: A fair persóne, · and stróng, and yóng of áġë*, but see also *The Erl of Tolous*, Lüdtke, p. 36, v. 2 : *Oónly gód and pérsons thré*.

The question of the legitimacy of the middle -ë- in *neih-e-bourę* involves the type of v. 535 : *ȝif þi néihëbóurę · misdoþ þé*, being in confliction with : *ȝif þi neih(e)bóurę misdoþ þé*, or *ȝif þi neih(e)bóurę · misdóþ þé*, the preferred form being *neihëbour*.

Illustrations of this character throughout the poem confirm the decision noted earlier, that the verse-types of the *Speculum* cannot be rigidly classified on basis of the accentual models of mediæval Romance poetry, but was adapted in rhythm to language susceptible to fluctuation through the influence of poetical aspiration and spiritual devotion.

In the study of the Bohemianism of this verse formation,[1] some attention is due to details in which the copyist was deficient in accuracy and faithfulness, and perhaps in intelligent understanding of his archetype. Although in some instances defect is incidental to the original, yet the scribe did not always understand the omission of the unstressed syllable. Thus the technique of verse 107, that stumbling-block to the scribe, illustrating the omission of the thesis in the fourth measure, is a dark mystery. MS. R tried to rectify the irregularity by the use of *vnto;* H_1 and H_2 tried to improve the metre by means of an adverbial modifier. Clearly the verse illustrates deficiency originating with the common archetype of all the MSS. MS. A_1 is to be unaltered.

Verse 341 reads in five MSS.: "But þu loue þyn cristene," *þyn* is wanting in A_1 alone. As exact translation, it is logically based on the Latin *proximum tuum* according to v. 338. Five MSS. recognize also the necessity logically if not metrically for *emcristene*, a form familiar to A_1 and D alone of the scribes. H_1 paraphrases *emcristene* with *neȝtbore*, 341 (*enemy*, 334). It is expanded to *euene crysten* by other copyists.

To the influence of the individual scribe,[2] with his varying sense of accuracy, must be reconciled some irregularity resulting in the omission of *here* v. 268, a reading preserved by H_1 and H_2. The error, that of haplography,[3] possibly originated through close associa-

---

[1] Among themselves the MSS. of this poem are peculiarly incongruous, increasing difficulty in determining the original form.
[2] Cf. Chaucer's *Wordes unto Adam, his owne Scriveyn*.
[3] *i. e.* lipography.

tion of two words distinct in meaning but the same in form. A_1 detected the incongruity, and attempted correction through the introduction of *here* in a second arrangement of the same line, later crossed out (cf. text, p. 14). Verso 269 is similar, where A_1 is also guilty of a careless substitution of *-es* (*fleshes*) for *-ly* of the original: *þurw sinne of fléschly · liking*. Five MSS. are answerable for *fleschly*.

In verse 89 the MSS. unite in the translation of *and* in the sense of *if* by the insertion of ӡ*ef*: *And* ӡ*éf þu wólt · haue gódes óre*, removing the verse from type D and re-classifying it as *A*. The latter reading seems to be correct.

Of hypotheses supplied by the scribe other examples are at hand. It has been deemed wise not to extend this discussion. Variants offer material for individual judgment. Textual notes will interest themselves in additional illustrations.

§ 4. *Treatment of the unstressed Syllable.*

It has been recognized, that the elemental measure contains one unstressed beat for every stressed syllable, but other combinations are employed. It is in this specific relationship that the verse distinguishes most sharply between standards of the poet Gower and those of the poet of the *Speculum*. Gower's rigid measurement of every syllable, forcing each to tally with its neighbour, found no sympathy even with Chaucer. But the better feeling of Chaucer did not permit him to introduce the double thesis with great frequency. Nor did the "halting metre" of Lydgate clog its steps with too heavy a burden of double thesis. The *Speculum* contains proof not only that a secondary unstressed syllable marks its rhythm, but that a measure may consist of arsis alone, the thesis being omitted for poetical effect or in the zeal inspired by the theme.

1. *The double thesis*. The double thesis is frequent in the first poetical measure, yet in this position as type E it may often clash with type D. That two unstressed syllables exist at the cæsura developing type B has been proved (*vide ante*). Two unstressed syllables are to be noted in other portions of the verse. The principal illustrations occur in the second measure.

v. 132. *hĕ nĕ mĭhtë;* 341, *þў̆n ĕmcrĭstenë;* 343, *mdĭtŏu lŏuĕ gód;* 356, *ŏf ă bŭsh;* 959, *ŏf þĕ cĭtë;* perhaps 670, *And who só bereþ poudre;* cf. also 255, 368?, 807? Probably to be read here are 92 and 474 (*vide ante*). 592 is excluded from the list, see Morsb. § 84, *Anm*.

Chapter XI.—Treatment of the Unstressed Syllable.

Probably to the fourth measure is to be traced the double thesis of verse 123 : *mourning in mód;* verse 150 (MS. A₁) is removed from classification in this division by slurring. Other conjectured instances of the double thesis in the fourth measure are generally not considered, on account of oft-quoted interference of elision, slurring, etc.; cf. verses 321, 469, 633, 873, 907, etc.

2. *Omission of the unstressed syllable.* An element of rhetorical significance characteristic of this verse is the omission of the unstressed syllable, emphasizing the narrative with dramatic picturesqueness through a "compensating pause," Guest, *Hist. of Engl. Rhythm.* The pause occurs:—

(1) In the first and second measures the conjunction being emphasized by accent as follows:

v. 563 : *Nóht, · if i dár it séië* (type D).

Compare other doubtful readings:

v. 398 : *Nay, nóman · mihtë dón þæt dédë.*
v. 973 : *Ne nóht · þát i mihte þe ʒíue.*

In Shakspere's time also the unemphatic monosyllable was permitted to occupy an emphatic place and to receive an accent, Abt, § 457. Shakspere strengthens a negative by the monosyllabic measure; cf. *Rich. II.* ii. 1. 148 : *Náy, · nóthing; áll is sáid.* And *Coriol.* iii. 3. 67 : *Náy · témperatelý; your prómise,* Abt, § 482, and p. 375. The first *virtue* prescribed for Guy of Warwick, verses 81 and 139, is conspicuous through the same medium:

Wís · dóm ‖ in gódës drédë (type D).

Continued exemplification of this dramatic canon designates significant passages : 86, 702, 734, etc.

(2) In the fourth measure. v. 673 : *Off mán hit fáreþ ‖ ríht · só;* 704 : *Dóþ a litël ‖ trés · pás.* Here the pause suggests the burden of responsibility and the seriousness of the preacher's message. v. 269 : *þurw sínne ‖ of fléschly lík · ing.* 502 with proper licence gains in emphasis when read: *Off hím ‖ and óf his gód · déde.* Compare also 85 (A₁), *miëknesse*? (inorganic -ë- is inserted in other MSS., cf. D *mekenes*); 86, *forʒíf · nés;* 390, *clér · té;* 107, *tó · mé;* 259, *tó · bé.* Fluctuating stress is possible, v. 259: *Hé þat wás woned to bé,* though the testimony of the copyists confirms *wóned* by the reading *wónt.* Compare also illustrations collected under type C. A₁ offers many instances of this type of verse, rectified in other MSS. through the insertion of an inorganic -ë- (cf. Sachse, *Das unorganische e im Orrmulum,* p. 63); cf. *sóþ-néssë,* 346, 411, 565.

Similar feature characterizes the versification of *The Erl of Tolous* (Lüdtke, p. 59), 83, 328, 403, etc.

The tonality of this application is indicative of power, giving in line 563 an impression of vigour, in 125 of sadness, in 81 of deep fervour, and in line 704 of solemnity. It is suggestive of the modern poetry of Robert Browning, infinitely dramatic in quality. It seems to be a deliberate purpose of the poet to embody through inner principle of language the character of the thought.

§ 5. *The Cæsura.*

The cæsura became an important factor in the hand of the poet. It seems to conform to two offices. Apart from its normal function, that of the metrical pause, it performs at the same time duties of emphasis. The effect of a pause after an emphatic monosyllable is similar to that of the omission of the unstressed syllable (*vide ante*), calling attention to the reading immediately preceding (cf. type C): 498, 517, *Iesu Crist;* 514, *lóue*, etc.; 494, *Óff þis wórd þat gód séide*, the emphasis marking *god*.

In general there exists considerable uniformity in the treatment of the cæsura. The epic cæsura (see type B) is not, as in Chaucer and Lydgate, of frequent occurrence. The cæsura may be discovered:

1. After the ictus of the first foot: 563. *Nóht, ‖ if i dúr it séie.* 697: *Hit sémeþ, ‖ þat hé haþ tréwe lóuë.* It occurs apparently in a colloquial usage, where the first measure is dissyllabic after *seide* 52, 68, 953; *seist* 555; *seiþ* 567; but also after a monosyllabic first measure: *Man* 481; *Lef* 866.

2. The cæsura in other positions. Lyrical cæsura occurs in some instances by the side of epic cæsura (see type B). The position of the typical pause is uniformly after the second ictus, but isolated exception, due rather to caprice than to deliberation, is exemplified, 520 *but Iblessëd; Coṁeþ* 423. Irregularity is to be noted in the following instances:

v. 617: Whij? ‖ fór þe kínde of þí manhódë.
v. 395: Mán, ‖ míhte hit éuere þánnë bé.
v. 523: Màn, ‖ íf þu wólt to mé herkný.

A pause offered by the cæsura seems demanded, though rarely, in two parts of the single verse: 431, 833, 982, etc.

§ 6. *Resolved Stress.*

Resolved stress,[1] fluctuating accent (*schwebende betonung, taktumstellung*), is determined on the one hand, objectively, through the natural accent of the individual word; on the other subjectively, through the rhetorical purpose of the specific verse. The rhetorical accent of the *Speculum* does not often clash with the rhythm, yet every measure cannot be regarded as a perfect unit, and stress must at times be divided between the word accent and the verse accent. This is exemplified particularly at the beginning of the verse and after the cæsura.

1. Beginning the verse:

   v. 43: Wìt óf clergíe · he hádde inóuh.
   v. 355: Hu Móyses hím sàuh, · wóltou héröʔ
   v. 950: Spàk tó Elíȝë · þe profétë.
   v. 972: Sìkér, she séide, · "bred háue i nón."

2. In the second section of the verse:

   v. 245: To sáuuö mán, · màn hé bicám.
   v. 349: þe fóurme · of þfe chìldrén he méttë.
   v. 414: þe cléne of hórte, · blòsséd þeih bé.[2]

The resolved stress is peculiarly applicable to individual words of Romance origin, where the accent was not at this period unalterably determined. Romance forms with the suffix *-aunce*, *-age*, etc., forms like *seruise, merci, res:un*, etc., where the primary word accent is no longer active, admit of fluctuation due to the conflict between English and French intonation. That *merci* of the present poem was subject to variable accent, is proved by metre. That the accent belongs at least once on the final syllable, is indicated by the riming form, *merci*[1]*: (herkny)* 524. To the contrary, *merci* in the following verses requires accent on the first syllable:

   v. 263: Mérci · néle he shéwö nón.
   v. 472: Gódës mércí · óf his sínnë.
   v. 532: Mérci wás þer · néuere uón.
   v. 545: Mérci gótestu · néuere nón.
   v. 567: Hé þat wóle · no mérci háuë.
   v. 568: On ýdel · dóþ he mérci cráuë.

[1] See Schipper, *Neuenglische Metrik*, vol. i., p. 32, natural emphasis is sacrificed to technical purpose.
[2] See also: "þe cléne of hértë, bléssęd þeih bé."

Verse 131, as illustration of type D, is open to speculation through variable accent:

v. 131 : Mercí he lés · þúrw þat sínnë.
Mérci hé lès · þúrw þat sínnë.

Resolved accent will be recognized also as hovering accent, and as wrenched accent was in use by Puttenham, *Arte of English Poesie*, and Gascoigne, *Notes of Instruction, Steel Glas*.

Consistent pronunciation is hardly possible at a time when laws were not more tangible, than is illustrated by Ben Jonson's rules, viz.: if a dissyllabic word be simple, it should be accented on the first syllable, but if derived from a verb, on the second; cf. *Abt*, § 490.

§ 7. *Slurring*.

Slurring[1] (*verschleifung*) in favour of the metre occurs, for instance:

1. At the cæsura: v. 934, *Fór so lítel · an álmesdédë.*—545. *Mérci gélestu · néuere nón.*—12. *Þu miht be siker · to héuene wéndë.* 264. *Ác, riht áfter · þat mán haþ dón.*—213. Also *after.*—Giving *after* two syllables: 876. *Ac riht áfter · þú hast dó.* A_1 and *R* preserve consistently the slurring and strengthen the claims of the verse to type A by the introduction of an additional syllable, *þat* following *after: Ác riht áfter · þat þú hast dó.* 345 illustrates slurring in a proper name: *þis séiþ sein Pówel · and béreþ witnéssë;* cf. Pogatscher.[2]

2. In the second measure: 218. *þe éuel to láte · and gód to tákë.* Parallel with *euere* (read *e'er*), *euel*[3] is monosyllabic through slurring, as was the Shaksperian usage, *Cymb.* V. v. 60 and I. i. 72 (*Abt*, § 466). Compare with *éuel*, in other measures (giving type A), 901, and *ýuël* (probably dissyllabic, type A) 15. Type C is confirmed by the slurred form *yuel* in verses 217, 228, 872, but the preferred reading gives two syllables. See also *evyll* in *Thomas of Erceldoune* (ed. Brandl) 379, *spéke none évyll of mé.* Other forms are also

---

[1] A moderated syncope resp. apocope, see Morsb., § 85, 5.
[2] Pogatscher gives explanation of *Powel* relatively to O.E. *au* in words of foreign origin, as follows: *Wenn Kons. + Liquida, oder Nasal. in den Auslaut tritt, kann im ae. aus silbebildender Liquida ein sekundärer Vokal entfaltet werden* (*Paulus*, O.E. *Páwel*, M.E. *Pówel*), § 275, and § 25 : *Vor silbebildendem r- oder -w im Auslaut, entsteht im ae. der Reibelaut w ; e. g.* M.E. *Pówel* < O.E. *Páwel* < *Paulus*, § 254.
[3] Compare the Elizabethan pronunciation of *devil* (Scotch *de'il*) with softening of the *-v-*; cf. Abt, § 466, with reference to *Macbeth*, IV. iii. 56 :
"Of hórrid héll can cóme · a dévil more dámn'd."

found: *wouder of* 149; *hunger and* 185; *Many a* 112, 369, 592; *Many and* 675; *Many on* 829.

3. In other measures: *euere omong* 186 occurs in the fourth syllabic measure; 44. *euere he* in the third measure. With a second slurring in the same verse occurs: *many on · euere amóng* 880.

Slurring is illustrated through inflectional forms: substantives: gen. in *-es: faderes* 254, 255; plu. in *-es: þewes* 97; in *en: children ifére* 978.—Verbs: in *-en: kepen his* 48; *comen him* 67; *comen* 240.—In *-est: louest* 13; in *-eþ: spekeþ* (cæsura) 275; *makeþ man* 124.

Wheiþer 219, 272, 536, 872, is to be read as a monosyllable, *whér;* cf. 219: *Wheiþer (whe'r) hé wole chése, · he háþ powér.* See Chaucer, *Monk's Prologue,* 3119; *Leg. of Good Women,* 1995; with Skeat's reference, l. 72, to Shakspere's 59th Sonnet, *Whe'er wé are ménded,* and Abt, *Sh. Gr.,* § 136 and § 466, with reference to *Tempest,* V. i. 111; *þider* 257; *Oþer* 175; *noþer* 862 are also to be regarded as monosyllabic.

§ 8. *Hiatus.*

The hiatus depends upon the preservation of unaccented final *-e,* before a word beginning with a vowel-sound, in positions where two vowels do not coalesce (cf. Skeat, *Leg. of Gd. Women,* 217), and where at times a conflict exists between type C or type A. The *Speculum,* availing itself of technical licence in favour of type A in distinction from type C, offers numerous examples of hiatus (*vide ante*); cf. as follows:

v. 266: To ióyë · ór to stróng turmént. (A)
v. 656: Þó to hóldë · ín þi pridë. (D)

The text is rich in such lines[1]; cf. 58, 68, 74, 109, 143, 145, 380, 409, 493, 495, 510, 651, 722, 743, 760, 792, 817, 845, 945, 1005. Elision (apocope) is not lost in the cæsura, as may be inferred from the following illustrations: 411, 413, 417, 721, 746, etc. Hiatus is possible in other measures:

v. 122: *Wickë ón · and wickë óþer.*
v. 1020: *Also ófte as þóu · maytȝ ȝéuë óuȝt.*

See 93, 106, 838, and possibly 600, 735, 904, etc.

---

[1] The association producing hiatus occurs before *h* as follows: 198, 419, 694, 789, 834, 895, 1028, 1029, etc. In this position the verse is to be distinguished from the Chaucerian system; cf. ten Br. § 270.

Inflectional -*n* retained in the infinitive excludes from consideration passages otherwise to be ranked in this class, for example: 181, 182, 188, 285, 292, 297, 405, etc. The introduction of final -*n* in the infinitive lessens the number of lines illustrative of hiatus; cf. 58, 74, 380, 743, etc. Verse 273 is improved by the addition of -*n*; *And þére biléuë[n] éuere mó.* See also 1005: *Now þu miht knówe[n] in þi mód.*

CHAPTER XII.
ON THE RIMING STRUCTURE OF THE *SPECULUM*.

§ 1. End Rime.

The rimes of the six MSS. of the *Speculum* are virtually the same, modified only in orthography through dialectical variations. They are in general adroitly handled, but are without great diversity or originality. Imperfect rimes occur through assonance.

Assonance.—The *Speculum* contains five illustrations of assonance: *ek* : *fet* 440; *cam* : *man* 590; *men* : *hem* 150; *wemme* : *brenne* 368; *vnderstonde* : *fonge* (corrected in D and R to *fonde*) 508. 826 offers in rime with *ariht*[1] (A_1), *white* A_2, *whiȝt* H_1, see Kluge, Pl. Grdr. I, p. 849. Compare also illustrations of Guy of Warwick (Ff. 2. 38), p. xiii., *hyt* : *nyght* 9505, and *ryght* : *ȝyt* 3209 (Zupitza's 3219, p. xiii.); str. 54: *delyt* : *plyt* (-*ght*) 93. : *spyt* 95. *Pearl* 90[7], and the *Rolandslied*, see Schleich, p. 26 *lyght* : *wit* 848; *erthe* : *hed* 101. Readily corrected by restoring the original reading is *þerwid* (read *þerwiþ*) : *griþ* 148.

Inexact rimes.—In some rimes practically perfect in the fundamental text, the vowels of corresponding syllables are dissimilar in instances, where the scribe's orthography and the author's do not correspond. The unimportant disagreement may be amended by a trifling change in orthography, since the consonants and consonantal groups following the vowel are identical. The accompanying forms are represented through illustrations from MS. A_1 : *e* : *i* (*y*): *forȝete* : *iwite* 194, : *wite* 764; *her* : *fyr* 452; *here* : *fire* 356; *seknesse* : *blisse* 188; *þisternesse* : *blisse* 114; *prest* : *Crist* 806.—*e* : *ei*: *drede* : *seide* 140, 494; *rede* : *scide* 168, 692.—*e* : *ie*: *answerede* : *heriede* 66.— *ei* : *i* : *eiȝe* : *liȝe* 828.—*u* : *e*: *turne* : *sterne* 436.—*a* : *o*: *gange* : *longe* 762.—*i* : *o*: *skile* : *wole* 712.—*i* : *u*: *gilt* : *ipult* 888; *aperteliche* :

---
[1] The poet undoubtedly spoke *riht* : *wiht*.

cxliv   Chapter XII.—Riming Structure of the Speculum.

muche 386 ; lihtliche : muche 672.—i : ui : flre : duire : 282.—o : u : worche : churche 860.—o : ou : noht : bouht 172, 226, : iwrouht 580, : souht 196, : þouht 32, 560, etc. These unimportant variations exist purely on the face of the MSS. and are without weight as regards the internal principle of the rime. A more or less successful attempt at correction of such errors has been offered by various scribes, who detected the inaccuracy.

Perfect rime.—Perfect rime is represented in both its classes; but this subdivision is to be modified in Teutonic words according to the interpretation of the syllabic value of final -*e*. If -*e* be regarded as silent, masculine rime predominates in the versification of the *Speculum;* while on the other hand, if -*e* be sounded, feminine rime is in excess in the proportion in general of 7 to 6. The discussion to follow will probably show that as in Chaucer (cf. Skeat, *Prioresses Tale*, p. lvii) and in contemporary poets (but see Schleich, *Ywain and Gawain*, pp. xxvii ff.) the dominant rime preserves the -*ë*, and in closer proportion relatively to the masculine rime than in the *Poema Morale* (Skeat, pp. lvii—lviii) and in *On God Ureisun of Ure Lefdi*, where the relationship of masculine rimes to feminine rimes stands perhaps as 10 to 150. Assuming that -*e* is to be pronounced, on basis of rimes recurring most frequently, perfect rime may be classified as follows :

1. *Masculine (strong, monosyllabic) rimes.*   (a) *Assonantal rimes.* In -*e :* be : þe 328, 334, 414, 536, 588 ; be : charite 96, 936, 1034 ; be : fle 834, 850 ; be : se 396, 534, 738, 752, 872, : (ise) 402, 730, : pite 260 ; me : se 190, : þe 108, 392, 550, 552, 556, 920, 1012 ; þe : bise 488 ; charite : me 56, 324, : þe 84, : be 96.—In -*i :* witerli : merci 458, 528 ; sikerli : empti 1002 ; lewedi : witerli 364.—In -*o :* also : do 10, 208, 898 ; do : to 68, 332 ; do : wo 484, 918 ; þo : mo 240, 1004. Numerous other examples might be included, in which this poem is prolific.   (b) *Consonantal rimes.*—In -*a :* al : þral 238 ; bicam : nam 246 ; cas : trespas 704 ; last : cast 636.—In -*e :* qued : ded 862, : red 48, 654 ; wel : katel 162, 578, 896, etc. ; power : ner 216.—In -*i :* wif : lyf 234, 702, 734 ; his : paradys 300 ; liht : niht 856.—In -*o :* forsok : tok 34 ; blod : rod 248 ; non : idon 546.—In -*oht :* bouht : noht 172 ; þouht : ouht 316 ; inouh : drouh 44. Here compare *Robert of Gloucester*, where *inou* rimes with *drou* 253, 269, 311, etc. (Wright's edition, *The Metrical Chronicle of Robert of Gloucester*, London). Compare also *Guy of Warwick*, Zupitza's fifteenth century edition, p. xiii : ynogh : too 10,859 ; ynowe : also 8953, and *Rolandlied*, enow : trowe 530, 1000 (Schleich, p. 28).

Chapter XII.—Riming Structure of the Speculum.

Feminine (weak, dissyllabic) rimes.—In *-a:* hauë : crauë 456, 530, 544, 568, 776; *take : forsake* 64, 100, 268, 498; *blame : shame* 778, 784, 812; *grace : face* 214, 904, *: place* 294.—In *-e:* clene : ene 366, 816; *clene : mene* 408, 824, 848; *sende : amende* 576, 952, *: spende* 990; *wende : ende* 12, 426; *leres : teres* 842; *here : ifere* 296, 978.—In *-i:* wille : stille 584, 594, 706, 892; *sinne : winne* 132, 472, 684, 694, 846, 1008; *sinne : biginne* 902; *sinne : widinne* 118; *sinne : inne* 732.—In *-o:* more : lore 24, 36, 740, 756, 854, 912, 928; *more : sore* 470; *broþer : oþer* 74, 122.—In *-ou:* mouþe : nouþe 420, 480; *founde : wounde* 774; *stounde : bounde* 710; *wrouhte : bouhte* 26.

Triple rime.—A single couplet in triple rime is preserved,[1] probably incidental to the poet: *dampnáción : sauuáción* 788.

Rimes in -y : -yë.—The *Speculum*, agreeing with the system of Chaucer, is free from the riming combination *-y : -yë;* cf. ten Brink, *Chaucer Studien*, pp. 22 ff., and Pabst, *Robt. of Gloucester*, pp. 99, 100. Distinction is here marked between this poem and texts of Lydgate (cf. Schick, p. lxii) and of *Guy of Warwick* (MS. Ff. 2. 38, cf. Zupitza, p. xiv), where rimes *charyté : sekerlyë* 5367; *companyë : thre* 3865, etc. are recorded. Concerning the rime *chivalry : Gy*, *The Rime of Sir Thopas*, v. 209, cf. Skeat's note.

Rimes of -cons. : -cons. + ë.—The poet was virtually accurate and logical in the use of final *-e*. The rime *goþ(e) : loþe* 448 is the most noticeable exception. The questionable *god : rod* 144, *goþe : loþe* 448, *quede : fede* 1026, are treated under inflection. *miht : sihte* 362 is withdrawn from discussion, because of the existing conditions of the poem, ascribing forms in *-ë (e)* to the dative of the substantive; cf. *Inflection of substantives*. The *Roland Lied* offers example to the contrary in the treatment of *cons. : cons. + ë;* cf. *shal : alle* 17; *place : has* 413, 714, and other examples. See Schleich, *Prolegomena ad Carmen de Rolando Anglicum*, p. 4.

Cheap rimes.—Cheap rimes are introduced in abundance in correspondences of identical riming suffixes :— *-aunce : -aunce* 92, 474, 572, etc.; *-é : -é* 96, 390, 678, etc.; *-hede : -hede* 372; *-(n)esse : -(n)esse* 306, 346, 412, etc.; *-liche : -liche* 146, 416, 442, 606, 718, 798, 822, etc.; *-ing : -ing* 278, 314, etc.; *-oun : -oun* 788, etc. Self-riming suffixes in *-ence* and in *-ful* are not represented in the system of the *Speculum*.

[1] The mediæval poet was rarely ambitious in his rhythmical composition to make current higher attainment than that of correspondences in feminine rime; cf. *Poema Morale*, *Guy of Warwick*, *Sir Beues*, *Patience*, etc.

cxlvi *Chapter XII.—Riming Structure of the Speculum.*

Double rimes.—*eiȝe* (O.E. *ēāge*) riming with *heie* (O.E. *hēah*) 388, on one hand, occurs also in rime with *liȝe* (O.E. *lēāȝ*) 828, suggesting a double form, but not proving its existence. Double forms of *have* are assured in rime *haue* : (*craue*) 455, 529, 543, etc., *haue* : (*saue*) 477 and *habbe* : (*gabbe*) 463 are preserved by the poet.

Rich rimes.—*acord* : *descord* 514 ; *anon* : *non* 972. Identical in form but different in construction are *mynë* (simple poss.) : *mynë* (absolute poss.) 340. The definite verb form *was* rimes with itself in the negative *nas* 360. Over this usage, as illustrated by Chaucer, compare ten Brink, § 330. The rime occurs in *R. of Gl.* (cf. edition of Wright) 254, 564, 656, etc. Many instances are recorded.

Of the numerous riming arts (cf. Kluge, *Zur Geschichte des Reimes im Altgermanischen*, Beiträge, vol. ix—x) lending richness and variety to the Chaucerian verse (cf. ten Brink, pp. 190 ff.), and to the systems of contemporary poets, the ten hundred rimes of the *Speculum* afford but limited scope for illustration. Of broken rimes, a class of which there are two illustrations in *Sir Beues* (see Kölbing, p. xii), v. 2928, 3423, two in *R. of Gl.* (see Pabst, § 4, with reference to *Anglia* IV, 479), v. 2481, 6575, several in *Guy of Warwick*, there occurs not an instance. No identical rime comes to light. The use of light endings by the poet, forms of *be, can*, etc., is attested to in the paragraph over *perfect rime*.

Although the dominant rime throughout is end rime, yet interior rime as illustrated by middle rime and sectional rime, and alliteration, are to be traced.

Middle rime.—It is illustrated as follows :

    v. 969 : Dó, he *seidë*,[1] · bé my *réd*[*ë*][2]
    v. 495 : þere í þe *findë*,[3] · i wólę þe *bindë*.
    v. 315 : Ne lát hit *nóht*[4] · come ín þi þóuht.
    v. 999 : Ne dréd þe *nóht*[4] womman, · ín þi þóuht.

Sectional rime.—A single instance of sectional rime is incidental to the verse of the *Speculum*, probably without the deliberate purpose of the poet :

    v. 174 : For *whán* a *mán* · haþ sínnë dó.

Read with fluctuating accent, verse 919 illustrates sectional rime :

    Lóuë frend, *herknè* to *mé*.

---

[1] Read *sede*, the poet's form ; cf. *se(i)de* : *rede* 168, 691.
[2] This is indeed questionable, but on some grounds justifiable.
[3] Read *findë*, the verse illustrating type B with hiatus at the cæsura.
[4] Read *no(u)ht*.

§ 2. *Alliteration.*

Alliteration, as embodying an underlying and elemental principle, a form of consonantal rime representative of the native English system, the direct correlation of Teutonic literature, has been lost in the verse of the *Speculum*. Not even sufficient mechanical link remains to connect this poem with that noble alliterative group of the " West Cuntre," whose " literary ancestors were Cædmon and Cynewulf," and whose latest minstrel was the Gawain poet; see Professor Thomas in her Zürich dissertation *Sir Gawayne and the Green Knight*,[1] and Dr. Trautmann,[2] *Ueber Verfasser einiger allit. Gedichte ;* see also Gollancz,[3] *Pearl*, p. xx.

But though the poet[4] cannot "geste—rom, ram, ruf—by lettre,"[5] yet his usage of alliteration occurs sometimes unconsciously, accepting formulæ common to the language of poetry and practical life in the century. Occasionally an example seems introduced deliberately according to literary standards for the purpose of ornament. As a rule one alliterative syllable occurs in the first half line, *i. e.* before the cæsura, one in the second. A line may have two alliterating syllables in the second half line and none in the first. In general, alliteration as here illustrated unites words connected by some normal syntactical relationship. The association is as in Chaucer based on metrical accent in preference to logical or word accent. The alliterative principle is illustrated in combinations as follows:

1. *Verb and object.*[6]—(*a*) Derived from distinct radicals: v. 28 *t*ale · ȝou *t*elle.—42 · *l*yf he *l*adde.—463 *h*ope · . . . *h*abbe (*h*aue). 477.—689, 690 *h*aue · *h*ope · to *h*euene blisse.—464 sey · þe soþ.— 983 · *m*ak me *m*ete. See also 35 *l*ouede (god · and) his *l*ore. (*b*) Presenting an etymological relationship between verb and cognate

---

[1] In *Sir Gawayne and the Green Knight.* 'A Comparison with the French *Perceval*, preceded by an Investigation of the Author's other Works, and followed by a Characterization of Gawain in English Poems.' By M. Carey Thomas (President of Bryn Mawr College). Zürich, 1883 (Zürich dissertation).

[2] *Ueber Verfasser und Entstehungszeit einiger alliterirender Gedichte des Altenglischen.* By Moritz Trautmann. Halle, 1876.

[3] Cf. *Pearl*, an English poem of the fourteenth century, edited by I. Gollancz, London, 1891, where the same topic receives attention, p. xlii.

[4] The *Speculum* would stand as a link of perhaps one hundred (at least fifty) years nearer this O.E. ancestry than the poet of *Pearl*, if Trautmann's theoretical date for the Gawain-group be final, 1370—80 (p. 33), or Gollancz's be preferred to Morris's (*Early English Alliterative Poems*, E. E. Text Society, 1864), in *Sir Gawain and the Green Knight*, whose title-page is dated 1320—30.

[5] *Prologe of the Persones Tale*, v. 43.

[6] A point indicates the position of the cæsura, marking the relationship of the alliterative syllable relatively to the half-line, in legitimate descent from the native alliterative construction.

noun : 50 · *s*ente his *s*onde.—549 *m*et · as þu *m*etest me.—859, 860 *w*orche Godes *w*erkes.—398 · *d*on þat *d*ede.—674 *d*edes · þouh he *d*o.—Verb and attribute : 45 · *w*as wel *w*ar.

2. *Verb with substantive limitation by means of preposition.*— v. 38 *l*iuede · in *l*awe.—232 (out of) *p*aradys · he was *p*ylt.—255 *s*it · on *s*ide.—411 *s*elf · *s*eide in *s*oþenesse.—719 *m*iht · in þi *m*od.—779 for *s*hame · . . . *s*hewe.—780, 781 *s*hewed · to *s*haftes.—804 for *s*hame · *s*howe.—812 *b*ringeþ · in *b*lame.—818 wid *w*ater men *w*assheþ. —831 *w*eneþ · *w*asshe wid þat *w*ater.—888 Into *p*ine · *i*pult.—978 mot *m*ake · of *m*ete.—1014 · *s*eide in *s*oþenesse.—1029 To þat *b*lisse · *b*ryng. Alliteration through cognate words : 19 at his *w*ille · he *w*ole.—405 *s*en · in *s*iht.—733 *l*iueþ · in *l*yf.

3. *Verb limited by the adverb.*—v. 145 *l*ate · al on*l*iche.—179 here · *h*olde *l*owe.—312 *w*ete þu *w*el.—637 *w*el *w*ite. 763.—895 *w*ot *w*el.—941 *w*ite it *w*el. 1017.—609 *s*eie · *s*oþeliche.—821 *s*eie · *s*ikerliche. Without direct grammatical relationship : 62 *l*ad · to *l*onge while.

4. *Verb and substantive.*—v. 368 þe *b*ush · mihte *b*renne. Alliteration uniting cognate forms : 879, 880 *g*ilour · *g*ileþ; cf. 431 *g*ostes, · *g*oþ. See also 447-8.

5. *Attributive adjective and substantive.*—v. 469 *s*innes · *s*ore.— 576 þi *s*eli *s*oule · .—744 þe *l*onge *l*yff · .—752 *g*iltes · *g*rete.—938 *m*ore · *m*ede.—980 *m*ete · *m*ore.

6. *Substantive in a relationship dependent on an associated word for its direction.*—v. 123 *m*ourning in *m*od.—211 *s*happere · of alle *s*haftes.—622 of *m*artyrdom · þe *m*ede.—690 *h*ope · to *h*euene blisse.—745 *d*rede · of *d*omes day.—770 *p*rest · tak þi *p*enaunce.— 868 *d*oiing · þi *d*omesday.—998 To þe *w*idewe · *w*ordes swete.

7. *Substantive and substantive.*—v. 158 · *p*ompe and *p*ride.—303 *k*unning · and *k*ointise.—400 *l*ered · and *l*ewed.—652 to *h*euene · or to *h*elle; cf. on · and oþer 74 and 122.

8. *Adjective and adjective.*—v. 381 *c*lene · and *c*ler.—574 *m*eke · and *þ*olemod. 666.

9. *Adverb and adverbial phrase producing tautology.*—v. 426 euere · widouten ende.

10. *Unclassified expressions.*—146 Nis nouht inouh.—157 *H*ele of *b*odi · in *b*on and *h*uide.—351 *t*okne · i *t*elle þe.—356 *f*ourme · al on *f*ire.—499 ofte · in orisoun.—618 *W*olde haue *w*reche · of *w*rongful dede.—669 *f*areþ · we *f*inde · .—742 ȝeueþ him grace · of *g*ostli.— 857 *l*yf · is cleped *l*iht.—858 *d*eþ · þe *d*erke niht.

CHAPTER XIII.
ON THE PHONOLOGY OF THE *SPECULUM*.

"that none miswrite þe."[1]

IN this study of the phonology of the *Speculum*, every riming couplet has been consulted. A verse-number refers to the single illustration or to both members of the strophe. In the latter instance it cites the line containing the second of the pair of rimes, irrespective of arrangement. If the rime quoted occur more than three times in the same combination, the fact is indicated by the sign *etc.* following the third verse-number. The investigation[2] begins always with the vowel of the text A_1. This vowel heads every sectional division of the argument. The study passes from the short sound of the vowel to the long, and concludes in each instance with its combination in diphthongs. Forms bearing secondary stress are not examined. The classification is not influenced nominally by the division "high vowels," "low vowels," and "mid vowels." Both members of each couplet are uniformly introduced, and marks of parenthesis inclose that element not immediately necessary to the subject under discussion. The orthography has for its basis MS. A_1, and reproduces the form occurring first in that text. Phonetical variations introduced by other scribes are not in general mentioned.

ă.

§ 1. Sources of short[3] *a* (*ă*) of the *Speculum* are English and Scandinavian.

A. Old English sources.

1. O.E. *a* (*ǫ*) corresponding uniformly to: (*a*) O.E. *a* (*ǫ*) before single nasals: *man* (cf. Brugmann, 180) : *bigan* 224 ; *man* : *can* 728 ; *cam* : *man* 590 ; *bicam* : *nam* 246 ; possibly also *ď* in *gange* : (*longe*) 761. In the study of *cam*, see *com* (O.E. *cóm* for *cwómon ;* Orrm, *cŭmm*) 250, 480, not confirmed by rime. Cf. Sweet, *Anglia,* vol. iii., p. 152 ; *Anglia*, vol. xiii., p. 214 ; Morsb., *Gram.*, § 90, Anm. 5 ; § 93, Anm. 2 ; p. 68, Anm. 4 ; ten Br., *Ch.*, § 12, Anm. 1 ; Menze, *O. M. Dialect*, p. 12 ; and Murray, *Engl. Dictionary*

---

[1] Chaucer, *Troilus* 1809.
[2] At the request of Professor Schick the arrangement of the following chapter is based upon the dissertation of Felix Pabst : *Lautlehre des Robert von Gloucester.*
[3] Criteria for determining the quantity of the vowels are not abundant in the *Speculum*. General laws of historical development rather than the immediate context have often governed the decisions of the editor.

Chapter XIII.—On the Phonology of the Speculum.

under *come*. (*b*) O.E. *a*, Gc. *a* in a closed syllable; Goth. *ai*-class, Morsb., p. 136, Anm. 2 : *habbe* : (*gabbe*) 463.

2. O.E. *a* (*ea*) : (*a*) Before *l* or *l* + a consonant : *alle* (O.E. *eall*) : *bifalle* (inf.) 292; *alle* : (*calle*) 521; *al* : (*smal*) 869; *al* : (*þral*) 237. (*b*) Following a palatal : *shaftes* (O.E. *gesceaft*[1]; cf. Sievers, *Gram.*, § 261) : (*craftes*) 211.

3. O.E. *æ* from Germc. *ă* in closed syllables : *faste* (adv.) : (*agaste*, inf.) 865; *was* : *nas* (*Pabst*, § 10 f.) 360; *hadde* (through assimilation) : (*ladde*) 41; *smal* (M.E. *smā-le* in open syllables; see ten Br., *Ch.*, § 27 β; *Sir Fir.* 2274) : (*al*) 870; *war* (uninflected adjective; cf. *Pabst*, p. 17) : *bar* (pret.; cf. *war* : *bar*, *Genesis and Exodus*, l. 1308, and *R. of Gloucester*, l. 6012) 46; *craftes* : (*shaftes*) 212.

4. O.E. *ǽ* shortened in open syllables before different consonant groups : *agaste* (inf. N.E. *aghast* pp., first used in 1700) : (*faste*, adv.) 866; *ladde* (ten Br., § 6 β) : (*hadde*) 42.

B. Scandinavian sources.

1. Scand.[2] *a* : *gabbe* (Ic. *gabba*, N.E. *gab*, *gabble*, *jabber*) : (*habbe*) 464; *calle*[3] (Ic. *kalla*, O.E. *ceallian*, cited once; cf. Murray's *Dictionary* under *call*; cf. Brugmann 585) : (*alle*) 522; *cast* (O.N. *kasta*) : *last* (cf. Ic. *löstr*, Goth. **lah-stus*) 636.

With *cast* compare *kest* (MS. A_1, *kast* in R) 992, not in rime, for illustration of interchange of *a* and *e*, sporadic in words of Old Norse origin; see Morsb., *Gram.*, p. 119, § 87, Anm. 2, and Schleich, *Carmen de Rolando Anglicum*, p. 9.

2. O.N. *ǽ* : *þral*, *tharll* H_2 (O.N. *þrǽll*) : (*al*) 238.

gange (read *gonge*) : (*longe*) 761, *vnderstande* : *honde* 1021, are discussed under *o*-rimes; *knowelache* (read *knoweleche*) : (*speche*) 509, *knowelaching* (not in rime) 725, under *e*-rimes.

ā.

§ 2. Long *a* (*ā*) corresponds :

A. In words of English origin.

1. To O.E. *ă* in open syllables, lengthened 1250 (?) : (*a*) Before a nasal (cf. Morsb., §§ 64, 90) : *agramed* (cf. *Guy of W.*; *King Alis.*) :

---

[1] Exceptional form without *i*-umlaut.
[2] Naturally the long vowel of an Old Norse word is marked by the acute accent (') in distinction from the diacritical marks indicating length classified, chapter V., § 3.
[3] See Kluge, "Sprachhistorische Miscellen," *Beiträge*, vol. x. p. 442.

Chapter XIII.—On the Phonology of the Speculum.

(*ashamed*) 794; *name* (O.E. *noma, nama*) : (*fame*) 30, 39. Here may be classed also *a* from O.E. *eo, ea*: *ashamed* : (*agramed*) 793; *ashamed* : (*blamed*) 766; *shame* (O.E. *sceomu, sceamu*) : (*blame*) 777, 783, 811. (*b*) Before a single consonant except nasals : *forsake* : (*take*) 64, 72, 99, etc.; *make* (O.E. *macian*, 1250 *māke*, 1650 *méke*) : *quake* (O.E. *cwacian*) 444; *make* : (*take*) 217, 582; *made* (O.E. *macode*) : *hade* (cf. ten Br., § 27 β) 244; *make* : *sake* 986; *sake* : (*take*) 595; *haue* (inflectional form; cf. Curtis, *Anglia* xvi., *Clariodus*, § 1) : (*craue*, inf.) 456, 530, 544, etc.; *haue* (2 sing.) : (*saue*) 477; *fare* (inf.) : þare (cf. Ѽra, Sievers, *Gram.*, § 321, Anm. 2) 954; *fare* (inf.) : (ȝare) 490. For the rime *fare* : þare see illustrations, *Sinners Beware*, str. 36; *Owl and Nightingale*, (ed. Stratmann) 995, 996, and additional references Morsbach, p. 86; Pabst, *Rbt. v. G.*, p. 20, Anm. 2; Carstens, *Sir Firumbras*, p. 22.

2. To O.E. *æ*: *water* : *later* (in *neuere þe later*) 832, 930. For the question of the influence of *r* in preserving this lengthening, cf. ten Br., § 16 β, 27 β 1; Morsb., *Gram.*, pp. 84, 92 *a*, and 93 *c*.

3. To O.E. *ea* : ȝare (O.E. *gearu*) : (*fare*) 489.

B. In loan-words.

1. Words of Old Norse origin : O.N. *a*: *take* (O.N. *taka*; cf. Goth. *tēkan*) : (*forsake*) 63, 71, 100, etc.; *take* : (*sake*) 596; *take* : (*make*) 218, 581; *craue* (equivalent cognate, Ic. *krefja*) : (*haue*) 456, 530, 544, etc.

2. Words of Romance origin :

(1) French[1] *a* in open syllables. (*a*) Before nasals : *blame* : (*shame*) 778, 784, 812; *blamed* : (*ashamed*) 765; *fame* : (*name*) 29, 40. (*b*) Before a single consonant except nasals : *face* : *grace* 214, 904; *grace* : *place* 294; *saue* (A.F. *sauver, saver* < L.L. *salvāre* < L. *salvus*; cf. Sk. II. 54. 1; 82. 5., p. 232; cf. *sauuacioun* (800), O.F. *au* > *a* + *lc*) : (*haue*) 478.

(2) French *a* in closed syllables. (*a*) Before mute + liquid : *profitable* : *fable* 4; *fable* : *merciable* 526. (*b*) Before a final *-s* (*-z*): *trespaz* : *solaz* 686; *trespas* : *cas* 704; *cas* : *solas* is employed by Chaucer, 23, 797, 798.

The rimes enumerated in § 2 indicate that M.E. *ă* had been lengthened before the composition of the *Speculum*, demonstrated as valid by the fact that stable *ā* of French origin rimes with *a* from

---

[1] In the study of the phonology of the *Speculum*, the abbreviation *A. F.* will represent Anglo-French, *O.F.* Old French.

clii Chapter XIII.—On the Phonology of the Speculum.

O.E. ă. 1250 is the date ascribed by Menze (p. 11) as in general the period, when the lengthening of ă occurred in English poems. The first half of the 13th century is given by Morsbach, § 64; and the second half of the 13th century by Curtis, *Clariodus*, § 42. This fact would determine relatively to the chronology of the *Speculum*, that the poem may be placed in a period later than 1250. The pronunciation of the vowel in this position is probably as in Chaucer a pure *a*-sound; see Morsb. § 88.

For ă before a lengthening consonant-group, the sporadic form *gange* in rime with *longe* 761 is no criterion. *gange* is explained by Morsbach, § 90, p. 123, as an exceptional instance in which the vowel-sound shifts easily to an earlier condition. In general O.E. *ā* had already developed a M.E. *ō*; cf. §§ 15, 16, 17.

ay.

§ 3. *ay* of the text is developed from:

1. O.E. *æ* + *g*: *day* : *lay* 250; *day* : *may* 492; *day* : (*nay*) 251; *domesday* : (*nay*) 257, 868; *domesday* : (*ay*) 745. A single link between *ai*- and *ei*-sounds of the poem is preserved in the couplet, *fain* (O.E. *fægen*; cf. Skeat, § 252) : (*aȝein*, O.E. *ongegn*, Merc. *ongægn*) 873, 965. *mait* : (*caiht*) 881 is probably to be classified in § 3, 1. *mait* seems to unite the grammatical forms (*ic*) *may* (*mæg*) and (*þu*) *miht*, combining the properties of both in the composite (*þu*) *mai(h)t*; cf. also *mait* (*mayt* in *D*) 342, and 882 in *D*, and *maytȝ* 1020, 1021. Compare Carstens, *Sir Firumbras*, p. 10, § 2; Schleich, *Carmen de Rolando*, p. 10.

2. O.N. *ei* : *nay* : (*day*) 252; *nay* : (*domesday*) 258, 867; *ay* : (*domesday*) 746.

3. Fr. Pic. *a* (*æ*) + *h* : *caiht* : (*mait*) 882. The double forms *caiht* and *ikauht* (cf. l. 17) are explained through analogy with *leiht* and *lauht*, *teihte* and *tăhte*, etc. (cf. Carstens, p. 10), depending upon a cognate development through *ā* and *ǣ*; cf. Morsb., *Gram.*, § 102, Anm. 5; ten Br., § 113 *δ* and § 182. *caiht* bears the relationship to *cauht* (pp. of *cachen*, written also *cacchen*, Pic. *cachier*), that *leiht* bears to its doublet *laught* from *geleaht* (inf. *lacchan*, (*ge*)*læccan*) and *teihte* to *tăhte* (O.E. *tǽc(e)an*); cf. Sievers, § 407, *a*, 4; *b*, 8; Skeat, II., § 140; Pabst, § :3, *d*; Carstens, pp. 21, 39; Schleich, *Carm. de Rol.*, p. 10. The development of the vowel is similar in *streight* < *streaht* and *eighte* < *eahta*; cf. Pabst, § 40, *a* and *b*. Compare *ikeiht*, *Ancren Riwle* (ed. Morton), pp. 134, 278, 332, etc.; *keihte*

Chapter XIII.—On the Phonology of the Speculum.

(pret.) p. 154; (*bi*)*keihte* : (*eihte*), *Poema Morale*, Trinity and Jesus MSS., 318, but *kehte* : (*aehte*), Egerton MS.; *R. of G. ycaʒt* : (*naʒt*) 4372, : *caʒte* 320; *Pearl*, *caght* : (*saght*), : (*faght*), str. 5^2, and *by-taghte* : (*saghte*, *naghte*), str. 101^7; *King Horn*, *taʒte* : *laʒte* 248.

au.

§ 4. *au*, written *aw* before a vowel, is developed from:

1. O.E. *a + g*: *dawe* (O.E. *dagum*, dat.) : (*lawe*) 37, 357; *drawe* : (*lawe*) 945; *drawe* : *plawe* (O.E. *plaga*) 16. *plawe* exists as cognate of *pleye* (O.E. *plega*), cf. *R. of G.* 11195, developed through O.E. *plagian* or O.N. *plaga*. See *plawe* : (*knawe*), *Havelok*, l. 950; but *pleye* : (*weie*), l. 953. The form is not frequent. It occurs in *King Horn*, MS. II (cf. Wissmann, *Quellen und Forschungen*, No. xlv.), *plawe* : (*felawe*) 1112, and *R. of G.* 5906; cf. Pabst, § 42, and Leo, *Angelsächsisches Glossar* (1872), column 92. Further, see Bosw.-Toller, *plagia, plagadun*, with reference to *Rush. Gloss.*, 11, 17; see Sievers, § 407, 5. Ettmüller illustrates derivatives from *plegan, *Lexicon Anglosaxonicum*, pp. 274-5. The riming form *knawe* : (*lowe*) 180 is classified under rimes in *ou*, § 18.

2. Of O.N. origin are: (*a*) O.N. *au* developed from *d* before *ht*: *drauht* (*draht*; cf. O.N. *dráttr*) : (*ikauht*) 18. (*b*) O.N. *a + g*, written *aw* before a vowel sound : *lawe* (O.E. *lagu* from O.N. *lǫg* < *lagu) : (*dawe*) 38, 358; *lawe* : (*drawe*, inf.) 946.

3. *au* in Romance forms : (*a*) O.F. *a + u* interpolated before a nasal group: *repentaunce* : *penaunce* 92, 474, 770, and 830 in H_2; *suffraunce* : *destourbaunce* 572. (*b*) Fr. Pic. *a + h*: *ikauht* (< *caht*, pp. O.F. *cacchen*, Pic. *cachier*) : (*drauht*) 17. *ikauht* is developed through analogy with the parallel form *ilauht* = *gelæht*, *ilacchen* < *gelæccan*; cf. *gelæhte* in *Samson*, *Ælfric's Book of Judges*, chap. xiv. 5, and see Skt., *Ety.* II. 140. Cf. *kacche* (*cage* in D) 903 and Varnhagen, *Anglia*, vol. III., p. 376.

ĕ.

§ 5. Short *e* (*ĕ*) is found:

A. *In words of O.E. origin.*

1. O.E. *e* < *a* (*i*-umlaut). (*a*) Before nasals or nasal-groups: *wemme* : (*brenne* in assonance) 367; *nempt* : (*dempt*) 135; *men* (assonance) : (*hem*) 149, but *mon* : *hom* in *R*. Probably *ĕ* characterizes the accented vowel of the following words: *ende* (inf.) : *wende* (inf.) 12; *ende* (sb.) : *wende* (inf.) 426; *sende* (3, sing. pret.) :

Chapter XIII.—*On the Phonology of the Speculum.*

(*amende*) 575, 951; *sende* (3, sing. pret.) : *spende* (inf.) < mediæval Latin *spendere*, but already O.E., 990. (*b*) In other combinations: *helle* (sb.) : *dwelle* (inf.) 450; *helle* : (*nelle*) 271; *dwelle* (O.H.G. *twaljan*) : *telle* (inf.) 28, 284; *answerede* (read *answéred* or *answérde*) : *heriede* (Goth. *hazjan*) 66. Possibly to be classed under this head are rimes in the suffix -*nesse* : *mieknesse* : *forʒifnes* 86; *fairnesse* : *þisternesse* 306; *witnesse* : *soþnesse* 346, 412, 566, 664, etc.; cf. concluding note and rimes in *i*. *e* before nasal groups (*vor dehnenden consonanten-gruppen*) is classified as long by various Anglicists, see Bülbring, *Eng. Stud.*, vol. xx., pp. 149 ff. and in *Litt. Blatt*, 1894, column 262; De Jong, *Eng. Stud.*, vol. xxi., pp. 321 ff.; Curtis, *Clariodus*, § 175; Morsb., *Gram.*, § 110, also p. 75 : Orrm seems to employ both *ĕ*- and *ē*- before -*nd*, but Robert of Gloucester illustrated only the short vowel, Pabst, § 14. In the *Speculum e* before *n* + *d* seems to be short, pronounced *ẹ̆*, decisive evidence being the rime *sende* : *amende* 575, 951.

2. O.E. (Germ.) *ë* : *werk* (sb.) : (*clerk*) 668; *wel* (adv.) : (*katel*, *catel*) 161, 578, 895, etc.; *wel* : *godspel* (see Bright, *Mod. Lang. Notes*, April 1889, Feb. 1890) 518, 548. To the study of *wel*, Bülbring has contributed, *Litt. Blatt*, 1894, p. 261; Pabst, § 15, m.

3. O.E. *ē* shortened before double consonants: *mette* : *grette* 350, 960; *dempt* : (*nempt*) 136.

4. O.E. *éā* before consonant groups: *hext* (O.E. W.S. *héahst*, *híehst* (from Angl.), *héhst* > *héxt* > *hĕxt*) : *next* (O.E. W.S. *néahst*, Angl. *néhst* > *néxt* > *nĕxt*) 326, 662; cf. Pabst, § 14, n), and Sievers, § 313 and Note.

5. O.E. *eo* (< *i*), breaking before the full vowel (*vor dunklem vocal*) in the following syllable: *henne* (O.E. *heonane*, *hinona) : (*kenne*) 297; *hem* (*heom*, him) : (*men*) 150.

6. O.E. *i* (*y*) : *nelle* : (*helle*) 272.

B. In loan words.

1. Of O.N. origin : *brenne* (through metathesis < O.E. *bærnan* caus. = *beornan*; cf. *brenna*) : (*wemme*) 368; *kenne* (O.N. *kenna*, see Skt. *Dict.*) : (*henne*) 298. Here belongs *eging* (Ic. *eggja*, Orrm. 11675) 229; see Brate, *Nordische Lehnwörter im Orrmulum, Beiträge* x., p. 37.

2. Of Romance origin. (*a*) Before *n* + consonant: *amende* : (*sende*) 576, 952; *iugement* : *turment* 266; *verreement* : *iugement* 878. *amende* is determinative in the conclusion, that *e* before -*nd*

Chapter XIII.—On the Phonology of the Speculum.

was not yet lengthened in the present text. (*b*) In words ending in -*el*: *katel* (*catel*) : (*wel*) 162, 577, 896, etc.

3. Ecc. Lat. *e*; *clerk* : (*werk*) 667, according to Skeat (*Dict.*) directly from Lat. *clericus*, or through O.F. *clerc*.

For the suffix -*nesse*, see rimes in *i*, the recurring couplet, *blisse* : -*nesse* removing these groups from the territory of the phonology of *e*- sounds. *witnisse* : *sopnisse* are probably the authorized forms for the poem; see Kluge, *Stammbildung*, and Morsb., § 109, Anm. 6. This transmission of the -*i*- sound, -*nisse* for -*nesse*, would classify the *Speculum* as belonging to the literature of the earlier M.E. period, see parallel instance in the early poem, *David the King*, where *meknisse* occurs in rime with *blisse*, l. 3, and *The Liif of Adam*, combining *thesternisse* : *lihtnisse* (proving no definite truth) 355 and 549.

Pabst, § 20, refers -*e*- (*e.g. u*), of *stede*, to a form, where the *e* was not yet lengthened, basing his conclusions on absolute riming formulæ. The lengthening seems to have occurred in the *Speculum*. *stede* : *dede* 598, 604, possibly to be treated as transitional forms in the development of language, may be read *stide* : *dide*, see Streitberg, *Urgerm. Grammatik*, p. 44, Anm. 1.

$\bar{e}$.

The riming system of the *Speculum* is characterized by two qualities in the development of long *e* ($\bar{e}$) and long *o* ($\bar{o}$). With reference to $\bar{e}$, the distinction is based on the development of O.E. *êa*, *œ* (umlaut of Germc. *ai*), and *ê* (lengthened from *ĕ*) on the one hand, and of O.E. stable *é*, *éo*, and *œ* (Germ. *á*, Goth. *ê*) on the other. The classification is recognized by the poet, the former division being extant in a long open $\bar{e}$ ($\bar{ę}$); the other $\bar{e}$ is, *à priori*, a long closed $\bar{e}$ ($\bar{ẹ}$). The uniformity of the observance of the law is not violated by the occurrence of a sporadic rime uniting the open and the closed vowel (cf. § 8), designating, according to Zupitza, an incident in rime-formation, rather than the violation of the purity of the rime. A third class of rimes in long *e* (cf. ten Brink, § 25) will not be considered in the following paragraphs. The O.E. *œ* (O.H.G. *â*, Goth. *ê*) was, it seems, closed in the language of the poet, rather than open, as it has naturally been noted by Pabst in the discussion of the southwestern (also West-Saxon territory) rimes of Robert of Gloucester; cf. p. 7, 2.

clvi *Chapter XIII.—On the Phonology of the Speculum.*

ẹ̄.

§ 6. Sources of long open *e* (*ẹ*), written *e*, are as follows:

1. O.E. *ǽ* (umlaut of *ai*, Gc. *ai*) : *mẹne* (1. sing.) : *clẹne* 408; *mẹne* (inf.) : *clẹne* 824, 848; *clẹne* : *ẹne* 366, 816; *bidẹne* : (*tene*) 191; *ẹuere* : *nẹuere* (with redundant -*e*- in both instances through svarabhakti) 280, 808; *tẹche* (inf.) : *rẹche* (inf.) 98, 142, : (*speche*, sb.) 2, 570, 754, : (*leche*) 70; *gẹþ* : (*unmeþ*) 616; *lẹde* (inf.) : (*drede*, sb.) 19, : (*rede*, sb.) 104. Here belong the composite forms with the termination -*hẹde* : *godhẹde* : *manhẹde* 372, : (*dede*) 397, : (*drede*) 379, 886; *manhẹde* : (*dede*) 617; *falshẹde* : (*dede*) 722; cf. Kluge, *Stammbildung* and Curtis, *Clariodus*, § 240, Pabst, § 15, o), also Paul's *Grundriss*, I. p. 874.

2. O.E. *ĕ* from various sources, lengthened in open syllables: *mẹte* (T. *mat-i*) : *iẹte* 984; *spẹke* : *brẹke* 810; *dẹle* : *wẹle* (cf. Bülbring, *D. Litt. Zeitung*, 1894) 1018; *stẹde*, Sievers, *Beiträge*, vol. xvi. pp. 235 ff : *dẹde* 598, 604; *stẹde* : *bẹde* 562; *forȝẹte* : (*iwite*) 193, : (*wite*) 764.

3. O.E. *ēä*, Gc. *au* : *dẹd* (O.E. *déäd*) : *quẹd* (or *quẹd*) 862 : *fede* 1025; *brẹd* : (*red*) 970; *vnneþ* (adv. MSS. A₂DH₁) : (*geþ* A₁A₂H₁) 615; *bilẹue* (also *bilēne*) : (*greue*) 201; *nẹr* : (*power*) 216; *ẹk* (Angl. *ēc*) : (*fet*) 439; *lẹs* : (*pes*) 519; *tẹres* (O.E. *tēär* < *teagar*, *h* to *g* by Verner's law) : (*leres*) 841; cf. Siev. *Beiträge*, vol. ii. p. 411. According to the interpretation *quẹd* < O.E. *cwéäd*, rimes in *quẹd* belong in this division, but cf. Pabst, § 15, *b*.

4. An *ǽ* lengthened from O.E. *æ* in other relationship : *sẹde* (< O.E. *sǽde* < *sægde*) : (*rede*, inf.) 168; *sẹde* (*seide*) : (*rede*, 3 plur.) 691, : (*drede*) 140, 494. For *seide* in rime with *rede*, etc., cf. Wilda, *Schweifreimstr*, etc., p. 12; Menze, p. 21, with reference to the same rime, Hausknecht, *Fl. and Blfl.*, pp. 111, 116, Libeaus, Octavius (Sarrazin), etc. *sede* is combined with *rede*, *King Horn*, 919; *R. of G.* 38; *Ed. I.*, p. 73.

5. O.F. *ai* developed into a monophthong before a dental : *pẹs* : (*les*) 520.

ẹ̄.

§ 7. Sources of long closed *e* (*ẹ̄*) are :

A. *Old English.*

1. O.E. *ē*. (*a*) Equivalent to O.E. *ē* (lengthened in monosyllabic words) : *me* : *þe* 108, 392, 550, etc., : (*be*, 3. sing.) 790, : (*se*, inf.) 189, : (*charité*) 56, 323, : (*meyne*) 1015; *þe* in rime with (*be*, 3. sing.) 328, 334, : (*be*, 3. plu.) 413, : (*be*, inf.) 535; 588, : (*se*, inf.) 863, :

Chapter XIII.—On the Phonology of the Speculum. clvii

(*bise*) 487, : (*charite*) 84, 932, : (*deite*) 373, : (*leaute*) 404, : (*trinite*) 351, : (*vilte*) 601. (*b*) O.E. *ê* in other significance : *her*(*e*) (O.E. *hêr*) in rime with (*ifere*, O.E. (*ge*)*fêra*) 296, 977, : (*elleswher*) 175, 779, : (þer) 321, : (*dere*) 1031, : (*fyr* for *fer*?) 452, : (*cler*) 375, 735, : (*power*) 220, 600, : (*manere*) 627 ; *mẹde* : *spẹde* 938, 1028, : (*fede*) 956, : (*almesdede*) 933, : (*goddede*) 622.

2. O.E. (*Anglian*) *ê*, W.S. *ǽ*, (*â*, Goth. *ê*) : *drẹde* (O.E. (*on*) *drǽda*, (vb. and sb.) : *dẹde* (O.E. *dǽd*) 696, 708, 748, etc., : *misdẹde* 830, : (*godhede*) 380, 885, : *rẹde* (sb.) 82, : *rẹde* (vb.) 648, : *louerẹde* 178, : (*seide*, read *sede*, O.E. *sǽde*) 139, 494, : (*lede*) 20 ; *lẹche* : (*teche*) 69 ; *speche* : (*teche*) 1, 569, 753 ; *dẹde* : (*godhede*) 398, : (*falshede*) 721, : (*manhede*) 618 ; *almesdẹde* : *rẹde* 922, : (*mede*) 934 ; *goddẹde* : *rẹde* (3. sing.) 466, : *rẹde* (1. plur.) 502, : (*mede*) 621 ; þer(*e*) : (*her*) 322, : (*were*) 354 ; *rẹd*(*e*) : (*seide*) 167, 692, : (*bred*) 969, : (*lede*) 103. Among rimes in O.E. *ê*, W.S. *ǽ*, is to be classed *qued*, according to Pabst (§ 15 *b*), illustrated in *quẹd* : *rẹd* 48, 654, : (*ded*) 862 ; *quẹde* : (*fede*) 1025 ; *speche* : *knowelache* for *kowelẹche* 510 ; Curtis, in *Clariodus*, *Anglia*, vol. xvi., p. 76. In *Clariodus*, *knowleʒe* is preserved in rimes with *rage* 1421, *langage* 10. *knowelaching* (725) occurs in the Southern texts: *Kath.* 1388 ; *Aʒenbite* 132 ; *Ancr. Riwle* 92 ; Gower II. 319, see Stratmann, *Dict.*

For *rede* (O.N. *rêdan*) *to read*, originally the same as *rede* (O.E. *rǽdan*) to counsel, cf. Cook, *Glossary to the Lindisfarne Gospels*.

3. Umlaut *ê* (from *ô*) : *fẹde* : (*mede*) 955, : (*quẹde*) 1026 ; *fẹre* : (*dere*) 423 ; *ifẹre* (O.E. *gefêran*) : (*here*, O.E. *hêr*) 295, 978 ; *fẹt* : (*ek*) 440 ; *swẹte* : (*profete*) 949, 998 ; *brẹme* (see Murray) : (*leme*) 383.

4. O.E. *ê*, Angl.-Kent *ê*, W.S. *îe*, *ý*, : *here* (O.E. *hýran*) : (*fire*) 355 ; *hẹre* : (*were*) 782.

5. O.E. *êò* developing later *ẹ*, pronounced *ẹ* : *bẹ* (inf.) : *sẹ* (inf.) 396, 534, : *isẹ* (inf.) 402, : *flẹ* (inf.) 834, 850, : (þe) 587, : (*charite*) 96, 935, : (*pite*) 259, : (*humilite*) 632 ; *bẹ* (3. sing.) : *sẹ* (inf.) 738, 872, : *isẹ* 730, : (þe) 327, 333, 536, : (*me*) 789, : (*charite*) 1034 ; *bẹ* (3. plur.) : *sẹ* (inf.) 752, : *isẹ* 288, 342, : (þe) 414 ; *sẹ* (inf.) : (*me*) 190, : (þe) 864, : (*clerte*) 389, (*humilite*) 657 ; *seþ* : *beþ* 818 ; *bise* : (þe) 488 ; *flẹ* (inf.) : (*humilite*) 678 ; *dẹre* (adj.) : (*fere*) 424, : (*here*) 1032 ; *dẹre* (adv.) : (*were*) 160 ; *tẹne* : (*bidene*) 192 ; *lẹme* : (*breme*, *beme* in R) 384 ; *lẹres* : (*teres*) 842 ; H_2 offers *frẹe* : (*me*) 323.

6. O.E. *ý*, umlaut of *û* : *fyr* (read *fẹr*) : (*her*, O.E. *hêr*) 451 ; *fire* : (*here*, O.E. *hýran*) 356, representing O.E. Kent. *ê*, also the rime of *Troilus* 111, 978 ; Danker, *Die Laut- und Flexions-Lehre der*

mittelkent. Denkmäler, etc., p. 11 ff.; Morsb., pp. 167, 174; and Wissmann, *King Horn*, p. 22, Kölbing, *Amis uud Amiloun*, p. xxvi., and ten Br., § 23 γ, Anm. with reference to *fere* : *dere*, *Tr*. I. 229. See the rime *fyer* (*fer*) : (*ner*) *Lybeaus Disconus* 571; *fyre* : (*Messangere*) *Duke Rowland* 94.

B. Loan-words of Romance origin.

1. O.F. *e*, Lat. *a* (cf. ten Br. *Ch.*, § 67, § 68, Anm.). (*a*) Through the ending -*atátem*: *charité* : *humilité* 680, : (*me*) 55, 324, : (*þe*) 83, 931, : (*be*, inf.) 95, 936, : (*be* 3. sing.) 1033; *humilité* : (*pite*) 88, : (*be* inf.) 631, : (*fle*) 677, : (*se* inf.) 658; *deité* : (*þe*) 374; *clerté* : (*se*) 390; *trinité* : *vnité* 206, 430, : (*þe*) 352; *vilté* : (*þe*) 602; *leauté* (*þe*) 403. (*b*) Through other formation: *cler* : (*power*) 915, : (*picher*) 976, 996, : (*her*) 376, 736; *greue* : (*bileue*) 202, : (*Eue*) 230.

2. Fr. *ié*, Anglo-Norm. *e*, Lat. *a* : *pite* : (*humilite*) 87, : (*be*, inf.) 260; *meyné* (O.F. *maisniée*) : (*me*) 1016; *manere* (cf. Pabst, *R. v. G.*, § 17, II. *b*) : (*here*) 628; *picher* (*pichier*, Körting, *Lat.-rom. Wört.*, no. 972) : (*cler*) 975, 995.

3. From other sources: *power* (O.F. *poër* for *poter, *e* < *ei* before *r* in monophthong, cf. A.F. *pouoer*) : (*cler*) 916, : (*ner*) 216, : (*her*) 219, 599, : (*ner*) 215.

4. *e* in loan-word from the French : *profete* (according to ten Br. § 67, β) : (*swete*) 950, 997, cf. *Handl. Syn.* 5158, 11,510.

Eue (O.E. *Éfe*) : (*greue*) 229, from the O.E. according to ten Br. § 23 x. Note the same rime in the unique poem, *The Liif of Adam*, verses 315, 419, and *Eue* : *bileue* 245; *Hand. Syn.* 1604. In the *Poema Morale*, *Eue* is in rime with *ileue* 174; *Har. of Helle*, *leue* : *Eue* 173.

For *prest* : (*Crist*) 805, and *sterne* : (*turne*) 436, refer to rimes in *i*.

ẹ̄ and ę̄.

§ 8. The distinction between the two systems of open and closed e-rimes (ẹ̄, ę̄), as outlined in the preceding sections, is rigidly adhered to in the *Speculum*. Some exceptions are incident to the verse, as in MSS. of other poems. For Lydgate's usage see Schick, *Temple of Glas*, p. lx; for *The Middle Scotch Romance Clariodus*, Curtis, *Anglia*, vol. xvi. p. 420; for *Editha and Ethelreda*, Fischer, *Anglia*, vol. xi. p. 190; see also Chaucer, ten Brink, *Ch.* § 25, where forms regarded as existing in two classes in Zupitza's strongly marked division, have been explained in three classes. The language of the

Chapter XIII.—On the Phonology of the Speculum.　clix

Speculum does not indicate the distinction *ę* and *ẹ* in the following instances[1] :

bidęne (*bidẹ̀ne*, see *Clariodus*, § 239 and Murray, *Engl. Dict.*) : *tęnę* 192 ; *lęres* : *tęres* 842 ; possibly *quęde*, *cwc̀ȧd*, *cwêd*, (or *quęde* ? < *cwêad*, *cwęd* ?) but *gnęde* in *R* (O.E. *gnéað* ; cf. *Havelok* 97) : *fęde* 1026 ; *spęche* : *tęche* 2, 570, 754, : *lęche* 70 ; *węre* : *dere* 160, : *here* 782 ; elsewhere : *here* 176, 780 ; *dręde* : *lęde* 20, : *seide* 140, 494 ; *rede* : *lęle* 104, : *seide* (i. e. *sęde*) 168, 692 ; *drędę* ; *godhęde* 886 ; *fęt* : *ęk* 440 ; *red* : *brę̄d* 970 ; *dęde* : *falshęde* 722, : *godhęde* 398, : *manhęde* 618 ; *gręue* : *bilęue* 200.

Were it possible that O.E. (Angl.) *ê*, W.S. *ǣ*, could give an open quality (*ẽ*), as in *R. of Gloucester* (cf. Pabst, p. 24), resulting in a neutral *e* having an open sound because riming with open *e*, many of the rimes cited would be not impure, but representative of the period and development of the language. Such rimes are the combinations of *rede* (to counsel, counsel), *rede* (to read, see Cook), *drède*, *spęche*, *lęche*, *dęde*. The quality of *e* in *qued* : *ded* (O.E. *déȧd*, Nh. *dēȯd*) 862, : *fęde* (*vide supra*) 1026 is uncertain. Granting validity to ten Brink's hypothesis, § 25, 2 that *lęde* is extant written with a closed *e* (*ẹ*), then the couplets, verses 20, 104, do not introduce an impurity in quality of the vowel. *were* : *þere* 354 belong properly under open *e*- rimes according to ten Brink.

ei.

§ 9. *ei* written *ei*, *ey*, is developed in the *Speculum* from :

1. O.E. *e* + *g* : *eiȝe* (O.E. *ege*, *e* umlaut of *a*) : *weye* 22, : *seie* (inf., *segan for *secg(e)an*, see Menze, p. 29) 796 ; *aȝein* : (*fain*, O.E. *fægen*) 874, 966 ; *leid* : (*misseid*) 592 ; *seie* : (*heie*) 445, : (*preie*) 563.

2. O.E. *œ* + *ȝ* : *misseid* : (*leid*) 591, : (*vbbreid*) 538. For *seide* properly *sęde*, see § 6.

3. O.E. *éȧ* + *g* : *eiȝe* (O.E. *éȧge*) : *heie* (adv. from inflected adj., see Siev., § 295, 1) 388 ; *eiȝe* (read *iȝe*, see rimes in *i*) : (*liȝe*) 827, see § 12, 7.

4. O.E. *ea*, *éȧ* before *h*, L.W.S. *êh* : *heih* : *neih* 634, : *iseih* 992 ; *iseih* (O.E. *geseah*, pret.) : *neih* 370.

5. O.F. *e* + *i* : *preie* : (*seie*) 564.

---

[1] A more symmetrical arrangement would place the open vowel uniformly before illustrations of the closed vowel.

clx *Chapter XIII.—On the Phonology of the Speculum.*

The diphthong has simplified itself to the monophthong *i(y)* in *eiȝe : liȝe* 828. This rime, although proving no definite truth, suggests for the poet of the *Speculum* the double pronunciation employed by Chaucer, in the forms *ye* and *eye*, but not known to Robert of Gloucester; see ten Br. § 21 *ε*, and Pabst, § 39, Anm. 1. *aȝein : fain* 874, 966, is the single link between the two riming systems represented by *ai* and *ei*.

eu.

§ 10. *eu*, written *ew* before a vocalic ending (cf. Ellis, § 302), represents:

1. O.E. *ĉe + w* producing an open *ew* sound (*ęw*) : *ręwe* (O.E. *rḗw*, sb.) : (*shewe*) 80 ; *lęwed* : (*ishewed*) 400. Here belongs *slęuþe* (O.E. *slẽwþ*) 116, *slęuþes* 121.

2. O.E. *éaw* : *shręwes* (O.E. *scréawa*) : *þęwes* (O.E. ðéawu ; cf. *Judith*, 129) 102 ; *shęwe : (rewe)* 79 ; *ishęwed : (lewed)* 399.

The remaining two classes of *ew*- sounds familiar to the student of Chaucer, are not illustrated in the rimes of the *Speculum.*

ĭ.

§ 11.—Short *i* (*ĭ*), written *y* in later MSS., occurs regularly corresponding to:

1. O.E. *i* unaltered. (*a*) In closed syllables. (1) Before nasal groups : *winne* (inf.) : *biginne* (inf.) 6, 78, : *þerinne* 650, : (*sinne*) 132, 471, 684, 694, etc.; *blinne* (inf.) : *biginne* (inf.) 200, : (*sinne*) 714 ; *inne* : (*sinne*) 731 ; *þerinne* : (*sinne*) 840 ; *widinne* : (*sinne*) 118 ; *biginne* : (*sinne*) 901. *i* before -*ng* or -*nk* is probably short : *þing* in rime with *biginning* 8, 884, : *bryng* 1030, : *shining* 382, : *speking* 330, : *wasshing* 836 ; *pining* : *brenning* 182, : (*king*) 899, : *liking* 270 ; *woniȝing* : *deseruing* 314, : *þing* 318 ; *ending* : *biginning* 210, : *deiing* 278 ; *mourninge* : *springe* 126 ; *prouing* : (*king*) 335 ; *noþing* : (*king*) 625 ; *drinke* : *swinke* 156. (2) In other combinations : *iwis* : *is* 504, 724, : *his* 338, : (*paradys*) 285, : (*prys*) 165 ; *þis* : (*amis*) 801 ; *his* : (*paradys*) 300 ; *iwisse* : (*blisse*) 309, 689 ; *misse* : *wisse* 120, : (*blisse*) 418 ; *þerwid* (read *þerwiþ*) : (*griþ*) 147 ; *churche* (practically *chirche*) : (*worche*) 860 ; *þisternesse* (for *þisternisse*) : (*blisse*) 114 ; *seknesse* (*siknisse*) : (*blisse*) 187 ; *sist : bist* 554 ; *wil* (O.E. *gewill*) : (*peril*) 169 ; *wille : spille* 198, : *stille* 584, 594, 706, etc. ; *shrift* : *ȝift* (cf. German *Mitgift*) 682. See also -*nesse* : -*nesse* 86, 306, 346, etc.   (*b*) In open syllables : *wole* (read *wille*, inf.) : (*skile*)

Chapter XIII.—On the Phonology of the Speculum. clxi

712; *liue* (inf.) : *shriue* (past p.) 758, 768; *liue* (3. pl.) : (ȝ*iue*, inf.) 184; *liue* (inf.) : (ȝ*iue*, inf.) 964, 974; *iwite* : (*forȝete*) 194; *wite* : *write* 926, : (*forȝete*) 763. On the possible length of the vowel in *-ing* and in *þing*, see Morsb., *Gram.*, § 55 and § 57 *d*, p. 73; on *king*, ten Brink, § 10, Anm. 1, and Morsb., § 55, Anm. 1, 5. *muche* for *miche* : (*aperteliche*) 386, : (*lihtliche*) 671, representing O.E. *micel, mycel* may be classified here, though in O.E. declension united with long stems, through analogy with O.E. *lȳtel;* see Siev., § 296, note 1, and Menze, p. 34, and compare *The Liif of Adam*, uniting *muche* : *sekerliche* 397; *miche* is the form supported by Langl., *Chr., Handl. Syn., Havelok, Gen. and Ex., Orrm*, etc.

2. O.E. *i* shortened in O.E.: *blisse* (O.E. *blīðs*) in rime with (*iwisse*) 310, 690, : (*misse*) 417, : (*þisternesse* for *þisternisse*) 113, and : (*seknesse, i. e. seknisse*, also *R. of G.* 7768) 188; *iliche* : *riche* (cf. Pabst, § 25; Morsb., *Gram.*, p. 145, Anm. 6) 312. Possibly might be classed here eighteen rimes in *-liche* : *-liche* (O.E. *-līce, -lice*, Siev. § 43,) 416, 442, 606, 610, 798, 822, etc.; *onliche* : *sikerliche* 146; *aperteliche* : (*muche*) 385; *lihtliche* : (*muche*) 672; and *swiche* : *reuliche* (O.E. *hrēowlīce*) 276; cf. ten Brink, § 52 ff., and *Beiträge*, vol. x. p. 504.

3. O.E. *y* umlaut of *u:* *sinne* in rime with (*biginne*) 902, : (*blinne*) 713, : (*inne*) 732, : (*þerinne*) 839, : (*widlinne*) 117, : (*winne*, inf.) 131, 472, 683, 693, 845, 1007; *agilt* : *fulfilt* 308; *gilt* : *pylt* 232, : *ipult* 888, although *pylt, ipult* is of uncertain origin. Under this heading may be classed *worche* (*wirche*, O.E. *wyrcan*) : (*churche*, O.E. *cirice*) 859; cf. *wirche* : *chirche, Fl. and Blancheflur.*

4. O.E., W.S. *ie, i, (y)* through influence of the preceding palatal (Siev., § 75, 3) : ȝ*iue* : (*liue*) 183, 963, 973; *forȝete* (to be altered to *forȝite* in conformity with the rime) : (*iwite*) 193, : (*wite*) 764.

5. O.E. late *i* for stable *y*, Sievers, § 36; ten Brink, § 10, Anm. 1: *king* : (*noþing*) 626, : (*prouing*) 336, : (*pining*) 900.

6. *ī* in loan-words. (1) O.N. *i:* *skile:* (*wole* for *wille*) 711; *griþ* (Ic. *grið*) : (*þerwid*(þ)) 148; *amis* : (*þis*) 802. (2) O.F. *i:* *peril* : (*wil*) 170. Of French origin but of uncertain etymology is *puite* (cf. O.F. *boter*) : (*luite*) 923, and *tirne* for *turne* (O.E. *tyrnan*, from the Latin) : (*sterne*) 435; cf. Steenstrup, *Daneleg*, p. 274 and Morsb., p. 167.

ī.

§ 12. Long *i* (*ī*), written also *y*, appears :

clxii *Chapter XIII.—On the Phonology of the Speculum.*

A. *In development from O.E. forms.*

1. O.E. *í* retained in M.E. (*a*) In open syllables: *side* : *abide* (inf.) 256, 676; *side* : (*pride*) 655; *liue* (O.E. *lif*, sb., dat., plu.) : *shriue* 486; *myne* : *myne* 340; *hie* (inf., O.E. *higian* or *higian*?) : (*crie*) 968; *while* : (*gile*) 62, *R. of G.* 3666, 11150. *wyse*, doublet of *guise*, borrowed through the French from the Frankish, Skeat, § 392 and *Dict.* : (*deuise*) 344. (*b*) In closed syllables : *wif* : *lyf* 234, 702, 734; *myn* : *Alquin* (O.E. *Ealhwine*, Latinized *Alcuīnus*) 52. To this class belong forms with the suffix *-li*, O.E. *lice* influenced by O.N. *-ligr* (*-liga*) : *witerli* : (*leuedi*) 364, : (*comforti*) 687, : (*merci*) 457, 527; *sikerli* : (*empti*) 1001, : (*forþi*) 468. Concerning the quality of the suffix *-liche* classified here § 11, 2, see Morsb. § 67.

2. O.E. *ĭ* in various relationships: (*a*) Before lengthening consonant groups, Morsb., § 67 : *finde* (1. sing.) : *binde* (inf.) 482; *finde* (1. plu.) : *winde* (sb.) 669; *binde* (inf.) : (*mynde*) 495. (*b*) Before O.E. *-g* (*-ig*) through vocalization of *-g* : *empti* : (*sikerli*) 1002; *herkny* : (*merci*) 523; *leuedi* (svarabhakti vowel *-e-*, O.E. *hlǣfdige*) : (*witerli*) 363; possibly *hie* : (*crie*) 968; *lyþ* 713 marks the development from *liþ* < O.E. *ligþ* ; *þre* (*þrie*) 349, 350 < O.E. *þriga*.

3. O.E. *y* umlaut of *u*, before lengthening consonant-groups : *minde* : *kinde* (O.E. *cynd*, Skeat, § 378) 620; *mynde* (O.E. (*ge*)*mynd*) : (*binde*) 496.

4. O.E. *ý* umlaut of *ú* : *pride* (O.E. *prýte* < *prút*) : (*side*) 656; *pride* : *huide* 158; *luite* : (*puite*) 924. Properly classified under rimes in *e* are *fyr* : (*her*, O.E. *hér*) 451; *fire* : (*here*, O.E. *hýran*, *hieran*, *héran*) 356; possibly under *u* (see Morsb., p. 176) : *fire* : (*duire*) 282. Further over *pride*, see Kluge, *Englische Studien*, vol. xxi. p. 33. For *lite*, see *Beiträge*, vol. ix. p. 365.

5. O.E. *ý* : *forð̄i* : (*sikerli*) 467.

6. O.E. *ēo* : *liȝe* : (*cumpaignye*) 637, : (*multiplie*) 1010; *liȝe* (O.E. inf. *lēogan*) : (*Eliȝe*) 947.

7. O.E. *ēa*. (*a*) Before *h* : *liȝe* (originally *leȝ*, N.E. *lye*) : (*eiȝe*) 828; cf. § 9. (*b*) Before ȝ : *eiȝe* (O.E. *éage*, read *iȝe*) : (*liȝe*) 827.

B. *In development from Romance forms.*

1. Generally developed from O.F. *i* are the following illustrations : O.F. *i*, Lat. *ī* : *crie* : (*hie*) 967; *Eliȝe* : (*liȝe*) 948; *deuise* : (*wyse*) 343; *medicine* : (*pine*) 771. O.F. *i*, Lat. *ia* : *cumpaignye* (cf. Lat. *com-pânis*) : (*enuie*) 437, : (*liȝe*) 638; *tricherie* : (*enuie*) 110;

glotonye : *leccherie* 116; *multiplie* : (*lye*) 1009; *clergye* (Latin *clēricia*, Greek κληρικός) : (*baylie*) 290. O.F. *i*, Lat. *ĭ*, before *i*- element: *kointise* : *feintise* 304. Combination *-idia* : *enuie* : (*cumpaignie*) 438, : (*tricherie*) 109. A.F. *-i*, Lat. *-ē-* : *merci* : (*herkny*) 524, : (*witerli*) 458, 528. Lat. *ĕi*-element: *prys* : (*iwis*) 166. In element: *prys* : (*iwis*) 166. In *i*- element: *paradys* : (*iwis*) 286; *paradys* : (*his*) 299. A.F. *i*, Germ. *ī:* *gile* : (*while*) 61. Under other formations are: *Crist* (see Pogatscher, §§ 143—144) : *prest* (Pogatscher, §§ 141—142, Wilda, p. 13) 806; *comforti* : (*witerli*) 688; *baylie* : (*clergye*) 289; *delit* : *profyt* 60; *prist*, represented by *prest*, in rime with *Crist* (with stable *i*) 805 belongs in § 12. Cf. Wilda, *Ueber die örtliche Verbreitung der 12-zeil. Schweifrime in England,* p. 13 ; Pogat., § 127. *duire* : (*fire*) 281 is to be studied under rimes in *u*. Inexactness in the quantity of the riming vowel, O.E. *ī* with O.E. *ĭ*, is to be noted for *his*, and *iwis*, each combined with *paradys*, 286, 300, and *iwis* with *prys* 166; cf. *pris* : *is*, Gen. and Ex. 326 ; *his* : *paradis*, Har. of Hell 5 ; and Menze, p. 65.

For *pine* see O.E. *pīn* < *pēna*, folk-Latin pronunciation of Lat. *poena ;* Kluge, *Wörterbuch ;* Siev., § 69 ; Pogat., § 127, *pine* : (*medicine*) 772. Cf. *peine* in H_2, O.F. *peine*, N.E. *pain*.

iht.

§ 13. *iht* of the *Speculum* represents:

1. O.E. *ih(t)*, Germ. *i, ë:* *siht(e)* (O.E. (*ge*)*sihð*) : (*almiht*) 742, : (*mihte*, sb.) 133, 254, 362, : (*niht*) 914, : (*briht*, O.E. *beorht*) 405, 905 ; *vnriht* : (*almiht*) 613 ; *ariht* : *wiht* (*R* reads *dight* < O.E. *i* < Lat. *ĭ*) 826.

2. O.E. *i* developed through palatal influence from *ea*: *miht(e)* (sb.) : *niht* 320, 516, : (*sihte*) 134, 253, 361 ; *almiht* : *niht* 476, : (*siht*) 741, : (*vnriht*) 614 ; *niht* (Orrm, *nahht*, 1904) : (*liht*) 856, 858, : (*siht*) 913.

3. O.E. *eo* or *ëo:* *briht* : *liht* (O.E. *lëoht*) 394, : (*flyȝte*) 639, : (*siht*) 406, 906 ; *liht* : (*niht*) 855, 857. *liht* occurs uniformly as substantive in the riming couplet of the *Speculum*, never as adjective.

ŏ.

§ 14. Short *o* (*ŏ*), written *o*, appears:

1. From O.E. *ǫ* (*a*) before nasal groups: *honde* : *londe* 586 ; *strong* (adj.) : *among* (adv. O.E. (*ge*)*mong*) 186, 880 ; *ilong* : *wrong* (sb.) 222 ; *long* : *wrong* (sb.) 750 ; *vnderstonde* : *sonde* 50, : *bonde*

clxiv *Chapter XIII.—On the Phonology of the Speculum.*

890, : *honde* 1022, : *fonge* (*fonde* MSS. DR) 508 ; *longe* : *gange* for *gonge* (cf. Morsb., § 90) 762. The quantity of this *o* is not certain, see Morsb., *Gram.*, p. 74, § 58 ; Sweet, *History of English Sounds*, § 395. Cf. also here *mon* : (*hom*) 147 of MS. R, but 149 A_1.

2. O.E. *o* in other combinations : *born* : *lorn* 130 ; *folewe* (O.E. *folgian*) : *swolewe* (< *swelgan* ?) 642 ; *lord* : (*acord*) 844, 894.

3. O.F. *o :* *acord* : *descord* 514 ; *acord* : (*lord* < O.E. *hláford* < *hláf-weard*, Siev. 43, 2 *b*, and ll. 4, Skt., § 257) 843, 893.

For *o* (*i*) in *wole* : (*skile*) 712, and in *worche* : (*churche*) 859, see § 11, 1, and 3. For short *o*, written *u*, see § 19, 1.

ǭ.

§ 15. The *Speculum* generally distinguishes in rime between long open *o* (ǭ), written *o*, and long closed *o* (ọ̄), written also *o*. Certain irregularities will be enumerated in § 17. Long open *o* (ǭ) has its origin in :

1. O.E. *á* in self-rimes or with derivations from O.E. *ó*. (*a*) At the end of a word : *þǫ* (O.E. *ðá*, pro.) : *mǫ* 240, : *wǫ* 112, : (*misdo*, pp.) 557 ; *þǫ* (adv.) : *mǫ* 1004, : *gǫ* (2. sing.) 982 ; *mǫ* : *sǫ* 204, : (*þerfro*) 128, : (*do*, inf.) 273 ; *alsǫ* : *wǫ* 434, : (*do*, inf.) 9, 207, 897 ; *gǫ* (inf.) : (*do*, pp.) 875 ; *sǫ* : (*do*, pp.) 173 ; *sǫ* : (*do*, subj. 3. sing.) 673 ; *wǫ* : (*do*, 3. plur.) 484, : (*do*, inf.) 917. (*b*) Before -*n :* *anǫn* : *euerychǫn* 432, : *gǫn* (inf.) 958, : *nǫn* (O.E. *nán*) 972 ; *nǫn* : *bǫn* (O.E. *bán*) 532, : *gǫn* (inf.) 652, : *gǫn* (pp.) 454, 726, : (*idon*) 545, : (*don*, pp.) 263 ; *vpǫn* : (*don*) 241 ; *ǫn* : (*don*, pp.) 838. (*c*) Before -*r :* *lǫre* (sb.) : *mǫre* (adv.) 24, 36, 740, etc., : *sǫre* (adv.) 236 ; *mǫre* : *ǫre* (O.E. *ár*) 90, : *sǫre* (adj.) 470, : *sǫre* (sb.) 980 ; *sǫre* (adv.) : *ǫre* 540. (*d*) Before -*þ* : *lǫþe* : (*bǫþe*) 76 ; *lǫþe* : *gǫþe* 448.

2. O.E. *ŏ* lengthened in open syllables : *ilǫre* : *wharfǫre* 716.

3. O.E. *o* or *a* (*ea*) before -*ld*. (*a*) O.E. *ŏ* lengthened in open syllables : *gǫld* : *bǫld* (O.E. *bold*, house) 154. (*b*) W.S. *ea*, Angl. *a :* *bǫld* (O.E. *beald*, adj.) : *cǫld* 820.

4. O.N. *á :* *þerfrǫ* (Ic. *frá*) : (*mo*) 127, and possibly in *bǫþe* (O.N. *báðir*, O.E. *báðá* ?) : (*lōþe*) 75.

ọ.

§ 16. Long closed *o* (ọ), represented by *o* in A_1, often by *u* in *D*, is derived from :

1. O.E. *ó* from various sources. (*a*) Final -*ó :* *dǫ* (inf.) : *tǫ* (prep.) 68, : *þertǫ* 332, : (*alsǫ*) 10, 208, 898, : (*mo*, adv.) 274, : (*wo*

918; *do̧* (3. sing.) : (*so*) 674; *do̧* (3. plur.) : (*wo*) 483; *do̧* (pp.) : (*go̧*, inf.) 876, : (*so*) 174; *misdo̧* (pp.) : (*þo*, pro.) 558. (*b*) Before -*n* : *do̧n* (pp.) : (*vpon*) 241, : (*non*, O.E. *nân*) 264, : (*on*, O.E. *ân*) 837; *ido̧n* : (*non*) 546; *so̧ne* (O.E. *sôna*) : *do̧ne* (gerund) 852, : (*bone*, O.N. *bón*, sb.) 987. (*c*) Before -*þ* : *bro̧þer* : *o̧þer* 74, 122. (*d*) In other relationships: *mo̧d* : *go̧d* (O.E. *gôd*) 14, 124, 164, etc.; *þolemo̧d* : *blo̧d* 574, 612, : *go̧d* 666; *go̧d* : *ro̧d* 144, : *vnderstọd* 462, 940; *blo̧d* : *ro̧d* 248; *forso̧k* : (*tok*) 33; *lo̧ke* : *bo̧ke* 460, 786.

2. O.N. *ó* : *to̧k* : (*forsok*) 34; *ro̧te* : *bo̧te* 94; *bo̧ne* (O.N. *bón*, sb.) : (*sone*) 988.

The tendency of M.E. *ō*, in course of the century, to approach a closed *o* sound, if, in its antecedent form, it had been preceded by *w*, was represented not merely by Chaucer, but, as is here illustrated by the preceding rimes, so early as the period of the *Speculum*. This *ǭ* was therefore in existence fifty if not a hundred years earlier than the period of Chaucer's more important works. But if, under other conditions, *w* began the word, then the open sound is to be regarded as unaltered; cf. § 15. Therefore *wo̧* riming with *do̧* (inf.) 918, and *do̧* (pp.) 483, but with *þǫ* (O.E. *ðâ*) 112, is excluded from this class distinguishing the closed sound of *ō*.

ǭ and *o̧*.

§ 17. The quality of the two *o* sounds of the poem is not always differentiated in rime. This inexactness was represented in the language of Chaucer and his school, as well as in the productions of earlier and later poets; cf. Menze, p. 68; Morsb., § 119. 3; ten Brink, § 25; Curtis, *Anglia*, vol. xvii., p. 137, etc. Open *o* (*o̧*) and closed *o* (*ǭ*) of the *Speculum* are combined in rime[1] as follows:

1. As final vowels: *do̧* (inf.) : *mo̧* (adv.) 274, : *wo̧* 918; *do̧* (3. plur.) : *wo̧* 484; *do̧* (pp.) : *go̧* (inf.) 876; *misdo̧* (pp.) : *þo̧* (pro.) 558.

2. Before a nasal: *no̧n* : *do̧n* (pp.) 264; *no̧n* : *ido̧n* 546; *o̧n* : *do̧n* (pp.) 838.

This list does not classify *also* : *do* 10, 208, 898; *so* : *do* 174; *so* : *do̧* (3. sing.) 674, rimes illustrating an accepted tendency to vacillate between high and low tone represented in open and closed qualities in sympathy with their environment, ten Brink, § 31; Morsb., § 119. 3. These have been treated § 16. In these

---

[1] In Section 1 *dǭ* occurs before the riming word illustrating *ǭ*, merely for convenience in arrangement.

clxvi *Chapter XIII.—On the Phonology of the Speculum.*

examples (*also, so*) ō represents an O.E. *á* preceded by *w*, and may be regarded as developing through that influence (see § 16) a mixture of both quantities of the vowel. This *o* might be regarded as presenting in M.E. a closed quality (Morsb., § 135, Anm. 4), or, on basis of a theory that ō (O.E. *á*) produces through influence of a preceding *w* in its O.E. form, both an open and a closed ō- sound (ǫ, ǫ) in a stressed syllable (Morsb., § 135. 4 ; ten Br., § 31), a third division of ō- rimes, including the preceding list (§ 17), might be recognized. The rimes are not impure, but embody to full degree phonological conditions of the language of the period; see Menze, p. 68.

ou.

§ 18. For the development of M.E. *ou*, see Luick, *Anglia*, vol. xvi., pp. 452—455. *ou* of the *Speculum* (MS. A₁) is written *ou* before a consonant, *ow* before a vowel-sound, but *o* (*i. e. o* before *ht*) in the single instance of *noht* 32, 171, 195, etc. In *R. of G.*, to the contrary, *o* (+ *ȝt*) predominates, Pabst, § 48. The open and the closed quality of *ou* (Pabst, §§ 50, 51) being treated under the same division *ou* of the *Speculum*, represents uniformly :

1. O.E. *ŏ* + *ht*, shortened in O.E., Sweet, § 403 : *wrouhte* (O.E. *worhte*, through *r*- metathesis of pret. of *wyrcan*) : *bouhte* (O.E. *bohte*, pret.) 26 ; *wrouht* (O.E. (*ge*)*worht*, pp. through *r*- metathesis) : (*þouht*, O.E. *þóht*, Orm. *þohht*, sb.) 759, 791 ; *iwrouht* : (*noht*) 580, 803 ; *bouht* (O.E. (*ge*)*boht*, pp.) : (*noht*) 172, 226.

2. O.E. *ó* + *ht*, early shortened through influence of *h* + *t* (Siev., § 125) : *þouht* (sb.) : (*wrouht*) 792, : *noht* (O.E. *ná*(*wi*)*ht*, *nó*(*wi*)*ht*, *nóht*) 32, 410, 560, etc. ; *þouht* : *ouht* (O.E. *á*(*wi*)*ht*, *ó*(*wi*)*ht*, *óht*) 316, 1020 ; *souht* (O.E. (*ge*)*sóht*, pp.) : *noht* 196 ; *noht* : (*bouht*) 171, 225, : (*iwrouht*) 579, 804. It is noticeable that O.E. *ná*(*wi*)*ht*, *nó*(*wi*)*ht*, as produced *noht* in rime with *bouht*, *wrouht*, *þouht*, and *souht*, the orthography showing a parasitic *-u-* as in *Clariodus*, § 60, while O.E. *á*(*wi*)*ht*, *ó*(*wi*)*ht* is represented by *ouht* in rime with *þouht*. This *o* is thus a link between the two riming systems representing O.E. *ŏ* and *ō*.

3. O.E. *á* + *g* (*ow* before a vowel) : *owen* (abs. poss.) : (*knowen*) 227.

4. O.E. *á* + *w :* *knowen* (O.E. *cnáwan*, inf.) : (*owen*) 228 ; *knawe* (*knowe*, inf.) : (*lowe*) 180, 629.

5. O.N. *á* + *g :* *lowe* (O.N. *lágr*, adv.) : (*knawe, knowe*) 179, 630.

Chapter XIII.—On the Phonology of the Speculum. clxvii

ŭ.

§ 19. Short *u* (*ŭ*), written *o* through influence of the Anglo-French (cf. Morsb., p. 90), represents O.E. *ŭ* not lengthened in open syllables (Morsb., p. 163 : § 126) *loue* (O.E. *lufu, lufe*) : *aboue* (O.E. *a-bufan* = *on-bufan*) 54, 512, 542, etc.; *shone* (2. sing.) : *wone* (O.E. (*ge*)*wuna*, sb.; cf. Zupitza, *Ælfric's Gram.*, pp. 252—6) 106 ; *shone* (inf.) : *wone* (inf.) 660 ; *wone* (inf.) : *sone* (O.E. *sunu*, sb.) 428 ; *some* (see Carstens, pp. 14, 15) : *inome* 644 ; *gome* (*grōme* in MS. R, for which see Morsb., § 65, Anm. 10; O.N. *grómr*) : *enome* 646.

For O.E. *i* (*y*) after *m*, written also *u*, see rimes in *i*, § 11 : *muche* (O.E. *micel, mycel*) : (*lihtliche*) 671 ; *muche* : (*aperteliche*) 386, the stressed vowel forming an intermediate stage between *i* and *u*.

ū.

§ 20. Long *u* (*ū*), written also *ou* and represented by *ow* before a vowel and often in a final syllable, occurs :

A. *In words of Germanic origin.*

1. From O.E. *ú* : *mouþe* (O.E. *múð*) : *nouþe* (O.E. *nú ðá*) 420, 480; *mouþ* : *couþ* (O.E. *cúþ*, pp., T. *kun-þo-*; cf. Sievers, § 185, 2) 814, : *vncowþe* 422 ; *hou* : *nowh* (O.E. *nú*, parallel with *nú*) 348, : *now* 378 ; *adoun* (O.E. *of dúne*, dat. *adún*) : (*lioun*) 261 ; *bour* (O.E. *búr, ú* from an older *ŭ* lengthened; cf. *neáhgebúr*, see Skt., § 217) : (*honour*) 152 ; *proud* (read *prout*) : (*stout*, cf. Kluge, *Engl. Studien*, vol. xxi., p. 337) 624.

2. O.E. *ŭ* before *n + d :* *stounde* : *bounde* 710 ; *founde* : *wounde* 774.

3. O.E. *ó* + final *h*, ten Brink § 33 ε : *inouh* (O.E. *genóh*) : *drouh* O.E. *dróh*, pret., Sievers's ablaut class vi.) 44 ; *inouh* : *wouh* (*wowe*, DH₂ ; *woghe* R O.E. *wóh*, sb. inflected *wowe*, Pabst, § 52, b ; O.S. *wáh*, Sievers, § 242) 302.

B. *In words of Romance origin.*

1. Representing Norman. *ú.* Through ending *-ōrem* (O.F. *-our*) : *honour* : (*bour*) 151. Through ending *-ōnem :* *orysoun* (*ureisun* < F. *ureizun* by false analogy < eccl. L. *ōrātiōnem*) : *fuisoun* 994 ; *orisoun* : *lesczoun* 500 ; *sarmoun* : *lesczoun* (Lat. *lectionem*) 58, 138. Rom. *o* before nasals : *dampnacioun* : *sauuacioun* 788 ; *croun* (A.F. *corone*, Lat. *corōnam*, ten Br., p. 5) : *sauuacioun* 800. Through other source : *lioun* : (*adoun*) 262 ; *myrour* : *socour* (Rom. *o̜*) 506.

clxviii *Chapter XIII.—On the Phonology of the Speculum.*

2. O.F. *ou:* *stout* (O.F. *(es)tout*) : (*proud (t)*) 623.

ŭ̆.

§ 21. *ŭ̆* written always *u*, spoken *i*, finds illustration in the *Speculum* as representative of *i:*

1. Through O.E. *y*, umlaut of *u:* *ipult* (O.E. *pyltan, Lat. *pultare*) : (*gilt*, Skt., § 337) 888 (cf. § 11, 3 under *i*-rimes for l. 232); *puite* (cf. O.F. *boter*. Perhaps read here *pŭtte* as in MS. R) : (*luite*, read *līte*) 923. Here belongs also *murie* 159, 905, *muryere* 284 of the text (MS. A₁). See Zupitza, *Engl. Stud.*, vol. viii., p. 465. Rimes in *gult : pult* are frequent in older M.E. poems; cf. *The Passion*, *ipult : gult* 190, 227; *agult :* (*i*)*pult*, *Pater Noster* 90, 129, but *agilt : pilt*, *Liif of Adam* 331, 337, 365, 555, 757.

2. O.E. *y* (*i*): *churche* : (*worche*, inf.; O.E. *wyrcan*) 860 (cf. *i*-rimes, § 11, for the reading *chirche*).

Under § 21 belongs *kudde* 178 of the text, O.E. *ӯ* (umlaut of *ū*) shortened before a consonant group.

ū̆.

§ 22. Written also *u*, spoken *ī* by the poet, the sources of *ū̆* are:

1. Germanic: O.E. *ӯ* (uml. of *ū*). The self-rime *huide* (O.E. *hӯd*, N.E. *hide*, sb.) : *pride* < *prӯde* < *prūt*, Siev. § 96, Skt. § 197; cf. Ic. *prýði*, O.N. *prýði*, O.E. *prӯt* 158 (cf. § 11, 2); *fure* (i. e. *fire*) : (*duire*) 282.

2. Romance: O.F. *u* written *ui:* *duire* (*dure*, *R. of G.* 3760, 6935, see Pabst, § 113, Morsb., p. 176) : (*fire;* cf. § 12, 4) 281. Possibly to be classified in this division, but difficult of classification is *turne* (Orm. *turrnenn*) : (*sterne*) 435. *turne* is equivalent to O.E. *turnian* < vulg.-Lat. *tornare* < Lat. *tornare*, loan-word from the Latin or O.F. before the conquest, explained by Pogatscher (*Zur Lautlehre der griechischen, lateinischen, und romanischen Lehnworte im Altenglischen*), §§ 159, 205, and 271 through *turnare* for *tornare*, *i*-umlaut of Lat. *o*, vulg.-Lat. *u*, hence *tyrnan*. Pabst, § 109, p. 102, accounts for *turne* as a hybrid development blending O.F. *torner* (Lat. *turbinare*), O.E. *turnian*, and O.E. *tyrnan;* cf. also Skeat II., 75. 2; 94. 25; 138. This interpretation explains the lengthening of *ü* before *r* + *n*.

The value of *üi* is represented in *anuied*, O.F. inf. *enuiier;* cf. O.F. dialectical parallel form *anoüer*, line 124 of the text, Pabst, § 122.

CHAPTER XIV.
THE INFLECTION OF THE *SPECULUM*.

THE discussion of the characteristics of the inflectional system of the *Speculum* assumes, that its conclusions have been, if possible, verified by rime or metre. Otherwise paradigms and synopses are completed from the body of the text. Conjectural readings are based upon the Auchinleck MS. The Auchinleck MS. contributes orthography, but an occasional note introduces graphical or phonetical emendations of the copyist. This chapter endeavours to collect testimony as to the development of the O.E. vowel in the unaccented inflectional syllable. It aims particularly to present a clear view of the poet's treatment of the M.E. final -ë in rime and in cæsural construction.[1] Its purpose is primarily to call attention to general characteristics,[2] rather than to establish any precise laws of grammatical structure.

I. DECLENSION.
§ 1. SUBSTANTIVES OF THE *SPECULUM*.
A. VOCALIC OR STRONG DECLENSION.
§ 1. MASCULINE AND NEUTER SUBSTANTIVES.
(a) *a- stems.*

Nominative and Accusative. The singular is without ending, corresponding to the O.E. archetype: *day* : (*may*) 492; *dom* 256, see also *fredom* 237; *god* 143; *word* (nom.) 519, (acc.) 420; *weye*?[3] (*way* in R) 651. Inorganic -ë seems to be demanded by *weië* (acc.) 298; compare *wegë*, *North. Gloss.*, *Mark* I., 2, and *weyë* also within the verse, the reading of *Orrm.*, Sachse, *Das unorganische ë im Orrmulum*, p. 7, of Chaucer, ten Brink, § 199, 5, Anm., and probably of Lydgate in his *Temple of Glas*, Schick, p. lxv, and in his *Guy of Warwick*, str. 37[7], and possibly also *weië*, str. 61[3] (cf. Zupitza). See also *pine* 176 and the dissyllable *almesse* (O.E. Lat. Greek? see Pogatscher, *Lautlehre*, pp. 38, 207, 218, and Cosijn. Gr., p. 97, 923).

---

[1] Difficulty must be conceded the interpretation of the value of a final -e at the cæsura, due to the existence of type C.
[2] These sections do not undertake to cite all illustrations of any specific subdivision of the material.
[3] The mark of interrogation designates the questionable value of final -e in syllabic arrangement; e. g. types A and C present rival claims to verse 651, owing to uncertainty regarding the metrical value of final -e in *weye :*

And óper wéyë · is per nón.
And óper wéyę · is per nón.

It is not possible to decide with exactness the value of this inorganic -e.

Genitive. The ending is -ës, continuing the O.E. ës: domës(day) 257, 745, 868; godës 38, 81, 89, etc.; lordës 892.

Dative. The old dative in -ë is preserved unaltered in the *Speculum*, but in many instances uninflected forms[1] occur also, when, as in Chaucer (cf. ten Brink, § 201) the dative is like the nominative: firë : (herë, inf.) 356; weyë : (ciȝe) 22; mouþë : (nouþe, O.E. nûþá) 420, 480; on liuë 859; yet without ending are mouþ : (couþ, pp.) 813, and on basis of metrical type A, mouþe̯ 94. Uninflected forms, as is indicated by rhythm or rime, are : wif : lyf 234; bon 531; dom 415, 766; day : (lay) 250, : (nay) 251; day 49, 475, 516; bon 157; bon : (non) 531; gold : (bold) 153; wil : (peril) 169. Owing to elision ȝate 959, is not determinative in the question of the development of the inorganic -e (cf. Sachse, § 25), through analogy with short fem. stems by means of O.E. plural forms in -u. day 250, it would seem, admits of explanation as nominative, subject of com, hit being pleonastic. The line recalls the idiom illustrated in the opening song of *Wilhelm Tell*, v. 1 : *Es lächelt der See !* O.E. derivatives from the Latin to be classified here end in -ë : pinë ? 772, but pine̯ 104.

Plural. The ending -ës (written often -is, -ys in other MSS.), O.E. -as, occurs uniformly for masculine substantives : gostës (type A, or goste̯s to produce type C) 431, but probably with syncope of the -e in goste̯s 447; nailës 439; terës 827; giltës 752; weyës 865. Dative forms are dawë (O.E. dagum) : (lawë) 37, 357; liuë : (shrine) 486. siþe̯ (with apocope) 394 is the plural contributed by H_1 and R. The termination of the masculine is carried over to the plural of other genders and other stems. Thus terës (O.E. hleór) occurs in rime with terës 842 and shaftës with craftës 212. Neuter nouns end in -ës : londës (Londys, H_2) 152, 163; wordës 276, 998; werkes 860; shaftes (creatures in D) 781 illustrate syncope of the second -e- ; for þingës (or þinge̯s) 141, see Pabst, *Anglia*[2] xiii., p. 247, Anm. 1. The plural of the neuter ends also in -ë : þingë (O.E. þingum, þinga) 284, and perhaps in þing[ë] : (biginning, biginning[ë] ?) 8, 883, : (speking[e]) 329. les : (pes) 519 is without ending. D and R offer bemë : (lemë) 383; god 163 is without ending. See also louere̯dë 177; bold 154; lyf 952, forms possibly to be regarded as plural, but through context uncertain.

---

[1] The principle was already illustrated by so early a linguist as Orrm (1200), representing, it must be remembered, the northern portion of the East Midland territory, and presenting northern peculiarities, often Scandinavian characteristics.

[2] *Flexionsverhältnisse bei Rbt. v. Gl.*

(b) *ja-* stems.

These stems reproduce O.E. final *-e* through *ë : ende* : (*wendë*) 426 ; *leche* (O.E. Angl. *léce*) 69.

(c) *wa-* stems.

Plural nouns illustrative of *wa-* stems are found : þewës 72 ; þewës : (*shrewës*) 101, but the syncopated form þewes 97.

(d) *i-* and *u-* stems.

i- and *u-* stems offer as representative of O.E. final *-e* (*-u*) a syllabic *-ë : stedë* : (*bede*) 561, : (*dede*) 597, 604 ; *metë* : (*iete*) 983 ; *eiʒë* (O.E. *eʒe*) : (*weye*) 21, : (*scie*) 795. A *u-* stem is *sonë* (O.E. *sunu*) : (*wone*, inf.) 428. Possibly to be classed here is the plural *metys* (H₂) 155, through analogy with O.E. *mettas* of the *ja-* declension, Siev. § 263, N. 3.

§ 2. FEMININE SUBSTANTIVES.

The endings of the feminine *jô-* and *i-* stems agree with those of the *ô-* stems.

Singular. Nominative. The termination is *-ë*, through weakening of O.E. *-u* for short stems, Sievers, § 252, or an inorganic *-ë* added through analogy with oblique cases for long syllables : *shamë* 799, 801 ; *shamë* : (*blame*) 811 ; *lorë* : (*more*) 755, 853 ; *dredë* : (*godhede*) 380 ; *Louë* (*Louę ?*, elision of *-ë* before a vowel in the following word) 87. The ending *-ę* is also to be noted : *louę* 304 ; *Streinþe* (before *i* of the following syllable) 305 ; *worldę* 17, 61 ; *Drede* 883. Characteristic of the period is the inorganic *-ë* affixed to the nominative singular of nouns ending with the suffix *-nes* (*-nis*), already to be noted in the English *Liber* (Camb. Univ. MS. Ii. 1. 33) of the 12th century. Cf. *soðfæstnysse* 28 ; *oncnawennysse* 20, 27 (Zupitza, *Anzeiger für deutsches Alterthum*, ii. 11) ; *fairnesse* : þisternesse 305.

Genitive. The ending is *-ës* through analogy with the masculine : *worldës* 13, 32, 113, 151, 195, etc. An old genitive is recognized in the adverb of time, *whilęs* 184.

Dative. *-ë* is the characteristic ending of the feminine dative, but uninflected forms are found here as in the masculine of the *a-* declension. (1) *-ë : louë* : (*aboue*) 53, 541 ; *louë* 243, etc. ; *trowþe* 1033 ; *spechë* : (*teche*) 1, 569, 753 ; *hondë* (dat.) : (*londe*) 585, : (*vnderstande*) 1022 ; *shame* 777, 779, 804, etc. ; *dredë* : (*dede*) 910, 943, : (*lede*, inf.) 20 ; *rotë* (Scand. loan-word) 93 ; *huidë* : (*pride*) 157 ;

rodë? 26; hellë : (nellë) 271. (2) -ę: louę 6, 21, 144, etc.; rod : (god) 144; rod : (blod) 248; sorwe (before initial e- in the following syllable) 769, but sorwę (with hiatus) 93; dredę 444, 914. To be classed here is Euë 229, according to ten Brink of O.E. origin, see also Siev., § 194.

Accusative. -ë is the normal ending : soulë 48, 576; whilë 62; louë : (aboue) 511; shamë 783; soulë 688; dredë : (dede) 695, 707, : (godhede) 885, but by the side of -ë occurs not infrequently the weakened -ę: worldę 64.

Plural. Plural feminine forms of substantives have the ending -ën, indicating the tendency to adopt in the plural the inflection of the weak or n- declension, already existing sporadically in the 12th century: woundën (acc.) 442; hondën 440; also -ës, sinnës (dat.) 469, (acc.) 803; synnys in H_2 91 and 830; dedës 674; probably hestę (singular?) 810.

B. CONSONANT DECLENSION.

§ 1. MASCULINE SUBSTANTIVES.

n- stems.

Nominative. The nominative ending is -ë in continuation of O.E. -a: bileuë 203; gomë (O.E. guma) 645; mone (before a vowel) 383; namë : (famę) 30, 39, but hopę 466.

Oblique cases are in -ë: hopë 463, 471, but hopę 477, 690; tenë 192; timę 703.

Plurals. In -ën is sterrën 383, retaining the old plural ending in -n, a plural not confirmed by rime. shrewës occurs in rime with þewës 102, and ferë with dere (O.E. dëore) 423.

§ 2. FEMININE SUBSTANTIVES.

Nominative. In -ë are widewë 965, 971, 987, 1003; (type B or with apocope?) 955 and the elided form sunnë 386.

Genitive. Ending in -ë is hertë (hertë rote, hertë blod) 93, 247; heuene (O.E. heofonan, gen. of fem. heofone, heuenð blisse, heuenë king) 336, 626, 690, 900. A_2 offers sonnës 393.

Dative. -ë characterizes hertë 87, 165, 208, 408, but hertę 414; eorþë 296, 375, 397, etc.; sidë : (abide) 255, 655; sunnę (dat. of indirect object) 393; widewë 951, 998.

Accusative. ʒemë 553; leuedi (O.E. hlǣfdige) : (witerli) 363 shows no inflection.

Chapter XIV.—The Inflection of the Speculum. clxxiii

§ 3. NEUTER SUBSTANTIVES.

Nominative and accusative end in *-ë: eiȝë* 396; *eiȝë* : (*heie*) 388. One plural form occurs : *eiȝen* (*eghen* in *R*, dat.) 841; *eiȝen* (acc.) 992.

C. OTHER DECLENSIONS.

§ 1. SUBSTANTIVES ILLUSTRATING MINOR DECLENSIONS.
(Sievers, §§ 281—290.)

(1) Irregular consonant stems. (a) *Masculines and Neuters*. The singular is represented by: *man* (nom.) : (*can*) 727 ; *man* (nom.) 37, 222, 223; Gen. *mannës* 388, 611, 723 ; *man* (dat.) 51 ; *man* : (*cam*) 590. Plurals of the same class with *i-* umlaut are : *men* (dat.) 149 ; *fet* : (*ek*) 440. (b) *Feminines*. These end in *-ë: bokë* : (*lokë*) 460, 785 ; *niht* (nom.) : (*liht*) 856 ; *niht* (dat.) : (*miht*) 320, 516 ; *niht* : (*liht*) 858, *niht* in this construction being an objective adverbial. (2) Stems in *-r:* voc. *fader* 52, dat. after *leue* 424 (O.E. *lēof*, cf. Chaucer) 428. The genitive is *faderës* 254, 255. *broþer* (nom.) : (*oþer*) 121 ; (voc.) 73. (3) Stems in *-nd*: *frend* 919 ; *fend* (dat.) 229 ; *fendë* (gen. in H_1) 696. (4) Stems in *-os*, *-es* (Gk. neuters in *-ος*, Lat. *-us*, *-eris*), Sievers's second class : *lomb* (nom. sing.) 260. The plural occurs in *children* (cf. Sievers, § 290, 2) (nom.) 287, (gen.) 986, (dat.) 349, 522. *childer* is the reading of *D* and *R*.

§ 2. SUBSTANTIVES OF ROMANCE ORIGIN.

Singular. In general, substantives of Romance origin retain a final syllabic *-ë*, preserved from the O.F. original: *gracë* : *facë* 214, 904; *gracë* 78 ; *gracë* : *placë* 294; *preië* 68 ; *blamë* : (*shame*) 778, 784, 812; *ioyë* (*ioye*) 295, 301, see also *croun* (A.F. *coroune*, *corone*?) 799, and *paunter* (O.F. *pantiere*?) 18, etc. Polysyllabic forms recur in Romance derivatives: *repentauncë* : *penauncë* 92, 474, 770 ; *suffrauncë* : *destourbauncë* 572 ; *manerë*? 628 ; *anguisse* 183 ; with accent thrown back: *séruise* 36 ; *séruage* 238 ; *citë*? 959 ; *Mérci* 131, 545 ; but also *mercí* 458, 524 ; *perìl* 170 : *myróur* 505. Representing a Romance original without final *-e* monosyllabic forms occur : *los* 158 ; *prys* 166 ; *voiz* 446 ; *cas* 703. In polysyllables : *katél* (*catel*) 162, 577, 896 ; *uertú* 922, etc.

Plural. The plural endings *-s* (*-z*) and *-e* occur for polysyllables of Romance origin, but seem to be generally without syllabic value : *deciples* 570 ; *uertuz* (*vertuys* in H_2) 71, 325, 661 ; *persones* 206 ; *manere* 785. Possibly to be regarded as plurals are : *vessel* 153 ;

Chapter XIV.—*The Inflection of the Speculum.*

tresor 154. Ending in *-es* occur *rentes* (*rentys*) 152, 163, and *ioyes* (syncopated form?) 286. H_2 reads *peynys* 176.

§ 2. ADJECTIVES OF THE *SPECULUM*.

The inflections of the poet agree with the O.E. forms through the weakening of unaccented full vowels. The twofold Germanic declension, the strong and the weak, is illustrated, but in the plural both declensions fall together in the uniform syllabic unaccented final *-ë*. Romance adjectives in inflected and uninflected forms retain unaccented *-ë*. Uninflected forms are also illustrated in adjectives of two or more syllables of Germanic or Romance origin.

§ 1. STRONG ADJECTIVES.

Strong adjectives of Germanic origin, in legitimate descent from the O.E., tend to drop the inflection except in *ja-* stems. Such adjectives of the strong declension find illustration as follows:

Singular forms: *gret, gretę* with apocope of the final *-e* 158, 214; *hot* 819; *god* 843. Used predicatively occur: *god* 105, 202; *vnmeþ* 615; *Wicke* (O.E. *wicca*) 122; *murie* 905; *fain* 965; *empti* 1002 show the vocalization of O.E. *g*. The dative is found corresponding to the uninflected nominative: *gret* 170, 899; *strong* 266, 274; *al* 319; *god* 571; *cold* 929. Yet sporadically the poem presents instances of inflection by means of *-ë*, in the dative. Cf. *godë* 29, 40; *heihë*, a form open to speculation on part of the copyists, 214; *hotë* 282, 451; and possibly *strongë* 282, 449. Datives having apocope of the final *-e* occur: *smale* 181; *hute* 182; *gode* 931. *ja-* stems are inflected with *-ë: trewë* 304, 697; *sternë* 446; *mildë* 594; *newë*?, used predicatively, 760.

Plural forms. The final *-ë* is retained: *Fairë* 71, 154?; *foulë* 72, 803; *Riche*? 153, 155; *oldë* 357; *allë* 239, 300, 329, 338, etc.; *gretë* 469; *godë* 674, and *godę* (dat.) 865. Stems in *-ja: bremë* 383; *kenë* 439; *swetë* 998. Predicative adjectives are: *loþë* 76; *foulë* 818; *gode* (with apocope) 287.

Words of more than one syllable are without inflection: *wraþful* 436; *ydel* 463, 466; *Holi(y)* 505, 701, 733, 755; *wrongful* 618; *Gostli* 715; *sinful* 751; *dedli* 774.

To the strong declension belong: *Wheiþer* (r. *Wher*) 219; *oþer* 74, 122, 651; plural: *operë* 135; *Tweię* (apocope) 141; *Tweye* 785; *aller* (*furst*) gen. plu. 70; the Scandinavian form *boþë* 75, 216; *Summë* 825, is a dissyllable as in Lydgate and Gower in distinction

Chapter XIV.—*The Inflection of the Speculum.* clxxv

from Chaucer's monosyllabic rendering *some* (except in rime; see ten Brink, §§ 255, 327). Compare also the riming form of the *Speculum*, *somë* : (*inome*), v. 643. Unaccented final -*e* is subject to apocope in *Boþe* 311, 400, 436 ?. Contracted forms are *next* : *hext* 326, 662.

§ 2. WEAK ADJECTIVES.

O.E. full-toned inflectional forms corresponding to *n*- stems of the substantive declension are represented in the *Speculum* by unaccented -*ë*. As in O.E. the weak adjective is employed:

α. After the definite article: *rihtë* 22; *gretë* 256; *strongë* 449; *heïë* 622, but *heie* (with apocope of -*e*) 415; *foulë* 654; *longë* 744; *derkë* 856, 858. Weak adjectives of more than one syllable are without inflection in this position: *holi* 352, 565, 687; *sinful* 727. Ordinals are declined as follows: *formë* (superlative in -*ma*) 223; *þriddë* 250, 251; *firstë* 358. A comparative occurs: *þe clannere* 826. To this division belongs *þilkë* (= *þe ilke*, O.E. *sê ilca*) 37.

β. After a demonstrative pronoun: *þat ilkë* 362; *þat foulë* 696; *þis ilkë* 799. *þat hotę* (acc.) 182, and *þat fairę* 914 occur with apocope of final -*e*. Adjectives of two syllables are found after a demonstrative, but are not inflected: *þat litel sinful* (dat.) 708; *þis seli* 987.

γ. After a possessive pronoun: *his rihtë* 39; *his gretë* 361; *his owen* (*owenë*?) 314; *hirę gretë* 390; *Hirę clenë* 364; *þin owën* (read *owenë*?) 620; *þi rihtë* 878; *ja-* stems: *Houre swetë* 569; *hourę . . . swetë* : (*profete*) 949. Adjectives of two syllables are illustrated: *þi seli* 576; *His gostli* 736; *Hirę litël* 990.

Plural forms are preserved: *þe wickë* 101; *þe richë* : (*iliche*) 311; *þe hotë* 827, 841; *þe leste* (*ę* through elision) 1016; *þise holi* 191; *His grisli* 442. Once the adjective precedes the vocative plural: *minë blessedë ferë* 423.

Of the weak inflection are probably *þiselfë* 10, 564, 579; *himselfë* 14; *onë* (O.E. *âna*) 239, see Sievers, 324, N. 1. In the weak declension are to be classified *Boxomere* (followed by *he*) 233; *muryere* 284; and *beyþere* 952.

Romance forms. Romance adjectives retain in inflected as well as uninflected forms final -*ë* : *porë* (?) 951; *doublë* 940, 1006; *merciablë* 526; see also *pore* (-*ę* through elision) 164; *cler* 381, 915; *stout* 623; *cruwel* (read with syncope of -*e*-, unless epic cæsura, metrical type B, be preferred) 559.

Vocatives. In this position the inflection is uniformly -*ë*.

Chapter XIV.—*The Inflection of the Speculum.*

Singular: *leuë* 73, 919; *Swetë* (*ja-* stem) 555. *ferssę* (sing.) 623 is the single Romance form. Plural: *corsedë* (*cursëd*?) 431, 447.

Before proper names occurs: *Sein* (*Powel*) 345; (*Daui*) 459, 691; (*Gregory*) 663. For *scint* 275 see ten Br., § 242.

§ 3. NUMERALS.

Numerals are employed in the *Speculum* as follows. They illustrate occasionally the value of an unaccented -*ë*:

Cardinals: on : (*don*) 838; *o* 204, 205, 354; *Tweie* (*two* R) 141, (*Tweyę*) 785; þre 206, 349, 350; *hundred* 394. *Onë* 239 preserves the form of the numeral with the meaning *alone*. Negative of *on* preserves -*ë*: *nonë* 344.

Ordinals: þe *firstë* (acc.) 358; þe *formë* (nom.) 223; þe *þriddë* 250, 251.

In orthography these forms reproduce MS. A$_1$. Decisive evidence through rime exists for numerals only in instance of *on*; vide *supra*.

§ 3. PRONOUNS.

§ 1. PERSONAL PRONOUNS.

The personal pronouns in use in the *Speculum* are as follows:

a. *First Person:* Sing. Nom. *i* (*I*) 2, 3, 27, 49, etc. Gen.—.Dat. *me* : (*charite*) 56 : (þe) 1011, etc. Acc. *me*, 62, 189, etc. Nom. *we*, 501, 504, 506, etc. Gen.—.Dat. *us* (*vs*) 54, 501, 1031, etc. Acc. *us* (*vs*) 1029.

β. *Second Person:* Sing. Nom. þu (þou) 5, 6, 8, 10, 11, 12, etc. Gen.—.Dat. þe : (*charité*) 84, : (*me*) 108, : (*be*) 328, 334, 588, etc. Acc. þe : (*bisë*) 487, : (*be*) 535, 588, etc. Plural. Nom. ʒe 177, 425, 447, etc. Gen.—.Dat. *ou* (Auch. MS.), ʒou (MSS. Arund. and Harl.) 2; ʒou 284; Acc. *ou* (Auch. MS.) 816, 824, 848.

γ. *Third Person:* Masc. Sing. Nom. *he* 19, 31, 33, etc. Gen. —.Dat. *him* (*hym*) 32, 227, 608, etc. Acc. *him* (*hym*) 34, 133, 369, etc. Fem. Sing. Nom. *she* (*ho*, MSS. D and R, or *scho* in R) 965, 968, 972, 990, 1004. Gen.—.Dat. *hire* (*hyre*) 981, etc. Acc. *hire* (*hore*, *hyre*, *hyr*) 960, 961, etc. The final *-e* (dat. and acc.) is uniformly silent.

Neu. Sing. Nom.: *hit* and *it* are found in A_1 and R (MSS. A_2DH_1 have *it*) 3, 16, 119, etc.; *hit* 123, 160, 161, etc. Gen.—.Dat. *him* (*hym*) 680. Acc. *hit* (*it* A_2DH_1) 15, 58, 175, etc.; *it* (A_1) 563, 575, 581, etc.

Plural. Nom.: *hij* (MSS. A_1 and R) 186, 277, 279, 309, etc.; þei (þeih A_1) 25, 80, 104, etc. Scandinavian forms are uniformly represented by the MSS. $A_2DH_1H_2$. Gen.—.Dat. *hem* (often written *hom* in MS. R) : (*men*, assonance) 150; *hem* (*hom* R) 159, 168, 316 etc. Acc. *hem* (*hom* R) 25, 100, 106, etc.

Possibly the most noticeable feature in the study of personal pronouns is the introduction of *hij* by the side of *þeih*, *hit*, and *ou*, the characteristic of MS. A_1; of *hij*, *hit*, *hom*, *scho*? and *hore*, of MS. R, and possibly for dialectical purposes of *ho* in MSS. D and R.

Scandinavian forms *þei*, *þeir* belong to later MSS., though A_1 has *þeih* sporadically. *þe*, *me*, *hem*, *him* are the personal pronouns absolutely warranted by the MSS. on basis of the rimes.

Possessives.

Simple possessives: *my* (generally before a consonant sound) 1, 59, 60, etc.; *myn* : (*Alquin*) 52; *ourę* 505, 916; *vrę* 363, 506, but *ourë* before the name of the deity 844; *vrë* 595, etc.; *Houre* 569, 949, whose syllabic character is lost by apocope. *þi* (followed by a consonant sound) 7, 14, 69, etc. *þin*[1] (before a vowel sound) 9, 93, 334, etc.; *his* (*hys*) 18, 19, 21, etc. *Here*[2] (fem,) 952; *hirë* 235 ?; *Hirę* 956, 990, 995; *mynë* : (*myne*) 339; *þin*[*ë*]? 841 and *þinë* (plu.) 842 retains its syllabic -*ë*, but *þinę* 841; *Hisę* (plu.) 570, 752; *His* 992; *here* 103, 169, etc. Otherwise plurals of possessives are often apocopated.

Absolute possessives: *mynë* rimes with *mynę* (simple possessive) 340, *his* with *paradys* 300, and with *iwis* 338.

Relatives and Demonstratives.

Relatives and demonstratives present no novel features. *þat* has the value of a *who*, lines 54, 317, (plu.) 424. Equivalent to *what* in lines 3, 73, etc., its use is substantive. *þat* serves also as a demonstrative 59, 82, 88, etc. *þis* 149 (= *þis is*) is the single instance of contraction. *þisë* 84 is used substantively. Without syllabic value is -*e* in *Whichę* (plu.) 76, 287, and in *þisę* 97, 191, etc.

§ 4. ADVERBS.

Adverbs following the history of the development of O.E. forms end in -*ë*, when formed from adjectives.

Adverbs from adjectives: *derë* : (*were*) 160 ; *derë* 172, 226 ; *sorë* : (*lore*) 236, : (*ore*) 539 ; but *sorę* through elision 766, 794 ; *lowë* 630 ; *foulë* 591 ; *stillë* : (*wille*) 584, 593, 706, etc.; *fastë* : (*agaste*) 865. As continuation of O.E. full endings occur : *aboutę* (elision) 190,

---

[1] Plu. 9, 334 ?   [2] *Here liue*, plural ?

clxxviii *Chapter XIV.—The Inflection of the Speculum.*

(apocope) 515; *aboutën* 196; *aboue* 908; *Oute* 490; *ofte* 493, 499, 1020. Through analogy *ekë* 436, 584, 681; but *ek* : (*fet*) 439. Assuming directly the form of an adjective ending in -e occurs: *swipë* 4, 236, 578, 630, 736, 879. Of another class are adverbs formed by composition of the simple adjective stem with O.E. -*līce*: *apertëlichë* 385; *soplichë* : *opënlichë* 442; *Kindelichë* 817, but *Hollichę* 353; *sikerlichę* 373; *Bodilichę* 375; *Rihtfullichę* 458. *witerli* : (*comforti*) 687; *sikerli* : (*empti*) 1002. Adverbs without corresponding adjectives: *ȝit* (O.E. *giēt*, *gȳt*) 851; *eftsonë* : (*done*) 851; *sonë* : (*bone*) 987; *sonę* 903. Oblique cases of adjectives employed as adverbs are from the accusative: *inouh* : (*drouh*) 43; *inouh* 305; *ful* 66, 517, 632; *heië* : (*eiȝe*) 387; *heię* 632.

A genitive as introductory element of a compound word occurs: *ellës* (*wher*) 176, 780. Derived from substantives are *alday* 342; *forsoþę* 391; *adoun* 842; *adoun* : (*lioun*) 261; *by day and niht* 475, represents adverbial construction of this class. *sorë* (original form with *i*- umlaut, Sievers, § 237, 2) offers illustration of an instrumental used adverbially. Adverbs from prepositions are: *innë* : (*sinne*) 731; *onne* 267. Adverbs of place are: *wherë* 176; *her* 197, 220; *herë* 296; *þer* 322. Of time *noupe* 107; *nowh* 348; *þannë* 199, 283, 395 is very frequent. A numeral adjective, *Enë* is used by the poet. Cf. *enë* : (*clenë*) 366, 815, and *bidenë* 191; *Enës* (gen.) 939.

Comparison of adverbs. Comparative: *betrë* 78, 937; *ererë* (comp. of *ar*, preserved by MS. A₁ alone) 140, 168; *inwardlicherë* 321; *clannerę* 820, 828; *lassë* 536; *morë* : (*ore*) 90, : (*lore*) 739, 854, etc.; *mo* : (*þerfro*) 128. Superlative: (*Aller*) *furst* 70.

Formal adverbial expressions occur: *ful iwis* 165, 285, 337, 503, 723; *mid iwisse* 309, 689; *on heih* 633; *On ydel* 568, 668; *for euere mo* 240; *widoute fable* 525; *widoute nay* 252, 258; *fer and ner* 216; *lude and stille* 584, 706, 891.

II. CONJUGATION.

THE VERB.

In the classification of strong and weak verbs with resulting methods of tense-formation, the *Speculum* does not differ materially from the normal text of the period, whose master was Chaucer. The study of the inflection of the verb with reference to the syllabic value of final -*ë* is of peculiar importance and interest. The copyists are often in disagreement regarding the poet's inflectional forms, and absolute proof is wanting for some specific illustrations.

Chapter XIV.—The Inflection of the Speculum.

§ 1. Forms that may be referred to the present stem.

The Infinitive. The final *-n* of the O.E. infinitive is almost universally dropped, sometimes with apocope of the final *-e*, resulting from the weakening of *-a* of the O.E. termination. Twice, remains of the O.E. *-ian* class occur in *-i (y)*, confirmed by rime.

α. Infinitives in *-ë* (*-in, -yn* of the MSS.): *techë* : (*speche*) 2, 570, 754; *drawë* : (*plawe*) 16; *ledë* : (*drede*) 19; *hauë* 455, 529, 543, 567, etc.; *folewë* : *swolewë* 642; *shewë* : (*rewe*) 79. Apocope of the *-e* occurs: possibly *nempnę* (or double thesis at epic cæsura?) 101; *hauę* 148; *comę* 331; *louę* 343; a contracted form is *seïë* 445, 796.

β. O.E. *-n* is retained: *don* 643; *gon* : (*non*) 652; *ben* (A_1) 938; *knowën*? : (*owen*) 228; *betën* 175; but *chastęn* (*Kast, H_1*) 181; an abbreviated form is *han* 295. In some instances the retention of final *-n* is conducive to smoothness of metre: *bileuën* 273; *wilnën* 279; *tellën* 292; *wantën* 316.

γ. Forms without ending through loss of *-n* : *do* : (*also*) 10, 208, : (*to*) 68, : (*mo*) 274; *be* : (*charite*) 96; *go* : (*do*, pp.) 875.

δ. Infinitives in *-i, -y* are : *herkny* : (*merci*) 523; *comforti* (not understood by the copyist of *R;* cf. *R*) : (*witerli*) 688; and within the body of the text *singy* 714; *wonÿë* 634; cf. *welny* (D) 280; *perty* (D) 298. This distinctively Southern inflectional characteristic is abundant in *Aȝenbite, Ancr. Riwle, R. of G.*, and the *Poema Morale,* but the infinitive in *-i (-y)* occurs also in the Southern Midland poems, *Horn* (see Wissmann) *werie* 1411, *chaungi* 1076, and in the Auch. *Reinbrun* (*Gy, sone of Warwike*): *norsy* : *servy* 151; *pasy* : *prouy* 972. For this infinitive in East Midland poems, see Stürzen-Becker, p. 71; Morris, *Spec. of E. Lit.*, p. xxi.; in Chaucer, ten Br., § 196.

ε. *Gerund.* Instance of gerund occurs : *to donë* 852.

ζ. Of Romance origin are a few infinitives in rime : *greuë* : (*bileue*) 202, : (*Eue*) 230; *deuisë* 343; *duirë* 281; *sauë* : (*haue*) 478. *vsë* occurs 90; *suffrë* 184, 583; *preïë* 564.

Present indicative, 1 pers. sg. The ending is *-ë*, occurring in rime : *findë* : (*binde,* inf.) 481; *vnderstondë* : (*sonde*) 49; *menë* : (*clene*) 407; *liȝë* : (*cumpaignye*) 637; *seïë* 467; with apocope of the ending, *gretę* 52; *sey* 464. Romance form : *preïë*, 53, 601. *willë* (anomalous form) is confirmed by rime : *willë* : (*skile*) 712.

2 *pers.* The ending in *-ëst* (MS. *-us, -ys, -es*); *-ëst, -ęst* is of frequent occurrence not confirmed by ryme. The couplet preserves only the contracted form : *sist* : *bist* (*bitst*) 554; cf. *Floris und Blauncheft.*

clxxx *Chapter XIV.—The Inflection of the Speculum.*

105. The vowel of the radical is in general not modified. In the body of the text are to be noted the following examples: *metëst* 549; *ʒeuëst* 936; *coupëst* 657. In -*ęst* occur: *louęst* 13, 321, 337, etc.; *leuęst* 189; *sparęst* 795; *seist* 555; *sext* 385, give contracted forms.

3 pers. sg. The third person ends in -*þ* (MSS. -*es*, -*ythe*, etc.) once in rime: *geþ* : *vnmeþ* 616, possibly *seþ* 817, and almost universally within the body of the text, where no criterion exists to determine that -*ëþ* be not the language of the copyist. The vowel of the radical is not modified. Examples are: *bringëþ* 114; *beginnëþ* 126; *ʒeuëþ* 212; *louëþ* 340; *ofþinkëþ* 539; *bitoknëþ* 363; *lastëþ* 426; *spekëþ* 501; *makëþ* 520; *berëþ* 566; *fondëþ* 655. In -*ęþ* occur: *spekęþ* 275; *beręþ* 345; *fallęþ* 585; *faręþ* 669; *beręþ* 670; *semęþ* 697; *liuëþ* 733; *ʒeuęþ* 742. Contraction of the ending is recognized in *seiþ* 276, 339, 345, 459; *haþ* (3 sing.) 386, 695; *halt* 166, 171; *tit* 807; *sit*[1] (one of the ten verbs preserving the present form with -*jo*-) 255; *fint*? 785; *fleþ* 672; *lyþ* (*jo*- stem) 710, 713.

Plural. Riming couplets preserve -*ëþ* in one instance: *beþ* : *seþ* (sing.? *men* = *one*, German *man*?) 818, but the verse contains additional illustration of forms in -*ëþ* (MSS. -*iþ*, -*yþ*): *louëþ* 23; *beþ* 23, 76, 80, 97, etc.; *bisekëþ* 504; *wasshëþ* 818; *Makëþ* 828. With syncope of -*e*-: *þinkęþ* 150; *wasshęþ* 825. Plurals in -*ën* (-*ęn*), -*ë* (-*ę*), are offered by rime: (*whiles þeih*) *liuë* : (*ʒiue*, inf.) 184; (*Wheiþer . . .*) *nellë* : (*helle*) 272; (*as men*?) *redö* : (*seidë*) 692; *dredë* : (*dedë*) 830; (*þeih*) *be* 287, 341?, 414. The rime contributes a plural in -*ë*: (*we*) *findë* : (*winde*) 669. Examples not verified by rime are: *fallën* 170; *findën* 518; *wolën* 272. *comęn* 240, 280, *sholęn* 416 occur with syncopated -*ę*-. Contracted plural forms are: *han* 384; *fint* (or sing.?) 785.

Subjunctive. Present endings are -*ë* and -*ę*, 2nd pers.: *shonë* : (*wone*) 105; *missë* : (*wisse*) 120; *þu knowę* 74; *berę* 671; 3rd pers. in -*ë*: *she turnë* 966; *hauë*? (with apocope) 837; *be* : (*se*) 872.

Imperative singular. The riming couplet introduces no example of the imperative, but the text affords illustration. Here the distinction active in Chaucer (cf. ten Br., § 189) of the preservation through weakened endings of the O.E. inflection remains. The subdivision into strong and weak imperatives seems still extant through ending in -*ë* for weak verbs: *Herknë* 137, 419; *louë* 329; *hauë* (Mätzner II., p. 29) : (*saue*) 477; *Lokë* 488; but *Loug* with apocope 113.

---

[1] *sit* = absorption of inflectional *þ* with *t* of the radical. See *halt*, *tit*, and *fint*.

Chapter XIV.—The Inflection of the Speculum. clxxxi

Making allowance for possible *hiatus*, e. g. *Hĕrknë*, and 328 ; *Herknę*? 348, 378 ; *Lokę* 758, 768. Often divergence from the strong verb is not marked, and the two classes fall together in forms without -*ë*. Singular, weak : *lef* 392, 866 ; *Put* 476 ; *þenk*? 493 ; *Cast* 647 ; *sped* 865 ; *Bring* 970. Strong : *lat* (possibly through contraction) 143, 777 ; *Nym* 553 ; *Forʒif* 541, 555 ; *tak* 770 ; *Go* (anv.) 855 ; *Do* 969 ; *ʒif* 1012. Romance imperatives end in *-ë* : *Vëë* 82.

Plural. Plural endings seem to be *-ëþ* : *Herknëþ* 1, 790 ; *Sittëþ* 790 ; *Comëþ* 423 ; *Listnëþ* 753 ; *Wasshëþ* 816, 824, 848. Remnant of an older form is illustrated in *goþ* 445 ; see Schleich, p. 6. Riming forms contribute no important testimony for the *Speculum*.

Participle. The present participle is wanting in MS. A_1 of the *Speculum*, but A_2.D.H_1.R read *suffrand* (Northern form) 587, and A_2.D.R offer *suffrande* 597 (H_2 *sufferynge*, A_1 *suffraunt*), the Anglo-Norman participle in adjective construction.

Verbal substantives in -ing (or *-ingë*). Verbals are of frequent occurrence in rime and text : *biginning* : (*þing*) 7, 884 ; *biginning* : *ending* 210 ; *deiing* : *ending* 278 ; *shining* 382 ; *speking* 330 ; *woniʒing* : *deseruing* 314, : (*þing*) 317 ; *pining* : *brenning* 182, : (*king*) 899. In *-ingë*?: *mourningë* (*mōurning*? 123) : (*springë*, inf.) 125.

§ 2. Forms that may be referred to the first and second preterit stems.

Preterit. Strong verbs. Ablaut variations of the O.E. are preserved in the *Speculum :* tok : *forsok* 34 ; *drouh* : (*inouh*) 44 ; *bar* : (*war*) 46 ; *bicam* : *nam* 246 ; *lay* : (*day*) 249 ; *steih* 253 ; *sauh* 347, 350, 355, 374 ; *iseih* : (*heih*) 369, 991 ; *vnderstod* : (*god*) 462, 939 ; *bad* 571 ; *cam* : (*man*) 589 ; *gan* (in pleonastic construction) 641, 642 ; *slowen* 438.

Preterit. Weak verbs. The second person ends in *-ëst :* *noldëst* 659, and the preteritive-present *coupëst* 657. Syncopation occurs in *haddęstu* 579 ; *woldęstu* 873 ; *maitou* 343. See also *mait* 881, *miht* 1005. Otherwise weak verbs end in *-ęd, -dë, -të*. *Singular verbs*. (a) In *-ëd :* *liuędę* 38 ; *birëdę* 133 ; *answerdę* 971 ; *Grauntëdę* 988. (b) The weak ending recurring more frequently is *-dë*, illustrated as follows : *louedë* 35 ; *answeredë* : *heriedë* (*i. e.* through analogy with the present, ten Br., § 162) 66 ; *hadë* : *madë* 244 ; *deiedë* 248, 528 ; *shewedë* 361 ; *dedë* : (*stedë*) 598 ; *answeredë* 981 ; *seidë* (i. e. *sedë*) 965 ; *liuedë* 1004. Variation of the radical vowel occurs in *laddë* 42. Plural verbs : *woldën* 268 ; *woldë* 530 ; *seruedë* (2 pers. pl.) 452 ; *dedë* : (*stedë*) 603. With apocope : *haddę* 454.

clxxxii *Chapter XIV.—The Inflection of the Speculum.*

Apocope and elision are also active in the following instances of singular verbs. With apocope : *kudde* 178 ; *made* ? 213 ; *wolde* 529. With elision : *birede* 133 ; *dede* 230 ; *seide* 411. Syncope and elision are both marked in *deiede* 144, 531, and *liuede* 192. The *d* of the ending is lost ? in *sende* : (*amende*) 575, 951 ; *sende* : (*spende*) 989.

(c) Forms in *-të : wrouhtë* : *bouhtë* 26 ; *þouhtë* 32. In *-tẹ : bouhtẹ* 236. Resulting from assimilation of the termination and the final vowel of the radical occur *grettë* : *mettë* 350, 960, but *grettẹ* (with elision) 353, *puttẹ* 994, and *sentẹ* (before *h*-) 50 ; *kest* introduces a contracted form 992. Preteritive-present forms are : *mihtë* (1. sing.) 292 ; (3. sing.) 368, 376, 398. With elision : *Mihtẹ* 291, 366, 367, 396.

Past Participle of strong verbs. The participle ends in *-ë*, but forms occur in *-ën*. (a) In *-ë* or with loss of *-n : inomë* 644, 646 ; *boundë* : (*stoundë*) 710 ; *ilorë* : (*wharfore*) 715 ; *shriuë* : (*liue*) 758, 768 ; *forȝetë* 764 ; *foundë* 773 ; *ietë* : (*mete*) 984 ; *do* : (*so*) 174, : (*go*) 876. (b) In *-n : born* : *lorn* 130 ; *don* : (*non*) 264 ; *idon* : (*non*) 546 ; *don* 802, 837 ; ȝ*oldën* 932. A syncopated form is *comẹn* 67 ; *nomẹn* 649.

Past Participle of weak verbs. The weak participle ends in *-ëd*, resp. *-ẹd* and *-t*. (a) In *-ëd : Ibiriëd* 249 ; *wemmëd* 366 ; *prenëd* (or *preuẹd*, type C ?) : *ishewëd* (?) 399 ; *ifilëd* 410 ; *dampnëd* 432 ; *chargëd* 468 ; *ashamëd* : *ayramëd* 794 ; *clepëd* 857 ; *irekenëd* 869. In *-ẹd : wonẹd* 259 (or *wonëd*, clerical form *wont*) ; ȝ*arkẹd* 300 ; *ashamẹd* 809. Romance forms are *anuïëd* 124 ; *Sauuëd* 128 ; *honurëd* 521, 632. (b) In *-t : ikauht* 17 ; (*i*)*bouht* 160, 172, 226 ; (*i*)*pylt* 232, 888 ; *agilt* : *fulfilt* 308 ; *gilt* 556 ; *iwrouht* : (*noht*) 580, 803 ; *caiht* : (*mait*) 882 ; see also *leid* 592 ; *aferd* 685. A contracted form is *misseid* 538, 591 ; and the- Fr. Pic. *kauht* 17. *couþ* occurs (O.E. *cúþ* ; Goth. *kunþ-s*) 814.

The prefix i- in the past participle. The prefix *i-* is undoubtedly to be read. Stürzen-Becker, p. 74, writes concerning the value of this prefix in East Midland poems. It is illustrated in *King Horn : iborn* 140 ; *inome* 160. Its value in the metrical verse is pointed out in the accompanying selections :

v. 17 : For, whán þe wórld · þe háþ ikáuht.
v. 546 : Off tréspas, · þát þu hást idón.
v. 580 : But ús hit wús · þurw gód iwróuht.
v. 715 : Góstli wít · he háþ ilóre.
v. 724 : þurw dédli sínne · ifílëd ís.
v. 803 : And fóule sínnes · háþ iwróuht.

Chapter XIV.—The Inflection of the Speculum. clxxxiii

Indication of inheritance from reduplicating verbs is to be noted in the *Speculum*. Derivatives from *lētan, rǽdan, feallan, healdan, gongan, cnáwan* find representatives in this poem, chiefly through infinitives. Cf. the contracted form *halt* 171; *held* 593; *lat* 315; *gange* : (*longe*) 761; *knowe* : (*lowe*) 180, 629.

Contracted participles are to be noted in *idempt* (O.E. *gedémed, gedémde*, Siev. 406, N.) : *nempt* (O.E. *genemde*) 136, but on the other hand gemination is not simplified in the weak participle *wemmëd* 366. A remnant of the old ending is marked in *goþë* (the *-ë* added through false analogy) : (*loþe*) 448 ; for *gothë* : (*sothe*), v. 469 of the *Rolandslied*, see Schleich, pp. 6 and 13 (*Prolegomena*), and Wülker's note *Anglia*, III., p. 402. The MSS. vary in the orthography of the inflectional terminations, the later MSS. contributing Midland and Northern forms.

The examples cited in the preceding pages show, it is believed, that the poet pronounced *e* in unaccented syllables, and particularly in unaccented inflectional syllables. This principle governed the composition of words. The *e*, organic or inorganic, standing between the parts of a compound word was sounded by the poet. MS. A_1 often omits this *e*, and thus places two accented syllables in immediate juxtaposition. Conclusions regarding *e* in the unaccented syllables have been collected in the two following sections.

Composition.

An unstressed *-ë-*, required by the rhythm between principal and subordinate syllables in words of Teutonic or of Romance origin and frequently written in that position by the later MSS.,[1] rarely by MS. A_1, has often the place of an unaccented syllable with its equivalent value. Orrm illustrates this phenomenon (cf. Sachse, p. 63), and it exists in Chaucer. Illustrations contributed by the *Speculum* are as follows: *louërede* 177; *soþënesse* 346, 411, 664?; *soþëliche* 525, 609; *mildëliche* 605; *trewëliche* 610; *forȝiȝënesse* 683; *apertëliche* 385, 416; *knowëlache* 509; *knowëlaching* 725; Fr. derivatives: *amendëment* 56; *iugëment* 265, 878; *verreëment* 877; the Eng. *dirkënessë* (MSS. $D.II_1$) 114, (MSS. $A_2.D$) 306. In opposition to these conclusions the following instances are to be cited, where *-e-* is not marked by distinctive syllabic value: *soþnesse* or *soþenesse* 722; *Wraþful* 262; *seknesse* 187; *Stedefast* 85; *lihtliche* 198; *Sodeyngliche* 882; *dedli* 710, 713; *soþeliche* 441.

[1] The MSS. show much divergence in the introduction of this inorganic *-e*.

It would seem, that distinction should be made between the verse omitting the unaccented syllable through the deliberate intent of the poet, and the verse corrupt through the scribe. This alternative renders some forms difficult of classification. Cf. notably: verses 81, 125, 305, 360, etc. Allowance must be granted type C in a few instances. To be noted possibly for fluctuating accent is *neiheboure* 535.

Final -e.

Conclusions involved in the discussion of the preceding sections, depending on the historical verification of phonological and inflectional classification, are approximately determinative with reference to the syllabic value of the final -e of the poem. Regarded from a position within the line as testified to by the rhythm, and at times confirmed by instances representing the riming system, it seems evident that the poet pronounced final -e and the -e of inflectional syllables, and that the final -ë of Romance words was still a distinct syllable. Double forms having the same syntax are attested to (cf. *mouþe, mouþ*, etc.) by the *Speculum*, and are reconciled by rime and metre. Evidence for the -e before the cæsura is subject to modification, due to the existence of the types C and E.

Conclusive in the history of the poem is the decision that the value of the -e in inflectional syllables has not been lost, that important dissyllabic forms have not been reduced to monosyllables; and, it is confirmed, that the poet, as master of language, availed himself with true æsthetic spirit of the license of the use of forms fluctuating in syllabic value within the verse and at the rime.

CHAPTER XV.
DIALECT AND CHRONOLOGY OF THE *SPECULUM*.
§ 1. *The Dialect of the Poem.*

"Is your own land indeed so far away,[1]
As by your aspect it would seem to be?"
"But trusteth wel, I am a sotherne man."[2]

THE phonological and the inflectional systems of the *Speculum* afford criteria for the investigation of the dialect of the poet. The following testimony is of value in the discussion:

1. Obvious is the Southern element in the language of the poet in rigid distinction from the Northern, as is indicated through the

---

[1] Rossetti's translation of Dante's *Vita Nuova*.
[2] Chaucer, *Persones Tale, Prologue*, v. 42.

Chapter XV.—The Dialect of the Poem.

following combinations. *Nōn* is embodied in rime with *dōn* (pp.) 263 and with *idōn* 545, etc. *alsō* occurs with *dō* 9, 207, 897. *gō* is united with *dō* (pp.) 875 ; *þō* with *misdō* 557 ; *mō* with *dō* 273 ; and *sō* with *dō* 173, 673. *wō* is in rime with *dō* 484 and 917.

2. The representative vowels *i, ī,* < O.E. *y, ȳ* (umlaut of *u, ū*), in rime with *stable i ī*, offer conclusive evidence for Midland dialect. Conclusive Midland forms are found in the following combinations: *mynde* with *linde* 496 ; and *pride* with *side* 656 ; *sinnë : winnë* 131, 472, 693, 845, 1007 ; *sinnë : widinnë* 117 ; *sinnë : blinnë* 713 ; *sinnë : innë* 732 ; *sinnë : þerinnë* 839 ; *sinnë : liginnë* 902 ; *puite : luite* 924. The self-rimes, *pride : huide* 158 ; *mindë : kindë* 620 ; *agilt : fulfilt* 308 ; *gilt : pylt* 232, and *gilt : ipult* 888, contribute nothing in the specification of the dialect, but confirm the testimony of decisive rimes.

3. Conclusive for Midland influence is the inflectional form in the plural of the present indicative. The ending -*ë* is uniformly returned by riming couplets : (*we*) *findë : (windë)* 669 ; (*men*) *redë : (seidë* for *sedë*) 692 ; *liuë* (3 plu.) : (*ȝiuë,* inf.) 184. The number of these forms is increased by the plurals of the regular text in its various MSS. Cf. *fallën* 170 ; *sholën* 281, 288, 295, 309, etc.

4. A Midland country in its Eastern division or a Southern neighbourhood is the evidence of *geþ : (unmeþ)* 616, third person singular, and possibly *seþ* (subject, *men = one*) *: beþ* (plu.) 818. Inflection by means of -*ëst* and -*ëþ* in the second and third persons singular is abundant in positions not supported by the rime. Indecisive is the form *sist : bist* 554. The text also affords plural verbs marked by the Southern ending -*ëþ : beþ* 23, 97 ; *louëþ* 23 ; *seiþ* 339 ; *lisekëþ* 504 ; *Makëþ* 828 ; *þinkëþ* 150 ; *wasshëþ* 825.

5. Apparently contradicting a claim to Midland origin through a form peculiar to the Kentish vocabulary but used by Chaucer, is the rime *fyr : her* (O.E. *hêr*) 451 ; *fire : here* (O.E. *hȳran, hîeran,* Angl. *hêran, i-* umlaut of *êa*) has no value in determining dialect, see Kölbing, *Sir Beues,* p. xvi. *dede : stede* 598, 603, may be read *dide : stide,* or *dude : stude. dide* (sing. or plu.) is explained by Morsb. § 130, Anm. 6, as representing an older *i (y)* ; *stede* preserves Kentish -*e-* ; see reference to Siev., *Beitr.,* vol. xvi., p. 235, Morsb., § 132, Anm. 2. This form is employed by *Rht. of G.,* v. 330, but it was found in all parts of England ; cf. *Gen. and Ex.,* 1298, 1836. For *styde,* see Streitberg, *Urgerm. Gram.,* p. 44, N. 1.

6. Southern is the infinitive in -*i, y: herkny : (merci)* 523 ;

comforti : (*witerli*) 688. The text offers: *singy* 714; *wonye* 634. These infinitives are not incompatible with Midland authorship, as will be recognized by comparison with *King Horn:* *werie* 1411; *chaungi* (Fr. origin) 1076.

7. Through the prefix *i-* (O.E. *ge*), required by the metre, and the loss of the inflectional final -*n*, the past participle is recognized as Southern in development: *inome* : (*some*) 644; *ilore* : (*wharfore*) 715. The Midland *King Horn* duplicates the phenomenon, verses 140, 162, 484, 500, 548, etc.

8. The normal form *sede* (O.E. *sǽde*) of frequent recurrence and verified by rime as follows : *sede* (MS. *seide*) : (*drede*) 140, 494, : (*rede*) 168, 691, characteristic of Southern poems, is, according to Sarrazin (*Octavian*), specifically a Kentish feature; cf. Wilda's note, p. 51, Pabst's, p. 26, Menze's, p. 21, and Brandl, *Anzeiger für d. Alt.* xix. 101. *sede* : (*rede*) 155, 223 ; *sede* : (*dede*) 131, occur in the *Poema Morale*. *sede* in rime with *drede*, *rede*, etc., is the reading of *Sir Beues;* see Kölbing, p. xv. *ful iwis* 285, 337, and *mid iwisse* 309, 689 occur in Southern poems; cf. *Poema Morale* 40, 141, 154, (*mid nane jwisse*) 236, 375, 391 ; *On God Ureisun of Ure Lefdi* 6 ; *De Muliere Samaritana* 37, 53. *henne* (O.E. *heonon*) : (*kenne*) 297, contributes a Southern rime, Sarrazin and Carstens, p. 8, Nessmann, p. 10.

9. Significant for Western origin is the couplet *fire* : *duire* (Fr. *duirer*) 282, see *Rbt. of G.* 3760, *dure* : *fure*, but *dure* : *fuire* occurs in *Alisaunder* 4322, a Southern poem with Kentish peculiarities. The *ui* represents the orthography of the *Ancren Riwle*, *Hali Meidenhad*, etc., Morsb., §§ 132, 133, 2 Anm. 2. The possibility of determinative value for dialectical purposes of the rime *puite* : *luite* 923, is weakened through the uncertainty of Anglicists regarding the specific etymology of *puite* (N.E. *put*). It is suggestive of *put* (read *pit*) : *wytte*, *Floris und Blaunchefl.*; cf. Hausknecht, p. 132, 1. The rime is probably *pitte* : *lîte* with unequal quality, see Morsb., § 129, Anm. 4, b, and p. 181.

Other couplets, calling to mind a South-western country, unfortunately do not occur in such connection as to become of value in the investigation. *ipult* : *gilt* 888 (cf. v. 232), *muche* : *aperteliche* 386, and : *lihtliche* 671, *churche* : *worche* 859, are not significant in dialectical study. They may be read with equal correctness *ipilt*, *miche*, *chirche* : *wirche*. *turne* : *sterne* 435, apparently characteristic of the Kentish dialect, is not impossible in Midland dialect, and is actually the form of Orrm. 961; cf. Morsb., p. 167.

Chapter XV.—*Chronology of the Speculum.*

Examining the conclusions derived from the foregoing paragraphs, the preponderance of testimony, contributed by the mass of phonetic and inflectional characteristics, argues for the poem a Midland nativity. Sporadic forms locate the poet in an East Midland territory, perhaps in the neighbourhood of *Floris and Blauncheflur* or *King Horn*, a poem also coloured with strictly Kentish characteristics. But this original home must have been far to the South, on proof of characteristic elements of the language. Some margin must be conceded in this judgment, for a poet of advanced culture in his age, as was illustrated in Chaucer, might have left the mark of the breadth of his culture in the variety of phonological elements represented in his speech. Still it would seem, that many Southern characteristics, and the combined value of the Southern features, would indicate that the environment of the poem was to some degree Southern.[1] The Western elements of the poet's language are not essentially farther to the West than are those of the *Hali Meidenhad*, *Katherine*, and other lives of saints, comprising Professor Morsbach's Katherine-group. With due regard, then, for rimes that might, *primâ facie*, indicate other locality, it would seem that the phonetic elements of the language of the *Speculum* combine in ascribing the *Speculum* to a country intermediate in position between the East and the West, but eastern rather than western. The poem has the colouring of the dialect spoken near the Midland boundary, possibly in a territory not far removed from the home of the legends of the saints, represented by the legend of Katherine, but in the associated neighbourhood of *Sir Beues;* see characteristics summarized by Kölbing, pp. xx., xxi.

§ 2. *Chronology of the Speculum.*

Absolute evidence affording even approximately an exact date for the composition of the *Speculum* has not been discovered. On ground of external test its ulterior terminus is naturally the limit of its oldest transcript. As an individual member of the Auchinleck collection, palæographical considerations suggest that the *Speculum* be regarded as a representative of the early decades of the 14th century. Important testimony is contributed by Zupitza, testing the

---

[1] In the early study of the dialect of the *Speculum*, in April 1894, the editor regarded the poem as a type of Middle-Kentish (borrowing Danker's phrase) literature. On later consideration it seemed that the rimes *i*, *í* (O.E. *y*, *ȳ*) : *i*, *í* (O.E. *i*, *í*) are sufficiently numerous to be evidence of Midland environment ; this a suggestion of Zupitza in 1894, later confirmed by Kölbing, both in personal communication with the editor.

Chapter XV.—Chronology of the Speculum.

age of *The Riming Chronicle, Liber Rerum Angliæ,* Auch. 40; see *Archiv für das Studium der neueren Sprachen und Litteraturen,* vol. lxxxvii., p. 90. He recognizes as determinative basis the period of King Edward the Second (Ed. II.), the Auchinleck list of kings continuing to 1327 through the reign of that monarch. Zupitza writes: *die in ihr (i. e.* the Auch. MS.) *gegebene Version der Chronicle of England geht bis zum Regierungsantritte Edward III.* Directly interpreted this specific transcript could not have been completed earlier than 1327, and, if Virgilian philosophy be valid, *ab uno disce omnes,* the *Speculum* on this proof could not be ascribed to a date earlier than 1327. The examination of the massive "Affleck" folio with its exquisite workmanship, and with the indication of the existence of large numbers of finely wrought illuminations belonging to the original volume, suggests that the mechanical execution of details of such delicacy could have demanded that an interval of a number of years intervene between the transcription of No. 10 and the completion of No. 40. The year 1325 might then be a generous limit *ad quem* for the *Speculum.* Considerable uniformity in the handwriting indicates that the transcripts were prepared at approximately the same general period. The *Speculum* bears, it is true, a different script. That change in text does not necessarily indicate a later interpolation, but rather the influence of another copyist, as seems confirmed in the fact that the ninth selection bearing the original number XIV., immediately preceding the tenth piece, original number XV., contains near the bottom of fol. 38 *d* instructions for the copyist, the first line of folio 39 *a* in the handwriting of the scribe of No. XIV: *Herkne al to mi spech* (cf. text), also the hand of text XVI. immediately following the *Speculum.* That this marks no irregularity, is further attested through the circumstance that the various articles follow[1] each other in orderly sequence,[2] apparently not disturbed by any irregularity in workmanship; cf. also Kölbing, *Englische Studien,* vol. vii., p. 183.

Various limits have been proposed dating this choice relic of Boswell's library. Numerous speculative periods, individual problems,

---

[1] "The poems regularly follow each other. There is no reason to believe that the alteration in script indicates earlier or later date than may be reasonably ascribed to the rest of the works;" see Scott, *Sir Tristrem,* pp. cvii., cviii.

[2] The Auchinleck MS. was, it will be recalled, the property of Alexander Boswell, father of Johnson's celebrated Boswell. The manuscript folio was a gift to the Faculty of Advocates in 1744. Interesting is the history of four of its leaves, the possession of David Laing. These precious parchments had served as covers for books and blanks, until purchased by Laing in 1750.

have been attributed to the Auchinleck texts by its various editors. Kölbing, *Sir Beues*, p. vii., dates the collection not younger than 1327; Scott, *Sir Tristrem* (1804), p. lxxxi., 1330; Ellis, *Early English Pronunciation*, vol. ii., p. 448, the beginning of the 14th century; Skeat, *Specimens of Early English*, vol. ii., p. xxxix., 1320—1330; Laing, *A Penni worth of Witte*, etc., p. i., "not later than the middle of the 14th century." "The *Speculum*," says a well-known Anglicist, "could have been copied into the collection so early as the 1310." Ritson, questionable authority, *A.E. Metrical Romancëes*, p. lxxxvi., mentioning the fact, that several poems of the folio refer to the reign of Edward the Second, believes that no romance was entered into the collective MS. before the time of Edward the First. Scott,[1] p. cvii., discusses the possibility of the earlier part of the 14th century, and p. lxxxi., has concluded that the date of the collection does not seem to be much later than 1330. The *Catalogue of MSS.* in the Advocates' Library, probably influenced by Scott, states indefinitely, about the middle of the 14th century. It would seem, from weight of general testimony, that the compilation of the Auchinleck texts was completed before 1340. That the common original of the MSS. of the *Speculum* could hardly have been transcribed later than 1325, is necessary, if the foregoing evidence be valid. On the other hand, there is nothing to dispute a greater antiquity or a more flowery youth. That the Auchinleck copies be a forgery of the 17th century, as Hazlitt[2] (*Remains of the Early Popular Poetry of England*, vol. i., p. 193) maintains, there is not the smallest proof.

Nor do the sources of the *Speculum* contribute material conducive in marking progress in the solution of the age of the poem recorded. Were the verses 355—368 to be considered as definitely an adaptation of stanza twelve of the fundamental poem underlying Chaucer's *A. B. C.*, and ascribable to the same source, de Deguileville (cf. chap. x.), then these verses written 1330—1331 (cf. Skeat, *Minor Poems*, 1888, p. xlvii.) contribute inferior date for the *Speculum*; but, although there is nothing seriously incompatible with this assumption, the evidence is not conclusive. The inference is not necessary, for the parallel metaphor was in existence so early as the 12th century, or earlier (cf. *Sources*, chap. x.), and Legends of Mary

---

[1] "The date of the MS. cannot possibly be earlier, and does not seem to be later than 1330," Scott, p. lxxxi.
[2] After examination of Hazlitt's note, I find a reference to the same statement in Mall's *Harrowing of Hell*, p. 5, in which he expresses opinion that Hazlitt's conclusion is *übertrieben*.

began to be recognized in English literature in the 13th century; cf. Lauchert, *Englische Studien*, vol. xvi., p. 124: *Erst am anfang des* 13. *jht. erscheint das Marienlied in der englischen litteratur.*

The solution of the question of the chronology is not advanced by the testimony of the MSS. The Guy legend was promulgated no earlier probably than the 13th century, as is the argument of its oldest MS., the Wolfenbüttel Codex, No. 87.4, *Augusteorum Guelferbyt.* of the 13th century. To this century belong the French MSS. of the Bodleian Library. The earliest English MS. does not permit the diminution of years from the history of the *Speculum*. It is a contemporaneous MS. of the Auchinleck collection. The remaining French MSS. and all the English MSS. belong to later centuries. The account of Guido in the *Gesta Romanorum*, ed. Oesterley, Berlin 1872, is of the late 13th century.[1] The *Dictionary of National Biography*, in a carefully discussed article over Guy of Warwick, grants literary form to the saga in the concluding years of the 12th century; ten Brink (*Eng. Lit.*, I. p. 246) believes that "Guy of Warwick and Bevis of Hamptoun were unknown to saga until they emerge as heroes of Anglo-Norman poems of the 12th century." An editorial note to Percy's *Folio MS.*, vol. ii., p. 509, allots the oldest literary form to the 13th century; Tanner (*Die Saga v. Guy v. Warwick*, p. 34), the 13th century; Jusserand (*Eng. Novel*, p. 39), the 13th century; Ritson, not later than the reign of Edward the First, and in the *Legendæ Catholicæ* (1840, cf. chap. ii., § 3), in the 13th or early 14th century; Morley (*Eng. Writers*, vol. iii., p. 276), the 13th century. That the Alexius saga was associated with an English hero in the 11th century (cf. G. Paris, p. 27, and Pannier, p. 340), opens the question as to whether the same germ could have become associated with Count Guido at an early stage of the development of the Alexius literature, and distinct from Guy of Warwick. The theological element in the *Speculum* points to a period of religious awakening,[2] such as was conspicuous in Southern England[3] in the 13th century.

[1] ten Br., I. p. 264. See also *Gesta Romanorum*, ed. of Wilhelm Dick, Erlangen 1890.
[2] Ritson, *Cath. Leg.*, ascribes the folio to "the gloomy fanaticism of a lazy monk" . . . "for the promotion of fanaticism," see pp. xi. and xii.
[3] Ritson, p. v. of *Cath. Leg.*, believes that the Auchinleck texts were written "in some North of England monastery," in opposition to Scott's view that the folio was written in South Britain. Scott's argument is, that every poem that introduces local reference concerns South England, and not a word refers to Scottish affairs. Scott locates the scriptorium of an Anglo-Norman convent as the scene of the workmanship of the Auch. texts (cf. p. cviii.). Laing confirms Ritson's conjecture, but places the location in the extreme North of Scotland.

Chapter XV.—Chronology of the Speculum.

Were it possible to ascribe connection with "Count Guido's Address to Guy of Warwick," Camb. MS. Ii. I. 33, the history of the *Speculum* could be conveyed to a more remote period. This MS. is attributed to the 12th century, but the text seems to represent virtually an 11th-century version. The language is archaic. Old forms are used intelligently. The weakening of unaccented vowels is not abundant. Full vowels are employed consistently. Such conditions would place the O.E. *Liber* so early as the year 1000 or 1025. Some points of coincidence could be traced more readily between the *Speculum* and the MS. *Vesp. D*, xiv., fol. 104 a ff., described in Hickes' *Thesaurus*, the *Wanley Catalogue*, pp. 246 ff.; cf. Assmann, *Anglia*, xi., p. 371, and *Homilien und Heiligenleben, Bibliothek der A.S. Prosa*, vol. iii., pp. 246 ff., probably the composition of one of the School of Ælfric, as Assmann suggests. This work has been ascribed to the last years of the 12th century; cf. Nehab, *Der altenglische Cato*, a Berlin dissertation, 1879, pp. 32—41. This premise would give the vantage ground of a hundred years to the earlier cited 13th century. The cogency of such a premise would be disputed; cf. Morsb. i., § 1, Anm. 1. The *Liber* is not of service in ascribing terminology to the *Speculum*, but internal tests, theological, æsthetical, metrical, phonological, ascribe to the poem an early composition.

The theology of the poem contributes no facts useful in establishing its exact age. Mediæval theories of hell fires, heaven's blisses, popular versions of the fall of Lucifer, reproduce tone and feeling of ages earlier than the 12th century, where these attributes of Christian doctrine are preserved; cf. *O.E. Homilies* edited by Morris (E. E. T. S.). It is possible that the hypothetical period allotted to the authorship of the *Speculum* finds terminus at one extreme by the date 1325. It is not probable that the poem was materially a later product, and it may be inferred that it was a much earlier composition. That conclusion will be in harmony with the history of associated Romance poems. Scott's protracted and tireless search for Thomas the Rhymer placed the composition of *Sir Tristrem* in 1250. *Sir Beues's* history begins with the 13th century, Kölbing, p. xxxviii.

Internal evidence of the poem, on basis of phonological and inflectional investigation, will probably demonstrate that the poem was not the product of a period earlier than 1250. Compare the chapters over *Phonology* and *Inflection*.

1. The lengthening of the short vowel in open syllables had already occurred. Whether this linguistic change immediately preceded or immediately followed 1250, the date of the composition of the *Speculum* must be associated with a later period.

2. O.E. *á* had passed into *ō*. This could not have occurred later than 1250; cf. Morsb., § 64, and Napier, *Compassio Mariæ*, p. 84.

3. In harmony with these conclusions is the retention of final *-ë* in the language of the poet. This recurs with a fair degree of constancy. Compare the section over final *-e*. The *Speculum* is an early production, yet naturally it does not represent a composition on the immediate boundary of the O.E. period, the weakening of the O.E. full vowel having occurred long before. On the other hand, it is to be conjectured that it may present an early phase in the history of the M.E. poetry.

4. Were the diphthongic character of *e + o* (*ëo*?), for example, to be regarded as an internal trait of the *Speculum*, that feature would attest to the antiquity of the original; cf. Napier, p. 86. The transition stage in the orthography *ei*, *Streinþe*, l. 305, suggests early condition of the language.

In conclusion,[1] it is to be said that the poem, the *Speculum*, must be ascribed to a period *circa* 1300. The limits seem certainly within the boundaries 1250—1325. The authority of the phonology of the text would justify the hypothesis of the existence of the poem even before the concluding years of the 13th century.

CHAPTER XVI.
AUTHORSHIP OF THE *SPECULUM*.
§ 1. *Conjectured Authorship.*

1. *Lydgate*. The *Library Catalogue* of the MSS. of the British Museum classifies the MS. Harley 525 (H_2) among texts of John Lydgate. Certain external evidence might tend to justify this arrangement. Metrical, grammatical, and dialectical features of the transcript preserved in MS. H_2, and particularly the name of the central figure of the narrative, suggest, at casual glance, Lydgate. Moreover, to ascribe the paternity of a M.E. poem to John Lydgate[2]

---

[1] A chapter on *The Style of the Speculum* could be appropriately introduced at this point; but the more conspicuous characteristics of the poem have demanded so full a discussion, that it seems wise to reserve the investigation for a special article.

[2] For the authentic works of Lydgate, see Schick, pp. cxii, and cliv, clv.

is a fallacy of the age.[1] It is a fallacy in this instance, for the author of the *Speculum* was probably dead before Lydgate was born. 1368 is the earliest year[2] to which the birth of the monk of Bury is ascribed; 1370 is probably the more correct limit.[3] The original poem of which MS. H_2 is a late transcript must certainly have been in existence in 1327, forty years and more before the advent into the world of "that approbate" priest, its reputed author. The poet must indeed be permitted the privilege of birth before that of authorship. *Poeta nascitur non fit.* Contrary to circumstantial evidence, history offers facts *à priori* not to be controverted. John Lydgate's claim to the authorship of the *Speculum* is ungrounded. The argument is *reductio ad absurdum* on proof of the earliest MS. of the poem. It might be intimated, that the *Catalogue* of the Harleian collection be placed "under correccioun."[4]

2. *Alquin versus Alcuin.* The *Speculum* testifies concerning its authorship. Thus it is learned who wrote the sermon for Guy: "Alquin was his rihte name," l. 39. Sir James Foulis, according to Ritson, *A. E. M. R.* I. p. xciii, explains that *Alquin* was "a Scotch Highlander." On investigation it might seem that Sir James is a myth, as is his Scotchman. History provides no direct personality for these two gentlemen. In the records of the family Sir James Foulis,[5] ancestor of the race, Burgess of London, died in 1549, and his grandson,[6] Sir James Foulis, the last Lord Colinton, two generations removed, died in 1688; cf. the interesting records made public in *The Account Book of Sir John Foulis of Ravenston,* 1671—1707, by Rev. A. W. Cornelius, Edinb. 1894. Yet if Sir James cannot be identified in person, it is not impossible that Ritson refers to some

---

[1] "The great names of literature have always been made the official fathers of unclaimed productions;" cf. Gollancz, *Pearl,* pp. xliv and xlv.
[2] Cf. also ten Brink, *Gesch. der Engl. Lit.,* ed. Brandl, Bd. II, p. 273 (Engl. ed.), where the dates 1371 and 1373 are offered for consideration.
[3] Schick, *Temple of Glas,* p. lxxxvii.
[4] The circumstance is worthy of Lydgate. His search after opportunity for self-deprecatory phraseology is in attempted imitation, perhaps, of Chaucer, his "maister"; cf. *Prologue to the Persones Tale,* v. 56 (v. 17367, Tyrwhitt's enumeration),
"(But natheles this meditacion)
I putte it ay vnder correccion."
Compare Schick's discussion of the question, pp. cxl and cxli, with quotation from *Troilus,* III, 1283, p. lxxxv, "alle under correccion."
[5] The figure of Sir James Foulis is to be recognized in the group of Scottish nobles, portrayed on the famous window adorning the parliamentary buildings, Edinburgh.
[6] Cf. Genealogical Tables accompanying the Foulis *Account Book.*

descendant of the family[1] Foulis, whose members have long been influential in the affairs of Scotland. Although no literary record authorizes the testimony of Foulis, still Ritson's quotation might be based upon some personal communication. The statement accredited to Sir James may be accounted for on various grounds. The *Speculum* could easily be regarded as the product of the authorship of that Alquin or Alcuin of Britain, *nom de plume* of Jacob Ilive, who " went on a Pilgrimage to the Holy Land," and whose pseudo-translation into English of the *Book of Jasher*[2] was published in 1751. Another hypothesis is, that Foulis might have been misled by the orthography. Finding a clue in a phonological test he might have conjectured the *-qu-* of Alquin to indicate Scotch origin. On the supposition of further investigation on the part of Foulis, Albinus, *Alcuin Albinus Flaccus*, could have suggested to him a native of Alban or a home in Alban. In this manner Alquin (Alcuinus) could have been converted into a Scotchman without having ever trod the Alban soil. But these conjectures are not supported, for the language and vocabulary of the *Speculum* do not indicate Scottish source for the original poem. Ritson attempts to correct the error[3] of Foulis, explaining that the Alquin here meant (*i. e.* in the *Speculum*) was Alquinus = Albinus Alcuinus, a Saxon-Engleishman at the court of Charlemagne; cf. *A. E. Metrical Romanceës*, p. xci. A blunder equally grave is involved in Ritson's explanation, for *Ealhwine* was, of course, no Saxon.

On the other hand, the underlying Latin text, *De Virtutibus et Vitiis Liber*, is by no means so conspicuous as source of the *Speculum* as to give to Alcuin, Alcuinus, Albinus Flaccus, who died in 804, preceptor of Charlemagne, any claim to the authorship of the present text. Rather the poem stands as an individual product. Its author, the poet, must be responsible for the entire composition.

3. *The poet of Ipotis as author of the Speculum.* Concerning alleged claim of the same authorship for the *Speculum* and for *Ipotis*, nothing is to be proved. On purely external evidence the personal

---

[1] There seems to be no connection between the family of Sir James and that of the eminent Glasgow printers to the University, which has identified the name Foulis with immaculate prints of the classics. Robert Foulis's *Demetrius Phalereus on Elocution*, 1742, the first Greek text printed in Glasgow, and the celebrated edition of *Horace*, 1744, have immortalized themselves in the memory of *literati*.
[2] Cf. *Holy Scriptures*, Josh. x. 13; 2 Sam. i. 18.
[3] No explanation occurs through Sir Henry Foulis's (Bart.) *Relation of a bloody fight*, etc.

character of the two poets is at the two diverging extremes of development. The same poet could have written the two poems only under different degrees of inspiration, or under varying conditions of life. *Ipotis* stands for a cruder nature, a narrower phase of experience. The artistic element is marked in the *Speculum*, but the poet of *Ipotis* permits all the machinery of his workmanship to be visible in rigid harshness.

As for internal tests, there are none of importance to cite. A few parallel passages are to be quoted; a few coincidences in construction can be traced. But no peculiar merit is to be ascribed to a common use of terms like the following (see Gruber, *Zu dem mittelenglischen Dialog 'Ipotis'*; Berlin, 1887): *hevene may wynne* (MS. D) 25, *Spec.* 5; *dedly synne* 26, *Spec.* 724; *hevene blysse* 30, *Spec.* 309—10; *in hys seruyse* B 612, *Spec.* 36. Prayer Book descriptions of God, ll. 35—36, *Spec.* 207—10, the Trinity, ll. 54—57, *Spec.* 204—6, an account of the fall of Lucifer, ll. 106—108, *Spec.* 635—44, point to nothing startlingly original in mental activity. The rimes are ordinary and do not contribute evidence marking connection with the *Speculum*. Both poems account for authorship on weirdly impossible grounds. It will be remembered that the *Ipotis* attributes its source to the apostle John, a theory fallacious on its surface, as well as assured by the crude verse. The assumption is without the grounds for possibility that must be permitted the hypothesis of the *Speculum*. The charming fantasy discovering a personality for Guy of Warwick in Count Guido is not reproduced in the awkward assurance of verses 613—616:

"Seynt Jon þe evangeliste,
þat ȝede in erþe with Jesu Cryste,
þis talle he fond in latyn
And dede it wrytte in parchemyn."—*Ipotis*, MS. B.

Nothing more striking can, it seems, be cited to clinch the argument of coincidence in the authorship of *Ipotis* and *Speculum*.

§ 2. *The Actual Author of the Speculum.*

"I know him by his harp of gold."[1]

History has not revealed the name of the poet of the *Speculum*. Whether he be called Lydgate or Alcuin, or whether he remain a nameless spirit, his name is of secondary interest. The man is to be recognized through his work. As to his individuality, as represented

[1] *Tristram and Iseult*, Part I, v. 19. *Poems by Matthew Arnold*, Macmillan, MDCCCLXXX, p. 132.

in his character and his personality, his mirror reflects his own features. The poet belonged to the clergy, but he was no ordinary priest. He lived no humdrum life of ascetic severity. His horizon was broadened by gifts of homely personal sympathy for his flock. His heavens had midsummer clearness through the beautifying dignity of love to humanity. The poet illustrates forcibly the application of the *Ars Poetica* that tuned the classic lyre of Penshurst and *Arcadia: sayde my Muse to mee, looke in thine heart, and write*.

The minstrel's songs peopled for him a glowing world of fancy, a vision of the hero in generous deeds. The knowledge that he uniformly displays of the Holy Scriptures and of the works of the fathers, suggests preparation for the priesthood and recalls hours of study at some monastic school, some English Abbey like that of the Holy St. Martin in France, with "quiet cloisters and gardens, in which the arts of peace[1] could be cultivated," and where a gentle and pious brotherhood could " illumine a martyrology or carve a crucifix."

The *Speculum* testifies to the worth and permanence of the individual; it reveals the story of a life. That life marks triumph over temptation, a longing for the mercy that the poet implores be given, a struggle after holy living, so that *In holinesse his lyf he ladde*, l. 42. The poet has learned the lessons that he would teach, of fortitude, of patience, of hope, of faith, of trust. He has lived through the humility of confession. He has found joy and peace. Alcuin's *Liber* is for him no collection of well-dried statistics. On the contrary, it reproduces his own experience. He has developed character, that gives as well as receives, in sympathy and helpfulness. He has grown not narrowly in mind alone, but in heart, in breadth of soul, in all that for this period could make true and intelligent manhood.

Did this modest country priest take part in church controversy, his attitude must have been that of the humanitarian. His argument would be primarily the doctrine of enforcing principle through laws of Christian brotherhood. He would become the apostle of gentleness, of culture, of kindly speech, the optimistic apostle of joy, the mind at peace, for,[2]

". . . gently comes the world to those
That are cast in gentle mould."

[1] Cf. Macaulay.
[2] It was not until a year after the present sketch had been completed, that the editor discovered that a similar theme had served as similar inspiration to Mr. Gollancz in his graceful "hypothetical biography" of the poet of *Pearl*. Cf. pp. xlvi, xlvii, xlviii.

Here gynneþ þe sermon
þat a clerk made þat was cleput Alquyn
To Gwy of Warwyk

Guy of Warwick, in deep remorse, would expiate his offences against God. He told his wish to Alquin, Dean of a religious brotherhood, and asked counsel for the welfare of his soul. The holy friar prepared a sermon, in which he instructed Guy how to discriminate between virtue and vice. The discourse unfolds principles of spiritual growth through a twofold medium, the renunciation of evil and the achievement of good. Alquin concludes with an appeal for benevolence, which is enforced by an account of the incident of the widow of Zarephath.

Speculum Gy de Warewyke.

Herkneþ alle to my speche, *39 a* Hearken!
  And hele of soule i may ou teche. I teach of the soul's health.
  Þat i wole speke, it is no fable,
  Ac hit is swiþe profitable. 4
  Man, if þu wolt heuene winne, To win heaven,
Þurw loue to god þu most biginne. love God and
Þus shal ben þi biginni*n*g :
Þu loue god ouer alle þing 8
¶ And þin emcristene loue also, thy fellow-Christian.
Riht as þi-self[e] þu most do.
If þu wolt þus bigi*n*ne and ende,
Þu miht be seker to heuene we*n*de ; 12
Ac, if þu louest more worldes god Flee the world.
Þan god him-self[e] in þi mod,
Þu shalt hit finde an yuel plawe :
To deþ of soule it wole þe drawe, 16 To death
¶ For, whan þe world þe haþ ikauht the world's
In[1] his paunter þurw his drauht, net drags the soul,

For the title, see the Introduction. The numbering of the folio follows the Auchinleck MS. The character ¶ reproduces the paragraphing of the Auchinleck text.   1 to] vnto DH$_2$.   2 And] om. D.   may] wyll A$_2$DH$_1$H$_2$R.   3 no] not R.   4 Ac] Bot DH$_2$R, For H$_1$.   swiþe] ful H$_1$R, very gode & H$_2$.   Between 4 and 5 the following three lines are interpolated in H$_2$:

  For the sowlys saluacyowne
  Who soo that herythe þis sermoune
  Inicium sapiencie timor domini   (Cp. H$_2$ in l. 138.)

6 Þurw loue] To loue H$_1$.   to god] of god A$_2$D, god H$_1$, om. H$_2$.   7 and 8 are omitted in H$_1$.   7 Þus] Þis A$_2$H$_2$R.   shal ben þi] ys the fyrste H$_2$.   8 Þu] To A$_2$, om. DH$_2$.   god ouer] wele god abovyn H$_2$.   9 emcristene] euen crystyn A$_2$DH$_1$H$_2$R.   loue] om. A$_2$H$_2$, þou loue H$_1$.   10 do] do so D.   11 and 12 are omitted in H$_2$.   11 If] And if R.   12 miht be] may R.   wende] to wende R.   13 Ac if] And ȝef A$_2$D, But and H$_1$, Iffe H$_2$, But if R.   worldes] þe worldes A$_2$, worldly H$_1$, þis worldis H$_2$, worldlis R.   15 an] for an H$_1$.   plawe] lawe (*The word was originally plawe. þ can be traced in the erasure.*) D.   17 ikauht] caught A$_2$DH$_2$R.   18 In] In to H$_2$.   þurw his] at a A$_2$.

   [1] *MSS. A$_1$ and A$_2$ have* and in.

and thou	Al at his wille he wole þe lede.	
	Ne shaltu spare for no drede,	20
	Ne for loue to god, ne for his eiȝe,	
shalt suffer.	To gon out of þe rihte weye;	
	¶ For swiche [þer] beþ, þat loueþ more	
	þe world and his foule lore,	24
	þan þeih don god, þat hem wrouhte 39 b	
	And on þe rode [hem] dere bouhte.	
	¶ Her-of i wole a while dwelle,	
I wish to tell	And a tale i wole ȝou telle	28
of an earl,	Off an eorl of gode fame—	
Guy of Warwick,	Gy of Warwyk was his name—	
	Hou on a time he stod in þouht:	
	þe worldes blisse him þouhte noht.	32
how he forsook the world,	þe world anon he þer[1] forsok	
	And to Iesu Crist him tok,	
and chose God.	And louede god and his lore	
	And in his seruise was euere more.	36
A devout man,	¶ A god man þer was in þilke dawe,	
	þat liuede al in godes lawe;	
Alquin,	Alquin was his rihte name,	
	And man he was of gode fame;	40
	Dekne he was, and þe ordre he hadde;	
lived then,	In holinesse his[2] lyf he ladde;	
	Wit of clergie he hadde inouh,	
	þerfore to godnesse euere he drouh.	44
of whom	¶ Off him þe eorl was wel war,	
Guy	þerfore his wille to him [he] bar,	

19 Al at] At R. wole] shall H₂. 20 Ne shaltu] þou shalt not R. 21 Ne for] For noo H₂. to god] of god A₂DH₁, om. H₂. eiȝe] awe R. 22 þe] his H₂. weye] lawe R. 23 For] om. DH₂. þer] it A₁DR, þei A₂. 24 and] þen D. foule] fals A₂. 25 þeih don god] Iesu criste H₂. 26 hem dere] dere A₁, dere hem A₂H₁, ful dere R. (D has hou dere.) bouhte] abouȝte H₂. 27 Her-of] Here R. wole] sall D. while] stounde H₂. 28 wole] sal H. 30 Gy] Sire Gy H₂. 31 Hou on] On D, Vppe on H₂, how in R. 32 þe] þis DH₂. 33 he þer] he A₂H₁H₂, þer he DR. 34 him] he hym DH₁. tok] bi toke H₁. 35 And] He H₂. his] all his A₂R, eke hys D (and and in H₂). 36 in his seruise was] serued hym after R. 37 in] be H₂. þilke] þat A₂H₂R. 38 liuede] leued R. al] wele A₂, wel alle R. in] om. R. 40 And] A A₂. And a D, A noble H₂. man he was] man DH₂. gode] riȝt gude D. 41 and] om. R. þe] om. H₁H₂. he] om. DH₂. 44 þerfore] and þerfore R. 45 Off him] þare of A₂DH₂. was wel] sone was full H₂. war] I war A₂D. 45 and 46 are omitted in R. 46 þerfore] And þarfore A₂, And alle H₂. he] om. A₁A₂.

[1] þer *is on erasure in MS.* A₁.   [2] MS. H₁ *has* his his.

And of him[1] he tok his red, — asked advice,
¶ To kepen his soule from þe qued.   48
¶   On a day, i vnderstonde,   39 c
Sire Gy þe eorl sente his sonde
To þe holi man Alquin
And seide : '[I][2] grete þe wel, fader myn,   52 and
And preie þe for godes loue, — begged
þat us alle sit aboue,
þat þu wole, par charite
And in amendement of me,   56
¶ Make me a god sarmoun — a sermon,
And don hit write in lesczoun :
þat were my ioye and my delit — to free his
And to my soule a grot profyt ;   60 soul from the
For þe world þurw his foule gile — world's guile.
Haþ me lad to longe while.
þer-of i wole consail take,
Hu i mihte þe world forsake.'   64
¶   Alquin þe eorl þo answerede, — Alquin
And Iesu Crist ful ȝerne he heriede, — with joy
þat swich a wit was comen him to
And seide : ' His preie i wole do.'   68 granted Guy's prayer,
' And, [sethen] i shal be þi leche,
Aller furst i wole þe teche, — and preached
Faire uertuz for to[3] take — of fair virtues
And foule þewes to forsake.   72 and ugly vices.
¶ þat maitou noht don, leue broþer,
Bote þu knowe on and oþer,

48 kepen] wyten D. qued] dede D. 49 On] Vpon H₂. 51 þe]' þat R. Alquin] sire alquyn A₂D, ffrere Alquyne H₂. 52 wel] om. H₂. 53 And] I A₂, anon I D. 54 us] ouyr vs H₂. 55 and 56 are omitted in A₂. 55 par] for H₁H₂. 57 Make me] Doo me make H₂. 58 don hit write] write hit R. lesczonn] a lessoun DR. 59 were] where D. my ioye] ioy A₂. my delit] grete delyte H₂. 61 foule] false H₂. 62 lad] lette H₁, be lyed H₂. while] A while H₂. 63 þer-of] þer for D. wole] wolde H₂. 64 þe world] hym H₂. 65 Alquin] þen Alquyne R. þe eorl þo] þen to þe erle D, sere Gy sone H₂, þe erle R. 66 And] And swythe H₂. ful ȝerne] ful werun D, om. H₂. he] om. A₂D. 68 His] þi A₂H₂. i wole] he wold DR. 69 And sethen] and whan A₁, Sythe that H₂, & sithen þat R. be] nu ben A₁A₂. þi] his H₁. 70 Aller] Alþere A₂H₁H₂, Erle D. furst] ferest H₁. wole] schal D. 71 for to] to þe D. 72 foule] lethere H₂. 73 þat] þis H₁, þus R. don] om. A₂, mynn H₂. 74 Bote] But ȝyffe H₂R. on] o þynge A₂, þat on D, bothe one R. oþer] þat oþer D (oþe in H₁).

[1] him *is above the line in MS.* A₁. *MS.* D *has* hys.
[2] *MS.* A₁ *omits* I.   [3] to *is above the line in MS.* A₁.

	I shal þe now shewe boþe,	
	Whiche beþ gode and whiche beþ loþe;	39 d 76
First,	¶ And at þe beste i wole biginne,	
to win grace	þe betre grace for to winne.	
he taught the virtues in order.	þe uertuz i wole first shewe,	
	Whiche þeih beþ, alle on rewe.'	80
Wisdom	'Wisdom in godes drede	
shall be thine,	Vse wel, þat be my rede;	
also faith, love,	Trewe bileue and charite—	
	þise sholen bileue wid þe—	84
steadfast hope, meekness, peace, mercy, forgiveness, patience, humility.	Stedefast hope and mieknesse,	
	Pes, merci, and forȝifnes,	
	¶ Loue of herte, ful of pite,	
	þat is verray humilite.	88
	And þu wolt haue godes ore,	
	Ȝit þu most vse more,	
Repent!	For þi sinne repentaunce,	
	And redi þerfore to don penaunce	92
In penitence	Wid sorwe at þin herte rote,	
confess.	And shrifte of mouþe shal be þi bote.	
Give in charity to thy life's end.	In almes dede and charite	
	þi lyf shal euere more be.	96
	¶ þise beþ þe þewes, þat i þe teche,	
	Whar-þurw þu miht to heuene reche,	
	And so þu miht þe world forsake,	
	If þu wolt hem to þe take.'	100

75 *and* 76 *are transposed in* A₂.   75 þe now shewe] shewe to þe now H₁, the shewe nowe hem H₂.   77 And at] And A₂, At H₁.   wole] sal D.   79 i wole] þat I wyll A₂, I sal D, fyrste I wylle H₂.   first] ȝow H₂.   shewe] chewe (*Before* chewe *space is left for an* s.) D.   80 Whiche] þe wyche D.   alle on] now o D, al in H₁, vppon A H₂, on a R.   82 be my] I þe D, is my R.   *Between* 82 *and* 83 *are the following two lines in* A₂ (*Cp.* A₂ *in ll.* 140, 141, *and* 142.):

Twey þynggys it wyll þe tech
Whare þorouȝ þou myȝt to heuen rech

83 bileue] loue R.   84 þise] þey H₁, þese thre R.   bileue] leue D, leeue R.   þe] me H₂.   85 hope] *om.* A₂, boþ H₁.   87 ful] *and* fulle H₂.   89 And] And ȝef A₂DH₁H₂R.   haue] *om.* R.   ore] lore D.   90 vse] doo welle H₂.   91 sinne] synne haue D.   92 þerfore] þare A₂.   94 And] Wiþ H₁.   mouþe] mowȝt D.   shal be þi] to A₂, with dede D, wyll be þi H₂.   95 charite] chaste D, in charyte H₂.   96 lyf] lyffe also H₂.   97 þewes] vertues A₂.   i] I wil R.   98 Whar-þurw] Where with H₂.   reche] Areche H₂.   99 so] thus H₂.   þu] þorow H₁.   miht] mayste H₂R.   100 wolt hem to] hem wolt to A₁, wylt heuen to A₂, wylt þese to D, wylte to thys goodnesse H₂.

And of Vices.

'Nu i wole nempne¹ þe wicke þewes, *Base vices*
þat beþ noht gode, ac muche shrewes,
For, if þu dost bi here red[e],
To strong[e] pine þeih wolen þe led[e]; 104 *lead to pain,*
¶ þanne is hit god, þat þu shone *therefore*
To drawe hem into þi wone. *shun*
Herkne nouþe to me,
And i hem wole nempne þe: 108
Pride, wraþþe, and enuie, *pride, wrath,*
Fals iugement and tricherie; *envy, injustice, faithlessness,*
Fals witnesse is on of þo— *false witnessing.*
Many a soule itt² doþ ful wo. 112
Loue noht to muche þis worldes blisse: *Avoid worldliness.*
Hit bringeþ man to þisternesse,³ *It induces*
¶ Auarice and glotonye, *avarice, gluttony,*
Wicke sleuþe and leccherie.' 116 *sloth, lechery.*
'Accedie is a wel foul sinne
To man, þat he may come widinne,
And, what it is, i wole þe wisse,
Vnderstond, þat þu ne misse: 120
¶ Accedie is (as) sleuþes broþer, *[Acedia], the brother*
Wicke on and wicke oþer; *of sloth,*
Hit is a derne mourni[n]g in mod
And makeþ man anuied to do god. 124
Ofte þurw swiche mourning[e] *attends*
Wanhope beginneþ for to spring[e], *despair of the mercy of God,*

101 wole] sall D. nempne] neuen A₂D (D has new, but the e is hardly distinguishable from o. There is a break in the parchment before wykyd.) H₁, telle H₂, þe nemen R. þe wicke] wykyd A₂D, þis worldly H₁, þe oþere H₂. 102 beþ noht gode] are swithe R. ac] bot A₂DH₁H₂, om. R. 103 here] there H₂. 105 is hit] it is A₂DH₁H₂, is R. 105 reads in H₁: Þerfor loke þou hem shoone. 106 To] For to H₁R. into] in H₁. 107 nouþe] now A₂DH₁H₂R. to] wele vnto D, bisily to H₁, Awhyle to H₂, vnto R. 108 i] om. R. hem wole] wyll hem D, hom I wil R. nempne] schewe A₂, neuen vnto D, neuen to H₁. 108 reads in H₂: And I wylle telle ȝow wheche þei bee. 109 enuie] enueny D. 111 and 112 are transposed in H₂. 112 ful] myche H₁, full moche H₂. 113 þis] om. D. 114 Hit] For it DH₁. bringeþ] lediþ H₁. man] a man A₂H₂, men DH₁, mony R. to] vnto R. þisternesse] theftnese A₂, dyrkenes DH₁, Vncerteynnesse H₂, merkenes R. 116 sleuþe] slownes R. 117 wel] ful R. 119 what] om. A₂. wole] sall D. 120 Vnderstond] vndirstond wel H₁, Vndyrstonde yt welle H₂. ne] not R. 121 as] om. A₂H₁H₂R. sleuþes] slownes R. 122 on] is on A₂R. 123 a] as a A₁D. 124 And] Hytt H₂. man] men D. anuied] vnneþe D, fro mynde R. 125 Ofte] Welofte H₂. swiche] swiche wicke A₁A₂R.

¹ The final e is above the line in MS. A₁.
² MS. A₁ has itc.
³ Read þisternisse.

	þat, bote man turne awey þerfro,	
	Sauued worþ he neuere mo.	128

through which Judas was lost.

¶ Wroþer hele was Iudas born,
For þurw þat sinne he was lorn ;   40 b
Merci he les þurw þat sinne,
Wher-þurw he ne mihte no ioye winne.   132

Hasten! ¶ Vch man birede him in his sihte
Flee that sin. To flen þat sinne bi his mihte
And alle oþere þat i haue nempt,
If he wole to ioye be dempt.'   136

Hearken to my sermon! **H**erkne now to my sarmoun,
What i wole telle in my lesczoun.
Wisdom Wisdom in godes drede,   *De Sapientia.*
Off which þat i erere seide,[1]   140

points two ways to heaven: ¶ Tweie þinges it wole þe teche,
Whar-þurw þu miht to heuene reche :
flee sin; do good. þat is, lat þi sinne and do god
For his loue, þat deiede on rod ;   144
¶ Ac to late þi sinne al onliche
Nis noht inouh, sikerliche.
The rewards are mercy and peace. þu most don god forþ þerwid,[2]
If þu wolt haue merci and griþ.   148

127 þat bote] Bot A₂H₁R, Butt yffe H₂. man] a man A₂D, men H₁. turne] flee H₂. 128 worþ he] worth þei A₂, shul he be H₁, maye he be H₂, bes he R. 129 Wroþer hele] In a carful tyme H₁, With wroþe hele H₂. 130 þurw] om. D. lorn] for lorne A₂DH₁H₂R. 131 þurw] for A₂. 132 ne] om. H₁H₂R. no ioye] heuen A₂. 133 birede] I rede A₂, be rede D, be redy R. him] om. R. 133 *reads in* H₁ *and in* H₂:
I counsel yche man with al his myȝte H₁.
Euyry man behouythe in hys syȝte H₂.
134 flen] flye H₁. bi] om. H₁, with H₂R. his mihte] all his myȝt DH₂R, boþ day and nyȝte H₁. 135 oþere] þe oþer DH₂. haue] here H₁. nempt] neuen H₁. 136 he wole] þai wil R. be dempt] idempt D, be demened R. 136 *reads in* H₁: If ȝe wil come to þe blisse of heuen. 137 sarmoun] lessounne H₂. 138 wole] shall A₂. telle] say A₂, þe tell D, rede þe H₂. in my lesczoun] be resounne H₂. *After* 138 *one line is interpolated in* H₂: Inicium sapiencie timor domini. (Cp. H₂ *after l.* 4 *and* A₁A₂DH₁ *after l.* 882.) 140 which] suche H₁. þat] om. D. erere] here D, eere of H₂, bifore R. 140 *reads in* A₂: Vse wele þat be my rede. (*l.* 82. Cp. A₂ *in variants.*) 141 it] I DH₂. 142 reche] Areche H₂. 143 þat] And þat A₂. lat] leue A₂H₁H₂R. þi] om. DR. 144 rod] þe rode D. 145 Ac] And A₂DH₁, om. H₂, But for R. late] leue A₂H₁H₂, loue R. þi] om. DR. sinne] om. R. al] om. A₂H₁H₂. (sekerlich *has been crossed out before* onliche *in* A₂.) onliche] onely R. 146 Nis] Es DH₁H₂R. sikerliche] sikerly R. 148 and] or H₁. griþ] greyþe D.

[1] *Read* sede.   [2] *Read* þerwiþ.

¶ Þis wonder of many sinful men,   The wicked
    þat þinkeþ it were muche[1] for hem.
    To haue gret worldes honour
    As londes, rentes, halle, and bour,   152
    Riche vessel of siluer and gold
    And grete tresor and faire bold,   value worldly possessions
¶ Riche mete and riche drink[e],
    And litel þerfore for to swink[e],   156
    Hele of bodi in bon and huide,   40 c
    And gret los of pompe and pride.   and fleeting glory, but
    A murie lyf hem þinkeþ þis were,
    But eft hit worþ ibouht [ful][2] dere,   160   earth's joy is bought dear.

Quia nihil[3] in-felicius, quam felicitas peccatoris.

Napeles hit may falle wel,
    þat, þouh man haue muche katel
    As londes, rentes, and oþer god,
    ȝit[4] he may be pore of[5] mod   164
    And low of herte, ful iwis,
    And halt þerof ful litel prys.
¶ Ac nu i wole speke and rede   Such sinful ones
    Of hem, þat i crere seide,[6]   168

149 þis] þis is A₂, It es D, Thys ys a H₂. of many] is of mony R. sinful] *om.* DH₂, a synful R. men] man DR. 150 it were] *om.* A₂. 152 As] As in D, *om.* H₂. 154 grete] oþer H₁. and faire bold] faire and bold A₂H₂, manyfolde H₁. 155 2d riche] goode H₁. 156 litel] lepe D. 157 Hele] Helthe H₂. in] *om.* A₂, and R. huide] hede H₁. 158 And] *om.* H₂AR. of] also of H₂. 159 þis] ytte H₁H₂. 160 eft] *om.* D, after H₁H₂. worþ] shal be H₁, wylle be H₂, mot be R. ibouht] abought A₂D, boȝte H₁H₂R. *After* 160 *are the following two lines in* H₂:

       Where be thoo þat thynkyþe þere vpon
       I cane nott telle be seynte John

Latin: *The Latin text is inserted between* 158 *and* 159 *in* R. Quia nihil] Qui R. in-felicius] infecelius A₂, felicius R. felicitas] fecilitas A₂, vita R. 161 Napeles] Neuer þe lese A₂H₂, but no þo lesse R. falle] be fall H₂, bifalle R. 162 þat] *om.* H₂R. (*Space is left for one word in* H₂.) man] a man A₂DR, men H₁, summan H₂. muche] ryȝt mochill H₂. 163 As londes] Londes londes (*The second* londes *is marked for erasure.*) D. 165 low] ful lowe DR. ful] *om.* DR, fully H₁, and fulle H₂. iwis] wyse H₂. 166 halt] haue H₂. ful] *om.* A₂H₂R. (lytyll *is over erasure in* H₂.) 167 *and* 168 *are transposed in* D. 167 Ac] And also A₂, and DH₂, But H₁R. nu i wole] now I sal D, I wil now H₁. and rede] *om.* A₂. 168 hem] whum D. crere] are A₂D, bifore H₁R, cere of H₂.

     [1] muchel *is in MS.* A₁.   [2] MS. A₁ *has* wel.
     [3] *The MSS. have* nichil.   [4] ȝit *is on the margin before* he *in MS.* A₁.
     [5] of *is above the line in MS.* A₁.   [6] *Read* sede.

	þat þurw here pride and here wil	
are in peril,	þeih fallen ofte in gret peril.	
	Seint Austin halt þer-mide noht	
	And seiþ, it shal ben dere bouht,	172
	And skilfulliche it mot be so,	
	For, whan a man haþ sinne do,	
and they must atone.	Oþer he mot hit beten here	
	Or suffre pine elles where.	176
The gracious love of God	¶ Wole ȝe here, what louerede	
	God kudde to¹ hem þat wole² him drede?	
	[He wyll hem here hold[e] lowe,	
	For þei schold hym þe better knawe³;]	180
grants chasteninges, anguish,	He wole hem chasten wid smale pining	
	And maken hem lese þat hote brenning;	
	And many anguisse he wole hem ȝiue	
	To suffre here, whiles þeih liue,	40 d 184
hunger, thirst,	¶ As hunger and þurst and trauail strong;	
	Hij sholen haue euere among	
earthly losses.	Lore of catel and seknesse,⁴	
These increase heaven's joys,	And al is to echen here blisse.	188
	Man, if þu (ne) leuest noht me,	

169 here] hyȝe H₁. wil] yll (*There is an erasure before* y.) D. 170 þeih] *om.* R. 171 halt þer-mide] þare with holdeth (*Two letters have been crossed out before* holdeth.) A₂, halde þer with DH₁, holte þere with ryȝt H₂R. 172 And] He DH₂. bouht] abouȝht A₂. 173 And] For H₂. skilfulliche] wilfullyche H₁. mot] moste H₁H₂R. 174 For] *om.* H₂. a man] man A₂H₂. sinne do] synn ido DR, mysdo H₁, A synne doo H₂. 175 mot hit beten] mot beten D, he motte be beten (*One letter has been erased before* h.) H₁, he mvste be betyn H₂. 176 Or] Oþer D, Or ellis R. pine] paynes A₂H₂. 177 ȝe here] þou here now R. louerede] I rede R. 178 kudde] kyþeþ H₁R, shewythe H₂. to] *om.* R. hem] man D, him H₁H₂. wole him] wold hyme A₂, hym wyll H₂. 179 *and* 180 *are omitted in* A₁. 179 hem] *om.* R. here holde] holde here D, hold meke & H₁, holdyn here full H₂, holde hom here R. 180 þe] *om.* H₁. 180 *has the following readings in* D *and in* H₂:

þe better for he sull hym knowe D.
The bettyr for þey shulde hym knowe H₂.

181 *and* 182 *are omitted in* A₂. 181 He wole] *om.* H₂. hem] hym DH₁, *om.* H₂R. chasten] kast H₁, Chastyse hem H₂R. 182 hem] hym D, hom to R. þat] þe DH₂. 183 And many] A man D, Many an H₂. hem] hym D. 185 As] *om.* DH₁H₂, *and* R. (And *is crossed out before* As *in* A₂.) 186 Hij] þei A₂H₁H₂R, he D. haue] suffri DH₂. 187 Lore] Losse A₂H₁H₂R. seknesse] stronge syknysse H₂. 188 And] *om.* H₂. al is] all it is A₂H₂, all D. here] þaire ioy *and* D, þeire H₁. 189 ne] *om.* A₂DH₁H₂R. leuest] be leue H₂.

¹ to *is above the line in MS.* A₁.
² *Before* w *one letter has been erased in MS.* A₁.   ³ *Read* knowe.
⁴ *Read* seknisse.

A Creed for Guy.

  þu sek aboute, *and* þu miht se
  þise holi men alle bidene,
  How þeih liuede *in* wo *and* tene.   192
  And, if my tale nis noht for-ȝete,[1]
  þanne maitou wel iwite,
  þat þe worldes blisse is noht,   *for the*
  Whan þu hast abouten souht;   196   *world's bliss*
                   is naught.
¶ For, ȝif[2] a man haþ her his wille,
  Wel lihtliche he may spille.
    Her i wole nouþe blinne.

De Fide.   Anoþer þing i wole biginne   200   *Believe in*
  To speke, man, of þi bileue,
  For hit is god, it[3] wole noht greue.
  Man, þi bileue shal be so:
  þat o god is and no mo,   204   *one God,*
  þat o god is *in* vnite,   *a God in*
  þre *per*sones *in* trinite.   *unity and in*
                  trinity,
¶ þu shalt, [man], bileue also
  And treuliche *in* þin herte do,   208
  þat god had neuere biginning   *without be-*
  Ne neuere (ne) shal haue ending,   *ginning,*
                   without end-
                   ing,
¶ And shappere[4] is of alle shaftes,   41 a   *Creator of all.*
  And ȝeueþ wit *in* alle craftes,   212

190 þu sek] Seek H₁R. þu miht se] by þe se A₂, bi se D, þou maist see H₁R, þe besye H₂. 192 liuede] lybbeþe D. wo] sorowe H₂. 193 if] if þou R. nis] es DH₁, þou H₂, *om.* R. 194 þanne] Now H₁. maitou] þou myȝt ful D. wel] þo better R. iwite] þerof I wyte H₁, wete H₂, witt R. 195 þe] þys H₂. blisse] wele DH₂. is] nys A₂. 196 abouten] all abouten DH₂, hit thorou R. souht] I soȝte H₁. 197 *and* 198 *are omitted in* H₂. 197 his] all hys D. 198 Wel] Ful DH₁R. lihtliche] lyȝtly H₁R. spille] hys saule spyll D, hymself spylle H₁. 199 Her i wole nouþe] Here I wyll not A₂, Now I wil here of H₁, Of thys now I wolle H₂, Here I wil a while R. blinne] be kenne (*The k is imperfectly formed.*) D, belynne H₂. 200 Anoþer] And oþere A₂, And anoþer D, And of othyre H₂. wole] sal D. 201 *and* 202 *are transposed in* D. 201 man] more R. 202 it] *and* DH₁R. wole] nyl H₁. 204 is] ther ys H₂. 204—206 *read in* H₁:

  þat þer is oo god & no moo
  Þe whiche is *in* persones þree
  And oo god *in* trinitee

206 þre] And þre D. 207 man] *om.* A₁A₂R, al so H₁. also] here to H₁. 208 treuliche] trewly A₂H₁H₂R. do] þenk so H₁, yt doo H₂R. 209 had] ne hadde H₂. 210 Ne] Nor A₂. ne] *om.* A₂DH₁H₂R. haue] haue noon H₁H₂. 211 shaftes] shappes A₂. (schaftes *is over erasure in* D.) 212 ȝeueþ] ȝif þe D, ȝifere of H₁, gaffe H₂.

---

[1] *Read* forȝite.
[2] *One letter has been erased before* ȝ *in MS.* A₁.
[3] *One letter is erased after it in MS.* A₁.
[4] re *is above the line in MS.* A₁.

	And made man after his owen face—	
	Nas þat gret loue of heih[e] grace?	
God bestowed freedom of will, but	And ȝaf to man fre power	
	To chese, boþe fer and ner,	216
	Off god and yuel shed to make,	
	þe euel to late and god to take.	
	Wheiþer he wole chese, he haþ power	
	þurw ȝifte of god, while he is her;	220
He is not at fault if man choose the wrong.	þanne is hit noht on god ilong,	
	If man wole chese to don wrong.	
Adam	¶ Adam was þe forme man,	
	þat euere singyn bigan,	224
	And þat was god to wite noht,	
bought sin dear.	þerfore hit haþ ben dere bouht.	
	God ȝaf him wit as his owen,	
	God and yuel for to knowen,	228
	Ac þurw eging of þe fend and Eue	
	He dede a sinne þat gan him greue.	
For disobedience he was thrust from paradise, but	¶ Vnboxomnesse was his gilt,	
	þerfore out of paradys he was [pylt].[1]	232
	Boxomere he was to his wif,	
	þan to god þat ȝaf him lyf;	
	And, for he dede after hire lore,	
	He bouhte hit siþþen swiþe sore.	236
	¶ His fredom was binomen him al	
	And put in seruage as a þral,	41 b

213 made man] man made A₁A₂R, shope man H₂. owen] om. H₂. 214 Nas þat] Was þer D, þat was H₁R, Was þat not a H₂. gret] for R. of heihe] and heȝe D, of his holy H₁, of hys H₂. 215 ȝaf] ȝif D. 216 To chese] Of thise A₂, to these R. 217 Off] And of D, om. H₂. yuel] of euel D. shed] for A₂H₂, cheyse D. 218 þe] þat D. late] leue A₂DH₁R. and] þe A₂DR. 219 Wheiþer] Whiche H₁. Too whether H₂. 220 ȝifte] might R. 221 is hit] it is A₂R. on] in A₂H₁. ilong] a longe A₂H₂, longe DH₁R. 222 man] he A₂DH₂. wole] wollen to D, om. H₁. 223 forme] first A₂H₁R, formeste H₂. 224 þat] In wham H₁. singyn] first synne DH₂, ony synne R. 225 wite] wyte ryȝte H₂. 226 hit] he D. haþ] was ful R. hen] om. DR. bouht] a houȝt A₂D. 227 his] is DH₂. 228 yuel] wicke R. 229 Ac] And A₂DH₁R, om. H₂. þurw] Thorowe þe H₂R. Eue] of eue D. 230 a] om. H₁. gan him] was ful D, dide hym H₁H₂R. 231 his] hit R. 232 he was] was he R. pylt] om. A₁, put D. 233 Boxomere] Buxom more D, Moore boxum H₁. 235 for] for þat R. hire] þeyre H₁. 236 bouhte hit] abouȝte D. siþþen] afterworde H₁, aftyr H₂. swiþe] ful H₁. 237 binomen him] bimonie hym H₁, fro hym tane R. 238 in] to D.

[1] pylt *is supplied from MS.* A₂. was *is the last word of the line in MS.* A₁. gilt *seems a deeper black than what precedes, suggesting that it may have been added later.*

¶ Noht one he, bute alle þo
  þat of him comen for euere mo.   240
  Ac for hit was þurw gile don,
  God ȝaf his pite þer-vpon,   *God's pity and love saved mankind.*
  And eke for loue þat he hade
  To man, þat he himselue made,   244
  To sauue man, man he bicam,   *God became man,*
  And pine for hem to him he nam,
  And ȝaf for hem his herte blod,   *and shed His heart's blood on the cross, died, was buried,*
  And deiede for hem on þe rod.   248
¶ Ibiried he was, in¹ toumbe he lay,
  Til hit com þe þridde day;
  Vp he ros þe þridde day   *rose the third day,*
  From deþ to liue wid-oute nay;   252
  To heuene he steih þurw his mihte, *ascended into heaven,*
  Riht in-to his faderes sihte,
  And sit on his faderes riht[e] side, *sits at His Father's right hand.*
  þe grete dom for to abide.   256
  þider he wole come on domesday,   *On Doomsday*
  Cruwel and sterne wid-oute nay,
¶ He þat was woned to be
  Meke as a lomb, ful of pite: 260
  þeder he wole lihten adoun   *He will come to earth to judge without mercy.*
  Wraþfful and sterne as a lioun.
  Merci nele he shewe non,

239 one] only A$_2$DH$_2$R, oonlyche H$_1$. alle] also al H$_1$. 240 for euere] euer A$_2$DH$_2$. 241 Ac] And A$_2$D, But H$_1$H$_2$R. þurw] for R. don] idon D. 242 God ȝaf] Almyȝty god had H$_1$, God had R. his] hym D, om. H$_1$R. 243 eke] also H$_1$H$_2$. for] for þe A$_2$H$_2$. 244 man] monkynde R. he] hem D. himselue] om. R. 245 To sauue man] To saue hym þan H$_1$, Man to saue H$_2$. man he] he man H$_2$. 246 pine] peyne & passion H$_1$, grete peyne H$_2$, pyne grete R. hem] man A$_2$H$_2$, hym R. to him] om. A$_2$H$_1$H$_2$R. 247 And] He H$_2$. hem] man H$_2$, hym R. 248 And] And þus H$_1$, om. R. deiede] with harde deth R. for hem] om. H$_1$R, for man H$_2$. on] opon A$_2$DH$_1$H$_2$R. 249 Ibiried] Biryed H$_1$H$_2$R. 250 Til hit com] Tyll it came to A$_2$H$_2$, Forto com D. 251 and 252 are omitted in H$_2$. 251 reads in A$_2$: And rose for soth als I ȝow say. 254 Riht] Ful ryȝt H$_1$, om. H$_2$. in-to] to D. faderes] awne fader D, ffadyrys ryche H$_2$. 255 And sit] þere he sittiþ H$_1$. 256 for] om. R. 257 þider] Hedere A$_2$, And hedyr H$_2$, om. R. he wole] shall H$_2$. on] at DH$_2$, sithen on R. 258 wid-oute nay] for soþe too saye H$_2$. 259 þat] þat afore H$_2$. woned] woned merciful H$_1$. 260 a] om. H$_1$H$_2$R. 261 and 262 are omitted in A$_2$. 261 þeder] þer DH$_1$, Hedyr H$_2$, þere þen R. lihten] þane lyȝte H$_2$. adoun] downe H$_2$. 262 and] om. R. a] ony H$_2$. 263 nele] þan wyll H$_2$, wil R.

¹ *There is an erasure after in in MS. A$_1$.*

¶ Ac, riht after þat man haþ don, 264
He shal fonge his iugement
To ioye or to strong turment.

¶ Allas! what sholen hij onne take,
þat wolden [here] her god forsake[1] 268
þurw sinne of fles[c]h[ly][2] liking,
And wolde hit bete wid no pining?
þer-fore þeih sholen in-to helle,
Wheiþer þeih wolen, or þeih nelle, 272
And þere bileue[n] euere mo,
In [as] strong pine as men may do.
Seint Austin spekeþ of alle swiche
And seiþ wordes [ful] reuliche: 276

**Habent mortem sine morte
et finem mortis sine fine.**

¶ "Hij sholen haue deþ wid-oute deiing
And point of deþ wid-outen ending;'
Here deþ hij sholen wilnen euere,
Ac to ende of deþ comen hij neuere; 280
Hij sholen euere more duire
In stronge pine of hote fire.
Her i wole nouþe dwelle,
And of mur[y]ere[3] þinge [i wole] ȝou telle. 284

Marginal notes: Those who forsook God / shall be driven / to hell. / The wicked in hell / shall suffer death without dying, / divers agonies, / sharp pain of fire;

264 Ac] Bot A₂H₁H₂R, And D. þat] om. A₂. man haþ] men haue H₂. 265 He shal] They shulle þan H₂, þai shal R. fonge] a fonge D, take H₂R. his] om. A₂. here H₂R. iugement] verament (MS. indistinct) A₂. 266 or to] or els H₁. turment] tournement DH₂. 267 what] how A₂DH₁H₂R. hij] þei A₂DH₁H₂R. onne] þan on H₂. 268 here her god] her god A₁A₂DR, here god here H₁, here here lorde H₂. 269 of] of here H₁. 271 sholen] shulle go H₁, shul wende R. into] til R. 272 or þeih] or A₂. 272 is omitted in R. In its place is the following line: nyl þai wil þai þere to dwelle. 273 bileuen] be leuyn H₂. euere] for euer H₁H₂R. 274 as] also A₁A₂, om. DR, als H₁. strong] strounger H₁. as] om. R. men] man A₂H₂, fend H₁, om. R. may do] & eke in woo R. 275 Austin] poul A₂, austyn he H₂. 276 ful reuliche] reuliche A₁D, rewefullich A₂. Latin: Through defacement of the page 'fine' is wanting in A₂. et] om. D. fine] morte H₁. 277 Hij] þei A₂DH₁H₂R. 278 point] apoynt D, ende R. 279 Here] þare A₂H₁. hij] þei A₂DH₁H₂R. wilnen] wyll A₂H₂R, welny D, feel H₂. 280 Ac] For A₂, And DH₂, But H₁R. ende] þe ende H₁H₂. hij] þei A₂DH₁H₂R. 281 Hij] þei A₂DH₁H₂R. duire] þere endure H₂. 282 In] In þe H₂. hote] hell A₂H₂. 283 Her] Herof H₁. i wole] sal I D. nouþe] a whill A₂ (before I wil) R, now D. 283 reads in H₂: [N]ow of þis tale I wylle dwelle. (A blank space has been left for a large N.) 284 muryere] a myrrier R. i wole ȝou] ȝou A₁R, om. D, I wil H₁.

---

[1] 268 is written twice in MS. A₁. The second time it is crossed out.
[2] MS. A₁ has fleshes. [3] MS. A₁ murszere.

The Blisses of Heaven

¶ Tellen i wole ful iwis
Off þe ioyes of paradys,
Whiche godes children, þat gode be,   *but God's children*
Sholen haue and ise ;   288
Ac, þouh i hadde in my bayli[e]
þe wit of alle clergy[e],
¶ Mihte hit neuere so bifalle,   *41 d*
þat i mihte telle[n] alle.   292
Ac, also god ʒif me grace,
I shal ʒou shewe in þis place,
What ioie þeih sholen han ifere,
þat seruen god on eorþe here.   296
Whan þeih sholen parten henne,
Ful wel þeih sholen here weie kenne   *shall know their way*
Riht to þe blisse of paradys,   *to paradise,*
þat god haþ ʒarked to alle his.   300
¶ þere is euere ioye inouh   *there to dwell in joy amid justice,*
And euere riht widouten wouh,
Wit and kunning and kointise,
And trewe loue widou[t]¹ feintise,   304   *love,*
Streinþe inouh and fairnesse,   *beauty,*
And liht wid-oute þisternesse.   *and light.*
þere sholen þeih noht ben agilt,
[For] al here wille shal ben fulfilt :   308
Hij sholen haue, mid iwisse,

---

285 Tellen] Telle ʒow H₂. wole] sal D. ful] ryʒt now A₂, om. D, su[m]what H₁, sone H₂, now forthe R. 287 Whiche] þo whiche R. 288 haue] þat ioye haue H₂. ise] eke see H₁, ytt see H₂, al so sene R. 289 Ac] For A₂, And DR, But H₁H₂. þouh] and H₁, of R. hadde] haue D. 290 alle] al maner H₁H₂. 291 Mihte hit] ʒit myʒt it H₁, Ne myʒt ytt H₂, hit might R. neuere] not H₁. 292 tellen] telle ʒow halffe ne H₂, thorouly telle hom R. 293 Ac] And A₂, om. D, But ʒit H₁, Butt H₂R. also] as H₁R. ʒif] wol ʒyf DH₁R. 294 shal] wylle H₂. 295—300 are omitted in H₂. 295 ifere] in fere DH₁R. 296 on] in A₂H₁. 297 Whan] When þat R. parten] departen A₂, perty D. henne] hethen R. 298 here] þair D. 299 to þe] in to A₂, to D. 300 þat] Whiche H₁. ʒarked] made A₂H₁. 301 euere ioye] ioye euere H₂. 302 wouh] vow (possibly for wowe of DH₂) H₁. 303 and 304 are transposed in D. 303 kointise] qweyntise A₂DH₂. 304 And] om. H₂. 305 and 306 are omitted in H₂. 305 Streinþe] þere is strenkþe H₁. 306 þisternesse] dirkenese A₂D, ony derknes H₁, merkenes R. 307 noht ben] fynde no A₂, haue no R. agilt] gylt A₂R, I guilde D. 308 For al] al A₁, For DH₂. here] þaire DH₂. 309 and 310 are omitted in H₂. 309 Hij] þei A₂DH₁R. mid] mende D, with a H₁, þer with R. iwisse] Wisshe H₁.

---

¹ MS. A₁ ou.

There poor and rich together,

each hath his dwelling, after his own deserving.

The least in God's kingdom hath perfect joy.

Love

is well pleasing to God.

Then love God well,

and

love thy fellow-man,

    Fulle ioye a*nd* fulle blisse,¹
¶ Boþe þe pore a*nd* þe riche,
  Ac, wete þu wel, noht alle iliche.   312
  Eu*er*ich shal haue his woniȝ[i]ng
  Riht after his owen deseruing ;
  Ac lat hit noht come i*n* þi þouht,
  þat any of he*m* shal wante*n* ouht,   316
  For he þat haþ lest i*n* þat woniing¹
  Haþ fulle ioye ouer alle þing.
¶ þerfore, man, i*n* al þi miht,
  þu loue wel god bi day a*nd* niht :   *42 a* 320
¶ þe inwardlichere þu louest hi*m* her,
  þe more shal ben þi ioye þer.
  Herkne nu alle to me,
  For i wole speken of charite.   324 *De uera Caritate.*
  Off alle uertuz hit is hext,
  And godes wille hit is next.
  Ȝif þu wolt wite [what] hit be,
  Herkne, a*nd* i wole telle þe :   328
  Hit is, loue god ou*er* alle þing,
  In þouht, i*n* dede, a*nd* in speking.
  And, if þu wolt euere come þerto,
  An-oþer þing þu most do :   332
  þu most loue, hu-so hit be,
  þin emcristene forþ wid þe.
¶ Man, woltou make a god prouing,

---

310 Fulle] Ful of D, Al man*er* H₁. fulle] ful of D, al man*er* H₁. 311 Boþe þe] Boþe A₂. þe] eke A₂, eke the H₂. 312 Ac] For A₂, and DH₁, But H₂R. þu] it D, þou it H₁. wel noht] wel *and* nauȝt D, wil noȝ H₁, wil not R. alle] *om.* A₂. iliche] elich A₂, in lyche H₂. 313 Eu*er*ich] Euere he A₂, For euery*che* H₂, Ilkone R. 314 owen] *om.* H₂. 315 Ac] And A₂D, But H₁H₂R. lat hit noht come] trow þou wel R. 316 any] non R. 317 he þat] who so R. 318 Haþ] He hathe H₂R. ouer] of A₂H₁R, in DH₂. 319 in] with A₂H₂R. 320 þu] *om.* DH₁H₂. wel god] god wel R. bi] *om.* D. 321 þe] þe more A₂. For so D, For the more þat H₂. inwardlichere] inwordelich A₂D, *om.* H₂. *Between* 322 *and* 323 *is interpolated in* H₂ : '*Deleccio es proximi.*' 323 alle] *om.* A₂. 323 *reads in* H₂ : Herken now my ffrende so free. 324 wole] sal now D. of] *om.* D. 325 hext] þo hext R. 326 godes wille] at goddys wyll þane (*The page is worn, so that the line is nearly crased.*) A₂. 327 wite] *om.* DH₂. what] hu A₁A₂. be] may be R. 328 wole] sall D. 328 *reads in* H₂: Sytte nowe stylle & herken me. 329 Hit is loue] Loue welle H₂. 330 in dede] & dede H₁R. a*nd*] *om.* A₂D. 331 euere] *om.* A₂H₂. 332 Anoþer] Ane oþer D. þing] *om.* H₂. þu] þe R. most] mvste nedys H₂. 334 emcristene] euene crystenn A₂H₂R, enemy H₁. forþ] ryȝt euen H₁. 335 Man] þan D. god] *om.* H₂.

¹ woniȝng *in MS.* A₁.

Of True Love.

Wher þu loue þe heuene king? 336
If þu louest god ful iwis,
þu [wolt] louen alle his. *so that*

**Si non diligis proximum tuum,
quem uides, deum quem non
uides, quomodo potes diligere?**[1]

For men seiþ soþ, bi wit[te] myne:
'Whoso loueþ me, he loueþ myne.' 340 *thou mayst see God.*
'But þu loue [þyn em][2] cristene þat bi þe be,
þat alday [þou][3] mait hem ise,
Hou maitou loue god, i ne can deuise,
Whom þu miht sen on none wyse!' 344
¶ þis seiþ sein Powel and bereþ witnesse,
As he may wel in soþ[e]nesse. *42 b*
Abraham him sauh, ac þu [nost] noht hou! *Abraham saw God*
Herkne, i wole þe telle nowh: 348
¶ þe fourme of þre children he mette, *in the person of three angels,*
þre he sauh, and (as) on he (hem) grette;
In tokne it was, i telle þe, *betokening the Holy Trinity.*
Off þe holi trinite. 352

336 Wher] Wheþere A₂D, If H₁H₂R.   þe] om. A₂.   337 If] For yſſe H₂.
ful] filly H₁, om. H₂, wel R.   338 wolt] most A₁, mvste nedys H₂.   his] þat
is hisse R.   *Latin: The passage is omitted here and is inserted between 345
and 346 in D.   diligis*] deliges A₂H₁.   *uides*] tu vides H₂.   *deum*] om. H₂.
'*quem non vides' is inserted after* '*deligere' in* H₂.   *quonodo*] commodo A₁,
quoniam A₂DH₁H₂.   *potes diligere*] diligere potes D, potes dilegere A₂H₁.   339
For men] Man H₁, Men R.   soþ] and soþ D, soþ for H₁.   339 *reads in* H₂:
In the gospelle I seye ȝow be ryme.   340 Whoso] He þat H₂.   myne] alle
myne H₂, my hyne R.   341 But] But yſſe H₂.   emcristene] cristene A₁,
euene crysten A₂H₁R, neȝtbore H₁.   þat bi þe be] þat by be þe D, þat dewllip
þe by H₁, be þe H₂, þat is by þe R.   342 *is omitted in* D.   342 alday] om.
R.   þou] om. A₁R.   mait] mast A₂.   hem] al day with eghen R.   ise] se A₂R.
342 *has the following readings in* H₁ *and in* H₂:

    Whom þou maiste see eche day wiþ yeȝe   H₁.
    That aldaye wythe hem mayste speke & see   H₂.

343 maitou] mast þou A₂, schuldest D, myxte þou H₁, þou R.   ne can] can
nouȝt A₂H₁H₂R.   344 Whom] That H₁.   miht] may not A₂H₁H₂, mait DR.
on] in A₂DH₁H₂.   345 þis] Thus H₂.   seiþ sein Powel] saint poul saiþ H₁,
seyþe poule H₂R.   346 As] Also A₂, Soo H₂.   wel] om. D.   in] in þe boke
of H₂.   347 him] om R.   ac] for A₂, om. D, but H₁H₂R.   þu] he R.   nost]
om. A₁, ne wost A₂, woste H₂, not wist R.   noht] om. A₂DH₁R.   348 i wole]
I sal D, and I wil H₁H₂R.   þe telle] tell þe A₂DH₁H₂R.   349 þe] In A₂.
þre] om. R.   350 and as] and A₂D, but H₁.   he] om. R.   hem] om. A₂DH₁.
351 tokne] tokenyng A₂H₂R.   telle] telle it D.   352 þe holi] god þat is in A₂,
þe soþfast holy H₁, alle the hole H₂, þe heghe holi R.

[1] *MS.* A₁ *has* dilegere.   [2] *MS.* A₁ *has* þe.   [3] *MS.* A₁ *omits* þou.

SPEC. WAR.   P

¶ Holliche as¹ ou he grette hem þere
In tokne of² o god, þat hij were.

Moses saw God

Hu Moyses him sauh, woltou here,
In fourme of a bush al on fire,³ 356
At þe mount of Synay bi olde dawe,
þar god him ȝaf þe firste lawe?

in the bush, burning but not consumed,

¶ Al on fire þe bush was,
And ibrent noþing it nas: 360
þere shewede god his grete miht
And himself in þat ilke sihte.

symbol of the pure maidenhood of Mary.

¶ Þat bush bitokneþ vre leuedi,
Hire clene maiden-hed witerli; 364
For hit was euere-iliche clene,
[Ne]⁴ mihtte hit noht be wemmed ene.
Hete of flesh ne mihte hire wemme,
No more þan þe bush mihte brenne. 368

Others have seen God,

And many anoþer him iseih
And wid [him] spak, þat was him neih,

but no man hath seen Him in His Divinity

¶ But noht alone in his godhede,
Ac i-meind wid þe manhede; 372
For, sikerliche i telle þe,
Man ne sauh neuere his deite

---

353 as on] om. A₂, as D, all oon H₂. grette] sawe A₂. hem] hym D, om. H₂. 354 tokne] tokenyng A₂H₂R. o] om. A₂. hij] þei A₂DH₁H₂R. 355 him sauh] says now D, sawe hym H₂R. here] now lere R. 356 of] al of D. on] of D, on a R. 357 *and* 358 *are omitted in* H₂. 357 At] And in H₁. 358 him ȝaf] ȝaf hym A₂, ȝaf H₁. 359 on] of D. was] ytt was H₂. 360 And] but R. ibrent] ebrynde A₂, brente H₂R. it nas] nas D, for soþe yt nas H₂, þo buske nas R. 361 grete] meche H₂. 362 And] In D. þat ilke] þulke D, þat H₁H₂R. 363 Þat] þe A₂H₂R. bush] boys D. bitokneþ] be tokenes of D, bi tokened H₁, tokend R. vre] one R. 364 Hire clene] In here H₂, with hir clene R. witerli] sykerly DR. 365 euere iliche clene] ilyche clene euere H₂. 366 hit] þer H₁. noht] om. A₂. be wemmed ene] ony wemme bene H₁, be weminyd neuere H₂, I nemed bene R (wemedene in A₂). 367 Hete of] he D. ne] om. R. hire] yt H₂, hir not R. wemme] warme H₁. 368 No] Ne D. þan] might R. mihte] did H₁, om. R. brenne] burne H₁. 369 anoþer] oþer H₁. him] that hym H₂. iseih] saiþe A₂, say DH₂, did sey H₁, seghe R. 370 wid him spak] wid spak A₁, spake with hym A₂, spake hym with R. þat] and D. 371 But noht] and D. alone] al on H₁, onely R. 372 Ac] Bot A₂DH₁H₂R. i-meind] I menged A₂H₂, imed D, it was mayned H₁, mynged R. þe] his H₁H₂. 373 For sikerliche] Sekyrly as H₂. telle] tell it D, now telle ytt H₂. 374 Man ne sauh] Man sawe DH₂R, þou mayst se H₁.

---

¹ liche a *is over erasure in MS.* A₁.   ² ne o *is over erasure in MS.* A₁.
³ *Read* fere.   ⁴ *MS.* A₁ *omits* Ne.

¶ Bodiliche on corþe her, *42 c*   here on earth.
　He mihte noht, it is so cler.　　　　　376
　And, if þu wolt witen hou,
　Herkne, i wole þe telle now ;
　For so heih a þing is þe god-hede,
　þer-of to speke it is drede.　　　　　380
　God is so clene and so cler a þing,
　þat heuene and erþe he¹ ʒeueþ shining,
　And sunne and mone and sterren breme,
　Off him þeih han al here leme.　　　384
¶ Þu sext, man, wel aperteliche,
　þat þe sunne haþ brihtnesse muche,²
　And, þouh he sitte so wonder heie,
　Hit greueþ euere mannes eiʒe,　　　388   We may not gaze on the sun.
　Inwardliche on hire to se
　For hire grete clerte.
　Nu, for-soþe i telle þe—
　And sikerliche lef þu me—　　　　　　392
　þat god, þat ʒaf þe sunne his liht,
　Is swich an hundred [siþe] so briht.　　God, its source, hath hundred-fold its brilliancy.
¶ Man, mihte hit euere þanne be,　　　　Can human eye
　þat bodilich eiʒe mihte him se　　　　396   behold that glory?
　Here on eorþe,—þe godhede ?

375 Bodiliche] Wit*h* bodily eyʒe H₁, Godlyche H₂, Bodily R.   on] in R. eorþe] herth D.   376 He mihte noht] Whilest þou art on lyue H₁, men might not R.   376 *reads in* D: No may noman haue þat power.   377 witen] I wyte D.   hou] now R.   378 Herkne] Herken and H₁R.   wole] sal D.   þe telle] tello þe H₁, telle ʒow R.   now] *om.* R.   378 *reads in* H₂: Sytte nowe stylle & herkenyþe nowe.   379 For] And D, *om.* H₁.   a þing] ys H₂, þing R. þe] his A₂.   380 þer-of to speke] þat to speke þer of D.   drede] no drede H₁, grete drede H₂R.   381 clene and so] *om.* A₂, cler and D, clene and D, clere and so H₂, cler] clene DH₂.   382 he] it D, *om.* H₂.   383 And] *om.* H₂.   breme] beme DR.   384 here] þaire D.   385 man wel] wele man D, man here H₁, man H₂R.   387 And] *om.* A₂.   þouh] *om.* R.   he] it A₂H₁.   sitte] schyne D, is sett R. so] neuer so A₂, *om.* DH₁.   388 Hit] ʒit it A₂.   euere] *om.* A₂R, euereche D, euere a H₁.   mannes] bodyly D.   389 Inwardliche] Inwardly H₂R. on] vppe to H₂.   hire] *om.* A₂, hit R.   390 hire] his R.   grete] moche H₂. clerte] charite R.   391 telle] tell it DH₂.   392 sikerliche] sekyrly H₂R. lef þu] þou mayste leue H₁, be leue H₂.   393 þat] *om.* A₂H₂.   ʒaf] *om.* A₂. sunne his] sonnes A₂, sonn here DH₂.   394 swich an] seche a D, an H₁R. hundred] hundreth A₂H₁.   siþe] *om.* A₁A₂D, tyme H₂.   395 Man] Man how D, þerfor man H₁, how þen R.   euere þanne] euer so A₂, euer DH₁R, þane euere H₂.   396 bodilich] bodelich wit*h* A₂, boldelyche H₂, bodily R.   eiʒe] *om.* H₂.   him] euer D, hym euer H₁, *om.* H₂.   397 on] in H₂.   þe] in his H₁.

---

¹ *One letter has been erased after* he *in MS.* A₁.　　² *Read* miche.

	Nay, noman mihte don þat dede :	
	þat is preued and ishewed	
	Boþe to lered and to lewed.	400
	þanne maitou þenke : 'Hu mai þis be?	
	Ne shal no man god ise?'	
Yes, yes,	¶ ȝus, ȝus, bi my leaute !	
	Herkne, and i wole telle þe :	404
	ȝif þu wolt sen in þi siht	
	God of heuene, þat is so briht,—	42 d
	¶ Vnderstond nu what i mene—	
the undefiled	'þu most ben of herte clene,'	408
	In word, in dede, and in þouht,	
	þat þu ne be ifiled noht;	
	For god self seide in soþ[e]nesse—	
	þe godspel þerof bereþ¹ witnesse :	412
shall see the infinite God of Heaven	Beati mundo² corde, quoniam ipsi deum uidebunt.	
	þis is to seie, i telle þe :	
	'þe clene of herte, blessed þeih be ;'	
	For, at þe heie dom sikerliche	
	'þeih sholen se god' aperteliche,	416
	In his godhede and in his blisse,	
and shall hearken to the joyous summons,—	Off which þeih sholen neuere misse.	
	¶ þanne sholen þeih here, herkne nouþe,	
	A blisful word of godes mouþe,	420

398 Nay] om. DH₂. 399 þat] and þat R. preued] I proued A₂, proued wele DH₂. ishewed] schewede DH₂R, wel shewede H₁. 400 lered and] lerned and eke H₁. 401 þanne] How D. (How is crossed out before þane in A₂. þane is above the line.) maitou] maste þoue A₂, myȝte þou H₂. hu] om. DH₁. mai þis] sal þis D, þis may not H₁, maye yt H₂. 402 Ne shal no man] þat noman sal D, þat any man here shal euer H₁, Shalle ther noman H₂, ne may no mou R. ise] see A₂H₁R, here se H₂. 403 and 404 read in H₁ :

ȝis for soþ wiþ outen ney
Herken & here what I wil say

404 wole] sal D. 407—475 are omitted in D. 407 nu] wel H₁H₂. 408 þu] For þou H₁. of] in H₁. 409 reads in H₁ : Of worde of dede & of þoȝte. 410 þat] So þat H₁. ne] om. H₁R. ifiled] fyled A₂H₁, fyled right R. 411 self] hym A₂, him self H₁H₂ (following sayed) R. seide] saiþe A₂H₁H₂. 412 þe] and þo R. 413 þis] þat A₂H₂R. telle] telle yt H₂. 414 þe] Al H₁R. þeih] om. H₂. 415 heie] daye of H₂, grete R. sikerliche] sekyrly H₂. 416 aperteliche] apertely H₂. 418 Off] þo R. 419 þanne sholen þeih] That shulle ȝe H₂. here] om. A₂. herkne nouþe] wiþ here ere H₁, þat bene couthe R. 420 godes mouþe] god þere H₁.

¹ MS. A₁ has bereþ þerof. ² MS. A₁ mondo.

[Which shal not be to hem vncowþe,
For god shal sey it with his mowþe:
Venite, benedicti[1] patris mei.]
'Comeþ, mine blessede fere,   *'Come, be-*
þat my fader beþ leue and dere!   424   *loved,*
                                                                dear to my
In-to my blisse ȝe sholen wende,   *Father!*
þat lasteþ euere wid-outen ende,   *In my bliss*
                                                                dwell ever-
And euere more þer to wone   *more.'*
Wid þe fader, and wid þe sone,   428
And wid þe holi gost in vnite,
þat is þe holi trinite.'

¶ 'And [ȝe],[2] cursede gostes, goþ anon,   *The doomed*
þat sholen ben dampned euerichon!'   432   *souls,*
þere hij sholen him sen also,
Ac al shal ben for here wo;
For toward hem he wole turne

¶ Boþe wraþful and eke sterne,   436
And namlich to þat cumpaignye   43 *a*
þat slowen him þurw enuie,   *who slew*
                                                                 Him with
And kene nailes driuen ek   *cruel nails*
                                                                 through
þurw his honden and his fet,   440   *hands and*
                                                                 feet,
¶ And þere þeih sholen se soþliche,   *shall see the*
His grisli wounden openliche,   *ghastly*
                                                               wounds they
þat þeih deden hemselue make.   *made.*
For drede hij sholen þanne quake;   444
þanne wole god to hem seie   *His angry*
                                                                 voice will
Wid sterne voiz and wid heie: *command:*

---

421 *and* 422 *are omitted in* $A_1A_2H_2R$. *The Latin is omitted in* $A_1A_2H_2R$. 423 Comeþ] Comes now R. fere] children in fere H_1, alle in ffere H_2, in fere R. 424 þat] þat to H_1H_2R. leue and] ful H_1. 426 lasteþ euere] euir shalle laste H_2. 428 and wid] and H_2. 429 And] *om.* H_1. 430 þat] whiche H_1. 431 And] *om.* H_1. goþ] þere H_1, *om.* H_2. 432 þat] þei A_2, *om.* H_1, ȝe H_2R. 433 hij] þei $A_2H_1H_2R$. him sen] se hym R. 434 Ac] For A_2, But H_1H_2R. al] yt H_2, þat R. for] to A_2, al for R. 435 turne] hym turne R. 435—444 *are omitted in* H_2. 438 þurw] þorouȝ here A_2H_1. 439 driuen] þey dryuen H_1. 440 and] *and* þorow H_1. his fet] fete did hom to seke (*þai is on the margin.*) R. 441 And] *om.* A_2. soþliche] opunlyche H_1, sothly R. 442 openliche] opnnly R. 442 *reads in* H_1: Al his woundis sicurliche. 443 hemselue] hym self A_2. 444 hij] þei A_2H_1R. (shul þai *follow* þen *in* R.) 445 god] he H_2. 446 and wid heie] *and with eye* A_2, *withoute neye* H_1, and angry eye H_2, & grete aie R.

---

[1] *MS.* benedicte.   [2] *MS.* A_1 *has* þe.

Of Unwavering Hope,

<small>'Accursed spirits, go! Depart into the tortures of hell!</small>

    'Corsede gostes, ȝe beþ me loþe!
Goþ anon, goþ nu,[1] goþe   448
¶ In-to þe stronge fyr of helle,
Euere more þer to dwelle,

<small>Burn eternally!</small>

And brenne þer in hote fyr![2]
Ȝe seruede non oþer her: 452

<small>For evermore</small>

Merci is al fro ȝou gon,
For whij on me hadde ȝe non!'
He þat nele no merci haue
Off him þat doþ him merci craue,   456

<small>'thou art judged!'</small>

He shal ben iuged, witerli,
Rihtfulliche, wid-oute merci.

¶ Sein Daui seiþ, if þu wolt loke
In a vers of þe[3] sauter boke: 460
Spera in domino, et fac bonitatem.   <small>De Spe.</small>

<small>Hope in God; do good.</small>

'Hope to god, and do god,'
Riht so i hit vnderstod;
Ac ydel hope man mai habbe—
I sey þe soþ wid-outen gabbe—   464
For alone to hope, widoute goddede,
¶ Is ydel hope, so god me rede.
Ac i ne seie noht forþi,   <small>43 b</small>

---

447 *and* 448 *have the following readings in* H₁ *and in* H₂:
    Ȝe cursyd gostis fro me goþ
    For to my fadire & me ȝe beþ ful loþ   H₁.
    Waryed gostys ȝe are me lothe
    Gothe in to sorowe & care bothe   H₂.

449 In-to þe] In to A₂R, And evene in to H₂. stronge] stynkynge H₁, om. H₂. fyr] payne A₂, pytte H₂. 450 Euere more] And euere more A₁H₁, Withowtyn ende H₂, for euer more R. þer] þeire In A₂, þere for to H₁. 451 *and* 452 *are omitted in* H₂. 452 ȝe] for ȝe han R. seruede] haue a seruid H₁. her] hyere A₂H₁. 453 al fro ȝou] now alle H₂. gon] I gonne H₂. 454 whij on] on A₂H₂. hadde ȝe] ne hadde ȝe D, ȝe haden R. *Between* 454 *and* 455 *are the following two lines in* H₂:
    Whan ȝowre power was full welle
    I sente I nowe of cuyry dele
455 nele] wil H₁H₂R. no] om. A₂. 456 Off] On R. him þat] hem H₁. doþ him] doþ A₂H₂, wolde hym R. 457 witerli] vtturly H₁. 458 Rihtfulliche] Skylffulliche H₂. 459 Sein] For seynt R. 459—814 *and the Latin text following are omitted in* H₂. 462 hit] *om.* R. 463 Ac] For A₂, But H₁R. man] a mon R. 464 þe] *om.* H₁. wid-outen] *and* not H₁. 465 *and* 466 *are inserted between* 470 *and* 471 *in* A₂. 465 alone to] all on to A₂, *om.* H₁, al onely R. goddede] ony good dede H₁. 466 rede] spede H₁R. 467 Ac i ne] For I A₂, But ȝit I H₁, But I ne R.

---

[1] nu *is above the line in MS.* A₁.
[2] *Read* fer.   [3] þe *is above the line in MS.* A₁.

þouh man be charged, sikerli	468 Though grievous the burden,
¶ Wid grete sinnes houie and¹ sore,	
He ne shal despeire neuere þe more,	be not in despair.
Ac soþfast hope haue, to winne	Be steadfast.
Godes merci of his sinne	472
þurw shrifte of mouþe and repentaunce,	
And redi þerfore to don penaunce.	
¶ 3if þu dost þus, bi day and niht,	Daily in confession and
Put al² þin hope in god almiht,	476 tears, hope for
And tristi hope to him þu haue,	mercy.
þat he þe wole helpe and saue.	
Herkne, what i wole seie nouþe,	
For hit com out of godes mouþe:	480
Ubi te inuenio, ibi³ te iudicabo.	
'Man, riht þere as i þe finde,	Delay not to do good.
Riht þere i wole þe iuge and binde.'	
Allas, what sholen hij þanne do,	
þat beþ ifounde in sorwe and wo,	484
þat wolde noht hemselue shriue,⁴	
While þeih mihte in here liue !	
Þerfore, man, i warne þe:	
Loke, þat þu þe bise,	488
þat þu be euere redi and 3are	Be ready.
Out of þis world for to fare ;	
For siker noman wite ne may,	
Whanne shal ben his ending day.	492
¶ Þerfore þenk ofte in drede	

468 þouh man] þou may R. 470 He] 3it R. ne] om. A₂DR, shal] shalt þou R. 471 Ac] And A₂, But H₁R. soþfast] stedfast R. haue] om. A₂, haue þou R. 472 Godes] And cry god H₁. his] þi R. *The MS. continues with* 476 *in* D. 476 in] to D. almiht] of might R. 478 þat] And H₁. helpe] boþ helpe H₁. 479 what] þat D. wole] sal D. seie] say þe D, om. R. nouþe] nowe D. 479 *reads in* H₁ : Loke þis be not to 3ow vnkowþe. (*Cp. l.* 421.) 480 out] om. A₂D. *Latin:* iudicabo] iudico A₂R. 482 þere] so D H₁. wole] sal D. 483 what] how A₂. hij] þei A₂DH₁R. 484 ifounde] I bounde A₂, fon D, confoundid H₁, founden R. sorwe] synne D. 485 wolde] nold D. hemselue] hem A₂. 486 While] þe whyle D. in here] in þeire A₂, *and were on* H₁. 488 bise] by þe so A₂, be se D. 488 *reads in* H₁ *and* R : Whilest þou maiste goo & see. þou] þat þou R. 489 þat] Loke H₁. euere] *om.* R. 490 þis] *om.* D. for] forþe D. 491 siker] sikurliche H₁, sikernes R. ne] *om.* H₁R. 493 þenk] haue it H₁. in drede] I þe reide R.

¹ and *is above the line in MS.* A₁.   ² al *is above the line in MS.* A₁.
³ *One letter has been erased before* ibi *in MS.* A₁.
⁴ 484 *and* 485 *are over erasure in MS.* A₁.

God said: 'Where I find, I bind.'	Off þis word,[1] þat god seide:[2] 'þere i þe finde, i wole þe binde:'	
Remember!	Lat ofte þat word ben in þi mynde!	496
	¶ Man, if þu wolt þe world forsake, And Iesu Crist to þe take,	43 c
Pray often.	þu most ben ofte in orisoun	
Read.	And in reding of lesczoun.	500 *De Scripturarum Lectione.*
In reading, God speaks with us;	Wid us god spekeþ, whan we rede Off him and of his goddede,	
in prayer,	And we wid him, ful iwis,	
we speak with God.	Whan we him bisekeþ þat riht is.	504
Holy Writ is our mirror, where is revealed	¶ Holi writ is oure myrour, In whom we sen al vre socour, And, if we hit wolen vnderstonde, þer we muwen sen and fonge,	508
knowledge of God.	To haue of god þe knowelache,[3] Boþe in þouht[e] and in speche.	
	¶ And, if þu wolt haue þe loue Off god, þat is in heuen aboue, þu most ben euere in god acord,	512
Seek peace.	In pes and loue, and hate descord, And ben aboute wid al þi miht, To make pes bi day and niht;	*De Præceptis Pacis.* 516
God hath proclaimed a blessing to the peacemaker.	¶ For Iesu Crist hit seiþ ful wel, As we hit finden in godspel: **Beati pacifici, quoniam filii Dei uocabuntur.**	

494 Off þis] þe H₁. word] world D. seide] bi fore saide H₁. 495 wole] sal D. 496 þat] þis H₁R. 497 wolt þe] wylt þen þe (þen *blurred*) A₂, om. D, wilt þis H₁R. 498 And] Aud to DH₁. to þe] holy þe D, þe H₁. take] bi take H₁. 500 And] And eke H₁. lesczoun] gods lessone R. 501 god spekeþ] to speke D. 502 goddede] godhede A₂H₁, blissed dede R. 503 we wid him ful] he with vs spekiþ H₁, we with hym R. 504 we] he D. him bisekeþ] him bysech A₂, hym bedes D, bi seche him H₁R. riht] riʒtful H₁. 506 sen] seken H₁. 507 hit wolen] willen it A₂D. 507 *and* 508 *read in* H₁:

If we vndirstond it welle
þere may we se euery delle.

508 we muwen] may we R. fonge] fonde D, vnderfonde R. 509 knowelache] knowleching R. 510 speche] speking R. 512 god] Iesu R. is in heuen] in heuen sittes R. 513 acord] wille H₁. 514 and loue] loue D. 514 *reads in* H₁: to hate synne boþ loude & stille. 516 bi] boþ H₁. 518 hit finden] fynde D. in] in þe A₂DH₁. *Latin: The text is inserted between* 522 *and* 523 *in* H₁.

---

[1] word *is corrected from* world *in MS.* A₁.   [2] *Read* sede.
[3] *Read* knowelche.

Of Peace and Mercy.

    A soþ word hit is and no les:
    'Iblessed be þat makeþ pes:'   520
    Hij ouhten to ben honoured alle,
    For 'godes children men shal hem calle.'

De Miseri-
cordia.

¶   Man, if þu wolt to me herkny,
    Nu i wole speken of merci.   524
¶ Soþ[e]liche, wid-oute fable,   43 d
    Man, þu most ben merciable.   *Be merciful.*
    On Iesu Crist þenk witerli,
    Hou he deiede for merci,   528   *Christ hath died*
¶ And al for he wolde merci haue
    Off hem þat wolde merci craue;
    For, ar he deiede in flesh and bon,
    Merci was þer neuere non.   532
¶ Bi þis ensaumple ȝe muwen se,   *for our sake,*
    Merciable for to be.   *example of mercy.*
    Ȝif þi neihboure misdoþ þe,
    More or lasse wheiþer hit be,   536
    Or in dede, or in vbbreid,
    Or wid word þe haþ misseid,   *Misdeeds against thee,*
    And he þer-after of-þinkeþ sore
    And þer-of crieþ merci and ore,   540
    For-ȝif hit him for godes loue,   *forgive for God's love.*
    Þat us alle sit aboue!
¶ And, if þu wolt no merci haue
    Off him þat doþ þe merci craue,   544
    Merci getestu neuere non
    Off trespas, þat þu hast idon;

---

519 hit is] is it H₁. no] not R. 520 Iblessed] Blessed H₁R. be] be þei A₂R, be he H₁. 521 Hij] þei A₂DH₁, hom R. ouhten to ben] owte be D, shul be H₁, oow to be R. 523 to me] come A₂ (*transposed after* herken *in* R). 524 Nu] *om.* H₁R. wole] sal D. speken] speke su[m]what H₁. merci] mercie to þe R. 525 fable] ony fable H₁. 527 witerli] entereli H₁. 528 for] oonly for H₁. 529 al for] for D. 530 Off] On H₁R. wolde merci] wyl it mekelyche D, wolde hym mercy R. 533 ȝe muwen] þou mast A₂. 534 *and* 535 *are omitted in* D. 534 Merciable] Ful merciable H₁. 535 þi] ony H₁. misdoþ] haue misdone to R. 536 lasse] lesse lasse H₁. hit] so hit R. 537 Or] Ouþer A₂DH₁R. or] ouþer D. in] with H₁, *om.* R. vbbreid] vnbroid D. 538 Or wid] Ouþer with A₂, Oþer in D, Or els with H₁. þe] þat he H₁ (*after* has *in* R). misseid] sayde H₁. 539 of-þinkeþ] for þynkkiþ A₂, a þenke it D, aþynkeþ H₁, forthinkus hit R. 540 crieþ] þe cry D. 541 For-ȝif] Forȝeued D. hit] *om.* A₂H₁. 543 if] *om.* R. wolt] nylt D. no] not A₂. 544 Off] On H₁R. him] hom R. 545 getestu] gestow DH₁. 546 Off] Of þe A₂. þu] þi selfe H₁. idon] done A₂DH₁R.

Of Forgiveness.

      For god it seiþ in his godspel—
      þere men may finde it ful wel—   548
¶ 'Alswich met as þu metest me,
      Alswich i wole mete to þe.'
      [For-ȝeue, þou man, for þe loue of me,   *De Indulgentia.*
      And I wyll for þe loue of þe.]   552
      Nym god ȝeme, man. þu sist
      In þi paternoster, what þu bist:
      **Et dimitte nobis debita nostra, sicut
      et nos etc.**

Pray: 'Sweet God, forgive my guilt,   þu seist: 'Swete lord, forȝiue þu me,   *41 a*
      þat i haue gilt aȝeines þe,   556
as I forgive.'   Riht as i do alle þo,
      þat me hauen ouht misdo.'

To the cruel   ¶ And þu, þat art so cruwel in þouht
      And wolt to merci herkne noht,   560
      What wole hit [þe] helpe in eny stede
the paternoster availeth nothing.   þe holi paternoster bede?
      Noht, if i dar it seie,
      For aȝein þiself[e] þu dost preie,   564
¶ And þe holi bok of soþ[e]nesse
      þer-of bereþ god witnesse
      And seiþ: 'He þat wole no merci haue,
      On ydel doþ he merci craue.'   568

547 For] *om.* D. it seiþ] seiþ it D. his] þe D. 548 men] *om.* H₁, mony mon R. ful] *om.* R. *The following text is introduced in R:* 'Eadem mensura qua messi fueritis remetietur vobis.' 549 Alswich] Also soch A₂, Sweche DR. met] mesure H₁. me] to me D. 550 Alswich] Also soch A₂, Soche H₁, right siche R. wole] sal D. to þe] þe A₂, vnto þe D, aȝen to þe H₁. 551 and 552 *are omitted in* A₁. 551 þou man] *om.* D, man H₁R. 552 wyll] sal D. for þe] for D, for ȝif for H₁. 553 Nym] Take A₂H₁, Take mon R. god ȝeme] now gome D, gode hede H₁. man] þer R. þu sist] þat þou sest A₂, þere þou sittest H₁, þou saiest R. 554 þi] þo R. what] þare A₂, whan H₁. bist] bedest A₂, biddest H₁, prayest R. *Latin: etc.*] *dimittimus etc.* A₂, *dimittimus debitoribus nostris* DH₁R. 555 þu] *om.* R. 556 gilt] trespased H₁, mysdone R. þe] *om.* A₂. 557 as] als D. do] do to DH₁R. 558 me] to me R. ouht] ony þinge H₁. 559 And] O D. þat] *om.* A₂. in þouht] in þy þouȝt A₂, *and* touȝt D. 560 wolt] nylt D. 561 þe helpe] helpe A₁, helpe þe A₂H₁, stonde R. stede] way H₁. 562 þe] þi D. bede] for to say H₁, þof þou hit bidde R. 563 Noht if] Nouȝt A₂, Ryȝt noȝt H₁. dar it] dare wele A₂H₁, doist (*for* dorst) D. seie] say *and* nay A₂, say for soop H₁. 564 aȝein] aȝenste H₁. dost preie] preyst wiþ mooþ H₁. 565 And] As A₂. 566 god] *om.* A₂R. 567 wole no] nelt D. 568 On] In D, ful R. doþ he] he doth A₂, may he R.

In patientia[1] bestra possidebitis[2] animas bestras.

De Patientia

Houre swete lord in his speche
Hise dociples began to teche
And bad hem ben of god suffraunce
In alle manere destourbaunce.   572

Our sweet Lord taught his disciples patience.

¶ ȝif þu art sek in flesh and blod,
þu most ben meke and þolemod
And þenk[e] þat god it þe sende,
þi seli soule to amende.   576

In sickness, be meek and content. Know that it is to help thy poor soul.

¶ ȝif þu hast lore of þi catel,
Biþenk þe þanne swiþe wel,
þat of þi-self[e] haddestu noht,
But as hit was þurw god iwrouht;[3]   580
And, if god it wole from þe take,
þu ne shalt þerfore no gruching make,

Mourn not loss of possessions. Of thyself hadst thou nothing; all is God's gift. What God hath ordered, must be right.

¶ Ac suffre al godes wille
Boþe lude and eke stille.   44 b   584

Be not regretful. God's will is best.

¶ And, ȝif þe falleþ trauail on honde,
Or pine of bodi, or shame in londe,
Off al þis þu most suffraunt be,
þouh þe þinke, hit greue þe.   588

In distress, pain, disgrace, be still.

þenk hou Iesu in-to erþe cam,
And þolede pine and shame for man,
And foule was þerto misseid,

Remember the agony, the vile words,

---

570 began to] he gan to A₂, he con R. 571 and 572 are transposed in R. 571 And] he R. bad] om. D. 572 alle] euery D. destourbaunce] of disturbaunce D, dissese or chaunce H₁. 573 and] or D. 574 most] salt D. and] om. R. þolemod] þole mod A₂, þole þi mode D, and lowe of mode H₁, in al þi mode R. 575 it þe] þe it A₂. 576 to] for to H₁. 577 lore] lose A₂H₁R, hire D. þi] om. A₂. 578 Biþenk] Loke & vmthink R. þanne] man H₁, om. R. 579 haddestu] hast þou (or Last in A₂) A₂D, þou haddest hit R. 580 iwrouht] ibouȝt D, wroght R. 581 it wole from þe] wyll it fro þe A₂R, wil fro þe it H₁. 582 ne] om. H₁R. þerfore] it þer of D. 583 Ac] Bot A₂H₁R, And D. 584 Boþe] What euer he do boþ H₁. eke] om. H₁. 587 Off al þis þu most] Of þis þou most D, þou muste in al þis H₁. suffraunt] suffrand A₂DH₁ (before most) R. 588 þouh þe] ȝe þoȝ þou H₁, þof þou R. 589 Iesu] Iesu Criste D. 590 þolede] suffrerd H₁, for mon he tholyd R. for man] om. R. 591 was þerto] þere was R. 591 and 592 are omitted in H₁. In their place are the following two lines:

    And many a fowle worde sufferd he þere
    Boþ scornyngis and lesinngis on hym þey bere

[1] MS. A₁ reads paciena.   [2] bitis is written below the line in MS. A₁.
[3] The line is punctuated here with a period in MS. A₁.

28 *Concerning Martyrdom*

the scorn laid on Christ. He was silent.	And many a skorn on him leid,	592
	Wid-oute gruching he held him stille,	
	And þolede hit al wid milde wille,	
	¶ And al¹ he dede for vre sake,	
	For we sholde ensaumple take	596
	To be suffraunt in eueri stede,	
	Riht as vre lord himselue dede.	
If man	And, ʒif a man þurw his power	
wrong thee, be not sad.	Doþ þe wrong on eorþe her,	600
	þenk in þin herte, i preie þe,	
	Off þe wrong and þe vilte,	
	þat men to Iesu Crist dede	
	Here on eorþe in many stede,	604
	¶ And hou he þolede hit mildeliche,	
	Al ffor þi loue, sikerliche.	
	On ensaumple of him þu nim,	
For love of Christ feel not ill will.	To suffre wrong for þe loue of him;	608
	For, i dar seie soþ[e]liche,	
He may be martyr without sword or flame, who is patient for the love of	He may be martyr, treweliche,	
	Wid-oute sheding of mannes blod,	
	þat may ben here þolemod,	612
	¶ To suffre wrong and vnriht	
God Almighty.	For þe loue of god almiht:	
The fight is hard, contrary to nature.	Ac swich a fiht is vnmeþ,	41 c
	For aʒein þe kinde hit geþ.	616

592 on him] vpon R. leid] was leid (*nearly erased*) A₂, lleide D. 593 he] *om.* R. held him] was ful H₁. 594 þolede] suffered H₁. hit al] it A₂. milde] good H₁. 595 al he dede] died D. 596 ensaumple] ensample of him H₁, at him ensaumpel R. 597 suffraunt] suffrande A₂DR, sufferynge H₁. eueri] ilk a R. 598 vre lord] criste H₁. himselue] hym D, for vs H₁. 599 a] ony R. 600 þe] ony H₁. 601 in] þus in D. þin] *om.* D. 602 Off þe] And of þe A₂, How myche H₁. and þe] and of þe A₂R, *and* H₁. vilte] wyte A₂, vilante (*perhaps for* vilanie) D. 603 þat men] Mankynde H₁. 604 on] in DH₁R. many] many a DH₁R. 605 þolede hit] it þoled A₂, þoled D, sufferid mekelych *and* H₁. mildeliche] mykelich A₂, stille H₁, myldely R. 606 sikerliche] sikerly R. 606 *reads in* H₁: For luf of man with good wille. 607 On ensaumple] onsample D. þu] now þou D. nim] take H₁. 608 þe] *om.* DH₁. loue of him] goddis sake H₁. 609 dar] dar wel H₁. soþeliche] sothly R. 610 He] þat a man H₁. martyr treweliche] martrid treuly R. 611 of mannes] of his D, here of his H₁. 612 may ben] wele may here D, is R. þolemod] þole (*verb*) mode (*substantive*) D, of meke mode H₁, of thole mode R. 615 Ac] For A₂, And D, But H₁R. vnmeþ] vnneþe A₂, wele vnneþ D, vn eþ H₁. 615 *reads in* R: But vnneth siche a faithe is þere. 616 þe] *om.* R. geþ] seþe D, were R.

¹ l *is above the line in MS.* A₁.

¶ Whij? for þe kinde of þi manhede
Wolde haue wreche of wrongful dede;
Ac of Iesu tak þi minde,
And fiht aȝein þin owen kinde,   620
And þu shalt haue for þi goddede
Off martyrdom þe heie mede.   *In crown of martyrdom haue meed.*
   Ac þu, fersse man, þat art so stout,
And heih of mod, and herte proud¹—   624 *God honoreth lowliness.*
He wole bowe for noþing
To man, ne to heuene king—
¶ And he þat wole him heinen here,   *The high He*
þat nele be meke in none manere,   628
In litel while he shal hit knowe
And falle þerfore swiþe lowe.   *draweth low;*

De Humilitate.

Qui se exaltat, humiliabitur, et qui se humiliat, exaltabitur.

þe milde þurw [her]² humilite   *the low He*
Ful heie honoured þeih sholen be;   632
For þeih³ sholen be drawen on heih   *lifteth high.*
And wonye⁴ god swiþe neih.
¶   And pride, it is so foul a last,   *The fairest angel was*
þat out of heuene he was cast.   636 *hurled from heaven*
þu shalt wel wite, þat i ne liȝe,
· For Lucifer [with] his cumpaignye,
[Out of heuen, þat was so bryȝte,
In-to helle for pride he toke his flyȝte.]   640

617 Whij] om. H₁. þe] þi D. þi] þe D, om. H₁R. manhede] mon R.
618 wreche of wrongful dede] vengaunce a non R. of] for A₂. 619 Ac] Bot A₂H₁R, And D. Iesu] Iesu criste D. tak] take þou H₁. 623 Ac] For A₂, But H₁R. þu fersse] þe ferþe (or ferye) D, þou H₁. art so stout] so proude art R. 624 And] om. A₂D. heih of] of hyȝe H₁. and herte] of herte A₂D, & stoute of hert R. proud] om. R. 625 He wole] He nyll A₂D, þou nylt H₁, he wil not R. 626 To] Neþere to H₁. 627 he þat] þat D. wole] wold A₂. him heinen] hym hye A₂H₁, hey hym D, heghe hym R. 628 þat nele] And wil H₁, and wol not R. be meke] bowe R. in none] in no A₂D, on noo H₁R. 630 þerfore swiþe] boþ fowle and H₁. Latin: exaltat humiliabitur] humiliat exaltabitur A₂R. et] om. A₂R. humiliat exaltabitur] exaltat humiliabitur A₂R. 632 heie] Wele A₂, lely R. þeih sholen] shall he A₂H₁R, he sal D. 633 þeih] he DH₁R. 634 wonye] wounne with H₁. 635 And] For A₂D, But H₁. it is] is DH₁. a] at A₂, boþ firste and H₁. 636 þat] om. D. heuene] paradys A₂. 637 ne] not R. 638 with] and A₁A₂DR. his] al his H₁. 639 and 640 are omitted in A₁A₂DR.

¹ *Read* prout.   ² *MSS.* his.
³ i *in* þeih *is in red ink above the line in MS.* A₁.
⁴ e *is above the line in MS.* A₁.

through pride.	þurw þe pride þat hem gan folewe,
	þe pine of helle hem gan to swolewe,
	¶ And so he wole don alle and some,
	þat in pride be inome. 644
Beware, proud man!	[Nowe be þou were, þou proude gome,
	þat þou ne be in pryde cnome :]
	Cast hit awey, i wole þe rede, "d
	Er of strong pine þe may drede ; 648
	¶ For siker, and þu be nomen þerinne,
	Heuene maitou neuere winne,
	And oþer weye is þer non,
Pride drags to hell.	Bute to heuene or to helle gon. 652
	þanne do bi consail and bi red,¹
	And ouercome þe foule qued,
	þat fondeþ þe on vch a side,
	þe to holde in þi pride. 656
	¶ Ac, if þu couþest knowe and se
	þe uertu of humilite,
	For noþing þu noldest shone,
Have contempt for vanities.	Ac hit sholde euere wid þe wone : 660
	Off alle uertuz it is hext,
	And godes wille it is next.
	Sein Gregory þerof bereþ witnes,
	þat muchel spekeþ of soþ[e]nes : 664
Without humility holy works are	**Qui sine humilitate uirtutes ceteras congregat, est quasi, qui in vento puluerem portat.**

641 *and* 642 *are omitted in* H₁. 641 gan] dyde D, con R. 642 pine] pytt D. hem] þeyme A₂. to] *om.* A₂R. 643 And so] So R. he] þei A₂, *om.* H₁. wole don] shalle do boþ H₁. and some] men R. 644 inome] takeu R. 645 *and* 646 *are omitted in* A₁D. 645 Nowe be þou] þen be H₁, Now be R. gome] grome R. 646 ne be] be not H₁, *om.* R. enome] I nome H₁, be not nome R. 647 wole] sal D, *om.* H₁. 648—653 *are omitted in* A₂. 648 Er of strong] Or of stronger H₁, Or ellis of strong R. þe] þou DH₁R. 649 siker] sikerly R. nomen] founde H₁, tane R. 650 maitou] myȝt þou D. 651 þer] þer neuer H₁. 652 to helle] helle þou must H₁, helle R. 653 þanne] Mau D. bi] be my D. and bi] aud be my D. 654 þe] þat A₂. 655 on] in A₂. vch] ilk R. a side] syde DH₁. 656 þe to holde] For to holdene A₂, Tho holde þe D, For to hold þe H₁R. þi] *om.* R. 657 Ac] For A₂, And DH₁, But R. couþest] kowdest H₁. and] or R. 659 þu noldest] noldest þou A₂, þou nost it D, woltest it H₁, þou woldist hit R. 660 Ac] For A₂, And D, But H₁R. 661 hext] þo hext R. 662 And] And at A₂. 663 þerof bereþ] bereþ þerof A₁, bereþ D. 664 soþenes] mekenesse D. *Latin: est*] *et* D, *om.* H₁R. *qui*] *om.* A₂R, *quem* D. *in vento puluerem*] *puluerem in vento* R.

¹ *MS.* A₁ bired.

Admonitions to

Man, þou[h] þu do muchel god,
But þou be meke and þolemod,
Sein Gregory seiþ, þat holi clerk,
þat muchel on ydel is þat werk. 668
Hit fareþ bi swiche, as we finde,
As who-so bereþ poudre in grete winde; *like dust in wind.*
For, bere he neuere so muche,[1]
Hit fleþ awey ful lihtliche. 672
Off man hit fareþ riht so,
For, gode dedes þouh he do, *45 a*
Many and fele in vch a side,
þer may non wid him abide: 676
Bute he haue humilite,
Awey þeih wolen fro him fle. *Away they fly.*

¶ A god þing is humilite :
Off him comeþ verray charite, 680 *From humility springeth penitence, of which*
And penaunce, and eke shrift—
De Compunctione cordis. þis is of god a wel fair ʒift—
And of him forʒif[e]nesse of sinne. *forgiveness is won,*
Wel is him þat hit may winne! 684

¶ Who-so is aferd of his trespaz,
He shal haue comfort and solaz
Off þe holi gost, witerli,
þat wole [his] soule comforti, 688 *the soul's comfort,*
And make men haue, mid iwisse,
Tristi hope to heuene blisse. *and everlasting delights.*
Sein Daui þer-of spak and seide[2]

---

665 do] *om.* D. muchel] ful meche D, neuer so mikel R. 666 meke and] lowe & meke of H₁. þolemod] þole (*verb*) mod (*substantive*) D, mode H₁, of thole mode R. 667 þat] þe A₂. clerk] chirche A₂D. 668 on] in A₂DR. þat] þi H₁, his R. 670 who-so] he þat H₁. grete] þe H₁. 671 bere he] þoʒ he bere H₁, of he bere R. 672 fleþ] fallepe D, flyeþ H₁R. ful] *om.* A₂. 673 and 674 *are transposed in* A₁, H₁, *and* R. 673 Off] Ryʒt be D. riht so] also A₂. 674 þouh] of R. 675 and] ane D. in] on H₁R. a side] syde A₂D. 676 him] oþer R. 677 Bute] But if H₁. humilite] verray humylite R. 678 *and* 679 *are omitted in* A₂. 678 Awey] Alle R. þeih wolen fro him] fro hym þay wyl D, þei wil al fro him H₁. fle] flye H₁. 679 *is omitted in* D. 680 him] him þat H₁. 681 And] In D. 682 þis] þat D. wel] *om.* A₂. ful R. 683 of him] of· hem D, *om.* R. sinne] hys synne A₂. 684 hit may] þat may A₂D, may it H₁. 685 Who-so] For who so A₂, He þat H₁. aferd] affred D. 687 witerli] vtterly H₁. 688 his] þi A₁R, man H₁. comforti] confort in hye R. 689 men] here D, men to R. mid] mynde A₂D, þer myd H₁, þer with R. iwisse] wysse D. 690 Tristi] Of tresty D. 691 þer-of] *om.* D.

---

[1] *Read* miche.   [2] *Read* sede.

In þe¹ sauter, as men rede : 692

**Secundum multitudinem dolorum meo-
rum in corde meo, consolationes tuæ
lætificauerunt² animam meam.**

Fear sin!
'[Þe]³ more man douteþ here sinne,
þe more ioye he shal winne ; '
For, who-so haþ of sinne⁴ drede
And nel noht don þat⁵ foule dede, 696
Hit semeþ, þat he haþ trewe loue
To Iesu Crist, þat is aboue.

¶ O þing is comen in my þou[h]t,
To shewe hit wole i spare noht : 700

The godly ¶ ȝif any þat is in holy lyf,
Man, maiden, oþer wif,
In any time, þurw any cas,

for a little trespass Doþ a litel trespas, 704
þat be aȝein godes wille,
Oþer loud[e] oþer stille,

grieveth more He wole haue more sorwe and drede
For þat litel sinful dede, 708

than doth for his sin þan many on wole in eny stounde,
þat lyþ in dedli sinne bounde.
ȝif ȝe wolen wite herof þe skile,
Herkne, and i ȝou telle wole :⁶ 712

the man lying in guilt þat man þat lyþ in dedli sinne,
And to singy wole noht blinne,

---

692 as men] boke men may D. rede] do rede H₁. *Latin:* meorum] om.
R. meo] om. D. consolationes tuæ] om. R. 693 man] a mon R. here] his
A₂H₁R, here of D. 694 he shal] shal he H₁. 695 sinne] his sinne A₁R. 696
And] He D. nel] wil H₁R. noht] no more R. þat foule dede] þe fende reed
H₁, hit in dede R. 698 is] sittiþe A₂H₁R. 699 comen] comyn now D. in]
to R. 700 hit wole] it nyl A₂H₁, nil D, hit I wil R. i] om. R. 701 þat is]
man be H₁, is R. 702 Man maiden] Man or childe made H₁. oþer] or A₂H₁,
wydow oþer D, childe or R. 703 any] one R. þurw] for D. any] a R.
704 Doþ] and dos R. a litel] gret or smale H₁. 705 be] is H₁R. 706 Oþer]
Erly or late H₁, be hit R. oþer] or H₁, be hit R. 708 litel] on H₁. 709 on]
om. DH₁. 710 lyþ] es D. bounde] I bounde A₂H₁R, iboude D. 711 ȝe
wolen wite] þou wylt A₂R, þou wolt nyt D, ȝe wil H₁. þe skile] skyll D, ony
þinge wite H₁. 712 i ȝou telle] I þe telle A₂R, tell þe I D, I wil tel ȝow H₁.
wole] ȝitte H₁. 713 þat] þe A₂DR. 714 And to singy] Fro day to day and
H₁, and þo synne he R. wole] wyll he A₂, nelo DH₁.

¹ þe *is above the line in MS.* A₁. ² *MS.* tue lctificaucront.
³ *MS.* A₁ *has so.* ⁴ *MS.* A₁ *has* his sinne.
⁵ *One letter has been erased after* þat *in MS.* A₁. ⁶ *Read* wille.

¶ Gostli wit he haþ ilore.
 Whi, i wole telle, [and] wharfore;   716   *He hath lost*
 For gostli siht, witerliche,   *discernment*
 Man, is þi resoun, sikerliche,
 Wher-þur[w] þu miht in þi mod
 Knowe boþe yuel and god,   720
 And shed to make in eueri dede
 Bitwene soþnesse and falshede.
¶ And, whan mannes soule, ful iwis,
 þurw dedli sinne ifiled is,   724
 His knowelaching is al gon;
 For wit no siht haþ [he]¹ non,
 Wherfore þe sinful man   *and*
 Noþer he ne may ne he ne can   728
 His owen stat [a]riht ise,   *cannot see*
¶ Ne knowe in what lyf he be
 For þisternesse, þat he is inne   *45 c*
 þurw þe filþe of dedli sinne.   732   *the filth of deadly sin; but the holy hath*
¶ Ac he þat liueþ in holy lyf,
 Man, mayden, oþer wyf,
 And serueþ god on corþe her,
 His gostli siht is swiþe cler;   736   *spiritual sight.*
 For þerwid he may knowe and se—
 In what lyf[e] þat he be—
 God and yuel, lasse and more,

715 wit] syʒt D. ilore] for lore A₂DH₁. 716 wole] sal D. telle] þe tell A₂. and] om. A₁A₂. how and D. 716 *reads in* H₁ *and* R : I wil ʒow telle whi & wharfore. ʒow] þe R. 717 gostli] þi gostly D. siht] witte H₁. witerliche] sikerlyche D, vtterlyche H₁. 718 Man is þi resoun] Is þi reson man H₁. sikerliche] soþelyche D. 719 Wher-þurw] wheire A₂R. 720 boþe] om. A₂, hoþe þe DR, þer bi H₁. and] and eke þe D, and þo R. 721 shed] partye H₁. to] om. DH₁. eueri] alle þi R. dede] stede A₂H₁. 722 Bitwene] Hyt wene D, bytwyx R. 723 And whan] When A₂. mannes soule] man is A₂. ful iwis] foule es D, fylid is H₁, I wis R. 724 þurw dedli] And þorouʒ A₂, þorow þe fende and H₁. ifiled is] fouled es D, I wisse H₁, fyled is R. 725 His knowelaching] Here knawlagyng D, gostly knowynge H₁, his knowing R. al gon] agone A₂, al agone D. 726 ne] nor A₂. 727 Wherfore þe] perfor þe sori H₁. 728 ne may] maye H₁R. ne he ne] nouþere he ne A₂, ne noþer he H₁, ne he R. 729 ariht] riht A₁R, ryʒt wel H₁. ise] see A₂R. 730 he] þat he R. 731 þisternesse] derkenes A₂, þe derknesse D, þe sternesse H₁, merkenes R. 732 filþe] fylyng R. 733 Ac] Bot A₂H₁R, And D. he] þoo R. 734 oþer] childe or R. 734 *reads in* H₁ : Be he man mayde or wyfe. 735 serueþ] serued D. on corþe] euer A₂, in erþe H₁. 736 is] om. D. swiþe] ful H₁R. 737—740 *are omitted in* H₁ *and* R. 737 se] sene D. 738 *is omitted in* D. 739 and] oþer D. and] oþer D.

¹ *MS. A₁ has* here.

The Almighty guideth him

Al he knoweþ þurw godes lore;
¶ For widinne him is god almiht
And ȝeueþ him grace of gostly siht
To sen and knowe in his mod
þe longe lyff, þat is so god, 740

744

to fear the day of eternity.

And þe drede of domes-day,
And þe pine þat lasteþ ay,
Wher-þurw hij sholen þe more drede
And flen sinne in al here dede. 748

¶ Here ȝe muwen se þe wrong
And knowe, wher-on [hit]¹ is long,
þat sinful man may noht se
Hise giltes, þou[h] þeih² grete be. 752

¶ Listneþ nouþe to my speche,

Needful is desire after righteousness, therefore

And of nedful þing i wole ȝou teche.
Off holi churche it is þe lore,
þat spekeþ to alle, lasse and more, 756
And seiþ: 'Man, while þu miht liue,
Loke þat þu be ofte shriue.'

De Confessione.

at once

¶ Anon, so þu hast sinne wrouht,
While it is newe in þi³ þouht, 760

proceed to confess.

Anon to shrifte þat þu gange,⁴
Ne dwelle þu noht þerwid to longe; 45 d
For, if þu dost, þu miht wel wite,
þat sumwhat shal be forȝete,⁵ 764
Wher-þurw þu miht be blamed,
And at þe dom sore ashamed.
¶ þerfore, man, while þu miht liue,

---

742 And ȝeueþ him] þat is R. 743 sen and knowe] know ande to se D. 747 hij sholen] þei scholen A₂R, he sal D, þei haue H₁. 748 And] to R. flen] flye H₁. in] and A₂, bi H₁. here] his (nede *has been crossed out after* his.) D, maner H₁. dede] rede H₁. 749 ȝe muwen se] we mow sene D. þe] boþ ryȝt and H₁. 750 knowe] se R. long] alange A₂. 751 þat] And D, þe H₁. may] om. D. 753 nouþe] now H₁R. 754 of nedful] mede H₁, nedeful R. wole ȝou] sal þe D, wil þo R. 755 churche] clerge D. 756 lasse] boþ lasse H₁. 757 miht] may DR. 758 ofte] clene R. shriue] Iscryue A₂H₁. 759 Anon so] als sone as R. wrouht] I wrouȝht A₂DH₁. 760 While] þe whyle D. 761 Anon] On on D. þat] loke þat H₁. 762 þu] om. A₂. noht þerwid] þerwith nauȝt D. 763 miht] maist A₂, may DR. 764 sumwhat] som gylt D. shal be] þu myȝte H₁. forȝete] for ȝete of hit R. 765 miht] maiste DR. 766 sore] þerof D, ful sore R. 767 miht] mayȝt DR.

¹ *MS. A₁ has* his.   ² *MS. D has* þay þay.   ³ *MS. A₁ reads* þi þi.
⁴ *Read* gonge.   ⁵ *Read* forȝite.

Loke, þat þu be [clene]¹ shriue, 768
Wid sorwe of herte and repentaunce,
And of þe prest tak þi penaunce.   *Penance from the priest is healing*
Þis is a riche medicine,
Hit shildeþ man fro helle pine. 772
A betre þing was neuere founde,—
For hit may hele dedli wounde—   *for deadly wound.*
And, who-so euere wole hit craue,
Wid-outen cost he may hit haue. 776
¶ Man, ne lat hit for no shame,   *In shame delay confession,*
Lest þu falle þerfore in blame.
If þu nilt for shame [shewe] hit her,
Hit shal ben shewed elle[s]wher² 780   *and all the creatures that ever were shall see and hear.*
To alle þe shaftes þat euere were,
And alle þeih sholen sen and here.

𝕹𝖎𝖍𝖎𝖑 𝖆𝖇𝖘𝖈𝖔𝖓𝖉𝖎𝖙𝖚𝖒,³ 𝖖𝖚𝖔𝖉 𝖓𝖔𝖓 𝖘𝖈𝖎𝖊𝖙𝖚𝖗,
𝖓𝖊𝖈 𝖔𝖈𝖈𝖚𝖑𝖙𝖚𝖒, 𝖖𝖚𝖔𝖉 𝖓𝖔𝖓 𝖗𝖊𝖚𝖊𝖑𝖊𝖙𝖚𝖗,⁴

And þer-of þu shalt haue shame
And þer-to wel muche blame. 784
   Tweye manere shame men fint in boke,
Who-so wole þerafter loke :
Þat on goþ to dampnacioun ;
Þat oþer, to sauuacioun. 788
¶ ȝif ȝe wole wite hou hit be,
Sitteþ stille, and herkneþ me :

---

768 shriue] I schryue A₂DH₁. 769 of] at þyne A₂. 770 þe] þy A₂. 771 riche] aryȝt D, a good & ryche H₁, rightful R. 772 man] þe right wys man D. helle] om. D. 773 was] nas A₂. founde] ifounde A₂DH₁. 774 may hele] makes holle R. 775 who-so] he þat H₁. 777 ne] no D. lat] late þou A₂ leue H₁. hit] þou R. 778 falle perfore] perfore falle R. blame] gret blame D. 779 nilt] lette H₁, wilt not R. shewe] om. A₁, to shew H₁. hit] hem H₁R. 780 Hit] þei H₁R. elles] als H₁. 781 shaftes] creatures D, folke H₁, men R. 782 And] om. D. sen] hom se R. and here] it per D. Latin: absconditum] occultum D, optatum H₁. scietur] reueletur H₁R. occultum] absconditum H₁. reueletur] sciatur H₁R. 783 per-of] þeire A₂. 784] wel] ful R. 785 manere] mauer of DR. 787 þat on] þe tone D. 788 þat oþer] þe toþer D. to] vnto D, goþ to H₁. 789 ȝe wole wite] he wytt D, þu wilt wite H₁R. hou] what H₁. hit] þis may R. 790 me] to me A₂. 790 *has the following readings in* D *and in* H₁R (l. 328):

   Harkeneþ alle now to me   D.
   Herken & I wil telle þe   H₁R.   (l. 328)

---

¹ *MS. A₁ has* ofte.   ² *MS. A₁* eller wher.
³ *MS. A₁* Nichil abscunditum.   ⁴ *MS. A₁* releuetur.

Be earnestly Penitent,

True shame,	¶ Man, þouh þu haue sinne wrouht	40 a
	In word, in dede, and in þouht,	792
In regret and sorrow,	If þu art þiself þerof ashamed,	
	And at þin herte sore agramed,	
	¶ And ne sparest for shame ne for eiȝe,	
craves pardon.	þat þu hit nilt in shrifte seie,	796
	Off god þu miht wel lihtliche	
Forgiveness wins	Forȝifnesse haue, sikerliche.	
	þis ilke shame, be my croun,	
eternal heaven.	Draweþ al to sauuacioun.	800
False shame	¶ þat oþer shame so is þis :	
	ȝif a man haþ don amis	
	And foule sinne[s]¹ haþ iwrouht,	
	And wole for shame shewe hem noht	804
	In his shrifte to þe prest,	
	He wrappeþ sore Iesu Crist.	
	For-ȝifnes, iwis, ne tit him neuere,	
	But in helle to brennen euere.	808
fears to show guilt.	¶ Whi artu more ashamed to speke	
	A word, þan godes heste to breke?	
This wicked shame brings death.	þis is foule, wicked shame,	
	þat bringeþ sinful man in blame.	812
	þe lore þat comeþ out of godes mouþ,	
	To alle men hit sholde be couþ :	
	Lauamini, et mundi estote.	De Pœnitentia.
	Iesu spak and seide ene :	

791 þouh] ȝef A₂DR. sinne] foule synne A₂D. wrouht] Iwrouȝt A₂D, don H₁R. 792 and] ouþere A₂, or D. 792 reads in H₁ and R : Loþly & fele manyoon. fele] foule R. (Cp. l. 838 in A₁.) 793 þiself þerof] þyself A₂, þerof H₁. 794 at] in D. sore] þerof D. 795 ne] om. R. for] ne for D, not for R. shame ne for eiȝe] loue ne ay R. 796 þat] But þat H₁. hit nilt] nylt it A₂D, wilt H₁, hom wilt R. 797 þu] þat H₁, om. R. miht] may D, þen may þou R. wel lihtliche] lightly R. 798 sikerliche] wole sykerlyche A₂, sikerly R. 800 al] þe R. 801 þat] þe D. so is þis] soch it is A₂, for soþ is þis H₁, for sothe hit is R. 802 ȝif] ȝif þat D. 803 foule] many fowle H₁. iwrouht] wroȝt DH₁R. 804 wole] nyl A₂D. hem] it D. 807 iwis] om. D. ne tit him] tydeþ hym A₂R, ne tydde D, tidde hym H₁. 808 to brennen] to brynne for A₂, to wou D, fyre burne for H₁, fire brenne R. 809 more] nere D. to speke] a word to speke A₂. 810 A word þan] þane þou art A₂. to] for to D. 811 is] is þe A₂D, ilke H₁R. 812 þat] om. H₁R. sinful] a synful H₁. man] men A₂D. in] iu gret D, to H₁, in mikel R. 813 out] om. A₂. *The manuscript continues with the Latin following* 814 *in* H₂. 815 Iesu] Iesu Criste D, Thus Iesu H₂. and seide] to hem al DH₁. ene] euene A₂H₂, bidene DH₁.

---

¹ *MS.* A₁ siuneþ.

    'Wassheþ ou, and beþ clene.'   816   *Wash there-*
    Kindeliche ofte men seþ,   *from.*
    Wid water men wassheþ, þat foule beþ,
¶ And¹ hot water, be þu bold,
    Makeþ clannere þan doþ cold.   820
    Al þis i seie sikerliche,
    For to speken openliche,
¶ What hit is for to mene :
    'Wassheþ ou, and beþ clene.'   824
    Summe wassheþ, ac noht ariht,
    For þe clannere beþ hij no wiht.
    Þe hote teres of mannes eiȝe²   *Weep, and*
    Makeþ clannere þan any liȝe.   828
    Many on wepeþ for his misdede,
    Ac to do sinne noht hij ne drede :   *leave sin.*
¶ He weneþ, wasshe him wid þat water,
    And he is foul neuere þe later.   832

816 beþ] be ȝe made H₁. 817 Kindeliche] Kendely H₂R. ofte men] often-tyme men H₁, menne ofte tyme H₂, of men R. 818 wassheþ] wasshe hem H₁. 819 and 820 are inserted between 828 and 829 in H₂. 819 And] For H₂. 820 Makeþ] wasshis R. doþ] þo A₂DH₂, dos þo R. 821 Al] And al H₁. þis i] I hyte H₂. sikerliche] sekerlye H₂. 822 speken] schew D. openliche] openlye H₂. 823—826 are omitted in H₂. 823 hit is] is hit R. 824 beþ] beþ made H₁. 825 wassheþ] wasshen hom R. ac] bot A₂H₁R, and D. 826 For] Neuere A₂. hij] þei A₂DH₁R. no] ne A₂, nauȝt DR. wiht] white A₂, ryȝt D, whiȝt H₁, diȝht R. 827 mannes] a mannes D. 828 Makeþ] þay makeþ D, wassheþ H₁. 829—840 read on fol. 53 a in H₂ :

         Sorowe of herte and repentawnce   (Cp. l. 769 in A₁.)
         And for ȝowre synnys doo penawnce (Cp. l. 474 in A₁.)
         Shalle graunte ȝowe myghte & space
832   Iesu cryste too sene hys ffacc   4
         Lady crownyd . heuene qwene
         Preye for vs alle be dene
         To thy sone . kynge of heuene
836   For hys holy namys seuene   8
         That he vs graunte . hys ryche blysse
         That we therof nott ne mysse
         And that hit soo mote boe
840   Amen . Amen for seynte charyte   12
         EXPLICIT SPECULUM GY DE WAREWYKE ⎤
         SECUNDUM ALQUINUM   HEREMITE ⎦

841—1034 are omitted in H₂. The manuscript ends with 840. For colophon, see the Introduction. 829 Many on] Many A₂R, And noman D. his] here A₂R. 830 Ac] Bot A₂H₁R, And D. noht] om. A₂H₁R, he nyl nouȝt D. hij ne] þei no A₂, om. D, he hav no H₁, þai han no R. 831 He weneþ] þei wene H₁R. wasshe him] þay wassh hym D, to wasshe hem H₁R. 832 he is] es D, ȝit þei beþ H₁, þai ben R. foule] foulid R.

    ¹ *In MS. A₁, d is in red ink above the line.*   ² *Read* iȝe.

Whij? For ȝit wole he noht sinne fle:
Iwis, vnclene he shal be.
Ac anoþer manere wasshing
Makeþ clene of alle þing: 836
Man, þouh þou haue sinne don,
Lodlich and foule many on,
¶ Ȝif þu hast wille to leue þi sinne,
þat þu no more ne come þerinne,   840

Hot tears of repentance

Of þin eiȝen þe hote teres,
þat goþ adoun bi þine leres,

make harmony between thy soul and God. They cleanse from sin.

Hij wolen make god acord
Bitwene þi soule and oure lord   844
And make þe clene of þi sinne,
Wher-þurw þu miht heuene winne.
¶ Nu ȝe muwe witen, what it is to mene:
'Wassheþ ou, and beþ clene;'   848
Ac he þat wole clene be,
Certes [synne] he mot fle.
¶ Wole ȝe here ȝit eft sone
Off þing þat nedful is to done;   46 c 852
Hit is godes owen lore,
þat spekeþ to alle, lasse and more:

De non Tardando Converti ad Dominum.

**Ambulate, dum lucem habetis, ne
tenebræ vos¹ comprehendant.**

Haste, lest night surprise.

'Go, man, while þat þu hast liht,
Lest þe of-take þe derke niht.'   856

Life is day: death is night.

þi lyf, man, is cleped liht,
And þi deþ þe derke niht.

---

833 Whij] *om.* R. ȝit wole he] ȝif he nyl D, þei wil H₁, if þai wil R. fle]
and fle A₂, flye H₁. 834 he shal] sall he D, þei shulle H₁R. 834 *reads in*
A₂: He was vnclene so schall he be. 835 Ac] Bot A₂H₁R, And eke D. 836
Makeþ] Clense D. 837 þouh] if R. don] idone D. 838 Lodlich] Dedelyche
(*Cp. l. 792 in* H₁R.) D, lodely R. (*The last word of line 838 is lost through a
hole in the parchment in* D.) 839 leue] lete D. 840—845 *are omitted in* A₂.
840 no more] more D. ne] *om.* H₁R. come] falle R. 843 Hij] þay DH₁R.
god] a good H₁. 846 miht] salt D. 847 ȝe muwe] may þou R. it is] is R.
848 beþ] be ȝe made H₁. 849 Ac] Bot A₂H₁R, And D. he] ȝe R. 850
synne] sum what A₁A₂R, deedly synne H₁. he] ȝe R. mot] moste A₂H₁R.
fle] flye H₁. 851 eft] efter R. 852 Off] One R. nedful] medeful D. to] to
be H₁. 853 godes owen] Iesu Criste D. 854 þat] *om.* D. alle] al men H₁.
855 þat] *om.* A₂H₁R. 856 of-take] oure take A₂H₁R. 857 is cleped] I clepe
þi D, is cald þi R. 858 þe] is þe A₂, þi D.

¹ *MS. A₁* te tenebre nos.

Craving God's Favor.

While þu art on liue, þu miht worche
Godes werkes of holi churche,¹   860   *While it is day, do works of love.*
And, certes, whan þat þu art ded,
þanne maitou don noþer god ne qued.

¶ þerfore, man, i warne þe,
While þu miht gon a*nd* so,   864
In gode weyes sped þe faste!   *Speed fast.*
Lef, þe niht þe wole agaste,   *The dark night brings terror.*
And sikerliche widoute nay,
At þi dei[i]ng² shal ben þi domesday,   868
For þere shal ben irekened al   *Then shall be counted all thy deeds.*
þat euere distu, gret a*nd* smal.
þere þu shalt knowe a*nd* se
God or yuel, wheiþer it be,³   872
And þanne, par aunter, wo[lde]stu fain
Biginne to worche a*nd* turne aȝein;

¶ Ac, certes, þu ne shalt noht go,
Ac riht after þu⁴ hast do,   876   *As thy deeds, shall be thy judgment.*
þu shalt fonge verrement
þare þi rihte iugement.

𝔈t ideo ambulate, dum lucem habetis.
    46 *d*

Deþ is gilour swiþe strong
And gileþ many on euere among,   880   *Death is a deceiver, and deceives many, therefore*
þerfore worch, while þu mait,

---

859 þu miht] a*nd* may D, þow maiste H₁R. 860 Godes werkes] To don warkes D, Good warki*s a*nd lawful H₁. 861 þat] *om*. A₂DH₁R. 862 þanne maitou] þou mayȝt D. don noþer] nouþere do A₂DR. ne] nor A₂. 864 While] þe while A₂, þat while D, whil þat R. þu miht] mayȝt þou D, þow maiste H₁R. 866 Lef] Les A₂, Laste DR, Els H₁. þe wole] wil þe R. 867 And] For D. 869 irekened] rekenyde A₂R, rekene D, rekkend H₁. 870 distu] dedest þou A₂, þou diste H₁, þou didist R. a*nd*] or A₂D. 872 or] a*nd* A₂, oþer D. it be] þay benn D. 873 A*nd* þanne] þen H₁. woldestu] þou woldest A₂, noldest þou D. 874 Biginne] By D. 875 Ac] Bot A₂H₁R, A*nd* D. ne] *om*. DH₁R. noht go] so A₂, not soo H₁R. 876 Ac] Bot A₂DH₁R. þu] þat þu A₁R. 877 shalt fonge] schalt A₂, afong D, shalt fynde þere H₁, shalt take R. 878 þare] Fong þeire A₂, For soþ H₁. rihte] *om*. A₂, owen H₁, rightwis R. 879 gilour] a gylour A₂. swiþe] *om*. A₂. 880 gileþ] be gyle D, bigiles R. many on] many A₂D (D *has an erasure of* m *before* man.), many men (*The* e *in* men *is defective through a small hole in the parchment.*) H₁. 881 worch] man wirch A₂, *om*. D. while þu mait] while mayt D, *with* out cessyngi*s* H₁, whil þat þou maght R.

---

¹ *Read* wirche: chirche.   ² *MS*. A₁ deijng.
³ wheiþer it be *is written on erasure in MS*. A₁.   ⁴ *MS*. A₁ þat þu.

For sodeyneliche þu miht be caiht.

Initium sapientiæ,[1] **timor domini:** *De Timore Domini.*

<small>fear God,</small>
'Drede of god in alle[2] þing
Off wisdom is þe biginning;' 884

<small>but not in dreud,</small>
And many hauen of god drede,
Ac noht for loue of his godhede,
But last þeih sholde for here gilt
In-to strong pine ben ipult.[3] 888

¶ Hit fareþ bi swiche, i vnderstonde,
As hit doþ here bi þe bonde:

<small>as the bondes-man before his lord.</small>
Þe bonde nele noþer loude ne stille
Don noht aʒein his lordes wille— 892
Ac þat nis for loue ne for acord,
Þat he haþ toward his lord—
For, if he dede, he wot wel,
He sholde lese of his catel; 896
And ʒit hit fareþ bi man also,
Þat spareþ more sinne to [do][4]

<small>Fear the King of Heaven, so that</small>
For þe doute of gret pining,
Þan for þe loue of heuen king. 900

<small>thou mayst catch grace</small>
¶ It is noht euel so to biginne,
For drede of pine to late þi sinne,
For sone after he may kacche grace
To biþenke him on godes face, 904
Hu murie hit were, to haue þe siht
Off godes face, þat is so briht!

<small>47 a</small>

882 For] Wyrche gude for D. miht be] may be A₂R, mayt D, miʒt han þyn H₁. caiht] endyngis H₁. 884 is þe] þis is þe first A₂. 885 And many hauen of] And many on haþe of DR, Man haue euer H₁. drede] in drede H₁. 886 Ac] Bot A₂R, And D, For H₁. noht for loue] lesingis of H₁. 887 But] And H₁. last] lat A₂, þat R. þeih sholde] þei shullen D, þat þou shalt H₁. here] þaire D, þi H₁. 888 strong] om. A₂. ipult] pute D, plyte H₁, pilt R. 890 As] Also A₂. þe] a H₁. 891 nele] wil H₁R. noþer] neuere A₂. 892 noht] om. H₁, oght R. *The manuscript ends with 892 in A₂.* 893 Ac] and D, But H₁R. nis] es DR, nowþer H₁. for] for no DR. ne for] no for no D, ne for non R. 894 toward] to R. 895 wot] wote ful D, wist hit R. 896 sholde lese] lese suld D. 897 ʒit] riʒt D. 898 þat] om. D. spareþ] lettes R. to] for to D. 899 þe] om. R. 900 þan] om. H₁. þe loue] loue DR. 901 biginne] gynne DH₁. 902 late þi] lete D, leue H₁, leeue his R. 903 sone after he may] he may sonn aftyr D, soon after þou myʒt H₁. 904 biþenke] be þenke DR. him on] hym of DR, þe in H₁. 905 þe] a D, þat H₁. 906 godes] þat D, his H₁. so briht] bryʒt so H₁.

---

[1] *MS.* Inicium sapiencie.   [2] *MS.* A₁ al alle.
[3] *Probably read* ipilt. *See l.* 239.   [4] *MSS.* A₁A₂ *have* go.

¶ And so he shal casten his loue
 To Iesu Crist, þat is aboue,   908
 And leten and flen sinful dede,   *to flee the evil world,*
 Boþe for loue *and* eke for drede.
 Ac, who-so wole don be my lore,
 Iwis he shal spare more,   912
 To flen sinne day and niht,
 For drede to lese þat faire siht   *lest thou lose the sight of God's glorious face.*
¶ Off godes face, þat is so cler,
 Off whom we han al oure power,   916
 Þan for drede of any wo,
 Þat any þing mihte hem do.
¶ Leue frend, herkne to me,
 And more i wole speke to þe;   920   *Be piteous to the poor.*
 For i*n* þe godspel i wole rede
 Off þe uertu of almesdede.
 Þin almesse þu shalt forþ puite,   *Put forth alms.*
 And spare hit noht, þouh hit be luite: 924
 [In þe godspel it es write,
 I sal, man, þat þou it wite.]
  God seiþ þus i*n* his lore:
 'Man, if þu miht 3eue no more   928   *Give but a cup of cold water in love,*
¶ But a dishful of cold water,
 Þu shalt hit 3eue neuere þe later
 Wid gode wille *and* wid charite,
 And ful wel it worþ 3olden þe.' *47 b* 932   *and it will reward thee.*
 And, whan þu shalt haue þank *and* mede
 For so litel an almesdede,
¶ Siker maiton þanne be,
 If þu 3euest muche i*n* charite   936
 To god, þu miht þe betre spede,

907 so] þus D. he] *om.* R. shal] may þen H₁, þen shal he R. 908 is] syttes DR. 909 leten and flen] lete flene D, leue *and* flye H₁, leeue & fle alle R. 910 eke] *om.* H₁R. *The manuscript ends with 910 in* H₁. 911 Ac] and D, But R. 912 spare] lett R. 913 day] bothe day R. 915 Off] And of D. 916 Off] And of D. 917 any] oure R. 918 mihte hem] hym my3t (*over erasure*) D, vs might R. 919 herkne] herken now D. 920 more i wole] meche I sal D. 921 þe godspel i wole] þis boke I sal D, þo gospel as we R. 923 almesse] almes dede R. puite] pitte R. 924 1*st* hit] *om.* D. luite] litte R. 925 *and* 926 *are omitted in* A₁R. 930 shalt hit 3eue] putt hit forth R. 931 wid charite] in pyte D, charite R. 932 worþ] wroþ D, bes R. 3olden] i3olde D. 933 whan] hou D. haue þank *and*] be þenke for þat D. 935 maiton þanne] þen may þou R. 937 To] Tho D. miht] salt D.

	And þe more shal ben þi mede.	
In almesdeed is double good.	Enes i it vnderstod,	
	þat in almesdede is double god:	940
	¶ It fordoþ sinne, wite it wel,	
	And hit wole eche þi catel.	
	And, if þu art her-of in drede,	
	Hu hit mihte so be in dede,	944
This learn of old law.	A god witnesse i wole drawe,	
	On ensaumple of þe olde lawe.	
	¶ Holi writ, þat wole noht liʒe,	
	Spekeþ of þe profete Eliʒe,	948
Christ sent Elijah to a widow to impart to her this twofold virtue.	Hou Iesu Crist, houre lo[ue]rd swete,	
	Spak to Eliʒe þe profete.	
	To a pore widewe he him sende,	
	Here beyþere lyf [for]¹ to amende.	952
	He seide: 'Eliʒe, þu shalt fare	
	In-to Sarepte and wone þare.	
	¶ þer is a widewe, þat shal þe fede,	
	And i wole ʒelde wel hire mede.'	956
Elijah	¶ þe profete Helie began anon	47 o
	Forþ in his weie for to gon.	
	At þe ʒate of þe cite þe widewe he mette,	
met the widow, and asked for	And faire anon he hire grette.	960
	He bad hire for godes loue,	
	þat us alle sit aboue,	
water and bread, to help him to live.	A di[sh]ful² water she sholde him ʒiue,	
	For to helpen him to liue.	964
	¶ þe widewe seide, she wolde fain,	
	And to serue him she turne aʒe[i]n.	
	After hire he gan to crie,	
	And bad hire þat she sholde lie.	968
	'Do,' he seide, 'be my red,	

938 more] more hym D.   939 i it] hit I R.   939 reads in D: Twys. I anderstand.   940 þat in] In R.   944 so be] be so DR.   945 A] I R.   wole] sal D.   946 On ensaumple of þe] In þe sample in D.   947 þat] om. R.   wole] nyl D.   liʒe] be leis R.   948 Spekeþ] It telleþe D, þat spekes R.   951 To] And to D.   he] om. D   952 beyþere] þore D, bothus R.   for to] to A₁R.   954 wone] lye D.   955 shal þe] þou sal D, wil þe R.   956 i wole] sal D.   wel] her ful wel R.   958 in] on R.   959 þe] þat R.   962 alle sit] sittes alle R.   963 dishful] disful of DR.   she] he R.   964 2nd to] vnto D, for to R.   967 he gan] began D, he bygan R.   969 be] aftyr D.

¹ for is supplied from D.   ² MS. A₁ has disful.

The Woman of Zarephath

Bring me wid þe a shiue bred!'
þe widewe him answere[de]¹ anon:
'Siker,' she seide, 'bred haue i non,   972   The widow had nothing
Ne noht, þat i mihte þe ȝiue,
For to helpe þe to liue,

¶ But an handful mele in o picher   but a handful of meal and
And a litel oyle, þat is cler,   976   some oil.
þat i mot make of mete here
To me and to my children ifere;
And seþþe we moten deie in sore,   She would eat and die.
For mete haue we no more.'   980

¶ þe profete hire answerede þo:
'Abid,' he seide, 'er þu go!   47 d   Elijah said: 'Give me
First, þer-of mak me mete,   first.
And, whan þat i hit haue iete,   984
Off þat bileueþ, þu shalt make   What remains, use
For þe and for þi children sake.'   for thyself.'

¶ þis seli widewe þo wel sone   The good woman
Grauntede² wel al his bone: 988
For his loue, þat him þider sende,   brought him food.
Hire litel mete she wolde spende.

þo þe profete þis iseih,   Then the prophet
His eiȝen he kest to god on heih: 992   turned his eyes to God.
To him he made an orysoun,
And anon god putte his fuisoun   Abundance came upon
Vp-on hire mele in hire picher   the meal and
And on hire oyle, þat is cler.   996   the oil.

¶ þo seide anon þe profete   He said
To þe widewe wordes swete:³   sweet words:

---

970 Bring] And brynge D. me] om. R. shiue] schyne D, shyuer of R. 971 him] þo D, om. R. 973 noht] nauȝt elles D. þe ȝiue] ȝeue D. 974 2nd to] for to D. 975 mele in o] of mele in a R. 977 of] in D, on R. here] now here D. 978 to] om. R. ifere] in fere DR. 979 deie in] die R. 980 haue we] ne haue D. 981 hire answerede þo] vnswerid hyr so R. 982 Abid] And badde her D, I bid þe R. 983 þer-of] he said D. 984 i hit] hit I R. iete] hete D, ete R. 985 bileueþ] þat leeues R. 987 þis] þe DR. þo wel] þen ful R. 988 al] to do R. 989 him þider sende] Iudas solde R. 990 she] he (*perhaps for* ho *of l.* 963) D. she wolde spende] shewe ho wolde R. 991 þo] When R. iseih] hym seghe R. 992 he kest to god] to god he kast R. 993 made an] mende his D. 995 hire] þe D. 996 on] in R. is] was so D, was R. 997 þo] þen R.

---

¹ *MS. D reads* answerd.   ² *MS. A₁ has an erasure after* t.
³ *998 and 999 are over erasure in MS. A₁.*

'*Fear not:*	' Ne dred þe noht, womman, in þi þouht!	
thy meal shall not diminish; thy oil shall increase.'	þi mele ne shal wante noht,	1000
	And þin oyle shal waxen: sikerli	
	þi lome shal noht ben empti.'	
	¶ Gret plente hadde þe widewe þo,	
	While she liuede euere mo.	1004
This proves, that in almsdeed lies twofold good. It removes sin, so that thou mayst win heaven.	Now þu miht knowe in þi mod,	
	þat in almesse dede is double god:	
	Almesdede for[doþe þi synne],	
	And þer-þur[w] [men may heuen wyn[ne]];	1008
It adds to earthly goods.	And þi god sh[al multiplie],	
	So seiþ þe bok, [þat nyl nauȝt lye].	
God says: 'Give, and men shall give to thee.'	¶ þe godspel sei[þe to þe *and* me]:	
	'Ȝif and men sha[l ȝefe þe].'	1012
	In anoþer stede, [I haue wytnesse],	
	þat god self se[ide] [in soþenesse]:	
	'Al þat þu dost [for loue of me]	
	To þe leste of m[yn meyne],	1016
	Riht to my-sel[fe, wete it wele],	
	þu dost þi pres[ent euery dele].'	
Be glad in thy gift;	¶ Glad maitou [be þan in þi þouȝt],	
	Also ofte as þ[ou maytȝ ȝeue ouȝt],	1020
thou	For, þu miht [wele vnderstande],[1]	
takest it to	þu takest hit [gode with þi honde];	
God with thy hand.	For godes w[orde in soþenesse]	
	þer-of bereþ [gude wyttnes]:	1024
Thou art not too vile to feed Christ.	'A man [may][2] b[e nouȝt to quede],	
	Iesu Crist for to [fede];'	
	For þer-wid þu [myȝt wele spede]	
Eternal joy will be thine.	And heuene h[aue vnto þi mede].	1028

999 Ne] no D. þi] *om*. D. 1000 ne] *om*. DR. wante] wane D, want right R. 1001 waxen] wereyn D. 1002 þi] and þi R. 1004 While she] And þe while ho D, whil þat ho R. 1005 miht knowe] knowest R. in] wele in D. 1006 þat] *om*. R. 1007–1031 *are defective in* A₁. *The page has been cut through the middle of folio* 48 a. *Folio* 48 b *is wanting. The lines have been completed from MS.* D. 1007 þi] *om*. R. 1008 men] þou R. 1010 nyl] wil R. 1011 þe] For þe D. 1014 self] hym selfe D, hym R. seide] saies R. 1015 for] for þo R. 1018 euery] ilk a R. 1019 be þan] be R. 1020 Also] Als DR. 1021 miht] maytȝ D, may nowe R. 1022 with þi] in his R. 1024 þer-of bereþ] Berþe þer of D. 1025 A] þer fore R. may] *om*. R. quede] gnede R. 1027 þer-wid þu myȝt] þou may þer with R. 1028 haue vnto] blis gete to R.

---

[1] *Read* vnderstonde.   [2] man man *is in MS.* A₁.

Thus ends the Sermon.

  To þa[t] blisse [he] [vs bryng],
 þat is king [ouer all[e] þyng],
¶ And 3eue us [grace, while we be here],
 [To serue hym *and* hys moder dere   49 b   1032
 In trowþe, loue, *and* in charite.
  Amen.   Amen.   So mot it be.]

Almighty King, show grace to us, that we may serve Him! Amen. Amen.

1029 he] *om.* A₁D.   1030 king] lord R.   1031 3eue] he gefe D.   1032—1034, *through loss of fol.* 48 *b, are not found in* A₁. *The text follows fol.* 179 *b in* D. 1032 *and* hys moder dere] *þat* vs boght dere R.   1033 trowþe] trewe R.   in] *om.* R. *The colophon reads in* R: EXPLICIT HIC SPECULUM VTILE ISTIUS MUNDI.

CRITICAL AND EXPLANATORY NOTES

TO THE

SPECULUM GY DE WAREWYKE.

Page 3. Lines 1—26: Introductory lines follow Romance models, conveying in a few words the purpose of the whole poem: *La moralité de tout un poëme* .... *exprimée dans ses premiers vers;* Gautier, *Les Épopées Françaises,* ed. 1865, vol. i., p. 233. See Hausknecht, *The Sowdone of Babylone,* note to l. 14.

Line 1. *alle:* i. e. *gode men,* according to *Harelok,* l. 1, *Pard. T.,* l. 904, and *A Lutil Soth Sermun,* l. 1 ; the hearers ordinarily addressed, *lordinges* of the M.E. romance, as annotated by Kölbing, *Sir Beues,* l. 1 ; Lüdtke, *The Erl of Tolous,* l. 7 ; Kaluza, *Libeaus Desconus,* l. 461. See *Gamelyn,* l. 343 ; *The Faerie Queene,* iii., ix., l. 3 ; the old play, *Mundus et Infans,* l. 236 ; and Chaucer in many of the *Tales.* Compare lines 1 and 2 with lines 1 and 2 of *The Harrowing of Hell:*

'Alle herkneþ to me nou,
A strif wille I tellen ou.'

l. 2. *hele of soule:* a *Kentish Charter* of 806 ?, *Cot. MS. Aug.* II. 79, l. 5 : 'fore uncerra *saula hela* . . . ðæt wit moten bion on ðem gemanon, ðe ðaer *godes* ðiowas siondan' ; *Arthour and Merlin,* l. 30 : 'God ous sende *soule hale*' ; *Ancren Riwle,* p. 300 : '*soule hele* is forloren vor eni deadlich sunne' ; Langl., *Piers the Plowman,* text B, v., l. 270 : 'bi my *soule hele*' ; A, vi., l. 22 : 'for my *soule hele*' ; *Homily,* ed. Small, p. 134, l. 66 : '*sawel hel*' ; but '*Hele of soule,*' *Speculum Vitæ,* l. 12. Compare *Gedicht aus der Hölle,* ed. Leonard, p. 51, l. 6, also cited by Halliwell, *Dict.,* p. 775 :

'. . . *soule hele* Y wyll yow teche.'

Orrm., l. 10,194, preserves *sawle bote:* 'To sekenn *sawle bote*' ; *Proverbs of Hendyng,* MS. Harl. 2253, l. 300 : 'Secheþ ore *soule bote*' ; *The Life of Saint Werburge,* Bk. I., l. 992 : '*soule helthe.*'

may ou: wyll ȝou on basis of MSS. $A_2DH_1H_2R$. Later texts fail of the beauty and seriousness of the verse in the loss of *may, am able:* 'I am able to teach you of salvation.'

l. 3. *no fable:* Compare Dr. Leonard's *Ged. Aus d. H.,* B note, l. 6 : *to fabille I wille you nought* (with reference to Einenkel, *Streifzüge,* p. 232 f.). For litotes in the *Speculum,* the following lines may be cited, l. 102 : *beþ noht gode,* i. e. very bad ; l. 193 : *nis noht forȝete,* is remembered ; l. 875 : *þu ne shalt noht go,* thou must go ; l. 892 : *Don noht aȝein,* carry out ; l. 1000 : *ne shal wante noht,* shall increase ; l. 1002 : *noht ben empti,* be full ; l. 947 and l. 1010 : *þat wole noht liȝe,* and l. 637 : *i ne liȝe,* tell the truth ; l. 132 : *he ne . . . no ioye winne,* he shall be condemned ; l. 360 : *noþing it nas;* l. 628 : *meke in none manere,* proud ; l. 651 : *oþer weye is þer non,* this is the only way ; l. 659 : *For noþing þu noldest shone,* should seek to obtain it at all costs ; l. 891 : *nele noþer,* will. Litotes strengthens a previous affirmation : l. 464 : *soþ,*

48   *Critical and Explanatory Notes. Page* 3, *lines* 3—15.

wiðouten gabbe;* l. 519: *soþ word .. no les;* l. 867: *sikerliche, widoute nay.* The *Speculum* thus testifies to the popularity of litotes in the M.E. period, as stylistic reaction from the French. See Tobler, *Beiträge* 165; Strohmeyer, *Stil d. me. Reimch. R. v. Gl.,* pp. 54 ff. and *Rbt.,* l. 1271: *he ne leuede noȝt bihinde,* he hastened, 4075, 6494, 11937; l. 1909: *he ne gan noȝt muche winne,* lost all, even life, 1488, 5015; l. 8081: *ne þoȝte noȝt be þe laste,* would be the first; l. 1718: *þer nas noȝt wel gret loue,* great hate, etc. See *Piers Pl.,* among many illustrations, A, I., l. 116: *his peyne haþ non ende; On g. Ureisun of Ure Lefdi,* l. 95: *wrom þine luue ne schal me no þing todealen,* love will continue, etc.

l. 5.   *heuene winne:* See lines 650, 846, and 1008; *grace .. winne* 78; *ioye winne* 132, 694; *merci .. winne* 471, 472; *forȝifenesse .. winne* 683, 684. Compare *Orrm.* (ed. White), 971: '*winnenn echc blisse*'; 1175: '*winnenn Godess are.*' *to win* is still in use in Scotland; see Jamieson, *Scotch Dict.,* under *win.*

l. 5 is to be classified under type D, giving emphasis to *þu*. Scansion according to type C, with emphasis on *if,* is not justified.

l. 6.   *to god: to god* is to be retained, as in l. 21, on authority of MSS. A_1R, the two oldest texts of group Z, in opposition to *of god,* extant in MSS. A_2D of group Y. It presents the true meaning of the passage.

l. 7.   *biginning:* Type A and type D both have claims to this verse on account of the variable accent ascribable to *biginning.* The scansion could be:

'þús shal bén þi bíginning' D.
'þus shál ben þi bigín 'nǐng' A.

The metrical and logical purpose of the author seems to be satisfied by the first reading, *biginning,* as in lines 209 and 884.

l. 9.   *emcristene:* see note to line 334.

l. 10.   *þiselfĕ:* Meter and inflection require the trisyllable authorized by MSS. H_1H_2R; read *þiselfĕ,* l. 564, 579; *himselfĕ,* l. 14; *himseluĕ,* l. 244, 598. L. 362 proves nothing. Final -*e (himselfe)* is lost through elision. See ten Br., *Ch. Sprachkunst,* § 255. The sounding of the final -*e* removes the line 10 from type C, where it is to be classified according to MS. A_1.

l. 11.   *biginne and ende:* suggested perhaps by '*qui perseveraverit* in bono, hic salvus erit ... bonum ergo *perfecisse,* virtus est,' Alcuin's *Liber, Caput* xxvi.: '*De perseverantia in bonis operibus,*' based possibly on *Matt.* x. 22: 'he that endureth firm *to the end* ...,' *Heb.* iii. 6, 14; 'be thou faithful *unto death,* and I will give thee *a crown of life,*' *Rev.* ii. 10. See *Poema Morale:*

l. 119: 'Ac drihte ne demð nanne man · æfter his bi ginninge.
ac al his lif sceal beo swich · se buð his endinge.'

l. 12.   *to heuene wende:* The infinitive employed without the introductory *to,* to avoid doubling the particle, see *to helle gon* 652; *paternoster bede* 562; and *Harrowing of Hell,* l. 244:

'And ȝif ous grace to liue and ende
In þi seruice and *to heuene wende.*'

l. 13.   *worldes:* The article is to be expected before *worldes.* Its omission called forth various scribal errors; see variants.

l. 14.   *himselfe:* read *himseluĕ.* See note to l. 10.

l. 15.   *plawe:* O.E. *plaga,* companion form M.E. *pleye, pleie* < O.E. *plega.* But one instance of *plagian* is recorded according to Bosworth-Toller, *A. S. Dict.* under *plagian;* cf. Sievers, § 391, Anm. 1; Pabst, § 42; Langl. A. Passus, xii., l. 295, ascribes to *play* the meaning pleasure: 'That thi *play* be plentevous.' *plawe* is not very frequent in M.E. texts, but see *Das Lied von King Horn* (ed. Wissmann), MS. H, l. 1112:

'þat trewe was in uch plawe'; *Havelok*, l. 950: *plawe* : (*knawe*) and *pleye* : (*weie*), l. 953; *R. of Gl.* 5906; *Trist.* 3101. See *Steenstrup*, pp. 15 and 190; *Svenska Språketslagar*, II. 99; Brate, *Beiträge*, vol. x., p. 48. Ettmüller, *Lexicon Anglosaxonicum*, pp. 274, 275, illustrates derivatives of *plĕgan. See also *Speculum*, 'Introduction' under *au*, chapter xiii on Phonology.

l. 16. *deþ of soule:* completing the antithesis begun with *hele of soule*, line 2: destruction of soul .. health of soul; condemnation .. salvation. The personification of the soul as a separate and independent being, thus ascribing to the living creature a sort of a dual existence, is a favourite conceit of the poet; see line 844.

l. 17. *þe world:* The account of the crafty fisherman *world* with his *paunter* for his victim, the soul, begins abruptly, l. 13, but the slender thread of the allegory is to be traced nearly to the end of the poem: lines 13—24, 33, 61—64, 99, 103, 151, 195, 222, 650—651, etc. See l. 882: *sodeyneliche þu miht be caiht*, and possibly *heuene blisse* 690, *helle pine* 642, and other references to heaven's glories and hell's torments.

ikauht: with *ikaȝte*, H_1, is to be retained. *caught* A_2 (*cauȝt* D, *cawȝte* H_2, *kaght* R) is contrary to the dialect of the poet; see *Inflection*. The metre and the language of the poet require the prefix *i-*. *icauht* and *cayt* are both employed by Chaucer and Wiclif. *Poema Morale* has *keht*(e), *keiht*.

l. 18. *and:* *and* is to be expunged. It does not occur in $D\ H_1H_2R$, MSS. preserving at times the best text.

paunter: paunter, as employed by the poet, is perhaps defined by a metaphor of F. G. Fleay, *Engl. Studien*, vol. vii., p. 87, 'Neglected Facts on Hamlet': 'inclosed in its *dragnet* this miraculous *draught* ... of *fish*,' and in *The Simonie* (Auch. MS.), l. 457:

'Pride hath in his *paunter* kauht the heie and the lowe,
So that unnethe can eny man God Almighti knowe.'

The *paunter, pantire*, is in its ordinary acceptance *a snare* or *net* for birds rather than for fish, as is made clear by Richard the Redeles, by Chaucer, and by Lydgate.

Richard the Redeless, II. 183, see Skeat:

'And ffell with her ffetheris fflat vppon the erthe,
As madde of her mynde and mercy be souȝte.
They myȝte not aschowne the sorowe they had serued,
So lymed leues were leyde all aboute,
And *panteris* preuyliche pight vppon the grounde.'

Leg. of G. W., l. 130: 'The smale foules, of the seson fayn,
That from the *panter* and the net ben scaped.'

T. of Glas, l. 604: 'But lich a brid, þat fleith at hir desire,
Til sodeinli within þe *pantire*,
She is Icauȝt . . . .'

See *Ancren Riwle*, p. 134 of the bird: 'heo beo *ikeiht* þuruh summe of þe deofles gronen.' In this usage of *paunter* the reader is referred to Schick's note to the *T. of G.*, l. 604, with its comprehensive list of examples of *pantire*, and its reference to Skeat, note to *Leg. of G. W., Prol.*, l. 130, and *Dict.* under *painter*, and to *Prompt. Parv.*, note to *pantire*.

Page 4. l. 21. *for loue .. for eiȝe:* a typical antithesis popular in M.E. See *Sir Beues*, text A, l. 1852: 'Wiþ loue or eiȝe'; *Sawles Ward*, ll. 25, 26: 'wiþ eie ant wiþ luue'; *Gamelyn*, l. 129: 'for Gamelynes loue .. for his eyȝe': *Wulfstan*, 'Address to the English,' Hatton MS. Jun. 99, ll. 168, 169: 'þá ðe riht lufiað and Godes ege habbað' ... Compare with *luue-eie*, *Ancr. Riwle*, p. 420: Skeat translates *his eiȝe*, 'for awe of him,' note to *Gamelyn*, l. 129, in harmony with *Gamelynes*, the genitive limiting *loue*, and in keeping with Stürzen-Becker, *Notes on Characteristics of E. E. Dialects*, p. 43; see *of god*, MSS. $A_2D\ H_1$, and note to l. 6.

R on its own authority alters the rime to introduce the more Northern form *awe* for *eiȝe* : *awe* : *lawe*.

l. 23. *þer:* demanded by the context and supplied by MSS. H_1H_2 and A_2, if *þei* be a scribal error for *þer*. Evidence of texts A_1DR would ascribe the anacoluthon of text A_1 to the poet.

l. 24. *worlde:* Hiatus is not justified before *and*. *worlde* is monosyllabic : *wórlde and;* see *world*, ll. 33, 64, 99, etc. The verse illustrates type C : *þe wórld and hís ∙ fóule lóre*.

l. 26. *hem:* *hem*, extant in MSS. $A_2H_1H_2$, and probably in the archetype of *D* is to be inserted to improve the metre. The added syllable was regarded necessary by *R;* see variants. Read *rodę* on authority of the riming couplet : *rod : blod*, l. 248. *dere bouhte:* see note to l. 160.

ll. 27, 28. *wole:* copyist's form throughout A_1 for *wyll(e)*, *wil*, in MSS. $A_2D\ H_1H_2R$; cf. rime *skile : wole*, l. 712, 'Introduction,' chap. III, § 1 and § 5, and *wole* in Langland, A. vii. 144, 208; II. 86; III. 265; V. 36; VI. 152, 193, 300, etc.

l. 28. *tale telle:* Compare Zupitza's note to *Athelston*, l. 153, and Chaucer, *Prol.* 731, 792, 831, 847; *D. L. Prol.* 22, 23, 48; *Pers. Prol.* 21, 25, 46, 66; *Duch.* 709, 1033, etc.

Reliquiæ Antiquæ, p. 241 (II.): 'ichow wol *telle*
                Of Crist aue litel *tale*.'

l. 29. *of gode fame:* Cf. Zupitza's note to *of gret renoun*, *Athelston*, ll. 19, 45; Leonard, *Ged. aus d. Hölle*, B l. 63; and *Spec.*, l. 40, where the *holy man* and the *knight* are described in the same class. Cf. as follows:

  Spec. Vit., l. 43: 'Ne of Beus of Hamtoun,
         Þat was *a knyght of gret renoun*.'
  Erl of T., l. 178: 'Syr Tralabas of Turky
          . . . . .
         A man *of gret renown*.'

l. 31. *bouht:* The sorrowful meditation of the love-poetry of the century, illustrated by Schick, *T. of Gl.*, note to l. 1. This meaning seems justified by the corresponding passages in the various *Guy of Warwick* MSS.

l. 35. Type C is confirmed by l. 35. It would be impossible to read *godę*, l. 35. See *Tundale*, l. 19. *all* of A_2R, or *eke* of *D*, are emendations of the scribe. Cf. *and hís—lóre*.

l. 41. *þe ordre he hadde:* For the history of the brotherhood, see Skeat, note to *Peres the Plowman's Crede*, l. 153.

l. 43. *Wit of clergie:* the understanding of books, book-learning, referring not merely to scholarship as an essential attribute of mediæval piety, but to Alcuin's ambition for an educated priesthood. See also *Hamlet*, I. i. 42.

l. 44. *to godnesse . . . drouh: Life of St. Dunst.*, l. 29. Cf. *R. of Gl.*, l. 252: *to . . . . prowesse he drou; toward þe deþe drou*, l. 1159; *to worse . . he drou*, l. 9242. See Strohmeyer, pp. 48, 49.

l. 46. *he: he* is to be supplied before *tok*. It is extant in $D\ H_1H_2$, two MSS. from one group, one from a second, in opposition to two MSS., A_1A_2, one of each group. Grammatically and metrically the sentence is strengthened by the introduction of the pronoun, though its omission as subject of the sentence is characteristic of the period; see Zupitza, note to *Guy of Warwick*, l. 10.

Page 5, l. 47. *tok .. red:* explained by *consail take*, l. 63, ordinary M.E. phraseology illustrated *Rbt. of Gl.*, *nime his rede* (or similar arrangement), as follows: ll. 609, 1685, 2137, 3562, 3846, 5280, 5853, 6263, 6422, 8215, 8230; text B: 11,850, 11,198; *nime ... conseil* 1111, 1245, 2170, 2187, 3040, 3139, 3470, 3516, 3528; B 11,004, 10,467, 10,493, 11,328, 11,837; *take* hire *to rede*, *Wm. of Palerne*, l. 133; *nime hom to rede*, *Rbt. of Gl.*[1] ll. 348, 6749, 7910; B 9758, 11,428; and *Gamelyn*, l. 683: *into counseil nome*; *O. Kent. Sermon*, ed. Skeat, l. 8: *nomen conseil.*

l. 48. *þe qued:* 'the evil,' 'the evil one,' 'the devil.' The etymology of *qued* is uncertain, O.E. *cwêad*? or *cwêad*?: Dutch *kwaad*; Fris, *qued*; G. *qwât, kât, kót.* See Mätzner, *Sprachproben*, I. p. 82; Grimm. *Gr.*, III. p. 606; Mall, *II. of II.*, note to l. 36; Pabst, *Lautlehre*, § 15 *b*; and the following illustrations:

Speculum, l. 654: '... ouercome þe foule qued.'
Rel. Ant., p. 16: 'Thus overkam ... the qued.'
H. of Hell, l. 36: 'For to lesen ous fram þe qued.'
Hand. Synne, l. 5605: '........ bode þe quede.'

For *qued* used in an adjective sense, refer to note, l. 1025.

l. 49. *i vnderstonde:* also l. 889 (see 507 and 1021), a popular construction to fill out the verse, *füllformel*, Lüdtke, *The Erl of Tolous*, l. 631 and l. 913, referring to Koch, II. § 399.

l. 49 illustrates type D on proof of five MSS. H_2 substitutes *Vpon* for *On*, restoring the line to type A:

'Vpón a dáye, · I vndyrstónde.'

l. 50. *sente his sonde:* an alliterating form profusely illustrated in M.E. See *Die Alliteration in Laʒamon*, Germ. Stud., vol. i. p. 182; Zupitza, note to *Guy of Warwick*, l. 10,477; Breul, note to *Sir Gowther*, l. 87; Schmirgel, 'Typical Expressions in *Sir Beues*'; *Sir Beues*, p. liv., referring to *Reinbroun*, str. 14, l. 7; *Arthour and Merlin*, l. 6733. Compare *Sir Beues*, text A, 3305; S 1277; M 2928, 4200; *Wm. of Palerne*, l. 64; Laʒamon, *Brut*, l. 14,200; *Gen. and Ex.*, ll. 2312-13; *King Horn*, l. 265; *Amis and Amiloun*, l. 625; *Man of Law's Tale*, l. 388; *Rbt. of Gl.*, ll. 363, 1835, 3273, 3291, 3727, 5958, 7860, 8037; B 10,211, 10,325, 11,354; C 223, 224.

sonde: explained by Zupitza's note as existing with two meanings, *the messenger* and *the message.* i. e. *what is sent*; cf. M.H.G. *santbote*, 'messenger'; see *Ancr. R.*, p. 190: 'was þes *sondes mon*'; p. 256: 'þes deofles *sondesmon*'; p. 190: 'Euerich worlich wo is *Godes sonde*'; *Guy of W.* text A: ll. 1929, 3751; text C, 3913, etc.

l. 52. '*I grete þe wel*': stereotyped expression in the sense of 'I send a salutation to.' See *Gamelyn*, l. 713: '*greteth hem wel*'; *Wm. of Palerne*, ll. 359, 360: '*greteþ wel ... alle my freyliche felawes*'; also *King Horn*, ll. 144, 145: '*Gret þu wel*'; *Gen. and Ex.*, l. 2382; Schmirgel, p. xlvii. with illustrations from *Sir Beues*, ll. 89, 117, 131, 164; *Guy of W.*, str. 289, l. 10; *Ipomedon*, B l. 1376; *Seven Sages*, A l. 3838; *Ywain and Gawain*, l. 1598; *Isumbras*, 532. See also *faire grette*, *Speculum*, l. 960; occurring also, *Wm. of Palerne*, ll. 369, 370; Laʒamon, 14,073; and Chaucer, *M. of L. T.*, l. 1051; but '*mekely grette*,' *Pard. Tale*, l. 714; 'reuerently and wysly ... *grette*,' *Clerkes Tale*, l. 952. See *Ancr. R.*, p. 430: '*greteð þe lefdi* mid one Aue Marie'; Orrm 2805, 2806: 'þu gann to *gretenn wiþþ þine milde wordess.*'

---

[1] For arrangement of references to *Rbt. of Gl.* indebtedness is due throughout the notes to Dr. Hans Strohmeyer's *Der Stil d. me. Reimchronik d. Rbt. v. Gl.*, Berlin, 1889.

Omission of I in A_1 is a scribal error. I is extant in five MSS., but compare with the Swiss salutation, *grüetze* used always without a pronoun; see Otfrid *gruazen*. H_2 attempts to restore the reading of type A by the omission of *wel*, reading:

'And séyd I gréte þe · fádyr mýnnë.'

l. 53. *for godes loue:* For this form of invocation to the deity see note to *Sir Beues*, text M, l. 344, with reference to Lange, *Die Versicherungen bei Chaucer*, p. 18; *for goddes loue, Gamelyn*, ll. 31, 55 ; *for Goddys loue, Handlyng Synne*, l. 5661 ; *Rbt. of Gl.*: *vor Godes loue*, ll. 428, 1886, 5006, 5801, 8890, 8968 ; B 9241, 11,355 ; also 828, 2610.

l. 54. Also lines 542, 962 ; cf. ll. 698 and 908. H_2 removes the verse from type D, placing it under type A, through the substitution of *ouyr us* for *us*:

'That óuyr vs álle · sýtte abóue.'

loue : aboue: also ll. 54, 512, 542, 698, 908, 962. See Kölbing's note to *Sir Beues*, text A, l. 1837, and to *Ipomedon*, text A l. 5.

l. 55. *par charite:* commented on by Zupitza, *Guy of Warwick*, l. 471 ; *Athelston*, l. 540 ; in Halliwell's *Dictionary* under *charity;* and *Speculum*, note to l. 840. See:

Langl., A. ix. 11 : 'And preiede hem, *par charite*.'
Spec. Vitæ, l. 15 : '*preyȝeth* alle now, *par charyte*.'
Prov. of Hend, 2, 12 : 'Amen, *par charité!*
God beginning makeþ god endyng ;
Quoþ Hendyng.'

ll. 56, 57. Cf. *Langl.* C. iv. 121, 122 ; B. III. 93 :

'Salamon the sage, a *sarmon* he made
In *amendement* of meyres.'

l. 57. *a god sarmoun:* Compare Mätzner, *Spachproben*, vol. i. p. 115 ; *Moralités et Sermones joyeux, Romania*, Tom. xv. pp. 414—416 ; *Life of Charlemagne*, pp. 85, 86, with reference to homilies prepared by Warnefried for Charlemagne ; Werner, *Alcuin et Charlemagne*, p. 252 ; Schick, *T. of G.*, l. 691 ; and, of course, Morley and ten Brink. See also *Ancr. Riwle*, p. 312 : 'in Uitas Patrum, þo me hefde longe iȝeildon him efter *sarmun*' ; Langl., C. vi. 201 : 'That suweth my *sarmon*' ; and *Hand. Syn.* l. 6936 :

'Seynt Ihoun to Troyle bygan to *sermun*
Wyþ ensamples of gode resun.'

l. 58. *in lesczoun: Speculum Vitæ*, l. 92 : 'And swyche a *lessoun* I schal ȝow ȝeue.' For *don write*, see *Old Song*, quoted by Robertson, *Glossary of Dialect Words in the County of Gloucester*, p. 37.

D and R alter the line, removing for their texts any question as to the value of *-e* at the cæsura.

ll. 61, 62. *gile : while:* a favourite rime of the author of *Gamelyn*, see ll. 370, 562, 580. *while* in the sense of 'a period of time' is used by Spenser in *Prothalamion*, l. 83.

l. 63. *consail take:* see note to l. 47.

l. 64. *forsake : take:* The rime occurs also in lines 72, 100, 268, 498. Line 64 is repeated in substance lines 99 and 497.

l. 65. See note to line 981.

l. 68. *His . . . i . . . do:* Four MSS. attempt to remove the anacoluthon. A_2 and H_2 alter the sentence so that it reads more logically in direct discourse through the rendering þi for *His*. D and R change the clause to indirect discourse by the substitution of *he* for *i*. The punctuation offered by the text seems to be in harmony with the reading of three good MSS., two of the best texts, and representatives of both groups of texts. *preie:* ordinarily in M.E. the prayer to the divinity: *Guy of W.*, B. l. 10,068; *Octavian*, l. 1089; *Sir Beues*, A, ll. 803, 2635; see Schmirgel, p. xlviii. *preie . . do:* This rendering in the sense of 'grant a request,' the editor has not yet discovered in other texts.

l. 69. *sethen i shal be:* On ground of four MSS. A_1 alone reads *whan*. Four MSS. remove *un* of text A_1. For *leche* see Introduction, 'Relation to the Guy of Warwick Romances, chap. vi.; *Faerie Queene*, I. x. 23, ll. 7 ff., and Chaucer:

The Pard. T., l. 916: 'And Iesu Crist, that is *our soules leche.*'
Somp. T., l. 184: 'With highe God, that is *our lives leche.*'
Bok of D., l. 920: '. . . that swete, *my lyves leche.*'
A. B. C., l. 134: 'Beth ye (*Mary*) . . *my soules leche.*'
2 N. T., l. 56: 'Thou (*Mary*) . . art *her lyues leche.*'

l. 70. *Aller(furst):* *Alþere* in MSS. $A_2 H_1 H_2 <$ O.E. *ealra*, 'of all;' see Skeat, *Leg. of G. W.*, l. 298 and Schick, *T. of Gl.*, note to l. 70.

l. 71. *Faire uertuz:* the moral graces, literally Alcuin's *virtutes*, the subject of the sermon of the *Speculum*.

l. 72. *foule þewes:* *De vitiis* of Alcuin, properly the seven deadly sins of the mediæval period; ordinarily *þewes* includes the virtues, or is limited to them, as in line 97, *2 N. T.*, l. 101, and *Conf. Amant.*, Bk. vii., l. 43. See *well-thewed*, Spenser, *Shep. Cal.* Feb., l. 96, annotated by E. K.: '*Bene moratæ*, full of moral wiseness.'

foule: translated *lethere* by H_2, a form popular with *Rbt. of Gl.*; see numerous examples: *luþer brod* 1595; *luþer duc* 4974, 5994, 6330; *luþer emperour* 1873, 1922, 1828; *luþer folc* 2689, 2693, 4637, 6086; *luþer gadeling* 6356; *luþer King* 2984, 6653; *luþer quene* 759, 5825, 5862, 5886, and many other examples. H_2 translates *foule*, l. 61, with *false*.

l. 73. *leue broþer:* nominally one of the brotherhood through Christ, in distinction from *leue brothyr*, an expression of good fellowship, as in *The Erl of Tolous*, l. 605.

l. 74. *Bote:* Bote *ȝuffe* of MS. H_2 improves the verse metrically, adding to the illustrations of type A.

on . . . oþer: i. e. *both*, quite common; see *Gamelyn*, l. 39.

Page 6, l. 79. The verse has been tampered with by the scribes of group Y, probably to restore the measure to the more evenly accentuated system of the classic verse.

l. 80. *on rewe: rewe* is, of course, O.E. *rēw*, to be distinguished from Hampole's *rowe* < O.E. *rāw*. See *in rewe*, *Gamelyn*, l. 867; *arewe*, *Sowdone of B.*, l. 390; *on a rewe*, Prol. to *Leg. of G. W.*, A, l. 285; *Kn. Tale*, l. 2008; *H. of F.*, l. 1692: *rewis* in Pecock's *The Repressor*, II. Chap. xi, l. 103; *on raw*, Douglas, Prol. to *Eneados*, l. 177; Minot, *Political Song.* l. 79; *a long rawe*: (*qlawe*) King. *Quhair*, str. 154, l. 3; *arowe*, *Hous of Fame*, l. 1835; *rowe*: (*loȝe*), *King Horn*, l. 1092. Line 80 recalls *Ancr. Riwle*, p. 198: 'Her beoð nu *areawe* itold,' etc.; p. 336: adunewardes *bi reawe & bi reawe*; Langl. C. II. 22: And rekene hem *by rewe*. *rowe*, *Spec.* MS. R, is the scribe's form for *rewe*, and is not to be referred to O.E. *rāw*.

l. 81, also l. 139. The list of the virtues follows, as based on the classification of Alcuin's *Liber*. They are *uertuz*, ll. 71, 79.

l. 82. *be rede:* The suggestion of MS. R as to the syntax of the line in the construction, *is my rede*, is not to be accepted. *rede* cannot be in the nominative case, but must be a dative, object of the preposition *be*.

l. 83. *bileue:* O.E. *geléafa*, N.E. *belief* through M.E. *bilẹ̄ue*. Compare with the verb l. 84, *bileue, to remain*, < *be-lifan*, M.E. *belȝue*, and Skeat's note to *Leg. of G. W.*, l. 10; *Gen. and Ex.*, l. 1332: 'Ysaac *bileaf* unslagen.'

l. 85. *mieknesse:* The spelling with *ie* in MS. A, is due, as in the case of N.E. *believe*, to Norman-French influence through analogy with such words as N.E. *grief*. The spelling *mieknesse* occurs in *Political Songs of England*, p. 335: 'So is *mieknesse* driven adoun, and pride is risen on heih.' In the later MSS. inorganic *e* unites the suffix with the root. The metrical quality of the verse is improved by the reading *mekẽnesse*.

l. 88. The verse describing true humility is to be read as follows:

'Þat ís verráy · humílité.'

l. 89. *And:* also l. 649, regular M.E. form for *if*. It is used by Lydgate, *T. of Gl.*, ll. 1002, 1289; Spenser, and of course by Chaucer; *Pearl*, str. 47, l. 8; *Tit. And.* II. i. 69; Bacon, Essay 23, l. 38. Cf. *an't, Macbeth*, III. vi. 19.

The rime *ore* : (*more*) occurs in *The Erl of Tolous*, ll. 586, 587: 'Y ask mercy for goddys *ore*': (*more*). Compare *Speculum*, l. 540: 'crieþ *merci and ore*': (*sore*). See Zupitza, *Guy of W.*, note to l. 8280.

l. 92. Line 92 is repeated l. 474. The rime *repentaunce : penaunce* occurs lines 474, 770, and l. 830 in H_2. Read l. 92 as follows:

'And rédi þẽrfóre · to dón penáunce.'

redi: vb. prepare? sb. readiness? or supplying *be : be ready*?

l. 94. *shrifte of mouþe:* also l. 473, a typical M.E. expression. See Zupitza, note to *Athelston*, v. l. 688; Leonard, note to the poem *Aus der Hölle*, l. 51; *Pers. T.*, l. 29; *Rel. Ant.*, p. 243. II.; and Skeat's note to *cordis contritione*, O.E. *Homily, Hic dic est*, l. 58, where the second step in contrition is described as 'confession of mouth,' *Oris confessione* of l. 56 of the same homily. See Skeat's illustrations and his annotation to the lines 55 ff.: 'he (i. e. *god-almihtin*) haueð geuen us to beon muð freo, þet we muȝen *mid ure muðe* bringen us ut of þisse putte' . . . 'þurh muðes openunge.'

l. 97. *þewes:* i. e. *god thewys, Ipotis*, l. 179; *heaued þeawes, Sawles Warde*, ll. 40, 41; *-clere*, 2 *N. T.*, l. 101; *Prov. of Hendyng*, ll. 4, 5:

'. . . . . monie þewes
Forte teche fele shrewes.'

Page 7, l. 101. *þe wicke þewes : foule þewes*, l. 72, and *gode þewes*, l. 97, make up the *þewes*, the mental qualities, discussed by Skeat, note to *Leg. of G. Women*, l. 2577. *wikked thewes* are described in *The Hous of Fame*, l. 1834, and, on ground of Alcuin's *Liber*, are limited to the vices as defined by the *Ancren Riwle*, p. 198 : 'þe seouen heaued sunnen,' popular everywhere in literature of the Middle Ages. See for *the seven deadly sins, MS. Cot. Ap.* 45; Stürzinger *Le Pelerinage de Vie humaine*, p. 332, 'the final assault of the seven deadly sins'; *Ancr. Riwle*, p. 198 ff.: 'Her beoð nu areawe itold þe seouen heaued sunnen': 1. þe Liun of *Prude*; 2. þe Neddre of *attri Onde*; 3. þe Unicorne of *Wreððe*; 4. þe Bore of *heui Slouhðe*; 5. þe Vox of *ȝicounge*; 6. þe Suwe of *ȝiuernesse*; 7. þe Scorpiun of *Lecherie*.

nempne: nempnẽ probably with double thesis at the cæsura, or *nempne* with apocope of *-e*, caused confusion with the copyist, as is proved by the variants. *nempne* was transcribed in various ways in l. 108.

l. 102. *muche shrewes:* very bad qualities. The *Speculum* employs the substantive *shrewes*, where the adjective is expected. This construction is not uncommon in M.E. See *A Poem on the Times of Edward II.*, l. 406, and *moche schrewe, The Tale of Gamelyn*, ll. 6, 230.

moche: Skeat discusses the use of *moche* as applied to size, *Gamelyn*, note to l. 230.

þewes : shrewes: The same rime occurs, *Prov. of Hend.*, ll. 4, 5, *Conf. Amant.*, Bk. vii., l. 44, and *Hous of Fame*, ll. 1834 ff. Compare line 102 with Chaucer's verses, ll. 1830 ff. :

> 'We ben shrewes, every wight,
> And han delyte in wikkednes,
> As gode folk had in goodnes;
> And loye to be knowen *shrewes*,
> And fulle of vice and wikked *thewes*.'

MS. R of the *Speculum* purifies the diction of the line by the removal of the redundant expression illustrative of litotes, *noht gode*, placing the verse in type D :

> 'þáte arc, swithe, mýkel shrówes.'

l. 103. *led : red :* of MS. A₁ is undoubtedly a scribal error. Read *rede* (dat. plu.) : *lede* (inf.) on authority of the other MSS., and according to the laws governing the inflection of the poem. Final *e* was pronounced. See Introduction.

l. 104. *stronge:* See Sievers, § 299, N. 1. The *e* is to be added on account of the metre. It seems to be authorized by the O.E. form.

l. 105. *is hit:* to be retained on authority of the oldest MS. Logically stress should be given to *is* rather than to *it*, as is required by group Y. The verse is unmistakably type C. It would be impossible to read *godë*. H₁ remodels the verse according to type D.

l. 106. *For: For,* H₁R, is to be cancelled. It exists only in one group of related texts.

l. 107. *Line* 107 is unsatisfactory in any of its readings. Refer to the Introduction, Chapter over Versification.

l. 109. *Pride: Pride* occurs in its normal M.E. position, standing first in the list of the vices. This is the arrangement of Alcuin in the *Liber*, Chap. XXVII., *De octo vitiis principalibus & primo de Superbia. Primum vitium est superbia*, de qua dicitur: Initium omnis peccati superbia, quæ regina omnium malorum ; Chap. XXIII., *Maximum diaboli peccatum fuit superbia*. It is the order usual in enumerations of this period. *Pride* is the first sin in Gower's *Confessio* and in *The Persones Tale*, as Schick has indicated in his note to *T. of Gl.*, l. 761. This view is confirmed by the old poem, *The Liif of Adam*, and in *Rel. Ant.* and Chaucer's *Pers. Tale*.

The Liif of Adam, l. 61 : '. . . . . for it com out of heuen,
    And was the form[est] sinne of seven.'

Rel. Ant., p. 166 : 'Pride is out and pride is ine,
    And *pride is rot of every sinne*,
    And pride will never blynne !'

Pers. Tale, l. 834: 'The *rote* of thise sinnes than is *pride*,' etc.

See Skeat's note, Langl., p. vi., l. 118, and Werner with reference to Hraban, Theodulf, Prosper, etc., pp. 253, 254. *Pride* is described in *The Simonie*, ll. 459, 460 :

> '*Pride* priketh aboute, wid withe and wid onde :
> Pes, loue, and charite hien hem out of londe.'

See also lists of Hampole, of the *Ancren Riwle*, etc. See note to l. 18. Cp. *R. of Gl.*, ll. 185 ff.:

> '. . turnde to sleuþe & to prude · & to lecherie,
> To glotonie, (& heye men · muche to robberie).'

Ipotis, l. 410 : '*Pryde* is a synne most of plyghte,
    þat wratteþ Iesus, ful of myghte.'

Compare l. 109 with Maundeville, p. 3: *Pryde, Covetyse, and Enrye, han so enflaumed the Hertes of Lordes of the world*, etc.

l. 111. *on of þo*: pleonastic also in *Ipotis*, D l. 171: 'Erþe .. *is on of þoo*.'

l. 114. The vocabulary of the *Speculum* is enriched by scribal interpretation of the *þisternesse*: *dyrkenes*, MSS. DH₁, *merkenes* MS. R. *myrkenes* is used also in *Tundale*, ll. 182, 437, 1122, 1205, and by Hampole, *Prick of Conscience*, see l. 7820: 'þare es, withouten *myrknes*, lyght.' Read here -*nissĕ*, to rime with *blissĕ*.

Tyndale, l. 181: 'þou shalte to fire withouten ende
And to *merknes* art þou frende.'
Macbeth, V. i. 40: 'Hell is *murky*.'

l. 116. *Wicke sleuþe*: *sleuþes*, l. 121. See Schick's note to *T. of Gl.*, l. 244. *Sleuþe* is translated literally by MS. R in the reading *slownes*, ll. 116 and 121. See Skeat, *Dict.*, under *sloth*, and in mediæval texts: *Langl. Prol.*, A, l. 45: '*Sleep and Sleuȝþe* suweþ hem euere'; *Leg. of G. W.*, l. 1722: 'To kepen her fro *slouthe and ydelnesse*'; *M. of L. T.*, l. 530: '*diligent, with outen slewthe*'; *Sec. N. T.*, l. 258: *withouten slouthe*; *Ancr. R.*, p. 208: 'nis hit *tricherie*, oðer ȝemeleaste *of slouhðe*'; *Pers. T.*, ll. 1687 ff.: '*slouthe . . . shendeth al that he doth*'; *Conf. Aman.* (ed. Morley), p. 176: *Slouth of lachesse*; p. 187: *Slouth of Negligence*; p. 188: *Slouth of Idelnesse*; p. 206: *Slouth of Slepe*; also *Pers. T.*, ll. 1738 ff.: *Conf. Amans*, p. 206, l. 41: '. . . he is cleped *Sompnolence*,
Which doth to *Slouth* his reverence,
As he which is his chamberlein.'

leccherie: See *Ipotis*, text D, l. 406: '*lecherye is þe devels net*,' recalling the world's *paunter*, l. 18 of the *Speculum*. The line is to be compared with *Ipotis*, D ll. 356, 357:
'And glotonye is þe furþe broþer,
Lecherye is þe ferþe,
On of þe wurste abowe erþe.'

l. 117. *Accedie*: normal form *accidie*; O.Fr. *accide*; Lat. *acedia*; the mental prostration of the recluse after fasting or other excess of asceticism. See Murray's *Dictionary* under *accidie*, and Langl., V. B, l. 366: C, l. 417: 'After al this excesse, he had an *accidie*.' *Accidia* is the lazy parson of Jusserand's *Piers Plowman*, p. 235. It occurs often as a synonym of sloth, e.g. *Ancr. Riwle*, p. 208: 'me not nout þeonne is hit ȝemeleste, under *accidie þet ich cleopede slouhðe*'; *The Persones Tale*, ll. 1649 ff.: 'the sinne of *accidie, or slouth*'; l. 1691: 'roten sinne of *accidie and slouthe*.' But thus *Aȝenbite*, l. 10: '*Sleauhðe þet me clepeþ ine clerȝie accidie*,' but this is not the application of the poet of the *Speculum*, as l. 121 distinctly tells us: '*Accedie is sleuþes broþer*.' See *Ancr. R.*, p. 286: '*Accidies salue is gostlich gledschipe*.' See also *The Seven Deadly Sins of London*, Thomas Decker, 1606. *Persones Tale*, ll. 1650 ff.: '*Accidie* maketh him hevy, thoughtful and wrawe'; 'bitternesse is mother of *accidie*'; '*accidie* the anguish of a trouble herte'; ll. 1827 ff.: 'ther ben .. *remedies ayenst accidie*,' etc.

as: is to be omitted on authority of four MSS. For the redundant *as* in the sentence, cf. Schick, *T. of Gl.*, l. 39. See also l. 121.

l. 119. *wisse*: O.E. *wissian*, to teach, see Schick's note, *T. of Gl.*, l. 637.

l. 123. *derne*: O.L.G. *derni*; O.H.G. *tarni*, hence archaic M.H.G. *Tarnkappe*. The mediæval poets liked the word *derne*. See Langl., A. x., l. 199: *deede derne*; B. II., l. 175: *derne rsurye*. Orrm uses *dærne*, verses 14,266, 18,864, 19,886.

Critical and Explanatory Notes. Page 7, lines 123—126. 57

> v. 14,266 : 'All was he *derne*
> Bilokenn & bilappedd.'
> v. 19,886 : 'Acc itt iss *dep & dærne*.'

derne is united with the history of *rune;* 'Godess *dærne rune,*' Orrm. 18,786, 18,864 ; 'God [scheawede] his *derne runes,*' *Ancr. Riwle,* p. 154, fol. 40; Godes *derne runes*, p. 96; *Spring Time* ('Specimens of Lyric Poetry,' II., p. 49), ll. 28 ff. :

> 'Deawes donkeþ þe dounes,
> Deores wiþ huere *derne rounes,*
> Domes forte deme.'

See *King Horn*, 1363 : 'He loucde Horn wel *derne*'; *Cursor Mundi,* v. 32 of 'The Visit of the Magi' :

> 'Þe thoghtfulest amang þam selue,
> and did þam in a montain *dern,*
> [Biseli] to wait þe stern.'

Compare *underne,* 'not secret,' *Ancr. Riwle,* p. 24 ; Wicl., *John* iv. 6 ; *Maund.* 163; *Shor.* 84. For its derived and secondary meaning see *Clerkes Tale* :

> l. 260 : 'The tyme of *vndern* of the same day.'
> l. 981 : 'Abouten *vndern* gan this erl alyghte.'

Orrm., l. 19,458 : 'Au daȝȝ at *unndernn* time.'

See also *Ancr. R.*, p. 24 : 'Fiftene psalmes siggeð abutan *undern deies.*'

l. 124. *anuied: anuied* occurs in the sense of wearied, troubled, or reluctant, in several instances in *The Persones Tale.* See *Havelok*, l. 1735, and Pers. T., ll. 1683, 1684 : '*Of accidie* cometh first that a man is *annoied . . . to do any goodnesse*'; l. 1656 : 'It [*accidie*] is *annoye of goodnesse.*'

l. 125. MS. H₂ places the line under type A by the substitution of *Welofte* for *Ofte*.

mourninge: Read *mourningĕ,* dative, to rime with *springĕ*. Final -e of the infinitive is pronounced in the verse of the *Speculum*. Read *swichĕ,* cancelling *wicke*, as Prof. Schick suggests, for the improvement of the metre.

l. 126. *Wanhope:* a fine English word, suggesting *unhope* of Langland's story of the cats and the mice, and described in *Ipotis,* text D, ll. 422 : *Wanhope is þe þridde broþer;* ll. 447 :

> '*Wanhope* it is anoþer synne,
> That many a man is bounden in.
> Yf a man be falle þerinne
> And doth it ever and wille not blyn,
> And troweth not god, ful of myȝt,
> The fende to wanhope hym plyȝt,
> That he wil no mercy crave,
> For he hopeth non to have.
> And for that *wanhope,* wrytyn I fynde,
> He goth to helle withouten ende.'

See also *T. of Gl.*, ll. 673 and 895, and the quotation cited in Schick's note to line 248, *Life of our Lady,* 1ₛ a :

> 'It is also the myghty pauyce fayre,
> Ageyn *wanhope* and dysperacion,
> Cristal shelde of pallas for dispayre.'

Ham. *Pr. of C.*, l. 2228 : 'Þai sal fande at his last endyng
Hym into *wanhope* for to bring.'

Kn. Tale, l. 391 : 'Wel oughte I sterve in *wanhope and distresse*'; *T. of Gl.*, l. 895 : *wanhop & dispaire ; The Persones Tale*, ll. 1705-6 : *wanhope*

58 *Critical and Explanatory Notes. Pages 7—8, ll. 126—139.*

. . *despeir of the mercy of God.* See Hampole, *P. of C.*, l. 2229. See also the last paragraphs of *The Persones Tale.* pp. 580 ff. (Tyrwh.), and *Confessio Amantis*, pp. 213, 214 of Morley's edition.

Page 8. l. 127. Type A is to be preserved on authority of three MSS., *þat bote* being supported by the oldest text.

l. 129. *Wroþer hele:* This beautiful old construction occurs in *Seinte Marherete*, l. 10, and was, therefore, in use so early as 1200. *Wroþer hele* was commonly made the object of a preposition, as in MS. H_2: *With wroþe hele*, or *to wroþer hele*, as in *O. E. Misc.*, p. 48 ; *The Life of St. Juliana*, text A, l. 47: 'tu seist *to wraðer heale*'; l. 92: '*to wraðer heale iwurðen*'; l. 118: 'sinken *to wraðer heale* ow to þe bale bitter deope into helle.' *Ancr. R.*, p. 102: 'Go ut ase dude Dina, Jacobes douhter *to wrother hele*.' *O. E. Hom.*, p. 33, has *wrether hele* and *ufele hele*. *Wroþer hele* is to be construed as the old gen. of the fem. adj. *wráþ* (O.E. ending -*re*) combined with *hele*, O.E. *hǽlu*, *wráþ* signifying bad, angry, *hǽlu*, health. See note to *Cursor Mundi*, l. 257, for explanation of the construction. *Wroþer hele* is found *Laȝamon*, l. 29,536; *Rbt. of Brunne*, ll. 104, 201, 291. See the related *goderhele* with parallel construction, *R. of Gl.*, l. 7570: 'þat goder hele al engelond was heo euere ibore.' See *vassail*.

Compare with the idiomatic phraseology of l. 129, verses 301 of *Piers Pl.* and *King Richard.*

Spec., l. 129: 'Wroþer hele was Iudas born.'
P. Pl., l. 301: 'For to wroþer hele was he iwrouȝt.'
K. Rich., l. 129: 'Why shope thou me to wroþer hele.'

l. 130. *lorn:* preserved on authority of the oldest and best MS., for logical and metrical smoothness in the verse.

l. 131. Line 131 may have two readings according to the stress attributed to *Merci*:

'Mérci hé les · þúrw þat sinne' D.
'Merci he lés · þúrw þat sinne' C.

The theology of verses 129—131 is not based on scriptural text. It finds parallel in *The Persones Tale*, ll. 1713 ff.: '. . . he that is despeired, ther n'is no felonie, ne no sinne, that he douteth for to do, as shewed wel by Judas.' The sin wanhope, despair of the mercy of God, is described in the next to the last paragraph of the *Tale*, ll. 3 ff.: 'The *first wanhope* cometh of that, he demeth that he hath sinned *so gretly and so oft, and so long lyen in sinne*, that he shal not be saved.' See also *Conf. Amant.*, p. 213:

l. 37 : 'Also whan he is falle in sinne.
Hem thenketh he is so coulpable,
That god woll nought be merciable
So great a sinne to foryive.'

l. 56 : 'Wanhope folweth atte laste,
Whiche may nought longe after laste.
. . . .
But god wot whider he shall wende!'

l. 133. *birede:* MSS. A_1D R, and perhaps A_2, support the reading *birede* through slightly corrupted forms.

ll. 137, 138. *sarmoun : lesczoun:* See notes to lines 57, 58.

l. 139. MS. A_2 supplies the ellipsis by which *Wisdom*, l. 139, is left without a predicate: *Wisdom vse wel*, etc. Otherwise there is no clue to the exact meaning intended by the poet. For mediæval interpretation of *wisdom*, see other M.E. texts, for instance, *The Owl and the Nightingale*, ll. 1755, 1756 :

'þar he demeþ manie riȝte dom,
And diht and writ *mani wisdom*,
And þurh his muþe and þurh his honde
Hit is þe betere into Scotlonde.'

See a MS. discourse over *wisdom*:
'There is no thynge better than wysdome, ne no þyng swetter than konnynge, ne no thynge lustyer than knowlege, ne no thynge worse than lewdenes. It is an highe godenes of god to knowe what þou schuldest do and eschew. And it is an high wrothidnes not to knowe where þou gost. þer for loue wysdome and it schall be schewed vnto þe. Go to it, and it schall come to þe. Be besy there aboute, and it schall lerne the.' Selected from 'the boke' 'to enforme man howe he schulde flee vice and folowe vertus by consideration of a man himself.'

l. 140. *erere:* also l. 168, not a common form; comp. of *ar*. It is not preserved in later MSS. of the *Spec*. It is retained on authority of MS. A$_1$. *seide:* Read *sede*. The rime demands *sede (drede : sede).* < O.E. *sǽde*. < O.E. *sǽyde*. See *Phonology*. *reed : seed* occurs *Fl.* and *Blfl.*, l. 52.

l. 143. *do god:* The preacher was eminently a philanthropist. He continually emphasizes the doctrine of good works, *gode dede*. See ll. 461, 674, 860—876, etc.

l. 144. *rod:* Chaucer would have spoken *rodĕ*. Final -*ĕ* is to be expected, but on basis of the co-ordinate rime, *rod : god* (adj. with subst. use) *rod* is to be read without a syllabic final -*ĕ*.

l. 146. *inouh : inouh* as well as *god* (N.E. *God*), lines 25 and 35 are argument in support of a type C. Neither can be read with the final -*ĕ* necessary to prevent the clashing of two stressed syllables at the caesura.

l. 147. *þerwid:* MS. A$_2$ preserves the correct form *þerwith* to rime with *griþ* in opposition to the false orthography *þer wid* of MS. A$_1$.

l. 148. *merci and griþ:* Examples of the juxtaposition of *merci* with *griþ* are not abundant. *Pes and griþ* are more commonly united. See Kölbing, *Sir Beues*, note to A, l. 849.

Page 9, l. 149. *þis :* i. e. *þis*) of MSS. A$_1$H$_1$, written in full *þis is* in MSS. A$_2$H$_2$, is to be regarded as monosyllabic as in A$_1$. The contraction occurs in Chaucer and Lydgate. See the illustrations cited by Schick, *T. of G.*, l. 496.

l. 151. *honour:* honors, *i.e.* the material conditions that are accompanied with honor, see ll. 152—158. The figure is metonymy.

l. 152, also 163. *londes : rentes : londis, rentis* in H$_1$; *Londys · rentys* in H$_2$; *R. of Gl.*, ll. 2462, 6628, 6630, 7585, 7686, 8565, 10,267, 10,268.

bour : *Bur* as inner and private department was distinguished from *hall*, O.E. *heall*, in the O.E. period. See *Beowulf*, l. 140: 'ræste sōhte bed æfter būrum,' see also ll. 1311 and 2456; Murray, *N. E. Dict.*, under *bower*. Illustrations from M.E. texts are as follows: *Orrm*, l. 8134: 'Onnfasst to *kingess bure*'; *bour* occurs in figurative usage, *Ancr. Riwle*, p. 34, fol. 8: 'þet *into ower breoste bur* is ililit of heouene'; p. 102, fol. 25: *þine heorte bur; K. Horn*, l. 386: 'al þe *bur* gan liȝte'; 729: *ut of bure* of lore; 1472: at Fikenhildes *bure;* also 273, 290, 400, and many additional instances; Langl. (redaction A. III.) 13, 14:

'. . . . . . the Iustise soone
Busked him into the bour, ther the buyrde was inne.'

And C. VII., l. 288; B. V., l. 222:

'The beste laye in my bour, and in my bed chambre.'

Harrowing of Hell, l. 31: 'He lihte of his heȝe tour
Into *seinte Marie bour*.'

Gamelyn, l. 405 : ' If I leete the goon out of his bour.'
Sir Beues, A, l. 160 : ' þe leuedi a fond in hire bour.'
Parl. of F., l. 304 : ' Of braunches were her *halles and her boures*.'

bour and *halle* are described together in *Guy of Warwick*, B. 102, *The Nonne Prestes Tale*, l. 12 ; Spenser has *in bowre or hall*, *Faerie Queene*, I. viii, str. 29, l. 9 ; *from inner bowre*, I. viii, str. 5, l. 6 ; *Guy of Warwick*, l. 2674: *mayde bryght in bowre*; *Pearl*, str. 81, l. 3—4 :

' Bryng me to that bygly bylde,
And let me se *thy blysful bor*.'

The word was still in use in Spenser's time. It occurs in the *Prothalamion* :

l. 14: '. . . . . daintie gemmes
Fit to decke *maydens bowres*.'

l. 91 : ' Ye gentle Birdes ! the worlds faire ornament
And heauens glorie, whom this happie hower
Doth leade into your lovers blissfull *bower*.'

L. Allegro, l. 87 : '. . . in haste her *bowre* she leaves,
With Thestylis to bind the sheaves.'

The original significance of the O.E. *búr* was lost early. It seems to be retained by Tennyson and Scott :

Godiva, l. 42 : ' Then fled she to her inmost *bower*.'
Minstrelsy of the Scottish Border, vol. ii. p. 144 (ed. 1802):

' There were twa sisters sat in a *bour*,
Edinborough, Edinborough.
Ther cam a knight to be their wooer,' etc.

Bayard Taylor retains a trace of the earlier significance in *The Poet of the East*, l. 3.

H_2 reads *halle and bowre*, *bowre* in rime with *honowre*. The *Speculum* does not preserve *honour* with variable stress, but retains the old accent *honoúr*. The alternative *hónour* is not found.

halle, A_2D *halles* : the public room characteristic of English life in this period, early the centre of social activity and the seat of conviviality, as described in O.E. poems, *Beowulf*, *Andreas*, etc. See Heyne, *Heorot* ; Grimm, *Andreas and Elene* xxxvii ; and illustration in *Gnomic Verses*, l. 28 f. :

'. . . cyning sceal on healle
beagas dælan . . . . . '

Distinction between *halle* and *bour* seems to be defined in Hartmann's *Iwein*, ll. 77 ff.

l. 153. *siluer and gold :* related terms often used conjointly in M.E. texts ; for example *Rbt. of Gl.*, A 285, 2609, 3552, 3559, 4013, 5543, 8292 ; *Sir Beues*, A l. 562: *al þe seluer ne al þe golde* ; A l. 2616 : *Naiþer for seluer ne for golde*; *Rich. C. de L.*, l. 3796 ; *Arthour and Merlin*, l. 128 ; *King of Tars*, V l. 81 ; *Seven Sages*, A l. 2719 ; *Alisaunder*, l. 403.

l. 154. *tresor . . . bold :* ' stores ? of treasure ' . . . ' buildings.' For *bold*, see *Riddle*, No. 16, ll. 8-9 :

' . . . . . þur ic wic búge,
bold, mid bearnum, ond ic bide þǽr . . .'

See Merlin's description of the sword of Arthour :

' Ich am yhote Escalibore,
Unto a king *a faire tresore*.'

Rbt. of Gl. l. 7133: *tresour . . . gold* ; *Sir Beues*, A l. 1504: *gold . . . tresor* ; *Rbt. of Gl.*, l. 372 : *Tresour . . . oþer god.*

l. 155. *mete . . . drinke*: another instance of juxtaposition of ordinary terms, illustrated with frequency; *Sir Beues*, A l. 2125: 'Mete and drinke þai hadde afyn'; also *Launfal*, l. 340; the litotes *Gamelyn*, l. 390: '*mete ne drynk* had he non'; *Rbt. of Gl.*, ll. 8808, 8848, 11,294, 11,997; *Sompnoures Tale*, l. 167: *Of mete and drinke*. See a poem *Aus der Hölle*, ed. Leonard, l. 57 of text A:

> 'In delycate metys I sette my delyte
> And myȝhty wynes vnto my pay.'

metys (plural in *-ys*): is the reading of H_2. The meaning is probably general for food, as l. 900 and Marlowe's *Faustus*, st. I, l. 164. See Kölbing's note, *Sir Beues*, A l. 1570 and A l. 1739.

drinke: This is a plural form to rime with *swinke*, inf. in *-ĕ*, the *swinkĕ* of later MSS. See Kölbing's note to *Sir Beues*, M, l. 1047.

riche: translated as 'delicious' by Kölbing, *Sir Beues*, O, l. 2846, '*A ryche souper there was dyght*.' It could appropriately have the same meaning here, but 'highly seasoned' is to be preferred. H_1 proposes *goode drinke*. *Riche* is to be distinguished from *Riche* l. 153, used in the sense of 'costly'; cf. *Richesses*, 'costly articles,' *P. Pl.*, A III., l. 24. See in note to l. 155 the qualities ascribed to *met* and *drink*, l. 57, A poem *Aus der H.*, perhaps equivalent to *riche*.

l. 156. *swinke*: to labour hard. Read *swinkĕ* according to the inflectional characteristics of the *Speculum*. *swinke*, a common word in M.E., is not to be found in Shakspere. See Skeat, *Leg. of G. W.*, note to l. 2041.

þerfore: 'for it,' as in Marlowe's *Faustus*, the last line of the first scene.

l. 157. *Hele of bodi*: also *Persones Tale*, l. 786. *huide*: here 'human skin.' See Breul's note to *Sir Gowther*, l. 33; *The Erl of Toulous*, l. 189: *hew and ek of hyde, hyde* in rime with *pryde*.

l. 158. *los*: 'renown' on account of vice as well as of virtue; see note, *Prompt. Parv.*, and reference to *Sir Gowther*, l. 186:

> 'His *loose* sprong ful wide
> because of sacrilogious deede.'

Maund., p. 108: 'Heroudes of gret name and *loos* for her crueltee.' In the meaning glory (*Ruhm*) *los* occurs in sense of good renown, *Langl.* viii, l. 109 (C), 'ȝoure goode *loos* to shewe'; xiv. l. 111: 'good *loos* of his hondes;' *Hous of Fame*, 1621, 1722, etc. Tobler in *Chrest.*, on 'Half Church Latin,' disclaims the derivation of *los* from the French: Church-Latin *laus*, Fr. *lōs*, M.E. *lōs*. See note to l. 166, and Skeat's note to *Leg. of G. W.*, l. 1514: 'Ercules, that had *the grete los*.' For the combined use of *los* in both senses, *Hous of Fame* gives example, ll. 1618 ff.:

> '. . . . . I graunte yow,
> That ye shal have a shrewed fame
> And *wikked loos* and worse name,
> Though ye *good loos* have wel deserved.'

See Kölbing's note to *los*, *Sir Beues*, M. l. 22.

l. 159. *murie*: also l. 905, and *muryere*, l. 284. Zupitza's explanation is to be referred to in *Engl. Stud.*, vol. vii, p. 465 ff., giving nominatives *myrge, mirge, merge* (M.E. *merge*). Chaucer naturally reproduces the three forms possible in M.E. See Stratmann, *M.E. Dict.*

hem þinkeþ: methinks of Shakspere, O.E. ðyncean, ðūhte, geðūht. *him þouhte*, l. 32, impersonal verb followed by O.E. dative, here *hem* or *hym*. See notes to ll. 521 and 648, and Zupitza's note to *Guy of Warwick*, l. 385, also l. 6223, *Gamelyn*, l. 398, and *Pearl:*

> str. 46, l. 12: '*Uss thynk uss oghe* to take more.'

str. 47, l. 1 : 'More haf we served *uus thynk* so.
. . . .
Then thyse . . . .'

l. 160. *ibouht . . . dere:* common M.E. phraseology for 'redeemed,' of *Is.* lxiii. 9, or '*bought* with a price,' 1 *Corinth.* vi. 20. See Kölbing's note to *Sir Beues*, A, l. 566, including Breul's to *Sir Gowther*, l. 3, and Skeat's to *Pard. Tale*, l. 501. Compare *bouhte . . . sore*, l. 236, and the following illustrations, where the application is sometimes different from the scriptural sense and is adapted to the language of ordinary life:

   Hymn on the Nativity, l. 152 : 'That on the bitter cross
                       Must *redeem* our loss.'
   Shep. Cal., *May*, l. 299 : '*set too dear a price.*'
       July, l. 148 : 'Whose love *he bought too dear.*'
   Pearl, str. 62, l. 1 :   'This maskellez perle that *boght is dere*,
          l. 3 :   Is lyke the reme of hevenes clere.'
   Townl. Myst., l. 244 : 'I have theym *boght agan*
                With shedyng of my blode.'
   Mundus et Infans, l. 291 : '*bonerly bought you* on the roode tree.'
   Pearl, str. 75, l. 5 : 'For thay *arn boght* fro the urthe aloynte.'
   Maund., *Prol. to Voiage*, l. 41 : 'how *dere he boughte . . .* and how dere he
                     aȝenboght us, for the grete love . . .'
   þe *Wohunge of u. Lauerd*, l. 120 : 'þe blod, þat *me bohte.*'
              l. 125 : 'siðen þat *tu bohtes* herte for herte.'
              l. 140 : 'mi liues luue, wið þi blod þu haues
                    me boht.'

The riming word is *bouhte*, ll. 26 and 226, as referred to in Kölbing's note and illustrated in that connection. See also as follows:

   Poema Morale, l. 184 : '*wel deore he us bohte.*'
   T. of Gl., l. 1258 : 'And more of pris, when *it is dere bouȝt.*'
   Comp. of Mars, l. 167 : 'I yaf my trewe servise and my thoght,
                For evermore—*how dere I have it boht!*'

ful: supplied from MSS. A_2DH$_1$H$_2$R. *wel* of A_1 illustrates skipping, the eye of the copyist probably catching the word from *wel*, l. 161.

be seynte John: l. 161 in MS. H$_2$. Common in Chaucer, *Somp. Tale*, l. 175 ; *Man of L. T.*, l. 1019 ; *Pard. T.*, l. 752 ; *Bok of the D.*, l. 1319 ; *Parl. of F.*, l. 451. See Kölbing's note, *Sir Beues*, M, l. 314, under illustrations of *was I nevere none* and *be sein Ion*, *Beues*, A, l. 2747 ; l. 4377 ; O, l. 3571 ; *The Erl of T.*, ll. 152, 517, 793, 931, 971, 1192.

Latin. nihil . . . quam: MS. A$_1$ reads 'nichil . . . quam.'

l. 161. *falle wel:* freely translated 'may happen perchance.' *Somp. Tale*, l. 5, 'And *so befell . . .* on a day'; also *The Erl of T.*, ll. 22, 181, 493, 997 ; *N. Prestes Tale*, l. 452, '*so byfel.*'

on a day is to be referred to l. 49 of the *Speculum* ; l. 61 of *Tundale*.

wel : catel: The same rime occurs ll. 578, 896, 942.

l. 163. *londes, rentes:* 'property and its revenues'; also l. 152 and *March. Tale*, l. 67. *Rbt. of Gl.*, l. 451, explains the terms:

'. . . . . . & þei *a lond* igranted were
To a man to bere þeruore *a certein rente* bi ȝere.'

The Nonne Prestes Tale expresses the idea, l. 7 : '*catel and rente.*'

l. 164. *pore of mod :* Compare the various expressions of humility as represented in M.E. interpretation and by the poet : '*low of herte*,' l. 165 ; '*halt þermide noht*,' l. 171 ; '*holde lowe*,' l. 179.

l. 165. *ful iwis:* See note to l. 723.

l. 166. *litel prys:* 'praise,' 'price,' = 'value,' recalling *los* l. 158, the two words perhaps synonymous in *Sir Beues;* M. 1. 22, 'For to wynne price and loos'; M. l. 3888, '*lose* ne of *price*'; *T. of Gl.*, l. 1381 : 'Now *laude and pris*.' *Gamelyn* increases the vocabulary growing from *pris* with the meaning valour, ll. 772 and 804 : 'ȝonge men of *prys*.' See also *T. of Gl.*, l. 1258, quoted in note to l. 160. Other M.E. meanings are as follows :

Pearl, str. 35, l. 11 : 'Hys prese, his *prys*, and hys parage.'
T. of Gl., l. 1380 : 'A litl tretise . . . .
In pris of women, oonli for hir sake.'
Minot, *Polit. Song*, l. 25 : 'Þan þe riche floure-de-lice,
Wan þaro *ful litill prise*.'

l. 168. *þat :* cf. l. 140, dat. 'of whom.' Cf. Zupitza's note to *Guy of Warwick*, l. 5462.

erere : See note to l. 140.

seide : Read *sede*, Southern form. See note to l. 140, and 'Introduction' under 'Inflection.'

Page 10, l. 173. *skilfulliche :* a form not often cited in M.E. Hampole employs *scilwisli*, Ps. xxxi. 6, with the meaning 'reasonable'; but *Aȝenbite*, l. 6, *skelvolliche*, 'skillfully,' and Chaucer, *Compl. of Mars*, l. 155, *skilfully* in the sense of particularly :

C. of M., l. 155 : 'The ordre of compleynt requireth *skilfully*,
That if a wight shal pleyne pitously . . .'
S. N. T., l. 320 : 'Men myghten dreden wel and *skilfully*' (= reasonably).

A corresponding adjective is to be found in *Gorboduc*, A, II. 2. 11, l. 762 :
'Lest *skillesse* rage throwe downe with headlong fall . . .'

The third *York Play*, l. 22 : 'A *skylfull* beeste þan will y make.' See *Orrm.*, l. 3715 ; *P. of C.*, l. 1818 ; *H. of F.*, l. 750; Mannyng, *Handl. Synne*, l. 5827 ; *Ancren Riwle* preserves the substantive in its normal meaning, p. 346, 'consent of the mind,' *skiles ȝettunge ; York Plays, The Ascension*, l. 113 : '*Anodir skill* forsoth is þis' ; *Pearl*, str. 5, l. 6, 'Wyth *fyrte skyllez*' (timid reasons, see note), etc.; *Thos. of Erceld.*, see Brandl., l. 288 : 'I sall þe telle þe *skille*.' Note the following combinations :

Lydg., *T. of Gl.*, l. 1382 : 'as it is *skil & riȝt*.'
Ch., *Leg. of G. W.*, l. 1392 : '*skille and right*.'
l. 385 : 'As hit is *right and skilful* that they be.'

The *Orrmulum*, l. 12,336 : 'Innsihht, & witt, & shæd, & *skill*.'

Sir Samuel Tuke (d. 1673) uses *skill* in its mediæval sense, 'reason,' in *The Adventures of five Hours*, v. 3, l. 25 :
'He is a fool, who thinks *by force or skill*
To turn the current of a woman's will.'

Tuke's lines are introduced in the *Examiner*, May 31, 1829, where *skill* is understood to mean in its modern character 'dexterity,' 'force.' They occur in paraphrases in Aaron Hill's *Epilogue to Zara*.

The meaning of Icel. *skilja*, to divide, occurs perhaps in *Taming of the Shrew*, iii. 2, l. 34 : 'it *skills* not much,' *i. e.* 'makes no difference.' See Skt., *Ety.*, § 277. The new English significance is illustrated in Shakspere's time, see *Cymb.* II. 5, l. 33 :

''Tis greater *skill*
In a true hate, to pray they have their will.'

See *Rich. III.* iv. 4. 116 ; *Henry IV*, Part I, v. 1, l. 133 ; Pope, *Essay on Criticism*, l. 1 :
''Tis hard to say, if greater *want of skill*
Appear in writing or in judging ill.'

l. 176. *pine:* 'torture'; *hell pine* described ll. 277-284. *pine* is derived from *pēna*, Folk-Lat. pronunciation of Latin *poena*, 'satisfaction,' 'punishment.' Gk. ποινή, penalty, according to Skeat, § 398. See O.H.G. *pína*, G. *pein*, in distinction from M.E. *peyne* from the Fr. *peine*, with the meaning 'trouble.'

The interpretation ending here recalls the terms of the Hebrew philosophy where wisdom is identified with goodness, wickedness with folly.

ll. 175-6, 187-188, 265-6, 876 suggest a fallacy of the mediæval wisdom philosophy, converting the law, that prosperity is a result of righteousness, destruction of wickedness, into a barter of religious consecration.

ll. 177-188. This portion of the poem attains its highest delicacy in the expression of the doctrine of God's chastening, illustrating with peculiar force *Heb.* xii. 6 and *Job* v. 17:

'Whom the Lord *loueth* he *chasteneth*.'

'Behold, blessed is the man whom God correcteth; Therefore despise not thou the chastening of the Almighty.'

The passage suggests a selection from Bede's *Eccl. Hist.*, ed. Miller, p. 68, l. 5 ff.: 'ond þeah ðe þat wiite hwene heardor & strongor don sy, þonne is hit of *lufan to donne* ... Forðon þaem menn þuth þa þrea þis bið gegearwod, þæt he ne *sy seald þæm ecan fyrum helle tintyres.*'

louerede: 'love tokens,' 'loving kindness,' *Is.* lxiii. 7, a word not common in the vocabulary of the period. It is found in *E. E. Psalter* C. viii. 5 of the thirteenth century, in *Metrical Homilies* of the fourteenth century, and also in *Aȝenbite*, see Strat. *Dict.* Cf. *luue eie*, p. 430 *Ancr. R.*

l. 178. *drede:* 'fear' in the sense of reverence, the line recalling *Job* iv. 6: 'Is not *thy piety* thy confidence?' where *piety* can be translated *fear of God*.

ll. 179-180. Not found in MS. A_1, probably a careless omission of the scribe. The lines are introduced here on authority of five MSS. The reading is that of MS. A_2.

l. 182. *maken ... lese:* 'deliver from,' see Zupitza's note, *Guy of Warwick*, l. 10,112.

l. 185. *hunger and þurst: Rev.* vii. 16: 'They shall *hunger* no more, neither *thirst* any more.' Conversely the mediæval poet includes *hunger and þurst* in ordinary enumerations of the tortures of hell, e.g. *Poema Morale*.

l. 229: 'On helle is *hunger end ðurst*, unele twa ifere.'

l. 197: 'þurst end hunger ... eche end eal un helðe.'

Pers. Tale, l. 286: 'They shul be *wasted with honger* ... and the gall of the dragon shal ben hir *drinke*.'

Orrm., l. 1614: '& pinenn þær þi bodiȝ a wiþþ chele & þrisst & hunngerr.'

The *Poema Morale*, in description of heaven, follows *Rev.* vii. 16.

l. 321: 'Né muȝen hi werien heom wið þurste ne wið hunger.'

l. 323: 'Ac ðer *nis hunger ne ðurst*. ne dieð. ne unhelðe ne elde.'

l. 186. *euere among:* 'from time to time,' 'continually?' see Zupitza, note to *Guy of Warwick*, l. 650; Lüdtke to *The Erl of Toulous*, l. 748; and Kirke's note to *Shep. Cal.*, Dec., l. 112 (str. 19, l. 4), introduced as 'ever and anon'; *King Horn*, l. 1565; *Sir Beues*, O, l. 606; *Two Noble Kinsmen*, iv. 3, l. 86.

l. 188. *to echen here blisse: Isaiah* liv. 8: 'With *everlasting kindness* will I have mercy on thee.' The graceful climax ending here shows the earnest *naïveté* of the preacher, one of the notable charms of the poem. The pictorial quality of the verse is peculiarly vivid in these couplets.

l. 189. *ne;* MS. A₁ preserves type D. Five MSS. authorize the omission of *ne*. The verse is then to be read according to types C and D:

Mán, if þú léuest noht mé.

Page 11. l. 190. *bidene:* derived by Zupitza from *mid êne*, note to *Guy of Warwick*, l. 2408, also ll. 8720, 8748, 11,637. See Murray's *Oxford Dictionary*, and Gollancz's note to *Pearl*, str. 17, l. 4. *bidene* is of frequent occurrence, for instance *Spec.*, l. 834 in *H₂*; Lüdtke, *Erl of Toulous*, l. 1217; *Havelok*, in the sense of 'forthwith,' ll. 730, 2841, with reference to *Tristrem*, p. 45; *Metrical Psalter*, Psalm ciii, l. 74; and *Orrmulum* as follows, l. 4793:

'onn an daʒʒ all *bidene*.'

The New English derivative of *bidene* occurs in *Blackwood's Magazine*, vol. xxviii, p. 738: 'Read our Bibles, pray *bedeen*.'

l. 194. *wel iwite:* a frequent expletive, often used merely to fill out an incomplete line, as in the *Speculum*, ll. 312, 637, 763, 895, 941, and Chaucer, *Prol.*, ll. 659, 711, 740, 771; *Rom. of Rose*, ll. 1355, 1904, 2018; *Havelok*, l. 2208; *Orrm.* l. 112. For *wel ywote* cf. Zupitza's note to *Guy*, l. 11,948.

l. 195. *is noht:* 'is worthless,' also the language of the Scriptures. See *Proverbs* xx. 14; 2 *Kings* ii. 19, etc.

ll. 196-198. *wille—spille:* 1 *Corinth.* v. 5: 'destruction of the flesh, that the spirit may be saved'; *Prov.* xix. 18: 'him spare to cause him to die.' See also *Prov.* xxiii. 14.

l. 196. *abouten:* 'everywhere,' 'to full extent'; in l. 191 *aboute*, 'around,' 'in the neighbourhood,' explained by *Rbt. of Gl.*: *aboute in ech side*, ll. 3962, 4550, 6153, 6766; *aboute in eche ende*, ll. 22, 3545, 7473.

l. 201. *þi bileue:* a specific *Credo* rather than a distinct quality of faith as described by Alcuin. *bileue* is used by *Rbt. of Gl.* in this sense:

St. Dunst., l. 27: 'To teche him his *bileue*, paternoster and crede.'

See *Credo* of the *Aʒenbite*, l. 1: 'Ich leue ine god ... makere of heuene and of erþe.'

ll. 204-206. *Eph.* iv. 6, reproduced in many M.E. texts, for example Chaucer, *The Seconde Nonnes Tale*, ll. 207 ff.:

l. 207: 'Oo Lord, oo feith, oo god withouten mo,
Oo Cristendom and fader of alle also. . . .'

l. 340: 'So, in *o being* of diuinitee,
Thre *persones* may ther ryght wel be.'

Conf. Aman., p. 344: 'The High Almighty Trinité,
Which is o God in Unité.'—l. 17.

Ipotis, l. 45: '. . . . . . . the sone
The fadyr and þe holy goste, togeder wone
Thre personys in trinite.'

ll. 203-212. See MS. *Arund.* 286: 'Of þe Sacrament of þe auter:' 'þe þridde poynt is of þe trinite, þat euery man owʒe studefastly to byleue inne þre þinges man oweþ to trowe of þo trinite: þe first þat þe fader *and* sone *and* þe holy gost is o god; þe secunde þat god is wiþoute bygynnynge *and* schal be wiþowte end *and* þat he made alle þinge; þe þridde is þat þe sone was euer fro þe bygynnynge wiþ þe fader *and* þe holy gost connynge fro hem boþe.'

l. 204. *o:* as in many MSS. of Chaucer's text. There seems to be no ground for the alteration of *o* (text A₁) to *oo* (text H₁) as is regarded desirable by Skeat, note to *Nonne P. T.*, l. 207, cited note to ll. 204-6.

l. 207. *man:* The interpolation of *man* is not justified by the MSS. This is an instance in which *H₂* preserves the most vigorous expression and the smoothest metre, and is in keeping with the general character of the poem.

l. 208. *in þin herte do:* 'enter it into thy heart,' 'imprint it on thy heart.' *do* is perhaps interpreted by the German *einprägen*.

l. 209-210. The substance of these lines is introduced freely in M.E. texts. See also *Rev.* i. 8; *Is.* ix. 6; *Heb.* vii. 3:

> *Conf. Amant.*, p. 344: 'Withouten ende and béginning
> And Creatór of allé thing.'—l. 19.

> *Ipotis*, l. 35: 'He is withowte begynnyng
> And also withowte endlynge.'

> *Poema Moral*, l. 85: 'He is ord abuten orde, end ende abuten ende.'

> *biginning : ending:* frequent rime. See *Poema Morale*, ll. 119, 120.

l. 210. Five MSS. require the omission of *ne*, giving illustration of type C instead of type A:

> 'Ne néuere shál · háue endíng.'

l. 211. *shappere ... shaftes:* frequent alliteration in this connection, based on *Col.* 1. 16:

> *þe Wohunge of u. Lauerd*, l. 62: 'schuppere of alle schaftes.'
> *Life of St. Jul.*, l. 8: 'þe lufsume lauerd þat schupte alle schaftes.'
> *Poema Morale*, l. 84: 'he scop ealle ȝe sceafte (sop alle safte, Tr. MS.).'
> *Hom. Good Shep.*, l. 8: 'ȝif ænig gesceaft is god ... seo gôdnys [is] of ðam scyppende.'
> Ælfred, *True Nobility*, l. 17: 'Gode is fader eallra *gesceafta* ... hi ealle *gesceop*.'

Minot, *Polit. Song*, l. 1: 'God, þat *schope* both *se and sand* ...'

Compare also as follows:

> *Destr. of Troy*, l. 1: '*Maistur* in mageste, *maker of alle*,
> endles and on, euer to last.'

l. 212. *shappere—made man:* See *Gen.* ii. 3: 'created *and made*,' King James's version.

Page 12, ll. 213, 214. Interpretation of the passage is difficult. Copyist's forms do not aid in a decision.

l. 213. *after his owen face:* See *Gen.* i. 27: 'created man in his own image'; l. 26: 'after our likeness.' The text is frequently quoted in M.E.

> *Ipotis*, B, l. 541: '. . . . . god made Adam,
> . . . .
> And schoppe hym *after hys owen face*.'

Nassington, *On the Trinity*, l. 96: '—— mad hym aftere thyne owene liknesse.'

Maund., *Voiage*, l. 41: 'man, that he made *after his owne image*.'

Aȝenbite, p. 87, l. 17: 'huer by we byeþ *yssaȝe to his ymage*.'
> l. 52: '*to þe ymage and to þe anliknesse of god*.'
> l. 10: '*ssop þe zaule to his anlycnesse an to his fourme*.'

l. 214. *heih:* 'holy,' *Almighty*.

l. 215. *fre power:* The doctrine of predestination seems settled with the poet in distinction from Chaucer, see *The Nonne Prestes Tale*, ll. 411-417, 422-430.

l. 219. *Wheiþer:* 'which of two.' Read *Whe'r* as monosyllable, see Skeat's note to *Leg. of G. W.*, l. 72, and *Whe'r*, ll. 272, 536, 872.

l. 223. *Adam ... forme man ... singyn began:* Common M.E. phraseology. See as follows:

Maund., *Prol. Voiage*, l. 26: 'for the synne of *oure formere fader Adam*.'

Poema Morale, l. 195: 'Vres *formes federes* gult we abigget alle.'
Pricke of C., l. 483: 'our *forme fader* ...' 'Our *forme fader* hit an byte.'
l. 224. *singyn:* See *Langl.*, C I, l. 109.
l. 227. *wit:* in the sense of the opening verses of *Pricke of Conscience* to be traced in other poems, see note to l. 339 and Add. MS. 11,304:

l. 1: 'þe might of þe fader alle myhty,
þe *witte* of þe oone alle *witty*,
þe grace and þe godenes of þe holy goste
on god of myht moste,
be wit us at þis begynnyng
And bryng vs to a gode endyng.
þe myht of the fader alle myhty
þe *witte* of the sone alle witty.'

his: is *D*, *ys H₂*; *Sir Gowther*, l. 55.
l. 229. *eging:* 'urging,' 'instigation,' another instance of the connection of this word with the story of the fall, noted by Skeat, *M. of L. T.*, l. 842:

M. of L. Tale, l. 842: '... thurgh wommanes *eggement*
Mankynd was lorn and damned ay to dye.'
The Deluge, l. 241: 'Bot þurʒ þe *eggyng of eue* · he ete of an apple.'
Ipotis, l. 515: 'And kepyn hem from fel *eggynge*.'
P. Pl., A I, l. 63: 'Adam and Eue he *eggede* to don ille.'
Chester Pl., The Creation: 'And, man, also I say to the,
"thou hast not done after me,
Thy wife's cownsell for to flee,
But *done so her bydding*."'

fend and Eue: 1 *Corinth.* xi. 3:
Gedicht aus d. Hölle, p. 62, l. 187: 'And that was thorow *Evys rede*
And þe *deuyll of helle*, wele y wott.'
Ipotis, D, l. 276 (*Adam speaks*): 'The *woman tysed* me þertylle.'
l. 280 (*Eve speaks*): 'Lord, *the edder* .. gart me with gylle.'
Pers. Tale, l. 655:
'The *fend* tempted *Eve*'; '*Adam consented* to the eting of the fruit.'

Eue : greue: The same rime is extant *Handl. Syn.*, l. 140; *P. Morale: eue : ileue*, l. 174; *Eue : leue, Pricke of C.*, l. 492.
l. 230. *dede:* 'committed.' *gan:* paraphrastic, to be omitted in translation.
l. 232. *pylt:* supplied from A_2. D reads *put*, H_2 *pylte*, R *pilte*; cf. l. 888; A_1 has *ipult*, A_2 *plyte*, D *pute*, H_1 *Ipylt*. The prefix *i-* of the participle is not demanded by the rhythm. For the combination *pult* + *paradys*, or *pyne*, see as follows:

Langl., B XV, l. 62: '*Pulte* out of *paradys*.'
Horn, l. 129: 'heo weren *ipult* ut of *paradise*.'
Adam and Eve, l. 123: '*Pulte out of paradys*.'
Langl., B XI, l. 157: '*Pulte* oute of *pyne*.'
Langl., B VIII, l. 96: 'to *pulte* adown the wikked.'

See further *Sir Beues*, A, l. 875; *Ancr. Riwle*, p. 366: 'hit wule *pulten* on him'; *Rel. Antiq.*, pp. 11, 244: 'to deþe .. *pulte*'; *Wm. of Palerne*, l. 381: '*pult* hire in hope to haue'; *K. Horn*, l. 1457: 'aʒen hire *pelte*'; *O.E. Homilies*, p. 197: 'hire oþer eare *pilteð* hire tail þerinne'; Halliwell, *Ashm. MS.* 61: 'I shalle hym *pelte*.' The modern English form is found in Bryant's *Cloud on the Way*, l. 18:

'Pleasantly between the *pelting* showers,' etc.

See other versions of the ever popular history of Adam's fall:

Ipotis, l. 547: '. . wer *dampned into helle*.'

Chaucer, *Monkes Tale*, l. 3203: 'Was *driue out* of his heih prosperitee
To labour, and to helle, and to meschaunce.'

Pard. Tale, l. 505: 'Adam our fader, and his wyf also,
Fro Paradys to labour and to wo
Were driuen.'

l. 511: '. . he was *out cast* to wo and peyne.'

Pers. Tale, l. 628: 'Adam . . *must nedes die*.'

l. 233. *Boxomere:* Cf. *Vnboxomnesse*, l. 231; *Paradise Lost*, II. l. 842: *buxom air*, also *Faerie Queene*, I. 11; IX. 37, 6; *Shep. Cal.*, *Sept.*, l. 149: 'they nould be *buxom* and bent.' *L'Allegro*, l. 24; *The Deluge*, l. 237: 'Adam in obedyent · ordaynt to blysse;' Ch. *Monkes Tale*, l. 3202: 'Adam . . for *misgouernaunce*.'

Tundale, l. 1861: 'That for goddis love wer *buxsum*.'

l. 1911: 'The whyche wer to god *luxsum* ay.'

l. 234. *him:* dat., indirect object.

l. 235. *lore: lore, instruction*, in sense of *persuasion*, as used by Kölbing, *Sir Beues*, M, l. 1386.

l. 237. *fredom:* freedom with added sense of privileges; also *Hom.*, ed. Morris, First Series, p. 41, l. 2.

was binomen him al: 'was taken away entirely,' he was deprived of. See O.E. *beniman*, governing the genitive. Cf. *al agon*, *Leg. of G. W.*, l. 1766; *al to-shake*, l. 1765.

l. 238. *put:* Supply *he was* for the sense. 'He was thrown into servitude.'

Page 13. l. 239. *one:* Read probably *only*, to agree with five MSS. For *one* see 'Introduction' under 'Inflection.'

l. 240. The same material is found in other texts:

Ipotis, D, l. 305: 'Thus Adam levedde in erthe here
. . . .
When he was dede, into helle nome
And alle, þat ever of hym come.'

Poema Morale, l. 173: '*Eælle ða isprungen beoð óf adam end of éue*.'

l. 196: '*eal his óf spring efter him*.'

l. 241. *gile:* 'beguiled' in the Bible, 2 *Cor.* xi. 3. See M.E. texts:

Ipotis, D, l. 343: 'But telle me, child, hit an þou can
Wharewith þe fend *begyled* man.'

Orrm., l. 1412: 'Forrluren ec forr heore *gillt*.'

The Deluge, l. 241: '. . . . . an apple
þat enpoysened alle pepleȝ.'

ll. 242, 243. *pite* . . *loue*: *Isaiah* lxiii. 9: 'In his *love* and in his *pity* he redeemed them.' Compare *Piers Plowman*:

A I, l. 141: 'He lokede on vs *with loue* · and lette his sone dye.'

l. 145: '*To haue pite* on þat peple, þat pynede him to deþe.'

l. 244. *man:* in general sense 'people.' See plural pronoun *hem*, lines 247, 248.

ll. 244, 245. See other texts as follows:

Orrm., l. 183 (l. 187 f.): 'þurrh þatt he comm to manne & þurrh
þatt he warrþ mann onn erþe.'

l. 1360: 'forr Crist iss baþe Godd & mann.'

Ipotis, l. 331: 'Godys sonne *wente in erþe* here.'

l. 245. *To sauue man:* See *Orrm.*, l. 1384: 'Forr uss to clennsenn þurrh hiss dæþ off sinness unnclænnesse.'

ll. 248, 249. See 1 *Cor.* xv. 3, and M.E. texts explaining *pine*, i. e. the penalty assumed in l. 246:

Orrm., l. 199: '. . . he ȝaff hiss aȝhenn lif
. . . . . .
to þoleun *dæþ o rodetre.*'

Pref., l. 31: 'forr þatt he *swallt o rodetre.*'
l. 9: 'forr Crist toc *dæþ o rodetre.*'

Ipotis, B, l. 335: 'He suffred *deth for oure gode.*'
D, l. 319: 'And dede hym *upon þe rode*
And bouȝt ous with his swet blode.'

Poema Morale (Jesus MS.), l. 187:
'Vre alre louerd for vs þrelles, ipyned wes *on rode.*'

Þe W. of u. Lauerd, l. 115: 'Nu deies mi lef for me *upo þe deore rode.*'
l. 120: 'cleues tat herte, and cumes flowinde ut of þat wide
wunde þe blod, þat me bohte.'

Pearl, str. 54, l. 9: 'Bot ther on-com a bote as tyt;
Riche blod *ran on rode* so roghe,
As wynne water . . . .'

Polit. Songs, p. 257: 'And for us *don on rode*
His swete herte blod he let.'

Orrm., l. 1368: 'þær Crist wass *uppo rodetreo*
naȝȝledd *forr ure nede.*'
,, l. 1374: 'drannc dæþess *drinnch o rodetreo*
forr ure woȝhe dedess.'

l. 248. *on:* Read *opon*, if five MSS. be authority for the correction.

ll. 248—250. See 1 *Cor.* xv. 4; *Luke* xxiv. 46. This material is drawn on freely in M.E. literature. The substance of this passage is to be traced in some form in most of the *Mass Books* and *Prayer Books* of the period.

The fundamental *Credo* is formulated by Michel in the *Aȝenbite*, l. 4: 'ynayled a rode . dyad . and be-bered . yede doun to helle. þane þriddo day aros uram þe dyade. Steaȝ to heuenes · zit aþe riȝt half of god þe uader al miȝti. þannes to comene he is to deme þe quike and þe dyade . . .'

ll. 249—257. *Ibiried he was:* Compare *Lay Folks Mass Book*, ed. Simmons, ll. 217 ff.:

Mass Book, l. 217: '. . . . . . deed he was,
layde in his graue,
þo soule of him went into helle
þo sothe to say;
Vp he rose in flesshe & felle
þo þyrd day.
He stegh til heuen with woundis wide,
thurgh his brouste;
Now sittes opon his fader right syde
In mageste.
Þeþ shal he come vs alle to deme.'

A Bestiary, l. 40: 'Do ure drigten ded was,
. . . . .
In a ston stille he lai
til it cam ðe ðridde dai
. . . . .
. . he ros fro dede ðo,
vs to lif holden.'

ll. 250, 251. See 1 Cor. xv. 4; *Homilies of Wulfstan* (ed. Napier), p. 105, and M.E. texts:

  Orrm., l. 167: '& off þatt he wisslike ras
    þe þridde daȝȝ off dæþe.'
  l. 215: 'Þurrh þatt he ras forr ure god
    þe þridde daȝȝ off dæþe.'

Þe *W. of u. Lauerd*, l. 130: 'his ariste þe þridde dei þer after.'

l. 253. *Steih*: See contrasting term *lihten adoun*, l. 261. *steih* occurs in this connection in many of the texts collected in the *Reliquiæ Antiquæ*, e.g. II., p. 23: '*stegh intil hevene, sitis on is fader richt hand*'; p. 38: '*steyet up to hevene*'; p. 42: '*steaȝ to hevenes*'; p. 57: '*steih into hevene*.'

 Ipotis, l. 345: 'And *styed to hevene*, þer he is kynge;
   On hys fader ryghte hond he set hym þan.'

Ancr. R., p. 250: 'he *steih* up to heouene.'
Faerie Queene, I. xi. 25, l. 8:
  'Thought with his wings *to stye* above the ground.'

 Orrm., l. 19,881: '. . . . . . *to stiȝhenn upp*
   To brukenn *heffness blisse*.'
 Orrm., l. 169: '& off þatt *he* wisslike *stah*,
   Þa siþþenn upp *till heffne*.'
  l. 233: 'Þurrh þatt *he stah* forr ure god.'

Spenser and Shakspere use *stye*; the *Ancr. R.*, pp. 19, 248, 250, *steih*; the *York Plays*, p. 424, l. 85: *stigh*.

l. 254. *mihtĕ* : *sihtĕ*: See Skeat, *Leg. of G. W.*, note to l. 50.

l. 257. *Rom.* xiv. 10, and M.E. texts:

 Orrm., l. 171: '& off þatt he shall cumenn efft
   to demenn alle þede.'
  l. 247: 'Þurrh þatt he shall o *Domess daȝȝ*
   uss gifenn heffness blisse.'

Poema Morale, l. 190: 'We ne þencheþ nouht þat *he schal deme* þe quyke . . .'

 Ipotis, l. 349: 'Schal come at þe day of iugement,
   To demen . . . .'

Rel. Ant., p. 38: 'he þon sal cume *to deme* þe quike an þe dede.'
Hymn on Nativ., l. 164: 'The dreadful judge shall *spread his throne*.'

l. 259. *woned*: Read *wŏned*. *woned* is not authorized by the MSS. A₂DH₁H₂R, all having *wont*. See *Prothal.*, l. 139: '*wont* to dwell'; *Hymn on the Nativ.*, l. 10: '*wont* . . To sit'; 1 *Henry VI.*, I. ii. 14: '*wont* to fear'; *Shep. Cal. Apr.*, l. 16: '*wonted* songs.' Cf. *wone*, subst., l. 106: '*custom*.' l. 259 illustrates type C.

ll. 260, 262. The same similes occur in substance in *The Second Nonnes Tale*, ll. 198, 199:

   'Ful *lyk a fiers leoun* she sendeth here,
   As *meke as euer was any lomb*, to yow!'
 l. 260: '*Meke as a lomb.*'

The figure is common property among the poets.

 P. Pl., A vi., l. 43: 'He is as *louh as A lomb*, louelich of Speche.'
 R. of Gl., l. 1321: 'þat in time worre *as a lomb* is boþe *mek* and milde.'.
 Rel. Ant., p. 243: 'Cryst com as *mocklyche as a lom*,
   He habbe for ȝou dethes dom.'
 Shep. Cal. July, l. 129: 'And *meek* he was, as meek mought be,
   Simple as simple sheep.'
 Hymn, Herebert, l. 1: 'Crist ycleped *hevene lomb*.'
 M. of L. T., l. 459: 'The *whyte lomb*, that hurt was with the spere.'

The comparison is based on Scriptural passages. The meekness of the lamb at sacrifice, Christ the lamb sacrificed, are suggested in *Isaiah* liii. 7 :

> 'He was oppressed,
> Yet he humbled not himself,
> And opened not his mouth ;
> *As a lamb that is led to the slaughter,*
> And as a sheep that before her shearers *is dumb ;*
> Yea, he opened not his mouth.'

Biblical references to Christ the lamb are as follows: *John* i. 29, 36 ; 1 *Pet.* i. 19 ; *Rev.* v. 6 and 12 ; xii. 11 ; xxii. 1 ; xiii. 8 ; the last, xiii. 8, recalling modern hymnology :

> 'Shout to the throne,
> Worthy the lamb.'

The graceful application of Biblical texts is to be noted in *Pearl*, str. 62 ff. ; the simile of the *Speculum* occurs str. 68, l. 11 :

> 'As *meke as lomb* that no playnt tolde,
> For uus he swalt in Jherusalem.'

The omission of the article recalls the reading of MSS. H_1H_2R of the *Speculum :*

> *Orrm.*, l. 1308 : '*wiþþ lamb* þu lakesst tin Drihhtin
> gastlike in þine þæwess.'
>
> l. 1312 : 'Forr *lamb* iss soffte & stille deor,
> & *meoc*, & milde, & lipe.'
>
> *M. of L. T.*, l. 617 : 'For as the lomb toward his deth is brought,
> So staut this Innocent bifore the king.'

l. 261. *lihten adoun :* 'alight,' completing the antithesis begun, l. 253. Cf. *Ancr. Riwle*, p. 248 : fol. 66 : '*alihte adun* to helle' ; and Pope, *Odys.*, xvii., l. 365.

An A. B. C., l. 161 : 'Xristus, thy sone, that in this world *alighte*.'

A Bestiary, ll. 29 ff. : 'vre louerd . . . . .
. . . . .
> wu ðo him likede
> to *ligten her on erðe*,
> Migte neure diuel witen,
> ðog he be derne hunte,
> hu he dun come.'

Orrm., l. 1398 : 'Forr whatt tc33 fellenn sone dun
off heoffne unntill helle.'

A pleonastic *doun* occurs with *lihten* in the colloquial language of the period.

Sir Fyr., l. 1122 : 'Bruillant . . . liȝte adoun.'
Squieres Tale, l. 169 : '*doun he lyghte*.'
Leg. of G. W., l. 1713 : '*doun they lighte*.'
H. of Fame, l. 508 : '*dounward* gan hit *lighte*.'
M. of L. T., l. 1104 : '*she lyghte doun*.'
King Horn, l. 519 : 'Horn *adun liȝte*.'
Beues, M, l. 3948 : '. . . light *adown*,
. . . *down lightyng*.'

Read l. 261 : 'Þéder he wóle · líhten adoún.'

l. 262. *sterne as a lioun :* as that of l. 260, a common figure illustrating the popularity of the simile in M.E., particularly such as 'move within narrow limit.' See Kölbing's note to *Sir Beues*, M, l. 772, and *Sir Orfeo*, p. 19.

Orrm., 1. 5978: 'He wass *tacnedd þurrh þe leo*.'
N. P. Tale, 1. 358: 'He *loketh*, as it were, *a grim lioun*.'
Gamelyn, 1. 125: 'he *loked as a wilde lyoun*.'
See *Bestiary*, before 1250, *Natura leonis, Significacio prime nature*, ll. 27 ff.:

> 'Welle heg is tat hil,
> ðat is heuen-riche,
> vre louerd is *te leun*,
> ðe liueð ðer abuuen.'

lioun: the most common orthography in M.E. according to Sturmfels, *Anglia* viii., p. 252. Auch. *Guy* has *lyoun*, 1. 3960; Caius *Guy, lyon*, 1. 4054.

Wraþful: Epithet ordinarily applied in figure to the lion. See Marlowe's *Faustus* in the 'examination of' the 'seven deadly sins,' sc. 6, l. 130: '*I am Wrath . . . I leapt out of a lion's mouth*,' etc.

Page 14. 1. 264. 2 *Corinth.*, v. 10: '*according to that he hath done*,' . . . (1. 265) 'every one may receive'; *Rev.* xx. 12: 'The dead were judged . . . *according to their works*'; v. 13: 'judged every *man* according to their works'; *Matt.* xvi. 27; *Rom.* ii. 6; *Rev.* ii. 23; xxii. 12.

ll. 264—266. *Poema Morale*, ll. 174—178:

> 'ealle hi sculen ðuder cume · for soðe wé hit ileue.
> þa ðe habbeð wel idon · efter heore mihte.
> to heuenriche scule faren forð mid ure drihte.
> þá ðe nabbeð god idón · end ðer inne beoð ifunde.
> hi sculen falle swiðe raðe in to helle grunde.'

Orrm., 1. 173: '& forr to ȝeldenn iwhille mann
     after hiss aȝhenn dede.'

Ipotis, 1. 350: 'to demen men *after here dedes*.'

ll. 266—274 recall *Gal*. vi. 7, 8.

l. 266. *turment:* MSS. DH$_2$ have *tournement*, to be attributed to the scribe of the text employed by copyists of *D* and *H$_2$*. A similar transposition is noted by Dr. Leonard in the Rawlinson MS. 118 of a poem *Aus der Hölle*, l. 105, where *tornament* is introduced instead of *turment*. See Dr. Leonard's note with reference to other instances, *Eng. Stud.*, vol. I., p. 118, 1. 390; p. 120, 1. 574. The confusion seems not uncommon. In *Cot. Cal. MS.* A II of the M.E. *Tundale*, *turnement* is supplied for *turment*, ll. 547, 1035, 1061, 1683. The error is readily explained as resulting from similarity in the form of the words. The meaning of *turment* is transferred to *tournement*.

l. 267. *onne take:* The most plausible interpretation of this interesting passage seems to be: 'What responsibility shall they assume,' i. e. *take on*, etc. Compare definitions for *take on* in the *Century Dictionary* and in Ogilvie's *Imperial Dictionary*, vol. iv., p. 299: '*to undertake the responsibility*.' See *Matt.* viii. 17: '*Himself took our infirmities*'; also *Rom. of Rose*, 1. 6107 and *Meas. for Meas.*, IV. ii. 10: 'If you will *take it on* you to assist him,' *i. e.* 'undertake.' Five MSS. modify the verse, introducing *how* instead of *what:* '*How shall they take on?*' to be rendered 'How shall they begin' (?) or *appear* (?). The beauty of this reading is marred by the suggestion of the modern colloquialism '*how . . take on*,' 'make a fuss over.' The vulgarism is not in keeping with the dignity of the poem. The modern 'take on' was used by Shakspere, but in connection with emotion of hysterical, sentimental, or humorous character. *The Merry Wives*, III. v. 40: 'She does so *take on* with her men'; also IV. ii. 22: 'he so *takes on* . . with my husband, so rails against,' etc.; *III Hen. VI.*, II. v. 104: 'How will my mother *take on* with me,' etc.,

'How will my wife .. shed seas of tears.' The meaning 'to be furious' is given by Alisaunder Schmidt at the conclusion of the discussion of *take*, *Shaks.-lexicon*, p. 1178, col. 2. See Halliwell, *Dict.* under *sterakelt*; *Volpone*, vi. The following illustrations have been contributed by Prof. Schick, suggesting the meaning 'How they behave themselves.'
Comedy of Errors, V. i. 242 : 'this pernicious slave took on him as a conjurer,'
    i. e. played the deceiver.
Mids. N. Dream, III. 2258 : 'take on, as you would follow .. yet come not':
    behave as if you would follow.

Various interpretations are thus placed before the reader, permitting the freedom of individual judgment. The MSS. are undoubtedly authority for the reading 'How .. on take,' but MS. A_1 in 'what .. onne take,' fulfils the conditions formulated by Sachse, see below. Shakspere lexicons contain numerous illustrations of the poet's use of *take on*. See also *Heb.* ii. 16; *Times' Whistle*, p. 24 ; and *The Bruce*, xii., l. 446 :
    'And quhen the king of England
    Saw the Scottis so *tak on hand*.'

onne: The inorganic -*e*, explained by Sachse, *Das unorganische e im Orrmulum*, pp. 61, 62, is peculiar to Orrm. It occurs in *onne*, according to Sachse, when the object of the preposition is a relative, as in MS. A_1 of the *Speculum*. *onne* is then written near the close of the sentence. The same law holds good for *in*, *of*, and *on*. See illustrations as follows :
    l. 6960 : 'þatt he wass *onne* i Beþþlecem.'
    l. 3752 : 'þatt hirdess wokenn o þatt nahht
        þatt Crist wass borenn *onne*.'
    l. 14,802 : '. . . . . þe sand
        All harrd to ganngen *onne*.'

Onne is not to be found in O.E. Inorganic -*e* is evidently added through analogy to *inne* and *uppe*, abundant in O.E. See *Havelok*, l. 341, '*onne* ride'; '*onne* handes leyde,' l. 1942.

l. 268. *here*: inserted for the sake of the metre at the suggestion of Professor Schick.

l. 269. *fleschly*: *fleshes* is to be rejected. It stands only in MS. A_1. Five MSS. have *fleschly*.

l. 270. *wolde*: 'were willing,' 'wished,' as in l. 268: 'They wished to forsake their Lord here on earth.' Note in contrast the force of l. 272, supported by l. 271. Individual consent, freedom in choice referred to ll. 216, 218, is no longer in question. A decisive judgment condemns to eternal torment.

l. 272. *wolen . . . nelle*: See Kölbing's note to *Sir Beues*, A, l. 3132.

l. 273. *bileuen*: -*n* is preserved as in case of *wolen*, l. 272, to preserve smoothness of metre and to prevent hiatus. Here as in the O.E. construction the present tense is used with the force of the future.

l. 274. *as*: introduced for metre at the suggestion of Prof. Schick. MSS. $A_1 A_2$ have *also*, H_1 *als*.

do: See l. 208 ; 'enter into,' 'experience.' *men*: 'people,' the human being.

l. 275. *Seint Austin*: i. e. Augustine favourite authority of Alcuin, and quoted in the *Speculum* by name, line 171.

l. 276. *ful*: authorized by four MSS. $A_1 R$ preserve the archaic verse, omitting the unstressed syllable in the fourth measure.
    'Ánd seiþ wórdes // réu · líche.'
Latin: MS. A_1 has: habent ... & ... See *Rev.* ix. 6.

l. 278. *point of death*: 'moment of death.' *point of death* is the language of the *Bible*, *John* iv. 47; *Mark* v. 23; *the point to die*, *Gen.* xxv. 32; *point of dawn*, *Hymn on the Nativity*, l. 86; *Richard the Redeless*, III. l. 142: '*in pointe ffor* to wepe.'

l. 279. *Rev.* ix. 6: '*shall desire to die.*'

ll. 279, 280. *Macbeth* IV. iii. l. 111: 'Died every day she lived,' etc.; *Apophthegms*, *Theological Remains of the Royal Martyr King Charles I., of Ever Blessed Memory*, p. 66: '*to die daily*,' in 'Conquering by a lively faith and patient hope those partial and quotidian *Deaths*, which kill us as it were by piecemeals.'

l. 279. *wilnen:* See *Pers. Tale*, l. 341: 'They shul folow deth, and they shul not finde him, and they shall *desire to die*, and deth shul flee from hem.'

l. 280. *ende of deþ:* the immediate crisis of physical death, the absolute death of the body, the end of life, explained *Ipotis*, l. 465: 'Or þe soule may partyn wythonne.' *ende*, subst. and vb., occurs frequently in M.E. texts, meaning 'death' or 'to die, as in ll. 278 and 492.

    Orrm., l. 19,325: '*ȝiff þatt himm likeþþ* ure lif
                    & ure *lifess ende.*'
     „   l. 3257: 'Att ure *lifes ende.*'
    Orrm., l. 8347: 'Affterr tatt Herode king
                    Was *endedd* inn hiss sinne.'
     „   l. 3254: 'uss ... *endenn* ure *lif.*'
     „   l. 17,465: '... he maȝȝ *endenn* hiss *lif*
                    Inn alle gode dedess.'
     „   l. 5033: 'sen *ifell ende.*'
    Rbt. of Gl., l. 1538: 'to his *ende* was *ido.*'
    Wohunge of u. L., l. 70:
       'bifore þin *ending* .... swa sare þat reade blod þu swattes for as.'
    Seven Sages (ed. Wright), V., l. 514 f.:
                'And ledis ȝe hym thare thyfys hyng
                Anon that he have hys *endyng.*'

l. 281. *duire:* Chaucer uses *dure* in rime with *assure*, etc. See Crome, *Rhyme Index to the Ellesmere Manuscript*, and *Tale of Man of Lawe*, l. 189: 'whyl his lyf may *dure*': (cure).

l. 284. *muryere:* Probably a copyist's error is preserved in A_1: *murszere. wole:* supplied from MSS. representing two groups.

Page 15, l. 286. *ioyes of paradys:* Compare with these lines other mediæval descriptions of paradise, notably that of the *Poema Morale*, *The Phoenix*, and *Sólar ljóð*, the Icelandic ideal of heaven. See *St. Patrick's Purgatory*, p. 59; *Sawles Ward*, pp. 259 ff.

l. 289. *baylie:* O.F. *baillie*, 'jurisdiction,' the word accented on its second syllable to rime with *clergye*. See Gollancz's note to *Pearl*, str. 37, l. 10. As in *Pearl* the word is not to be confused with *bayly*, 'fortress,' as is indicated here by the added *-e* : *baylie.*

l. 290. *wit of clergye:* 'the understanding of all science.'

l. 292. *tellen:* *-n* is added for metre to avoid hiatus or the omission of the unstressed syllable in the fourth measure.

l. 296. *on eorþe here:* See note to l. 375.

ll. 295, 296. *Colossians* iii. 24 is recalled here.

l. 297. *parten hence:* 'depart hence,' as affirmed by MS. A_2. Compare *parting day*, l. 1 of Gray's *Elegy* (written in a country churchyard), and *parting soul*, l. 89: *parting Genius, Hymn on Nativity*, l. 186; and *henne wende*, *Poema Morale*, l. 396.

l. 299 ff. Suggest Hampole's description of heaven, *The Pricke of Conscience*, ll. 7814 ff.:

    ' Þare es ay lyfe withouten dede ;
     Þare es yhowthe ay withouten elde,
 l. 7817 : Þare es rest ay, withouten trauayle.
 l. 7819 : Þare es pese ay, withouten stryf ;
 l. 7821 : Þare es, withouten myrknes, lyght ;
     Þare es ay day and neuer nyght,
     Þare es ay somer fulle bryght to se,
     And neuer mare wynter in þat contre.'

See also *The Phœnix*, ll. 50 ff.:

    ' Nis þær on þām londe lāðgeniðla,
    ne wôp ne wracu, weatâcen nân
    yldu ne ynnðu, ne se enga dēað,
    ne lifes lyre, ne lâþes cyme,
    ne synn ne sacu, ne sâr wracu.' . . .

These recall the *Poema Morale*, ll. 369 ff.:

 l. 369 : ' Þer is wéle ábute gane · end reste abuten swincho '
 l. 371 : ' Þer is blisse a buten treȝe · and lif a buten deaþe.'
 l. 373 : ' Þer is ȝeoȝeðe bute ulde · and hele a buten vn helðe.
    nis þer so(re) we ne sor · ne neure man vn sealþe.'

ll. 302, 304. *riht* . . . *trewe loue:* 'unvarying justice,' 'ever faithful love.'

 feintise: 'dissimulation,' 'feigning,' explained by Lydgate in the words of l. 1971 of the *Rom. of the Rose*, and in distinction from the use of *P. Pl.* See below :

  Compleynt, l. 477 : ' With oute *feynynge or feyntyse.*'
(also *Rom. of R.*, l. 1971.)

P. Pl., A. V. l. 5 : ' Er I a Furlong hedde I fare A Feyntise me hente,
    Forþer mihti not afote · for defaute of Sleep.'

 l. 303. Intelligence, and skill, and knowledge.

  kunning: *T. of Gl.*, l. 538 :
     'And eke I want *kunnyng* to deuyse.'

Spiritus Guidonis, l. 3 : '. . . men grete nede may wyn
    and nameli clerkes þat can of lare
    if þai þaire *cunyng* will declare.'

Wm. of Palerne, l. 120 : ' Of *coninge* of wicche-craft · wel y nouȝ ȝhe couȝde.'

And Marlowe's Faustus, the first Chorus, l. 20 :
    'Till swoln with *cunning* . . . .
    His waxen wings did mount above his reach.'

See Skeat's note, *Leg. of G. W.*, l. 68 ; *Psalm* cxxxvii. 5.

 l. 305. *Streinþe*: interesting form, *ei* marking the intermediate stage in the transition of *e* to *i* before *n* + a consonant. The interrupted growth is to be noted in *Horn*, l. 1169, and in *strenþede*, Böddeker, *Ae. Dichtungen*, p. 257. See Stratmann. The transition is completed in *Bruce*, but see *Octovian*, *strenþe*; *Poema Morale*, *strenþe*; but *strynth* < O.E. *strengð* in the *Bruce*, l. 87, p. 106 of Zupitza's *Übsbuch*. The transition is not marked in N.E. as in *string* < O.E. *streng*, in the N.E. pronunciation of *England*, or in Old Norse words of the same nature. See Noreen, *Grammatik*, § 143 *Anm.*, and the list of illustrations collected by Dr. Leonard in *Zwei me. Geschichten aus d. Hölle*, p. 69, and in Wilda's dissertation, *Über die ört. Verbr. d. Schweifr.-Strophe in Engl.* See other forms illustrating the history of *e* + *i* before *n* + consonant : *Lib. Disc.*, l. 338, *flyng* (Icel. *flengja*) ; *Emare*, l. 794 : *unhende kynge.*

 Pr. of C., l. 675 :   'springes,
    . . . hares, þat on þe heued *hynges.*'

Cursor Mundi, l. 291 : 'And sagh a frut þar on *hingand.*' (See *Flight into Egypt.*)
Woh. of u. L., l. 17 : 'swa rewliche *hengedes* on rode.'
,, ,, l. 55 : 'he *henges* bituhhen,' etc. (See ll. 53, 63.)
,, ,, l. 111 : '*henges* o rode.'
Havelok, l. 43 : 'And heye *hengen* on galwe tre.'

l. 306. *þisternesse:* suggesting *Eph.* v. 8 and 13; *liht widoute þisternesse* = 'everlasting light,' *Isaiah* lx. 19, *i. e.* 'uninterrupted light'; 'one day... at evening song time ... light,' *Zechariah* xiv. 7; 'There shall be no night there,' *Revelation* xxi. 25; xxii. 5; *þisternesse* = 'thickness '?, *Zech.* xiv. 6. See *Poema Morale*, l. 366 : 'dei a buten nihte'; and l. 378 : 'ði nabbed hi nouht iliche · alle of godes *lihte.*'

l. 308. *For:* inserted on authority of five MSS., producing type A instead of type D.

Page 16, l. 311. *Poema Morale*, l. 66 : 'þe ðe mare hefð end ðe þe lesso · þaðe mei iliche.'

l. 313. *woniȝing:* 'dwelling-place,' as in 2 *Corinthians* v. 1 : 'An house not made with hands, eternal in the heavens,' suggestive also of *John* xiv. 2.

l. 314. *his ... deseruing: Poema Morale*, l. 63 :

'þer me sceal ure weorkes we ȝen, be foren heue kinge.
end ȝieuen us ure swinches lien œfter ure earninge.'

l. 319. *in al þi miht:* ll. 134, 253, 515. See *Schmirgel*, p. xlvii.

ll. 324, 325. *charite ... hext: Col.* iii. 14 : '*Charity the bond of perfectness.*' Charity here is 'love,' distinguished from charity, ll. 95, 936, '*benevolence*,' 'almsdede' :

Orrm, l. 2998 : 'Godess Gast iss *kariteþ.*'
Pearl, str. 40, l. 2 : 'And *charyte grete* be yow among.'

hext : next: See *Two Noble Kinsmen*, III. ii. 33 : 'The *best* way is the *next* way to a grave.'

l. 327. *what:* supplied from four MSS. for the context.

ll. 328, 329. Compare the Vulgate text, *Luke* x. 27 : *Diliges Dominum Deum tuum toto corde tuo, ex tota anima tua, et ex omnibus viribus tuis.* Also *Poema Morale*, l. 305 : '*Luuie we god mid ure heorte · end mid al ure mihte.*'

ll. 333, 334. *Matt.* xix. 19 : '*Diliges proximum tuum sicut teipsum,*' of the Vulgate text; *Poema Morale.*

ll. 329, 334. See 1 *John* iii. 10 and 23 ; *Poema Morale*, ll. 305 f.:

'Luuie we god mid ure heorte . end mid al ure mihte.
end ure émcristen eal us sulf . swa us lerde drihte.'

See the old poem *On the king's Breaking his Confirmation of Magna Charter*, p. 256, *Polit. Songs* :

'Love clepeth ech man brother.'

l. 334. *emcristene:* Assimilation from *cristene*, in works of the 12th and 13th centuries in MSS. of the South and West. Cf. M.E. texts: *Poema Morale*, l. 306, 'and ure *emcristene* eal us sulf'; Second series of homilies : 'To luuien god and al his *emcristen;*' p. 5; 'bicherð his *emcristen*'; 'here *emcristen* bicharen,' p. 193; 'and his *emcristen* also himseluen,' p. 54 ; '*Vre emcristene* ben alle þo þe hered ore Louerd,' p. 9; 'togenes ure *emcristene,*' p. 63; *emcristen* occurs in the *Aȝenbite* (dating 1340): 'þou sselt zigge non ualse wytnesse aye þine *emcristene,*' l. 10; 'Hou þat god deleþ his *emcristen*, he ys acorsed of god,' p. 66. See First Series of *Homilies, Sermo* cxxiv. 6, p. 157, l. 6. *Emcristen* is used by Langland, and thus its history is traced chronologically to 1362.

Even cristen occurs in the later MSS. of the *Speculum*. From the time of *Piers. Pl.*, 1362, the full forms *efen (euen) cristene* are abundant.

Euencristene may be dated at least so early as 1320 through the *Castel of Loue*, l. 976. See the *Persones Tale*, l. 855; Wiclif (1380); Sir Thomas More, p. 83: 'Proudly judging the lives of their *even Christians*,' and p. 277, 'And where thei men not fihte ... against their *even christen*';

Ipotis, l. 1. 522: 'And wolde helpyn al oþere,
Hys *evenne* cristen, þat ben þowere.'

The word is no longer to be found after its famous appearance in *Hamlet*, V. i. 27. The readings of the first folio and of the first quarto are identical. 'And the more pitty, that great folke should haue countenance in this world to drown or hang themselves more than *their euen Christian*.' The passage stands in the first quarto, l. 25:

'Mary more's the pitty, that great folke
Should haue more authorite to hang or drown
Themselues, more than other people.'

Efen abounds in compounds of this period: *Hom.* I. p. 175; *efennextu*, Wiclif, *Phil.* ii. 25; '*euene knyght*,' *Phil.* ii.; '*euen discipilis*,' *John* ii. 16: '*euen seruant*,' *Apoc.* xix. 10; *Matt.* xviii. 29; *efenneche*, 'coeternal,' *efennmete*, 'commensurate'; *efenrike*, 'equal in power,' etc. *Prompt. Parv.* has *Evynhoode*, 'equality'; *Evenholde*, 'of equal age.'

Page 17, l. 336. *Wher:* here the conjunction, 'whether or not'; see note to line 219 of the *Speculum*.

l. 338. *wolt:* introduced from four MSS. H_2 is without weight in textual arrangement. *must* in A_1 is probably the scribe's error.

Latin: 1 *John* iv. 20. 'For he that loveth not his brother, whom he hath seen, how can he love God whom he hath not seen?' Cf. also 1 *Peter* 1. 8: 'Whom having not seen, ye love.' MS. A_1 reads: '... proximum tuum ... deum qu[em] ... quomodo potes dilegere.'

Compare *O. E. Homilies* 1, p. 100: 'þe þat ne lufeþ his broþer, þene þat he isihð, hu mei he lufian God, þene þat he ne isihð licomlice.'

l. 339. *seiþ soþ:* See *Rbt. of Gl.*, ll. 713, 720, 2734, 3046, 6261, 6368, 6414, 6420.

witte: dative in -e regularly formed according to the inflectional characteristics of the poem.

l. 341. *þyn emcristene:* See Latin text, l. 338, *proximum tuum*, 'brother,' in the scriptural foundation, and the reading of four MSS. The fifth contributes *nextbore*. For *emcristene* see note, line 334.

l. 342. *þou:* supplied for sense and metre: 'So that thou mayst see them every day.' It occurs in four MSS. The arrangement: *þat [þou] alday mait hem ise*, is supported by MSS. A_2R.

ll. 340—344. These lines recall *Leg. of G. W.*, B, ll. 14, 15:

'For ... thing is never the lasse soth,
Thogh every wight ne may hit nat ysee.'

l. 345. *Sein Powel:* The preacher evidently did not verify his reference. His text is to be ascribed to John, 1 *John* iv. 20, see reference above. Strangely enough H_2, whose mission it was to set things right, did not correct the error.

l. 347 ff. See 'Introduction' with Scriptural sources.

l. 347. *nost:* supplied from MS. D, and necessary to the sense according to all the MSS. The reading *noht* of A_1 could be interpreted as a scribal error for the poet's *not = ne wot*. A_1 could possibly have written *noht* (N.E. *not*) for *not* (*ne wot*) of other MSS. An instance of double thesis would then be eliminated, and type A would occur: *Abrahám him sáuh, ac þú not hóu*.

l. 348. *nowh:* inorganic final *-h* a peculiarity of MS. A₁. For *nost hou*, see Schick's note, *T. of Gl.*, l. 17.

l. 350. *as . . . hem:* are to be omitted on authority of three MSS., representatives from both groups.

Page 18, ll. 355 ff. Numerous illustrations of this comparison are to be found in the 'Introduction' under 'Sources.' Cf. *Cal., July*, l. 157 ff.:

'Sike one . . . Moses was,
That saw his Maker's face,
His face more clear than crystal glass,
And spake to him in place.'

ll. 356, 359. *on fire:* See Koch, *Historische Grammatik der englischen Sprache*, II, p. 377, l. 7. *al on fire:* Spenser's *Prothol.*, l. 56: *all in haste; Hymn on the Nativity*, l. 207: *all of blackest hue; Il Pens.*, l. 33: *All in a robe*, etc.

l. 358. The *York Plays* (ed. L. T. Smith), pp. 47, 73, and the *Towneley Mysteries* (Surtees Society, 1836), pp. 55 ff., record the exact words of the dialogue between Moses and the Lord; see the mystery ascribed to the Hoseers, No. XI of the *York Plays*, No. 8 of the *Towneley*. *þe firste lawe:* naturally the ten commandments.

l. 361. Compare sc. 2, l. 92 of the eleventh *York Play:* 'Thus has god shewed his myght in me.'

Town. Myst. xxxvii, l. 86: 'To me, Moyses, *he shewed his myght.*'

l. 363. *bush: boys* in MS. D, the French expression for *bush*, mentioned in Halliwell's *Dictionary*. *boys* is defined in *Promptorium Parvulorum* as *scurrus*, 'a clump of bushes,' but according to the Hebrew term a single bush.

The significance of the bush as emblem of Mary seems suggested in the *Cal. Jul.*, l. 73, although Kirke explains 'Our Lady's bower' as 'a place of pleasure':

'Of Sinah can I tell thee more
And of our Lady's Bower.'

lenedi: See Pabst, *Lautlehre, Reim. Ch. Rbt. of Gl.* § 15.

l. 365. *clene:* MS. Bibl. *Bod. Jun.* 23, fol. 79: 'Ðurh *clæne mæden* Crist wearð ȝeboren'; *The Seconde N. Tale*, l. 225: 'With body *clene* and with vnwemmed thought . . .'; l. 47: 'and thou, virgin wemmeless' . . . 'mayden pure.' Cf. note to l. 367.

l. 366. *Ne:* required by five MSS.

l. 367. *wemme:* In the dialect of Norfolk *wem* (as explained by the *Prompt. Parv.*) 'is a small fretted place in a garment.' In figurative meaning *wem* is applied to religion. Cf. Wiclif, *Song of Sol.*, III. 7: 'My frendesse, thou art al faire, and *no wem is in thee*'; *James* i. 27: 'A *clene religion and vnwemmed*'; quoted in the *Ancren Riwle*, p. 10, fol. 2 b: '*cleane religiun wiðuten wem.*' The application to the Virgin is made by Chaucer, 2 *N. T.*, l. 47; *withouten wemme* is translated in the *Cursor Mundi*, l. 11,226, 'immaculate,' but in Hereford's version of *Psalm* xiv. 2, it represents N.E. 'uprightly' as in *Isa.* xxxiii. 15, and is equivalent to *wemles* in the same passage of the *North. Psalter.* See also Michel's *Sermon on Matt.* xxiv. 43, l. 149: *wyþoute wem:* 'uram alle heresye wy oute wem habbeþ yclenzed.'

Pearl, str. 19, l. 5: 'Bot a wonder perle *withouten wemme.*'

Ipotis, l. 556: 'Of þe mayde Mary, (also 315, 316 in D, 478, 479 B)
Withowten wem of hyr body.'

See *Pearl*, str. 62, l. 5: 'For hit is *wemlez*, clone and clere.'

See Kölbing's note to *Sir Beues*, E. l. 385: '*Wemme ne wunde.*'

l. 370.   *him :* necessary to sense and metre.
l. 371.   *noht alone :* Compare *Acts* xix. 26.
l. 372.   *imeind :* See *Ancr. R.*, p. 332: 'Auh hope and drede shulen euer beon *imeind* togederes.' The word is not uncommon, for instance: *Shep. Cal. Nov.*, l. 203: '. . . how bene thy verses *meint*,
      With doolful plesaunce . . . . .'
Owl and Night, l. 18: ' *Imeind* mid spire and grene segge.'
      l. 428: '*Imeind* bi toppes and bi here.'
Poema Morale, l. 144:
  'betere is wori weter í drunke · þene atter í *meng* mid wine.'
l. 374. See 1 *Tim.* vi. 16: 'Whom *no man hath seen* nor can see.' *St. John* i. 18; 1 *John* iv. 12: '*No man hath seen God* at any time'; *St. John* vi. 46. Cf. *Speculum*, l. 395 ff.

Page 19, l. 375. *on eorþe her :* a similar redundancy is found in *Rbt. of Gl.*: '*he in þis lond*,' ll. 866, 1694, 1833, 2165, 4097, 4836, 6674, etc. See *in erþe here, Ipotis*, ll. 318, 331, but *aboven erþe*, l. 413.

corþe : This orthography for *erþe* is also that of the poem *De Muliere Samaritana*, l. 1 ; *Alisaunder*, l. 3853; *Homily*, ed. Zup., *Uebsbuch*, p. 72, l. 9: *grið on eorðe*; *On god Ur. of U. Lefdi*, l. 159 ; '*on heouene and on eorðe*'; *Poema M*, l. 75, and *eorles*, l. 320, as in the *Speculum*, ll. 45, 50, 65; *Langl.* V. A. 18. *Merlin* preserves *earþ*, l. 1523.

Bodiliche : i. e. 'in human form,' 'in person.'
l. 376. *it is so cler : i. e.* 'it needs no proof,' 'it is evident,' 'not to be doubted.'
l. 381. *clene . . . cler :* The same tautology of alliterating adjectives occurs *Pearl*, 62⁵, *Rbt. of Gl.*, 180:
      'England is *so clene* and *so cler*.'
l. 6802: 'heo was so *clene* maide . . . of so *clene* liue.'
Mass Book, l. 3 (of Mass): 'graunt alle, þate hit shal here,
      of conscience be *clene & clerc*.'
      l. 7: '. . . *clene* in dede & þoght.'
      l. 10: 'with *clenc* herte & gode intent.'
l. 382. See *Hom., post Pascha*, ll. 66—8 and the following selections:
Poema Morale, l. 75: 'Heuene end eorðe he oue sihð . . . .
      Sunne . mone. . . . bið þustre to ȝeanes his lihte.'
See 2 *N. T.le*, l. 108: ' *The sonne and mone and sterres* euery weye.'
  Pearl, str. 88, l. 1: 'Of *sunne ne mone* had thay no nede;
      The self god wacz her lompe lyght.'
l. 387. *wonder :* intensive equivalent to 'exceedingly,' common as an adverb: *wonder sory, Gamelyn*, l. 732; *wonder grete, Tundale*, l. 573.
l. 388   *mannes :* 'human,' 'mortal.' See *Pearl*, str. 19, l. 7: 'A *mannes* dom,' and *Ipotis*, l. 464: '*mannys* body.' See Gollancz's note. Cf. *bodilich*, l. 396.
l. 391. *forsoþe . . . þe :* one idea is presented here as in Orrm's: 'þat witt þe *wel to soþe*,' as Prof. Kölbing kindly suggests.
l. 394. *siþe :* necessary for meaning and preferable to *tyme* of MS. H₁. See also *Shep. Cal. Jan.*
      str. 9, l. 1: 'A thousand *sithes* I curse that careful hour.'
      l. 3: '. . . . thousand *sithes* I bless the stoure.'
M. of L. T., l. 1155: 'She herieth god an *hundred thousand sythe*.'
l. 396. *bodiliche :* See *Ipotis*, B, l. 462: 'þat on deth is *bodylyche* here.'
l. 397. *godhede :* H₁ preserves what would seem to be the preferred meaning : 'in his godhede'; but the version of a single MS. in this connection is not sufficient reason for alteration of the verse.

Page 20, l. 398. *don þat dede:* The common Hebrew idiom linking a verb with its cognate noun. It is noted in the terse wisdom literature of the Book of Job; see *Job* iii. 25: 'I *feared a fear*, and it hath overtaken me.'

l. 400. *lered ... lewed:* Common linking of terms. *Sir Beues*, A. 4020: '*lewed .. lered*'; *Orrm.*, l. 967: '*to lœred, to lœwedd*'; *Tund.*, ll. 413, 593.

l. 403. *bi my leaute: lytylle feythe* in *Prompt. Parv.* under *lewte*. See *Polit. Song of The Reign of Ed. I.*, l. 1, also *Song on the Flem. Insurrection*, p. 192; '*by ȝour lewte*,' *Gamelyn*, l. 657; '*bi mi leaute*,' *Rich. of Almaigne*, l. 2; '*By my faith*,' *Gamelyn*, ll. 95 and 301, '*Par ma foy*,' l. 367, etc.

ll. 398, 402. 1 *John* iv. 12: 'No man hath seen God at any time.' See note to l. 374.

l. 407. A different interpretation of the passage would demand a colon after *mene*.

l. 410. *ifiled:* See *Macbeth* III. i. 65, 'defiled,' 'made foul':

'For Banquo's issue have I filed my mind;
.... the gracious Duncan have I murdered.'

l. 412. *Latin* and ll. 414—416. See *Matt.* v. 8. MS. A₁ reads: 'mondo .... quoniam.'

l. 413. *þis is to seie:* Frequent in Lydgate and Chaucer, illustrated in Schick's note to *T. of Gl.*, l. 311.

l. 416. *aperteliche:* The adjective *apert* is in modern usage. See Sir G. Buck, *Hist. Rich. III.*, p. 79: 'open and *apert*.' See Stratmann-Bradley and Murray for illustrations. See *Shep. Cal. Sept.*, ll. 160 and 162:

'Or privy or *pert* if any bene.'

l. 417. *godhede:* 'divinity' and 'glory,' in distinction from *manhede*, l. 372.

ll. 417, 418. Compare *Tundale*, ll. 2107, 2108:

'... what joy here is and blis,
þat þai ... shalle never mysse.'

Page 21, ll. 421, 422 and Latin. It is to be conceded, that these lines are of doubtful origin, possibly spurious. On later thought they would probably not have had place in the main text.

l. 422. *sey with mowþe:* common 'fill-gap.' See *Ipotis*, B. l. 281.

Latin and l. 423. *Matt.* xxv. 34: 'Come, ye blessed of my father ...' Compare *York Plays*, xlviii. l. 277:

'Mi blissid childre on my right hand,
. . . .
Commes to þe kyngdome ay lastand,
þat ȝou is dight for youre goode dede.'

Town. Play, l. 365: 'Mi chosyn childer, commes to me,
With me to dwelle now shalle ye weynde,
Þere ioie and blis schalle euer be.'

Tundale, l. 1778: 'The voyce of god shall saye: "Come nere,
My fadres blissed childer fre,
And resceyve the kyngdom with me."'

l. 423. *fere:* in the 17th cent., still used. *The Two Noble Kinsmen*, V. l. 116: 'his young fair *fere*.'

l. 424. *fader:* dat. after *leue*, O.E. *lēof*, O.E. construction.

leue and dere; also Chaucer, *Mil. T.*, l. 3051; *L. of G. W.*, l. 1978: *leve suster dere*; *The Seconde Nonnes Tale*, l. 257: *leue brother dere*, etc.; *Hand. Syn.*, l. 5744: 'þey are with God boþe *lefe and dere*.'

l. 425. *Matt.* xxv. 34 : 'Inherit the kingdom,'
l. 426. 'prepared for you from the foundation of the world.'
wende : ende : See Kölbing's note to *Sir Beues*, A. l. 4569.
l. 426. *widouten ende :* See *euere mo*, l. 450; phrases with the rime *wende : ende* are often used in descriptions pertaining to the decrees of the final judgment.

Tundale. l. 827 : 'And þe sonner fro alle payne *wende*
To gret joy *withouten ende.*'

l. 187 : 'Therfor with us shalle þou *wende*,
To brenne in helle *withouten ende*.'

l. 1197 : 'For þou shalt now with us *wende*
To payne of helle *withouten ende*.'

l. 181 : 'Þou shalte to fire *withouten ende*,
And to merknes art þou frende.'

See also l. 2234.

l. 427 ff. *Matt.* xxv. 46: 'the righteous into life eternal.'
l. 431. *Matt.* xxv. 41: 'Depart ... ye cursed (and 449), into everlasting fire.' Biblical passage and *Speculum* recall Browning in *Ferishtah's Fancies :*

'How,
Enormous thy abjection, hell from heaven.
Made tenfold hell by contrast ! . . . . .'

cursed gostes, see *Sir Beues*, A. l. 781, and l. 362.
ll. 436—444. These lines suggest *Zech.* xiii. 6, and *John* xx. 25. See *Wraþfful and sterne*, l. 262.
l. 438. Type C exists on authority of two MSS., A_1 and R, in opposition to the remaining two texts. D and H_2 are omitted here. A_2 and H_1 preserve type A, reading :

'þat slówen hém · þurw [hére] enúie.'

enuie : 'ill-will,' 'hatred.' See *The Two Noble Kinsmen*, V. iii. 21 :

'There is but *envy* in that light, which shows
The one the other.'

l. 439. *kene :* sharp. This meaning is also found in *Pearl*, str. 4, l. 4 : *crokez kene ; Sir Beues*, M. 3401 : '*spere kene*' and S. l. 4168, '*swerde keene*'; Chaucer's *Genl. Prol.*, l. 104, has '*arwes kene*'; in figurative application, *Shep. Cal.*, Feb. l. 3 : 'The *keen* coldblows.' See note by Kirke and Robertson, *Glossary of Dialect of Gloucester*, p. 191.

l. 442. *grisli wounden :* Kölbing, *Sir Beues*, note to A, l. 724, enumerates illustrations of *grisli* as epithet to *wounden* with reference to Mätzner, *Wörterbuch*, II. p. 322 ; *Guy of Warwick*, A. str. 224, l. 9, recalling also *grieslie ghostes, Cal.*, Nov. l. 55.

l. 444. *drede . . . quake :* Compare Schmirgel's collection of expressions for grief, p. xlvi, where *Guy of Warwick*, *Guy* B., l. 3756, *Sir Beues*, ll. 1367, 1389, *Libeaus Desconus*, l. 604, offer illustrations of *quake* for *drede*.

l. 445. Type C is confirmed by all the MSS., additional proof of the existence of the type. *gode* and *voize*, l. 446, are historically impossible. Under any conditions one unstressed syllable must be regarded as lost in these verses, whether in the third or fourth measure.

Page 22, l. 447: *beþ loþe :* perhaps based on *Luke* xiii. 27 : 'I know you not.'

l. 448 ff. *Goþ :* 'Depart from me,' *Matt.* xxv. 41 ; *Luke* xiii. 27 ; *Ps.* vi. 8.

Compare l. 431 ff. of the *Speculum*. See also *O. E. Hom.* (Second Series), p. 5: *Ite maledicti in ignem eternum.* 'Witeð, ȝe awariede gostes, into þat eche fir on helle'; *Hom.* xii, *The first Sunday in Lent*, p. 69, reads; 'witeð ȝe aweregede gostes in þat eche fur þat is ȝarked to deuules and here fereden to wuniende eure and ó abutan ende;' *York Play*, xlviii. l. 369:

'ȝe cursed kaitiffis, fro me flee,
In helle to dwelle withouten ende.'

30*th Towneley Pl.* l. 369: 'Ye warid wightes, from me ye fle,
In helle to dwelle withouten ende.'

See notes to ll. 426 and 431 ff.

The repetition ll. 447 ff., in almost identical words, suggests a *naïvete* of the poet common in ancient narrative. He was not reluctant to indulge in frequent repetition. Perhaps he regarded the construction as a grace. It was not at the period a crudeness in structure.

ll. 450, 451. *dwelle . . . fyr: Isaiah* xxxiii. 14: 'dwell with the devouring fire.' *euere more: i. e.* in 'everlasting fire,' *Matt.* xxv. 41. See note to ll. 431 ff.

l. 451. *hote fyr:* 'pytte of helle' in H_2; *Pers. Tale*, l. 452; *Ipotis*, l. 388 (D); *Tundale*, l. 1298. See *Generides*, l. 2129.

fyr : her: See *Lybeaus*, 571 : *fyer : destrer; Duke Rowland*, l. 94 : *fyre : Messangere; Sir Otuel of Spayne.*

l. 452. *non oþer:* virtually *hell* according to context. The *devil* is the expected taskmaster for the condemned soul.

ll. 453—458. See *James* iii. 13.

ll. 457—458. *Matt.* xxv. 46: 'And these shall go away into everlasting punishment.'

l. 460. *a vers:* This verse is not to be cited. The poet probably united two texts to advance his doctrine of good works, see ll. 148, 465, 502, 621, etc.

Latin: domino et. MS. A_1 domino et.

l. 461. *Hope to god: Psalm* xlii. 5 and xliii. 5: '*Hope in God.*' *do god:* not authorized by the scriptural text or the *Liber*, but suggesting confusion with *James* ii. 26: 'Faith without works is dead'; *Liber, Camb. MS. Ii. I.* 33: 'Witodlice þe ȝeleafa bið unnyt butan þam ȝodum weorcum.' *Seconde Nonnes Tale*, l. 64: 'And, for that *feith is deed withouten werkes.*'

l. 463. *ydel hope:* In contrast with *soþfast hope*, l. 471. *hope* is often classified by the mediæval theologian as referring to the expectation of evil; for instance *The Erl of Tolous*, ll. 815, 823, 835. See Lüdtke's note, *Gowther*, ll. 202, 212, 227, and note to l. 208, and Wagner's note to *Tundale*, l. 90.

l. 464. *widouten gabbe:* See *A Treatise on Dreams*, *Rel. Ant.*, p. 266:
'God tydynge *withoute gabbe.*'
'Apeyrement, *y nul nout gabbe.*'

See *Sir Beues*, S, l. 1492 and 1854: 'Y wyl noȝt *gabbe*'; Chaucer, *The Nonne Prestes Tale*, l. 246; *The Book of the Duchesse*, l. 1075.

l. 466. *so god me rede:* 'God help me.'

Page 23, l. 468. *charged . . . sore:* 'burdened.' See *Macbeth* V. I, l. 60: 'The heart is *sorely charged.*'

l. 471. *soþfast hope:* in contrast to *ydel hope*, ll. 463, 466, *unsure hope, Macbeth* v. 4. 19. It seems to be equivalent to the 'good hope' employed by Lydgate, *T. of Gl.*, and described in Schick's note to l. 892. *Hope* and *dread* ('fear,' anxiety) are at times contrasted in the same passage by the M.E. poet, as for instance:

T. of Gl., l. 641: 'Hanging in balaunce bitwix *hope* & *drede*.'
  l. 892: 'And al biforne late *hope* be þi guide,
          And þouȝe þat *drede* woulde with þe pace
          It sitteþ wel.'
  l. 1197: 'So þat goode *hope* alway þi bridel lede,
           Lat no despeire hindir þe with *drede*.'
Ancr. R., l. 332: '*hope and drede* ... imeind,' etc.; see note, l. 372.

l. 473. *shrifte of mouþe:* See note to l. 94.

l. 474, also l. 92. *redi* suggests Kölbing's 'aim' applied figuratively here in the sense of 'purpose'; see *Sir Beues*, l. 3101:
  'A þrew is knif, & kouþe nouȝt *redi*.'

l. 475, 476. 'If thou doest thus, then put all thy hope in God Almighty.' See *Romans* viii. 24.

ll. 480—483. See note to l. 495.

ll. 483, 484. Cf. lines 267, 268.

l. 484. *sorwe and wo:* Suggesting *Job* iv. 21: 'They die, even *without wisdom*,' recalling in wisdom philosophy; 'They die in sorrow and woe.' See Genung, *The Epic of the Inner Life*, p. 156.

ll. 491, 492. This serious truth weighed on Ælfred, as is evident in the wisdom literature contributed to his *Witenagemôt*, collected in *An O.E. Miscellany* (E.E.T.S., 1872):
  l. 172: 'Not no mon þene tyme.
          hwanne he schal heonne turne.
          Ne nomon þene ende.
          hwenne he schal heonne wende.'

l. 492. *ending day:* 'death-day'; 'þat is elces mannes *endedeie* þat he stepð ut of þese life into þan oðre,' as is explained in an O.E. *Homily*, *An Bispel* (edited by Morris), l. 137. *ending day* is used by Chaucer in *The Compleynt of Venus:*
  l. 55: 'And therfore certes, to myn *ending-day*
          To love him best ne shal I never repente.'
See *ending*, l. 278; *ende of deþ*. l. 280; and *Orrm*.
  Orrm., l. 8108: 'þatt daȝȝ þatt he *tok ende*.'

Page 24, l. 495. See also ll. 481—482. An early proverb seems either to have been in existence, or to have been formulating itself at this time. '*Fast find, fast bind*,' occurs in Heywood's *Proverbs* of 1546, in *Jests of Scogin* of 1565, and in *Merchant of Venice*, II. 5, l. 50:
  '*Fast bind! fast find!*
  A proverb never stale in thrifty mind.'
'*Safe bind, safe find*,' in *Washing*, by Thomas Tusser, of 1523—80. The underlying scriptural text referred to in line 494, *þis word, þat god seide*, is probably *Matthew* xvi. v. 19: 'Whatsoever thou shalt *bind* on earth, shall be *bound* in heaven'; also *Matthew* xviii. v. 18. See *Poema Morale*, ll. 215, 216:
  'þe ðe godes milce sechð. jwis he mei his *finde*.
   ac helle king is are lies. wið ða þe he mei binde.'
Homily, Post Pascha A. ed. Morris, l. 44: 'demd to deaðe and þerto bunden. swo is þe maan þe halt his sinne. he is demd fro heuene to helle.'

l. 496. *ben in mynde:* 'be in remembrance,' 'be borne in mind.' See *Leg. of G. W.*, l. 18, and note, *Spec.*, l. 619, and *New Engl.* 'bear in mind.'
  Sec. Non. T., l. 123: '*bar in hir mynde*.'
  M. of L. T., l. 1127: '*bere ... in mynde*.'
  Ipotis, D, l. 152: 'The soneday *to haue in mende*.'

l. 498. The present text is supported by the best MSS. and by MSS. of the two groups. Read with metre like l. 446, type C:
> 'And Iésu Crist · tó þe táke.'

'If you will accept Jesus Crist,' rather than 'turn to him,' or 'call upon him,' according to the reading of MSS. D and H_2, type D:
> 'Ánd to Iésu Críst þe táke.'

l. 500. *lesczoun:* Compare with l. 505 below.
> *Spec. Vit.*, l. 92: 'And swyche *a lessoun* I schal ȝou ȝeue
> þat *myrour* of lyf to you may be.'
> *Der eng. Cato* (ed. Goldberg, p. 14), v. 81:
> 'Let holi writ beo þi *mirour*
> In word and eke in dede.'

l. 502. *goddede:* preserved by the two oldest MSS., by the best MS., and by a MS. of the opposing group, in distinction from the plausible reading *godhede* of the two remaining texts, also representatives of both groups. The meaning '*good deed*' seems to be specifically the suffering and death of Christ upon the cross.

l. 505. *myrour:* a very common usage. The passage explains itself. For various M.E. interpretations of the term *mirror*, see Schick's note to *T. of Gl.*, l. 292, and ll. 754 and 974, and Spenser's usage:
> *Shep. Cal.*, *Oct.*, str. 16, l. 93: 'Such *immortal mirror*, as he doth admire,
> Would raise one's mind above the starry sky.'
> *Gorboduc*, I. 3, l. 798: 'Happie was Hecuba, the wofullest wretch
> That euer lyued to make *a myrour* of.'
> *P. Pl.*, C. xix. l. 175: 'Thou shalt be *myrour* to menye men to deceyue.'

Cf. also *Henry V.*, 2. Chorus, l. 6.

l. 508. *fonge: fonde*, extant in *D* and *R*, MSS. of two distinct groups, is probably the correct reading, not only as is indicated by the rime but by the sense: 'here (in holy writ) must we look (see) and seek (trust to it) to obtain knowledge of God.' See *John* xxi. 3, MS. Otho 1, C 3: 'ne fengon nan þing on ðære nihte'; *Pref. Cura Past*, l. 22: 'ðâ ðâ ic tó ríce *féng*,' in comparison with *Aȝenbite*, the story of the monk, *Uebsbuch*, p. 99, ll. 104, 105: 'huer he hedde yby uourti yer uor *to uondi* ane monek . . .'

l. 514. *pes and loue:* See *The Seconde Nonnes Tale*, l. 44:
> '. . . . the eternal *loue and pees*.'

The passage is to be traced in Dante's *Paradiso*, Canto xxxiii, l. 44:
> '*Per lo cui caldo nell'* eterna pace.'

l. 515. *ben aboute:* 'be astir,' 'be actively striving to secure peace.'

l. 516. *To make pes:* See l. 520, and Chaucer in *An ABC*:
> l. 69: 'Than *makest* thou his *pees* with his sovereyn.'

make is linked with *pes* in illustrations cited by Kölbing, note to *Sir B.* l. A, l. 879.

l. 518. *godspel:* See Kirke's note to *spell*, *Shep. Cal.*, *Mch.*, l. 54. Latin: *Matt.* v. 9.

Page 25. l. 519. *no les: The Bruce*, l. 419, *vithouten less*; the *Erl of T.*, l. 472; *The Life of St. Juliana*, A, ll. 76, 77: *wiðuten les*; *Wallace*, Bk. I., l. 321: *but less*; also *Leg. of G. W.*, ll. 1022, 1128, 1518.

l. 520. *les : pes:* tho rime of *Erl of T.*, ll. 472, 473. See the lines:
> 'I trowe *wythoute lees*
> let us lyfe *in pees*.'

makeþ pes: See note to l. 516.

l. 521. *hom oow to be* of MS. R: *hom* is a dative with the impersonal verb *oow* in the present tense. See Skeat's note, *Leg. of G. W.*, l. 27, and note to *Spec.*, l. 159; *Pearl*, str. 46, l. 12 : '*uus oghe* to take more.'

l. 525. *widoute fable = widoute les*, l. 518, a common expletive often useful in filling out an incomplete line. See illustrations collected by Zupitza, note to *Guy of Warwick*, l. 3254, explained by *wythowt lesynge*, l. 550 of *Guy of Warwick*; by *withoute layne*, l. 2994 ; and by the more emphatic *withouten gabbe* of the *Speculum*, l. 464. See Kölbing's *no doubt*, l. 2027 of *Sir Beues*. Examples in *Sir Beues* are : A, l. 1672, 2027, 2219 ; M, l. 1933 ; S, l. 2612; O, l. 2381 ; *Ipotis*, l. 436 ; *Seven Sages*, l. 1558. Compare the usage of other writers :

Spense, *Rhymes of Rome*, 7 : 'Alas, by little ye to nothing flie,
　　　　　　　The people's *fable* and the spoyle of all.'
Ben Jonson, *Volpone*, l. 1 : 'Know you not, Sir, 'tis the common *fable*.'
Marlowe, *Faustus* vi., l. 62 : ' But is there not *cœlum igneum et crystallinum* ?'
　　　　　No, Faustus, they are but *fables*.'
Pearl 50, l. 4 : 'Other holy wryt is bot a *fable*.'

l. 526. *merciable:* also l. 534. The suffix -*able* has not the force of modern English here, but is used in an active sense *to show*, 'inclined to *mercy*,' as is indicated by Abbott, *Shaks. Gr.*, § 3, § 445, and illustrated by Schick, *T. of Gl.*, l. 1266. *profitable*, l. 4 of the *Speculum*, is to be interpreted 'is capable of yielding profit.' *Merciable* has an active force in Chaucer's texts :

An A. B. C., l. 1 : 'Almighty and al *merciable* quene . . .'
　　　l. 182 : ' Ben to the seed of Adam *merciable*,
　　　　　　So bring us to that palais that is bilt
　　　　　　To penitents that ben to *mercy able*.　Amen.'
Leg. of G. W., l. 347 : 'And therto gracious and *merciable*.'
　　　l. 410 : 'Yow oghte been the lighter *merciable*.'
Prioresses Tale, l. 1878 : 'That of his mercy god so *merciable*
　　　　　　On vs his grete mercy multiplye.'

l. 531. *flesh and bon:* Generides, A, l. 1348 ; *Monkes Tale, Hercules*, l. 10, another common circumlocution used instead of 'body,' found in Job ii. 5 ; *bone and flesh*, xix. 20 ; *Sir Beues*, A, ll. 628, 4044, 4407 ; *Chron. of Engl.*, l. 675, etc.; *nother flesshe ne bones, Tundale*, l. 910. See also *flesh and blod* 573.

l. 539. *of þinkeþ:* for *þynkkiþ* of A_2 and *R*, is used probably in sense of *gives displeasure*, according to Zupitza's note to *Guy of Warwick*, l. 984.

l. 540. *crieþ merci:* See *Gamelyn*, 874 ; *Tundale*, ll. 233, 234 ; *Rbt. of Gl.*, also in Chaucer and Shakspere :
　　Rbt. of Gl., A, l. 288 : ' crie on hom *no mercy þer nis*.'
　　　　　　l. 499 : '& *criede* him *milce and ore*.'
Tale of M. of L., l. 1111 : '*mercy* I yow crye.'
Merry Wives, III. v. 25 : 'I *cry you* mercy.'
Cf. on the other hand *Two N. Kinsmen*, I. ii. 13 : 'Cried up with example,' *i. e.* enforced by experience.

Page 26.　l. 547.　*gospel:* i. e. *Matt.* vii. 1 ; *Mark* iv. 24 ; *Luke* vi. 38.

ll. 549, 550.　*Piers Plowman*, 1, A, ll. 151, 152 :
　　　　' For þe same *Mesure* þat ȝe *Meten* · Amis oþer elles,
　　　　　　ȝe schul be weyen þer with · whon ȝe wenden hennes.'
See Latin preceding, l. 150, for the text incorporated in MS. R : '*Eadem mensura qua mensi fueritis remeci[e]tur uobis*.' For *mete*, see Zupitza's note to *Guy of Warwick*, l. 6954.

ll. 551, 552: omitted in A_1 probably through fault of the scribe. The lines are contained in all the other MSS., and are in keeping with the style of the poem, where *man* is addressed often in personal exhortation. The text follows MS. A_2. See ll. 201, 203, 319, etc.

l. 551. *þou:* The desirability of inserting *þou* in this position is questionable. It is omitted in two MSS.

l. 552. *forȝeue:* occurs in one MS. only; see variants. It is of no weight in the construction of the text.

l. 553. *Nym god ȝeme:* common linking of terms explained by MS. H_1: 'take gode hede.' See *Ancr. R.*, p. 100: '*Nimeð* nu *gode ȝeme*'; *O. E. Hom.* (ed. Morris, p. 89 ff.), l. 62: '*Nime we . . . geme*'; also MS. *Hom. Dominica Palmarum*, l. 62; *Owl and N.*, l. 727; *Rbt. of Gl.*, Harl. 2277, fol. 511, l. 29; *Gamelyn*, l. 825. See *Ancr. R.*, p. 416 ff., l. 324: 'ȝe nimen to ham *gode ȝeme*.'

l. 554. *bist*, i. e. *biddest, bitst:* normal form connected with the *Pater Noster*. See *Rom. of Rose*, l. 772: '*Biddeth* a Pater Noster'; *Spec. Vit.*, l. 18; *Orrm.*, ll. 5404, 5454, 5465.

Orrm., l. 5454: '. . . bede þatt mann bitt
Uppo þe Paterr Nossterr.'

Promptorium Parvulorum, p. 35: '*byddyn bedys* or seyn prayers'; *Book of Curtasye*, Sloane MS. 1986, f. 22 b, note over byddyn bedys:

'Rede, or synge, or byd prayeris
To Crist for all thy Cristen ferye.'
'. . . . .
Byddynge, or praynge.'

For *bid*, to call to a specific devotion as to the *Pater Noster*, see *Bidding Prayer*, I., *The Lay Folks Mass Book*, p. 62, with explanation on historical basis.

bist : sist : Cf. *byst : ryst*, Bonaventura's *Meditations on the Sorrows of our Lady Mary*, ll. 1015, 1016.

Latin. See *Matt.* vi. 12; *Luke* xi. 4.

See poem 'On the King's breaking his Confirmation of Magna Charter,' p. 257 of *Polit. Songs:*

'For if that he to blame be,
For ȝif hit him par charite.'

l. 555. *Swete lord:* also ll. 569 and 949, the language of the mediæval love-song to the Redeemer. See *A prayer of Loue vnto þe swete herte of Jesu*, Add. MS. 22,283, and similar construction in Morris's *O. E. Hom.*; *Tundale*, l. 234: '*Swete fader, mercy!*'

l. 556. Cf. *Pard. Tale*, ll. 130, 131:

'for a man hath *agilted* his lord . . . *agilted* his father celestial . . . *agilted* him that boughte him,' etc.

ll. 557, 558. The golden rule of Christ: 'Whatsoever ye would that men should do to you, do ye even so to them.'—*Matt.* vii. 12; *Luke* vi. 31.

l. 559 ff. Cf. *Isaiah* lv. 7.

l. 561. *þe:* authorized by three MSS.

l. 562. *bede:* 'to pray.' See *bede*, a prayer of the bead roll, hence 'peir of bedes,' Shak. *Rich. II.*, iii. 3. 145; *Ipotis*, l. 156: *bydde bedys*; 'on which that she hir bedes bede,' *Rom. of Rose*, l. 7371. See Kirke's note to *Shep. Cal. Sept.*, l. 1: 'For to bid is to pray, whereof cometh beads for prayers . . "To bid is beads, to say his prayers."'

l. 563. *dar it seie: S. Nun's Tale*, l. 214. The effect of the denial is in harmony with the other characteristics of the poet's vigorous style.

l. 564. *aȝein:* 'in opposition to,' used in the same sense in the *Prothalamion*, l. 17. See Halliwell's *Dict.*

l. 567. *seiþ:* i.e. in *James* ii. 13. Read: 'And séiþ: He þat wóle no mérci háve.'

Page 27. l. 568. *Latin:* See *Luke* xxi. 19.

l. 569. *speche:* i.e. the Sermon on the Mount, *Matt.* v. ff.
Houre: See l. 949; inorganic *H* as in *nowh*, l. 348.
lord: or *louerd* as in l. 949, to read by type A. See 'Introduction.'

l. 572. *in alle manere:* 'In every kind of.' See *in none manere*, l. 628, *Beues*, l. 565, note to l. 835, and Zupitza's note to *Guy of Warwick*, l. 1228. *on al manere* = 'by all means'; *in this manere, The S. N. T.*, l. 273.

l. 573. *flesh and blod:* See *flesh and bon*, l. 531; *bon and huide*, l. 157; *Aȝenbite* (ed. Morris), p. 87, ll. 6 ff.: 'We byeþ children of one moder ... huer of we nome *vless and blod*'; *S. N. Tale*, l. 42: 'His sone *in blode and flesshe*'; *Gamelyn*, l. 491:

'Cursed mot he worthe, *bothe fleisch and blood.*'

The meaning of l. 573 is purely in physical sense, 'physical illness to effect spiritual good' (l. 576: '*þi seli soule to amende*'). See *Homily*, ed. Small, p. 144, l. 255 f.:

'Bot for his *fleis* was pined here,
His *sawel* es now *til godd ful dere.*'

No trace is to be found here of the figurative use of the O.E. homily. See *Homily* (ed. Morris, Second Series), *Dominica Palmarum*, l. 51: 'bruken *his fles and his blod*, þat is þe *holi husel*'; *In die Pascha*, l. 71: 'to his *holi fleis* and to *his holi blod.*'

l. 574. *þolemod:* The copyist of *D* did not understand *þolemod*. He regarded it as two distinct words, a verb *þole* and a substantive *mode*. See *Ancr. Riwle*, p. 158, fol. 40 b: 'two endie wordes (þeawes, MSS. C and T) ... *þolemednesse* ... edmodnesse. Vor *þolemod* is þo þet *þuldeliche abereð* wouh, þet me deð him.'

l. 576. *seli soule:* according to *Cursor Mundi*, 'blessed soul.' 'Sely saule' occurs in *York Plays*, xlv., l. 171. *Ancr. R.*, p. 108: 'tu *seli ancre*, þet ert his *seli* spuse'; p. 352: 'þis is a *seli* deað, þet makeð .. mon oðer wumman vt of þe worlde.'

The Death of Mary: as 'the happy soul.' See note to l. 987.

l. 582. *gruching:* 'murmuring,' 'grumbling.' See 'Widoute grucching,' l. 593, and *Ancr. Riwle*, p. 418: 'wurche þet me hat hire *wiðuten grucchinge*'; *Owl and Night.*, l. 423:

'Grucching & luring him beoð rade.'

The advice of l. 582 is contrary to the doctrine of *Gorboduc*, V. v. 1:

'With *grudging mind* to damne those he mislikes.'

l. 584. *lude and eke stille:* also ll. 706, 891. Cf. Zupitza's note to *Guy*, l. 792.

l. 585. *falleþ on honde:* happens 'to be your lot,' 'falls to you.' *on honde* is used with various verbs in metaphorical sense: *Der. engl. Cato*, V., l. 397: 'ȝif þe bifallen serwe on honde.' *Owl and Night.*, l. 1651: '*gest an honde*'; *M. of L. T.*, l. 348: '*ytake on honde*'; *Beues* 25 and *Rbt. of Gl.* 2321 (A): '*take on honde*'; also 10,511; 10,817; C 267; *nim an honde* 61, 62, 113, 114, 743, 796, 882, 1344, 1365, 1894, 2062, 2073, 2133, 2146, 2154, 2351, 2612, 2760, 2871, 3476, 3872, 4052, 4366, 4620, 4711, 4880, 9463, 9964, and other instances.

Page 28. l. 592. *leid:* MS. D preserves the more exact inflectional form, *lleide*.

l. 594. See *Ipotis*, B 520: '[He] takyth the povert *myldelych and stylle*,' and *P. Pl.*, A 1, l. 141 : 'lette his sone dye .. *Mekeliche* for vre misdede .. have pite on þat peple, þat pynede him to deþe.'

ll. 596, 607. *ensaumple:* N.E. *example*, a compromise between M.E. *ensaumple* and the Latin, according to Sturmfels, *Afr. Vokalismus im M.E.*, *Anglia*, vol. viii., p. 243. See Zupitza's *Six-Text Oxford edition of the Pardoner's Prologue*:

> p. 25 : 'þenne telle y hem ensamples many oon,
> of olde stories longe tyme agon.'
> p. 60 : 'There may ye lerne, / and by ensample teche,' fol. 488 b, Sloane 1686, leaf 2.

See Sloane MS. 1686, leaf 221, and Harl. MS. 7333.

l. 609. *i dar seie: The Seconde Nonnes Tale*, l. 214: *I dar wel say*. The form is to be contrasted with the N.E. expression, where the M.E. sense is entirely lost.

seie soþeliche: The *Speculum* frequently assures its reader of its veracity : l. 519 : 'A soþ word hit is and *no les*'; l. 480 : 'For hit com out of godes mouþe'; l. 3 : 'it is *no fable*'; ll. 346, 411, 1014, 1023 : '*in soþnesse*'; l. 464 : 'I sey þe soþ, *widouten gabbe*'; ll. 947, 1010 : 'Holi writ, þat *wole noht liȝe*'; l. 565 : 'þe holi bok *of soþnesse*'; l. 637 : 'þu shalt wel wite, þat *i ne liȝe*.'

l. 613. See 608. The required number of unstressed syllables for the measure is to be provided by the reading *wrongé*, but historically the form can be only *wrong*.

l. 615. *unneþe:* the reading of three MSS. giving the meaning 'scarcely.' See Spenser, the *Shep. Cal. Jan.*, l. 6 :

> 'That now *unncthes* their feet could them uphold.'

Page 29. ll. 617, 618. 'Why? Because human nature desires revenge for injury.'

l. 619. *tak þi minde:* See note to l. 496.

l. 622. *martyrdom:* See *Tundale:*

> l. 1861 : 'That for goddis love were buxsum,
> In erthe to suffur *martyrdom*.'

martyrdom . . . mede: i. e. *the palm of martirdom, The Seconde Nonnes Tale*, ll. 240 and 274.

ll. 623—625. The poet seems responsible for an anacoluthon in the transition from þu, l. 623, to *He*, ll. 625 ff., þeih in l. 632 ff.

ll. 623 ff. See *Isaiah* v. 15 : 'And the mean man is bowed down, and the great man is humbled, and the eyes of the lofty are humbled.'

l. 624. *heih of mod:* 'proud,' in contrast to *pore of mod*, l. 164, and *low of herte*, l. 165. See note to l. 164.

l. 626. *heuene:* O.E. fem. *heòfan*. The feminine is indicated here by the gen. ending -e. The feminine is recognized in *The Hymn on the Nativity*, ll. 145, 146.

> 'And *Heav'n*, as at some festivall,
> Will open wide the gates of *her* high palace hall.'

ll. 626—630. These lines recall *Isaiah* xxvi. 5 :

> 'For he hath brought down them that dwell on high,
> (the lofty city):
> He layeth it low, he layeth it low, even to the ground;
> He bringeth it to the dust.'

l. 627. *heinen: heynyn, heinin*, translating *exaltare* (l. 630), occurs in *Promptorium Parvulorum*, p. 233. No other instance of this word has been discovered. It is equivalent to Swedish *höjna* (*hauhnjan* > O.E. *héhnan*). See Stratmann-Bradley. The lists of the *Prompt. Parv.* contain other allied words: *heighthyn, hawneyn, Heynynge*. See *Ancr. Riwle, iheied*, pp. 154, 174, 380, 430.

See M.E. translation of Lat. *exalto*: *Ancr. Riwle*, p. 154: 'beon ine heort gostliche *iheied* touward heouene'; p. 174: 'nout one *heinesse*, auh *heinesse* of folke, vorte scheawen soðliche, þet heo þet hudeð ham ariht in hore ancre huse, heo schulen beon ... ouer oðer kunnes folke wurðliche *iheied* '; p. 430: 'He beo euer *iheied* from worlde to worlde'; p. 100: 'Wend ut . . .', 'Hwuder?' 'Vt of mine *heihschipe* '; p. 86: 'he hit heued to *heie* up.'

ll. 629 ff. *he, his, þeih:* over inconsistency in the use of number in personal pronoun, see Zupitza, note to *Guy*, l. 100.

l. 630. Latin: MS. A₁ has exaltabit*ur*.

l. 631. *her:* MSS. *his*, altered in text to remove anacoluthon.

ll. 631, 632. See *Moral Prov.*, MS. Harl. 3810:

'Ever the hiere that thou art,
Ever the lower be thy hert.'

Ancr. R., p. 130: 'Fleo *heie*, and holdeð . . . þet heaued *euer lowe*.'

l. 634. *wonye:* according to Gollancz's note to *Pearl*, str. 24, l. 8, *-y-* representing the secondary suffix *i* of O.E., and not nominally the inf. characteristic. For inf. in -*ie*, see Skeat's *Langl.*, p. lviii.

l. 636. *he:* he refers already to Lucifer.

l. 638. *Lucifer:* The apocryphal legend was known and introduced into literature so early as the fifth century. See James Rothschild, *Mistere du Viel Testament*, I. p. xlii., and *Speculum Ecclesiæ* of Honorius. It became the subject of at least two miracle plays, *York Play*, No. I., and *Chester Play*, No. I. It was rarely omitted in religious literature from the earliest period. See *Henry VIII.*, III. ii. 371, and Skeat's note to *M. T.*, ll. 3189, 3192. In *The Myroure of our Ladye*, p. 189, the accepted version has suffered modification: 'The north wind signifies Lucifer; by the northe is vnderstondeð the fende Lucyfer, that by coldnesse of hys malyse caused other aungels that are lykened to fayre flowers to falle from blysse.' See Longfellow, *Epilogue to Golden Legend:*

'Lucifer!
The son of mystery, . . .
He, too, is God's minister
And labors for some good' . . .

Isaiah xiv. 12: 'How art thou fallen from heaven, Lucifer' . . .

Langl. A. I., l. 115: 'Bote *Lucifer* louwest liȝþ of hem alle;
For pruide þat he put out. . . . . . .'

Monke's T., l. 3192: '. . . . . *fel* he for his sinne
Doun into helle, wher he yet is inne.'

Meph., Marlowe's *Faust.*, 5. 93: 'I swear by *hell* and *Lucifer*.'

See also *Ipotis*, l. 108: 'In heven . . . .
Þat *Lucifer* fel oute *for pride*.'

ll. 639, 640, and *with* 638. Questionable reading. The appropriateness of the lines seemed reason for inserting them in this connection. Compare other texts:

Tundale, l. 1393: 'Fro heven *throw pride* he felle downe
Heder into þis depe dongowne.'

l. 639. *The Liif of Adam*, l. 52:

'In heauen *Pride* first began,
In angels ar it cam in man.'

l. 640. *toke flyȝte:* touching upon the trait (in Satan's character) of restlessness as represented, *Job* ii. 2—5, and as incorporated in the Introduction to Goethe's *Faust*.

Page 30, ll. 641, 642. *gan:* paraphrastic, written *can* in MS. R as in *Sir Gowther*, see ll. 49, 60, etc. and *Pearl*, 87, 135, etc.; the auxiliary is not to be translated.

l. 643. *alle and some:* See *Cent. Dict.* A formula exceedingly frequent to the present day. In the sense of *universi et singuli* it occurs as follows:

R. Cœur de Lion, l. 2283 : ' We are betrayed and ynome
                 Horse and houses, lords, *all and some.*'
Clerkes Tale, l. 941 : 'And in the peples eres *alle and some.*'
Mirror for Mag., p. 91 : 'In armour, the souldiers *all and some.*'
See also *Herrick*, p. 84 : 'Something made of thread and thrumme,
            A mere botch *all and some.*'

rede: See Zupitza, note to *Guy of W.*, l. 313 ; Kölbing, *Sir Beues*, l. 360.

ll. 645, 646. These lines are contained in the three MSS. A_2H_1R, probably from the original text. They are in harmony with the style of the poet.

l. 648. *þe drede:* impersonal use of *drede*, see Abbott, *Sh. Gr.*, § 297, note to l. 159, and Spenser, *Prothalamion*, l. 60.

strong : *strongë*, dative, a questionable form. See *strong*, ll. 266, 274 ; but *strongë*, l. 282 ; *þe strongë*, l. 449.

l. 649. *siker:* expletive 'certainly,' an adverb used instead of *sikerliche.* The question arises as to the desirability of the comma between *For* and *siker*. These words form a single expression. *and:* here *if*.

l. 653. *bi consail and bi red:* See Kölbing's note to *Sir Beues*, M. l. 360, and Ch., *Genl. Prol.*, l. 665.

þe foule qued: The customary alliterative combination is *foule fend*. See *Sir Gowther*, l. 4 ; *Orrm.* 12,335 : 'þuss *fandeþþ* deofell Godess folle.'

l. 654. *þe qued:* See notes to lines 48 and 1025.

l. 657. *Ac:* Southern adversative, German *sondern; ac* preserves a previous negative, cf. Mätzner, *Wörterbuch* under *ac*. Cf. O.E. use through *Elene*, l. 355 ; *Beowulf*, l. 109 : '*ac* he hine feor forruc' ; l. 1991 : '*Ac* þu ... gebéttest inærum þeodne,' where the significance is adversative, Latin : *nonne, num quid*. $A_2DH_1H_2R$ do not use *ac*, see variants. See *Rbt. of Gl.*, p. 4681, l. 657 :
        'If thou hast any intelligence, any knowledge,' etc.

l. 658. *uertu:* 'efficacy.'

l. 661. *hext:* also the attribute of *charity* in the sense of 'love,' l. 325.

l. 664. *Latin:* MS. A_2 reads: *Qui* . . . ceteras congregat . . . *qui* . . . puluerem*, recalling Isaiah xvii. 13 : the description of *A Doom Song*, the *Doomsday* : '[They] shall be . . . like *the whirling dust* before the storm.' The Latin is quoted in the *Ancren Riwle*, p. 278, with translation : 'þe þet is umhe, wiðouten hire' (edmodnesse) 'worte gederen gode þeawes, he bereð dust iðe winde.'

Page 31, l. 665. *þouh:* See note to l. 752.

l. 672. Read possibly, as in l. 797, *lihtëliche* with inorganic *e* between suffix and stem, according to laws described in the Introduction. Thus type A is preserved instead of either type C or A with the unstressed fourth measure of MS. A_1 :
        'Hit fléþ awéy ful líhteliche.'

l. 674. *dedes . . . do:* verb with cognate substantive occurs frequently; *Rbt. Gl.*, ll. 1107, 1649, 1655, 3845, 4499, 5273, 5876, 7047, 7459. Also 1602, 2192, 2246, 3082, 5436, 5820, 6333, 5483, 6545, 6849, 7175, 7346, 7436, 7448, 9036. See Strohmeyer, p. 23, and note to l. 398.

l. 676. *abide:* See Darlington, *The Folk Speech of South Cheshire*, p. 105.

l. 685. *aferd:* See *ferd*, l. 17 of *A Poem on the Times of Edward II.*, *Gamelyn*, l. 854, and Skeat, pp. xii, xiii. *aferd of:* 'affected with fear on account of.' Cf. *Dict. of the Kentish Dialect*, etc., p. 2; Halliwell's *Dict.* With MS. D *affred* note the reading of Chaucer, *The Shipman's Tale*, l. 403 :
'This wif was not *aferde* ne *affraide*.'
Macbeth, I. iii. l. 96 : 'Nothing *afeard* of what thyself didst make.'
V. i. 41: 'a soldier, and *afeard*.'

ll. 689, also 309. *mid iwisse:* See *Poema Morale*, ll. 40, 141, 154, 375, 391; *On god Ureisun of ure Lefdi*, l. 6; *De Muliere Samaritana*, ll. 37, 53; *mid nane jwisse*, *Poema Morale*, l. 236.

See *Monograph* of M. Jacoby, *Vier me Gedichte aus dem 13, Jahrhundert*, p. 43, l. 47; 'þo þi sone al *mid iwisse*.'

mid: occurs in Southern poems. See note to l. 689 and *Pearl*, *Rbt. of Gl.*, and other Southern poems. For the W.S. *mid* cf. Miller's well-known discussion, Bæda's *Eccls. History*, pp. xliv., xlvii. See also compounds of *mid*, *þer mid*, etc.

Page 32, l. 692. *Latin:* MS. A_1 reads: 'S[e]c[un]dum multitudunem dolor[um] meor[um] in corde meo consolationes tue letiticaueront animam meam.'

l. 693. *þe:* so in A_1 is a copyist's error.

l. 698, also 512 and 908. *is aboue:* See *sit aboue*, ll. 54, 962, the heavenly ruler symbolized through the attributes of an earthly monarch. The conception is very old, a notable characteristic of the O.E. See *heofoncyning*, *Exodus*, l. 410; *Elene*, l. 621; *Héliand* : *hôhon himile*, l. 656; *bi himile themu hôhon*, l. 1509; *heah heofon*, *Genesis* B, 476, 736; *Riddle* 41, l. 22. See the *gloria in excelsis* and modern hymnology, e. g. Seagrave's :
'Rise, my soul, to seats prepared *above*,
Exalted high at God's right hand.'
See illustrations from the M.E. collected by Schmirgel, p. xlix.

aboue : *loue:* a rime exceedingly frequent everywhere, as Kölbing notes, *Sir Beues*, A l. 1837, and illustrates in *Ipomedon*, A l. 5. See 'Willie's emblem,' *Shep. Cal.* for *March* :
'To be wise, and eke to *love*
Is granted soarce to *Gods above*.'

l. 705. Type A can be secured by the reading *aȝeinës*, but this form is not justified by the MSS. The scansion is as in l. 446 according to type C.

l. 710. *stounde : bounde:* For rimes with *stounde*, see Schmirgel, pp. lxi, lxii.

l. 712. *wole:* owing to a scribe who has spoiled the form. Read *wille*.

Page 33, l. 716. *and* : *and* is important to metre and sense, and has the support of three MSS., viz. DH_1R.

l. 721, also l. 217. *shed:* O.E. *gescéad*, O.H.G. *sceit*, N.E. *shed*, 'choice.' Cf. *Kath.* l. 240 : 'schead ba of god & of uvel, nis bitwenen ȝunc & hein nan shed'; *Orrm.*:
l. 5533 : 'þe fifte ȝife iss *shed* & *skill*,
& weorelld like þiness.'
l. 12,336 : 'Innsihht & witt, & *shœd*, & *skill*' (see *skifulliche*, l. 173).

l. 722. *falshede:* *falseness* in antithesis to *soþnesse*.
'Bitwénë soþnésse · ánd falshéde.'

l. 723. *ful iwis:* also ll. 165, 285, 337, 503. See *mid iwisse,* note to l. 689; O.E. *Homilies* (ed. Morris), 'Hic dic ... de Propheta,' l. 17; *Orrm.,* l. 1356; Laʒamon's *Brut,* text A. l. 14,234, and text B. l. 21,561 :

l. 14,234 : 'He hæhte heo *ful iwis.*'
l. 21,561 : 'and an hiʒende wende *foliwis.*'

Cf. *Gen. and Ex.,* l. 2521 : 'to *ful in wis*' and '*wele iwyss,*' *Pearl,* str. 33, l. 10.

l. 726. *wit:* See note to l. 227, and other M.E. texts :

Poema Morale, l. 2 : 'mi *wit* ah to ben more,' etc.

Destr. of T., l. 4 : 'wysshe me with *wyt* þis werke for to ende.'

l. 25 : 'to ken all the *crafte* . . . .'

Recalling l. 212 of the *Speculum:* 'ʒeueþ *wit* in alle *craftes.*'

he: from four MSS. *he* is necessary to the sense. *here* is a scribal error in A_1.

l. 728. *can:* See note to *Sir Beues,* E. l. 3963 : 'He is neither able nor knows how to perceive his own condition.' See Skeat's note to *The Prioress Tale,* l. 1650.

l. 738. This line is to be regarded as parenthetical, whether the break be indicated by the mark of parenthesis or by the comma.

l. 739. *God . . . more:* all, 'the larger and the smaller,' 'good and bad,' *i. e.* righteousness and wickedness.

Page 34, l. 744. *þe longe lyff:* eternity in heaven contrasted with *pine þat lasteþ ay,* l. 746.

ll. 745, 746. See *Persones Tale,* ll. 197, 198 : '*drede of the day of dome and of the horrible peines of helle.*'

l. 746. *domesday : ay:* For this rime see Kölbing, note to *Sir Beues,* A. l. 2643.

l. 750. *hit:* emended from four MSS. *his* of MS. A_1 is a scribal error. The line admits of the punctuation : *long:* instead of *long,.*

l. 752. *þouh: þou* of A_1 is quite possible, see Stratmann, *Dict.* The scribe probably intended to write *þouh.* The final *-h* is added here for symmetry.

l. 756. *lasse and more:* 'everybody.' See Skeat's note to *The Clerkes Tale,* l. 940; *Tundale,* l. 1852; *Beues,* ll. 453, 499; also Auch. *Guy,* str. 38, l. 4 ; and Caius, *Guy,* l. 3160.

l. 758. *ofte shriue:* based on MSS. A_2DH_1. Two texts give the more plausible form *Iscryue. clene* in MS. R alone occurs probably from comparison with l. 768.

l. 759. *wrouht: I wrouht* of MSS. A_2DH_1 is the more exact text, according to the standards of the poet.

l. 761. *þat:* without verb on which to depend has here the character of a kind of substitute for the imperative.

Page 35, l. 768. Also l. 758 in MS. A_1.

clene: through MSS. A_2DH_1R. *ofte* of A_1 is probably retained from l. 758.

shriue: better *I schryue,* MSS. A_2DH_1, according to the participial forms peculiar to the *Speculum.*

l. 769. Approximately l. 829 in H_2.

l. 771 : Cf. *Der engl. Cato,* v. 603 : '*serwe* is *medicine* of þi guld.'

l. 773. *founde:* MSS. A_2DH_1 have the preferred form *ifounde.*

l. 776. *Widouten cost:* recalling Isaiah lv. 1 : *Without money and without price;* Rev. xxii. 17 : *take freely.*

l. 779. *shewe:* The verb is wanting in MS. A_1. *shewe* is not necessary for the meaning, because it could be understood from *shewed,* l. 780 ; it is supplied because found in all the MSS. except MS. A₁. It seems probable that the omission was due to the scribe alone.

l. 779 ff. See *Persones Tale*, p. 581 (ed. Tyrwhitt, Routledge edition), l. 11: 'to him *may nothing be hid ne covered*. Men should eke *remember hem of the shame that is to come at the day of dome. for all the creatures in heven, and in erthe, and in helle, shal see apertly all that they hiden in this world.*' See also *Tundale*:

  l. 2124: 'Thay se alle thyng, both evell and goode.'
  l. 2128: 'And al creatures, þat ever god made.'
  l. 2131: 'Thare may no thyng in this worlde be,'
  l. 2134. 'þat has sene god almyghty.'
  l. 1934: '. . . . . throw þat sight
    Of alle, þat thay in the worlde dyde.'

l. 782. MS. A₁ reads: 'Nichil abscunditum quod non scietur nec occultum quod non relenetur.'

l. 784. *shame* : *blame :* also ll. 778, and 812. See Kölbing's note, *Sir B. A*, l. 469.

ll. 785 ff. '*Tweye manere shame*': See *Persones Tale*, p. 581, quoted l. 779, for the *two maners* of shrift, and l. 4 for *ayenst the shame that a man hath to shrive him*.

Page 36, l. 794. *ashamed* : *agramed :* common rime, see note to *Sir Beues*, SN, l. 408, and A, l. 1135, with reference to Mätzner, *Wörterbuch*, I, p. 42.

l. 799. *be my croun :* *Sir Beues*, text S, l. 1004 ; O, ll. 1923, 1987 : see Kölbing's note to text C, l. 131, with reference to Lange, *Die Versicherungen by Chaucer*, p. 39, and Zupitza's note to *Guy of Warwick*, B. l. 974. Lange cites illustrations from *The Reeves Tale*, ll. 121, 179, etc.

ll. 803—804. See other texts as follows:

  Tundale, ll. 211, 212: 'Thy wykked thoughtes in thy breste.
    Woldest þou never schewe to þe preste.'

l. 806. *wraþþeþ :* Here *wraþþeþ* is used in the original sense of the word, 'make angry,' 'annoy.' See Zupitza, note to *Guy of Warwick*, l. 77.

l. 807. Read 'Forȝifnes, iwis, ne tit him nenere.'

l. 808. Note ellipsis, to be supplied in modern English: 'he will be condemned.'

l. 814. *couþ :* See pret. used by Spenser in the *Shep. Calendar, Jan.*, str. 2, l. 4, with Kirke's reference to Sir Thomas Smith's *Book of Government*, lent him by his 'very singular good friend Master Gabriel Harvey.'

Latin. The Vulgate text, *Is.* i. 6, reads: *Lauamini, mundi estote*. The poet follows Alcuinus ; see Introduction.

Page 37, ll. 816, 824, 848. See *Isaiah* i. 16: '*Wash you, make you clean*,' followed by H₁ in the reading *be ȝe made* or *beþ made clene*. See also *Jer.* iv. 14 ; *Eph.* v. 26 ; See Engl. texts *Ipotis*, l. 618 : '*To whasschen and to mak clene*' ; *þe Wohunge of ure Lauerd* (ed. Zup.), l. 7 : 'he cleues tat herte, and cumes flowinde ut of þat wide wunde . . . þe water, þat te world of sake and of sunne' ; '*wasche mi sawle and make hit hwit*' ; *M. of L. T.*, l. 453 : '*wesh the world fro the olde iniquitee.*'

  Tundale, l. 1860: 'holy men, þat god loved ryght.'
    l. 1863: 'And that *washyd* hor stolys *in the blod*
     Of the lombe, wyt myld mod,
    And thay lefte the world holy,
    For to serve god allemyghty.'

l. 817. *men seþ :* men used in a general sense, equivalent to 'people' with a singular verb, common in Chaucer. See Skeat's note, *Leg. of G. W.*, l. 12.

l. 826. *no wiht:* Cf. N.E. 'not a whit.'

ll. 827-828. See the Modern English poem *A Flower of a Day*, D. L. Muloch: '*Wash them clean with tears.*'

ll. 829, 830. The transition from singular to plural is unexpected, yet it seems supported by the MSS. MSS. A_1R preserve, it is true, the better and smoother reading. An alteration *misdedes : he dredes* is impossible according to the dialect of the poem.

l. 833 (in H_2). *heuene qwene:* Compare *The Book of Common Prayer:* 'O Queen of Heavens, incline thine ear to us.' The coronation of Mary was a popular theme in the *York Plays*. See play xlvii. *The Coronation of Mary, Speech of Jesus*, ll. 7 ff.

    p. 491, l. 7: '*Off heuene* I haue hir chosen *quene*
        In joie and blisse that laste schall aye.'

    p. 493, l. 75: 'We schall þe bringe in to his sight,
        To croune þe quene . . . . .'

    p. 496, l. 155: 'Ressaye þis *croune*, my dere darlyng,
        þer I am kyng, þou shalt *be quene.*'

The subject of the crowning was prominent in two plays at York, Beverley, etc. See Tischendorf, *Apocalypses Apocryphæ*, Text N, 135; Mrs. Jameson's *Legends of the Madonna*, pp. 328, 329; L. Toulmin Smith, *York Mystery Plays*, p. xlix and l.

l. 834 in H_2. *be dene:* See note to l. 191.

l. 836. *namys seuene* in H_2, l. 8, of the independent reading: The meaning is not decided upon by Zupitza, note to *Guy of Warwick*, l. 2682, nor by Kölbing, note to *Sir Beues*, A, l. 2191, with references to *Seynt Mergarete*, l. 68, and *Octovian*, ll. 194, 993. It may possibly be simply an additional illustration of the introduction of the mystical seven so common at this period. For the *Uses of Seven* see MS. Harl. 45. The name of Christ called on seven times within a specified period is the suggestion of the words. See a prayer, *Rel. Ant.* I, p. 22, str. 2: 'halged be þi name with *giftis seuene*'; also the *Burney MS.* 356. 5: 'In þe pater noster beth *seuene biddyngges* that God hym sylf ordeyned on erthe.' See other expressions of the same idea:

    Spec. Vitæ, l. 99: 'And specially of þe *seuene askynges*
        þat on þe Pater Noster henges.'

    Eng. Stud. vii., p. 469: '. . . . þe seuene ȝyftes of þe holy gost,
        þat þe seuene askynges may to vs haste.'

    Ancr. Riwle, p. 28: 'þe *scoue bonen* i þe Paternoster aȝein þe *scouen heaued*
        deadliche sunnen.'

    An ancient Pat. Nos.: '*Seven oreisouns* ther beth inne.
        That helpeth men out of Dedli Sinne.'

Thus are recalled the seven daily petitions enjoined on inmates of cloister and monastery, the seven orisouns often referred to in M.E. See *The Myroure of oure Ladye* (ed. Blunt), p. 11: Seven prayers daily were the formal duty of the sisters of holy Sion, the 'seven appeals' 'to heal the seven deadly sins' and to assure 'the seven gifts of the Holy Ghost.'

l. 840. *Seynte Charite* in MS. H_2: Charity figured as a saint in the Roman Calendar according to Halliwell's *Dict.*: but see also Skeat, note. Compare Zupitza's note to *Guy of Warwick*, l. 1060; Lange, *Die Versicherungen bei Ch.*, p. 39; *Gamelyn*, ll. 451, 513, and numerous illustrations in other M.E. texts.

    On g. *Ureisun of u. Lefdi*, l. 161: 'nu ich þe bisecche *ine Cristes cherite*.'

The saint is invoked with frequency even to the sixteenth century: *Hamlet*, IV. v. 26;

> *Gam. Gur. Needle* 52: 'And helpe me to my neele, for God's sake and
> St. *Charitie*.'

J. R. Lowell, *Godminster Chimes:* 'Chime of *Sweet Saint Charity*,
    Peal the Easter morn.'

Keble, *Christian Year*, st. 6: 'Steals on *soft handed Charity*.'

Page 38. ll. 833, 834. The MSS. themselves mark an uneasiness over this difficult passage. Both language and context seem to yield the following rendering: 'Why? If he will thus continually persist in sin, then he must assuredly remain unclean' (*i. e.* 'unpardoned').

l. 834. Cf. *Rich.*, II. iv. 253: 'And water cannot *wash away* your sin.'

l. 835. *manere:* generally written without *of*, expected in N.E. because replacing O.E. *cun*, 'kind,' as explained by Morris, *O. E. Hom.; Hic Dic. est*, l. 90, and Zupitza, note to *Guy of Warwick*, l. 4346. The pleonastic use of '*manere*' according to French models (Strohmeyer, p. 8) is common in M.E. texts. See *Spec.*, l. 785; Tyndale's *Bible, Rev.* xviii. 12: 'Al *maner vessels* ivery'; *M. of L. T.*, l. 519: 'A *maner latyn* corrupt'; Shoreham:

> 'þre *maner peyne* man fange
> For his senne nede.'

Rbt. of Gl., A 2644: 'wiþoute eni *maner harme*'; 2750: 'A *maner gostes*'; also ll. 3081, 4524, 5561, 7392, 8004, 8331, 8342.

l. 836. *Makeþ:* MS. D *Clense*, 'purifieth.'

l. 838. Also l. 792 in MSS. H,R.

l. 843. *acord:* See the following illustrations:

Prothalamion, l. 101: 'Let endlesse Peace your steadfast hearts *accord*.'

Pearl, str. 31, l. 11: 'Of care and me ye made *acorde*.'

Maund. *Voiage*, l. 75: 'temporel lordes and alle worldly lordes weren at gode *acord*.'

l. 851. *ȝit eft sone:* 'now soon again,' 'immediately,' in Spenser's phrase:

> *Prothalamion*, l. 55: '*Eftsoones* the Nymphes,' which now had Flowers
>   their fill,' etc.

Two N. Kinsmen, III. i. 12: 'That I, poor man, might *eftsoons* come between,
    And chop on some cold thought.'

eftsone is of ordinary occurrence in earlier texts. See *Mark* iii. 1; Wiclif *Bible:* 'And he entride *eftsone*,' *eftsone* corresponding to *again* of King James's version.

l. 853. *godes lore:* i. e. *John* xii. 35. Cf. *John* xi. 9, 10.

l. 854. *lasse and more:* see note to l. 756.

Latin MS. A₁ reads: 'lucem ... comprehendant.' With this passage compare the text quoted in the *Ancr. Riwle*, p. 326: '*Fili, ne tardes converti ad Dominum*,' and the old book, *Vehiculum Vitæ*, p. 107: '*Ne tardes converti ad Dominum, et ne differas de die in diem, nam subito rapit miseros inclemencia mortis.*'

l. 856. See also *John* ix. 4, recalling *Isaiah* xxi. 11, 12: 'Watchman, what *of the night?*'

> 'The morning cometh,
>   And also *the night*.
> If ye will inquire, inquire ye.'

l. 858. *þe derke niht:* common expression in M.E., *Sir Beues*, A, l. 2790; *Partonope*, l. 1182; *Alisaunder*, l. 6097, see Schmirgel, p. lxiii. The *Poema Morale* preserves þustre nihte.

Poema Morale, l. 78 : 'nis hit na swá durne idón · né aswa þustre nihte.'
Shep. Cal. Nov., l. 165 : 'She hath the bonds broke of *eternall night*.'
See *Persones Tale*, l. 255 : 'Covered with the *derkenesse of deth* . . defaute of the sight of God,' through 'the sinnes that the wretched man hath don.'

Page 39. l. 859. *While þu art on liue:* recalling *whil he was on lyue*, *Gamelyn*, ll. 20, 58, 157, 225, 228, as noted by Skeat, p. xxxiv.

on liue : See Skeat's note to *Gamelyn*, l. 20.

Compare the passage with *John* ix. 4 : 'While *it is day*,' . . . 'I must work the *works* of him that sent me,' i. e. *Godes werkes of holi churche*, *Spec.*, l. 860. See *Vulgate* text quoted, *Ancr. Riwle*, p. 326 : *Fili, ne tardes converti ad Dominum*.

ll. 859, 860 : *worche . . . werkes :* 'do works of love,' as explained by Zupitza, note to *Guy of Warwick*, l. 6675, und Kölbing, note to *Sir Beues*, A, ll. 58—60, and A, l. 3230, quoting Guy's advice to the old earl :

> 'Hyt were better for þe to be in *churche*,
> And *holy werkys for to wyrche*.'

The rime in this favourite passage of the M.E. poet is uniformly *worche* : *churche*, as is illustrated in numerous passages from different mediæval texts :

Tundale, l. 29 : 'The *werkes of mercy* wolde he not *wyrke*,
He lovede not god ne holy *kyrke*.'
l. 209 : 'þou lovedest not god *nor holy kirke*,
Ne *workes of mercy* woldest non *wyrke*.'
Owl and Night., l. 720 : 'Vorþi me singþ *in holi chirche*
And clerkes ginneþ songes *wirche*.'
The Miller's Tale, l. 196 : 'Than fell it thus, that to the . . . *cherche*
(Of Cristes *owen werkes* for *to werche*)
This god wif went upon a holy day.'
The Sompnoures Tale, l. 269 : '. . . to bilden Cristes owen *chirche*,
. . . if ye wol lernen for *to werche*.'
Ipotis, B, l. 216 : 'Lowen god and *holy cherche*,
And oþer god *werkes for to werche*.'

See also *The Marchantes Tale*, l. 237 ; *Gamelyn*, l. 507 ; *Ipotis*, D, ll. 431, 432.

See *King Horn*, l. 1407 : 'Horn let sone *wurche*
Chapeles and *chirche*.'

l. 862. *qued :* See notes to the *Speculum*, lines 48 and 1025.

ll. 866, 867. *John* ix. 4 : 'The night cometh when no man can work.' See modern hymnology : 'Work, for the night is coming.'

l. 866. *agaste :* This early form was used by Milton in the past participle :

Hymn on Nativ., l. 160 : 'The aged earth *agast*
With terror of the blast,' etc.

See also *Wm. of Palerne*, 1778 : 'and him *agast* maked . .' The *h* of N.E. *aghast, pp.*, is inorganic and unauthorized on historical basis. Cf. Murray, *Dict*.

faste : agaste : rime of *Gamelyn*, ll. 288, 384.

l. 867. *widoute nay :* 'it cannot be denied.' See Zupitza's note to *Guy of Warwick*, l. 3054.

ll. 869, 872. See 2 *Corinth*. v. 10.

l. 872. *wheiþer :* See note to l. 219.

l. 873. *par aunter :* i. e. *peradventure* read as a trisyllable for the metre, also noted by Schick, l. 233. See Wiclif, *Matt.* v. 25: 'Lest peradventure thin adversarie take the to the domesman,' and *Pearl*, str. 49 :

l. 12: '*Paraunter* noght schal to-yere more.'

See Skeat's note to l. 935 of the *Pardoner's Tale*.

ll. 876—878. *Rev.* xxii. 12. See *Poema Morale*, l. 171:

'End éfter þet hé heavet i don, scal ðer ben ídemed.'

l. 876. þat of A_1 : omitted in this text on authority of three MSS. from two groups in opposition to the reading of a single MS., and because securing possibly a better metre. Compare the two readings with l. 264, where the MSS. do not admit of the loss of the þat:

l. 876: 'Ác riht áfter · þú hast dó.'
'Ác riht áfter · þat þú hast dó.'
l. 264: 'Ác riht áfter · þat mán haþ dón.'

l. 878. *Latin:* MS. A_1 reads *dum*. See note to l. 854.

ll. 879, 880. *gilour . . . gileþ:* Compare *Hand. Syn.*, l. 5975, and other texts:

Reves Tale, l. 4219: 'A *gilour* shal himself *begiled* be.'

P. Pl., A, II., l. 162: 'Boto *gyle* was forgoere and *gilede* hem alle.'

See also:

King Horn, l. 1488: 'He haþ *giled* þe twie.'

Prov. of Hend., l. 304: 'Hope of long lyf *gyleþ* mony god wyf.'

l. 880. *euere among:* See note to l. 186.

l. 881. *þerfore worch:* 'Go work,' *Matt.* xxi. 28. *worche* is a correct form in this connection historically and according the syntax of the passage. See O.E. *wyrce*. The line belongs then properly to type A:

'þérfore wórchë, while þu máit.'

mait: For this curious form see Introduction, the explanation advanced by Professor Schick.

Page 40. l. 882. *caiht:* See 'Introduction' under 'Phonology.' This orthography is not common. It is given approximately in the *Ancr. Riwle*, p. 154: 'neuer ȝet i monne floc ne *keihte* he swuche biȝete'; p. 278: 'hwo mei wið þeos witen him, þet he ne beo mid summe of þeos *ikeiht*'; p. 134: 'leste heo beo *ikeiht*.'

miht be caiht: M.E. expressions for *death* or *to die* are curious and interesting. See the *Ancr. Riwle*, p. 62: 'þurh eie þurles deað haueð here ingong into þe soule'; p. 110: 'al his bodi deaðes swot swette'; p. 274: 'ȝiueð deaðes dunt'; Aȝen. 130: 'deaðes drench'; l. 30: 'his licham of erðe he nam.'

Orrm., l. 8111: 'Ær þann he ȝaff his fule gost
to farenn inntill helle.'

l. 7781: 'Forr sinness draȝhenn sinnful mann
Till helle dæþ onn ende.'

l. 15,436: 'ȝe shulenn deȝenn ifell dæþ
To dreȝhenn helle pine.'

l. 1381: 'Wiþþ dæþess pine o rode.'

P. Pl., B, xviii., l. 53: 'bede hym *drynke* his *deth yuel*.'

R. of Gl., l. 9128: 'king henri þen deþ *nom*.'

l. 131: '*deþ* com him þus to.'

l. 5320: 'þen *wey of deþe nom*.'

Cf. with 490 '*out of þis world for to fare*.'

Orrm., l. 7010: 'þo wende heo *out of þisse liue*.'

Sir Beues, l. 3656: '*ibrouȝt of þe lif dawe*.' 209, 317, 481, 1064, 1594, etc.

Latin and ll. 883, 884. MS. A₁ reads: 'Inicium sapiencie timor domini,' to be found *Psalms* cxi. 10; *Proverbs* i. 7; ix. 10. See also *Job* xxviii. 28; *Deut.* iv. 6; *Eccles.* xii. 13. H₂ quotes the Latin in two other instances, ll. 4 and 138, where it is not cited in other MSS. See *Moral Proverb*, Harl. MS. 3810:

'For *the begynnyng of wisdom is*
For *to drede Goddys* ryʒtwysnes.'

See *The Persones Tale*, l. 1752 ff.

l. 883. *þing:* Originally a neuter noun, *þing* is preserved unchanged in the plural, but the orthography *þinge, þinges* is to be noted. The final -e of *þingĕ* occurs through analogy with the dative plural, O.E. *þingum*. See Sachse, *Das unorganische e im Orrmulum.* Cf. *þing, Leg. of G. W.*, l. 11; 'and tatt alle *þinge* seþ.' *Orrm.*, l. 13,664. Final *-es* of *þinges* indicates analogy with the plural of the masculine. See *Orrm.*, l. 11,895: 'eorþlic · *þingess* (gen.) lusst'; l. 13,749: 'seʒʒde swilkke *þingess*'; l. 18,798: 'lasstenn alle *þingess*.' See also l. 19,692: 'mikell *þing* to tacnenn,' and l. 12,347: 'Inn alle, kinne *þinge*.' See also 'Introduction' under Inflection of substantives.

l. 888. *ipult:* See l. 232, and *Ancr. Riwle*, p. 366: 'hit *pulteð* up,' ... 'hit *wule pulten* on him.'

Rel. Ant., p. 244, II.: 'To dethe a wolde hym *pulte*
for Adames *gulte*.'

Langl., A, l. 125: '*pryde* that he *pult* out.'

gilt : ipilt: rime frequent in the *Liif of Adam* and an old *Pater noster*. See *Gamelyn*, l. 894.

l. 889. *i vnderstonde:* See note to l. 49.

l. 898. *do:* From three MSS. instead of *go* of two.

l. 903. *kacche:* See pp. *ikauht*, l. 17, and *Ancr. Riwle*, p. 324: 'Ase ofte ase . . . *kecheþ* toward þe.'

ll. 905, 906. See *The Persones Tale*, ll. 259 f., and *Tundale*.

Tundale, l. 1836: 'So *fayre a sight* as he saw than.
The *grete bryghtnes of goddis face*.'

l. 2113: 'Thay beheld faste *his swete face*,
þat *shone bryght* over al þat place.'

Page 41. l. 910. *loue : drede:* See l. 21: *loue . . eiʒe*; l. 795: *shame ne eiʒe*. See *The Tale of Melibeus*, l. 85: 'did him *reverence more for drede than for loue*.'

l. 924. *luite : puite:* This interesting rime is not common. I have not met with it in other texts.

ll. 925, 926. Lines of doubtful authenticity, probably on later consideration not to be introduced in this connection. See 1 *John* iv. 17, 18.

l. 927. *in . . . lore:* i. e. *Matt.* x. 42; *Mark* ix. 41. See *Matt.* xxv. 40.

l. 928. ·*Man:* This term of address, strikingly frequent in the *Speculum*, is of rare occurrence in other homilies of the Old and Middle English literature, without some qualifying adjective, often *Leofemen*, as in *O. E. Hom.* 41, l. 1 (see ed. Morris, First Series), or *good men, Pard. Tale*, l. 904, as in the modern sermon. See Skeat's note to l. 904.

l. 931. *gode wille . . . charite:* 'in my name, because ye belong to Christ.' *Mark* ix. 41.

wid: The *d* in *wid* stands for þ. See Breul, *Sir Gowther*, p. 18. The poet pronounced *wiþ*. Cf. *wiþ : griþ*, l. 148. See Napier's note to *A Middle English Compassio Mariæ*, ll. 3 and 19.

l. 932. ʒolden þe: 'he shall not lose his reward,' *Mark* ix. 41.
l. 937. See *Prov.* xxviii. 27.
þe betre: See Zupitza's note to *Guy of Warwick*, l. 5205. Cf. Lat. *eo melius*. þe is O.E. þý, M.H.G. *diu*.
Page 42. l. 938. *mede*: *Matt.* vi. 12; *Luke* vi. 38. Rewards of the Lord, *Prov.* xxv. 22; according to works, *Hos.* iv. 9; *Matt.* xvi. 27; *Luke* xxiii. 41; 1 *Cor.* iii. 8; 2 *Tim.* iv. 14.
l. 939. *Enes*: MS. D preserves a corrupt reading. The form seems to be *Twys*, but it may possibly stand *Iwys*. Cf. *ene*, ll. 366, 815, and Gollancz's note to *Pearl*, str. 25, l. 3; see str. 80, l. 5.
l. 946. *olde lawe*: 1 *Kings* xvii. 8—16. For influence of Gregory and Augustine on the poet, see the 'Introduction,' p. cxiv. Scriptural texts alone will be consulted in the preparation of the notes. See also *Ancr. R.*, p. 402 : 'mid þe *poure wummon of Sarepte*.'
See l. 637 : *i ne liʒe*. See *P. M.*, l. 287 : 'nelle *ich cow naht leoʒen*'; 'if I shal nat lye,' *M. of L. T.*, l. 1007.
l. 952. *beyþere*: gen., a form hitherto not discovered in any other M.E. text. Although the etymology of M.E. *boþe* is yet in question, yet it is probable that this genitive cannot represent the Scandinavian *báðir*. It seems, as Prof. Schick has pointed out, that the second half of the word is a form of O.E. *þá*. The development may be traced as follows :
O.E. Nom. *bá*   *þá*   : M.E. *bā*, *þe* = *bōþe*.
O.E. Gen. *bēg(r)a þára* : M.E. *beire*, *þere* = *beyþ(e)re*.
for: inserted from D for the sake of metre. The verse is thus transposed from type C to type A. *beyþere* suggests the emendation *liue*, the plural form as used in line 486. The insertion of *for* is not necessary, if the verse be read as follows : 'Her béyþere líue tó aménde.'
l. 953. *seide*: 'saying,' *Script.* v. 8; *þu shalt fare*: v. 9 : 'Get thee . . .'
l. 954. *Sarepte*: 'Sarepta,' *Luke* iv. 26, the reading of Gregory and Augustine. More correctly Zarephath (v. 9 of 1 *Kings* xvii., and *Obadiah* 20), from which *Sarepte* is a corrupted form.
wone þare: v. 9 : 'dwell there.'
l. 955. *widewe*: 'a widow woman'; *þe fede*: 'to sustain thee.'
l. 957. *began anon*: v. 10 : 'So he arose.'
l. 958. *to gon*: 'went.'
l. 959. *ʒate of the cite*: 'gate of the city'; *widewe he mette*: 'widow was there.'
l. 960. *he grette*: 'he called to her there,' *faire grette*.
faire grette: See *grete wel* of l. 52. Usual form of greeting in M.E. texts. See note to l. 52, and as follows :

Ipotis, l. 14 : 'þe emperour *ful fayr* he *grette*.'
Brut., A, l. 288 : '& *fœire* hine gon *greten*.'
l. 36 : '*fœire* heo hine igrætten.'

M. of L. T., l. 1051 : '*fayre* he hir *grette*.'
See Schmirgel, p. lv., for the rime *mette* : *grette*, *Leg. of G. W.*, ll. 977 and 1485; *King Horn*, l. 1040.
ll. 961, 963. *bad hire . . ʒiue*: 'Fetch me'; *for godes loue*: 'I pray thee.'
l. 963. *a dishful water*: 'water in a vessel.' *dishful water*: a cup of cold water. *Matt.* x. 42. For the omission of the preposition see note to *shiue*, l. 970, and to *manere*, l. 835.
l. 964. *helpen (him) to liue*: 'that I may drink.'
l. 966. *serue . . . aʒein*: v. 11 : 'she was going to fetch it.'

turne: subjunctive, 'she would turne again'; the syntax seems justified by the meaning.

aȝein: to rime with *fain:* O.E. *ongœgn:* O.E. *fœgen.*

l. 967. *After* ... *crie:* 'he called to her.'

l. 969. *he seide:* v. 11: 'and said.' Read *sede.*

Page 43, l. 970. Scriptural narrative v. 11: 'Bring me ... a morsel of bread in thine hand.'

shiue bred: 'shive,' 'slice,' 'morsel.' See also *hundful mele,* l. 975, *dishful water,* l. 963, Skeat's note to *Morsel breed, Monkes Tale,* l. 3624, and the readings of MS. R *shyuer of brede,* D and R *disful of water,* R *hondful of mele.* Cf. *Sir Beues*:

A, l. 1825 : 'Nowich wolde ȝeue hit kof
For a *schiuer of* a lof!'

M, l. 1826 : '*Of a lofe to haue a shyuer.*'

l. 972. *she seide, bred haue i non:* Script. v. 12: 'And she said ... I have not a cake.'

siker: See *Shep. Cal., Mch.,* l. 7: 'Sicker, Willie, thou warnest well.'

ll. 975-976. 'but an handful of meal in a barrel, and a little oil in a cruse.'

ll. 977, 978. 'That I may go in and dress it for me and my son, that we may eat it and die.'

l. 979. *deie:* See Napier's note to *A M.E. Comp. Mariæ,* l. 14, and Chaucer, *T. of Melib.,* l. 159: '*live in sorwe.*'

l. 981. *answerede þo: Script,* v. 13: 'And [he] said unto her.' See also l. 65, and *Sir Beues,* A, l. 1841: 'þe leuedi *answerde him þo.*' Ordinary language of the period.

l. 982. *Abid:* also conversational form common with the poet of the period. See *Owl and N.,* ll. 837, 845.

l. 983. 'But make me thereof a little cake first,' *Script.* v. 13. See *Sir Beues,* l. 1837: 'Dame, a seide'; l. 1840: 'ȝeue me ... a *meles met.*'

l. 986. *make : sake:* See Kölbing's note to *Sir Beues,* M, l. 4317.

l. 987. *seli:* 'kind'? as in *Compl. of Mars,* l. 89. The sense suggests 'innocent,' 'unsuspecting.' See Skeat's note to *Leg. of G. W.,* l. 1157; note to l. 576 of the *Speculum,* and texts as follows:

M. of L. T., l. 682: '*sely innocent* Custance.'

Leg. of G. W., l. 1254: 'O *sely* woman, ful of innocence.'

l. 2713: 'This *sely* woman is so wayk, allas!'

Chan. Yem, T., l. 1076: 'O *sely* preest! O *sely* Innocent!'

Ancr. Riwle, p. 108: 'tu *seli* ancre, þet ert his *seli* spuse.'

Ancr. Riwle, p. 352: 'þis a *seli* deað þet makeð þus ... mon oðer wuman ut of þe worlde.' Compare also another usage, that of Spenser, *Shep. Cal., Sept.,* Diggon's speech, l. 62:

'My *seely* sheep (ah, *seely* sheep!)'

Chaucer uses *sely* as epithet in connection with proper names: *sely John, Reves T.,* l. 188; *sely Venus, Compl. of M.,* ll. 89, 141; *sely Progne, Leg. of G. W.,* l. 2346; *sely Dido, Leg.,* ll. 1157, 1336; *sely poure Grisildis, Clerkes T.,* l. 948.

l. 988. *Grauntede* ... *bone:* probably stereotyped expression in M.E. See *Rbt. of Gl.,* 'Life of St. Dunstan,' l. 37; Ch. *Kn. Tale,* l. 1411; *Parl. of F.,* l. 643; *H. of F.,* l. 1537; *Gamelyn,* l. 153-4: 'aske me *thy boone* ... I it *graunte sone.*'

l. 993. *orysoun:* prayer to Almighty God, but also naming supplication to heathen gods. See Schick, *T. of Gl.,* note to l. 460. Cf. a sixteenth-century MS.: 'Ane *deuoit orisoun* to be said in the honour of the sevin wordis that our saluiour spak apoun the croce,' *Arund.* 28 b, fol. 165.

l. 994. *fuisoun:* See Gollancz's note to *Pearl*, str. 89, l. 2; *Two Noble Kinsmen*, v. i. l. 53: 'the teeming Ceres' *foison*'; *Macbeth* iv. iii, l. 88. Compare l. 994 with l. 504, *M. of L. T.*:

'God sente his *foyson* at hir grete nede.'

Page 44, l. 999. *Ne dred þe noht:* also *The Seconde Nonnes Tale*, l. 324 = 1 *Kings* xvii, 13: 'Fear not.'

l. 1000. *Script.*, l. 14: 'The barrel of meal shall not waste.'

l. 1001. 'neither shall the cruse of oil fail.'

l. 1002. *lome:* N.E. *loom*, here a vessel, and applicable either to the Scriptural 'barrel' or to the 'cruse.' *lome* admits of varied application, the *ark* in the poem *The Deluge*, ll. 314, 412; *tools* in the *Parable of the Labourers*, l. 15. See a song in MS. Harl. 2253, and various illustrations in Skeat's *Dict.*

l. 1003. *Script.* v. 15: 'and she ... and her house did eat.'

l. 1004. *While she liuede euere mo:* v. 15 'many days'; marginal note: 'a full year.'

l. 1006, also l. 940: *almesse dede is double god:* See Lowell, *The Vision of Sir Launfal*, Part II, str. 8, l. 14:

'In what so we share with another's need;
Not what we give, but what we share,—
For the gift without the giver is bare;
Who gives himself with his alms feeds three,—
Himself, his huugering neighbor, and me.'

l. 1008. *þur[w]:* conjectured orthography, not authorized by MS. D providing the completed line. *þur[w men...*] would be the preferred arrangement, were MS. D not consulted as standard.

l. 1012. *Luke* vi. 38. 'Give, and it shal be given unto you'; *Prov.* xix. 17; 2 *Corinth.* ix. 7.

l. 1014. *sei[de in soþenesse]* is to be preferred. *seide* is not, however, the orthography of *D*, the MS. supplying the deficiency in MS. A₁.

soþenesse: Inorganic -*e*- uniting radical with suffix, is to be noted here, as illustrated in MS. D. See 'Introduction.'

ll. 1015-1018. *Matt.* xxv. 40: 'Inasmuch as ye have done it unto one of the least of these my brethren, ye have done it unto me.'

l. 1016. *meyne:* 'brethren,' *vide supra*. See Skeat's note *Leg. of G. W.*, l. 1059; Gollancz's to *Pearl*, str. 46, l. 2. See str. 94, l. 11; str. 96, l. 5; *The Deluge*, l. 331; *Wm. of Palerne*, l. 184; *Occleve, De R.*, str. 620, l. 5; *Chevy Chase*, l. 6; *Gamelyn*, l. 575.

l. 1019-1022. Reference is here possibly to *Prov.* xix. 17: 'He that hath pity upon the poor, lendeth unto the Lord.'

ll. 1020, 1021. *mayt3:* unique form found only in MS. D, perhaps a scribal inaccuracy for *may3t*, ll. 863, 864. See rime *mait : (caiht)*, l. 881.

l. 1025. *quede : gnede* in *R*, O.E. *gneað*. For *qued* as substantive, 'the devil,' see note to l. 48, and Mull's note to *The Harrowing of Hell*, l. 36, reading 'For to lesen ous fram þe *qued*.' The various substantive meanings are developments representing the adjective *qued*, 'evil.' See *The Pater Noster* according to Michel, *Aȝenbite of Inwyt*, p. 262, l. 5: 'no vri ous vram *queade*.' The same occurs in the *Ancr. Riwle* and in *Rel. Ant.* I, p. 42. See also *Ancr. R.*, p. 72: 'Moni mon weneð to don wel þat he deð al to *cweade*'; p. 336: 'ofte we weneð wel to donne & do al to *cweade*.' The *Dutch Testament* of 1700 translates *Matt.* vii. 17: 'Eur *quade* boom brenghi voort *quade* vruchten.' Cf. *Engl. Psalter, Psalm* xvii. 12 (Cotton MS. Vesp. D vii): 'Vmgriped me weeles of *quede*' (=

iniquity); and lines 654 and 862 of the *Speculum*. Cf. *On g. Ureisun of u. Lefdi*, l. 42 : 'lif cleane urom alle *queadschipe*.'

Page 45, l. 1034. Compare for this conclusion Zupitza's note to *Guy of Warwick*, l. 11,973 ; Breul's to *Sir Gowther*, l. 763 ; *Erl of T.*, l. 1222. Auch. *Guy* ends : 'Amen, par charite.' *Meditations by Bonaventura:*

'Sey amen, amen, pur charyte,'

with which is to be compared note to l. 840 in H_2, various forms of benediction collected by Schmirgel, p. xlvii, and the Biblical models, *Jude* 24, 25 ; 1 *Tim.* i. 17.

EDITIONS OF MIDDLE ENGLISH TEXTS

REFERRED TO IN THE NOTES

Professor Kölbing's list of Middle English texts on pages 361, 362, and 363 of *Sir Beues*, specifies those used in the compilation of the notes to the *Speculum Gy de Warewyke*. Some of these works have been employed with greater frequency than others, and the volume is indebted to publications and manuscripts not mentioned by Professor Kölbing. The subjoined list enumerates editions particularly useful in the arrangement of the *Speculum*. The abbreviations introduced in the *Speculum* will be recognized by reference to these pages as follows. In general Kölbing's comprehensive editions, Zupitza's editions of Guy of Warwick MSS., Morris's and Skeat's editions, especially of Chaucer texts, Zupitza's six-text editions of Chaucer published for the Chaucer Society, and Furnivall's Chaucer texts have often been consulted. It will not be necessary to classify them a second time.

Ancren Riwle, a Treatise on the Rules and Duties of Monastic Life. Camden Society, Number 57.

Arthur. A short Sketch of his Life and History, edited by Frederick Furnivall. London, 1864.

Athelston, edited by Julius Zupitza, *Englische Studien*, vol. xiii, pp. 331 ff.

Canterbury Tales. From the Text and with the Notes and Glossary of Henry Tyrwhitt. Routledge edition. London.

Cato, Der englische, edited by M. Goldberg, 1883.

Confessio Amantis. Tales of the Seven Deadly Sins, edited by Henry Morley. London, 1889.

Erl of Tolous, and the Emperes of Almayn, eine englische Romanze aus dem Anfange des 15. Jahrhunderts, edited by Gustav Lüdke. Berlin, 1881.

Floris and Blauncheflur, edited by Emil Hausknecht.

Harrowing of Hell, Das altenglische Spiel von Christi Höllenfahrt, edited by Eduard Mall.

Gamelyn, The Tale of, edited by Walter W. Skeat. London, 1884.

Ipotis, text B, edited by H. Gruber, 1887.

King Horn, Das Lied von, edited by Thomas Wissmann. Strassburg, 1881: also *King Horn, Untersuchungen zur mittelenglischen Sprach- und Litteraturgeschichte. Quellen und Forschungen*, vol. xvi.

Monk of Evesham, The Revelation to the, edited by Edward Arber. London.

Ormulum, edited by R. M. White. London, 1878.

Pearl. An English Poem of the fourteenth century, edited by Israel Gollancz. London, 1891.

Poema Morale, generally the text of Zupitza, *Uebungsbuch,* pp. 49 ff., rather than the editions of Furnivall, Morris, or Lewin.

Promptorium Parvulorum, edited by Way for the Camden Society.

Robert of Gloucester, edited by W. H. Wright, London, 1887; also *Der Stil der mittelenglischen Reimchronik Roberts von Gloucester; eine Untersuchung zur Ermittelung der Verfasser dieses Werkes,* by Hans Strohmeyer. Berlin, 1889.

Shepherds' Calendar, edited by Henry Morley.

Sir Beues, The Romance of, edited by Eugen Kölbing. London, 1885—94.

Sowdone of Babylone, edited by Emil Hausknecht. London.

Speculum Vitæ, edited by Ullmann, *Englische Studien,* vol. vii, p. 469.

Temple of Glas, edited by J. Schick. London, 1891.

Thomas of Erceldoune, edited by Alois Brandl. Berlin.

Tundale. Das mittelenglische Gedicht über die Vision des Tundalus, edited by Albrecht Wagner. Halle, 1893.

Uebungsbuch, Alt- und mittelenglisches, edited by Julius Zupitza, Fourth edition. Wien, 1889.

York Plays. The Plays performed by the Crafts, or Mysteries on the day of Corpus Christi, in the 14th, 15th, and 16th centuries, edited by Lucy Toulmin Smith. London.

GLOSSARY

[*The Glossary serves also as an index to the* Speculum. *It includes all words important in the evolution of the poem. The N.E. derivative often appears among the meanings distinguished, showing direct or cognate form of the root specified. Discussion of the more archaic or rare words will be found in the Notes.*

The sign † *marks an obsolete form;* etc. *indicates that the word cited is used more than three times with the same meaning. Other abbreviations will be readily understood from the context. A notation for grammatical classification is frequently omitted.*]

abide, *inf.* to await (*tr.*), 256; to abide, remain (*intr.*), 676; **abid,** *imp.* 982.
aboute, *adv.* about, on every side, 190; astir, 515; **abouten,** 196.
ac, but, 4, 13, 102, etc.
accedie, accidie† (*see note to line* 117), 117, 121.
acord, *sb.* accord, agreement, 513; good will, 893; reconciliation, 843.
aferd, *pp.* afeard†, afraid, 685.
after, *prep.* after, in imitation of (*Gen.* i. 25—27), 213; in conformity to, 235; in proportion to, 264, 876; according to, 314.
agaste, *inf.* to affright, terrify, 866.
agilt, *pp.* aguilt†, offended, 307.
agramed, *pp.* grieved, irritated, 794.
aȝein, *prep.* against, in opposition to, 564, 620; contrary to, 616, 705, 892; **aȝeines,** 556.
alday, every day, at any time, 342.
alle, all people, all hearers, 1, 54, 323, etc.; **alle and some.** *See* some.
allerfurst, *adv.* first of all, first, 70; **alþere,** MSS. A_2 H_1 H_2.
almes dede, alms-deed, the practice of alms-giving, 95; deeds of mercy, 922, 1007; a gift, 934; **almesse dede,** 1006.
almesse, alms, a charitable act, 923.
almiht, *adj.* almighty, 476, 614; omnipotent, 741.

alone, only, merely, 465; **alone—ac,** 371-2.
amende, *inf.* to amend, bring to a more perfect state, 576, 952.
amendement, amendment, correction, 56.
amis, *adv.* amiss, wrong; **don amis,** erred, 802.
among, *adv.* **euere ——,** from time to time, continually, 186, 880.
and, if, 89, 387 ?, 649.
anon, at once, immediately, 33, 431, 448, etc.; as soon as, 759; quickly, 761.
anguisse, anguish, excruciating pain, 183.
anuied, *pp.* annoyed, disturbed, hence reluctant, 124.
aperteliche, *adv.* plainly, openly, 385, 416.
ar, *adv.* ere, before, 531.
ariht, *adv.* aright, correctly, 729; in a right way, 825.
auarice, avarice, greediness of gain, 115.
aunter, par ——, adventure, perchance, 873.

bar. *See* bereþ.
baylie, jurisdiction, control, 289.
bede, *inf.* to pray, 562.
behouythe, 3. *sing.* behooves, needs, 133 (*reading of* H_2).
bereþ, 3. *sing.* bears, carries, 670, (*subj.*) 671; **—— witnes(se),** tes-

Glossary

tifies, 345, 412, 566, etc.; **bar**, *prt.* 46.

bete(n), *inf.* to make amends for, atone for, 175, 270.

beyþere, *plu. gen.* both (= two-fold?), 952.

bidene, *adv.* in one company, together, 191.

bifalle, *inf.* to befall, come to pass, 291.

bileue, *sb.* belief, faith, 83; creed, 201, 203.

bileue(n), *inf.* to believe, 207; to remain, 84, 273; **bileueþ**, 985.

binde, *inf.* to bind, imprison, 482, 495; **bounde**, *pp.* 710.

binomen, *pp.* taken away from, 237.

birede, *refl.* take thought, deliberate, 133.

bise, see, provide, give heed to, 488.

bisekeþ, 1. *plu.* beseech, call on in prayer, 504.

bist, 2. *sing.* biddest, prayest, 554.

bitokneþ, 3. *sing.* betokens, typifies, 363.

biþenk, *imp.* bethink, consider, 578.

blame, *sb.* blame, censure, 784, 812; **falle in blame**, become culpable, 778.

blamed, *pp.* blamed, reproved, 765.

blinne, *inf.* to leave off, 199; to cease, 714.

blisse, *sb.* bliss, pleasure, 32, 113, 188, etc.; supreme delight, 299; glory, 417.

bodiliche, *adv.* bodily, in person, 375; *adj.* human (*i.e.* man's physical), 396.

bold, *sb.* house, dwelling, 154.

bold, *adj.* bold, certain, 819.

bonde, *sb.* the bondsman, the vassal, 890, 891.

bone, boon, request, 988.

bote, *sb.* boot, expiation, 94.

bouhte, *prt.* bought, paid for, 236; redeemed, 26; **ibouht**, *pp.* 160; **bouht**, *pp.* 172, 226.

bounde. *See* **binde**.

bour, bower, inner apartment, chamber, 152.

boxomere, *adj. comp.* more obedient, 233.

breme, *adj.* bright, shining, 383.

brenne, *inf.* to burn, be consumed, 368, 451, 808; **ibrent**, *pp.* 360.

brenning, burning, conflagration, 182.

briht, *adj.* bright, glorious, 406, 639.

caiht, *pp.* *See* **kacche**.

calle, *inf.* to call, name, 522.

can, *vb.* can, am able to, 343; has the skill, 728; **couþest**, 2. *sing.* 657; **couþ**, *pp.* 814.

cas, *sb.* case, chance, 703.

cast, *pp.* *See* **kest**.

catel, *sb.* chattel, property, goods, 187, 577, 896; **katel**, 162.

certes, *adv.* of a certainty, assuredly, 850, 861.

charged, *pp.* charged, burdened, 468.

charite, *sb.* charity, Christian love, 55, 83, 324; giving of alms, 95, 680.

chasten, *inf.* to chasten, afflict, discipline, 181.

chese, *inf.* to choose, select, 216, 219; prefer, 222.

clene, *adj.* clean, 816, 824, 848, etc.; unblemished, 364, 365; bright, glorious, 381; pure, 408, 414; **makeþ clene**, cleanses, purifies, 836, 845; **clannere**, *comp.* 826; **makeþ clannere**, 820, 828.

cleped, *pp.* called, 857.

cler, clear, evident, 376; discerning, 736; unclouded, 976, 996; **clene and cler**, glorious, 381.

clergie, *sb.* clergy, learning, science, 43, 290.

clerk, *sb.* clerk, clergyman, 667.

clerte, *sb.* clearty†, splendour, brilliancy, 390.

comen, 3. *plu.* descend, 240; 3. *sing.* 680. **come** (*inf.*) **widinne**, 118.

comfort, *sb.* comfort, relief, 686.

comforti, *inf.* to comfort, encourage, 688.

consail, *sb.* counsel, 63, 653.

cost, expense, 776.

couþ, *pp.* known, 814. *See also* **can**.

craftes, *plu.* crafts, forms of human skill, 212.

craue, *inf.* to crave, beg earnestly, 456, 530, 544, etc.

crieþ, 3. *sing.* cries, implores, 540.

croun, *sb.* crown, tonsure, 799.

Glossary. 107

cruwel, *adj.* cruel, pitiless, 258; merciless, 559.
cumpaignye, company, multitude, 437; retinue, 638.
cursede, accursed, condemned, 431, 447.

dampnacioun, damnation, spiritual ruin, 787.
dampned, *pp.* damned, consigned to hell, 432.
dar, 1. *sing.* dare, am bold enough to, venture, 563, 609.
day, 250, 251, etc.; **on a day**, once, 49; **in þilke dawe**, at that time, 37; **bi day and niht**, always, 320, 475, 516; **alday**. *See* al.
deite, deity, 374.
dekne, dean, 41.
dele, deal, part; **euery dele**, every bit, entirely, 1018.
dempt, doomed, assigned, 136.
dere, *adv.* dearly, at great price, 26, 160, 172, etc.
derne, secret, intense, 123.
deseruing, deserving, merit, 314.
destourbaunce, disturbance, agitation, 572.
deþ, death, 858; **deþ of soule**, condemnation, destruction of the lost soul, 16.
deuise, *inf.* to devise, tell, conceive, 343.
do in, to enter into, imprint on, 208.
dom, doom, judgment, 256, 415, 766; **domesday**, 257, 745, 868.
doute, *sb.* doubt, fear, 899.
douteþ, 3. *sing.* doubts, is anxious about, 693.
drauht, draught, haul, 18.
drawe, *tr. inf.* to draw, drag, 16, 106; to deduce, 945; **draweþ**, 3. *sing.* 800; drawen on heih, *pp.* exalted, 633; **drouh**, *intr.* 44.
drede, *sb.* dread, fear, *i. e.* apprehension, 20, 493, 695, etc.; fear, *i. e.* reverence, 81, 139, 883, etc.; awe, 380.
drede, *tr. inf.* to dread, fear, *i. e.* reverence, 178; to terrify, 648; **dred**, *imp.* 999; *intr. inf.* to fear, be alarmed, 747; 3. *plu.* 830.
drinke, *sb.* drinks, 155.

duire, *inf.* to endure, continue to exist, 281.
dwelle, *inf.* to dwell, leave off, 27, 283; to remain, 450; to delay, 762.

echen, *inf.* to eke (out), increase, 188.
eft, *adv.* afterward, 160; **eft sone**, soon again, 851.
eging, egging†, instigation, 229.
eiȝe, fear, awe, 21; terror, 795.
eiȝe, eye, 388, 396, 827; **eiȝen**, *plu.* 841.
eke, ek, *adv.* also, 243, 436, 439, etc.
elleswhere, elleswher, 176, 780.
emcristene, even Christian, fellow-Christian, 9, 334, 341.
empti, *adj.* empty, 1002.
ende, *sb.* end, instant, 280; **widouten ende**, eternally, 426.
ende, *inf.* to continue, 11.
ending, *sb.* ending, 210; death, 278; **ending day**, last day, death, 492.
ene, *adv.* once, 366, 815; **enes**, 939.
enome, *pp. See* nim.
ensaumple, example, pattern, 533, 596, 607.
enuie, envy, 109; hatred, ill-will, 438.
eorþe, earth; **on eorþe her(e)**, 296, 375, 600, 735; **here on eorþe**, 397, 604; **erþe**, 382, 589.
er, *conj.* ere, before, 648, 982.
erere, *comp.* earlier, before, 140, 168.
euel. *See* yuel.
euere, *adv.* ever, always, 44, 279, 388, etc.; at any time, 331; **euere more**, for ever more, from this time, 36, 96; **euere mo**, always, 240, 1004; eternally, 273; **euere among**, 186, 880. *See* among.
euerich, each, every, 313; **eueri**, 597; **euery**, 1018; **euerichon**, every one, 432.

fable, *sb.* fable, idle talk, 3; **widoute fable**, without falsehood, certainly, 525.
face, *sb.* face, image, likeness (*Gen.*

i. (26), 213; countenance, presence, 904, 906.
fain, *adj.* fain, gladly, 873; with pleasure, 965.
fair(e), *adj.* fair, spotless, 71; beautiful, 154; pleasing, 682.
fairnesse, *sb.* fairness, beauty, 305.
falle(n), fall, 170; befall, happen, 161; falleþ on honde, 3. *sing.* 585; falle lowe, *inf.* to fall low, be humiliated, 630.
fals, *adj.* false, unfair, 110; untrue, 111.
falshede, *sb.* falseness, 722.
fame, *sb.* fame, renown, 29; reputation, 40.
fare, *inf.* to fare, journey, 490; fareþ, 3. *sing.* fares, comes to pass, 669, 673, 889.
feintise, *sb.* feigning, hypocrisy, 304.
fele, *adj.* many, numerous, 675.
fend, fiend, the serpent (*Gen.* iii. 4, 13), 229.
fer, *adv.*; fer and ner, everywhere, 216.
fere, *sb.* companions, children, 423.
fersse, *adj.* fierce, proud, 623.
filþe, *sb.* filth, pollution, 732.
fire, *sb.*; al on fire, burning with fire (*Ex.* iii. 2), 356, 359.
firste, *adj.* first; þe firste lawe, the ten commandments, 358.
flen, fle, *inf.* to flee, run away from, 134, 748, 833; escape, 850; to fly, 678; fleþ, 3. *sing.* 672.
flesh, flesh; in flesh and blod, in the body, physically, 573.
fleschly, *adj.* of the flesh, carnal, 269.
folewe, *inf.* to follow, pursue, 641.
fondeþ, 3. *sing.* tempts, 655; *the reading of D and R,* 508.
fonge, *inf.* to receive, 265, 508 ($A_1 A_2 H_1$), 877.
for, for, on account of, by reason of, 20, 21, 91, 243, etc.; for the sake of, 246, 247, 248, etc.; for to, *with the infinitive,* 71, 78, 126, 156, etc.; *conj.* for, because, 17, 61, 174, etc.; for whij, wherefore, 454; forþi, on this account, for this reason; noht forþi, 467.
fordoþ(e), 3. *sing.* does away with, destroys, 941, 1007.

forȝete, *pp.* forgotten, 193, 764.
forlorne, *pp.* lost, condemned, 130 (*See variants*).
forme, *adj.* first, 223; formeste (*reading of* H_2).
forsoþe, forsooth, in truth, 391.
forþ, forth, forward, 958; forþ (þer)wid, forthwith, without delay, at the same time, 147, 334.
foule, *adj.* foul, base, 24, 61, 117, etc.; ugly, 72; wicked, 635, 654; guilty, 811.
foule, *adv.* abusively, 591.
fourme, form, person, 349; appearance, 356.
fre, free, unlimited (voluntary?), 215; generous, 323 (*reading of* H_2).
fredom, freedom, liberty, 237.
fuisoun, foisont, profusion, 994.
fulle, ful, *adj.* full, filled with, 87, 260; much, 112; perfect, complete, 310, 318.
ful, *adv.* full, very, 66, 166, 298, etc.; ful iwis, assuredly, 165, 285, 503; completely, 337; ful wel, 503, 517, 548.
fulfilt, *pp.* fulfilled, carried out, 308.

gabbe, *sb.* gabble; widouten gabbe, without lies, without deception, 464.
gan, *prt.* began (*used pleonastically*), did, 230, 641, 642.
gange, 2. *sing.* go, proceed, 761.
getestu, gettest thou, obtainest thou, 545.
gile, *sb.* guile, wiles, 61; deceit, fraud, 241.
gileþ, 3. *sing.* beguiles, deceives, 880.
gilour, *sb.* beguiler, deceiver, 879.
gilt, *sb.* guilt, offence, 231; giltes, *plu.* 752.
gilt, *pp.* sinned, 556.
glad, *adj.* glad, joyful, 1019.
glotonye, *sb.* gluttony, greed, 115.
gnede, *adj.* sparing, stingy, 1025 (*reading of MS. R*).
god, *sb.* goods, wealth, property, prosperity, 13, 163; do god, 124, 143, 461, etc.
goddede, *sb.* good deed, good works, 465, 502, 621, etc.
godhede, *sb.* godhead, divinity,

Glossary.

371, 379, 397; glory, 417; divine qualities, 886.
godnesse, *sb.* goodness, piety, 44.
gome, *sb.* man, 645.
gostes, *sb.* spirits, souls, 431, 447.
gostli, *adj.* ghostly, spiritual, 715, 717, 736, 742.
grete, 1. *sing.* greet, salute, 52; grette, *prt.* 350, 960.
greue, *inf.* to grieve, cause pain, 202, 230, 588; greueþ, pains, 388.
grisli, grisly, horrible, 442.
griþ, *sb.* peace, security, 148.
gruching, *sb.* grudging, murmur, complaint, 582, 593.

ȝaf. See ȝeue.
ȝare, *adj.* yare (*Shak.*), ready, 489.
ȝarked, *prt.* prepared, 300.
ȝate, gate, 959.
ȝelde, *inf.* to yield, pay, 956; ȝolden, recompense, 932.
ȝeme, *adj.* care, heed, 553.
ȝerne, *adv.* joyfully, eagerly, 66.
ȝift(e), gift, grace, favour, 220, 682.
ȝit, yet, 90, 164, 851.
ȝiue, ȝeue, *inf.* to give, 183, 963, 973, 1020; ȝefe, 1012; ȝeueþ, 3. *sing.* 212; ȝaf, *prt.* 215, 227, 234, etc.; ȝif, *imp.* 1012.

habbe. See haue.
halle, hall, large building, 152.
halt. See holde.
han. See haue.
handful, handful, a little, 975.
haue, *inf.* to have, receive, 89, 148, 186, etc.; to possess, 151, 309, 471, etc.; to show, 455, 529, 543, etc.; han, 295; habbe, 463; hauen, 3. *plu.* 558; han, 384; hadde, *prt.* 41, 43, 289, etc.; hade, 243; haddestu, 579.
heie. See heihe.
heih(e), *adj.* high, almighty, 214; exalted, 379; heie, noble, 622; *adv.* 632; on heih, on high, above, 633; heih of mod, haughty, 624; hext, *sup.* 325, 661.
heinen, *inf.* to make high, exalt, 627.
held. See holde.
hele, *sb.* health, 157; salvation, 2.

hele, *inf.* to heal, 774.
helle pine, hell torment, 772.
helpe, *inf.* to help, relieve, 478; to avail, 561.
henne, *adv.* hence, from this place, 297; hethen (*reading of R*).
here, *inf.* to hear, 355.
heriede, *prt.* herried†, praised, glorified, 66.
herkny. to hearken, listen, 523; herkne, 560; herkne, *imp.* 107, 137, 323, etc.; herkneþ, *imp.* 1, 790.
heste, *sb.* behests, commands, 810.
hete, heat, passion, 367.
heuie, *adj.* heavy, grievous, 469.
hie, *inf.* to hie, hasten, 968.
holde, *inf.* to hold, 656; holde lowe, to humiliate, 179; halt, 3. *sing.* values, considers, 166, 171; held, *prt.* 593.
holliche, *adv.* wholly, entirely, 353.
honde, *sb.* hand; honden, *plu.* 440; on honde, 585.
honour, *sb.* honour, possessions, 151.
hote, *adj.* hot, raging, 282.
huide, *sb.* hide, human skin; in bon and huide, physically, 157.
humilite, *sb.* humility, 88, 631, 658, etc.
hunger, *sb.* hunger, famine, 185.

ibiried, *pp.* buried, 249.
iblessed, blessed, 520.
ibouht. See bouhte.
ibrent. See brenne.
idon, *pp.* done, committed, 546.
iete, *pp.* eaten, 984.
ifere, together; in fere (*reading of D II, R*), 295.
ifiled, *pp.* defiled, 410, 724.
ifounde, *pp.* found (surprised?), discovered, 484.
ikauht. See kacche.
iliche, alike, equally, 312, 365.
ilke, the same, 362, 799.
ilong, depending on, 221; long, 750.
ilore. See lese.
imeind, mingled, 372.
inome. See nim.
inouh, enough, sufficient, 43, 146, 301, 305.
inwardliche, *adv.* intently, 389;

inwardlichere, *comp.* more earnestly, 321.
ipult, thrust, 888; **pylt,** 232.
irekened, reckoned, estimated, 869.
ise, *inf.* to see, 288, 342, 402, etc.; **iseih,** *prt.* 369.
ishewed, *pp.* showed, revealed, 399.
iuge, *inf.* to judge, 482; **iuged,** *pp.* judged, condemned, 457.
iwis, certainly, truly, 807; **ful iwis,** 337, etc. *See* **ful;** **mid iwis(se).** *See* **mid.**
iwite, *inf.* to know, 194.
iwrouht. *See* **worche.**

kacche, *inf.* to catch; —— **grace,** to have the inclination, choose, 903; **ikauht,** *pp.* 17; **caiht,** *pp.* 882.
katel. *See* **catel.**
kene, *adj.* keen, sharp, 439.
kenne, *inf.* to ken, know, perceive, 298.
kepen, *inf.* to keep, guard, 48.
kest, *prt.* cast, turned, 992. *See* **cast,** *pp.* hurled, 636.
kinde, *sb.* kind, nature, 616, 617, 620.
kindeliche, naturally, according to nature, 817.
knowelaching, knowledge, intelligence, 725.
kointise, *sb.* skill, 303.
kudde, *prt.* made known, showed, manifested, 178.
kunning, *sb.* cunning, knowledge, 303.

lad, ladde. *See* **lede.**
lasse, last. *See* **litel.**
last, *sb.* last†, vice, 635.
last, *conj.* lest, for fear that, 778, 887; **lest,** 856.
lasteþ, 3. *sing.* lasteth, endureth, 426.
late, *inf.* to let, give up, 145, 902; to leave, reject, 218; **lat,** *imp.* 143, 315, 496, 777.
later, neuere þe ——, 842.
lawe, laws, decrees, 38; commandments, 358.
leaute, faith, 403.
leche, physician, 69.
leccherie, lechery, lewdness, 116.
lede, *inf.* to lead, drag, 19, 104;

ladde, *prt.* passed, 42; **lad,** *pp.* guided, 62.
lef. *See* **leuest.**
leid, *pp.* laid, 592; **lay,** *prt.* 249.
leme, light, brightness, 384.
lered, the learned, the clergy.
leres, *sb.* cheeks, 842.
les, *sb.* lies, 519.
lesczoun, lesson (*the Liber*), 58; a passage of Scripture, 500.
lese, *inf.* to lose, 182, 896, 914; **les,** *prt.* 131; **ilore,** *pp.* 715; **lorn,** *pp.* 130.
lest, *adj. See* **litel;** *conj. See* **last.**
leue, *adj.* dear, 73, 919.
leuedi, *sb.* lady, the Virgin, 363; **lady,** 833 (*reading of H*$_2$).
leuest, 2. *sing.* believest, 189; **lef,** *imp.* 392, 866.
lewed, the lewd, the unlearned, the laity, 400.
liʒe, *sb.* lye, 828.
liʒe, lie, 637, 947; **lye,** *inf.* 1010 (*reading of D*).
lihten, *inf.* —— **adoun,** to descend, 261.
lihtliche, *adv.* lightly, easily, 198, 672, 797.
liking, *sb.* liking, pleasure, 269.
lioun, *sb.* lion, 262.
listneþ, *imp.* listen, attend to, 753.
litel, *adj.* little, small, 166, 629, 704, etc.; **luite,** 924; **lasse,** *comp.* 536, 739, 756, etc.; **þe leste,** 1016.
lodlich, loathesome, hateful, 838; **lodely** *in R.*
loke, *inf.* to look, 786; *imp.* take heed, 488, 758, 768, etc.
lomb, lamb, 260.
lome, *sb.* vessel, 1002.
londes, *plu.* lands, property, 152, 163.
long. *See* **ilong.**
longe, long, 62, 744; *adv.* 762.
lore, lore, teaching, 24, 35, 740, etc. persuasion, 235; (*the Scriptures*), 755.
lore, *sb.* loss, 185.
lorn. *See* **lese.**
los, *sb.* glory, 158.
loþe, bad, hateful, 76, 447.
loude, lude. *See* **stille.**
louerede, love counsel (= *tokens of love*), loving-kindness, 177.

Glossary. 111

lyff, eternal life, 744; **liue**, 252, 952.

maidenhed, maidenhood, virginity, 364.
mait, 2. *sing.* art able, 342, 881; **maitou**, 73, 194, 343.
make, *inf.* to make, compose, 57, 217, etc.; **maken**, to cause, 182; **made**, *prt.* created, 213, 244.
manere, kind, 835; *plu.* 572, 785; way, 628.
manhede, human, 372.
martyrdom, martyrdom, 622.
mede, meed, reward, 622; recompense, 933, 938, 956, etc.
medicine, remedy, 771.
meke, *adj.* meek, 666; gentle, 260, 824.
mele, meal, 975, 1000.
mene, 1. *sing.* mean, 407; *inf.* 823, 847.
merci, mercy, 86, 148, 263, etc.; pardon, 131, 567?, 568?.
merciable, merciful, 526, 534.
met, *sb.* measure (*Mark* iv. 24), 549.
mete, meats, food, 155; **metys** *in II₂*.
mete, *inf.* to measure, 550; **metest, metest** (*Mark* iv. 24), 549.
mette, *prt.* met, 349, 959.
meyne, company, brethren (*Matt.* xxv. 40), 1016.
mid, with; **mid iwisse**, assuredly, 309, 689.
mieknesse, *sb.* meekness, 85.
miht, *sb.* might, strength, 134, 253; power, 361.
mildeliche, mildly, patiently, 605.
minde. See **mynde**.
misdede, *sb.* wrong-doing, offence, 829.
misdoþ, injure, treat with unkindness, 535; **misdo**, *pp.* 558.
misse, miss, make mistake, fail, 120; want, lack, 418.
misseid, *pp.* missaid, spoken evil against, slandered, 538, 591.
mod, mood, heart, 14; mind, spirit, 123, 164, 624.
mourning, *sb.* mourning, 123, 125.
muche, much, important, 102, 150.
muchel, much, 664, 665, 668.
multiplie, to multiply, increase, 1009.

murie, merry, joyous, 159, 905; **muryere**, *comp.* 284.
mynde, mind, remembrance, 496; **minde**, 619.
myrour, mirror, 505.

nailes, nails, 439.
nam. See **nim**.
namlich, namely, specially, 437.
naþeles, nevertheless, notwithstanding, 161.
nay, nay, no, 398; **widoute nay**, without denial, 252, 258.
ne, not, 20, 189, 343, 367, etc.
ne, nor, 21, 626, 862, etc.
nedful, needful, necessary, 754, 852.
neih, near, 370, 634; **fer and ner**, 216; **next**, *sup.* 326, 662.
neiheboures, neighbour, 535.
nele, will not, 263, 455, 628, etc.; **nelle**, 272; **noldest**, 659.
nempne, to name, enumerate, 101, 108; **nempt**, *pp.* 135.
ner. See **neih**.
neuere þe more, never again, 470.
newe, new, fresh, 760.
nim, 2. *sing.* take, 607; **nym**, *imp.* 553; **nam**, *prt.* 246; **inome**, *pp.* 644; **enome**, 646; **nomen**, *pp.* 649.
nis, is not, 146.
noht, not, 225, 239; naught, of no worth, 32, 171, 195, etc.; nothing, 579.
nost (*ne wost*), dost not know, 347.
noþing, not at all, 360.
nouþe, now there, 107, 199, 283, etc.

o. See **on**.
oftake, 3. *sing.* repents, 539.
ofte, *adv.* often, many times, 170, 493, 496, etc.; **offte**, 125.
olde, *adj.* old, ancient, former, 357.
on, one, 111, 122, 350, etc; **o**, 204, 205, 354; **one**, alone, only, 239.
onliche, *adv.* only, 145.
on liue, alive, 859.
onne. See **take**.
openliche, openly, publicly, 442; plainly, 822.
ordre, monastic order, 41.
ore, mercy, compassion, 89, 540.
orisoun, orison, prayer, 499; **orysoun**, 993.

oþer, other, 4, 52; oþere, *plu.* 134; *conj.* or, 702, 706, 734, etc.; oþer —or, 175.
ouercome, overcome, vanquish, 654.
ouht, aught, anything, 316, 558.
oyle, oil, 976, 996, 1001.

par, through, for (*reading of* $H_1 H_2$), 55; by (*See* aunter), 873.
paradys, paradise, 232, 286, 299, etc.
parten, *inf.* to depart; —— henne, to die, 297.
paunter, *sb.* panter†, net, 18.
penaunce, penance, penitence, 681; penalty, 770; **to don ——,** to meet penalty, 92, 474.
peril, peril, danger, 170.
persones, persons, individuals, 206.
pes, peace, 86, 514, 516, 520.
picher, pitcher, cruse (1 *Kings* xvii. 12, 16), 975, 995.
pine, pain, suffering, 586, 902; torment (in hell), 176, 642, 746; **helle pine,** 772; **strong(e) pine,** 104, 274, 282, 888; **peyne,** penalty, 246 (*reading of* $H_1 H_2$), 590?.
pining, pining, suffering, 899; pain (preparatory miseries), 181, 270.
pite, pity, 87, 242, 260.
place, *sb.* place, 294.
plawe, *sb.* play, pleasure, 15.
plente, plenty, 1003.
point, point, the instant, 278.
pompe, pomp; **pompe and pride,** ostentation, 158.
pore, *adj.*; **pore of mod,** humble, 164; þe **pore,** *sb.* the poor, 311.
poudre, powder, dust (l. 664, '*puluerem*'), 670.
power, power, 215; freedom, 219; influence, 599.
preie, *sb.* prayer, request, 68.
preie, to pray (to God), 564; 1. *sing.* ask (of man), 53, 601; **preye,** *imp.* (*the reading of* H_2), 834.
present, present, gift, 1018.
preued, proved, 399.
pride, pride, 109, 158, 170, 635, etc.; **pryde,** 646.
profete, prophet, 948, 950, 981, etc.
profitable, *adj.* profitable, beneficial, 4.

profyt, profit, advancement, 60.
proud, proud, 624, 645.
prouing, proving, test, 335.
prys, price, value, 166.
puite, *inf.* to put; **forþ puite,** to offer, 923; **put,** *pp.*? 238; **putte,** 994; *imp.* 476; thrust (*reading of D*), 232.
pylt. *See* ipult.

quake, *inf.* to quake, tremble, 444.
qued, *sb.* the evil one, the devil, 654.
qued, *adj.* bad, evil, 862; **quede,** vile, 1025.
qwene, qween, Mary (*see* H_2), 833.

reche to, *inf.* to reach, arrive (at), 98, 142.
red, *sb.* counsel, advice, 47, 82, 653.
rede, *vb.* to counsel, advise, 647; take care of (*see Zupitza, Guy,* 7187), 466; read, 167, 501.
redi, *inf.* to make ready, prepare, 92, 474.
redi, *adj.* ready, prepared (*see also Kölbing, Sir Beues,* 3101), 489.
rentes, rents, income, revenue, 152, 163.
repentaunce, repentance, 473, 769; penitence, 91.
resoun, reason, 718.
reuliche, rueful, sad, 276; **rewefulliche,** *reading of* A_2.
rewe, *sb.* on ——, in order, one after another, 80.
riche, rich, costly, 153, 771; highly seasoned, 155; the rich, 311; **ryche** (*see* H_2), 837.
riht, *sb.* right, justice, 302.
riht, *adj.* right, straight, 22; correct, 39; righteous, 504.
riht, *adv.* right, exactly, in the same proportion, 10, 264, 314, etc.; straight, directly, 254, 299, 1017.
rihtfulliche, rightfully, justly, 458.
rod, rood-tree, cross, 26, 144, 248.

sarmoun, sermon, discourse, 57, 137.
sauh. *See* se.
sauter, Psalter, 460.
sauuacioun, salvation, deliverance from sin, 788, 800.
sauue, *inf.* to save, to atone for,

245; **sauued,** saved, delivered from sin, 128.
se, sen, to see, 190, 344, 405, etc.; to look, 389; **knowe and se,** 657, 737, etc.; **sext,** 2. *sing.* 385; **sist,** 553; **sauh,** *prt.* 347, 350, 355, etc. **seþ?,** 817.
seie, *inf.* to say, 413, 445, 479, etc.; **seist,** 2. *sing.* 555; **seiþ,** 3. *sing.* 172, 276, 345, etc.; **seiþ,** *plu.?* 339; **seide** *for* **sede,** *prt.* 52, 68, 140, etc.
seke, *inf.* to seek, search for; **sek,** 2. *sing.* 190; **souht,** *pp.* 196.
seker, *adj.* sure, certain, 12.
seknesse, disease, 187.
seli, blessed, happy, 987; weak, 576.
seruage, servage, servitude, 238.
sethen, *conj.* since, 69.
serue(n), to serve, 296; to minister to, 966; **serueþ,** 3. *sing.* 735; **seruede,** *prt.* 2. *plu.* 452.
shaftes, creations, creatures, 211.
shame, *sb.* shame, mortification, 777, 779, 785, etc.; disgrace, 783; *tristitia* (*Liber*), 799.
shappere, Shaper, Creator, 211.
shed, distinction, 217, 721.
sheding, shedding, 611.
shewe, to show, exercise, 263; to point out, describe, 75, 79, 700; reveal, 294; disclose, 779, 804; **shewede,** *prt.* manifested, 361; **ishewed,** *pp.* 399; **shewed,** *pp.* 780.
shildeþ, shields, preserves, 772.
shining, shining, radiant, 382.
shiue, slice, piece, 970.
shone, shun, avoid, 105, 659.
shrewes, shrews, evil beings, 102.
shrift, shrift, confession, 681, 761, 796, etc.; **shrifte of mouþe,** 94, 473.
shriue, *inf.* to shrive, make confession, 485; *pp.* 758, 768.
side, side, 655, 675; **riht side,** 255.
siht, sight, presence, 133, 254; appearance, 362, 405.
siker, surely, 491, 649.
sikerli. *See* **sikerliche.**
sikerliche, surely, 146, 373, 392, etc.; **sikerli,** 468, 1001.
sinful, sinful, 149, 708, 727, etc.

singyn, *inf.* to sin, 224; **singy,** 714.
sist. *See* **se.**
siþe, times, 394.
siþþen, *adv.* afterward, 236.
skile, reason, 711.
skilfulliche, reasonably, 173.
skorn, scorn, derision, 592.
sleuþe, sloth, 116; **sleuþes,** *gen.* 121.
slowen, *prt. plu.* slew, 438.
smale, small, a little, 181; **gret and smal,** 870.
sodeyneliche, suddenly, unexpectedly, 882.
solaz, solace, relief, 686.
some. *See* **summe.**
sonde, sending, message, 52.
soþ, *adj.* true, 519.
soþ, *sb.* truth, 464.
soþfast, soothfast†, true, 471.
soþliche, in truth, 441; truthfully, with truth, 525, 609.
soþnesse, truth, 346, 411, 1014; righteousness, 565.
spare, *inf.* to spare, refrain, 20, 700, 912; withhold, 924; **sparest,** 2. *sing.* 795; **spare,** 3. *sing.* 898.
speche, speech, discourse, 1, 753; sermon (*on the mount*), 569.
spede, *inf.* to speed, prosper, 937, 1027; **sped,** *imp.* 865.
spende, *inf.* to expend, bestow, 990.
spille, *inf.* to be destroyed, perish, 198.
springe, *inf.* to spring up, grow, burst forth, 126.
stat, estate, condition, 729.
stede, stead, place, 561, 597, 604, etc.
stedefast, steadfast, unwavering, 85.
steih, *prt.* ascended, 253.
sterne, stern, 446; unrelenting, 258, 436; fierce, 262.
sterren, *plu.* stars, 383.
stille, still, silent, 593, 790; **lude and stille,** under any circumstances, at any time, 584; **oþer loude oþer stille,** 706; **noþer loude ne stille,** 891.
stounde, stound, time, 709.
stout, stout, proud, boastful, 623.
strong, strong, agonizing, excruci-

ating, 104, 266, 274, 282, 449, 888; hard, exhausting, 185.
suffraunce, sufferance, patience, 571.
suffraunt, sufferant, patient, 587, 597.
suffre, *inf.* to suffer, experience, 176, 184; to be submissive to, 583; to bear patiently, 608, 613.
summe, some, certain ones, 825; alle and some, all without exception, 643.
sumwhat, somewhat, a little, 764, 850 (*see* $A_1 A_2 R$).
swete, sweet, beloved, 555, 569; gracious, 949; consoling, 998.
swiche, swich, such, 23, 67, 125, etc. *See* alswich, 549, 550.
swinke, *inf.* to swink (*Spenser*), toil, 156.
swiþe, *adv.* very, exceedingly, 4, 236, 578, etc.
swolewe, *inf.* to swallow, engulf, 642.

take, *inf.* to take, accept, 71, 100, 498, etc.; to choose, select, 218; onne take, to assume (be grieved?, appear?), 267; tok, *prt.* 47; *refl.* betook, 34; tak, *imp.* 770; tak minde, 619; consail take, 63; ensaumple take, 596.
tale, *sb.* tale; tale telle, to give an account, 28.
teche, *inf.* to teach of, 2; to instruct, direct, 70, 570, 754; show, point out, 97, 141.
telle, tellen, to tell, relate, 138, 284, 285, etc. *See* tale.
tene, teen (*Shak.*), grief, 192.
teres, tears, 827, 841.
til (*MS. R*), to, 271.
time, time; on a time, once, 31.
tit, avails; —— him, falls to his lot, 807.
tok. *See* take.
tokne, token, symbol, 351; evidence, 354; tokenyng (*reading of MSS.* $A_2 H_2 R$).
toumbe, tomb, 249.
trauail, *sb.* travail, labour, 185; trouble, 585.
tresor, treasures, stores of treasure, 154.

trespas, trespass, sin, 546, 704; trespaz, offence, 685.
treuliche, truly, faithfully, 208; treweliche, in truth, 610.
trewe, true, constant, 83; real, genuine, 304, 697.
tricherie, treachery, perfidy, 110.
trinite, Trinity, 206, 352, 430.
tristi, trusty, trustful, 477, 690.
trowþe, faith, 1033.
turment, torment, 266.
turne, *inf.* to turn, 127, 435.
tweie (*things*), 141; tweye, 785.

þank, thanks, expression of gratitude, 933.
þar. *See* þer.
þeder. *See* þider.
þenke, to think, 401, 575; þenk, *imp.* 493, 527, 589; þenk in herte, 601.
þer, there, 23, 33, 37, etc.; þere, 273; þar, 358; þare, 954; þerfore, for it, 92, 582, 630; þermide, 171; þerwid, 147, 762.
þewes, moral qualities, habits, 72, 97, 101.
þider, thither, 257; þeder, 261.
þilke, those same, 37.
þing, theme, 200; being, 381; þinge, *plu.* 284; þinges, 141; þing, 836, 883; ouer alle þing, 8, 318, 329, etc.
þinkeþ, *impers.* seems, 150?, 159; þinke, 588; þouhte, *prt.* 32.
þisternesse, darkness, 114, 306, 731.
þo, *adv.* then, 65, 981, 1003.
þo, *dem. pro.* those, 111, 239, 557, etc.
þolede, *prt.* suffered, experienced, 590; endured, 594, 605.
þolemod, patient, 574, 612.
þouht, *sb.* thought, meditation, trouble, 31; thought, 315, 409, 559, etc.
þouhte. *See* þinkeþ.
þral, thrall, slave, 238.
þridde, third, 250, 251.
þurst, thirst, 185.
þurw, *prep.* through, 6, 18, 61, etc.

uertu, virtue, power, 658; uertuz, *plu.* moral virtues, 71, 79, 325, 661.

Glossary. 115

vbbreid, *sb.* upbraid, reproach, 537.
vch, each, every, 133, 655, 675.
verray, very, true, 88, 680.
verreement, verily, truly, 877.
vers, verse, 460.
vessel, vessels, plate ?, 153.
vilte, vility†, contempt, 602.
vnboxomnesse, disobedience, 231.
vnclene, unclean, defiled, 834.
vncowþe, uncouth, unknown, 421.
vnite, unity (i. e. *organic totality*), 205; in one, 429.
vnmeþ, difficult, 615.
vnriht, wrong, injustice, 613.
voiz, voice, 446.
vp, *adv.* up, 251.
vpon, *prep.* upon, 995.
vre, our, 363, 506, 595, etc.
vse, use, practise, 82, 90.

wanhope, despair, 126.
wanten, to want, be lacking, 316; waste (1 *Kings* xvii. 14), 1000.
war, *adj.* aware, 45.
warne, 1. *sing.* warn, 487, 863.
wasshe, *vb.* wash, 831; **wassheþ**, 816, 818, 824, 825.
wasshing, washing, cleansing, 835.
waxen, *inf.* to wax, increase, not fail (1 *Kings* xvii. 14), 1001.
wel, well, 45, 52, 82, etc.; very, 117, 160, 198, etc.
wemme, *inf.* to wem, blemish, 367; **wemmed**, *pp.* 366.
wende, *inf.* to wend, go, 12, 425.
weneþ, weens, believes, 831.
wepeþ, weeps, sorrows, 829.
were, *adj.* be —— were, beware, 645. *See* **war**.
wete, *imp.* know, consider, 312, 1017. *See* **wite**.
wheiþer, which of two, 219, 536.
wher, whether, 336; **wheiþer —— or**, 272.
wherþurw, by reason of which, 132.
while, *sb.* while, time, 27, 62; **whiles**, *conj.* during the time that, 184.
wicke, wicked, evil, 101; base, 116, 122.
wid, with, 84, 93, 181, etc.
widewe, widow, 951, 955, 959, etc.
wil, wilfulness, 169.
wille, *sb.* will, liking, 19, 326, 662;

etc.; desire, 46, 197, 308, etc.; yielding, 594.
wilnen, to desire, long for, 279.
winne, to win, acquire, 5, 78, 132, etc.
wisdom, wisdom, 81, 139, 884.
wisse, to point out, teach, 119.
wit, *sb.* wit, knowledge, 43, 67, 212, etc.; discrimination, 227, 290; witte, 339.
wite(n), *inf.* to know, 225, 327, 377, etc.
witerli. *See* **witerliche**.
witerliche, truly, surely, 717; witerli, 364, 457, 527, etc.
witnesse, witness, evidence, 111, 345, 412, etc.
wo, woe, injury, 112, 434; sorrow, pain, 192, 484.
womman, woman, 999.
wonder, *adv.* exceedingly, marvellously, 387.
wone, wont, habits, 106.
wone, *inf.* to dwell, remain, 427, 660; wonye, 634; woned, *pp.* accustomed, 259.
woniȝing, dwelling, 313; **woning**, 317.
worche, *inf.* to work, 859, 874; **wrouhte**, *prt.* wrought, created, 25; **iwrouht**, *pp.* done, 580; committed, 803; **wrouht**, *pp.* 759, 791.
worþ, becomes (i. e. *will be*), 128, 160, 932.
wouh, wrong, 302.
wounden, *sb.* wounds, 442.
wraþfful, wraþful, wrathful, angry, 262, 436.
wraþþe, wrath, anger, 109.
wraþþeþ, 3. *sing.* angers, 806.
wreche, wreak, revenge, 618.
wrong, wrong, 222; injury, 600; injustice, 602, 608.
wrongful, harmful, 618.
wroþer hele, misfortune, 129.
wrouhte. *See* **worche**.
wyse, wise, manner; **in none wyse**, 344.

ydel, idle, vain, 463, 466; **on ydel**, 568, 668.
yuel, evil, pernicious, 15; **god —— yuel**, 217, 228, 720, 739; euel, wrong, 901; þe euel, 218.

INDEX OF NAMES.

Abraham, 347.
Adam, 223.
Alquin, 39, 51, 65.
Austin, *Seint* ——, Augustine, 171, 275.

Daui, *Sein* ——, David, 459, 691.

Eliȝe, Elijah, 948, 950, 953; **Helie,** 957.
Eue, Eve, 229.

Gregory, *Sein* ——, 663, 667.
Gy of Warwyk, 30; **Sire Gy,** 50.

Iesu Crist, 34, 66, 498, etc.
Iudas, 129.

Lucifer, 638.

Moyses, 355.

Powel, *Sein* ——, 345.

Sarepte, Zarephath (1 *Kings* xvii. 9, 10), 954.
Synay, þe *mount of* ——, 357.

www.ingramcontent.com/pod-product-compliance
Lightning Source LLC
Chambersburg PA
CBHW030754230426
43667CB00007B/968